ACCESS TO LAND, RURAL POVERTY, AND PUBLIC ACTION

UNU WORLD INSTITUTE FOR DEVELOPMENT ECONOMICS RESEARCH (UNU/WIDER)

was established by the United Nations University as its first research and training centre and started work in Helsinki, Finland in 1985. The purpose of the Institute is to undertake applied research and policy analysis on structural changes affecting the developing and transitional economies, to provide a forum for the advocacy of policies leading to robust, equitable, and environmentally sustainable growth, and to promote capacity strengthening and training in the field of economic and social policy-making. Its work is carried out by staff researchers and visiting scholars in Helsinki and through networks of collaborating scholars and institutions around the world.

Access to Land, Rural Poverty, and Public Action

Edited by
ALAIN DE JANVRY
GUSTAVO GORDILLO
JEAN-PHILIPPE PLATTEAU
and
ELISABETH SADOULET

A study prepared for the World Institute for Development Economics Research of the United Nations University (UNU/WIDER)

OXFORD
UNIVERSITY PRESS

OXFORD
UNIVERSITY PRESS

Great Clarendon Street, Oxford OX2 6DP

Oxford University Press is a department of the University of Oxford.
It furthers the University's objective of excellence in research, scholarship,
and education by publishing worldwide in

Oxford New York

Athens Auckland Bangkok Bogotá Buenos Aires Calcutta
Cape Town Chennai Dar es Salaam Delhi Florence Hong Kong Istanbul
Karachi Kuala Lumpur Madrid Melbourne Mexico City Mumbai
Nairobi Paris São Paulo Shanghai Singapore Taipei Tokyo Toronto Warsaw

with associated companies in Berlin Ibadan

Oxford is a registered trade mark of Oxford University Press
in the UK and in certain other countries

Published in the United States
by Oxford University Press Inc., New York

World Institute for Development Economics Research of the United Nations University
(UNU/WIDER) Katajanokanlaituri 6B, 00160 Helsinki, Finland

First published 2001

British Library Cataloguing in Publication Data
Data available

Library of Congress Cataloging in Publication Data
Access to land, rural poverty, and public action / edited by Alain de Janvry . . . [*et al.*].
p. cm. — (WIDER studies in development economics)
'A study prepared for the World Institute for Development Economics Research of the United Nations University (UNU/WIDER).'
Includes bibliographical references and index.
1. Land use, Rural—Developing countries. 2. Land reform—Developing countries.
3. Land tenure—Developing countries. 4. Rural poor—Developing countries. 5. Rural development—Developing countries. I. De Janvry, Alain. II. World Institute for Development Economics Research. III. Studies in development economics.
HD1131.A25 2001 333.3′09172′4—dc21 00–050426

ISBN 0-19-924217-8

1 3 5 7 9 10 8 6 4 2

Typeset by Graphicraft Limited, Hong Kong
Printed in Great Britain
on acid-free paper by
Biddles Ltd., Guildford & King's Lynn

FOREWORD

The 1950s, 1960s, and 1970s were characterized by a lively debate about unequal agrarian structures, rural poverty and land redistribution. During this period, land reform figured prominently on the policy agenda of several developing countries. Changes over the last two decades have taken much wind off the sails of land reform. In some countries, rapid rural–urban migration and the decline in land rents moderated the pressure for land redistribution. In others, the difficulties met in managing its political-economic impact led to its gradual dismissal. And the advent to power of authoritarian regimes further reduced its political viability, particularly in Latin America. Because of all this, during the last twenty years, the 'land issue' has been conspicuously absent from the research and policy agenda of most developing countries.

The issue of access to land has re-emerged forcefully in recent years due to the persistence of pervasive inefficiencies in land distribution, an aggravation of environmental problems caused by misuse of land by rural households with restricted access to it, and the widespread persistence of rural poverty (which accounts for over half of the world's 1.3 billion poor). Recent political changes, such as the end of apartheid in South Africa, the return to democracy in Latin America, and land privatization in transitional economies, have contributed to the renewed interest in the land issue. Finally, the importance of a broad-based access to land has been underscored again by mounting evidence that limited institutional innovation in agrarian structures severely constrains long-term growth and poverty alleviation.

This renewed emphasis on access to land has generally led, however, to more eclectic interventions than in the past, which have transcended traditional redistributive land reforms. These new interventions focus on ensuring access via gradual measures rather than one-off massive redistributions, place greater emphasis on new forms of access such as community titling, intra-family and intra-community land transfers, and regulated land markets. They also explicitly seek greater complementarity between land interventions and supportive measures in the field of rural development. This book underscores that there are alternative paths of access to the land and that, in most cases, simplistic universal solutions are unlikely to provide an efficient response to local land access needs.

The study is the first comprehensive assessment of new land policy interventions. It covers this vast new field through twelve topical chapters, each discussing alternative mechanisms of access to land, combined with five detailed country case studies that span Africa, Asia, Latin America and Eastern Europe. Its original findings offer considerable food for thought to those scholars, policy makers and practitioners seeking to enhance access to the land, alleviate rural poverty and promote broad-based growth in developing and transitional countries. I strongly recommend it to them all, as well as to the general reader interested in development issues.

Giovanni Andrea Cornia,
Director, UNU/WIDER

CONTENTS

TABLES

FIGURES

NOTES ON CONTRIBUTORS

Dr. J.E. Michael Arnold is a Consultant in Oxford, UK.

Dr. J. Bahati is a Lecturer in the Department of Forestry at Makerere University in Kampala, Uganda.

Dr. Jean-Marie Baland is a Professor of Economics, CRED in the Faculté des Sciences Economiques, Sociales et de Gestion at the Université de Namur, Namur, Belgium.

Dr. A.Y. Banana is a Senior Lecturer in the Department of Forestry at Makerere University in Kampala, Uganda.

Dr. Hans Binswanger is Senior Agricultural Policy Advisor in the Agriculture and Natural Resources Department of The World Bank in Washington DC.

Dr. Michael R. Carter is a Professor in the Department of Agricultural and Applied Economics at the University of Wisconsin in Madison, Wisconsin.

Azeta Cungu is a Research Associate in the Policy Research Group of the Department of Agricultural and Environmental Economics at Katholieke Universiteit in Leuven, Belgium.

Dr. Alain de Janvry is a Professor in the Department of Agricultural and Resource Economics, University of California at Berkeley.

Dr. Klaus Deininger is an Economist in the Policy Research Department of The World Bank in Washington DC.

Dr. Marcel Fafchamps is a Professor in the Center for the Study of African Economics in the Department of Economics at Oxford University.

Dr. W.S. Gombya-Ssembajjwe is a Senior Lecturer in the Department of Forestry at Makerere University in Kampala, Uganda.

Dr. Gustavo Gordillo de Anda is the Regional Director for Latin America and the Caribbean for the Food and Agriculture Organization of the United Nations (FAO) in Santiago, Chile.

Dr. Tomas Doucha is the Director of the Research Institute of Agricultural Economics (VUZE) in Prague, The Czech Republic.

Dr. Erik Mathijs is an Assistant Professor in the Policy Research Group of the Department of Agricultural and Environmental Economics at Katholieke Universiteit in Leuven, Belgium.

Dr. Rinku Murgai is an Economist in the Development Research Group (DECRG) at The World Bank in Washington DC.

Dr. Elinor Ostrom is Co-Director and Professor in the Workshop in Political Theory and Policy Analysis at the University of Indiana in Bloomington, Indiana.

Dr. Keijiro Otsuka is a Professor in the Department of Economics at the Metropolitan University in Tokyo, Japan, and is also a Research Fellow at the International Food Policy Research Institute in Washington DC.

Dr. Jean-Philippe Platteau is a Professor of Economics, CRED in the Faculté des Sciences Economiques, Sociales et de Gestion at the Université de Namur, Namur, Belgium.

Dr. Agnes R. Quisumbing is a Senior Research Fellow at the International Food Policy Research Institute in Washington DC.

Dr. Elisabeth Sadoulet is a Professor in the Department of Agricultural and Resource Economics, University of California at Berkeley.

Mandira Saha is Manager at the State Bank of India in New Delhi, India.

Dr. Uday Shankar Saha is Assistant General Manager at the National Bank for Agriculture and Rural Development in Mumbai, India.

Dr. Ramón Salgado is the Vice Rector at the Universidad Pedagogica Nacional Francisco Morazan and Profesor de Sociologia Rural at the Universidad Nacional Autonoma de Honduras in Tegucigalpa, Honduras.

Dr. Johan F.M. Swinnen is Economic Advisor for the Directorate-General for Economic and Financial Affairs of the European Commission in Brussels, Belgium and is also Associate Professor in the Policy Research Group of the Department of Agricultural and Environmental Economics at Katholieke Universiteit in Leuven, Belgium.

Wendy Wolford is a Graduate Student in the Department of Geography at the University of California at Berkeley.

1
Access to Land and Land Policy Reforms

ALAIN DE JANVRY, JEAN-PHILIPPE PLATTEAU,
GUSTAVO GORDILLO, AND ELISABETH SADOULET

The persistent issue of access to land: questions and hypotheses

In most developing countries, the problem of optimum access to farm land—i.e., access for whom and under what conditions—remains a serious unresolved issue, frequently with high efficiency and welfare costs, environmental consequences, and explosive political manifestations. Land is typically misallocated among potential users and worked under incomplete property or user rights that create disincentives to efficient use. In the current economic context, the implication is that macro-economic reforms implemented as part of structural adjustment policies have often induced only weak supply response in agriculture, undermining one of the main objectives of the reforms. Many poor rural households are unable to gain sufficient access to land when this could be their best option out of poverty. The result is the reproduction of rural poverty and inequality, which further add to inefficiencies through disincentive effects and negative externalities (Bardhan, Bowles, and Gintis 1998; Kanbur and Lustig 1999). As countries move beyond the macro-level implementation of structural adjustment to concerns with micro-level reforms to enhance producer response (Stiglitz 1998), the need to address the issue of optimum access to land has led many countries to reopen the dossier of land policy reforms. While large-scale expropriative and redistributive land reforms are generally no longer compatible with political realities, there are many alternative paths to access to land and forms of property rights and tenure that can be explored to improve efficiency and welfare. A rich agenda of land policy interventions can consequently be defined to alter access to land. This is what we explore in this book.

The book focuses on the following fundamental questions, providing answers that often run counter to conventional wisdom.

1. For whom and under what conditions is gaining access to land, as a productive asset, important for efficiency gains and poverty reduction compared to access to other productive assets, i.e., when is it important for governments to address the issue of access to land? Available evidence (see later in this chapter) shows that redefining access to land for particular categories of households and communities, under particular configurations of market failures and institutional gaps, can create efficiency and/or welfare gains. Examples are landless households with family labor and other productive assets that

cannot be put to use through the market, but can be used productively when applied to working land; and communities that do not have exclusion rights on the land they use and hence cannot efficiently manage resources, but could do so if they had collective titles. When these circumstances hold, there is a role to play for land policy reforms that alter access rights. Hence, even if traditional expropriative land reforms are off the current policy agenda, there is logic for intervention on a broad array of land policy issues that codify access to land.

2. What property rights over land are necessary to achieve efficient use? We start here from the proposition that property over a resource is composed of a multiplicity of rights that include access, appropriation of resources or products, provision of management, exclusion of others, and alienation by selling or leasing (Ostrom, Chapter 5). These different rights over a particular land parcel may be held by different actors (Bromley 1989). It is only ownership that conveys the cumulation of all of these rights. Access to land and resource use can thus occur under property rights that are far from complete in the sense of including the right of alienation. In many situations, secure access to land can be achieved under incomplete rights, and the benefits of alienation (e.g., as a means of securing access to formal credit) may be immaterial to the levels of efficiency achieved in using the land. Hence, it is not correct to think that the full range of rights associated with private ownership should be implemented in all circumstances (Ostrom, Chapter 5; Otsuka and Quisumbing, Chapter 4). In that perspective, individual titling programs, which represent the ultimate development in making private ownership complete, may be neither necessary nor sufficient to achieve efficiency in land use (Deininger and Binswanger, Chapter 17).

3. What form of tenure is optimal for giving access to land to the rural poor and achieving efficient use? The studies in this book show that, in terms of efficiency, there is not one dominant form of tenure. Common property resources (CPR), access to land in usufruct via community membership and lineage, tenancy contracts, and ownership (private, community, corporate, or public) all have their relative merits under particular conditions. In general, land policy reforms have overstressed the need to give private ownership rights over the need to give user rights (Sadoulet, Murgai, and de Janvry, Chapter 8). Clearly, it is always better for an individual to own more assets (land and others) than not, and as a result, to be less poor and less vulnerable. Thus, in terms of welfare, ownership rights do matter since they determine the costs and risks of access to land. Reforms that give access to land in ownership as opposed to usufruct and tenancy should thus be pursued when feasible (Deininger, Chapter 13). However, gaining access to assets in ownership through subsidized transfers is a remote possibility for most rural households if the cost of these programs is high, and if market failures and institutional gaps persist after the transfer.

4. What are the conditions under which land markets can be made to perform efficiently? Clearly, well functioning land markets are fundamental in allocating land efficiently among potential users, both under rental contracts and purchases. In general, the conventional wisdom is that property rights need to be formalized through land titling and registration in order for land rental and land sales markets to

perform efficiently. Evidence in this book shows that this is not necessarily the case (Otsuka and Quisumbing, Chapter 4). When communities are vested with high levels of social capital, informal procedures can be effective in solving moral hazard problems (see Baland *et al.* 1999 for Uganda; Katz 2000 for Guatemala). Under these circumstances, transaction costs can be held low, and land markets grounded in community norms can be very effective without any formal legal support system. André and Platteau (1998) observed that this holds true in Rwanda, even under conditions where land sales are illegal. Local land conflict resolution mechanisms, grounded in the social capital and the structure of authority of communities, can be effective for this purpose. When this is missing, however, formal titling becomes necessary to sustain land markets.

5. Are land sales markets necessarily hostile to the poor? While the answer will generally be yes (Otsuka and Quisumbing, Chapter 4 for Sumatra; Carter and Salgado, Chapter 10 for Latin America), and the conditions that create this outcome can be identified, this is not always the case. It is possible that anti-poor biases in the operation of land sales markets only come with increasing land scarcity and formalization of property rights, while freely operating informal land markets under relative land abundance can help mitigate initial inequalities in land endowments. For instance, households with less land received through the family or the community can compensate their initial disadvantages by purchasing land on the market (Otsuka and Quisumbing, Chapter 4 for Ghana; Baland *et al.* 1999 for Uganda). Hence, while land sales markets are rarely level playing fields for the poor (Carter and Barham 1996), there are circumstances where these markets can work progressively.

6. Can land rental markets serve as more effective instruments to access land than land sales markets for the rural poor? While land rental markets are extraordinarily active in the more developed countries and in the Indian subcontinent, these markets have been greatly suppressed by land reform legislation and a lack of enforcement of property rights in other parts of the world, especially Latin America, the Philippines, and several African countries including Rwanda, Uganda, Zimbabwe, Kenya, and South Africa. Yet, evidence in this book shows that land rental contracts can be effective entry points for the poor in accessing land, particularly if contracts are drawn to compensate for the market failures and institutional gaps that affect them (Otsuka and Quisumbing, Chapter 4; Carter and Salgado, Chapter 10; Sadoulet, Murgai, and de Janvry, Chapter 8). Hence, an effective anti-poverty strategy that focuses on access to land for the rural poor should seek to reactivate land rental markets where they are not functioning, assist tenants in obtaining more favorable contracts, and promote access to contracts for the poorer households.

7. Do we know enough to design effective land policy reforms? At the conceptual level, if all other markets could be assumed to work, the issue of optimal land policy reforms would be relatively straightforward. In practice, however, the contexts and conditions under which these reforms are implemented are highly diverse and complex, with missing markets, institutional gaps, and government failures. We still know very little about the wide range of conditions under which land is accessed, and the

determinants of efficiency in resource use under alternative forms of access. Hence, we still need more definitive research on land issues to design effective land policy interventions. This includes fundamental factors such as the determinants of inheritance practices, how land rental and sales markets operate, the impact of evolving land tenure systems on women and other vulnerable social categories, the determinants of communities' abilities to manage common property resources and deliver local public goods, and the political economy of land policy reforms. This book consequently not only provides a set of answers, but also raises questions for future research on access to land and land policy reforms.

Why is access to land an important policy issue?

We start by analyzing the welfare and efficiency effects of gaining access to land by considering the most neutral tenure situations, namely when land is used under either fixed rent or ownership with fully mortgaged land. We then analyze the advantages and shortcomings of accessing land under other forms of tenure relative to these two.

If all markets were perfect and there were no economies of scale, optimal factor use would be equally achieved under the two forms of tenure. A fixed-rent contract would also be equivalent to ownership from a welfare point of view, since rent paid to the landlord under the first is equal to the interest paid to the bank under the second. Returns to labor for a landless household would be identical under either form of access to land and also to earnings on the labor market. If the outcomes in terms of poverty and inequality are not as socially desired, the optimal distribution of income could be reached either by *ex ante* reallocation of land and other factor endowments (at zero efficiency cost due to separability between efficiency and equity under perfect markets), or *ex post* through lump-sum taxation and transfers.

In a second-best world where there are transaction costs on markets and many markets fail, this happy result no longer holds. In this case, reallocating access to land across households can have both welfare and efficiency effects, and the two are not separable. Non-separability implies that there can be win-win situations where both efficiency and welfare can be jointly increased, or win-loss situations where gain in one is achieved at the cost of a loss in the other.

We consider here the potential welfare and associated efficiency effects of giving access to land to a landless household under fixed rent or fully mortgaged ownership. These advantages are as follows.

1. Access to land, when land is combined with variable inputs and with other assets, provides beneficiary households with a source of income. While not the only pathway out of poverty, ample evidence suggests that access to land is effective in helping rural households generate higher incomes. At the same time, access to land is neither the only strategy out of poverty, nor is it sufficient to guarantee escaping poverty. Hoddinott, Haddad, and Mukherjee (2000) review empirical studies for China, Chile, Ethiopia, Côte d'Ivoire, Kenya, India, the Philippines, Tanzania, and Zimbabwe that

evidence the positive role of access to land in household income. Income equa estimated for households in the Mexican *ejido* sector show that access to land makes a significant contribution to income (de Janvry and Sadoulet 1999). Lopez and Valdés (1997) similarly find that land plays an important role in determining the per capita income of farming households in El Salvador and Paraguay. The income effect of access to land via land reform programs has also been documented in studies for Taiwan, Zimbabwe, and the Philippines (Hoddinott, Haddad, and Mukherjee 2000). Tenancy reforms have also been important. Besley and Burgess (1998) find that 10% of the decline in the Indian poverty gap can be attributed to tenancy reforms and the abolition of intermediaries. Who in the household has access to land also affects welfare outcomes. Studies by Haddad, Hoddinott, and Alderman (1997) and by Quisumbing and Maluccio (1999) show that when access to land is controlled by women, child welfare in terms of nutrition, health, and education is improved. Agarwal (1994) shows how important control over land is in empowering women within the household, on the labor market, and in local political life.

Access to land is, however, not sufficient to secure higher household incomes. This is the case when the policy context is adverse to farm profits, competitiveness is undermined by a lack of supportive institutions, assets transferred are not valorized by complementary public goods (e.g., access roads), and investment is deterred by insecurity regarding the conditions for access. Beneficiary households may not have control over the necessary complementary assets. Access to land may thus not be the best pathway out of poverty for some households. For instance, educated landless household members may find greater rewards in off-farm non-agricultural employment and in migration. Households with capital endowments and easy access to markets may be better advised to invest in commerce rather than in farming. Households with insufficient complementary assets may be better off renting out their land to others who can use it more productively (see Sadoulet, Murgai, and de Janvry, Chapter 8).

A puzzle that has repeatedly been observed is that the income of small farmers tends to be inferior to that of landless households, suggesting that access to a small plot of land may not be effective for poverty reduction (Cornia 1985; Lopez and Valdés 1997). These households would expectedly be better off abandoning farming for the labor market. Possible explanations in defense of the role of land are that lower income is met by higher security, that food prices are lower for small farmers, and that data tend to underestimate home consumption. This puzzle clearly requires further research.

2. Access to land helps give value to assets held by a household with zero or low opportunity cost outside the land. These assets typically include captive family labor such as children, elders, women in reproductive phases of their life cycles, adults during weekends, and unemployables due to legal restrictions. They also include draft animals (there is moral hazard on the bullock market, preventing their rental to others), labor supervision capacity, and managerial skills. If the fixed set-up costs to enter farming can be incurred, access to land allows rents to generate on a household's otherwise idle or low productivity asset endowments that are complementary to land, and can thus

help a household escape poverty traps. In this case, for the household that obtains access, there are both social efficiency gains through mobilization of otherwise idle resources and individual welfare gains.

3. Access to land allows direct use of factors of production held by the household at a lower cost than for buyers of these factors. This is the case for family labor with an opportunity cost outside the farm. Adverse selection and moral hazards in hired labor (and hence the need to incur screening and supervision expenditures when hiring) are avoided since family labor is self-motivated by being the residual claimant on profits. Transaction costs on labor markets give a labor cost advantage to small holders using family labor. If farming is labor intensive, this creates an inverse relation between farm size and the reservation price of land on the land sales market. This inverse relation allows win-win effects of land redistribution: as land is shifted from large to small farms, access to land for landless households creates both efficiency and equity gains, offering the classical justification for redistributive land reform (Lipton 1993).

4. Access to sufficient land to avoid being a buyer of food provides cheap food when there are food market failures. The existence of large transaction costs on food markets makes food produced by self-sufficient households, and food retained for home consumption by net sellers, cheaper than food bought on the market. Hence, access to land creates welfare gains for the household via cheap food. In addition, since there is typically hidden information in the quality of food products transacted on informal markets (e.g., white corn in Mexico and rice in West Bengal), production for home consumption secures access to better quality food.

5. Access to land is a source of insurance against price shocks on the food and labor markets. Positive shocks to food prices create welfare losses for landless households as their real incomes fall. Consumers may insure themselves against food price risk by directly producing some of their needs (Finkelshtain and Chalfant 1991). These food-price, risk-management strategies are permitted by access to land, creating welfare gains for net buyers of food compared to landlessness. Risks of unemployment on the labor market are similarly mitigated by access to land that allows self-employment on the farm. Small holders who are net sellers of labor will work more on their own farm as a risk-management strategy if they perceive employment and wages as risky.

6. Access to land allows mobilization of farm-financed social welfare, creating social efficiency gains (Owen 1966). Land transfers to poor landless households in communities that practice mutual insurance are more efficient than income or food transfers since they allow these households to mobilize otherwise idle captive assets. Hence, communities are observed to engage in periodic redistribution of land according to need (China) and to make land grants to newcomers in the community (Sub-Saharan Africa). Household heads are similarly motivated in making *inter vivos* transfers to able family members who would otherwise be dependants.

7. Access to land serves as a component in an income strategy based on a portfolio of activities that include wage labor, self-employment in microenterprises, and migration. Complementarities between these activities and land arise when there are low correlations among sources of income so that farm earnings help insure non-farm revenues, when liquidity earnings obtained in one activity are used in another (e.g., remittance

incomes that relax liquidity constraints in farming, giving a high shadow value to off-farm earnings), and when there are learning effects across activities (e.g., farm worker experiences are transposed to the adoption of new practices on the home farm). Hence, access to even small amounts of land can prove to be extraordinarily valuable for pluri-active households and for female-headed households (Agarwal 1994). This materializes in very high reservation prices for land on small, pluriactive farms (Carter and Barham 1996). This suggests that land reform programs should not always aim at creating 'viable family farms' where farming is expected to be the only source of income for the household. When active labor markets and other sources of off-farm income exist, access to sub-family farms may be both socially efficient and effective to reduce rural poverty, and may be landless households' preferred options over full-scale family farms.

Household-specific asset endowments, idiosyncratic market failures, and specific institutional and policy contexts imply a particular schedule of reservation prices for land associated with farm size and other asset endowments (see Carter and Salgado, Chapter 10). To start with, land is not optimally allocated across households in terms of this schedule. Second, this schedule is constantly changing as households travel through their life cycles, are exposed to random shocks, and are faced with new opportunities both on farm (e.g., technological change) and off farm (e.g., higher wages on the labor market, new migration opportunities). For this reason, access to land that is flexible and with low transaction costs is essential to allow maximum efficiency in land use.

We conclude that both welfare and efficiency gains can be achieved if flexible and low-cost channels of access to land exist and are usable by the rural poor. There exists a wide array of paths through which access to land can be secured, opening possibilities for a wide array of policy interventions. The following access paths are explored in this book.

1. Intra-family transfers
   - Inter-generational transfers: inheritance (Chapter 2)
   - *Inter vivos* transfers: land gifts, anticipated inheritance (Chapter 2)
   - Intra-household allocation of land plots to women (Chapter 3)
2. Intra-community access
   - Membership in communities endowed in common property resources (Chapters 5 and 6)
   - Devolution from state to community control (Chapter 7)
   - The transition from community to land markets (Chapter 4)
3. Land markets
   - Land sales markets (Chapter 10)
   - Land rental markets (Chapters 8 and 9)
4. Land reform
   - Parcelization and titling in Latin America (Chapters 11 and 12)
   - Decollectivization: Eastern and Central Europe (Chapters 14, 15, and 16)
   - Land market-assisted land reform (Chapter 13)
   - Land policy reforms as pursued by the World Bank (Chapter 17).

This chapter reviews the issues involved in securing access to land for the rural poor through these different paths and at the same time serves as a summary and conclusion for the book.

Intra-family transfers

Inheritance and inter vivos transfers

Access to land via intra-family transfers is of fundamental importance, particularly when land markets are poorly developed. Indeed, it is likely the case that, where land frontiers are closed and large-scale redistributive land reform programs are not feasible, most farmers access land through intra-family transfers. These transfers can be *inter vivos*, for instance grants of land to sons when they get married, or *post mortem*. The questions here are: (1) who gains access to land, and who is marginalized, and hence what are the poverty and equity implications of these transfers; and (2) under what terms and conditions is the land received, and hence whether or not it will be possible for the new users to cultivate the land efficiently.

In a broad historical survey, Platteau and Baland (Chapter 2) observe that there is a universal tendency for transfers from parents to children to be done on an egalitarian basis, at least among sons. Unequal *inter vivos* transfers, for instance to older sons, tend to be compensated through subsequent unequal transfers at the time of inheritance; or land transfers to some tend to be compensated through transfers of other assets or through educational expenditures. This egalitarian vision is, however, far from universal and suffers many exceptions, either because it is in the best interest of the household as a unit of survival not to divide the land; because there are attempts by landlords, the community, or the state to restrict division; or because there are exclusionary processes at work within the family under acute land pressure which result in lesser benefits for some or outright marginalization of weaker members.

Even if there are constant returns to scale in farm production, ownership of a large estate may be a source of external gains, creating a logic not to divide land through inheritance. Thus, under a de-centralized feudal system where social and political functions are tied to ownership of a land estate, there are powerful incentives to follow the rule of primogeniture not to dissipate the benefits of these functions. Among non-aristocratic classes, there sometimes exist external constraints to division. They can be imposed by landlords who prohibit peasants from transmitting the land to more than one descendant in order to make tax collection easier. The community itself may restrict transmission to more than one heir of rights of access to common property resources (e.g., the *ejido* in Mexico) to contain over-extraction. In other situations, there exist internal advantages to preserving a large unit that implies limiting inheritance to unigeniture. This happens when there are economies of scale. In this case, heirs are better off dividing the proceeds of the farm than dividing the farm itself. When patriarchy is an important source of cohesion of a family clan, land may be transmitted to only one son to ensure reproduction of this status. Finally, there are situations of extreme population pressure on the land (e.g., in Rwanda) where the farm has already reached a minimum size to sustain a household. If the household has other assets, those who do not inherit the land can be compensated, for instance through education. When there are no other assets, serious conflicts are bound to occur and the result is highly inequitable by default. Categories that tend to be excluded from access to land are the weaker household members: girls in general, divorced women who must return to their father's family pending remarriage, illegitimate children, orphans, return migrants, and women who were married without bride price and are prevented by brothers from being given land when they return, since their marriage did not generate benefits for the household.

In Sub-Saharan Africa, as land markets tend to develop with the individualization of property rights, access to land via inheritance is also altered. Land that has been acquired through the market, instead of being inherited through lineage relationships, is not subjected to traditional inheritance rules. This new freedom is a source of discretion in transmitting land that can be used to exclude some and favor others. Fathers can transmit freely, including to daughters if they choose to do so, and sons who want to set up their own households cannot pressure them to distribute land early (as they can with lineage land). If land is very scarce, intra-household conflicts may be enhanced. Fathers can resist demands for land by sons at the time of marriage; and older sons can resist demands by younger brothers for adjustment in *pre mortem* land distribution.

In general, it is fair to say that not enough is known about what determines access to land through *inter vivos* and inter-generational transfers. Within the household, land gifts are not uncommon, would it only be to mobilize the labor of landless members instead of having to share food with them post-harvest. Inheritance laws, particularly for land, are frequently discriminatory against women, particularly land acquired via land reform programs, although significant gains have recently been made in reducing this bias (Deere and León 1997). Much more attention needs to be given to facilitating equitable land transfers. When the land cannot be divided, access to mortgage credit is needed to help the one who inherited the land compensate other siblings to avoid decapitalization of the farm. Decentralization of economic activity, by providing off-farm sources of income, allows further subdivision of the land and avoids intra-household conflicts and the pressure to exclude siblings. Indeed, off-farm sources of income have been shown to be extraordinarily important for the landed poor throughout the world (Reardon *et al.* 1998). In this case, access to even a small plot of land via inheritance can be a significant contribution to reproduction of the household unit and to food security in a context of profitable but risky off-farm activities.

Allocation of land to women in Africa

Use of separate plots by different family members is an anomaly that characterizes much of Sub-Saharan Africa compared to the rest of the world (Fafchamps, Chapter 3). In this case, the household jointly cultivates family plots under the authority of the man, and women (plural if there is polygamy) additionally cultivate separate plots. Food produced on the family plots is used to feed the family. Income from the food surplus sold and from cash crops produced on the family plots is under the jurisdiction of the man. This income is used to cover the household's major expenses and investment expenditures, as well as the man's needs. Women have control over the product obtained from their own plots. They use it to improve the family diet and to cover the costs of their own needs. Why are there separate plots? This is an interesting puzzle since this separation is not observed in the rest of the world, even where there is polygamy as in Bangladesh and other Muslim countries. In addition, recent observations (Udry 1996) indicate that resources such as fertilizer are inefficiently allocated between the family and women plots, suggesting cooperation failure. While this inefficiency is small, it signals that the household's objective achieved via separate plots does have an opportunity cost in terms of efficiency. Why is allocation eventually inefficient? To a large extent this remains unexplained. The following are potential logical explanations.

If there are diseconomies of scale or if specialization among family members is by activities (crops), then separate plots are possible from an efficiency standpoint. In this case, women can have separate access to land in addition to the family plots. A better explanation is that land is allocated to women because of commitment failures in sharing the rewards from effort on the family plots beyond basic food that is consumed jointly. In this case, enforceable contracts are impossible. To mobilize the effort of women, land is allocated directly to them and inefficiencies may follow if fertilizer is allocated in priority to the family plots to cater to family food security, or because the man has greater bargaining power in achieving his own needs beyond food.

Why are there commitment failures in the African household more than anywhere else? After all, the household is a long-term institution, and commitment should simply derive from the repeated nature of the distribution of rewards from effort on the family plots. A possible source of commitment failure not discussed by Fafchamps (Chapter 3) that is typically African is the pressure to share that is exercised on the household head by the extended family and clan members. If the man cannot commit that he will be able to resist pressures so that sharing is not at the cost of the woman's return to effort, he cannot enforce a contract to reward her efforts on the family plots. Hence, the separation of plots is needed to mobilize her effort for any output beyond basic food necessities, which are the only product that cannot be extracted by others through redistributive demands.

Another possible explanation when there is polygamy is that distributive struggles among women beyond basic food (which is insured by production on the family plots that is collectively worked) would be impossible to resolve by the man. Hence, even at the cost of some inefficiency in the allocation of resources across plots, land is allocated to women for them to generate directly the income needed to satisfy their own needs beyond basic food. Clearly, both the reasons women cultivate separate plots and the eventual efficiency costs that this separation implies are in need of further research.

Access to land via community membership

Management of common property resources

Access to land via membership in communities that have control over resources remains very important, most particularly lands for grazing and forestry. If user rights are so incomplete that the community cannot exclude others from encroaching on the land, the open access nature of the resource leads to the well-known tragedy of the commons, with under-provision of services (e.g., for maintenance of irrigation canals) and over-appropriation of resources (e.g., an excessive number of animals per hectare in herding and over-logging in forestry) leading to exhaustion of the resource. We do not consider this case since nothing can be done to protect the resource until either entry is limited, making it a common property resource, or access is individualized (Ostrom, Chapter 5).

When entry is limited to a well-defined set of users over a well-delineated set of resources through formal or informal community titling, rational management becomes possible if cooperation among community members can be achieved. CPR are non-excludable for community members and rivals in use (i.e., the forage or the trees disappear with appropriation by one member). Community management of natural resources has assumed renewed importance in the last decade. Following structural adjustment, the reduced capacity of the state to directly manage resources (most particularly forests and irrigation systems) has led to widespread devolution of control to local communities, often in co-management arrangements with the state (Arnold, Chapter 7). The impact of devolution on efficiency, welfare, and sustainability in resource use depends on the ability of the community to cooperate, the managerial capacity of the state agency, and coordination between the two.

Access to land through itinerant farming (slash-and-burn, swidden) on community land also responds to CPR logic (Lopez 1998). While the product of cleared plots is individually appropriated, soil fertility is a common property resource. Hence, unless the community is able to cooperate in setting rules for the amount of land to be opened to cultivation (which reduces fallow land and the reconstitution of soil fertility) and the management of soil fertility in plots under use, the individual incentive is to deplete soil fertility.

There are well-defined potential advantages to maintaining resources under common property rather than individualizing access. They include efficiency and equity reasons. Efficiency gains derive from potential economies of scale and indivisibilities (e.g., water holes for animals), possibility of internalizing externalities over a larger geographical unit (e.g., watershed with joint upstream and downstream interests for soil erosion), geographical risk spreading (when there is high variance of yields on any one parcel and low correlation of yields across parcels, see Nugent and Sanchez 1998), high cost of dividing the resource, and high cost of enforcing individual property rights. Equity reasons derive from greater access to resources for the poor than in private regimes, flexible reallocations according to life cycle and outside opportunities, the risk that individualization could have strong negative equity effects if there is uncontrolled appropriation, and preservation of community relations that have other benefits such as mutual insurance, information sharing, and political representation.

The risks of holding resources under CPR are, however, well known: they tend to induce defection on provision and appropriation as the dominant strategy in prisoner's dilemma-type behavior, and they can lead to inefficient levels of cooperation if cooperation is costly, or if cooperation is achieved only in a subcoalition of cooperators while the rest of the community members free-ride on cooperators. Failure to cooperate at the optimum level has both static efficiency (rent dissipation) and dynamic efficiency (resource depletion) costs.

This consequently raises the very important issue of identifying the determinants of cooperation leading to rational and efficient CPR management (Ostrom, Chapter 5; Arnold, Chapter 7). Successful community cooperation is indeed demanding as it requires the following four achievements: (1) a positive individual present value of expected gains from cooperation (participation constraint); (2) observability of the others' actions and third party verifiability (monitoring); (3) ability to enforce (punish in case of default); and (4) time to learn to cooperate. Whether these conditions hold depends on a complex coincidence of characteristics of the resource, the community, and the institutional and macroeconomic framework explored by Ostrom and Arnold (see also Baland and Platteau 1996).

Success stories in cooperation show that resource management under this form of tenure can indeed be efficient, sustainable, and equitable. These successes have been used by advocates of CPR forms of tenure to argue for community titling as opposed to individualization of access to land since it allows the advantages of CPR to be preserved (Ostrom 1990; Platteau 1992). At the same time, this potential of CPR remains largely unrealized, with many communities failing to cooperate. This is particularly serious when there is extensive devolution of CPR management to communities in the context of structural adjustment and descaling of the role of state agencies, leading to uneven outcomes (Arnold, Chapter 7). With forest departments in Africa typically underfunded and ineffective in protecting illegal encroachment, turning over the management of forest resources to local communities, and assisting them in performing this task efficiently is high on the policy agenda (see Uganda case study by Gombya-Ssembajjwe, Banana, and Bahati, Chapter 6). Evident is that insufficient attention has all too often been given to assisting communities to acquire a clearer idea of the potential gains from cooperation (often, villagers know a lot of relevant things for cooperative management, yet are unable to articulate these facts into a genuine body of knowledge), and to learn to cooperate, frustrating the purposes of devolution. Traditional administrative structures (Ministries of Agriculture, Forest Services) are typically unequipped to perform these tasks. This leaves an important unattended area of opportunities to improve the efficiency of accessing land in CPR where identification and promotion of best practices could have huge payoffs.

From community to market: access to land in emerging land markets

Under increasing population pressure, a more mobile population, and growing market integration, access to land via family lineage and community membership tends to give way to individualization of property rights, and to access to land via land sales and land rental markets. Otsuka and Quisumbing (Chapter 4) analyze this transformation in forest frontier areas in Ghana and Sumatra. They find that, even though property rights are informal, active land rental and land sales markets can exist. This finding confirms observations made by Katz (2000) in Guatemala and the

Procuradoria Agraria (1998) in Mexico where communities with high endowments in social capital can sustain active land markets without formal titling by contrast to communities of recent colonists: social capital is sufficient to deter moral hazards in land transactions.

In addition, land sales markets operating in traditional settings need not be regressive. In Ghana, Otsuka and Quisumbing (Chapter 4) find that land purchased serves to compensate for low levels of land received through lineage or community transfers, or carved from the forest when frontiers increasingly close. Hence, population pressure stimulates the emergence of land sales markets, and these markets can serve as equalizers of access to land. This finding is confirmed by Baland *et al.* (1999) in a study of the land market in Uganda: poorer sons with less inherited land from their fathers succeeded in partly compensating their initial disadvantage by purchasing land on the market. This progressive role of land markets is, however, far from general: in Sumatra, Otsuka and Quisumbing (Chapter 4) found that those who own more paddy land can purchase more land for agroforestry. In Rwanda, André and Platteau (1998) observed that operation of the (illegal) land market has led to increasingly unequal land distribution and rapid dispossession of many household members. As we shall see below, land sales markets in Latin America also tend to perform regressively (Carter and Salgado, Chapter 10). Hence, the conditions that make land sales markets act progressively or regressively remain very much in need of further research. Care must be taken to control for selectivity biases in observing a presumed progressive effect of land markets since households who failed to gain access to land, under conditions where local labor markets and off-farm sources of income are weak, are simply no longer there to be observed.

The other very important result from these studies of emerging land markets, in a context of strong community relations, is that intensification of land use can occur without formal property rights. Trees are planted in land accessed through informal family and community mechanisms as a way of strengthening individual property rights (see also Sjaastad and Bromley 1997). Yields are unaffected by tenure: traditional rights give enough security that trees are equally productive (cocoa in Ghana and cinnamon in Sumatra) as those planted on lands with strongly individualized rights. Brasselle, Gaspart, and Platteau (1998) similarly found that the traditional village order in Burkina Faso provides enough security of access to land to stimulate small-scale investment. These results are important because they challenge the traditional wisdom according to which land titling programs are necessary to enhance investments in agriculture because they offer security of continued access to land and collateral to qualify for formal credit. In many situations, titling may increase transaction costs in the circulation of land, create new sources of conflicts if formal land rights are assigned without due recognition for the customary arrangements that previously codified rules of access to land (e.g., in Honduras, see Jansen and Roquas 1998), and not add anything to efficiency in resource use. In Cotopaxi, in the Ecuadorian Sierra, a program of land registration and individual titling (CATIR) did not help improve the security of access to land relative to traditional guarantees offered by the community. As a result, titling per se did not improve land use, nor did it help reduce poverty (World Bank-FAO

1999). Complementary programs to remove market failures in credit and to increase access to technical assistance would have been needed. In Cameroon, the 1974 Land Ordinance that introduced formal private titles similarly did not improve security of access to land, and introduced new conflicts in situations where multiple actors have rights over a single parcel of land (Firmin-Sellers and Sellers 1999). Lessons from these experiences indicate that titling programs may be premature (due to lack of complementary markets), detrimental if improperly administered, and unnecessary if customary law is sufficient to secure rights and ratify transactions. When conditions are ripe for individual titling, effective programs should seek active involvement of the community for local conflict resolution prior to titling (as was done in the Mexican *ejido*), be accompanied by programs to remove failures on the other markets that determine the competitiveness of beneficiaries, and provide access to cheap and reliable conflict resolution mechanisms.

Land sales and land rental markets

In a first-best world, land sales and land rental markets should be equally effective in providing access to land to the rural poor. However, in a second-best world of market failures and institutional gaps, land sales markets are quite ineffective for this purpose. And, even if access to land in ownership is achieved, the continued existence of market failures and institutional gaps jeopardize the competitiveness of beneficiaries, compromising their survival. Land rental markets, by contrast, can be friendlier to the poor. And access to land via idiosyncratic contracts allows mitigation of many market failures and institutional gaps, making competitiveness and survival more likely. Via land rental, poor households can eventually progress toward the desirable goal of land ownership. Hence, the land rental market can offer a step toward entry into the land sales market as income generated through rental is gradually capitalized into land ownership.

Land sales markets

There are powerful reasons why formal land sales markets are not 'level playing fields' (Carter and Barham 1996) for the rural poor, with the result that they have a hard time using these markets to access land, and the dynamics of these markets tend to play regressively on small holders (Carter and Salgado, Chapter 10). The main reasons that explain these outcomes are:

1. For all buyers, land is overpriced for agricultural use because its ownership generates side benefits due to failures in other markets (Binswanger, Deininger, and Feder 1995). Hence, even a loan against the full present value of agricultural profits (which represents ability to pay the loan) would be insufficient to buy land, since the land price exceeds this amount for the following reasons: (1) land serves as a store of wealth against inflation; (2) land serves as a source of self-employment if there are labor market failures, and a source of food security if there are food market failures; (3) land serves as collateral for credit; (4) land serves as a source of insurance

as it can be sold, rented out, or pawned for liquidity; (5) land has speculative value as urban demand rises; (6) land serves to access credit subsidies; (7) land offers tax breaks; and (8) land provides political and social capital.

2. Land is even more overpriced for poor, small buyers since many of these side benefits of land ownership apply to large but not to smallholders.
3. Long-term mortgage loans to buy land are generally not available to the rural poor.
4. If long-term credit is available using the land as collateral, fully mortgaged land does not allow access to further loans for working capital. Hence, poor buyers with no additional resources cannot be competitive, unless they achieve competitiveness by reducing consumption.
5. Land sales markets are segmented by farm size due to the overpricing of land for small holders (as above) and higher transaction costs for downside sales. As a result, large farmers tend to sell to large farmers, smallholders tend to sell to large farmers under distress conditions, and buyers of small farms cannot acquire land from large sellers.
6. High transaction costs on land sales markets imply low participation. Transaction costs originate in bureaucratic hurdles, imperfect information, and costly and inaccurate registration of land transfers. Households are also reluctant to part with their land in conditions of risky labor markets and uncertain prospects for the future, especially the future lot of their children. As a result, land sales markets tend to be thin and sluggish.
7. There is a high positive correlation between agricultural profits and land prices. As a result, random shocks in agricultural profits widen price bands on land sales markets: land prices fall for a particular household precisely when it would like to sell land, and they rise when it would like to buy. The result is to extend the range of non-participation to land sales markets by small holders, except for distress sales.

Land rental markets: fixed and share rent contracts

Land rental markets tend to be friendlier to the rural poor than land sales markets in allowing them access to land for the following reasons.

1. There are lower transaction costs in land rental than in land sales markets. Hence, land rentals allow: (1) flexibility to adjust farm size to shocks and to life cycle stages; and (2) regaining access to the same plot of land for subsequent use by the current owner, with obvious locational advantages.
2. Idiosyncratic rental contracts can be designed to mitigate the market failures to which the poor are exposed.

Empirical support for the greater friendliness of the land rental market for the rural poor, in contexts where formal land markets are well developed, is provided by Carter and Salgado (Chapter 10) with data from Chile, Honduras, and Paraguay. They find that the market failures and institutional gaps (particularly for access to credit and insurance) that affect smallholders are more detrimental to their participation in the land sales market than in the land rental market. In the cases they analyzed, land rental markets have helped land-scarce households gain access to land.

Fixed rent tenancy gives full incentives to the tenant, but high risks and liquidity constraints reduce demand for the contract while the risk of asset mismanagement (Hayami and Otsuka 1993) reduces its supply, limiting access to land under this form of tenancy for the rural poor. Share rent has the disadvantage of creating a Marshallian disincentive for the inputs that are fully provided by either the tenant or the landlord, while the product is shared. This disadvantage can, however, be compensated by the following (qualified) advantages (Sadoulet, Murgai, and de Janvry, Chapter 8):

1. Share tenancy allows liquidity saving compared to fixed rent since payment of rent is postponed until after harvest, and purchased input costs are shared with the landlord.
2. Share tenancy offers risk reduction. In determining optimum share for the tenant, the landlord faces a trade-off between the negative effects of the Marshallian disincentive on effort (resulting from a lower share) and the positive insurance effect on effort (also resulting from a lower share).
3. Share tenancy can overcome market failures for non-tradable inputs that can be provided by either the landlord or the tenant according to their comparative advantages (Eswaran and Kotwal 1985), in spite of Marshallian disincentives implied by exclusive provision. Examples include: (1) provision of management skills and/or market information by the landlord in which he is more efficient than the tenant; (2) provision of supervision skills, captive family labor, and draft animals by the tenant in which he is more efficient or better endowed than the landlord.
4. Share tenancy allows interlinking land rental with other transactions. The land rental contract can bundle other arrangements that help the tenant to overcome market failures and institutional gaps to which he is subjected. This is made possible because the contract allows enforcement (if the tenant defaults on any component of the multiple contract, he loses the advantage of all the other components of the contract) and low transaction costs in monitoring.
5. The Marshallian inefficiency of sharecropping has never been observed to be very large. Shaban (1987) estimates a 16% difference in yields; Hayami and Otsuka (1993) find, on average across a large number of studies, a 17% difference in gross output. In addition, there exists a whole array of conditions under which the Marshallian inefficiency can be made to disappear, for instance via close monitoring of the tenant's effort, long-term contracts, interlinked transactions, and social norms on effort.
6. Share tenancy can be the entry point in accessing land, leading toward land ownership through an 'agricultural ladder.' Sharecropping allows capitalization of rent accrued to the tenant's non-tradable assets which are given value by access to land. It also allows the accumulation of managerial experience. This can help the tenant shift to better contracts and capitalize savings in land purchases following the sequence: farm worker, sharecropper, fixed rent tenant, owner-tenant, and landowner.

Share contracts can thus be effective in providing access to land for the rural poor. The contract can be designed to mitigate idiosyncratic market failures for credit, insurance, and non-tradable inputs that plague poor rural households, even if they would receive land in ownership through 'incomplete' redistributive or land market-assisted land reforms. Sharecropping has, however, been denounced as detrimental to long-term maintenance of the assets (although less so than fixed rent contracts) as well as a contract that gives too much power to the landlord to exploit the tenant (Bardhan 1984). This can be mitigated by proper design of the contract and altered norms of negotiation. Incentives to invest in land improvements and to use resources sustainably can be provided by full contracts with termination clauses and a minimum level of tenure security. The terms of the contract can be made more favorable for the tenant by raising his bargaining power in negotiating with landlords, and by defining menus of standard contracts from which the two parties can choose. And sharecropping can be an effective entry point toward better contracts and land ownership. However, as agriculture becomes more capital and management intensive, landlords prefer to select tenants from among the non-poor, reducing the promise of vertical mobility offered by sharecropping.

Land rental markets, both fixed rent and share rent, are extraordinarily active in the more developed countries (Swinnen 1998) and in parts of the developing world such as the Indian subcontinent. In general, however, these markets have been suppressed by land reform legislation that has weakened property rights and given occupancy rights to tenants. In a few rare cases such as West Bengal, massive interventions have improved sharecroppers' rights (U. Saha and M. Saha, Chapter 9). In much of the rest of the world, and Latin America, Africa, and the Philippines most of all, restoring the dynamics of land rental markets to help poor rural households gain access to land remains an unfulfilled promise.

The ultimate advantages of access to land in individual ownership

Use of the land under the status of owner-operator is by far the most heralded form of property rights in agriculture (Deininger and Binswanger, Chapter 17). The advantages of land ownership over other forms of property rights are the following:

1. For rural households, land is an effective instrument to accumulate wealth and to transfer wealth to the next generation.
2. Land ownership serves as collateral for access to credit if formal credit exists. Even in accessing credit through informal financial institutions, land ownership may be important: in Rwanda, the landless are systematically excluded from local rotating savings clubs (André and Platteau 1998).
3. Land ownership (in a portfolio of assets) is a source of self-insurance and old-age social security: land can be sold, rented out, or pawned for consumption smoothing in response to shocks and life cycle stages.
4. Land ownership is a source of security in continued access to the same plot of land, offering the possibility of capitalizing in long-term investments, and a source of local social capital.
5. Land ownership is a source of social status and bargaining power.

Short of inheritance, *inter vivos* transfers, enclosures of community lands, and direct appropriation of frontier land, we have seen that access to land in ownership can be achieved through purchase on the land market. It can also be obtained through government interventions in redistributive land reform programs, such as parcelization and titling of land reform cooperatives and state farms in Latin America (de Janvry, Sadoulet, and Wolford, Chapter 11), and through decollectivization and individualization of tenures in Eastern and Central Europe (Swinnen, Chapter 14), both of which are one-time historical events. In a sustained fashion, access to land in ownership for the rural poor can be achieved through programs of land market-assisted land reform (Deininger, Chapter 13).

Parcelization and titling in Latin America

In Latin America, access to land in ownership through state-managed redistributive land reforms occurred in two phases. In a first phase, land was expropriated on the basis of maximum farm size or minimum land-use standards, and organized in reform sectors, usually as production cooperatives or as individual farms in usufruct with centralized management of relations with the outside world (*ejidos* and *asentamientos*). In a second phase, land was parcelized (cooperatives) and titled (*ejidos* and *asentamientos*), creating in countries such as Chile, Mexico, Peru, Honduras, El Salvador, and Nicaragua large numbers of independent, small owner-operators. Subsequently, these smallholders were either largely bankrupted (such as in Chile due to unfavorable market conditions, a high agrarian debt, inability to enter the booming fruits sector due to credit market failures, and high demand for land by commercial farmers and new entrants into agriculture), became semi-proletarians with an agriculture oriented toward home consumption (as in Peru, following what Carter and Alvarez (1989) called 'disorganized decollectivization'), or became competitive capitalized smallholders (some beneficiaries in Chile and Mexico). However, few of the small owner-operators that emerged from sixty years of land reform in Latin America became viable entrepreneurs. The main tasks left to complete are: (1) to secure the competitiveness of remaining beneficiaries through rural development interventions in a context of liberalized commodity and land markets; and (2) to develop new ways of providing access to land for the remaining landless and minifundists in a context where state-managed redistributive land reforms are no longer politically feasible. Only in a few countries such as Brazil is land reform still in progress with grassroots initiatives (the Landless Movement, MST) pressing for government intervention to ratify expropriation of under-used lands following invasions by potential beneficiaries. This process has induced violence as a way of securing support of the federal government over the power of local courts (Wolford, Chapter 12).

Decollectivization in Central and Eastern Europe

Decollectivization in Central and Eastern Europe opened different paths of access to land in ownership in different countries (Swinnen, Chapter 14). Collective farm lands, that were in general still legally owned by pre-collectivization owners, were either restituted (Central Europe, Baltic countries), distributed to workers in ownership shares

(Ukraine, Russia), or physically distributed in individual farms (Albania). State farm lands, which had been legally expropriated from previous owners, were sold in the Czech Republic, East Germany, Hungary, Poland, and Slovakia. Individualization of land tenure was the highest in Albania, Armenia, the Baltic countries, and Romania. In general, individualization was higher where collective farm productivity was the lowest and where the share of agriculture in total employment was the highest. In Albania, land was distributed as individual family farms that were allocated to former workers of collectives and state farms (Cungu and Swinnen, Chapter 15). In this case, there were no restitutions because there was no possible return to the feudal structure that preceded collectivization, land had been fully expropriated in the transition to socialism, the labor-intensive nature of farming made large farms highly inefficient, and lack of off-farm employment options made it politically necessary to absorb labor in agriculture. In the short run, the incentive effect of residual claimancy by family workers created strong output gains. However, land fragmentation and highly imperfect capital markets now threaten the sustainability of these gains.

Decollectivization in the Czech Republic was the polar opposite (Doucha, Mathijs, and Swinnen, Chapter 16). Most of the land was restituted to former owners and only 24% of the land ended up in private farms. The rest was held in large-scale organizations under the form of joint stock companies and cooperatives. In these farms, 95% of the land is rented from former owners to whom land was restituted. Making the choice of large-scale organizations was due to the capital intensity of farming, high start-up costs with missing capital markets, and high exit costs for individuals to pull land and other farm capital out of the large farms that succeeded the collectives.

With redefinition of property rights well advanced, the important next steps for these reforms to be successful are: (1) to consolidate the competitiveness of those who obtained access to land via reconstruction of a set of institutions that can service them, particularly for credit, insurance, technical assistance, and low transaction costs access to product and factor markets; and (2) to get land markets to work so land can be reallocated, from the way it was assigned by the reforms, to the most efficient users and consolidated in optimum farm sizes.

Land market-assisted land reform

With the declining political feasibility of state-led expropriative land reforms and the consolidation of property rights, the logical approach to maintaining open access to land for the rural poor is to seek doing this via the land sales market. Since the market, left to itself, is as we have seen generally hostile to the poor once land becomes scarce and property rights formalized, the state can devise a set of interventions to alter market performance in favor of the rural poor. This is the land market-assisted land reform approach that has been sponsored by the World Bank in Colombia, Brazil, and South Africa (Deininger, Chapter 13).

Following this approach, land transactions occur between a willing large seller and a number of small buyers assisted by the local government and the community. We have seen that the land market fails the poor because there are a number of benefits to ownership that are internalized in the price of the land, and a number of costs involved in the transaction, that even a fully mortgaged transfer will not cover. Since the poor have no accumulated savings to cover these costs, a subsidy is needed. This subsidy must cover the overpricing of the land relative to its productive value, plus the set-up costs and the working capital costs for the first year, minus the liquidity that the household can generate with labor supplied on the labor market. The subsidy can be costly. It has been set equal to 70% of the land price in Colombia. In Brazil, the allotment per household is a US $11,000 lump-sum transfer, where the cost of land is a loan and the rest a pure cash transfer. The advantage of a set transfer is that it creates incentives to acquire low-priced, under-used land, and to save the rest of the transfer to invest in improving the land. However, little land has yet been acquired through this mechanism compared to capture under organized grassroots pressures (Wolford, Chapter 12).

The innovative component of the land market-assisted approach is the heavy involvement of the local government and the community in organizing the transfer and assisting the beneficiaries. In Colombia, the municipality must develop a comprehensive and well-publicized land reform plan to identify potential sellers of land and potential candidates for acquiring land, leading to an expected match between the two. This information on potential sellers and potential beneficiaries is broadly circulated in the community to avoid corruption and favoritism. Potential beneficiaries are offered training in farm management and assistance in developing land use plans. These plans serve the important functions of helping to select candidates, train beneficiaries, and establish the land price on an objective basis. Land use plans must be approved in public meetings of the municipal council. This allows the screening of candidates on the basis of potential competitiveness, as opposed to the rent seeking and political motives that typically dictated selection of beneficiaries under state-led land reforms. The municipality participates actively in negotiating a just price for acquisition of the land. Rural development assistance is provided in an attempt to mitigate the market failures to which beneficiaries are exposed and to develop institutional support to secure the competitiveness of beneficiaries. The private sector is actively involved in implementation. Technical assistance is provided by private service firms and is paid for with vouchers that are part of the subsidy. The commercial bank, which made the loan to purchase the land, supervises land use by beneficiaries and provides technical assistance to avoid defaults. While expensive, and hence likely of restricted applicability, the approach is highly innovative and worth monitoring carefully in order to extract lessons from the on-going experiments and to adjust the design of best practices for application in other contexts.

Policy framework to make land sales and rental markets work

We have seen that, under conditions of relative land abundance, and/or in communities with strong social capital that helps establish a working informal order based on community trust-enforcement mechanisms (e.g., in Rwanda where land is scarce), land markets can work efficiently and be progressive without formal definition of property rights and without formal registration of transfers. When these conditions do not hold, formalizing the legal definition of property rights and introducing the modern institutions necessary to make land markets work both efficiently and equitably become essential. Deininger and Binswanger (Chapter 17) identify necessary measures for this purpose.

1. Provide well-defined, transparent, and secure land rights through land registration, land titling (individual or communal), the continuing updating of locally accessible records, and low-cost legal enforcement of property rights. Increasing the security of land titles has the potential of raising the value of the land (and hence wealth, the collateral value of land, etc.); decreasing risks in sales and contracts; reducing costly investments in protection and reducing the cost of disputes; and decreasing inefficient use of the land due to under-use because of risk of loss and over-use (e.g., deforestation in frontier areas) to show ownership.
2. Introduce a progressive land tax to eliminate rents deriving from non-agricultural benefits of land ownership that differentially accrue to large farmers. With decentralization, municipalities have direct interest in enforcing land taxation since real estate taxes are their major source of autonomous revenues, creating a new political economy for land taxes that have historically met with fierce opposition from landed elites.

Specifically for land sales markets:

3. Decrease distortions and lower transaction costs on land markets: role of land banks to mediate acquisition of land in large farms by small holders; role of land market-assisted land reform programs to mediate relations between sellers and buyers.
4. Decrease other market failures: role of mitigating institutions for accessing credit, insurance, and factor and product markets. Otherwise, land markets can neither be efficient nor equitable (Carter and Salgado, Chapter 10).
5. Availability of long-term mortgage credit and subsidies. Even with full credit available, purchasing households need savings as fully mortgage-based land purchases leave no access to working capital loans. Hence, the poor with no savings are excluded —'fundamental financing problem of the poor' (Carter and Mesbah 1993). This is why an element of subsidy is needed in support of market-assisted land reforms.

Specifically for land rental markets (Sadoulet, Murgai, and de Janvry, Chapter 8):

6. Introduce low-cost, reliable, local, land conflict-resolution mechanisms.
7. Registration and enforcement of contracts. Set a legal lead time for the termination of contracts, and compensations for residual value of investments if terminated.
8. Definition of standard contracts to increase the bargaining power of tenants.
9. No direct interventions on rents (rent control) except briefly under emergency situations or under powerful and comprehensive programs of government intervention (U. Saha and M. Saha, Chapter 9).
10. Facilitate direct access to capital and management advice by the tenant to make as many inputs as possible jointly provisionable. This is particularly important to

avoid increasing exclusion of poor potential tenants as the capital and managerial intensity of agriculture rises.

Conclusions: an agenda for land policy reforms

Land reform was high on the development agenda in the 1950s (particularly in Asia and the Middle East, see Warriner 1969) and in the 1960–70s (particularly in Latin America, see Dorner 1992). It subsequently largely fell off the agenda, neither for lack of demand by the rural poor nor for lack of agreement on the importance of the issue among development scholars and practitioners, but due to the difficulty in managing the political economy of the reforms as conceptualized at the time (de Janvry and Sadoulet 1989). It may thus seem surprising that the issue of access to land has returned in full force in development debates in the 1990s, but this time as a more eclectic set of propositions and interventions that are still very much in the design phase. The World Bank, for instance (Deininger and Binswanger, Chapter 17), has extensively revised its philosophy in addressing land policy issues, and, through loans and advice, assisted in a set of experiments in formulating and implementing new approaches to favor access to land for the rural poor via subsidies on the land sales market. The FAO (Platteau 1992) has championed the potential of community titling as opposed to individual titles under a wide range of situations where communities have high levels of social capital and leadership. In Latin America, possibly under the pressure of a growing feminist movement (Deere and León 1997), many countries have been revising legislation codifying women's rights in land titling programs toward greater gender equity. The turning point in placing the issue of access to land back on the development agenda has been to seek implementation of continuous mechanisms of adjustment as opposed to one-time and generally dramatic historical events, to place greater reliance on traditional forms of access to land in potentially achieving efficiency and equity, to seek greater use of land markets properly regulated and assisted for the purpose of facilitating access to the poor, and to seek compatibility between land policy proposals and the forces of the political economy. This is opening a new era of land policy reforms that we are exploring in this book. The controversies on the subject reveal that we are still missing good theories of land policy reforms and solid empirical studies on many of the questions that are raised. This book is an attempt to highlight a non-exhaustive set of critical issues, to suggest ways of conceptualizing them to provide partial answers, and also to trigger more intellectual and experimental efforts in this field.

The chapters in this book show that there are many alternative roads of access to land, some totally informal and others rigidly formalized, some spontaneous and others relying on extensive government intervention. The efficiency and equity effects of each of these roads are idiosyncratic in context and in the types of rural households concerned. For instance, access to land in individual ownership is not the panacea that simplistic Western views all too often hold. There can exist advantages to access to land as common property resources according to the characteristics of the resource, the community, and the institutional and macro contexts. Access to land through rental contracts, share arrangements in particular, can be effective for the poor under conditions of extensive market and institutional failures. Informal land markets can be both efficient in reallocating land across users, and equitable in compensating for low endowments obtained by inheritance or community assignments, if land is sufficiently abundant and/or communities are endowed with enough social capital. An important message of the book is that we should be wary of simplistic and universal solutions, seeking instead idiosyncratic approaches and flexibility in arrangements.

The chapters also show that, to be effective, land policy reforms need to be embedded in comprehensive policy and institutional reforms, and to be complemented by effective rural development interventions in support of the competitiveness of beneficiaries. This is not a new result, since Doreen Warriner (1969) had arrived at the same conclusion in the 1960s with her concept of 'integral' land reform. What is new is the more thorough, if still highly incomplete, understanding that we have of the role of market failures and institutional gaps for the competitiveness of beneficiaries, and the experience with effective institutional design, for instance in microfinance, local governance, the determinants of cooperation, and the mobilization of social capital to remedy these deficiencies. Devolution of resources to community management can be effective if complemented by assistance to the capacity to cooperate and manage (Arnold, Chapter 7). Land reforms following decollectivization in Eastern and Central Europe need extensive institutional reconstruction to insure the international competitiveness of beneficiaries (Swinnen, Chapter 14). Yet, the book is an exercise in humility in identifying huge knowledge gaps in efficiently designing land policy reforms. We clearly need to know a lot more about inheritance and *inter vivos* transfer practices for both sons and daughters; about why land is sometimes allocated in separate plots to women and why this may have efficiency costs; under what conditions common property regimes can be efficient and devolution of control over these resources to communities can work; about when and why land sales markets can be efficient and equitable; about the types of land rental contracts that favor the poor; about the determinants of competitiveness of land reform beneficiaries; and about the political economy of the trade-offs that particular societies may be willing to accept in redefining access to land when win-win outcomes for efficiency and equity may not be achieved. The book is thus as much a set of answers as a set of questions for a rich agenda of research and experimentation on this important agrarian question.

REFERENCES

Agarwal, Bina. 1994. *A Field of One's Own: Gender and Land Rights in South Asia.* Cambridge: Cambridge University Press.

André, Catherine and Jean-Philippe Platteau. 1998. 'Land Relations Under Unbearable Stress: Rwanda Caught in the Malthusian Trap.' *Journal of Economic Behavior and Organization* 34(1): 1–47.

Baland, Jean-Marie and Jean-Philippe Platteau. 1996. *Halting Degradation of Natural Resources: Is There a Role for Rural Communities?* Oxford: Oxford University Press.

Baland, Jean-Marie, François Gaspart, Frank Place, and Jean-Philippe Platteau. 1999. 'Poverty, Tenure Security, and Access to Land in Central Uganda: The Role of Market and Non-Market Processes.' Working paper, Cahiers de Recherche du CRED, Faculty of Economics, University of Namur, Namur, Belgium.

Bardhan, Pranab. 1984. *Land, Labor, and Rural Poverty: Essays in Development Economics.* New York: Columbia University Press.

Bardhan, Pranab, Samuel Bowles, and Herbert Gintis. 1998. 'Wealth Inequality, Wealth Constraints, and Economic Performance.' Working Paper C98-097, Center for International and Development Economic Research, University of California, Berkeley, CA.

Besley, Timothy, and Robin Burgess. 1998. 'Land Reform, Poverty Reduction, and Growth: Evidence from India.' The Development Economics Discussion Paper Series No. 13, London School of Economics, London.

Binswanger, Hans, Klaus Deininger, and Gershon Feder. 1995. 'Power, Distortions, Revolt, and Reform in Agricultural Land Relations.' In *Handbook of Development Economics*, Volume 3B, J. Behrman and T.N. Srinivasan (eds.). Amsterdam: North-Holland.

Braselle, Anne-Sophie, Frédéric Gaspart, and Jean-Philippe Platteau. 1998. 'Land Tenure Security and Investment Incentives: Further Puzzling Evidence from Burkina Faso.' Working paper, Faculty of Economics, Social, and Management Sciences, University of Namur, Namur, Belgium.

Bromley, Daniel. 1989. *Economic Interests and Institutions: The Conceptual Foundations of Public Policy*. Oxford: Basil Blackwell.

Carter, Michael and Elena Alvarez. 1989. 'Changing Paths: The Decollectivization of Agrarian Reform Agriculture in Coastal Peru.' In *Searching for Agrarian Reform in Latin America*, William Thiesenhusen (ed.). Boston, MA: Unwin Hyman.

Carter, Michael and Brad Barham. 1996. 'Level Playing Fields and Laissez-Faire: Postliberal Development Strategy in Inegalitarian Agrarian Economies.' *World Development* 24(7): 1133–49.

Carter, Michael and D. Mesbah. 1993. 'Can Land Market Reform Mitigate the Exclusionary Aspects of Rapid Agro-Export Growth?' *World Development* 21(7): 1085–1100.

Cornia, Andrea. 1985. 'Farm Size, Land Yields, and the Agricultural Production Function: An Analysis for Fifteen Developing Countries.' *World Development* 13(4): 513–34.

de Janvry, Alain and Elisabeth Sadoulet. 1989. 'A Study in Resistance to Institutional Change: The Lost Game of Latin American Land Reform.' *World Development* 17(9): 1397–1409.

—— 1999. 'Asset Positions and Income Strategies Among Rural Households in Mexico: The Role of Off-farm Activities in Poverty Reduction.' Working paper, Department of Agricultural and Resource Economics, University of California, Berkeley, CA.

de Janvry, Alain, Gustavo Gordillo, and Elisabeth Sadoulet. 1997. *Mexico's Second Agrarian Reform: Household and Community Response, 1990–1994.* La Jolla, CA: University of California Center for US-Mexican Studies.

Deere, Carmen Diana and Magdalena León. 1997. 'Women and Land Rights in the Latin American Neo-Liberal Counter-Reforms.' Working Paper 264, Women in International Development, Michigan State University, East Lansing, MI.

Dorner, Peter. 1992. *Latin American Land Reforms in Theory and Practice: A Retrospective Analysis.* Madison, WI: The University of Wisconsin Press.

Eswaran, Mukesh and Ashok Kotwal. 1985. 'A Theory of Contractual Structure in Agriculture.' *American Economic Review* 75(1): 352–67.

Finkelshtain, Israel and James Chalfant. 1991. 'Marketed Surplus Under Risk: Do Peasants Agree With Sandmo?' *American Journal of Agricultural Economics* 73(3): 557–67.

Firmin-Sellers, Kathryn and Patrick Sellers. 1999. 'Expected Failures and Unexpected Successes of Land Titling in Africa.' *World Development* 27(7): 1115–28.

Haddad, Lawrence, John Hoddinott, and Harold Alderman. 1997. *Intra-Household Resource Allocation in Developing Countries: Models, Methods, and Policy*. Baltimore, MD: The Johns Hopkins University Press.

Hayami, Yujiro and Keijiro Otsuka. 1993. *The Economics of Contract Choice*. Oxford: Clarendon Press.

Hoddinott, John, Lawrence Haddad, and Sanjukta Mukherjee. 2000. 'Assets and Rural Poverty.' Working paper, International Food Policy Research Institute, Washington DC.

Jansen, Kees and Esther Roquas. 1998. 'Modernizing Insecurity: The Land Titling Project in Honduras.' *Development and Change* 29(1): 81–106.

Kanbur, Ravi and Nora Lustig. 1999. 'Why is Inequality Back on the Agenda?' In *Annual Conference on Development Economics 1999*. Washington DC: The World Bank.

Katz, Elizabeth. 2000. 'Social Capital and Natural Capital: A Comparative Analysis of Land Tenure and Natural Resource Management in Guatemala.' *Land Economics*, forthcoming.

Lipton, Michael. 1993. 'Land Reforms as Commenced Business: The Evidence Against Stopping.' *World Development* 21(4): 641–7.

Lopez, Ramón. 1998. 'The Tragedy of the Commons in Côte d'Ivoire Agriculture: Empirical Evidence and Implications for Evaluating Trade Policies.' *The World Bank Economic Review* 12(1): 105–31.

Lopez, Ramón and Alberto Valdés. 1997. *Rural Poverty in Latin America: Analytics, New Empirical Evidence, and Policy*. Washington DC: The World Bank.

Nugent, Jeffrey and Nicolas Sanchez. 1998. 'Common Property Rights as an Endogenous Response to Risk.' *American Journal of Agricultural Economics* 80(3): 651–7.

Ostrom, Elinor. 1990. *Governing the Commons: The Evolution of Institutions for Collective Action*. Cambridge: Cambridge University Press.

Owen, Wyn. 1966. 'The Double Developmental Squeeze on Agriculture.' *American Economic Review* 56(1/2): 43–70.

Platteau, Jean-Philippe. 1992. 'Land Reform and Structural Adjustment in Sub-Saharan Africa—Controversies and Guidelines.' Economic and Social Development Paper No. 107, Food and Agriculture Organization of the United Nations (FAO), Rome.

Procuradoria Agraria. 1998. *Los Tratos Agrarios en Ejidos Certificados*. Mexico City: Procuradoria Agraria.

Quisumbing, Agnes and J. Maluccio. 1999. 'Intra-Household Allocation and Gender Relations: New Empirical Evidence.' Working paper, International Food Policy Research Institute, Washington DC.

Reardon, Thomas, Kostas Stamoulis, A. M. Balisacan, Maria-Elena Cruz, Julio Berdegue, and B. Banks. 1998. 'Rural Nonfarm Income in Developing Countries.' In *The State of Food and Agriculture 1998*. Rome: FAO.

Shaban, Radwan A. 1987. 'Testing Between Competing Models of Sharecropping.' *Journal of Political Economy* 95(5): 893–920.

Sjaastad, E. and Daniel Bromley. 1997. 'Indigenous Land Rights in Sub-Saharan Africa: Appropriation, Security and Investment Demand.' *World Development* 25(4): 549–62.

Stiglitz, Joseph. 1998. 'Distribution, Efficiency, and Voice: Designing the Second Generation of Reforms.' Paper presented at the Conference on Asset Distribution, Poverty, and Economic Growth, sponsored by the Ministry of Land Reform, Brazil, and the World Bank, Brasília, Brazil, 14 July.

Swinnen, Johan. 1998. 'Land Leasing in Western Europe: A Historical Perspective.' Policy Research Working Group Paper, Katholieke Universiteit, Leuven, Belgium.

Udry, Christopher. 1996. 'Gender, Agricultural Production, and the Theory of the Household.' *Journal of Political Economy* 104(5): 1010–46.

Warriner, Doreen. 1969. *Land Reform in Principle and Practice.* Oxford: Clarendon Press.

World Bank-FAO. 1999. *Regularización Predial en Ecuador: Caso Cotopaxi.* Washington DC: The World Bank.

2

Impartible Inheritance Versus Equal Division: A Comparative Perspective Centered on Europe and Sub-Saharan Africa

JEAN-PHILIPPE PLATTEAU AND JEAN-MARIE BALAND

Introduction

Although not denied, the equity and insurance effects of various land tenure systems have been relatively neglected by economists—barring a few exceptions such as Michael Carter and a few others (see, e.g., Carter, Wiebe, and Blarel 1994)—but not by other social scientists. The same can be said of non-market mechanisms of land allocation that so far have been the almost exclusive province of lawyers and anthropologists (Bassett and Crummey 1993; Downs and Reyna 1988; Le Roy, Karsenty, and Bertrand 1996), except for some recent theoretical attempts by economists to understand the effects on wealth distribution of inheritance practices in general, and of primogeniture in particular (Blinder 1973; Menchik 1980; Tomes 1981; Bernheim, Shleifer, and Summers 1985; Cyrus Chu 1991). To the extent that traditional social protections are embodied in customary rules that do not use the market, the two questions, that of equity and that of non-market mechanisms, are obviously intertwined.

Since non-market mechanisms continue to play a significant role in the allocation of land in many developing countries, their neglect is hardly justifiable. The major mode of land acquisition in most African countries is inheritance. This is true even in countries where this mode of land access is more likely to lose importance, namely countries where land titling programs have been more or less systematically implemented in the countryside (Kenya, Zimbabwe, Uganda, Zambia) and in countries characterized by high population densities (Kenya, Rwanda, Burundi, Malawi).[1] It is therefore important to know whether and how non-market mechanisms of land

Thanks are due to Marcel Fafchamps, Kaushik Basu, Alain de Janvry, Robert Frank, Elisabeth Sadoulet, and David Easly for their helpful comments in the course of seminars in which preliminary versions of this chapter were presented and discussed. Also much appreciated is the research assistance of Anne Cherton.

[1] Thus, from a survey of sixteen different areas belonging to six countries with titling programs and/or high population densities (Kenya, Rwanda, Burundi, Uganda, Malawi, Zambia), it comes out that, on average, 63% of the land parcels are obtained through inheritance and various kinds of gift transfers, 16% are acquired through market purchases and the rest through other means among which state allocation stands foremost. Median figures are very close to the averages yet the ranges can be quite large, reflecting contrasted situations between Uganda, where the incidence of market purchases is quite important, and other countries in the sample (see André and Platteau 1998).

allocation evolve when land pressure increases as a result of population growth and/or agricultural commercialization.

Since it deals with exclusionary processes, the present contribution is clearly concerned with equity issues arising in the process of evolution of land tenure systems towards increasing individualization. The focus is put on the transformation of non-market modes of land allocation, including inheritance rules and practices. In a first stage, various intra-family exclusionary processes will retain our attention, with special emphasis on inheritance rules (Sections 2, 3, and 4). That such rules tend to differ between social classes will be evident from the discussion, particularly when addressing the issue of primogeniture versus equal sharing. In fact, Section 2 deals specifically with the custom of primogeniture in the upper class (the nobility) whereas Section 3 is concerned with inheritance practices as they prevailed in the lower rural classes of Europe since pre-industrial times.

As for Section 4, it will specifically deal with the situation prevailing in present-day developing countries, particularly Sub-Saharan Africa. Reference to the latter continent is apposite because it suffers from growing land scarcity, is known to have undergone a rapid process of individualization of land tenure, and has witnessed the multiplication of non-agricultural activities during the last decades. It is therefore interesting to know whether and to what extent inheritance rules evolve in a manner similar to that observed in Western Europe in pre-industrial and proto-industrial times. It will be argued that there are some striking differences between the patterns of evolution in these two regions, because Africans seem to have a more systematic and deeper attachment to the equal sharing rule and because strong intra-family solidarity ties continue to prevail in the lineage-based societies of Africa.

In a second stage (Section 5), again referring to the Sub-Saharan experience, it is argued that rapid population growth under a system of partible inheritance, to the extent that it activates the land market, may not only make for a more unequal land distribution and for the emergence of a landless class in the countryside, but may also lead to an erosion of the inheritable base of land assets and give rise to serious intra-family conflicts. This applies not only to land but also to other productive assets (e.g., cattle). Finally, Section 6 concludes the paper.

Empirical material for the study to follow will be essentially (yet not exclusively) drawn from the contemporary situation in densely populated countries of Sub-Saharan Africa (particularly, Rwanda, Kenya, Uganda, and Botswana), and from the historical experience of Europe, both western and eastern. The latter actually presents the advantage of being rich enough in contrasted pictures to permit comparative analysis.

A final remark is in order. The topic addressed in this paper is vast, as witnessed by its length. This is due not only to the comparative approach followed, but also to the complexity of the issues involved. In order to keep this complexity within manageable bounds, however, attention will focus on the situation of male children only. It is evident that a complete picture of the inheritance problem can be obtained only if the situation of the daughters is simultaneously considered. This forms a wider research project that is presently in progress but clearly beyond the scope of a single chapter.

Single-heir devolution in upper classes: a retrospective outlook

Evidence from feudal Europe

Under primogeniture, family land is entirely devolved to the first-born male child upon the parents' death. The endogenous emergence of this single-heir devolution system in Europe around the eleventh to twelfth centuries is best explained by scale economies in military expenditures and the indivisibility of political power associated with land.

The idea of the indivisibility of landed estates originated in the early Carolingian period when 'the king bound to himself by the ties of vassalage those to whom he entrusted the chief responsibilities of government.' The fief was indeed 'the office in its entirety, the indivisible source of power and wealth . . . the superior authority, by allowing it to be divided, would run the risk at once of weakening the executive power exercised in its name and of making control more difficult' (Bloch 1965*a*: 192–3, 203; see also Roberts 1995; Poly and Bournazel 1980).

Vassals had simply no right to divide or alienate this property which was a revocable gift made in return for strictly personal services. However, as the Carolingian Empire disintegrated, estate holders were prompt to transform fiefs into genuine family properties (including heritability).[2] The vacuum of central order also enabled them to appropriate regal powers at the local level, in particular the powers to issue money, exercise justice, and recruit peasants for the defense of local territories. They became simultaneously the genuine owners of big estates (over which they only had rights of conditional tenure in the vassalage era), political leaders, administrators, and military commanders.[3] Feudalism was thus born out of the fusion between property and power (Kriegel 1995).

Starting in Normandy around the year 1066, the principle of heritability of the fief became dominant in many parts of Europe by the twelfth century (Bloch 1965*a*, *b*).[4] It then took a few decades for landed aristocracies to choose the principle of single-heir devolution over the traditional rules of succession that favored equality of heirs of the same degree, especially in Germany (Thirsk 1976; Le Roy Ladurie 1976). In France, provincial chiefs soon realized that the size of their landed property determined their political and military clout. Subdividing land estates to give each of the sons a share of the inheritance created a real risk of disintegration by causing a proliferation

[2] New lords were in many cases former holders of public office in the demised empire. In France, for example, all, or almost all, the families that founded the territorial principalities originated from the imperial aristocracy, meaning that they had parenthood ties with Charlemagne's lineage (Poly and Bournazel 1980; Bloch 1965*a*, *b*).

[3] It is not until the thirteenth century that many rulers, usually kings, were able to partly restore their power over those they ruled. This was often because 'they could keep up large armies and arm them with the most effective weapons' (Roberts 1995: 485–6; Lopez 1971; Tilly 1990; Tilly and Blockmans 1994).

[4] In the words of Henry Maine: 'European society decidedly retrograded during the dissolution of the Carolingian empire. . . . The great characteristic of the period was the feebleness, or rather the abeyance, of kingly and therefore of civil authority. The lord with his vassals, during the ninth and tenth centuries, may be considered as a patriarchal household, recruited, not as in the primitive times by Adoption, but by Infeudation; and to such a confederacy, succession by Primogeniture was a source of strength and durability' (Maine 1861: Chap. 7).

of noble titles and the scattering of the related powers in the economic, judicial, and military spheres (Bloch 1965*a*, *b*; Neveux, Jacquart, and Le Roy Ladurie 1975). The experience of Wales attested that partible inheritance could destroy the nobility by causing excessive partition of estates and exacerbating strife between brothers (David Powell 1584, quoted from Thirsk 1976: 188).

The integrity of the land and mansion became the physical symbol of the unity and indivisibility of the political and military functions associated with the lord's estate. As pointed out by Adam Smith, 'when land was considered as the means, not of subsistence merely, but of power and protection, it was thought better that it should descend undivided to one. In those disorderly times, every great landlord was a sort of petty prince. . . . The security of a landed estate, therefore, the protection which its owner could afford to those who dwelt on it, depended upon its greatness. To divide it was to ruin it, and to expose every part of it to be oppressed and swallowed up by the incursions of its neighbors' (A. Smith 1776: 382; see also Pipes 1995; Mill 1848; Maine 1861; McCulloch 1848; Bergstrom 1994).

The above considerations explain why rulers in many European countries adopted legal forms of settlement for their upper classes—from at least the early fourteenth century in parts of France and Italy, from the late fourteenth century in Castile, and later, in the course of the sixteenth century in Germany (Cooper 1976). To keep large landed estates whole, the principal instrument consisted of the entail system of England, the Pactes de Famille of France, and the Haus-Gesetze of Germany, 'which universally stipulated that lands held by knightly service should descend to the eldest son' (Maine 1861, Chap. 7: 6).

Primogeniture was applied most rigorously in England[5] (and in the district of Caux in Normandy, France, from where the system was imported) (Thirsk 1976; Le Roy Ladurie 1976). Among the conquered population of England, the existence of practices already closely resembling vassalage facilitated the adoption of feudalism. For instance, conditional tenure prevailed (allod, a medieval antecedent to private property in land, was not permitted) and, therefore, the king's or superior lord's prescription that fiefs should remain undivided was more easily enforced. As a result, 'the old Carolingian principle of "coercion" by the lord was applied, in these lands which had never known the Carolingian Empire, with almost ideal precision' (Bloch 1965*a*: 188, *b*: 329–30).

It is true that the practice known as 'parage' was imported from France after the Conquest, implying that 'the eldest son, who was under a moral obligation not to leave his brothers without support, could and indeed must make some provision for them from their father's estate.' Nonetheless, the disadvantages of such partition became obvious after several generations and the 'parage' system was abandoned in England toward the middle of the twelfth century in favor of strict primogeniture. In the Caux district, the dukes had never admitted the 'parage' system, yet, as aptly pointed out by Bloch, such strict application of the primogeniture rule was 'only possible under the influence of a territorial authority of exceptional strength and organizing capacity' (Bloch

[5] Note that exceptions existed even within England: partible inheritance was allowed to continue in Kent after the Conquest, by permission of the Norman Kings, and it continued in Wales (Thirsk 1976).

1965*a*: 205). In the rest of France, by contrast, primogeniture was not observed in all its rigor, and some partition of family property took place.

Non-inheriting sons were often confronted with a harsh fate since they were compelled to look for alternative occupations outside the family estate and to accept a late marriage or, worse, a state of permanent celibacy (Cooper 1976).[6] In the words of Maine, the younger brother 'sank into the priest, the soldier of fortune, or the hanger-on of the mansion' (Maine 1861, Chap. 7: 9). In the best case, a younger son could become the head of an abbey and thereby come in possession of a large land domain that his own family could not directly provide him. Unless they could enroll themselves into the Crusades' armies, many nonheirs from noble families 'formed themselves into turbulent bands who were bound together by the chivalric ideal, by the impossibility of marriage, and by the practice of "courtly love"' (Goody 1983: 184). Some of these bands, such as the so-called 'seigneurs brigands' (brigand lords) in France, were having a definitely adverse effect on peace and order by roaming the countryside and committing numerous acts of looting or plundering. In this way, they were partly defeating the very purpose for which primogeniture was established.[7]

In later periods, the system of male primogeniture was often mitigated by the payment of portions, *alimenta*, or annuities to younger children. Thus, in England, whether male or female, non-heir children could receive annuities or cash gifts when they reached twenty-one or upon marriage, whichever came first. These sums were usually raised out of income 'by assigning part of the estate to trustees for a period of years to pay the annuities or raise the capital' (Stone and Fawtier Stone 1984: 69). As the heir was often obliged to use the future proceeds of the farm to service the mortgage entered into on behalf of his non-inheriting siblings, impartible inheritance was often achieved by burdening the family estate with heavy long-term debts. According to Cooper (1976), this situation prevailed, from at least the sixteenth century, in parts of England, Spain, Italy, and France, with the effect of increasing the dependence of great nobles on creditors and monarchies, and of discouraging agricultural investments.

Some historians contend that the hardships of the primogeniture system were most keenly felt among the gentry because, unlike the situation observed for the nobility, their means were not sufficient to provide decently for younger sons. 'The practical problems of younger sons of gentlemen almost begging in the streets' were at least evident in the sixteenth century when standards of living had risen sharply among the gentry and 'elder brothers had greater expectations, and could not spare so much for

[6] According to Stone and Fawtier Stone, 'the absence of nunneries in Protestant England undoubtedly encouraged marriage' among daughters of upper-class families. In England's late eighteenth century, three-quarters or more of all sons of peers did get married, 'which is in striking contrast to parts of Europe such as Sweden or Florence where a majority remained unmarried.' As a result of these relatively high nuptiality rates by younger sons and daughters, the English elite was provided with 'a reservoir of nephews and cousins who were essential for the maintenance of family continuity, on the frequent occasions when there was a failure of the direct male line' (Stone and Fawtier Stone 1984: 71). On the other hand, it is interesting to note that in Germany some Protestant rulers 'feared that by espousing primogeniture they would drive their disinherited children into the arms of the Catholic church, for it alone offered the refuge of a monastic life' (Thirsk 1976: 190).

[7] In order to fight against the 'seigneurs brigands' and bring some security back to the countryside, the church mobilized and organized peasants into a self-defense movement known as 'La paix de Dieu' (Peace of God) (information personally obtained from Stefan Platteau).

their younger brothers' (Thirsk 1976: 186–7; see also Mutel 1976 for detailed observations regarding the Caux district in France).

Evidence from feudal Japan and from India

The indivisibility of political and symbolic functions attached to family landed property in upper social classes appears to have also determined the emergence of a discriminatory system of inheritance in feudal Japan. The Japanese system rested upon the indivisibility of family headship: 'Along with heirlooms, the main dwelling, ancestral graves, and plaques—headship of the family passed to a single heir.' (Note incidentally that the heir was not necessarily the eldest son and could even be a nephew of the previous head.) 'It was this heir who perpetuated the family and through whose issue descent was traced, who performed the ancestral rites that linked the family to the remotest past and projected it indefinitely into the future' (T. Smith 1959: 37).

Since 'no member of a family had birthright to an individual share of the family patrimony, or even to freedom to separate from the group in order to establish a family of his own,' a member could be held indefinitely in the family, as part of its labor force, without individual property, if that were advantageous to the group. If, on the other hand, a man were given land and freedom to set up his own household, 'it was an act of generosity for which eternal gratitude to the family head was the only proper sentiment.' His new family would be established as a branch family, a collateral line of descent clearly subordinated to the main family. Branch families were rarely autonomous: they were not necessarily granted the right to put up their own dwelling, and the land and capital equipment at their disposal were clearly not enough to make a living.[8] While providing labor to the main farm when asked, branch households 'received in return housing, tools, animals, water, fertilizer, firewood, and protection' (T. Smith 1959: 45–6).

Japan is far from being a unique case. Laura Betzig (1993) has thus contended that noble classes in great ancient civilizations such as Mesopotamia, Egypt, Aztec Mexico, Inca Peru, and China—all characterized by highly stratified societies with extreme inequality of wealth—practiced primogeniture and monogamous marriage (plus polygamous mating). In South India, primogeniture was the hallmark of the Nambudiripad Brahmines of Kerala, among whom only the eldest son could marry and inherit so as to ensure that the family property, including the temple, would be kept whole. Younger sons were traditionally allowed to have sexual relations with Nair women (from a non-Brahmine caste) but not to marry them. Many Brahmine women remained unmarried and stayed with their family of origin. They eventually revolted against this unjust custom that was abandoned only in the twentieth century.[9]

In North India, as is well known, the British colonialists followed the practice of transforming agents who acted as fiscal intermediaries under the former empire into full-fledged landlords of the English kind, thus considerably enhancing their wealth

[8] 'There was reluctance on the part of the main line to relinquish any of the physical symbols of family continuity' (T. Smith 1959: 38, 42–3).

[9] Thanks are due to Anita Abraham who supplied us with this information.

and power (Wolf 1982). In the case of the Taluqdars of Awadh, primogeniture was made compulsory for all of their families, whether Hindu or Muslim, through the Taluqdari Succession Act of 1869 (Jassal 1997). In this instance, clearly, the aristocratic logic aimed at preserving the integrity of an estate domain was successfully imposed by the British colonial power on a rural elite that was somehow artificially constructed.

The contrasting experience of Russia

The Russian nobility could never pretend to the same predominance as their European counterparts since in Russia land property and control of manpower were clearly dissociated from political or symbolic functions. Indeed, from the mid-fifteenth to the mid-seventeenth century, the tsars transformed Russia into a strongly centralized royal domain that was to endure throughout most of the twentieth century. Following the domainial practice, the empire's population was divided into the 'big men' (*muzhi* or *ludi*), a service class in the administrative and military sector, and the 'little men' (*muzhiki*), commoners who, after their enserfment,[10] owed both taxes and labor to the rulers of Moscow (Pipes 1995: 86; Anderson 1974).

Allodial property was eliminated on a large scale in the second half of the fifteenth century to be replaced by tsar property. As a result, 'the Russian state grew and took shape without having to contend with entrenched landed interests' (Pipes 1995: 172).[11] The 'big men,' the Russian equivalent of the nobility, held both their land and their control over the serfs on royal sufferance in exchange for services to the tsar. Those 'nobles' were thus 'transformed into nothing less than the serfs or servants of the sovereign' (Raeff 1984: 10). Peasant serfdom in Russia 'was not an exceptional condition, but an integral aspect of an all-embracing system binding the entire population to the state . . . (it) was only the most widespread and most visible form of bondage which pervaded every layer of Muscovite society creating an interlocking system without room for personal freedom' (Pipes 1995: 105, 1998: 17–18; see also Worobec 1995).

To get a complete grip on the localities, the rulers of Moscow prohibited their provincial administrators from holding office in any area where they had estates and rotated them at annual or biannual intervals, even at the highest levels of the service class. In this way, service nobles were prevented from linking land property to their

[10] Before, the commoners had complete freedom to move in space and a certain amount of social mobility was possible (Hosking 1997). In fact, it is only between 1550 and 1650, approximately, that the bulk of the Russian rural population ceased to be tenants and turned into serfs, at the very time when the monarchy emerged as the absolute master of the country. This is in contrast to Western Europe where serfdom appeared much earlier, in the wake of the collapse of law and order in the early Middle Ages, to disappear mostly in the course of the thirteenth and fourteenth centuries with the liquidation of the feudal order. In other words, while in western Europe the 'fief' came into being during the age of 'feudal decentralization' and vanished when royal power consolidated, in Russia things went the other way round: serfdom was the deliberate creation of the Muscovite monarchy acting as a centralized power (Pipes 1995: 100).

[11] The pedigreed families and clans (usually known as *boyars*) who originally owned *votchiny* (a *votchina* is a land estate which was the legal property of the *boyar*) were gradually uprooted, especially under Ivan IV. Their estates were transformed into so-called *pomest'e* lands, which they and their descendants could retain only for as long as they continued to render satisfactory service to the tsar. Their status thus began to resemble that of the more humble *dvoriane*, who were initially employed as domestic servitors of the appanage princes (and most of whom were actually slaves) to be later transformed into nobles by the tsar to counterbalance the pedigreed families and clans (Pipes 1995).

administrative and political functions, and never knew for certain in advance what obligations they would have to discharge from one year to the next (Hosking 1997), a predicament that left them at the complete mercy of the central rulers. Compared to the European experience, there did not exist any meshing of landed wealth with administrative functions in the hands of a concentrated hereditary rural elite that enabled the latter, wherever it existed, to withstand the autocratic rule (Pipes 1995; Anderson 1974). Even when the tsar's grip over them lessened, under Peter III and Catherine II, the Russian nobles chose to solidify their economic and social privileges instead of attempting to acquire political rights and increase their contribution to the country's political life.

In 1714 Peter the Great issued an edict requiring landlords to bequeath their immovable properties to a single heir (not necessarily the eldest, however). His objective was double: (1) to buttress the material capacity of the nobility to perform state service hereditarily by preventing landed properties from becoming subdivided until they were no longer able to provide a sufficient living for a nobleman; and (2) to compel non-inheritors to earn both their livelihood and noble status by entering the many fields of endeavor which his reforms had opened up, including the civil or military service (Hosking 1997; Pipes 1995).

The new law ran against a long-established custom of equal sharing of land property that led, for instance, to the gradual shrinking of the northeastern principalities in the Volga-Oka region from the mid-twelfth to the mid-fifteenth century. By introducing 'almost surreptitiously' a system of royal succession based on primogeniture during the fourteenth century, the rulers of Moscow principality (descended from Alexander Nevsky) acquired 'an immense advantage over rival princes who continued to split properties into equal shares among their heirs' (Pipes 1995: 42, 64; see also Martin 1995, Chap. 8). The Muscovy state, which would govern Russia in modern times, was born. Thereafter, the noble class continued to equally divide their estates among their sons, as 'there was hardly anything that young men deprived of their share of the landed estate could draw income from.' Land was thus 'relentlessly cut up into ever smaller lots, with the result that the overwhelming majority of *dvoriane* lacked economic independence and could not afford to live in the style of landed gentry. . . . The roots of this class were not in the land, as was the case with nobilities the world over, but in the royal service' (Pipes 1995: 98, 132, 176; see also Raeff 1984; Hosking 1997; Waldron 1997). The noble class therefore resisted Peter's edict to the effect that, in 1730, Empress Anne had no other choice than to repeal an edict that had turned out to be unenforceable.

Impartible versus partible inheritance in non-noble classes: the European experience

General considerations

As has been amply documented above, impartible inheritance was a pervasive practice among European nobles, and legal provisions often supported this practice to that effect. As indivisibility considerations underlying primogeniture among nobles are not pertinent for the lower social classes, we should not expect this system of inheritance to prevail among these classes. Maine confirmed this prediction when he wrote: 'As to lands held by servile tenures . . . the system of succession prescribed by custom differed greatly in different countries and different provinces. The more general rule was that such lands were divided equally at death among all the children' (Maine 1861: Chap. 7: 6).

The argument can actually be extended to lesser nobles who are not rich enough to have realistic pretensions to status and power. To return to the experience of Russia, it is interesting to note that in this country, where primogeniture never took root, the large majority of nobles were 'exceedingly poor' (Raeff 1984: 74; Pipes 1995) and the economy was at a low level of economic development. In Western Europe, the law of primogeniture was frequently violated among the lower nobility for precisely the same reason that Russian *dvoriane* resisted it. In Poland, for example, 'the middling and lesser nobles continued to follow partible inheritance while the magnates entailed their lands from the late sixteenth century' (Cooper 1976: 198–9). In actual fact, the condition of many poor nobles was closer to that of peasants than to that of the high aristocracy.

It is noteworthy that in the aforecited excerpt, Maine duly qualifies his statement regarding partible inheritance among lower social classes. He indeed makes the extremely important point that inheritance customs varied greatly between countries and regions. This qualification is amply justified in light of the most recent historical research and the mapping of inheritance customs in Western Europe.

Just take the example of France. As can be judged from ancient regional custumals, this is a region characterized by a wide spectrum of inheritance customs (Le Roy Ladurie 1976). At the two polar extremes of this spectrum, we find the strongly egalitarian practices that are a crystallization of Norman customs (with the notable exception of the Caux district), on one side, and impartible inheritance or discriminatory devolution in which there is a preferred heir (not necessarily the eldest son),[12] on the other side. The former pattern was mainly observed in the western part of the country—especially in Normandy, Brittany, the Touraine, and the Angevin domain where egalitarianism used to prevail in its purest form—but also in Champagne and in Brie to the east of the Paris–Orléans zone. As for the latter system, it characterized the Provençal-speaking south and some regions situated in the north and the northeast, including the Lorraine, the Verdun area, and especially Picardy and Wallonia. In between these two extremes lies the so-called Capetian domain with its core in the Paris–Orléans region.

Contrasts may not only be stark but also occur within small areas. In the words of H.J. Habakkuk (1955: 3), 'there might be considerable variations within a single region: islands of inheritance by a single heir in areas where the predominant rule was division, and vice versa.' This is for example evidenced by the opposition between the egalitarian inheritance customs of the Flanders and the discriminatory devolution practices of Wallonia in what are today the two sides of Belgium's linguistic border. Or,

[12] As noted by Lutz Berkner, 'impartible inheritance does not specify *which* child will become the heir, or *when* that child may marry and take over the farm. Peasant customs may favor the eldest (primogeniture), the youngest (ultimogeniture), or leave the choice open' (Berkner 1976: 89).

to take another example, while property went to a single heir in the western part of Czechoslovakia—in Bohemia, Silesia, and northern and western Moravia, equal division was the rule in the eastern part—in southwestern Moravia, Ruthenia, and Slovakia (Habakkuk 1955). More striking still is the variation observed between the territories of Calenberg and Göttingen in Lower Saxony (in the upper part of Germany), two neighboring territories with quite similar geographical features but characterized by different inheritance customs—impartible holdings in Calenberg and partible ones in Göttingen (Berkner 1976). The inheritance system in non-noble rural classes could vary not only geographically but also over time. Unigeniture emerged in some circumstances and a reversal to partible inheritance could ensue if there was a return to conditions congenial to subdivision of landholdings (Howell 1976).

Before attempting to understand the causes or the origins of the above variations, it is important to bear in mind that an unequal division of the family land does not necessarily imply an unequal division of the inheritance (Mill 1848). As a matter of fact, provisions for other siblings often accompanied the transfer of the main part of the family land to a privileged heir, which could possibly be the responsibility of the advantaged son. Or, alternatively, division of the land in favor of one son could be combined with the division of movables in favor of the other sons. For this reason, the distinction between impartible and partible inheritance may not be as decisive as it appears at first sight (Howell 1976; Spufford 1976), as attested by the situation observed in some parts of England such as Cambridgeshire, to which we shall return.

This point is closely related to the previous one inasmuch as, in England, there exist well-documented variations not so much in the basic principle of inheritance (which is impartible), but in the accompanying features that may have an important impact on the dynamics of asset distribution. As will be explained later, when the system of impartible inheritance is seriously altered by mitigating clauses, the economic consequences are likely to be very similar to those achieved under partible inheritance. Contrary to appearances, therefore, the situation in some parts of England (or in some social categories) may not be very different from that reported for regions of continental Europe known as egalitarian.

Two last general remarks are in order. First, regarding common people, the term unigeniture or single-heir devolution does not necessarily refer to the practice of primogeniture whereby family land descends to the eldest son. Although less widespread, ultimogeniture (the land descends to the youngest son), or free selection of the exclusive inheritor (the family head freely chooses which one of his sons is to be his heir) were also observed to exist in England and Ireland (Homans 1941).[13] Second, much of what will be said below draws heavily from recent advances in the so-called new history, which essentially relies on detailed examination of micro-level data. Among the most useful historical sources exploited by these new historians, we can mention the following: parish registers (containing a wealth of demographic information), court rolls (where tenures and land transactions are registered), contemporary wills, estate surveys, and local or regional custumals (when they exist).

[13] The reader will find in the cited work of Homans a brief discussion of the comparative advantages of the three systems of exclusive devolution.

The circumstances conducive to single-heir devolution

Why is it that single-heir devolution, or unigeniture, was the rule in some parts of Europe whereas the principle of equal division, which seems to be such a natural norm of sharing family property, prevailed in other areas? To raise that question is to ask why peasants wanted to keep their farm intact in some circumstances and not in others. Several answers come to mind that are explained in detail below. Yet, unigeniture is not the only possible way to maintain the farm intact; other solutions may indeed be available and, in some instances, implemented. Some of these solutions will be examined in the course of the discussion. Once this is done, a number of special topics will be addressed with a view to completing our understanding of this inheritance system as it was applied in pre-industrial and industrial Europe. More precisely, attention will be lent to the systems of compensations provided to non-inheriting children as well as to the dynamic effects of unigeniture on population, technical progress, and entrepreneurship.

By reviewing the various circumstances under which impartible inheritance arose among non-noble classes of Europe, attention will necessarily be drawn to different rationales underlying its emergence. Such rationales can be essentially regrouped into the following five categories: (1) savings in administrative costs of tax collection; (2) production conditions reflected in scale economies, physical indivisibilities, and coordination requirements with respect to land use; (3) symbolic indivisibilities and the maintenance of patriarchal relations; (4) restrictive membership rules at the community level; (5) economic viability (as distinct from profitability) of the farm. All these motives will become clearer as the discussion proceeds.

Savings in administrative costs of tax collection

Historical evidence converges to show that the areas that adopted unigeniture coincide 'remarkably faithfully' with areas of widespread manorialization (Howell 1976: 117; Le Roy Ladurie 1976). In general, therefore, 'the areas of impartibility in western Europe were those with a strong manorial control over land tenure and settlement rights.' The situation did not differ in central Europe 'where the lord often required the peasant holding to remain intact' (Berkner and Mendels 1978: 212). It is particularly interesting to note that, while a much larger part of the surface was fully in the hands of the lords (demesne) in England than in France—the English lords throughout the whole of the medieval period 'enjoyed a far stronger position vis-à-vis their peasants than did their French counterparts' (Brenner 1985: 295–6)—single-heir devolution was much more widespread in the former than in the latter country.

We have already noted the striking difference in the inheritance systems adopted in the two neighboring areas of Calenberg and Göttingen in Lower Saxony, Germany. What needs to be added now is that this difference may be apparently traced back to different forms of agricultural organization. As a matter of fact, in Calenberg where impartible holdings were the rule (as observed in the course of the seventeenth century), 'most of the land fell under the strictest manorial controls': the dominant type of tenure was the so-called *Meierland* which was 'owned' by the lord but held under secure hereditary rights by the peasants (the land was held by a written, periodically renewable, contract from the landlord) and fell under all possible manorial restrictions. In Göttingen, the opposite was true: most lands were either *Erbzinsland* (something like copyhold)—on which only minimal manorial dues were paid and which could be more freely disposed of by the peasants—or *Eigenland*, which the peasants owned outright, free of all manorial controls. In this latter area, parcels of land used to be divided into smaller fragments with each passing generation (Berkner 1976: 77, 80–2).

In the Paris–Orléans region of France, the property of a villein 'generally remained entire except for the removal of a few minute fragments previously subtracted by the parents to provide portions for those of their children who had left to make their home under another roof' (Le Roy Ladurie 1976: 43). Revealingly, the Normandy region was uniformly characterized by equal division of peasant land properties among all descendants. This is because 'Norman law was not born under the abject conditions of villeinage; it is more the creation of a superior stratum of free yeomen' who are sure of their right and 'not much in danger of encroachment by the seigneur on their rural holding.' Likewise, Flemish inheritance customs reflected 'the habits of a stratum of free men, accustomed to more liberty of action' than their more dependent Walloon neighbors 'because they are not imprisoned by the iron constraint of the seigneurial system' (Le Roy Ladurie 1976: 60, 68).

In so far as the areas most susceptible to the processes of manorialization were typically areas of land shortage, the above relationship between the manorial system and unigeniture implies that this system of inheritance tended, other things being equal, to arise where land–man ratios were relatively low (Howell 1976). This bears out the standard hypothesis that a discriminatory mode of inheritance is more likely to emerge when population presses on scarce land resources, yet, in this case, the relationship between relative resource endowments and the inheritance system is mediated by an estate-based form of agricultural organization.

A characteristic feature of the manorial system that is directly relevant to our topic lies in the fact that a lord usually had 'the legal right to approve every transfer effected through a marriage contract, inheritance settlement, or sale, and could deny any provisions that threatened to reduce his income.'[14] As can be inferred from the foregoing examples, lords of manorial domains often forbade their peasants to divide their landholdings, presumably because 'large impartible farms provided the most effective base for taxation' (Berkner 1976: 77; Brenner 1976; Hilton 1985).

There are several reasons large farm units could be advantageous for the lord of a manor from a fiscal point of view. First, anecdotal evidence suggests that the rate of taxation increased with the size of the farm. Apparently, the labor services required from the peasants or villeins were indeed proportionally more important when the farms were larger (Goody 1983). Moreover, the holders of sizeable landholdings could be asked to provide additional services that poorer tenants were not expected to furnish, say, due to their inability to reap the benefits of scale economies or to obtain a surplus over their subsistence needs. In Lower Saxony (Calenberg), for instance, smallholders

[14] Contrary to the views expressed by some historians, it has now become clear that manorial customs generally recognized the fundamental right of the villeins to leave land to heirs and to inherit land (Howell 1976).

owed only hand labor services to their lord while large holders were also required to provide a team of horses (Berkner 1976).

Second, by imposing taxes and labor or other services on large, undivided farm units, the owners of manorial estates were able to minimize the risk of tax defaulting. As a matter of fact, large households (say, an eldest son with his wife and children together with his unmarried brothers and, possibly, old parents) living on sizeable landholdings, by allowing the pooling of idiosyncratic risks, such as risks of human or animal disease, could ensure a more stable provision of taxes and services to the lord than the same number of villeins dispersed over many small households living off tiny landholdings. Third, the per unit administrative cost of collecting taxes or calling for labor services was obviously smaller when the lord could deal with a more restricted number of taxable units.

In Russia, too, it may be noted, serfowners and the Ministry of State Domains attempted to obstruct fissions in serf and state peasant households lest they should default in their military and tax obligations. Serfowners thus feared that only large peasant households had sufficient labor to work their own lands as well as their serfowner's demesne, and they also believed that household divisions jeopardized the sanctity of patriarchal relations within families. They therefore instituted a variety of paternalistic measures to ward off fissions and maintain large serf families with several conjugal units. In particular, they punished offenders who dared set up new households without first seeking the bailiff's permission. As for the Ministry of State Domains, it allowed household divisions only when the original household was so large that the new units would have at least three male laborers each (Worobec 1995). However, for reasons to be elucidated shortly, the norm of equal inheritance among the peasants was so strong that the restrictive measures adopted by the Russian ruling class did not succeed in establishing anything close to unigeniture.

Production conditions with respect to land use

Of course, the presence of technical indivisibilities can directly lead to impartible inheritance even though there is no authority structure able to bring them to bear owing to the fiscal advantages involved. A simple illustration contrasting two neighboring areas with different technologies will suffice. The contrast is between the region of the Polders and that of the interior within Flanders (in today's Belgium). In the Polders during the eighteenth century, land fragmentation was curtailed and large commercial farms were maintained owing to the presence of substantial indivisibilities: 'the heavy soils of the Polders required large plows pulled by several horses which were expensive and practical only on large holdings.' By contrast, the land continued to be divided in the interior, a region characterized by sandy light soils that were well suited for labor-intensive agriculture on small family farms (Berkner and Mendels 1978: 218; Mendels 1970, 1972, 1975).

It must be emphasized that a relationship between scale economies (which imply an increase in all production factors) and impartible inheritance can exist (whether or not it is mediated by an agrarian ruling class with extensive fiscal prerogatives and power attributes) only if households under this system of inheritance tend to have a larger size than under the system of partible inheritance. Insofar as households run by a privileged son typically comprise unmarried siblings (in addition to elderly parents) working with him on the undivided family land, this condition is actually fulfilled (Goody 1976).

Not only scale economies but also coordination needs may determine an inheritance system based on the principle of single-heir devolution. In his detailed study of English villages in the thirteenth century, George Homans observed that in areas where the custom was the descent of a villager's holding to one of his sons, only open-field agriculture predominated (such as it did in the so-called champion country which occupied a broad band stretching from the North Sea coast to the Channel). In these areas, the fields of a village were divided up into two or three great sectors submitted to a customary rotation of winter corn, spring corn, and fallow; when lying fallow the fields were used as the common pasture of all the cattle of the village. Instead of making up one compact plot, a villager's holding lay in the form of a number of strips scattered all over the fields, intermingled with the similar strips of his neighbors. Moreover, big and concentrated villages were the common type of human settlement in open-field areas (Homans 1941, 1953, 1957–8).

Unfortunately, Homans does not provide any explanation for the above phenomenon. A plausible reason the rule of exclusive inheritance prevailed in manors where open-field agriculture was practiced is that partible inheritance, besides multiplying the number of landholders, would have caused an excessive fragmentation of the village lands given the scattering of family fields over the different sectors. The coordination required among all landholders to ensure proper rotation of land uses at the village level would have been made more difficult under such conditions. In contrast, this problem did not arise in areas belonging to the so-called woodland (Devon, Cornwall, Wales, Suffolk, Kent, and Essex) where more individualized forms of agriculture were found, with fenced-in fields and relatively scattered settlement. In these areas, therefore, land customarily descended jointly to all the sons.

Note that, for Homans, and contrary to what has been said under the previous point, variations in inheritance practices existed even within areas under manorial control, implying that manorialization is not the only variable at play: where cultivation systems were different from the two- and three-field systems, partible inheritance tended to be the custom of the manor. It is, however, likely that manorial rule was more assertive where the need for coordination was stronger, so that the aforementioned relationship between manorialization and unigeniture remains broadly valid.

Symbolic indivisibilities and the maintenance of patriarchal relations

Internal forms of hierarchical relationships, rather than external forms (such as lord-villein relationships), may also provide the right context for single-heir devolution. The patriarchal structure, where the father yields a lot of authority over an extended family group, is a case in point. As a matter of fact, the preservation of such a structure implies that the family farm is kept whole and that authority is transmitted to a single son who will become the new patriarch for the next generation (Neveux, Jacquart, and Le Roy Ladurie 1975).

A well-documented example is that of southern France (the Provençal-speaking Midi) where patriarchal and paternalist ideas had been directly implanted on the people by the renaissance of Roman law at the end of the Middle Ages (Le Roy Ladurie 1976; Kriegel 1995). There, the favored descendant (not necessarily the eldest son) succeeded to virtually the whole of the family land, often after a period of co-residence during his parents' lifetime. As for the other children, they had to be content 'with portions of varying degrees of meagerness . . . with crumbs distributed in the will, [or] with a custom-prescribed hand-out of a few sous' (Le Roy Ladurie 1976: 62–3). This tradition was so strongly rooted in the culture of southern France that it remained alive even after the French Revolution and the Civil Code seriously restricted testamentary freedom in favor of nearly equal inheritance (Berkner and Mendels 1978). As for the central provinces of France (Auvergne-Marche, Poitou-Angoumois-Saintonge, Berry-Bourbonnais-Nivernais, Burgundy), they formed a 'disputed battleground' between the influences of the egalitarian north and those of the patriarchal south.

It is worth noting the similarity between the forces that led to primogeniture among noble classes, on the one hand, and the rationale underlying impartible inheritance in the patriarchally oriented peasant classes of southern France, on the other hand. In both cases, indeed, it is the indivisibility of authority and the strong determination to perpetuate the family name, power, and prestige that seem to have caused the emergence of an inegalitarian system of land transmission.[15]

The authority element undeniably present in the patriarchal family system, as well as its continuity under an indivisible form, are obviously crucial factors conditioning the feasibility of any strategy aimed at keeping the family farmland whole over successive generations. This can be best understood by contrasting the family structure of southern France with that of Russia.

In the latter country, newly married couples used to be incorporated into the patriarchal household to form an extended family structure. In this structure, the patriarch (the *bol'shak*) held absolute power over management of the household economy and the labor input of family members within limitations set by the commune and the local community. In general, this situation lasted until the patriarch's death when authority was devolved to the most senior member of the family in the male line, either his eldest brother or his eldest son. According to Christine Worobec (1995: 81), 'It was at this point that other male family members had to decide whether to remain in the household or to split off from the household, taking their rightful shares of the patrimony with them.' In actuality, the normal tendency was for the brothers and sons to divide the family property (land and movables) and set up independent households.

The fact of the matter is that 'if a son became household head upon his father's death, he could not command authority over his brothers as had his father.' Internal family tensions were the chief reason accounting for household fissions in peasant Russia. Thus, even the relative size of each conjugal unit was a source of dispute: 'a brother

[15] Some historians have stressed the fact that, in England during the eighteenth century, an imitation effect was at work in the countryside, ensuring that the habits of the nobles did not remain confined to a small circle: 'the aspirations of the gentry filtered down to the next class below, and produced yeomen who followed the rule of primogeniture . . .' (Thirsk 1976: 191).

resented having to work twice as hard, or so he believed, because one of his brothers had twice as many children . . . he doesn't want to have to work for someone else's children' (Worobec 1995: 81–2). For example, household division cases in Moscow and Tambov provinces in the early 1870s mainly involved disputes between brothers, uncles, and nephews, and collateral relations (Worobec 1995: 88; see also Dixon 1999: 106–7 and, above all, Hoch 1986).

It would be wrong to believe that household divisions were necessarily *postmortem*. Sometimes, but increasingly frequently during the post-emancipation period, sons (and their wives) refused to wait until the patriarch's death to leave the family household and set up on their own. This is because they 'naturally resented having to take orders well into their 30s, 40s, or even 50s before their fathers' deaths permitted them to ascend to the headship of the household' (Worobec 1995: 83). If they decided to part with the father's household against his will, they faced the risk of being disinherited, not a negligible threat in the absence of alternative resources and employment opportunities.[16]

In southern France, by contrast, the existence of a more undisputed mechanism of devolution and transmission of family authority or headship from the father to a chosen son could ensure simultaneously a strong integration of the multiple family structure and the impartibility of the ancestral property.

In Russia, inasmuch as married sons stayed a long time within the parental household, there is a high likelihood that when they set up their own independent household, they would have already had several children of working age with them. At every point of time, therefore, provided that no splitting occurred before the father's death, a given peasant household could rely on a sizeable workforce. This enabled it, or its ruler(s), to reap reasonable gains from scale economies and risk-pooling. Yet, on the other hand, since family land was destined to be eventually divided, savings on administrative costs per unit of tax collected were lower than what would have obtained under a system of impartible inheritance, such as was observed in southern France.

Clearly, an important lesson from the Russian experience is that, absent a strong tradition of authority lineage, co-ownership and co-management of family property between brothers are difficult to achieve in practice.[17] It seems a general feature that 'joint family households are in precarious equilibrium, constantly threatened by fission' (Cooper 1976: 300). The problem is that such arrangements are extremely vulnerable to internal quarrels and tensions which make them a rather unreliable method to benefit from risk-pooling, scale economies, or various forms of savings in administrative costs. All this being said, the question remains entirely open regarding whether the hierarchical family with several conjugal units has emerged with the purpose of achieving the gains of large size, or with that of maintaining a patriarchal structure thought to have its own merits irrespective of economic considerations.

[16] In the latter part of the nineteenth century, however, sons could more easily ignore their fathers' threats of disinheritance given the option of pursuing nonagricultural employment (Worobec 1995). In fact, it is the availability of wage labor opportunities, especially in the central industrial provinces, that had the effect of exacerbating strained relations between fathers and sons. Indeed, 'wage-earning sons resented having to contribute cash to the common family coffers' (Worobec 1995: 83).

[17] John Stuart Mill saw in such cooperative arrangements a ready-made alternative to primogeniture given the presence of genuine economies of scale (Mill 1848).

Restrictive membership rules at the community level

There is still another type of circumstance, in itself highly indicative of a situation of population pressure on land resources, which is likely to induce peasant households to opt for unigeniture, namely the existence of membership rules regarding access to the village commons. Indeed, if a rural community has set up rules to the effect of limiting such access, there is a high likelihood that drastic steps will be taken to prevent the formation of new (branch) households that would be deprived of access rights. This would in turn imply that family farms are passed to a single heir in order to avoid dividing the farms into several parts managed by separate households.

For example, in the Canton of Zürich during preindustrial times, the *numerus clausus* of the general right of using the common property and being a member of the community 'was used as legitimation for setting up regulations that no new house could be built either in the village settlement or outside, unless an old one was torne down. These regulations prevented an uncontrolled expansion from within too' (Braun 1978: 299).

At this point, it is useful to draw a parallel with villages of Tokugawa, Japan where the development of fixed rights to using the village commons and to being a member of the community acted as a powerful factor controlling the subdivision of holdings and the formation of new households. As a matter of fact, villages possessed the power to determine which households could be granted rights of access to the commons. Especially noteworthy is that large households could not obtain advantages by splitting into several households, since permission to form a branch household from the main household had to be obtained from village authorities who were usually reluctant to grant such permission in order not to increase pressure on the available commons. Records from some villages actually show that, about midway through the Tokugawa period, the number of formally constituted households did not increase 'because no new households were permitted unless an old one died out for lack of heirs' (McKean 1986: 551–3; see also T. Smith 1959).

The economic viability of the farm

High population pressure in conditions of heavy dependence on agricultural incomes is the last circumstance that needs to be examined in a more general context. At least till the seventeenth century, demographic conditions in many European countries were such that the average number of children per family to escape infant and juvenile mortality and eventually reach marriageable age was rarely more than two, typically a brother and a sister (Le Roy Ladurie 1976). In this typical household, the parents would find a husband for their daughter who would leave home 'with a dowry of varying meagerness.' As for the boy, he was destined to live with his father and mother, serve his apprenticeship as a farmer and, when the time came, take possession of the family farm (Le Roy Ladurie 1976: 44).[18] The land property of a peasant or villein could thereby remain entire over successive generations through a sort of natural process of single-heir devolution. However, when population growth started to accelerate and the expected

[18] If there was no son, the practice was to invite a son-in-law to settle under the parental roof.

number of surviving children exceeded two, the question of how to divide the family property among the potential heirs inevitably arose.

In the absence of scale economies, risk-pooling considerations, symbolic indivisibilities, and other advantages of large farm size, partible inheritance appears as the most natural solution to adopt by relatively rich households whose members entirely depend on agriculture for their survival. If, on the other hand, non-agricultural income opportunities are available, the tendency is for rich families to bequeath the land to one or several sons who remain in agriculture. The other sons receive compensation, by way of education, in cash, or in the form of other assets that may help them to start a gainful career, generally in an urban setting.

The situation is, of course, entirely different regarding poor households that do not have a holding large enough to support all their male children. For them, the choice of the mode of inheritance is a thorny question that cannot be solved in any satisfactory manner. There are two possible paths. In some regions, typically those with a strong manorial or patriarchal tradition, preventing the fragmentation of the land to ensure that the privileged son can make a decent living from the parental farm was the preferred solution. Non-heirs were then compelled either to migrate permanently in search of an alternative way of living in the outside world, or to postpone their marriage and work in the native village with their inheriting brother or as an agricultural laborer. In the former case, it can be said that primogeniture generated long-distance migrants who were to provide in due time the raw recruits for industry: it is only exclusive inheritance that 'provides the steady, long-term migration necessary to a modern industrial labor force—one that will stay in cities long enough to learn a skill and then remain to use it' (Parish and Schwartz 1972: 156). In the meantime, the life of the 'penniless and unskilled sons' sent out by very small holdings was truly hard since they 'joined the vagabond class of the pre-industrial era, for whom there was seldom sufficient employment' (Howell 1976: 154).

For example, in the primogeniture area of Calenberg (Germany), inheritance was 'a highly inequitable settlement.' The non-heirs 'received only a small fraction of the total property of their parents and were to stay in the household only until the age of 14, when they could be asked to leave. If they remained as servants, their inheritance portions could not be claimed until they left home' (Berkner 1976: 78). In a German hamlet in the Franconia region, it appears that, as a result of impartible inheritance, the number of holdings remained more or less constant, yet not less than one-third of the children were excluded from local marriage and succession (Planck 1967—cited from Berkner and Mendels 1978: 219–20).

In the canton of Zürich, likewise, extreme pressure on the land was noticeable, at least until the eighteenth century, and the response of the inhabitants was to give preference to one heir and to limit the fragmentation of the land (Braun 1978). In southern France, 'younger sons who wanted to become independent were practically excluded from the inheritance and, if they stayed in the parental roof, their marriage was subject to the approval of the household head' (Neveux, Jacquart, and Le Roy Ladurie 1975: 278—our translation). To take a last example, in the western part of Czechoslovakia, before the advent of industrialization, the tendency was for the younger sons to remain unmarried and to work with the head of the family farmstead, or to become agricultural wage-earners (Habakkuk 1955; see also Le Play 1871; Goody 1983; Macfarlane 1978, for the case of England). Permanent migration made its appearance with the development of new industrial employment in the cities.

The second path is that of equal partition of the family estate, a solution that inexorably led to the emergence of increasingly small holdings in the countryside.[19] The inability of children to sustain themselves and their families from the inherited patches of land forced them to migrate, generally on a seasonal basis. They worked as wage laborers with a view to complementing their meager farm incomes and, in the best of cases, to purchasing additional land in the native village, possibly from their very brothers so as to maintain or reconstitute the family property (Braun 1978). In general, the inhabitants of areas of partible inheritance 'were not likely, in the absence of such severe pressure (a succession of poor harvests), to respond readily to demands for permanent industrial labor in regions distant from their homes' (Habakkuk 1955: 7).[20]

Not surprisingly, the 'involutionary' path of increasing fragmentation through equal division triggered a process of increasing differentiation of the peasantry, and ultimate concentration of land through the multiplication of distress sales and land foreclosures in conditions of an increasingly active land market (Spufford 1976: 164; Habakkuk 1955). Thus, in Languedoc, an acceleration of population growth accompanied by widespread practices of partible inheritance in the seventeenth century, unleashed profound changes that caused great landowners to progress, small ones to proliferate, and middle ones to retreat prodigiously (Le Roy Ladurie 1966).

The appearance of small-scale industrial establishments in the countryside, such as cottage or putting-out industries, brought considerable relief to rural inhabitants suffering from a shortage of land. Not only could rural proto-industrialization slow down or stop the process of economic and social differentiation of the peasantry under conditions of partible inheritance—since 'the partition of the land could continue beyond the limits set by considerations of purely agricultural viability' (Berkner and Mendels 1978: 216); it could also cause a shift of the inheritance system from discriminatory to equal devolution of family land. A vivid illustration of the latter possibility is provided by Rudolf Braun (1978) in his study of the canton of Zürich in the seventeenth and eighteenth centuries. It is worth quoting him in detail, including some original sources that he has used:

> The tendency to give preference to one heir and to limit the fragmentation of the land was strengthened in the Zürich countryside in the seventeenth century by the development of fixed rights to using common property and to being a member of the community as well as of regulations forbidding the building of new houses. . . . The earning possibilities generated by the putting-out

[19] This reality has led some historians to believe that 'every western European society that has continued to be a peasant society has eventually been forced to adopt some type of preferential partibility to prevent the fragmentation of land below a level of minimum subsistence' (Berkner and Mendels 1978: 214).

[20] In Slovakia, 'where division had created extremely small holdings,' the sons of a peasant household, once married, used to leave their homes and wives and emigrate with the purpose of earning enough money to set themselves up as farmers or to supplement the family earnings at home' (Habakkuk 1955: 9).

industry of Zürich, however, created an entirely new situation . . . there were now entirely new possibilities of marriage and founding a household. Industrial earnings could make a substantial contribution to a peasant enterprise. With this transformation of the basis of peasant existence, the circumstances of inheritance rights were transformed. . . . In the end, people found that it was even enough to have a corner in the house for a spinning wheel or a loom and enough land for a vegetable garden. Hirzel went on to tell us of 'a brave and worthy farmer' whom he had come to know that year (1792), 'who is cultivating only one-eighth of the holding of his grandfather and yet is living happily and well.' In his letters on Switzerland (1791), C. Meiners wrote: 'The increased and sure income offered by the combination of cottage manufacture with farming hastened and multiplied marriages and encouraged the division of holdings, while enhancing their value. . . . Previously fathers and sons avoided dividing fairly large and, even more, modest holdings, for they were concerned that each piece be able to nourish its holder. This fear vanished entirely with the diffusion of manufactures and cottage industry; and now the sons redivided the parcels received from their fathers, themselves the product perhaps of several divisions, because people are convinced that even a small field is enough to feed a diligent holder along with wife and children.' (Braun 1978: 311)

By creating new employment possibilities that peasants could avail while staying in their villages, the development of rural industries had the effect of easing the consequences of partible inheritance, thereby making this system more practicable. Hence the presupposition that partible inheritance is more likely to be found 'in areas where a scanty agrarian income may be supplemented by developing domestic industries and crafts' (Thompson 1976: 342; see also Habakkuk 1955). The expansion of urban-based industries, it may be noted, is expected to generate entirely different effects. As a matter of fact, by creating new income prospects outside of the agricultural sector, urban industrialization tends to increase the returns on education and to induce more permanent migratory movements. This should prompt rural household heads to change their inheritance practices by moving from equal to unequal partitioning of family land.

Compensations

Under systems of single-heir devolution, compensations were frequently given to non-inheriting sons (and to daughters upon their marriage). When the size of the provision for the younger children was left to the discretion of the heir—such as was the case, for example, over most parts of Germany outside the Rhineland and Thuringia (Habakkuk 1955)—land pressure could easily lead him to reduce the inheritance portions of his siblings in order to avoid de-capitalization of the family property. However, when the succession and the provision for the children were determined by the parents—e.g., they were specified in detail in a settlement made on their marriage—the privileged heir was much more restricted and, under conditions of acute land scarcity, economic consequences could be rather similar to those produced by a system of partible heritance.

For example, in the area of Cambridgeshire, which was 'nominally one of primogeniture,' fathers made provisions for their younger children in their wills in the form of fragments of land and cash sums for younger sons, and dowries for daughters, as well as maintenance for the widow.[21] Yet, all these provisions 'did not come out of the savings, if any, of the testator,' and therefore amounted 'to a very considerable burden on the main holding and on the inheriting son.' It is to this burden that we must ascribe the breakdown of holdings of 15 to 45 acres that occurred in spite of the rule of primogeniture (Spufford 1976: 157). In Chippenham, in particular, the granting to younger sons of small portions of land which were not in themselves adequate for support 'merely weakened the main holding.' For one thing, these small bequests of land often ended up in the hands of rural moneylenders-cum-landowners (enterprising yeomen who 'built up their holdings by acquiring mortgages while they were still farming') because they were not viable economic concerns and could not weather bad harvests or other adverse shocks. And, for another thing, the main holding could not be maintained intact and could even be brought close to ruin because it had to support the burden of compensations that could not be provided without eroding the farm's capital. The same effect frequently occurred when, instead of receiving portions of the family land, the younger sons received a cash sum 'to start them off in life' (Spufford 1976: 161–6; see also Schofield 1989 and Todd 1990). The same phenomenon has also been noted by E.P. Thompson: 'the outpayments to be made by the heir sometimes appear as unrealistic,' such as is typically the case when 'mortgages must be taken up or debts incurred to meet the legacies' (Thompson 1976: 346).

Things need not turn out that way, though. Thus, the aforecited study by Homans (1941) suggests that in thirteenth-century England, the claims of non-inheriting children (in open-field areas) were limited to equal portions of non-land assets (goods and chattels) that were not required by the heir for the operation of the family farm. Endowed with these portions, non-inheriting sons would then go out into the world and seek their fortunes outside agriculture—by going to school and then into religious orders, by going to the wars, by entering households of noblemen, or by working as apprentices in towns—or, alternatively, they would cling to an agricultural occupation either by staying and living on the family holding in a celibate state or by working as wage laborers for another landholder (Homans 1941).[22]

When favorable conditions prevailed, the situation was easier to manage: agriculture was more prosperous and ample compensations could therefore be paid to non-inheriting children without threatening the economic viability of the family landholding. A good illustration of this is provided by the study of Cicely Howell (1976) on the English Midlands. According to this study, indeed, the 'drastic culling of village families which took place during the plague period' caused a sudden increase in the size of holding, accompanied by a decrease in household size. This change made possible the accumulation of savings in the form of cash or capital equipment such as had hardly been possible so far, a process that underwent a rapid acceleration during the

[21] In the Paris–Orléans region, the property of a villein 'generally remained entire except for the removal of a few minute fragments previously subtracted by the parents to provide portions for those of their children who had left to make their home under another roof' (Le Roy Ladurie 1976: 43). Often, the non-inheriting children agreed to be compensated in other ways, under the form of cash, apprenticeship or other types of education (Braun 1978).

[22] Marrying an heiress (a daughter without surviving brothers) was, of course, a much better solution since it allowed non-inheriting sons to gain access to land.

inflationary years of the sixteenth century. As a result, younger children could be endowed with cash portions in place of the livestock and gear, which they typically received as compensations for the land that accrued to their eldest brother.[23]

Thanks to capital accumulation and the growing prosperity of yeomen and husbandmen, the main family holding was preserved intact, and 'every effort was made to improve its profit so that larger cash portions could be distributed among the children.' In point of fact, the effect of the shift from legacies in kind to legacies in cash 'not only ensured the continuance of large farms but stimulated long-term improvements in agricultural practices, and provided the motivation for commercial, rather than subsistence, farming.' As for the younger sons of these prosperous yeomen families practicing primogeniture, they were not slow to take advantage of the opportunities open to them in the form of occupations in trade, the professions, and the universities. Moreover, since they had received their portion, they did not return to the native village, unlike what was observed in France and other countries where child portions continued in kind, 'bringing children back at regular intervals to collect their sack of potatoes or to claim maintenance' (Howell 1976: 139, 153, 155).

The dynamic effects of exclusive inheritance on population growth, technical change, and economic entrepreneurship

Population growth

The impact of the inheritance system on population growth is obviously a crucial question since, as documented above, it is under conditions of acute population pressure that adoption of impartible inheritance seems to be most cruel.[24] On *a priori* grounds, it is not easy to predict whether single-heir devolution stimulates or discourages population growth compared with the alternative system of partible inheritance. Two effects may indeed be at work. On one hand, fertility is expected to be higher in stem families typical of regions of impartible inheritance. (Stem families are composed of the privileged heir, his wife and children, his parents, and 'a penumbra of celibate uncles and aunts, younger brothers and sisters.') This is because, being assured of keeping the whole family property, the heir has 'relatively slight inducement to limit the number of his children' (Habakkuk 1955: 6). On the other hand, the nuptiality rate should be significantly lower in single-heir areas since non-heirs are explicitly discouraged to marry early (since they have to leave their home if they want to establish families of their own).[25] This is in contrast to areas of equal division where it is easier for all the

[23] 'In those times, the heir could then either buy out his brothers and sisters, or could continue to support them on the tenement in return for the use of the livestock and the gear, at any rate for the first few years' (Howell 1976: 146).

[24] That was clearly the opinion of Adam Smith (and John Stuart Mill after him): '. . . as of all institutions it (the right of primogeniture) is the fittest to support the pride of family distinctions, it is still likely to endure for many centuries. In every other respect, nothing can be more contrary to the real interest of a numerous family, than a right which, in order to enrich one, beggars all the rest of the children' (A. Smith 1776: 383–4).

[25] As pointed out by Homans, 'a man's status as a landholder or a landless man is in close relation with his status as married or single' (Homans 1941: 136).

sons to marry once they are set up on their own inherited plot, a tendency which should counteract their presumed proclivity to limit the number of their children (if they are able to do so) in order to avoid progressive fragmentation.

The prediction of H.J. Habakkuk is that, 'other things being equal, the higher proportion of marriages under the latter system was likely to produce in the aggregate more children than the fewer but more productive marriages of the former.' As a result, it is hypothesized that 'the single-heir system tended to retard population growth and division to promote it' (Habakkuk 1955: 6; see also Parish and Schwartz 1972; Tilly 1978). From a comparison of two regions belonging to late seventeenth-century Lower Saxony—one which practiced impartible inheritance (Calenberg) and the other the equal division rule (Göttingen and Grubenhagen)—it comes out that both the number of households and total population increased more than twice as rapidly in Göttingen and Grubenhagen as they did in Calenberg between 1689 and 1766 (Berkner and Mendels 1978). Such a finding therefore bears out Habakkuk's above hypothesis that partible inheritance results in fragmentation of the land and rapid population growth through multiplication of local nuclear households and a high nuptiality rate.[26]

If this empirical finding can be taken seriously, there is ground to believe that impartible inheritance has the advantage of attacking the ill that has perhaps caused its emergence, acute population pressure on the land. On the contrary, partible inheritance would accentuate the very problem that makes it an unsatisfactory solution, possibly leading to a total impasse.

Technical change

Regarding technical change, the impact of the inheritance system seems relatively clear. As a matter of fact, in areas of equal division, the peasants were unable to generate savings or, when they could do so, they used them not to improve their properties but to counter the fragmentation of their lands by purchasing additional parcels thrown on the market by the less fortunate members of their own class. In areas of unigeniture, the same outcome could be obtained if the privileged heir was charged with an obligation to compensate the younger children with sums of money calculated on the market value of the property. In these circumstances, indeed, the family property might become heavily burdened with debt and thereby starved of capital (Habakkuk 1955). By contrast, when the heir was not so compelled to provide for his siblings, he could devote more resources to productive investment in the inherited farm.

Economic entrepreneurship

The effect of inheritance practices on economic entrepreneurship is a fascinating question on which very diverse opinions have been expressed but scant empirical evidence is available. A starting point is provided by John McCulloch who contended long ago

[26] The empirical study on rural France by Parish and Schwartz (1972) has concluded that stem households had fewer children than nuclear families. The explanation given by the authors for this rather unexpected result is that stem families may have controlled fertility out of a fear of the new inheritance law imposing equal division of the family property (under the Napoleonic Code).

that primogeniture could stimulate the development of new economic opportunities. For him, indeed, the desire of the younger children to escape from their predicament and to achieve the same standard of living as their elder brother would inspire them 'with an energy and vigor they could not otherwise feel' (McCulloch 1864—cited from Mill 1848: 891). In other words, powerful incentives to start economic ventures in untrodden paths would result from the presence of large and concentrated hereditary fortunes that generate push or demand pressures. According to this view, the positive effect of primogeniture on industrial entrepreneurship depends 'not so much on the poverty of the younger children as on the contrast between that poverty and the riches of the elder' (Mill 1848: 891).

It is, however, hard to believe that industrial development can be triggered off in such a mechanical way. More realistically, a supporting environment must exist for available energies to be willing to invest themselves in new and risky endeavors. To say it otherwise, pull or supply factors must exist that are susceptible to attracting young available energies into non-agricultural occupations, such as was apparently the case in England since the sixteenth century.

A recent thesis, propounded by the French historian Emmanuel Todd (1990), actually goes in the same direction as that of McCulloch although the causal mechanism is quite different. Todd has indeed argued that a strong correlation existed between the type of prevailing agrarian system, in which the rules of inheritance play an important role, and the probability of diffusion of Protestantism and, thereby, of modern capitalism within Europe. The more inegalitarian agrarian systems, such as those embodying inheritance customs based on primogeniture or ultimogeniture, tended to be more open to the influence of Protestantism, a central tenet of which is the essentially inegalitarian idea of predestination. In the words of Todd: 'The idea of predestination of elected people, of a selective access to salvation, remains understandable and acceptable in all the regions where only one brother is entitled to inherit the father's property' (Todd 1990: 143—our translation).

If impartible inheritance is thought by some authors to have stimulated urban entrepreneurship, Habakkuk has put forward the idea that equal division has likewise encouraged entrepreneurship and employment in rural industries: 'the practice of division of property was favorable to the development of local industry in the home or small workshop, for it tended to create a population with time for by-employments.' Yet, the extremely careful wording used by this historian when citing examples reflects his awareness of the shaky empirical foundations of his thesis. He thus writes that it is 'perhaps not entirely a coincidence that the medieval woolen textile industry should have flourished in East Anglia, a region of partible inheritance.' In some other cases, also, it is 'a reasonable conjecture' that the practice of division directly promoted the development of local domestic industry (Habakkuk 1955: 10).

Habakkuk is on much more solid ground when he argues that, whatever may have been the effects of the inheritance system on the distribution of industrial activities, if any, the rule of equal division seems at least to have greatly influenced the capacity of rural domestic industries to withstand the competition of factories in the nineteenth century. The reason is that, as has been pointed out earlier, partible inheritance has

the effect of maintaining a profound link between all (or most of) t
family land, while at the same time forcing them to look for alternative s
As a consequence, labor is readily available for local industrial employ
to attract permanently to urban employment opportunities. 'This fact limited the of operations over which the factory could successfully compete with domestic industry, decentralized in the small workshop and the home, and drawing its labor from local peasant families of the neighborhood' (Habakkuk 1955: 10).

Since, on the contrary, primogeniture areas are characterized by their capacity to send forth their younger sons to become part of a permanent industrial labor force, we have a clue to understanding the differential patterns and rhythms of industrial growth in England and in France, for example. In the words of Habakkuk (1995: 11): 'The persistence of old forms of industry in France, and the wide geographical diffusion of French industry are also, in considerable measure, to be ascribed to immobilities arising from the structure of the French family. It is significant that England, the country of the earliest factories and regions of industrial concentration, was the country where, with a few minor exceptions, young children had no claim at common law to any share of their father's estate.'

Unigeniture versus equal division in developing countries (with special reference to Sub-Saharan Africa)

In light of the above analysis, it is certainly interesting to ask how land is shared in African communities subject to acute land pressure and confronted with the additional difficulty of a lack of industrial development. In fact, Africa constitutes a genuine living laboratory to examine how human societies respond to pressures arising from a scarce natural environment. Yet, before turning to Africa, it is useful to point out that the Asian situation does not apparently differ much from the picture we have painted for Europe.

As a matter of fact, exclusionary tendencies as embodied in primogeniture systems are sometimes found in Asian countries. Thus, in the Garo Hills dominated by matrilineal inheritance practices (Meghalaya state, India), we learn that 'parents with a modest holding usually gave the bulk or even the whole of the land to the heiress-daughter' while 'those with extensive holdings sometimes gave small plots to non-heiress daughters and even to sons, although for the most part, this practice was restrained.' Garos from wet rice areas expressed the feeling that 'it was much better to keep the land together because if it split up, everyone would become poor.' Excluded children were in fact advised to open up new land elsewhere or to work hard and purchase some (Agarwal 1994: 160). Nonetheless, the general picture in the Indian subcontinent seems to be very different as attested by the revealing fact that when British administrators suggested the introduction of primogeniture as a solution to land pressure, 'the scheme was eventually shelved because of enforcement difficulties and the recognition that excluding other children, especially younger sons, would be unacceptable in a system where all children traditionally had inheritance rights' (Agarwal 1994: 182).

In the Philippines as well, we find the same picture of a dominant tendency towards partible inheritance mitigated by some striking exceptions to the rule (e.g., the system of bilateral primogeniture—the eldest son inherits the land of the father and the eldest daughter the land belonging to the mother—prevailing in the Cordillera).[27] Finally, the matrilineal societies of Western Sumatra have devised an ingenious solution to maintain the integrity of the family land estate, by organizing systematic rotation of the right to manage it among the heir daughters (see Otsuka and Quisumbing in this volume).

The situation in Sub-Saharan Africa reveals a deep attachment to the equal division rule. To begin with, this region does not have a tradition of association between land and political power (manifested in indivisible titles and functions) as Western Europe had developed since the early Middle Ages. In that sense, it is correct to say that noble classes, and their custom of impartible inheritance, have not existed in most of the African continent. Village chiefs, and so-called chiefs of the land, masters of the fire, or masters of the axe, had admittedly crucial powers to decide allocation of village lands, yet they were always acting on behalf of the whole community conceived as the corporate owner of the land. Under their responsibility, land was managed in ways that allowed for genuine multitenure systems with different land uses calling for different tenures.

It must now be reckoned that the land tenure system in Sub-Saharan Africa has undergone profound transformations during the last century and particularly during the last decades. In point of fact, under the combined pressures of population growth and increased market integration, landholders have increasingly asserted individualized use rights to given plots: the right to resume cultivation of a specific plot after a period of fallow; the right to assign the plot to an heir or to a tenant; the right to prevent holders of group or secondary claims (e.g., the right of pastoral herders to graze their animals on crop stubble) from exercising their traditional prerogatives; and the right to dispose more freely of the land. In other words, with increasing land pressure and concomitant evolution towards more intensive agricultural practices, community controls over land use and allocation have been reduced, and corporate ownership of the lineage land has gradually given way to more individualized forms of land tenure (see, in particular, Boserup 1965, 1981; Noronha 1985; Bruce 1988; Atwood 1990; Migot-Adholla *et al.* 1991; Platteau 1992, 1996, 2000).

An important manifestation of the above process of individualization of land tenure in Africa is the fact that male children may receive land upon marriage (a so-called *inter vivos* transfer) which they can work within the framework of an independent household. In most cases, however, it is only upon the death of their father or their mother that the definitive partition of the family land takes place with the distribution of all the parcels which the parents had kept for themselves for subsistence during their old age. Frequently, parcels held by the sons are pooled together again with those used by parents and, on that basis, a definitive allocation is realized. It is the customary practice in many areas, and particularly in the densely populated regions of Eastern Africa, that when the father is dead, the mother or, more generally, the eldest son acts as the custodian of the land destined for still unmarried sons.

[27] See Van de Gaer and Crisologo-Mendoza (1996).

The fundamental principle guiding the distribution of family land in Africa is that all male children are entitled to receive more or less equal shares when the property is definitely partitioned (daughters are expected to obtain use rights over their husband's land). Shares of the father's land need not be strictly equal, though. In many countries, for example, the eldest son is customarily entitled to an additional share on account of his special duties, such as custodianship of family land to be distributed later in favor of younger brothers and other family duties, including the power to settle intra-family conflicts. The youngest son may also be granted one or several additional shares when the custom requires that he takes care of his parents during old age. In northwestern Rwanda (and also in western Kenya), characterized by exceptionally high population densities, nonetheless, André and Platteau (1998) have found that these privileged shares are increasingly called into question by the other brothers, hence the rising practice of strictly equal shares. Such a trend towards between-son equalization of status—which has also been reported for Botswana within the context of a herder society (Peters 1994)—seems to be at least partly due to the declining caretaking role of the youngest brother vis-à-vis his old parents.

In addition, a recent study conducted in about forty villages of southeast Uganda by Baland *et al.* (1998) reveals that the dominant pattern of inheritance is that of strictly or almost strictly equal shares among all the male children. Not infrequently, one son, usually the eldest, obtains a higher share than his brothers, yet the difference is rarely substantial given the fact that he may have land in custody on behalf of younger brothers.

In Kenya, another example of a very densely populated region of Africa, people also attach great importance to the principle of equal sharing of family land between all sons. This is so much true that government's attempt to limit the subdivise impact of indigenous inheritance systems through its land registration system led to an enormous amount of evasions which undermined the whole of that system (Bruce 1986). The fact of the matter is that customary law (such as subdivision of land among all the sons) 'in fact continues to govern the way in which most people deal with their land, making tenure rights ambiguous. The land law failed to gain popular understanding or acceptance, individuals continued to convey rights to land according to customary law, and a gap developed between the control of rights as reflected in the land register, and control of land rights as recognized by most local communities' (Barrows and Roth 1989: 7). Likewise, in Rwanda, an official decree (1976) attempting to prohibit the sale, fragmentation, or subdivision of parcels by households owning less than a minimum amount of land (of two hectares) has proved equally unenforceable (for more details, see Ruhashyankiko 1985; Gasasira 1993).

The above evidence is impressive as all the countries covered are confronted with acute problems of access not only to land but also to other sources of subsistence. Equality in inheritance seems to be maintained at the price of reducing landholdings to minuscule sizes that cannot ensure decent livelihood for the rightsholders. It is interesting to note that when access to non-agricultural income opportunities is possible, the erstwhile rule of more or less egalitarian distribution of family property is not modified. Platteau has conducted recent field enquiries in Central Burkina Faso and the Senegal River valley (in the northernmost part of Senegal), and it indeed appears that apportionment of family land is made irrespective of whether a son has received advanced education and obtained a permanent job outside the agricultural sector as a result.

Such a practice is not unjust, as it may seem at first sight. As a matter of fact, there is a sort of implicit contract according to which an educated member of the family who enjoys access to a non-agricultural source of income has a duty to help his brothers who have remained in agriculture whenever the need arises, but more particularly when cash expenditures have to be incurred for purposes of education or health. A majority of respondents still maintain that the rule of equal sharing of family land is applied unconditionally to all the sons, yet deeper probing reveals that there are strong and natural expectations of mutual assistance among educated and non-educated brothers: a son remaining in agriculture may help a brother living in a city by cultivating his rightful share of the father's land (against a share of the harvest) or overseeing its cultivation by other workers; on the other hand, the educated son comes to the help of his brother by providing him with gifts in cash, supporting his children while they are studying in town (e.g., by providing accommodation), etc.

It is noteworthy that in Burkina Faso and Senegal where land pressure is much less impressive than in Kenya, Rwanda, or southeastern Uganda, parents have become acutely aware of the need to diversify sources of income and to encourage their children (including daughters) to attend school with the explicit purpose of gaining access to employment outside agriculture. Unlike what was observed in preindustrial Europe, such employment is available in presently developing countries, and education is an effective strategy opened to those willing and able to leave agriculture. Yet, probably because educated men have special responsibilities toward their farming brothers, the multiplication of these new job opportunities has not led to a questioning of the principle of equal sharing of family land property as has been observed in some European regions.

Now, if state policies or other conditions have the effect of hindering the development of non-agricultural activities—such as has been the case in Rwanda—too many people are compelled to draw their livelihood from a narrow agricultural base. In these circumstances, exclusionary forces acting through the market or through non-market channels will be set off and will negate the egalitarian effects achieved by partible inheritance practices. Let us first consider the nature of such forces when they operate outside the market before turning to the next subsection on market mechanisms proper.

In their aforementioned study of a Rwandan village in Gisenyi Prefecture, André and Platteau have shown that when conditions of living are extremely precarious, weaker categories of rights holders tend to be discriminated against as land becomes scarcer. These vulnerable categories typically comprise women (especially when they are widowed, separated, or divorced, or wives under polygamous arrangements), return migrants, handicapped children, orphans, illegitimate children, or offspring of broken marriages whose father has remarried.

For example, orphans are still accommodated by their grandparents, yet upon the death of the latter they risk being excluded from the (patrilineal) succession. Not very dissimilar is the situation of children of broken marriages: they also live with their paternal grandparents but they suffer from their half-brothers' attempts to evict them from access to the lands of the patrilineage. Or, separated women who come back to their native village along with their children may find their brothers opposing their return lest there should be too little land left for patrilineal descendants. Widows seem to be in an especially difficult position; they often express feelings of insecurity and continuous fear of reprisals from their brothers-in-law who tend to view their children as competing claimants for the lineage's land (a phenomenon which we also observed in Kenya and Uganda).

Another noteworthy feature is the increasing severity with which indigenous marriage customs are enforced with a view to rationing the demand for land (André and Platteau 1998). This is an effective device in so far as a growing number of young residents evade erstwhile marriage customs because their parents are too poor to make the wedding gifts traditionally pledged to the wife's family in order to seal the alliance thereby contracted (the *inkwano*). It was estimated that roughly two-thirds of the couples in the study area of the Rwandan Gisenyi Prefecture were married without payment of the brideprice, and the proportion is obviously much higher among young couples.

Also in the recent past, although on a smaller scale, unions formed in the area were not necessarily accompanied by the brideprice payment. It is noteworthy that the non-fulfillment of this customary obligation did not make the unions illegitimate in the eyes of the local population and, as a result, the rights of access to land of those involved (parents and children) were safely maintained. The only unions that were systematically disapproved of were those resulting from the abduction of a girl by her lover against the will of all parents (a practice known as *gucikira*).

Recently, however, unions performed outside the *inkwano* system are increasingly considered as illegitimate precisely when they have become a widespread practice, owing to rising poverty in the context of acute land pressure. Under these conditions, the stricter reference to custom appears as a convenient stratagem to define new rationing devices to allocate the scarce land resource. The consequences of an illegitimate union may thus be quite serious for the woman in the event of separation from her husband. This is because her bargaining power within the lineage of origin (to which she would then return under the well-established custom) is weak due to the fact that her marriage did not bring material advantages to the lineage's elders and also because she did not perform her traditional role as the instrument through which inter-lineage alliances are sealed under the elders' auspices. Further, if her husband dies, continued access to his land may be denied to her and her children by paternal uncles, a second (legitimate) wife, half-brothers, and other rival relatives competing for the land.

As is evident from the above, the consequences of non-customary unions are quite perilous for the children because they are less recognized as legitimate descendants either by the father's or the mother's lineage. Traditionally, these children were considered to belong to the mother's lineage. Yet, under conditions of growing land scarcity, their customary rights are increasingly called into question by maternal uncles. This is why, for example, it has become common practice for the separated mother to return to her lineage accompanied only by her daughters (since they do not compete for land). The sons are thus left with their father with all the attendant risks of being denied access to his lineage's lands. If the father passes away, they may be rejected from all sides and quickly driven into a landless state. A genuine vicious circle of poverty is therefore at work: children of poor parents cannot get married according to the custom, which makes them more liable to lose the security of access to land and become landless, thereby perpetuating or accentuating the poverty of the last generation of the family.

Impact of land market development on inheritable assets and timing of inheritance

In conditions of acute land scarcity, if family land is divided more or less equally among all sons upon the father's death, population growth has the obvious effect of reducing the land endowment accruing to each male descendant. In the case of a country like Rwanda with an annual population growth rate of about 3.5%, simple calculations show that one holding would fragment into 8.17 parcels in the time span of only two generations and into 66.72 holdings after four generations (120 years)![28] Under these circumstances, as has been argued above, exclusionary processes and resulting conflicts are highly likely to occur. Land market transactions may also be expected to multiply when land becomes so rare that landholdings become economically nonviable. Land parcels are then likely to be sold under distress conditions (or mortgaged and later seized by creditors), entailing the risk that landlessness and land inequality increase (see André and Platteau 1998).[29]

Bearing special emphasis in the context of this study is the influence of land market transactions on non-market mechanisms of land acquisition. Thus, in the Rwandan village studied by André and Platteau, an explicit distinction is drawn between ancestral land that has been obtained through inheritance and land that has been added to inherited wealth by using personal savings. Being considered as rewards for the buyer's own efforts, parcels of land purchased in the market may be freely disposed of by their owner without regard for customary rules of inheritance, an observation which has also been made for northern Ghana (Lastarria-Cornhiel 1997).[30] As a consequence, it is possible that the lands acquired by well-to-do persons will not serve to enlarge the inheritable property of their children.

[28] We have assumed that a generation lasts thirty years. The number of children surviving to age 30 has been found to be 5.715. The formula used is simply: $R = (e^{xp})^G$, where R is the ratio of the number of holdings in terminal year to the number of holdings in initial year; G is the number of generations over which the multiplication of holdings is contemplated; p is the annual rate of population growth; and x is the age at which succession occurs and the family landholding is divided among all the surviving sons. Note that the number of surviving sons to age x is given by e^{xp}.

[29] Historical evidence about medieval Europe points to a relationship between partible inheritance and the activity of the land market (Goody 1983; Le Play 1871; Habakkuk 1955; Parish and Schwartz 1972).

[30] The same practice was also found in England. As early as the thirteenth century, the head of a household was indeed free, subject to the consent of the lord of the manor, to grant or to leave to whom he pleased any land he had acquired outside hereditary succession. 'Only such land descended to the heir as had descended to a line of heirs before him. A family holding, villagers felt, was not to be diminished by alienation, nor was it to be increased by acquisitions' (Homans 1941: 132). In Norway, heirs were actually protected by custom against sale decisions that could reduce their inheritance. Thus, according to the Gulathing Laws, there are two types of land, hereditary or odal land, and money land. Money land was a relatively insecure form of possession since, at any time within twenty years of purchase, the seller's heirs were entitled to redeem it. Moreover, the land purchased did not become hereditary until it had remained in the buyer's family for five generations. By contrast, land transferred by gift immediately became hereditary land (Howell 1976).

Interestingly, when improvements are brought to the land by a household head, the resulting increment in the value of the land is not deemed to be at his free disposal. Therefore, personal efforts and savings are not the only factors that account for the difference in status between inherited and purchased lands; there is also the fact that, contrary to incremental values to existing parcels that cannot be realized separately from the value of the base asset, the value of newly acquired parcels can be easily assessed from the purchase price.

In addition, and more importantly, the household head has to incur out-of-pocket expenditures to acquire land through the market, whereas improvements to inherited lands typically involve labor efforts. And, as we know from several socio-psychological experimental studies, out-of-pocket costs are not equivalent to opportunity costs: the latter tend indeed to be under-weighted relative to the former (Thaler 1991). As a result, landowners insist that the outcome of their out-of-pocket expenditures be under their complete control while simultaneously agreeing that improvements to inherited land parcels, brought about by their labor efforts, obey customary rules of inheritance.

Parcels of land acquired in the market can be freely disposed of by the owner. This implies that he may sell them if he so wishes, or otherwise give them to any person of his choice (including his daughters), thus preventing his sons from inheriting them. But the father may also refuse to grant more land parcels on the occasion of the marriage of his son(s) on the ground that he has acquired them by means of his own savings.[31] In other words, a household head may more easily postpone the devolution of land to his descendants if he has purchased it than if he has inherited it.

To understand all the potential for conflict involved in such situations, it is useful to recall that, if land inheritance can be completed only on the father's death, the practice of *pre mortem* apportioning of family parcels among sons on the occasion of their marriage has become quite widespread. As is evident from recent field inquiries in Burkina Faso and Senegal by Platteau, the emergence of this practice has been caused by the growing desire of young people to emancipate themselves from their father's authority and to run their farm as they wish. Fathers tend to increasingly yield to such pressures because they realize that granting more autonomy to their sons as they enter into adulthood is the only way to provide them with proper incentives to apply labor efforts, and to avoid the sort of intra-family tensions and disputes that arise from working in a team and sharing output according to needs.

Two types of risk continue to exist as long as definitive division of family land takes place only on the father's death. The first risk comes from the fact that the land kept by the father for his own use may be sold by him and therefore ceases to be available for distribution at the time of his death. As we have pointed out above, such risk is especially great when the land has been acquired through market purchases. The

[31] The household head can obviously use the same argument to refuse to abide by other traditional obligations, e.g., the duty to grant use rights over some land to women in difficulty. In their study, André and Platteau thus report that a resident refused to give a parcel of land to his sister who came back to her village after having separated from her husband. He thus violated a custom aimed at preventing social destitution among women who have lost access to land (bear in mind that women are allocated land for usufruct as wives in their husband's lineage), and this he did on the ground that he built up his whole property by purchasing land on the market.

second risk is that the father may decide to take an additional wife (bear in mind that polygamy is a widespread practice in many African countries) to whom he will allocate personal parcels for her own sustenance and that of the newly born children who will one day be additional claimants to the family land.

As a rule, the father is entitled to take land away from his elder sons and redistribute it in favor of younger sons if it appears, say at the time of the latter's marriage, that such transfer is required for the implementation of the equal division rule. (If no transfer takes place, the younger sons would not get as much land as their elder brothers.) Such redistribution can also occur upon the father's death on the same equity ground.[32] These processes of wealth reshuffling are thus grounded on *ex post* assessments since neither the number of claimants nor the inheritable land base can be known at the time of the first apportionments. Yet, for understandable reasons, elder sons tend to resist such attempts at redistribution, especially so if they arise from what appears to be inconsiderate behavior on the part of their father, whether reflected in marriage or in land sale decisions. Of course, such resistance creates room for severe conflicts, not only with the father but also with the younger brothers who risk being disadvantaged.

As illustrated in the case study of Rwanda, resistance by the father against demands for land by his sons, particularly at the time of their marriage, as well as resistance by elder sons against attempts at land redistribution in favor of younger brothers later in their family life cycle, unavoidably give rise to serious arguments and conflicts (André and Platteau 1998). Such conflicts tend to poison intra-family life and destroy co-operation both between father and sons, and among siblings.

Tensions and disputes are especially bitter if married sons live under distress conditions and consider that the land retained by their father for his use (or that of his wives) is too large given his present subsistence needs. It must be pointed out that, in both Rwanda (André and Platteau 1998) and Uganda (Baland *et al.* 1998), the farm area owned or operated per household member has been found to be significantly smaller among young than among old households. Likewise, children may contest the right of their father to rent out land to a stranger while they are themselves short of production means. When the land disputed between father and sons has been purchased by the former instead of having been inherited, the father typically argues with his sons that if they need more land they just have to fend for themselves and emulate his own success in acquiring additional land through purchases.

Mutual understanding is all the more difficult to achieve as the father's strategy is likely to be influenced by feelings of insecurity which drive him to retain some land as precautionary savings. Such feelings are actually encouraged by the erosion of arrangements of old age support following the equalization of status among all the sons. As a

[32] It is interesting to note that a similar practice existed in Normandy, a western region of France characterized by strongly egalitarian tendencies. In the words of a well-known French historian: 'There, in accordance with the rule that after the father's death cancels the arrangements he made for his children during his lifetime, the heirs are obliged to restore to the common stock of property subject to division by inheritance, all the liberalities, gifts, portions and advantages granted to them by the deceased before his death' (Le Roy Ladurie 1976: 55). The habit of returning gifts made *inter vivos* to the common pool upon the death of the father was apparently also in force in ancient England (before the Conquest) (Howell 1976).

matter of fact, the duties of the youngest son in this regard have largely fallen into disuse as well as the land privileges attached to this function.

There are thus many occasions liable to cause suspicions, frustrations, and antagonisms to grow between the two generations. When scarcity of land is extremely acute, such as it was in the Rwandan community studied by André and Platteau, the passing away of parents brings considerable relief to the successors, and parents have painful feelings of neglect and abandonment during their old age. Dominique de Lame has confirmed this impression on the basis of her own observations in another area of Rwanda: there is a tendency among old and weak persons to just let themselves die out of sheer desperation, or out of a feeling that they should make way for younger members of their lineage (de Lame 1996).

As hinted at above, emancipation from indigenous social customs through market transactions can be claimed not only by the older but also by the younger generation. This is illustrated by the study of herder communities of south Botswana (Kgatleng district) by Pauline Peters (1994). In this study, the frustration of elders is emphasized, not a surprising fact given that youngsters are in a privileged position thanks to their access to non-agricultural income opportunities in neighboring South Africa. The traditional system of cattle property inheritance is identical to that observed above for agricultural lands. This system indeed provides that 'cattle are inherited not only on the death of the father but through a *pre mortem* disposition of earmarking animals for children born. . . . On the establishment of the son's own household, the father sets aside the earmarked cattle of his son and a field for the use of the new household' (Peters 1994: 101–2). When the father dies, the unallocated portion of the herd is divided among his children, 'usually with senior members of the deceased's family officiating at the distribution.' During the time the herd remains undivided, either the widow or the eldest son acts as the caretaker. Yet, as the author points out, things are not so simple in actual practice:

> This process is smooth only in description; in practice, the intense competition over the allocation of property is a dominant theme in Kgatla discourse on family and property and is a major source of conflict . . . elder brothers are stereotyped as 'eaters' of their younger siblings' inheritance. Additionally, *pre mortem* inheritance entails conflict between father and son(s). A father faces a dilemma that has moral and tactical aspects. A mark of a proper father is his ability to set up his sons in independent compounds, but of course he must also come to terms with relinquishing control over some of his wealth, with loosening his authority over his sons, and with the foreshadowing of his death. . . . While the animals remain in the same *kraal* with the undivided family herd, they are the responsibility of the father. A son may not sell or otherwise dispose of his earmarked beasts without the permission of his father. His doing so may be treated as theft by his father and pursued as such in the chief's court. Yet the son does have claims on his earmarked cattle: they are recognized to be his, though subject to his father's decisions until he is able to establish his own compound and herd. . . . Disputes arise between father and son over the definition and interpretation of these reciprocal claims. . . . Some fathers, recognizing that to assign animals to an heir is to give a stronger basis for claims of disposition over the animals, are reluctant to engage in this *pre mortem* inheritance, despite custom. (Peters 1994: 102–4)

In the words of a local elder resenting the growing assertion of economic independence by the young generation: 'If a man does earmark animals and later sells an ox, his son may sue him in court for theft! The son forgets that you have brought him up, given him everything he needed. Now he says he wants to be independent and forgets about his younger brothers and sisters whom the father is struggling to bring up' (cited from Peters 1994: 104). The fact of the matter is that 'a son who purchases cattle from his earnings as a mineworker in South Africa can claim that these are solely his and do not come under the authority of his father. The same holds for a daughter who buys cattle from her wages as a housemaid or civil servant. A father, as noted, may remind his children of the past care bestowed on them and of the younger siblings still to be reared. The father's claims are based on the premise that he is the caretaker of the family's corporate property. His child's claim is antithetical to this, founded upon ideas of individual, exclusive rights. Kgatla sometimes describe these conflicts in shorthand as the ways of the whites (*ka sekgoa*) as against those of the Kgatla (*ka sekgatla*)' (Peters 1994: 104–5).

As in the case of western Rwanda, pervasive uncertainties tend to make the practice of *pre mortem* distribution of property conducive to bitter conflicts both between father and sons and between brothers or siblings. As a matter of fact, owing to unpredictable expenditures requiring the sale of animals or to uncertainty about the exact number of heirs, the future stock of inheritable wealth available per claimant cannot be known for sure. Elder brothers therefore strive to have their share not simply earmarked for them but also put at their disposal and under their complete control as soon as possible. They thus hope to avoid situations in which their share is eroded as a result of market sales decided by their father and the additional claims of yet unborn children. On the other hand, the young generation is able to guard itself against such future contingencies by earning monetary incomes through migration and investing the savings thus accumulated in cattle wealth. This is resented by the older generation which considers that this newly acquired wealth ought to be used for the benefit of the whole lineage, including younger siblings.

To sum up, when they acquire assets through the market with the help of personally earned money, family members (whether father or children) tend to claim the rights to use and dispose of these assets at their own discretion without having to submit to customary allocation rules. Those who do not have access to newly acquired assets tend to call the above claims into question and to position themselves as defenders of the 'true' tradition. The outcome of this struggle is, of course, undecided since it depends on the bargaining strength of the contending parties that is not derived from economic position alone. In the long term, however, there is little doubt that economic strength gained through participation in the market will force deep changes in the balance of power between father and sons or between siblings. Where new income opportunities are numerous, particularly in non-agricultural activities, the status of the younger generation is going to be enhanced relative to that of the elders. In other circumstances, the latter's position may remain more unchallenged, especially if they are able to use old and new networks of political patronage to accumulate assets and secure access to the market.

Conclusion

The focus of this chapter is on non-market processes of exclusion from access to land, particularly under conditions of acute land pressure. Among such processes, intra-family exclusionary mechanisms have received primary attention. Yet, as has been argued at length, the borderline between market and non-market mechanisms is not as neat as one might think because owners of self-acquired land tend to consider that such land is exempt from any customary obligation, thus affecting intergenerational transfers of landed wealth.

One of the most well-known intra-family exclusionary mechanisms is that of impartible inheritance which has the advantage of avoiding the fragmentation of family property. The comparative perspective on Europe and Sub-Saharan Africa, which reveals the importance of this mechanism, leads to a number of salient conclusions.

To begin with, the rule of primogeniture has been widely applied in the upper, aristocratic classes of Western Europe since the early Middle Ages, apparently because of the indivisibility of the titles and political functions associated with landownership under the feudal system born of the dissolution of the Carolingian empire. In countries where such a system has never taken roots, such as in Russia and Sub-Saharan Africa, primogeniture in land transmission is not observed among the elites.

Among the lower classes, exclusive or preferential inheritance was much less widespread, especially when due account is taken of the fact that written (customary) laws of primogeniture were frequently circumvented or ignored. The principle of equal transmission of land was nevertheless not universally followed in Western Europe. Impartible inheritance has been observed in some regions and in some periods, and to account for such variations of inheritance patterns throughout the European countryside is a challenging research project that is far from being completed to this date. Yet, an interesting finding that comes out of available studies is that unigeniture was not necessarily associated with conditions of acute land scarcity. Thus, with fiscal advantages in mind, it could be imposed on villeins by local lords who wielded significant power within the purview of their demesne. Or, it was determined by material conditions, such as scale economies and coordination requirements under the open-field system.

On the other hand, unigeniture was found in highly integrated and complex families run by a well-established headship. In this case, the same rationale might have been at work (as among the nobility): the indivisibility of authority and a strong determination to perpetuate the family name, power, and prestige. The desire to reap the benefits of scale economies was still another consideration that could justify the establishment of exclusive inheritance rules.

This said, there is ample evidence that exclusive inheritance tended to develop in regions subject to extreme population pressure, whether under the influence of village-level regulations regarding community membership or not. Even admitting a strong, historically rooted preference for partible inheritance, the question therefore arises as to how far this system can be maintained under conditions of continuous land pressure. The European experience suggests that exclusive patterns of devolution may become unavoidable if such pressure reaches critical thresholds beyond which subsistence from tiny, subdivided holdings becomes impossible. In these circumstances, unless they are ready to go through the ordeal of a prolonged celibacy and accept all the tensions arising from co-residence with a favored eldest brother, youngest sons are compelled to migrate and seek employment and income sources outside the agricultural sector.

Note that when unigeniture in land transmission is accompanied by mitigating clauses under the form of mandatory provisions for non-heir siblings, it may have consequences that are not very different from those yielded by partible inheritance: the family estate may be de-capitalized and possibly dissolved. In these circumstances, the border between the two systems of inheritance becomes blurred.

For another thing, evidence on the so-called proto-industrialization in Western Europe indicates that the expansion of industrial and commercial opportunities in the course of the eighteenth and nineteenth centuries has provided a well-needed safety valve to farming households. In so far as these new opportunities took the form of domestic or cottage industries localized in the villages, they enabled poor rural households to increase (as well as to diversify) their income. As a result, subdivision of landholdings as required by the custom of partible inheritance became possible again, or could be pursued without leading to economically unviable plots of land. According to this story, therefore, rural non-agricultural employment goes hand in hand with partible inheritance.

What can we learn from situations of acute land pressure in present-day Sub-Saharan Africa? Here is a broad region where equal partition of family land upon the death of the father is a sacrosanct social norm that seems able to resist not only the pressure of population on land resources (legislation attempting to prohibit land fragmentation beyond some critical point has been bypassed by rural households of both Kenya and Rwanda), but also the advent of education and the multiplication of non-agricultural activities. When population pressure becomes acute and non-agricultural occupations are poorly developed, the continuation of partible inheritance cannot prevent discriminatory practices from occurring, yet they take on a more concealed or indirect form than under impartible inheritance. As the experience of Rwanda reveals, behind the egalitarian tendencies embodied in the equal sharing rule of inheritance, powerful exclusionary forces are at work that operate within the core of family life. These forces are immensely divisive because they have the effect of setting sons against their father, brothers against sisters and other brothers, rights holders against in-laws, etc.

It is, of course, not an original conclusion to say that, when the natural resource base is too narrow to provide a decent livelihood to all family members, the adoption of an equal sharing rule is bound to create problems and to lead to behind-the-door exclusionary processes. However, how these subtle processes operate and which categories of the rural population are most at risk are worth exploring. Only then can public actions be devised with the aim of alleviating the lot of these people.

On the other hand, when employment opportunities exist outside the agricultural sector that villagers with a sufficient level of education can gain access to, the persistence of the norm of equal sharing of family land has to be seen in light of the implicit obligation of employed educated sons to help their farming brothers whenever feasible. It is presumably because such solidarity ties were not as strong in pre-industrial or proto-industrial Europe than in present-day Africa that the development of urban non-agricultural activities seems to have encouraged the shift from partible to impartible inheritance in Europe while strengthening equal division in Sub-Saharan Africa. The fact that in Africa the social structure is still essentially based on lineage probably goes a long way towards explaining this persistence of active intra-family networks of solidarity.

A possible advantage of impartible inheritance, as suggested by Habakkuk, lies in its capacity to slow down population growth by lowering nuptiality rates. Under a system of equal division of inherited lands, indeed, young men have more incentives to form nuclear households and have children than under a system where access to land is reserved for only one male member of the family. To the extent that all African rural societies adhere to the rule of partible inheritance, it is unfortunately impossible to further test this hypothesis on the basis of African material. Habakkuk has also advanced the hypothesis that equal division encourages entrepreneurship and employment in rural industries. This hypothesis is impossible to test rigorously for Africa, again due to lack of counterfactuals.

Yet, records of rural industrialization in Africa are unimpressive and there seem to exist many infrastructural and other obstacles to such a process that have nothing to do with the kind of prevailing inheritance system (Platteau 2000). Rather than being induced by the inheritance system, availability of non-agricultural employment opportunities in the countryside appears as an exogenous phenomenon that has allowed the equal division principle to survive in a context of strong intra-family solidarity ties.

REFERENCES

Agarwal, B. 1994. *A Field of One's Own—Gender and Land Rights in South Asia.* Cambridge: Cambridge University Press.

Anderson, P. 1974. *Lineages of the Absolutist State.* London: Verso.

André, C. and J.P. Platteau. 1998. 'Land Relations under Unbearable Stress: Rwanda Caught in the Malthusian Trap.' *Journal of Economic Behavior and Organization* 34(1): 1–47.

Atwood, D.A. 1990. 'Land Registration in Africa: The Impact on Agricultural Production.' *World Development* 18(5): 659–71.

Baland, J.M., F. Gaspart, F. Place, and J.P. Platteau. 1998. 'The Roles of Market and Non-Market Mechanisms in the Allocation of Land: The Case of Southern Uganda.' Working paper, CRED (Centre de Recherche en Économie du Développement), University of Namur, Belgium.

Barrows, R. and M. Roth. 1989. 'Land Tenure and Investment in African Agriculture: Theory and Evidence.' LTC Paper 136, University of Wisconsin-Madison, Land Tenure Center, Madison, WI.

Bassett, T.J. and D.E. Crummey (eds.). 1993. *Land in African Agrarian Systems.* Madison, WI: University of Wisconsin Press.

Bergstrom, T.C. 1994. 'Primogeniture, Monogamy and Reproductive Success in a Stratified Society.' Technical Report, University of Michigan, Economics Department, Ann Arbor, MI.

Berkner, L.K. 1976. 'Inheritance, Land Tenure and Peasant Family Structure: A German Regional Comparison.' In *Family and Inheritance—Rural Society in Western Europe, 1200–1800*, J. Goody, J. Thirsk, and E.P. Thompson (eds.). Cambridge: Cambridge University Press.

Berkner, L.K. and F.F. Mendels. 1978. 'Inheritance Systems, Family Structure, and Demographic Patterns in Western Europe, 1700–1900.' In *Historical Studies of Changing Fertility*, C. Tilly (ed.). Princeton, NJ: Princeton University Press.

Bernheim, B.D., A. Shleifer, and L.H. Summers. 1985. 'The Strategic Bequest Motive.' *Journal of Political Economy* 93(6): 1045–76.

Betzig, L. 1993. 'Sex, Succession and Stratification in the First Six Civilizations.' In *Social Stratification and Socioeconomic Inequality*, L. Ellis (ed.). New York: Praeger.

Blarel, B. 1994. 'Tenure Security and Agricultural Production Under Land Scarcity: The Case of Rwanda.' In *Searching for Land Tenure Security in Africa*, J.W. Bruce and S.E. Migot-Adholla (eds.). Dubuque, IA: Kendall/Hunt Publishing Company.

Blinder, A.S. 1973. 'A Model of Inherited Wealth.' *Quarterly Journal of Economics* 87 (November): 608–26.

Bloch, M. 1931. *Les Caractères Originaux de l'Histoire Rurale Français*. Paris: Armand Colin (reprinted 1952).

—— 1965*a*. *Feudal Society—Volume I: The Growth of Ties of Dependence*. London & New York: Routledge & Kegan Paul Ltd.

—— 1965*b*. *Feudal Society—Volume II: Social Classes and Political Organization*. London & New York: Routledge & Kegan Paul Ltd.

Boserup, E. 1965. *The Conditions of Agricultural Growth: The Economics of Agrarian Change under Population Pressure*. London: Allen and Unwin.

—— 1981. *Population and Technology*. Oxford: Basil Blackwell.

Braun, R. 1978. 'Early Industrialization and Demographic Change in the Canton of Zürich.' In *Historical Studies of Changing Fertility*, C. Tilly (ed.). Princeton, NJ: Princeton University Press.

Brenner, R. 1976. 'Agrarian Class Structure and Economic Development in Pre-Industrial Europe.' *Past and Present* 70 (February). [Reprinted in Aston, T.H., and C.H.E. Philpin (eds.), 1985, *The Brenner Debate—Agrarian Class Structure and Economic Development in Pre-Industrial Europe*, Cambridge: Cambridge University Press.]

—— 1985. 'The Agrarian Roots of European Capitalism.' In *The Brenner Debate—Agrarian Class Structure and Economic Development in Pre-Industrial Europe*, T.H. Aston and C.H.E. Philpin (eds.). Cambridge: Cambridge University Press.

Bruce, J.W. 1986. 'Land Tenure Issues in Project Design and Strategies for Agricultural Development in Sub-Saharan Africa.' LTC Paper 128, University of Wisconsin-Madison, Land Tenure Center, Madison, WI.

—— 1988. 'A Perspective on Indigenous Land Tenure Systems and Land Concentration.' In *Land and Society in Contemporary Africa*, R.E. Downs and S.P. Reyna (eds.). Hanover, NH and London: University Press of New England.

Carter, M.R., K.D. Wiebe, and B. Blarel. 1994. 'Tenure Security for Whom? Differential Effects of Land Policy in Kenya.' In *Searching for Land Tenure Security in Africa*, J.W. Bruce and S.E. Migot-Adholla (eds.). Dubuque, IA: Kendall/Hunt Publishing Company.

Cooper, J.P. 1976. 'Patterns of Inheritance and Settlement by Great Landowners from the Fifteenth to the Eighteenth Centuries.' In *Family and Inheritance—Rural Society in Western Europe, 1200–1800*, J. Goody, J. Thirsk, and E.P. Thompson (eds.). Cambridge: Cambridge University Press.

Cyrus Chu, C.Y. 1991. 'Primogeniture.' *Journal of Political Economy* 99(1): 78–99.

de Lame, D. 1996. 'Une Colline Entre Mille ou le Calme Avant la Tempête—Transformations et Blocages du Rwanda Rural.' *Annales des Sciences Humaines*, Volume 154, Musée Royal de l'Afrique Centrale, Tervuren.

Dixon, Simon. 1999. *The Modernisation of Russia, 1676–1825*. Cambridge: Cambridge University Press.

Downs, R.E. and S.P. Reyna (eds.). 1988. *Land and Society in Contemporary Africa*. Hanover, NH & London: University Press of New England.

Dubuisson, J.F. 1998. 'Ampleur et Effets des Transactions Foncières dans un Village Béninois.' Working paper, Mémoire de Maîtrise en Sciences Économiques et Sociales, Faculté des Sciences Économiques, Sociales et de Gestion, Namur University, Belgium.

Gasasira, E. 1993. *Manuel de Droit Rwandais: Droit des Biens et Droit Agraire*. Bruxelles: Bruylant.

Goody, J. 1976. *Production and Reproduction—A Comparative Study of the Domestic Domain*. Cambridge: Cambridge University Press.

—— 1983. *The Development of the Family and Marriage in Europe*. Cambridge: Cambridge University Press.

Habakkuk, H.J. 1955. 'Family Structure and Economic Change in Nineteenth Century Europe.' *The Journal of Economic History* 15(1): 1–12.

Hilton, R.H. 1985. 'A Crisis of Feudalism.' In *The Brenner Debate—Agrarian Class Structure and Economic Development in Pre-Industrial Europe*, T.H. Aston and C.H.E. Philpin (eds.). Cambridge: Cambridge University Press.

Hoch, S.L. 1986. *Serfdom and Social Control in Russia: Petrovskoe, a Village in Tambov*. Chicago, IL: Aldine.

Homans, G.C. 1941. *English Villagers of the Thirteenth Century*. Cambridge, MA: Harvard University Press.

—— 1953. 'The Rural Sociology of Medieval England.' *Past and Present* 4(1): 32–43.

—— 1957–58. 'The Frisians in East Anglia.' *Economic History Review* (2nd Series) 10: 189–206.

Hosking, G. 1997. *Russia—People and Empire, 1552–1917*. London: HarperCollins Publishers.

Howell, C. 1976. 'Peasant Inheritance Customs in the Midlands, 1280–1700.' In *Family and Inheritance—Rural Society in Western Europe, 1200–1800*, J. Goody, J. Thirsk, and E.P. Thompson (eds.). Cambridge: Cambridge University Press.

Jassal, S.T. 1997. 'Primogeniture in Awadh—Sociological Implications for Class and Gender.' *Economic and Political Weekly* 32(20): 1255–64.

Kriegel, B. 1995. *The State and the Rule of Law*. Princeton, NJ: Princeton University Press.

Lastarria-Cornhiel, S. 1997. 'Impact of Privatization on Gender and Property Rights in Africa.' *World Development* 25(8): 1317–33.

Le Play, F. 1871. *L'Organisation de la Famille*. Paris: Téqui.

Le Roy Ladurie, E. 1966. *Les Paysans du Languedoc*. Paris: SEVPEN.

—— 1976. 'Family Structures and Inheritance Customs in Sixteenth-Century France.' In *Family and Inheritance—Rural Society in Western Europe, 1200–1800*, J. Goody, J. Thirsk, and E.P. Thompson (eds.). Cambridge: Cambridge University Press.

Le Roy, E., A. Karsenty, and A. Bertrand. 1996. *La Sécurisation Foncière en Afrique—Pour une Gestion Viable des Ressources Renouvelables*. Paris: Karthala.

Lopez, R.S. 1971. *The Commercial Revolution of the Middle Ages, 950–1350*. Englewood Cliffs, NJ: Prentice-Hall.

Macfarlane, A. 1978. *The Origins of English Individualism—The Family, Property and Social Transition*. Oxford: Basil Blackwell.

Maine, H.S. 1861. *Ancient Law*. London: Oxford University Press (pub. 1931).

Martin, J. 1995. *Medieval Russia, 980–1584*. Cambridge: Cambridge University Press.

McCulloch, J.R. 1848. *A Treatise on the Succession to Property Vacant by Death.* London: Longman, Brown, Green, and Longmans.

—— 1864. *The Principles of Political Economy.* New York: Augustus M. Kelley (Reprint of the 5th edition, 1965).

McKean, M.A. 1986. 'Management of Traditional Common Lands (Iriaichi) in Japan.' In *Proceedings of the Conference on Common Property Resource Management*, National Research Council. Washington DC: National Academy Press.

Menchik, P.L. 1980. 'Primogeniture, Equal Sharing, and the U.S. Distribution of Wealth.' *The Quarterly Journal of Economics* 94(2): 299–316.

Mendels, F.F. 1970. 'Industry and Marriages in Flanders before the Industrial Revolution.' In *Population and Economics: Proceedings of Section V of the IV Congress of the International Economic History Association*, P. Deprez (ed.). Winnipeg: University of Manitoba Press.

—— 1972. 'Proto-Industrialization: The First Phase of the Process of Industrialization.' *Journal of Economic History* 32(1): 241–61.

—— 1975. 'Agriculture and Peasant Industry in Eighteenth-Century Flanders.' In *Economic Issues in European Agrarian History*, W.N. Parker and E.L. Jones (eds.). Princeton, NJ: Princeton University Press.

Migot-Adholla, S., P. Hazell, B. Blarel, and F. Place. 1991. 'Indigenous Land Rights Systems in Sub-Saharan Africa: A Constraint on Policy?' *World Bank Economic Review* 5(1): 155–75.

Mill, J.S. 1848. *Principles of Political Economy.* New-York: Augustus M. Kelley (Reprint of the 7th edition 1871, 1965).

Miller, C.T.C. 1992. 'The Governance of Real Property in England from Henry I to the Second Reiteration of Magna Carta.' Working paper, Webster University, St. Louis, MO.

Montesquieu, Charles de Secondat. 1834. *De L'Esprit des Lois.* Paris: Didot.

Mutel, A. 1976. 'Recherches sur les Coutumes d'Aînesse Absolue: Ponthieu et Boulonnais.' *Revue Historique de Droit Français et Étranger* 4(54): 321–47.

Neveux, H., J. Jacquart, and E. Le Roy Ladurie. 1975. *Histoire de la France Rurale, Tome II: L'âge Classique des Paysans, 1340–1789.* Paris: Seuil.

Noronha, R. 1985. 'A Review of the Literature on Land Tenure Systems in Sub-Saharan Africa.' Working paper, Research Unit of the Agricultural and Rural Development Department, The World Bank, Washington DC.

Obeyesekere, G. 1967. *Land Tenure in Village Ceylon.* Cambridge: Cambridge University Press.

Parish, W.L. and M. Schwartz. 1972. 'Household Complexity in Nineteenth Century France.' *American Sociological Review* 37 (April): 154–73.

Peters, P.E. 1994. *Dividing the Commons—Politics, Policy, and Culture in Botswana.* Charlottesville, VA & London: University Press of Virginia.

Pipes, R. 1995. *Russia under the Old Regime.* London: Penguin Books.

—— 1998. *Three Whys of the Russian Revolution.* London: Pimlico.

Planck, U. 1967. 'Hofstellenchronik von Bölgental 1650–1966: Strukturwandlungen in einem Fränkischen Weiler.' In *Wege und Forschungen der Agrargeschichte. Festschrift zum 65. Geburtstag von Günther Franz*, H. Haushoferand and W. Boelcke (eds.). Frankfurt am Main: DLG Verlag.

Platteau, J.P. 1992. 'Land Reform and Structural Adjustment in Sub-Saharan Africa—Controversies and Guidelines.' FAO Economic and Social Development Paper No. 107, FAO, Rome.

—— 1996. 'The Evolutionary Theory of Land Rights As Applied to Sub-Saharan Africa: A Critical Assessment.' *Development and Change* 27(1): 29–86.

—— 2000. *Institutions, Values and Economic Development.* Harwood Publishers, forthcoming.

Poly, J.P. and E. Bournazel. 1980. *La Mutation Féodale—X–XII Siècle.* Paris: Presses Universitaires de France.

Raeff, M. 1984. *Understanding Imperial Russia.* New York: Columbia University Press.

Roberts, J.M. 1995. *The Penguin History of the World.* London: Penguin Books.

Ruhashyankiko, N. 1985. 'Réflexion sur Quelques Aspects du Problème Foncier au Rwanda.' *Revue Juridique du Rwanda* 9(1): 1–20.

Schapera, I. 1970. *Tribal Innovators: Tswana Chiefs and Social Change, 1795–1940.* London: Athlone Press.

Schofield, R. 1989. 'Family Structure, Demographic Behaviour, and Economic Growth.' In *Famine, Disease and the Social Order in Early Modern Society*, J. Walter and R. Schofield (eds.). Cambridge: Cambridge University Press.

Smith, A. 1776. *An Inquiry into the Nature and Causes of the Wealth of Nations.* Indianapolis: Liberty Classics. [Reprinted 1979, Clarendon Press, Oxford, R.H. Campbell and A.S. Skinner (eds.).]

Smith, T.C. 1959. *The Agrarian Origins of Modern Japan.* Stanford, CA: Stanford University Press.

Spufford, M. 1976. 'Peasant Inheritance Customs and Land Distribution in Cambridgeshire from the Sixteenth to the Eighteenth Centuries.' In *Family and Inheritance—Rural Society in Western Europe, 1200–1800*, J. Goody, J. Thirsk, and E.P. Thompson (eds.). Cambridge: Cambridge University Press.

Stone, L. 1977. *The Family, Sex, and Marriage in England 1500–1800.* Harmondsworth: Penguin Books.

Stone, L. and J.C. Fawtier Stone. 1984. *An Open Elite? England 1540–1880.* Oxford: Clarendon Press.

Thaler, R.H. 1991. *Quasi-Rational Economics.* New York: Russell Sage Foundation.

Thirsk, J. 1976. 'The European Debate on Customs of Inheritance, 1500–1700.' In *Family and Inheritance—Rural Society in Western Europe, 1200–1800*, J. Goody, J. Thirsk, and E.P. Thompson (eds.). Cambridge: Cambridge University Press.

Thompson, E.P. 1976. 'The Grid of Inheritance: A Comment.' In *Family and Inheritance—Rural Society in Western Europe, 1200–1800*, J. Goody, J. Thirsk, and E.P. Thompson (eds.). Cambridge: Cambridge University Press.

Tilly, C. (ed.). 1978. *Historical Studies of Changing Fertility.* Princeton: Princeton University Press.

—— 1990. *Coercion, Capital, and European States, AD 990–1992.* Cambridge, MA & Oxford: Blackwell.

Tilly, C. and W.P. Blockmans (eds.). 1994. *Cities and the Rise of States in Europe, A.D. 1000 to 1800.* Boulder, CO: Westview Press.

Todd, E. 1990. *L'Invention de l'Europe.* Paris: Editions du Seuil.

Tomes, N. 1981. 'The Family, Inheritance, and the Intergenerational Transmission of Inequality.' *Journal of Political Economy* 89 (October): 928–58.

Van de Gaer, D. and L. Crisologo-Mendoza. 1996. 'Inheritance Rules and the Distribution of Land: Customary Law in the Cordillera, Philippines.' Working paper, Department of Economics, Katholieke Universiteit Leuven, Belgium.

Waldron, P. 1997. *The End of Imperial Russia, 1855–1917.* London: Macmillan Press.

Wolf, E.R. 1982. *Europe and the People Without History.* Berkeley, CA: University of California Press.

Worobec, C.D. 1995. *Peasant Russia—Family and Community in the Post-Emancipation Period.* DeKalb, IL: Northern Illinois University Press.

3

Intrahousehold Access to Land and Sources of Inefficiency: Theory and Concepts

MARCEL FAFCHAMPS

The literature on women and development has documented women's lack of access to land, credit, and farm inputs in many developing countries (Boserup 1970; Gladwin and McMillan 1989; von Braun and Webb 1989). It also has provided evidence of gender casting and other restrictions on female labor (Brown and Haddad 1995; Fafchamps and Quisumbing 1998). This situation has been identified as a source of inequality between men and women, and as encouraging abuse (Jones 1983, 1986). In addition, it has been claimed to be inefficient (Jiggins 1989; Udry 1996*b*). In response to these claims, aid agencies have set up targeted programs to deliver credit and inputs to women and, to a lesser extent, to open their access to land. This chapter proposes a framework that integrates efficiency and equity issues and identifies conditions under which intrahousehold allocation of resources can be inefficient.

Implicit in much of the lay literature is the assumption that women's unequal access to land is a source not only of inequality but also of inefficiency. For instance, it is often claimed that poor countries cannot develop unless women are granted equal access to productive resources (Boserup 1970).[1] The rationale behind these claims is not entirely clear, however.[2] The main objective of this chapter is to clarify the debate by identifying conditions under which inequality is indeed a source of inefficiency. To do so, we must distinguish between access to land within households and across households. Although the two are often discussed interchangeably, conceptually they are quite

I benefited from comments on an earlier draft from Agnes Quisumbing, Lawrence Haddad, Chris Udry, Elisabeth Sadoulet, and participants of the WIDER conferences on access to land held in May 1997 in Helsinki and April 1998 in Santiago de Chile.

[1] Calls for better female access to land have been strongest in Sub-Saharan Africa (Gladwin and McMillan 1989). This is somewhat surprising because relative to other regions of the world such as South Asia or Latin America, women in Sub-Saharan Africa have a comparatively easier—though by no means equal—access to land.

[2] Some claim that women produce 'all the food' and thus should be given more land (Gladwin and McMillan 1989; Jiggins 1989). Jiggins (1989), for instance, claims that in Sub-Saharan Africa '[women] produce approximatively 60% of the food that is consumed by rural households.' It is unclear how women could produce all the food if they do not have access to land, however. Others argue that women should be given better access to credit so that they can hire enough manpower to cultivate their fields. Egyir (1998), for instance, points out that Ghanaian women who farm independently '[hire] male labor to take on strenuous activities.' Playing the devil's advocate, it looks like these women have more land than they can cultivate—i.e., that they were given too much land for an efficient allocation of factors of production, not too little.

separate. Access to land for male and female dependents is determined within the household; access to land for female-headed and female-operated households is determined outside the household.[3] The processes for allocating resources vary between the two.

Allocation within the household resembles what takes place within a firm. Most households have a hierarchical structure, with much of the control over household resources such as land and capital concentrated into the hands of the head (Haddad, Hoddinott, and Alderman 1997; Egyir 1998). Conflicts over the division of welfare between dependants and the head are somewhat reminiscent of labor disputes between workers and employers—and potentially as bitter and unpredictable. In addition to a hierarchical structure, households often institute an explicit division of labor together with systems of delegation of authority (Cleave 1974; Egyir 1998; Shapiro 1990; Fafchamps and Quisumbing 1998). This is particularly true of rural households in poor economies where self-provision of food, shelter, water, fuel, child and elderly care, and most services is the rule—and thus where the tasks undertaken by households are both numerous and complex.

In contrast, the allocation of land across households typically takes either the form of a gift or a market transaction, with occasional hybrid combinations of the two such as rental to a friend at below market price (Egyir 1998, Table 2). Land sales, rentals, and sharecropping are market transactions: they involve two-way contractual obligations that are mutually balancing. Inheritance, transfer at marriage, and other transfers *inter vivos* are examples of allocation mechanisms based on the gift principle. In this chapter we focus exclusively on intrahousehold allocation; interhousehold allocation is discussed in other chapters of this volume. As we shall argue in the conclusion, access to land by female-headed and female-operated households can be fully understood only after making sense of intrahousehold allocation issues. This is important because the proportion of such households appears to be on the rise in certain African countries (for Ghana, see Egyir 1998).

This chapter is organized as follows. After a brief review of the literature, we construct a model of intrahousehold allocation of labor and land, and we derive conditions for allocative efficiency. We show that, depending on returns to scale, specialization, and experience, efficiency in production may require land and other productive inputs to be centrally managed and individuals to specialize in certain tasks or activities. Intrahousehold equity in welfare, however, need not be achieved. We also propose an explanation for the observed heterogeneity in the allocation of tasks by age and gender across regions. We then explore conditions under which commitment failures arise, that is, when household members are unable to pre-commit their future actions and hence find it difficult to enforce intrahousehold agreements regarding land and labor. In this case, we show that imperfect factor markets prevent households from achieving allocative efficiency and that access to land and other productive resources is likely to be conflictual. We argue that the West African practice of letting female

[3] Female-headed households are defined as households headed by widows, divorced, and single women; female-operated households are those where the male head is absent and participates little or not at all in household production activities.

and male dependents cultivate their own plots of land can be understood as a way of motivating dependents to work harder and of resolving commitment failure between heads of household and dependents. Implications for empirical research are summarized at the end.

A brief survey of the intrahousehold literature in economics

Much of the economic literature on intrahousehold issues has focused on the distribution of consumption among household members (McElroy and Horney 1981; Manser and Brown 1980; Haddad and Kanbur 1990; Haddad, Hoddinott, and Alderman 1997; Browning *et al.* 1994). Production decisions are often ignored and, with the exception of Becker (1981), the emphasis is exclusively put on gender issues, with little consideration for intergenerational issues. Such treatment may suffice for developed countries where small nuclear households dominate, most people work for a wage, and children go to school and leave their parents afterwards. Indeed, thanks to household equipment and public utilities, the time devoted to household chores has drastically been reduced. Meal preparation and childcare services are increasingly purchased on the market instead of being self-provided.

This fundamental transformation of family life has not yet reached much of the Third World, especially rural areas. There, households are large, occasionally encompassing several couples with their children. Household members are engaged in a multiplicity of income generating activities, both on their own account and in collaboration with others. Self-employment is the rule—in farming, livestock raising, crafts, trade, and services. Household chores are many and time-consuming; they fall overwhelmingly on the shoulders of women. Children, of whom there are plenty, spend less time in school and more time helping around the house or the farm. It is customary for young adult males to remain on their father's farm until they are allowed to marry—and often to stay after marriage in the case of vertically integrated households (Binswanger and McIntire 1987; Rosenzweig and Wolpin 1985). Third World households are thus more complex than present day households in developed economies. A proper understanding of their functioning requires a conceptual framework tailored to their characteristics.

Much of the descriptive literature on intrahousehold issues in developing countries—and much of social tension and political activism—focuses on access to productive resources such as land, capital, and farm inputs (Kumar 1994; De Groote and Kebe 1995; Goetz and Gupta 1996; Smith 1994). This is hardly surprising given that the predominant avenue to financial independence—and thus to the freedom to choose one's consumption and privately enjoy it—is by engaging in an individually managed income-earning activity such as a farm or business (Egyir 1998). Third World societies have evolved detailed laws and customs governing the transfer and use of productive resources such as land and capital, and specific tasks and roles are assigned to household members according to their status (Fafchamps and Quisumbing 1998). These rules restrict individual choice and impose financial and work obligations that contribute to the joint welfare of the household as a group.

Financial independence is usually granted in exchange for assuming specific responsibilities. In many Sahelian villages, for instance, the head of the household manages the main cereal fields and disposes of the output, but is responsible for feeding the family. Married wives often are granted small plots that they cultivate on their own, but they must provide the 'sauce,' that is, the vegetables and condiments that spice up family meals. Unmarried sons may earn pocket money by cultivating their own field, but they must first work on the household's main fields. Tension between household members therefore arises from the allocation of labor among competing income-generating activities with distinct residual claimants (Jones 1983, 1986; Boe 1996). Some suspect that tension over labor allocation may even be the source of economic inefficiency (Udry 1996*a*; Balsvik 1995). Gender inequality in the acquisition of schooling, experience, and skills opening the door to wage employment is also widespread (Rosenzweig and Evenson 1977; Adams and He 1995; Alderman and Christi 1990; Khandker 1988; Jacoby 1991; Filmer 1996), together with occasional accusations that male heads of household collude to exclude women or young adults from remunerative activities (see Kevane 1996; Anderson and Francois 1996). Domestic violence and social stigma are cited as additional pressures that certain heads of household bring to bear on recalcitrant members. Jones (1986), for instance, reports that if a wife refuses to work on her husband's farm, the husband is allowed by custom to beat her (see also Lilja 1996; Lilja *et al.* 1996; Kevane 1996).

While some of the themes that run through the intrahousehold literature in developing countries are similar to those that animate the feminist discourse in developed economies, the emphasis on access to productive resources and on the allocation of household labor to individual income-earning activities is original (Haddad, Hoddinott, and Alderman 1997). Issues of welfare equity within Third World households are also not limited to gender distinctions (Haddad and Kanbur 1990, 1993; Kanbur and Haddad 1994; Quisumbing, Haddad, and Peña 1995; Dercon and Krishnan 1997). They encompass adult dependents, mostly young males.

Early formalization of intrahousehold allocation is couched in terms of a unitary model of the household (Becker 1965). Labor supply response and nutrition outcomes are interpreted as results of the maximization of a single utility function. The works of Rosenzweig (1986), Rosenzweig and Evenson (1977), Pollak and Wachter (1975), Jacoby (1991), and Skoufias (1993) fall within this category. If applied wisely, this approach can yield interesting results, even if the underlying assumptions can be criticized as unrealistic. For instance, it can explain why parents prefer to send boys to school because returns to education are higher than for girls (Rosenzweig and Schultz 1987); why food, when it is scarce, goes to adult males because they are the prime income earners of the household (Pitt, Rosenzweig, and Hassan 1990); or why women concentrate on house chores because their wage outside the household is lower than that of men (Evenson 1978; Becker 1965; Low 1994).

Seminal contributions by Manser and Brown (1980) and McElroy and Horney (1981) challenged the unitary model of the household and proposed its replacement with a collective model in which household members bargain over the distribution of consumption among themselves. They show that the bargaining power of individuals depends on the resources they command, and thus on their individual incomes. Consumption thus depends not only on the household's total income but also on which member earns it. Individual payoffs in case of breakdown of cooperation serve as threat points in the negotiation over household expenditures, thereby helping to shape the allocation of leisure and consumption among household members. Several possible determinants of these threat points have been suggested in the literature, such as land ownership, education, entitlement programs, laws and customs about the sharing of household assets in case of divorce, and social norms regarding gender-specific tasks and parenting responsibilities (McElroy 1990; Lundberg and Pollak 1993). Tests of income pooling have usually rejected the unitary model (Manser 1993; Thomas 1993).

Intrahousehold modeling has recently been rejuvenated by the work of Chiappori (1988, 1992, 1997) and co-authors (Browning *et al.* 1994; Bourguignon *et al.* 1993; Bourguignon, Browning, and Chiappori 1995). Chiappori's idea is a simple but powerful one. Even though there is no commonly accepted model of bargaining, most such models discussed in the economic literature—whether cooperative or not—generate Pareto-efficient outcomes (as do unitary models which are a special case of collective models; see Haddad, Hoddinott, and Alderman 1997). Efficient allocations within the household exhibit certain characteristics that can serve as a basis for a test of allocative efficiency without assuming any particular form of bargaining. The application of these ideas to household consumption data from developed countries has failed to reject allocative efficiency while rejecting income pooling (Browning *et al.* 1994; Bourguignon *et al.* 1993; Thomas 1993; Manser 1993; Fortin and Lacroix 1993). Using data from Taiwan, Thomas and Chen (1994) nevertheless reject Pareto efficiency for some allocations. Taken together, these results constitute evidence in favor of the collective model of the household, leading Alderman *et al.* (1995) to urge analysts to think seriously about collective model alternatives to the unitary model.

Early work by Jones (1983, 1986) and a recent paper by Udry (1996*a*) nevertheless suggest that farming households in Africa fail to efficiently allocate productive resources within the household. Rather than relying on the complicated consumption-based tests proposed by Chiappori and co-authors, Udry (1996*a*) focuses on the production side and tests whether yields are equalized across plots managed by different household members. He finds conclusive evidence that plots in the hands of women and young adult males have lower yields than those operated by male heads of household. His results and those of Jones, obtained in African farming households where individual members are known to operate in separate spheres (Lundberg and Pollak 1993, 1994; Katz 1994; Carter and Katz 1997), cast doubt on the efficient collective model of the household.

The reason for allocative inefficiency is unclear, however. Balsvik (1995) suggests that it may be due to commitment failure. Because the head of the household is unwilling or unable to credibly commit to reward the work of his wife and dependents after harvest, the latter prefer to divert their labor to their own fields and income earning activities. Similar ideas permeate the works of Jones (1983) and Lundberg and Pollak (1994). In a repeated long-run union, the threat of future non-cooperation should in principle induce voluntary collaboration and solve the commitment failure problem.[4] If, however, certain promises are not credible and certain Pareto-improving trades are not feasible, the achievement of allocative efficiency may be prevented. One of the objectives of this chapter is to examine the precise conditions under which a commitment failure may arise. We leave for future work the enforcement difficulties arising from the presence of multiple wives or nuclear households within the production unit, as in the case of polygamous or vertically integrated households (Jacoby 1995).[5]

A neo-classical model of intrahousehold allocation

To capture the essence of the allocative issue, consider the following stylized model of a collective household operating in separate spheres. The household is assumed comprised of N members, each of whom is endowed with total time T_i, land A_i, and labor efficiency e_i, representing schooling, skills, and experience (Becker 1981). (Without loss of generality, variable A_i can also be thought of as a vector of land qualities and productive assets including farm equipment, working capital, and livestock.) For the moment, individual land endowments and the mapping of individuals into households are taken as exogenously given. Non-productive members of the household are ignored for simplicity. Individual household members allocate their time between work on their own account and work for other members of the household, outside wage work, and leisure. They choose how to spend their income.[6] Individual consumption expenditures are financed through income from their own production and wages, the net of transfers to and from other household members.

We begin by assuming that factor markets are totally absent. This assumption is lifted later on. Formally, the decision problem facing each individual member of the household can be denoted as follows:

$$\underset{c_i, L_{ij}, g_{ij}}{Max}\, U^i(c_i) + V^i\left(T_i - \sum_j L_{ij}\right), \tag{1}$$

subject to a budget constraint

$$pc_i = F\left(A_i \sum_j e_j L_{ji}\right) + \sum_j g_{ji} - \sum_i g_{ij}, \tag{2}$$

[4] Indeed, in many societies, laziness is often an accepted motive for divorce.

[5] It is immediately apparent that many concepts developed for firms can be applied to complex household structures, such as multiple-agent models, theory of hierarchies, information circulation issues, etc. Patrimonial law—e.g., rules of devolution of assets upon death or dissolution—also becomes more complicated in multiple households.

[6] In other words, we rule out paternalism, that is, the possibility that a particular household member may decide the consumption of another member against his or her will. How individual consumption is decided is irrelevant, as long as individual preferences dictate how money is spent on someone's consumption bundle. The production and consumption of household public goods singularly complicates the analysis without adding to our results; it is not considered here (see, for instance, Bergstrom 1995).

and non-negativity constraints $L_{ij} \geq 0$ and $g_{ij} \geq 0$. Variable c_i stands for consumption (possibly a vector); L_{ij} is the labor time provided by individual i on j's income earning activity; and g_{ij} is the transfer from individual i to individual j. Utility is assumed non-altruistic and separable between goods and leisure. Preferences may vary across individuals but all have access to the same production technology $F(\cdot)$, which depends on total effective labor $\sum_j e_j L_{ji}$ and land A_i. Leisure l_i equals total time T_i minus total labor $\sum_j L_{ij}$. When deciding their own labor and consumption, individuals take transfers from others L_{ji} and g_{ji} as given. First order conditions yield the usual

$$\frac{\partial U^i}{\partial c_i} = \lambda_i p, \tag{3}$$

$$\frac{\partial V^i}{\partial l_i} = \lambda_i e_i \frac{\partial F}{\partial L_i}, \tag{4}$$

where $L_i = \sum_j L_{ji}$. Variable λ_i is the Lagrange multiplier associated with the budget constraint; it measures the marginal utility of income. Voluntary transfers of labor and money are against an individual's self-interest since they subtract from his own consumption. In equilibrium therefore, $L_{ij} = 0$ and $g_{ij} = 0$ for all $i \neq j$.

In this world of isolated individuals, production efficiency is not achieved. Individuals with low land A_i and thus low returns to labor would be better off exchanging labor for consumption with better-endowed individuals who would themselves benefit from hiring other people's labor. The absence of market implies that production decisions are a function not only of individual assets A_i but also of tastes $U^i(\cdot)$ and $V^i(\cdot)$ and of individual efficiency of labor e_i. This result is a well-known feature of unitary household models with missing markets (Singh, Squire, and Strauss 1986; de Janvry, Fafchamps, and Sadoulet 1991).

Suppose now that a complete competitive market exists in which individuals can freely exchange labor at the same wage w per unit of effective labor. The production and consumption choices of individuals operating in their separated spheres becomes:

$$\underset{c_i, L_{ij}}{Max}\ U^i(c_i) + V^i\Big(T_i - \sum_j L_{ij}\Big), \tag{5}$$

subject to a budget constraint

$$pc_i = F\Big(A_i, \sum_j e_j L_{ji}\Big) + \sum_j we_i L_{ij} - \sum_i we_j L_{ji}, \tag{6}$$

and the usual non-negativity constraints, $L_{ij} \geq 0$. First order conditions yield the usual

$$w = \frac{\partial F(A_i, L_i)}{\partial L_i}. \tag{7}$$

Labor use and thus output no longer depend on individual preferences and labor efficiency, but they still are a function of individual land endowments A_i. The wage rate w clears the market for labor. Labor flows from resource-poor to resource-rich individuals. Everybody is at least as well off and many are strictly better off, although better-endowed individuals continue to enjoy a higher level of welfare. How gains from trade are divided across buyers and sellers of labor depend on labor supply and demand elasticities.

The existence of a competitive labor market implies that labor resources are allocated efficiently within the household as well. Since all household members face the same opportunity cost for effective labor, workers are efficiently allocated to individual production units. There is no need for intrahousehold bargaining. Intrahousehold labor transactions need not, however, take the form of an explicit wage contract. Household members may be compensated for the work they provide to others in an implicit manner, e.g., through gifts or a larger share of household consumption expenditures. Formally, this situation can easily be represented in our model by letting the size of the gifts from other household members to i be a function of the labor provided to them:

$$g_{ji} = we_i L_{ji}. \tag{8}$$

As long as the 'brownie points' that individuals gain by helping out other household members are commensurate to the wage they would earn outside the household, their labor is allocated efficiently within the household. In equilibrium, if households are sufficiently similar, labor transactions between households may be infrequent without necessarily implying that labor is not put to the best use.

The existence of a labor market does not, by itself, ensure productive efficiency, however, unless A_i is not a vector but a single land input and the production function $F(A, L)$ exhibits constant returns to scale (CRS). In this case, the existence of a competitive labor market ensures that expected yields are the same for all individuals on all plots—maintaining our assumption of common technology. Evidence that yields differ then constitutes an indication that labor markets are inefficient (Gavian and Fafchamps 1996; Udry 1996*b*). When A_i is a vector of inputs, however, markets for all factors of production except one must exist for production efficiency to be achieved. Short of that, output will continue to depend on individual resource endowments.

If production is not CRS, efficiency in production requires that markets exist for all factors of production.[7] Exchange can take a variety of forms (e.g., rentals, sales, or partnerships) that, for our purpose, is largely irrelevant as long as efficiency is achieved. Assume that it is. What will efficient production look like? The answer depends on returns to scale. If they are decreasing, the atomization of production is optimal:

[7] There are many reasons why production techniques may not be perfectly replicated from field to field and thus why returns to scale in agriculture may not be constant. All ultimately have to do with the presence of imperfectly traded inputs, such as credit, management, experience, and rental services of indivisible equipment and infrastructure (Feder 1985; Eswaran and Kotwal 1986).

each individual should be an independent producer. If they are increasing, all production should be undertaken by a single individual who will buy and rent all factors from the market. If returns to scale are first increasing then decreasing, the optimal size of the production unit may require that several, though not all individuals pool their productive resources together; individual production will be sub-optimal.

These results, although hardly original, seem to have been overlooked in much of the lay discourse on intrahousehold allocation. Efforts by heads of household to centralize farm management and gather control over land and other productive resources are customarily interpreted as a devious ploy to deprive women of their rights. This may very well be the case, as we shall argue when we discuss commitment failure. But one should also be open to the possibility that centralization is in fact efficient, especially, as von Braun and Webb (1989) suggest, when new technologies are introduced. Financial outlays for fertilizer, improved seeds, and pesticides raise marginal returns to labor and increase the penalty for untimely performance of agricultural tasks, especially if the household is risk averse. New agricultural technologies may also raise the returns to education, and hence the comparative advantage of better educated household heads as farm managers (Jamison and Lau 1982). In these cases, technology adoption is expected to trigger a concentration of control over household labor into the hands of a single individual, typically the head of household (von Braun and Webb 1989).[8] If concentration is efficient, then it should be possible for household heads to improve everyone's lot while at the same time compensating other members for their loss of individual output. From an economic point of view, such compensation can be regarded as a payment for the use of productive resources controlled by individual household members.

The structure of production is also likely to be affected by returns to experience (Becker 1981). Suppose that production requires that various tasks be performed, e.g., planting, weeding, harvesting, threshing. Further suppose that, thanks to learning by doing, individuals with a lot of experience in a certain task k are more proficient in that task so that:

$$e_{ik}^{t} = g_k\left(\sum_{s=1}^{\infty}\sum_{j}\gamma^{s}L_{ijk}^{t-s}\right), \tag{9}$$

where e_{ik}^{t} denotes the labor efficiency of individual i in task k at time t, $\gamma \leq 1$ is a depreciation factor, and $g_k(\cdot)$ is some increasing function. In the presence of returns to experience, it is in society's interest to encourage individuals to specialize in particular tasks and to make sure that a task is always performed by the person most experienced to undertake it. To achieve this result, individuals may have to work in each other's fields, e.g., men clearing women's fields and women weeding men's fields. Alternatively, they may become exclusively responsible for particular activities

[8] This of course begs the issue of who in the household is the most suitable person to assume management responsibilities. For instance, if schooling and experience raise effectiveness in management, the better-schooled and most experienced member of the household ought to be the one to take over management duties. Some of these issues are addressed below.

involving closely connected tasks, such as food preparation or beer brewing, for instance (Fafchamps and Quisumbing 1998).

From the point of view of efficiency, how tasks are distributed among people is largely irrelevant as long as gains from learning by doing are achieved. This may account for the existence of extremely wide variations in the distribution of agricultural tasks by gender and age. In northern Nigeria, for instance, women do not participate in field work (Hill 1977; Fafchamps 1986); in much of Zaire, they perform almost all agricultural tasks with the exception of land clearing. Individual comparative advantage in learning and performing particular tasks may nevertheless dictate who specializes in what. It would be unwise, for instance, to assign children to tasks that require much physical strength, such as clearing fields. But they are perfectly adapted to herding livestock. In countries where women bear many children and breastfeed them for extended periods of time, one may argue that activities around the home constitute their comparative advantage. In stable pre-industrial societies where the range of tasks and activities undertaken does not change over time, the allocation of people to specific tasks is achieved largely through age and gender casting. Gender-specific role models often reinforce gender casting (Collier and Yanagisako 1987). Certain societies push this principle even further by restricting particular tasks or activities to individuals belonging to a specific lineage or caste (e.g., the caste system in India or Yemen; marabouts, griots, and blacksmiths in Africa).

Age and gender casting to match individuals with particular tasks also dictates a particular pattern of land allocation, and thus, of land inheritance and disposition *inter vivos*. For instance, when men are responsible for clearing the land and do most of the land preparation while women do most of the weeding, harvesting, and processing, as is true in parts of South Asia, there is no need to allocate land by gender; it is optimal for men and women to farm together under the management of a single head. In this case, inheritance customs are expected to ensure that households have a viable farm size without much concern for gender. Of course if farm management itself is a task that is the full responsibility of the household head, the devolution of land, either by inheritance or *inter vivos* transfer, should be tightly linked to household formation: land will be passed from heads of households to heads of households.[9] To the extent that household heads are married men, access to land by women will be *de facto* restricted.

In contrast, when women are responsible for growing vegetable crops while men cultivate staple food crops, as is the case in Burkina Faso for instance (Matlon and Fafchamps 1989), most land should go to men; women should only receive small vegetable gardens, which is precisely what we observe. When women take care of producing the staple food while men produce a cash crop, as occurs in Central Ghana for instance, then one would expect women to have larger plots and more equal access to land. The contrast that Egyir draws between Central Ghana and Northern Ghana, where

[9] It is so natural to think of a farm as being managed by the household head that survey questionnaires often assume this to be the case. This stands in sharp contrast with off-farm activities such as crafts and trade which are often undertaken by dependents and are not linked to household formation: while the creation of a new farming unit occurs simultaneously with the creation of a new household, the creation of a new trading or craft enterprise does not.

little cash crop production takes place, is consistent with this pattern: women have less access to land and are more subordinate to their husbands in the North. Finally, if women are not participating in crop production at all but look after livestock in and around the house, as is the case in Ethiopia and Pakistan (Fafchamps and Quisumbing 1998), all cultivable land ought to go to men. Women may nevertheless hold grazing rights as a result of their involvement in livestock production. The same is true for secondary land rights that women derive from their responsibilities for firewood and water collection. What gender casting cannot explain, however, is why male and female members of the same household would grow the same crops on different, individually managed plots, as reported by Udry (1996*a*).

In the presence of learning by doing, sorting people among multiple activities cannot easily be achieved in a decentralized manner. Letting individuals decide what to specialize in may lead to over or under provision of certain skills.[10] Age and gender casting thus can be seen as a means of solving the coordination problem involved in achieving gains from specialization. It nevertheless raises two serious objections. First, it seldom is equitable. Certain tasks are more pleasant than others, and the return from certain skills higher than others. Those forced to undertake unpleasant and undervalued tasks are likely to resent the allocation process and oppose it if they can. Second, age and gender casting is unlikely to be fully efficient because it prevents many individuals from expressing their full potential. The efficiency loss will be larger when new economic opportunities arise and traditional casting rules no longer ensure a match between the supply and demand for task specific skills. This may explain why age and gender casting have been more successfully challenged in modern societies than in traditional ones.[11]

It would be erroneous to assume that economic growth necessarily leads to a loosening of gender roles, however. In many societies, a sizeable gap exists between ideal gender casting as specified in the dominant ideology, and the actual division of tasks by gender. Local culture may, for instance, stipulate that women should not work in the field because such work is thought demeaning. Yet many poor households may fall short of the social ideal simply because they cannot afford to abide by it (Hill 1977; Matlon 1977). In such an environment, increased prosperity is likely to result in a closer match between social ideals and social realities and thus to reinforce gender casting in practice. Good examples of such processes can be found in many Islamic countries where higher standards of living translate into a tighter separation of the sexes (e.g., Saudi Arabia, Pakistan).[12] Efforts by trade unions and other progressive political forces to have strenuous jobs declared unsuitable for women in turn-of-the-century Europe can be seen in a similar light. A complete discussion of these issues is left for future work.

[10] See Matsuyama (1991) for an illustration of how occupational decisions can lead to multiple Pareto ranked equilibrium paths in the presence of sunk costs.

[11] Gender casting may be less rigid than sometimes assumed. von Braun and Webb (1989) showed, for instance, that the introduction of modern irrigation methods along the Gambia River led men to rapidly replace women in rice cultivation in spite of strong taboos regarding male involvement with rice.

[12] I observed similar trends in rural Morocco and Northern Nigeria (see also Matlon 1977).

Missing land and labor market and voluntary exchange

In the previous section we argued that land and other productive resources are allocated efficiently within the household if outside markets exist and are competitive. In practice, however, factor markets are notoriously subject to transaction costs, information asymmetries, and enforcement problems. Can the household efficiently allocate resources within its confines even in the absence of outside markets? The answer is yes, provided traditional gender casting rules ensure a perfect match between the demand and supply of skills and rewards for work on household enterprises equate the marginal return to labor. In the absence of an outside market to set clearly identifiable wage rate w and factor prices r_i, household members may, however, disagree as to how gains from resource reallocation ought to be shared among themselves.

To see this, consider the model presented earlier and suppose for a moment that the economy is limited to the household. Formally, nothing has changed. There exists, therefore, a wage rate w and land price r_i that equilibrate the household factor markets and ensure allocative efficiency within the household. Given the small number of people involved, however, it is unlikely that the household will resort to explicit wage labor transactions. It can, in principle, achieve the same outcome through implicit contracts. Furthermore, the household economy being small, perfect competition is unlikely; there is scope for parties to bargain over the distribution of the gains from resource reallocation. If bargaining is efficient, however, productive resources will nevertheless be allocated such that their marginal returns are equalized across all activities undertaken by the household.

Thanks to the second welfare theorem, any Pareto efficient resource allocation can be represented as a price system combined with lumpsum transfers. Any efficient bargained outcome can thus be written as the solution to a series of individual maximization problems of the form:

$$\underset{c_i, L_{ij}}{Max}\ U^i(c_i) + V^i\left(T_i - \sum_j L_{ij}\right), \tag{10}$$

subject to a budget constraint

$$\begin{aligned} pc_i = {} & F\left(A_i + \sum_j \hat{A}_{ji} - \sum_j \hat{A}_{ij}, \sum_j e_j L_{ji}\right) \\ & + \sum_j (we_i L_{ij} - we_j L_{ji} + r\hat{A}_{ij} - r\hat{A}_{ji} + G_{ji} - G_{ij}), \end{aligned} \tag{11}$$

and the usual non-negativity constraints $L_{ij} \geq 0$, $G_{ij} \geq 0$, and $\hat{A}_i \geq 0$. Variable $\hat{A}_{ij}$ denotes a temporary transfer of productive resource A_i from i to j and G_{ij} is a lumpsum transfer from i to j. The wage rate w and the rental price r can be thought as the shadow cost of labor and resource A_i that individuals face in their bargaining over consumption with other household members. ($\hat{A}_i$, w, and r can be vectors without affecting the argument.)

For a bargaining equilibrium to be both efficient and voluntary, individuals must internalize the true opportunity cost of the land and labor they command. This is achieved by providing rewards or transfers $we_i L_{ij}$ and $r\hat{A}_{ij}$ for labor and land contributed to other members' productive activities, and by demanding rewards and transfers equivalent to $we_j L_{ji}$ and $r\hat{A}_{ji}$ for labor and land contributed by others to i. In practice, of course, these transfers are netted out, so that they are not separately observed.[13] What matters is simply that household members perceive that, at the margin, an additional unit of labor or resource that they provide to others or receive from others is matched by an increase or decrease in individual consumption equivalent to the economic usefulness of these assets in household production. In an efficient bargaining framework, differences in bargaining power only determine the size of lumpsum transfers G_{ij} between household members, not shadow prices w and r.[14]

Without specifying the bargaining process, we now examine the conditions under which individual household members will voluntarily agree to an incentive scheme $\{w, r, G_{ij}, G_{ji}\}$. For readers familiar with general equilibrium or cooperative game theory, this is akin to constructing the core of the household economy (Hildenbrand 1974; Friedman 1990). We consider three possible threat points: (1) non-cooperation within the household, (2) separation from the household, and (3) domestic violence (Lundberg and Pollak 1993; Kevane 1996). In the case of non-cooperation within the household, we assume that individual members can refuse to exchange labor and land with others and choose to rely on their own labor and land A_i. In the case of separation from the household, we allow for the possibility that laws and customs may request that land A_i and other resources be redistributed and that compulsory transfers be imposed on one of the parties (e.g., alimony and child support).[15] Finally, we examine how the threat of domestic violence may induce someone to 'voluntarily' agree to a distribution of the gains from resource reallocation that they would otherwise reject.

Let W_i^a be the discounted utility of a non-cooperating household member i:

$$W_i^a = \sum_{t=0}^{T} \delta_i^t U^i(c_i^a) + V^i(T_i - L_{ii}^a), \tag{12}$$

where c_i^a and L_{ij}^a are the levels of consumption and labor that solve equations (1–2) and δ_i is the discount factor of individual i. Let W_i^c be the discounted payoff of a cooperating household member:

$$W_i^c = \sum_{t=0}^{T} \delta_i^t U^i(c_i^c) + V^i\Big(T_i - \sum_j L_{ij}^c\Big), \tag{13}$$

[13] Jones (1983, 1986) nevertheless reports that Cameroonian women who work in their husbands' fields customarily receive a share of the harvest that is proportional to the work they have contributed. In Papua-New Guinea, it is customary for all household members to receive a share of crop revenue that is commensurate to their contribution to output (private communication from John Gibson).

[14] The size of lumpsum transfers may nevertheless affect the supply of labor and thus the equilibrium wage rate w.

[15] Some customs specify that the bride price must be returned in case of repudiation.

where c_i^c and L_{ij}^c are the solution to the individual's optimization problem when facing incentive scheme $\{w, r, G_{ij}, G_{ji}\}$. Individual i will voluntarily agree to the incentive scheme if:

$$W_i^c \geq W_i^a. \tag{14}$$

This condition, called the household participation constraint, sets limits to the redistribution of welfare that can credibly take place within the household.

Since cooperating households allocate resources more efficiently than non-cooperating ones, individuals can be made to cooperate to incentive schemes that specify lumpsum transfers to others. Lumpsum transfers can be thought of as an entry fee that individuals have to pay to join the cooperating entity. Some household members may be able to capture most of the gains from better resource allocation even if participation by others is voluntary. The maximum size of voluntary transfers is large when gains from cooperation are large, e.g., in the presence of returns to scale and specialization.

Individuals may object to transfers G_{ij} that would make them worse off than what they could guarantee themselves by leaving the household. For this reason, rules regarding access to land are likely to have a paramount effect on the intrahousehold distribution of welfare. Let W_i^l represent the discounted payoff after separation. Depending on current asset endowments A_i (themselves a function of patterns of inheritance and *inter vivos* land transfers), and on laws and customs regarding the rights and obligations of separating household members (e.g., laws regarding divorce, minors, support to the elderly; see Egyir 1998), W_i^l may be larger or smaller than W_i^a. If $W_i^l > W_i^a$, individual i can credibly threaten to separate from the household unless the intrahousehold distribution of consumption is such that $W_i^c \geq W_i^l$. What happens if $W_i^l < W_i^a$? Can the household member credibly threaten to refuse to cooperate without leaving the household? This depends on what happens upon separation. Suppose that separation only entails a redistribution of household land A_i and direct transfer obligations. In this case, $W_j^l > W_j^a$ for some j whenever $W_i^l < W_i^a$: taking resources away from one must make the other better off. Consequently, any threat by household member i to refuse to cooperate without leaving the household will be met by j's threat to leave the household. In this case, all that matters are the W_i^a payoffs. Threats to remain within the household while refusing to cooperate have no power.

The situation is different if household members must relinquish control over some of their land A_i and other assets upon household separation. For example, upon repudiation the bride price may have to be returned to the wife's parents, not to the wife herself. Court fees in case of divorce also subtract from the household assets.[16] In these cases, it is possible that $W_i^a > W_i^l$ for all i's in the household. If this condition is satisfied, no household member can credibly threaten to separate from the household; W_i^a payoffs are the relevant bounds to the houschold participation constraints. If, however, $W_i^a < W_i^l$ for *any* household members, then the relevant payoffs are the W_i^l's.

[16] Another example would be if a young adult who has received land from the chief must return it to the community in the case of a dispute with his father.

Household members may also try to affect the distribution of gains from cooperation through the threat or use of verbal and physical violence (e.g., Egyir 1998; Kevane 1996). Domestic violence is unfortunately too common for this possibility to be discounted. Let P_{ij} denote the pain and suffering that i can inflict on j and let $W_i^a - \sum_j P_{ji}$ be the payoff of a non-cooperating household member who is 'punished' by the others through domestic violence. Whether or not the threat of violence is credible depends on social attitudes and on the legal protection (or lack thereof) that is granted to victims. Clearly, if the threat of violence is credible, $W_i^a - \sum_j P_{ji} < W_i^a$ and the threatened household member is more amenable to intrahousehold distributions of leisure and consumption that are detrimental to himself or herself.

Depending on the social context,[17] a household member may be able to escape violence by leaving the household, provided of course that violence ceases once the victim leaves. This is not always true, as numerous cases of ineffective restraining orders against violent spouses amply demonstrate in the US. If the threat of violence after separation is credible, the payoff upon separation becomes $W_i^l - \sum_j P_{ji}$, thereby further reducing bargaining power. If violence against runaway household members is not credible, perhaps because of physical distance, it is then possible that $W_i^l > W_i^a - \sum_j P_{ji}$. If the above inequality holds, the threat of violence to non-cooperating household members is ineffective—provided individuals can flee the household fast enough to avoid ever incurring P_{ji}.

Given that most domestic violence takes place behind closed doors, deterrence by outside institutions is only feasible if victims choose to report it. Reporting is not problematic after separation since, by definition, $W_i^l - \sum_j P_{ji} < W_i^l$. In the case of violence to non-cooperating members within the household, however, complaining to an external agency may not be individually rational if it leads to the dissolution of the household (e.g., husband or father arrested) and if life after separation is not an attractive option, i.e., if $W_i^c > W_i^l$. As a corollary of this principle, a poor wife might optimally choose not to report a beating rather than starve. If this is the case, the threat of domestic violence is credible and effective even though external deterrence is available at no cost. In other words, household members can only be protected against the threat of physical violence if their outside payoff W_i^l is high enough. This reasoning explains why poor, illiterate women in environments characterized by widespread unemployment might more readily tolerate domestic violence.

We have seen that bargaining power partly determines intrahousehold transfers and thus the relative influence that household members have on household decisions. Credible threats thus affect whose preferences have the largest weight in consumption choices (what Chiappori calls the sharing rule). This idea is implicitly behind much of the discourse about the potentially beneficial consequence of empowering women. For instance, it is often argued that women are more concerned about child nutrition

[17] In some societies runaway wives are hunted down and brought back to their husbands (Kevane 1996). The same treatment is reserved to runaway children almost anywhere.

and education than men. If true, this implies that child nutrition and education can be improved by raising the bargaining power of women within the household. Women have similarly been assumed to care more about vegetables and less about beer and cigarettes than men. To the extent that policy makers identify more readily with (supposed) female preferences, they may choose to increase women's bargaining power even if they do not care about female welfare *per se*.

We argued earlier that age and gender casting are a convenient way of capturing gains from specialization but that, judging from the wide diversity of rules encountered in practice, the allocation of tasks by age and gender is largely arbitrary. In other words, in any given society, there are many different ways of dividing tasks among men and women, the young and the old, all of which capture returns to specialization and are equally efficient. We also pointed out that the choice of age and gender-casting rules dictates a particular set of rules regarding access to land. The arguments presented in this section indicated that access to land (and other income earning opportunities) is expected to have a dramatic impact on the intrahousehold distribution of welfare. Putting the two sections together implies that combinations of rules of gender casting and access to land that are equivalent from an efficiency point of view need not yield the same intrahousehold distribution of welfare. An immediate policy implication is that the relative welfare of a particular group, e.g., women or young adults, can be modified by redefining the rules of role casting and access to land (and other income earning opportunities). To be successful, however, efforts to challenge the status quo need to satisfy two requirements. First, rules regarding role casting and access to land must remain 'in sync.' There is little point insisting that women inherit land if they are not allowed to cultivate it, and vice versa. Second, the new rules must ensure that returns to specialization are achieved. In this respect, efforts to eliminate age and gender casting altogether and replace it with a Jeffersonian ideal of equal opportunity for all may be ill suited to traditional societies with little economic progress. Replacing one role casting system by another that is more beneficial to the target group may be more acceptable by all than the 'chaos' of equal opportunity for all.

Discrimination and collusion in labor and land markets

Throughout the previous section, we assumed that markets do not exist for labor, land, and other productive resources so that the only way efficiency gains from resource reallocation can be achieved is for individuals to form households.[18] In this section we investigate the effect of various market configurations on intrahousehold allocation. We begin by noting that, if complete markets exist and there are no household public goods, there are no efficiency gains to be made from the formation of households.[19] There is, therefore, no room for the cooperative payoff W_i^c to be higher than the

[18] Or other, looser structures such as co-residence units (compounds) and social networks.

[19] This simple but powerful observation may account for the erosion of the family in developed countries. See Binswanger and McIntire (1987) on vertically integrated households.

non-cooperative payoff W_i^a for all i. The only way W_i^c can be greater than W_i^a for some i is for W_j^c to be below W_j^a for some j. In this case, if separation is costless[20] and domestic violence cannot be exerted on separated household members, cooperative payoffs must equal autarky payoffs:

$$W_i^c = W_i^l \tag{15}$$

for all i's. If separation is costly for the household, there is room left for negotiation on the distribution of household leisure and consumption. But if it is not, individual welfare is entirely dictated by factor prices and the distribution of household resources after separation.

The above suggests that legal provisions governing the attribution of household assets and providing for alimony and child support should have a direct effect on the relative welfare of household members (see Egyir 1998 for a description of these provisions in Ghana). In a world of complete markets, however, individuals should refuse to voluntarily join households unless they are guaranteed a payoff after separation that is equivalent to their expected payoff, should they remain on their own. Once laws and customs affecting intrahousehold welfare are fully anticipated, they should result in side payments (e.g., bride price, dowry) at the onset of the union itself, making it difficult for an equity-minded policy maker to durably affect the intrahousehold distribution of welfare (Becker 1981; Lundberg and Pollak 1993).

We just saw that the existence of perfect markets makes it harder for a particular household member, e.g., the male head of household, to appropriate the efficiency gains from the redistribution of land and productive resources. It may, therefore, be tempting for, say, male heads of household to collude and deny their wives and dependents the right to get land of their own and to work outside the household (Kevane 1996; Egyir 1998; Fafchamps and Quisumbing 1998). So doing, they lower females' W_i^a and W_i^l and more easily extract transfers from them. The prohibition to get land and work outside the home or farm further raises the bargaining power of household heads if the members who specialize in domestic or household-based chores become less well informed about possible exit options, less able to secure a job through job market contacts, and thus become more fearful of the consequences of dissent.[21]

The allocation of labor resulting from collusion among male heads need not be inefficient, however, provided that heads of household spend at least part of their time on their own farm or business.[22] Indeed, as long as captive and non-captive workers work together on the same production activity, the opportunity cost of captive labor

[20] i.e., if household members do not have to incur costs to separate (legal costs), they do not have to relinquish household assets to non-household members (e.g., bride price returned to wife's family), and they do not lose entitlement benefits (e.g., tax break).

[21] Formally, the lack of information about job market opportunities translates into flat (i.e., high variance) priors which, if the person is risk averse, lower the expected utility of exit. The lack of network contacts has the same effect by reducing the probability of finding a job. See also Schaffner (1995) for evidence that servility shifts preferences against exit.

[22] As Basu and Van (1996) argue in the case of child labor, prohibiting certain household members from working outside the household may also be efficient if the withdrawal of their labor raises total wages. See also Anderson and Francois (1996).

is the same as the market wage. Aggregate labor resources can thus be allocated efficiently by ensuring that captive workers are given an implicit incentive to work equivalent to we_i. Only when non-captive workers spend all their time outside the household is the allocation of labor inefficient: the household is no longer at an interior solution and the marginal return to captive labor falls below the market wage. In this case, all could be made better by letting underemployed captive workers rent in land or hire themselves out for a wage. If Pareto gains from letting women and children work for other households are large enough, the redistributive gain that household heads obtain by colluding not to rent land or hire each others' dependents is smaller than the efficiency gain that they could achieve by letting them work as laborers or independent farmers. Such a situation is likely to arise in villages and regions with many landless workers and sub-marginal farmers. Collusion to keep dependents out of the land and labor markets then loses much of its attraction and can reasonably be expected to collapse or take another form. Heads of household may, however, continue to extract transfers from dependents by colluding to restrict access to the best land and to pay women and dependents a low wage. Formally, the situation is akin to forming a cartel of employers and is discussed in Akerlof (1976).

Both types of collusive arrangements among heads of household—captive labor or lower wage and bad land—are, of course, vulnerable to free riding. In both cases, it is in the interest of a single employer or landlord to circumvent the collusive arrangement. Employers could attract captive workers by paying them a wage below the market rate or by renting them land at higher than market price because, by securing an independent source of income, captive workers would avoid paying the lumpsum 'tax' imposed by the household[23] and could thus be better off. Similarly, by raising the wage paid to women and children slightly above that paid by others, employers could attract a larger number of low wage but equally productive workers and thus make more profit. Cartel-like arrangements are thus not self-enforcing and require a meta-punishment to be sustained. The form that the meta-punishment may take is unclear, although one can imagine things like social ostracism by other male heads of household, sabotage, violence, poisoning, etc. (Platteau 1996; Kevane 1996). Women and children who work in violation of social prohibition may also face various forms of harassment, including sexual harassment by co-workers.[24]

Another, more subtle way to lower the wage of dependents and thus their exit payoff is to lower their e_i by restricting their access to education and by inciting them to learn tasks with low potential for wage employment, such as household chores. As we noted earlier, age and gender casting of this type need not be inefficient, even though they clearly have detrimental effects on equity.[25] Finally, in places where

[23] Either directly by leaving the household, or indirectly by renegotiating their obligations within the household.

[24] In such a setting, non-discriminatory employment opportunities for women can be created by setting up rural public works programs open to all (e.g., Deolalikar and Gaiha 1992, and the references cited therein show that women often constitute an important proportion of public works employees).

[25] With the same caveat as before, namely that age and gender casting are restrictions to the freedom of opportunity and prevent individuals from achieving their full economic potential, e.g., as entrepreneurs, leaders, researchers, inventors, and the like.

income-earning opportunities mostly take the form of farming and self-employment, access to individual income requires personal finances. In that case, another way of lowering the compensation for dependents' labor is to restrict their access to credit and hence to remunerative uses of their time other than collaboration to household production (Egyir 1998; De Groote and Kebe 1995; Goetz and Gupta 1996; Smith 1994). Udry (1996*a*) gives yet another example in which access to organic fertilizer is the key factor for which women have unequal access.

Time and commitment

In the two preceding sections we argued that individual household members will object to a distribution of gains from resource reallocation that makes them worse off than what they could guarantee themselves by leaving the household or refusing to cooperate. This idea was captured in a household participation constraint of the form $W_i^c \geq W_i^k$ where W_i^k denotes the credible threat point of household member i, which is either W_i^a or W_i^l with or without violence, depending on circumstances. We now examine how participation constraints are affected by the passage of time between the reallocation of land and other productive resources, and the enjoyment of consumption. Throughout this section we assume that households first allocate labor, land, and other productive resources to production (period one). Output is then realized and the proceeds used to finance consumption (period two).

Consider the following arrangement between household members: i agrees to work on j's field in period one in exchange for a share of output in period two, i.e., a 'gift' at harvest time (Jones 1986; Boe 1996). As we have seen in the preceding section, it is rational for i to accept such an arrangement if $W_i^c \geq W_i^k$. For j to voluntarily compensate i, however, the agreement must be self-supporting, that is, it must also be rational for j to fulfill his or her promise in period two:

$$U_j(q_j^c) - U_j(q_j^c - e_i L_{ij} + G_{ij} - G_{ji}) \leq \delta(W_i^c - W_i^k). \tag{16}$$

In other words, for j's promise to be credible, it must be in j's interest to share output with i afterwards. As the above equation shows, j will do so only if the short-term loss from having to compensate i is smaller than the long-term gain from a continued relationship. (We have implicitly assumed that if j fails to pay i, individual i responds by not transferring G_{ij} and refusing to cooperate in the future.) This is unlikely to be true if the promised compensation $e_i L_{ji} + G_{ij} - G_{ji}$ is large, the gain from cooperation $W_i^c - W_i^k$ is small, or j's time horizon is short, i.e., δ is low. If equation (16) is not satisfied, j is unable to credibly commit to compensate i and the agreement will not be fulfilled. Anticipating this, i should refuse to cooperate. There is commitment failure: a Pareto improving transaction does not take place because one party cannot credibly commit to honor the contract (Coate and Ravallion 1993; Balsvik 1995).

Clearly, the possibility of commitment failure puts additional constraints on the type of resource reallocation and compensation schemes that are self-supporting (Pollak 1985). First, for a household member to credibly commit to any *ex post* payment that member must not have been pushed to his or her exit payoff; he or she must derive some benefit from participating within the household. Put differently, for the household head to credibly commit to compensate dependants for participating in farming or household chores, the head must be strictly better off in a functional household than outside of it. If the welfare gains from the household formation are small, this may require that most if not all these gains go to the head for intrahousehold labor transfers to take place. When this condition is not satisfied, members are likely to insist on operating in strictly separate spheres with little or no labor exchange—a feature that many would associate with dysfunctional households. Of course the refusal to collaborate on a common project further reduces gains from household formation and makes the household even more fragile.

Second, for any distribution of the gains from collaboration $W_i^c - W_i^a$, there are limits to the *ex ante* redistribution of productive resources. If equation (16) is binding, production efficiency may be impossible to achieve: i may refuse to work more than a certain number of days L_{ij} on j's field because any promise of payment in excess of $we_i L_{ij}$ is not credible. Of course, it may be possible to redistribute the gains from cooperation differently and raise $W_j^c - W_j^k$ so as to satisfy equation (16). But this would mean taking something away from i, a prospect i is likely to object to.

Third, allowing for an external enforcement mechanism may mitigate commitment failure. One possible mechanism is for household members to pass among themselves market transactions that are at least theoretically enforceable by courts.[26] One conceivable mechanism is reliance on legal institutions, such as nuptial agreements, business partnership agreements, joint ownership of assets, joint holding of bank accounts, etc. When small amounts are involved, however, court action is seldom attractive because it is too costly and time consuming. Alternative legal institutions at the village or community level, such as chiefs and marabouts, may exist that have jurisdiction to adjudicate matrimonial disputes and can put pressure on a recalcitrant spouse to honor a promise. Proving that a promise has been breached and that one spouse is at fault is often difficult to verify, given that households often engage in complex implicit arrangements. If breach of promise cannot be established, external agents may choose to rely on general standards of fairness instead. Given the paucity of data on these issues, providing empirical evidence of what these standards are and how matrimonial disputes are adjudicated in practice is a promising area of research.

Fourth, agreements are more difficult to enforce if compensation is promised only in a distant future (i.e., δ low). In some cases, compensation may be delayed until the death of the spouse or until dissolution of the marriage (Egyir 1998). In this case, rules and customs about the devolution of assets limit the forms that compensation may take, while at the same time making some forms of credible commitments possible. For instance, if laws and customs stipulate that the wife inherits half of the household assets upon death or divorce, it will be easier for the husband to convince his wife to

[26] Market transactions among spouses are common in parts of Sub-Saharan Africa, notably the coastal areas of Ghana and Nigeria. It is, for instance, frequent for women traders to purchase the output of their husband farmers or fishermen.

help build up joint assets than if the wife has no right upon them. In this case, asset devolution rules can be seen as providing a crude commitment mechanism. For such a commitment mechanism to be effective husbands must have no discretion to change the devolution of joint assets; efforts to circumvent rules must be regarded as a form of fraud and punished accordingly.

Credit constraints also matter. Household members who are credit constrained may be unable to promptly pay for labor services and may have to wait until sufficient output has been generated before doing so (Egyir 1998). Their production activity may also be subject to shocks, in which case they may be unable to pay in period two. One would therefore expect commitment problems to be more severe and the intrahousehold allocation of resources to be less efficient in poor, credit constrained households. Finally, commitment failure is more likely when j's time horizon is short, as would be the case if j expects to leave the household in the near future. Implicit agreements among household members are thus less likely to be made and more likely to be broken in households that are dysfunctional or are breaking apart.

For the same reason, commitment failure is more problematic for individuals who expect to migrate, exit, or marry out of the household: these individuals are more likely to free ride and less likely to take a long-term interest in the prosperity of the household. Laws and customs about inheritance, bride price and dowry, etc., can be regarded as an effort to mitigate this form of free riding. Societies in which daughters marry before they are old enough to rationally choose to free ride, also typically deny daughters a right to inherit. In contrast, sons often continue to contribute to household production until they are much older and are typically given, through customs regarding inheritance and *inter vivos* transfers, a stake in their fathers' farms (Egyir 1998).[27]

Another possible way that commitment problems can be solved is by trading labor against land or other productive resources.[28] Suppose j tries to convince i to work full time on his field but i objects that she does not believe she will be fully compensated for her effort—i.e., equation (16) is violated. Given this state of affairs, it may be in j's interest to let i cultivate part of his land and keep the proceeds in exchange for a payment after harvest $r\hat{A}_{ji}$. The transfer of user right over land can then be seen as a way of giving an immediate payment and thus of bypassing commitment failure (see Egyir 1998 for an illustration). Since the land transfer partly or fully cancels out the implicit wage payment we_iL_{ij}, equation (16) is more easily satisfied and the exchange of labor can take place.

Whether or not this arrangement is efficient depends on returns to scale and specialization: if returns to scale are increasing, it is inefficient to divide the farm into distinct units. Even so, the efficiency gain from a better allocation of labor may compensate the efficiency loss from a worse allocation of land, so that the net effect of the

[27] For a discussion of how the concentration of land into the hands of the elder affect family organization and sectoral employment, see for instance St.-Amour and Vencatachellum (1996).

[28] Other give-and-take arrangements can be found as well, e.g., letting women take some of the grain to brew into beer and sell (e.g., Haggblade 1987).

arrangement is beneficial. Udry's (1996*a*) finding that women work harder on their fields than on their husband's is consistent with the existence of incentive problems such as the ones generated by imperfect commitment. Other features described by Udry are also more consistent with commitment problems than role casting. For instance, Udry finds that dependents often grow, on their individual fields, the same crop as the head on the household fields; this is inconsistent with a pure role casting rationale for dependants' plots. Descriptive accounts also point out that dependants who cultivate their own plots are entitled to use the money as they wish—provided they contribute to household expenditures.[29] This is in line with the role of dependants' plots as financial compensation devices: capturing gains from specialization does not require financial independence but commitment failure does. Finally, the fact that dependants' plots are only granted on a temporary basis, mostly by the head of the household, is further indication that commitment failure is the motivation. If role casting were the rationale, there would be little reason for dependants' plots not to be allocated on a permanent basis. All in all, the preliminary evidence is thus highly suggestive that the practice of dependants' plots, which is widespread in much of Western and Central Africa, is primarily an effort to overcome commitment failure within the household. More work is nevertheless needed before we reach a definitive conclusion.

Conclusion and prospect for empirical work

This chapter has examined the conditions under which land, labor, and other productive resources might not be allocated efficiently within (and across) households. We noted that, depending on returns to scale, specialization, and experience, efficiency might require the centralization of production—and thus land—under the authority of the head, and the specialization of individual household members in certain tasks and activities. In this context, age and gender casting can be understood as an institution meant to resolve the allocation of tasks among household members. Because gender and age seldom confer a strong comparative advantage in any particular task, role casting is largely arbitrary, as indicated by the wide variety of task allocation rules that one finds in poor rural areas.

Role casting can thus be seen as an efficiency enhancing institution that attempts to capture gains from specialization by providing a focal point for intrahousehold task allocation. So doing, however, it introduces a potential mismatch between the tasks allocated to particular individuals and their innate talent. The welfare loss from such

[29] The anthropological literature often argues that the reason women receive individual plots is *because* they have responsibilities for providing 'sauce' ingredients and for helping their parents in need; only what is left after these obligations have been met can be used for personal consumption (e.g., Guyer 1981, 1984; Jones 1986; Davison 1988). I propose that causality be reversed, namely that the financial responsibilities of women are nothing but a tax that is imposed upon them *given* that they cultivate their own plot. Since women remain residual claimants of the product of their labor, this is a tax that does not distort incentives. If women did not cultivate their own plot, they would be 'taxed' in labor instead.

a mismatch is probably low in unspecialized, undifferentiated societies such as poor rural areas of the Third World. But it is likely to be high in highly diversified, rapidly evolving societies. Consequently, we expect role casting to become increasingly costly and ill adapted as societies become more differentiated—and thus to be progressively repealed as development takes place. More work is needed on this issue.

A good grasp of role casting is necessary before one can make sense of rules of access to land because role casting often dictates a particular pattern of land allocation across individuals and, thus, of land inheritance and disposition of *inter vivos*. For instance, when women are responsible for certain crops such as vegetables or food crops, it is natural that they be granted access to a commensurate piece of land. In contrast, when women do not participate in crop production—or where participation is restricted to certain agricultural tasks, not certain crops—then female access to land is not required to capture returns from specialization. In that case, one would expect only household heads to receive land.

Role casting and access to land do not only affect intrahousehold efficiency, they also are important determinants of intrahousehold welfare through their effect on exit options and bargaining power within the household. Combinations of rules of gender casting and access to land that are equivalent from an efficiency point of view need not yield the same intrahousehold distribution of welfare. An immediate policy implication is that the relative welfare of a particular group, e.g., women or young adults, can be modified by redefining role casting and rules of access to land (and other income earning opportunities). To be successful, however, efforts to challenge the status quo need to ensure that returns to specialization are still achieved.

We also investigated the relationship between intrahousehold land allocation, voluntary participation constraints, efficiency, and equity and showed that commitment failure within the household may lead to inefficiency. Granting dependants temporary rights to cultivate their own plot of land, as discussed for instance in Udry (1996*a*), may be used to mitigate intrahousehold commitment problems. If this is the case women and other dependants are expected to apply more labor to their farm and business than is efficient. Udry's (1996*b*) results are consistent with this prediction. Second, the head of household is expected to mitigate commitment problems by allocating individual plots and other productive resources on a discretionary basis, as documented by Egyir (1998). Third, inefficiency is expected to be fostered by factors that exacerbate commitment failure, such as short time horizon (sons and daughters who expect to leave the household; dysfunctional families), low assets (low gains from intrahousehold exchange), unequal stakes in the household (some members have low welfare gains from household participation), and poor external enforcement. This is consistent with the observation that adult dependants work in general less hard than the household head and his wife (Cleave 1974; Fafchamps 1986; Fafchamps and Quisumbing 1998). Finally, our framework predicts that the allocation of consumption and leisure should reflect participation constraints. It therefore provides the basis for a test of the effect of determinants of exit options—such as access to land—on the intrahousehold allocation of leisure and nutrition. Providing empirical verification for these predictions is the object of future research.

We finish with a few words about a topic that was ignored here, that of female-headed households. As pointed out by many authors (Egyir 1998; Gladwin and McMillan 1989; Jiggins 1989), female-headed households have unequal access to land and credit. Similar problems, although not as severe, afflict female-operated households. The question is: why? One possible answer is that denying women access to land and credit is a way to lower their exit payoff. Making exit less attractive for women has two effects. First, it reduces their bargaining power within the household, and thus is likely to affect women's welfare even in male-headed households. This issue was discussed in the previous section. Second, it also makes commitment failure less likely and thus mitigates incentive problems and inefficiency within households. This is because allocating most of the welfare gains from household formation to male heads gives them a stake in the preservation of the household. As a result, household heads have an incentive to honor their commitment to redistribute part of the joint output to dependents in exchange for their participation in household activities.

If the above interpretation is correct, denying women access to land and credit indirectly serves to stabilize households—although it does so, arguably, at women's expense.[30] This opens another question, namely, what is the reason for the existence of female-headed households and for the apparent rise in the proportion of female-headed and female-operated households in some African countries? Is it a result of efforts to empower women? Is it a consequence of male migration to cities, mines, and plantations? These issues deserve empirical investigation as they undoubtedly have serious implications on the welfare of children and other social issues (see Akerlof, Yellen, and Katz 1996; Korenman and Neumark 1991; and Akerlof 1998 for a similar emphasis in the US). Before encouraging equal access to land and credit for women, one would like to know what impact this will have on household stability.

To make this clear, consider the following stylized example. Suppose that all land goes to male heads of household, that heads marry to get access to female and child labor, and that they can credibly commit to compensate their dependants because they gain from marriage. Suppose further that a reform grants women half of their husband's land upon divorce. While this reform would probably raise the welfare of wives in existing households, its net long-term effect may be null or negative. For instance, men may respond by refusing to marry and by hiring women and children as wage-workers instead. In this case, the long-term net welfare impact of the reform on women is essentially zero but its effect on out-of-wedlock birth and thus on illegitimate children is likely to be very negative.[31] Only by simultaneously ensuring that daughters gain equal access to land through inheritance and transfers *inter vivos* can this negative effect be avoided. This example serves to illustrate that tampering with family law should not be attempted without considering the effect on household formation.

[30] Because households with two or more adults benefit from cost savings in the provision of household public goods, it is conceivable that women benefit in the absolute sense from being denied access to land if, without it, there would be many more households headed by a single adult, male or female. A thorough treatment of this issue is left for future research.

[31] In equilibrium, the wage women get as workers is equal to the intrahousehold compensation they get when their only asset is labor.

REFERENCES

Adams, R.H. and J.J. He. 1995. 'Sources of Income Inequality and Poverty in Rural Pakistan.' Research Report 102, International Food Policy Research Institute (IFPRI), Washington DC.

Akerlof, G.A. 1976. 'The Economy of Caste and of the Rat Race and Other Woeful Tales.' *Quarterly Journal of Economics* 90(3): 599–617.

—— 1988. 'Men Without Children.' *Economic Journal* 108(447): 287–309.

Akerlof, G.A., J.L. Yellen, and M.L. Katz. 1996. 'An Analysis of Out-of-Wedlock Childbearing in the United States.' *Quarterly Journal of Economics* 111(2): 278–317.

Alderman, H. and S. Christi. 1990. 'Simultaneous Determination of Household and Market-Oriented Activities of Women in Rural Pakistan.' *Research in Population Economics* 7: 245–65.

Alderman, H., P. Chiappori, L. Haddad, J. Hoddinott, and R. Kanbur. 1995. 'Unitary Versus Collective Models of the Household: Is It Time to Shift the Burden of Proof?' *World Bank Research Observer* 10(1): 1–19.

Anderson, S. and P. Francois. 1996. 'Unequal Access and the Detrimental Impact of Development on Women.' Working paper, Department of Economics, University of British Columbia, Vancouver.

Balsvik, R. 1995. 'Production Decisions in Nonpooling Households.' Working paper, Department of Economics, University of Oslo, Oslo, Norway.

Basu, K. and P.H. Van. 1996. 'The Economics of Child Labor.' Working paper, Department of Economics, Cornell University, Ithaca, NY.

Becker, G.S. 1965. 'A Theory of the Allocation of Time.' *Economic Journal* 75(299): 493–517.

—— 1981. *A Treatise on the Family*. Cambridge, MA: Harvard University Press.

Bergstrom, T.C. 1995. 'A Survey of Theories of the Family.' CREST Working Paper 93(13), Department of Economics, University of Michigan, Ann Arbor, MI.

Binswanger, H.P. and J. McIntire. 1987. 'Behavioral and Material Determinants of Production Relations in Land-Abundant Tropical Agriculture.' *Journal of Economic Development and Cultural Change* 36(1): 73–99.

Boe, T. 1996. 'Access Regimes, Loss Avoidance and Institutions: The Mandinka Household Economy.' Working paper, Chr. Michelsen Institute, Bergen, Norway.

Boserup, E. 1970. *Women's Role in Economic Development*. London: Allen and Unwin.

Bourguignon, F., M. Browning, and P. Chiappori. 1995. 'The Collective Approach to Household Behaviour.' Working Paper No. 79, Centro Studi Luca d'Agliano, Queen Elizabeth House, Development Studies, Oxford University.

Bourguignon, F., M. Browning, P. Chiappori, and V. Lechene. 1993. 'Intra Household Allocation of Consumption: A Model and Some Evidence from French Data.' *Annales d'Economie et de Statistique* 29: 137–56.

Brown, L. and L. Haddad. 1995. *Time Allocation Patterns and Time Burdens: A Gendered Analysis of Seven Countries*. Washington DC: International Food Policy Research Institute.

Browning, M., F. Bourguignon, P. Chiappori, and V. Lechene. 1994. 'Income and Outcomes: A Structural Model of Intrahousehold Allocation.' *Journal of Political Economy* 102(6): 1067–96.

Carter, M. and E. Katz. 1997. 'Separate Spheres and the Conjugal Contract: Understanding the Impact of Gender-Based Development.' In *Intrahousehold Resource Allocation in Developing Countries: Methods, Models and Policy*, Lawrence Haddad, John Hoddinott, and Harold Alderman (eds.). Washington DC: Johns Hopkins University Press for the International Food Policy Research Institute.

Chiappori, P. 1988. 'Rational Household Labor Supply.' *Econometrica* 56(1): 63–90.

—— 1992. 'Collective Labor Supply and Welfare.' *Journal of Political Economy* 100(3): 437–67.

—— 1997. '"Collective" Models of Household Behavior: The Sharing Rule Approach.' In *Intrahousehold Resource Allocation in Developing Countries: Methods, Models and Policy.* Lawrence Haddad, John Hoddinott, and Harold Alderman (eds.). Washington DC: Johns Hopkins University Press for the International Food Policy Research Institute.

Cleave, J.H. 1974. *African Farmers: Labor Use in the Development of Smallholder Agriculture.* New York: Praeger Publishers.

Coate, Stephen and Martin Ravallion. 1993. 'Reciprocity Without Commitment: Characterization and Performance of Informal Insurance Arrangements.' *Journal of Development Economics* 40(1): 1–24.

Collier, J.F. and S.J. Yanagisako. 1987. *Gender and Kinship: Essays Toward a Unified Analysis.* Stanford, CA: Stanford University Press.

Davison, Jean. 1988. 'Land and Women's Agricultural Production: The Context.' In *Agriculture, Women, and Land: The African Experience*, Jean Davison (ed.). Boulder, CO: Westview.

De Groote, H. and D. Kebe. 1995. 'The Impact of Credit on Women's Income, or: Is Credit Targeting in South Mali Justified?' Paper presented at the Annual Conference of the American Agricultural Economics Association in Indianapolis, IN, August.

de Janvry A., M. Fafchamps, and E. Sadoulet. 1991. 'Peasant Household Behavior with Missing Markets: Some Paradoxes Explained.' *Economic Journal* 101(409): 1400–17.

Deolalikar, A.B. and R. Gaiha. 1992. 'Targeting of Rural Public Works: Are Women Less Likely to Participate?' Working paper, University of Washington, Seattle, WA.

Dercon, S. and P. Krishnan. 1997. 'Risk-Sharing within Households in Rural Ethiopia.' Working paper, Oxford University, Oxford.

Egyir, I. 1998. 'Intra-Household Access to Land and Sources of Inefficiency: A Case Study of Ghana.' Working paper, Department of Agricultural Economics, University of Ghana at Legon, Accra.

Eswaran, M. and A. Kotwal. 1986. 'Access to Capital and Agrarian Production Organization.' *Economic Journal* 96(382): 482–98.

Evenson, R.E. 1978. 'Time Allocation in Rural Philippine Households.' *American Journal of Agricultural Economics* 60(2): 322–30.

Fafchamps, M. 1986. 'Labor Use and Productivity and Technological Change in African Smallholder Agriculture: Synthesis Report.' Report for Jobs and Skills Programme for Africa, International Labor Organization, Addis Ababa.

Fafchamps, M. and A.R. Quisumbing. 1998. 'Human Capital, Social Roles, and the Division of Labor: Evidence from Pakistan.' Working paper, Department of Economics, Stanford University, Stanford, CA.

Feder, G. 1985. 'The Relation Between Farm Size and Farm Productivity.' *Journal of Development Economics* 18(2–3): 297–314.

Filmer, D. 1996. 'Gender Differences in the Intrahousehold Allocation of Schooling and Preventive Medical Care in Developing Countries: Estimates from Ghana.' Working paper, Department of Economics, Brown University, Providence, RI.

Fortin, B. and G. Lacroix. 1993. 'A Test of the Neoclassical and Collective Models of Labor Supply.' Working paper, Université Laval, Quebec.

Friedman, J.W. 1990. *Game Theory with Applications to Economics.* Oxford: Oxford University Press.

Gavian, S. and M. Fafchamps. 1996. 'Land Tenure and Allocative Efficiency in Niger.' *American Journal of Agricultural Economics* 78(2): 460–71.

Gladwin, C.H. and D. McMillan. 1989. 'Is a Turnaround in Africa Possible Without Helping African Women to Farm?' *Economic Development and Cultural Change* 37(2): 345–69.

Goetz, A. and R.S. Gupta. 1996. 'Who Takes the Credit? Gender, Power, and Control Over Loan Use in Rural Credit Programs in Bangladesh.' *World Development* 24(1): 45–63.

Guyer, Jane. 1981. 'Household and Community in African Studies.' *African Studies Review* 24(2–3): 87–137.

—— 1984. *Family and Farm in Southern Cameroon*. Boston, MA: Boston University, African Studies Center.

Haddad, L. and R. Kanbur. 1990. 'How Serious Is the Neglect of Intra-Household Inequality?' *Economic Journal* 100(402): 866–81.

—— 1993. 'The Value of Intrahousehold Survey Data for Age-Based Nutritional Targeting.' *Annales d'Economie et de Statistique* 29: 65–81.

Haddad, L., J. Hoddinott, and H. Alderman (eds.). 1997. *Intrahousehold Resource Allocation in Developing Countries: Models, Methods, and Policy*. Baltimore, MD: Johns Hopkins University Press for the International Food Policy Research Institute.

Haggblade, S. 1987. 'Vertical Considerations in Choice-of-Technique Studies: Evidence from Africa's Indigenous Beer Industry.' *Economic Development and Cultural Change* 35(4): 723–42.

Hildenbrand, W. 1974. *Core and Equilibria of a Large Economy*. Princeton, NJ: Princeton University Press.

Hill, P. 1977. *Population, Prosperity and Poverty: Rural Kano 1900 and 1970*. Cambridge: Cambridge University Press.

Jacoby, H.G. 1991. 'Productivity of Men and Women and the Sexual Division of Labor in Peasant Agriculture of the Peruvian Sierra.' *Journal of Development Economics* 37(1–2): 265–87.

—— 1995. 'The Economics of Polygamy in Sub-Saharan Africa: Female Productivity and the Demand for Wives in Côte d'Ivoire.' *Journal of Political Economy* 103(5): 938–71.

Jamison, D.T. and L.J. Lau. 1982. *Farmer Education and Farm Efficiency*. Baltimore, MD: Johns Hopkins University Press.

Jiggins, J. 1989. 'How Poor Women Earn Income in Sub-Saharan Africa and What Works Against Them.' *World Development* 17(7): 953–63.

Jones, C.W. 1983. 'The Mobilization of Women's Labor for Cash Crop Production: A Game Theoretic Approach.' *American Journal of Agricultural Economics* 65(5): 1049–54.

—— 1986. 'Intra-Household Bargaining in Response to the Introduction of New Crops: A Case Study from North Cameroon.' In *Understanding Africa's Rural Households and Farming Systems*, Joyce L. Moock (ed.). Boulder, CO: Westview Press.

Kanbur, R. and L. Haddad. 1994. 'Are Better Off Households More Unequal or Less Unequal?' *Oxford Economic Papers* 46(3): 445–58.

Katz, E.G. 1994. 'Gender and Trade Within the Household: Observations from Guatemala.' Working paper, The World Bank, Washington DC.

Kevane, M. 1996. 'Determinants of Women's Time Allocation Between Home, "Family" Field, and Market Production in South-Western Burkina Faso.' Working paper, Department of Economics, Santa Clara University, Santa Clara, CA.

Khandker, S.R. 1988. 'Determinants of Women's Time Allocation in Rural Bangladesh.' *Economic Development and Cultural Change* 37(1): 111–26.

Korenman, S. and D. Neumark. 1991. 'Does Marriage Really Make Men More Productive?' *Journal of Human Resources* 26 (Spring): 282–307.

Kumar, S.K. 1994. *Adoption of Hybrid Maize in Zambia: Effects on Gender Roles, Food Consumption, and Nutrition*, Research Report 100. Washington DC: International Food Policy Research Institute.

Lilja, N. 1996. 'Technological Change in Agriculture and the Welfare of Women in Southern Mali.' Ph.D. Thesis, Department of Agricultural Economics, Purdue University, Lafayette, IN.

Lilja, N., J.H. Sanders, C.A. Durham, H. De Groote, and I. Dembélé. 1996. 'Factors Influencing the Payments to Women in Malian Agriculture.' Working paper, Department of Agricultural Economics, Purdue University, Lafayette, IN.

Low, J.W. 1994. 'The Effect of Household Structure and Inter-Household Income Transfers on Child Nutritional Status in Northern Malawi.' Working paper, Department of Economics, Cornell University, Ithaca, NY.

Lundberg, S. and R.A. Pollak. 1993. 'Separate Spheres Bargaining and the Marriage Market.' *Journal of Political Economy* 101(6): 988–1010.

—— 1994. 'Noncooperative Bargaining Models of Marriage.' *American Economic Review* 84(2): 132–7.

Manser, M.E. 1993. 'The Allocation of Consumption by Married Couple Families in the US: An Analysis Conditioning on Labor Supply.' *Annales d'Economie et de Statistique* 29: 83–108.

Manser, M. and M. Brown. 1980. 'Marriage and Household Decision-Making: A Bargaining Analysis.' *International Economic Review* 21(1): 31–44.

Matlon, P.J. 1977. 'Income Generation in Three Villages of Northern Nigeria.' Ph.D. Thesis, Cornell University, Ithaca, NY.

Matlon, P.J. and M. Fafchamps. 1989. 'Crop Budgets in Three Agro-Climatic Zones of Burkina Faso.' ICRISAT Progress Report, Hyderabad.

Matsuyama, K. 1991. 'Increasing Returns, Industrialization, and Indeterminacy of Equilibrium.' *Quarterly Journal of Economics* 106(425): 617–50.

McElroy, M.B. 1990. 'The Empirical Content of Nash-Bargained Household Behavior.' *Journal of Human Resources* 25(4): 559–83.

McElroy, M.B. and M.J. Horney. 1981. 'Nash-Bargained Household Decisions: Toward a Generalization of the Theory of Demand.' *International Economic Review* 22(2): 333–49.

Pitt, M.M., M.R. Rosenzweig, and M.N. Hassan. 1990. 'Productivity, Health, and Inequality in the Intrahousehold Distribution of Food in Low-Income Countries.' *American Economic Review* 80(5): 1139–56.

Platteau, J.P. 1996. 'The Evolutionary Theory of Land Rights as Applied to Sub-Saharan Africa: A Critical Assessment.' *Development and Change* 27(1): 29–86.

Pollak, R.A. 1985. 'A Transaction Cost Approach to Families and Households.' *Journal of Economic Literature* 23(2): 581–608.

Pollak, R.A. and M.L. Wachter. 1975. 'The Relevance of the Household Production Function and Its Implications for the Allocation of Time.' *Journal of Political Economy* 83(2): 255–77.

Quisumbing, A., L. Haddad, and C. Peña. 1995. 'Gender and Poverty: New Evidence from Ten Developing Countries.' FCND Discussion Paper No. 9, International Food Policy Research Institute, Washington DC.

Rosenzweig, M.R. 1986. 'Program Interventions, Intrahousehold Distribution and the Welfare of Individuals: Modeling Household Behavior.' *World Development* 14(2): 233–43.

Rosenzweig, M.R. and R. Evenson. 1977. 'Fertility, Schooling, and the Economic Contribution of Children in Rural India: An Econometric Analysis.' *Econometrica* 45(5): 1065–78.

Rosenzweig, M.R. and T.P. Schultz. 1987. 'Fertility and Investments in Human Capital: Estimates of the Consequences of Imperfect Fertility Control in Malaysia.' *Journal of Econometrics* 36: 163–84.

Rosenzweig, M.R. and K.I. Wolpin. 1985. 'Specific Experience, Household Structure, and Intergenerational Transfers: Farm Family Land and Labor Arrangements in Developing Countries.' *Quarterly Journal of Economics* 100 (Supplement): 961–87.

Schaffner, J.A. 1995. 'Attached Farm Labor, Limited Horizons, and Servility.' *Journal of Development Economics* 47(2): 241–70.

Shapiro, D. 1990. 'Farm Size, Household Size and Composition, and Women's Contribution to Agricultural Production: Evidence from Zaire.' *Journal of Development Studies* 27(1): 1–21.

Singh, I., L. Squire, and J. Strauss. 1986. *Agricultural Household Models: Extensions, Applications and Policy*. Washington DC: World Bank.

Skoufias, E. 1993. 'Labor Market Opportunities and Intrafamily Time Allocation in Rural Households in South Asia.' *Journal of Development Economics* 40(2): 277–310.

Smith, L.C. 1994. 'Structural Adjustment and Welfare in Rural Africa: The Role of Resource Control in Households.' Staff Paper Series No. 368, Department of Agricultural Economics, University of Wisconsin, Madison, WI.

St.-Amour, P. and D. Vencatachellum. 1996. 'Family Organization, Retirement and Sectoral Employment in Developing Agricultural Economies.' Working paper, Department of Economics, Laval University, Quebec.

Thomas, D. 1993. 'The Distribution of Income and Expenditure within the Household.' *Annales d'Economie et de Statistique* 29: 109–35.

Thomas, D. and C. Chen. 1994. 'Income Shares and Shares of Income: Empirical Tests of Models of Household Resource Allocation Labor and Population Program.' Working Paper 94–08, The Rand Corporation, Santa Monica, CA.

Udry, C. 1996*a*. 'Gender, Agricultural Production and the Theory of the Household.' *Journal of Political Economy* 104(5): 1010–46.

—— 1996*b*. 'Efficiency and Market Structure: Testing for Profit Maximization in African Agriculture.' Working paper, Department of Economics, Northwestern University, Evanston, IL.

von Braun, J. and P.J. Webb. 1989. 'The Impact of New Crop Technology on the Agricultural Division of Labor in a West African Setting.' *Economic Development and Cultural Change* 37(3): 513–34.

4

Land Rights and Natural Resource Management in the Transition to Individual Ownership: Case Studies from Ghana and Indonesia

KEIJIRO OTSUKA AND AGNES R. QUISUMBING

Introduction

The allocation of land to forests, pasture, and crops, and its subsequent use and management, are governed by property rights institutions. Incentives to preserve natural resources and to invest in the planting of trees and other land improvements for future benefits will be dampened without well-established property rights, be it individual, family, or group ownership, simply because the future benefits will not otherwise accrue to those who manage them (Mendelsohn 1994). Thus there is a direct link between the nature of access rights to land and the quality of land use.[1]

Under customary or communal tenure, uncultivated forest land is owned by the community and controlled by the village chief, whereas land that is cleared for cultivation is traditionally 'owned' by the extended family whose members cleared the forest. While usufruct rights are usually well established, individual rights to transfer and inheritance are limited and controlled by community and lineage leaders.[2] Given unclear and

This chapter is based on ongoing work at IFPRI funded by the Government of Japan, the United Kingdom's Department for International Development, and the U.S. Agency for International Development, Office of Women in Development, Grant No. FAO-0100-G-00-5020-00, on 'Strengthening Development Policy through Gender Analysis: An Integrated Multicountry Research Program.' The research was undertaken in collaboration with the Land Tenure Administration Centre, University of Science and Technology, Kumasi, Ghana, and the International Center for Research on Agroforestry. We would like to acknowledge the input of J.B. Aidoo, Frank Place, S. Suyanto, Towa Tachibana, and Thomas Tomich. We thank Marcel Fafchamps and Jean-Philippe Platteau for comments and suggestions. Ellen Payongayong provided excellent research support. The usual disclaimers apply.

[1] This does not necessarily imply that the private ownership system with clear land title is socially most desirable. For example, negative externalities, such as soil erosion, may arise under the private ownership system, when forest lands are opened up and newly brought into cultivation. Private ownership may create inequitable distribution of the benefits from natural resources. Furthermore, farmers may not be able to cope effectively with covariate risk of agricultural and livestock production under the private system, in the absence of well-developed insurance and credit markets. In these cases, common property regimes with communal rules and regulations on the use and extraction of natural resources may be more desirable (Gardner, Ostrom, and Walker 1990).

[2] As will become clearer, there are more similarities than dissimilarities between land tenure institutions in Sub-Saharan Africa and Sumatra. See, e.g., Shepherd (1991) and Bassett (1993) for an overview of land tenure institutions in Sub-Saharan Africa.

uncertain individual rights, incentives to invest in land and tree resources may be thwarted (Besley 1995). Generally, relatively strong individual ownership rights are granted to those who clear communal forests for cultivation and to those who plant trees. However, if land use is limited to food crops grown under shifting cultivation (slash and burn), individual land rights acquired through clearance of communal forests tend to diminish over time. In particular, when land is fallowed, other members of the extended family or the community can claim the right to use this 'unused' land. Under such institutional rules, an individual community member who has cleared forest land would have strong incentives to plant trees in order to establish secure land rights.

Communal land tenure seems to be designed to achieve the equitable distribution of land (and hence income) among community members, thereby assuring communal solidarity and food security. Such an institution works when land is abundant. As population increases, investment in land improvement, such as terracing, irrigation, and tree planting, is often required in order to intensify land use (Boserup 1965). Yet, distortions to individual incentives under customary land tenure may cause serious under-investment in land. Customary land tenure institutions consequently may evolve towards greater individualization with more secure individual land rights (Ault and Rutman 1979).[3] Feder and Noronha (1987) and Feder and Feeny (1993) strongly argue for the efficiency of secure private ownership in providing appropriate incentives to invest in land improvement. Empirical evidence is, however, deplorably weak.

This chapter explores the causes of the evolution of land rights from communal to individualized systems and the consequences of this change on natural resource management, specifically investment in tree planting and the decline of slash and burn agriculture. We base our discussion on household- and community-level surveys from two areas: (1) a major cocoa growing area in Ghana, and (2) the buffer zone of a national forest in Sumatra. We chose these two sites for in-depth case studies because preliminary investigations and field observations revealed similar changes in land tenure institutions in the two geographically separate areas. In particular, traditional systems of communal ownership and inheritance are giving way to individualized property rights in both areas. We attempt to quantify the effect of population pressure and other exogenous variables on the structure of property rights, even though we recognize the difficulty of identifying the impact of population pressure, which is often endogenously determined. Once changes in property rights are determined, we examine the effects of individualization on the sustainable use of the environmental resource base through the adoption of agroforestry. Based on our results, we discuss the implications of policies promoting: (1) the further individualization of land tenure institutions, including the feasibility and desirability of land titling, (2) agroforestry, and (3) market development.

[3] Articles included in an edited volume by Bruce and Migot-Adholla (1993) provide ample evidence that individualization of ownership rights to farm land growing annual crops has taken place in various parts of Sub-Saharan Africa. Yet, comparable evidence has not been supplied for tree crop areas converted from forest areas. See, however, Besley (1995) for the case of cocoa tree management in Ghana, and Place and Otsuka (2000*b*) for the case of woodland management in Uganda.

Methodology and data

Analytical methodology

We conduct our analysis of changing land tenure institutions at the village level, the household level, and the plot level. Following the evolutionary model of farming systems by Boserup (1965), a theory of property rights developed by Demsetz (1967) and Alchian and Demsetz (1973), and a theory of induced institutional innovation developed by Hayami and Ruttan (1985) and Hayami (1997), we postulate that population pressure on land induces changes in customary land tenure institutions from communal and extended family ownership to individualized ownership. However, the autonomous process of evolution of land rights institutions to provide incentives for investing in perennial tree crops rather than shifting cultivation does not necessarily lead to the establishment of a complete private ownership system with land titling which would completely internalize externalities associated with incomplete or insecure land ownership (Platteau 1996).

Village-level analysis

In traditional areas characterized by communal ownership, the agreement of the community must often be obtained in order to convey individualized rights. Since the incidence of different forms of land tenure is determined by the characteristics of the community, we use village-level data on population pressure and the incidence of various land tenure systems to test our hypotheses. We construct estimates of the proportions of land under different degrees of individualized rights at the village level, and estimate the following reduced-form functions explaining the incidence of the various land tenure institutions using a common set of explanatory variables:

$$\begin{aligned} S_i = a_{0i} &+ a_{1i}\,(\text{population pressure indicators}),\\ &+ a_{2i}\,(\text{proportion of migrant population}),\\ &+ a_{3i}\,(\text{a vector of other village characteristics}),\\ &+ a_{4i}\,(\text{regional and area dummies}), \end{aligned} \tag{1}$$

where S_i stands for the proportion of *i*th type of land, a_{ji} are parameters, and all explanatory variables are village-specific except for regional dummies.[4] Land types are indexed by *i* and cover the range from communal to individualized forms of land tenure and usually correspond to the mode of acquisition.[5] Indicators of population pressure include the man–land ratio as a proxy for population density and the population growth rate. We also include the proportion of migrants or other ethnic groups in the population, and other village characteristics such as distance or walking time to the forest or nearest market town, the proportion of nonfarm households, and school

[4] Since the sum of S_i is unity, it is redundant to estimate the four share functions except to show the significance of coefficients directly.

[5] In Ghana, the land tenure types are: family land, gift, village forest land, and acquired nonforest land. In Sumatra, the categories are: land cleared from forests, purchased land, and tree planted area.

attendance ratios. We hypothesize that the man–land ratio or population density has a positive effect on the incidence of individualized forms of land tenure.

Household-level analysis

Having identified the effects of exogenous forces on the choice of land tenure institutions at the village level, we use household-level data to analyze the behavior of households regarding land access. We can reasonably assume that the acquisition or clearance of forest land, the rental and purchase of land, and the development of agroforests reflect choices made by an individual household, while the acquisition of land through inheritance and family allocation is determined primarily by the extended family. Our field observations in both sites suggest that land acquisition generally follows this pattern: if forest land is available, a man acquires such land through clearance when he is young; he receives family land through inheritance, temporary allocation, or gifts, either when he gets married or upon the death of a parent; and he acquires additional land through renting and private purchase. The sequence will vary across cultures and may, of course, reflect idiosyncratic variation. In some societies such as Ghana, forest clearance occurs as a right of passage for young males, and family land is allocated at the time of marriage or upon the death of a parent. In Sumatra, on the other hand, inheritance occurs only upon a parent's death. If potential inheritance or family allocation is correctly anticipated, young farmers may adjust their land acquisition behavior accordingly.

It is therefore reasonable to specify a recursive system of equations in which: first, the acquisition of forest land is determined by exogenous forces; second, the acquisition of family land is determined by the amount of forest land acquired during one's youth, as well as exogenous forces; and finally, the acquisition of land through market transactions is explained by the predetermined forest and family land areas and other exogenous factors.[6] That is:

$$\text{Forest land acquired by farmer} = b_0 + b_1 \text{ (Vector of exogenous variables)} + e_1. \quad (2)$$

$$\text{Transfers of family land or Inheritance} = c_0 + c_1 \text{ (Vector of exogenous variables)}, + \gamma \text{ (Forest land acquired by farmer in his youth)}, + e_2. \quad (3)$$

$$\text{Purchased or rented land} = d_0 + d_1 \text{ (Vector of exogenous variables)}, + \delta_1 \text{ (Forest land acquired in youth)}, + \delta_2 \text{ (Transfers of family land)}, + e_3. \quad (4)$$

The exogenous variables in our estimation include characteristics of the household head (such as age, years of schooling, and place of origin), measures of initial wealth, and measures of family labor endowments. If extended families operate to equalize wealth

[6] If inheritance is perfectly anticipated, the order of equations (2) and (3) may be reversed.

among heirs, *inter vivos* transfers by the extended family may be negatively correlated with initial household wealth. We hypothesize that if land acquired through forest clearance and transfer of family land is insufficient for subsistence, additional land will be acquired through renting and purchase. Population pressure may also affect inherited land per household. We hypothesize that, as population pressure increases, the size of inherited land per household decreases, and farmers clear more forests or purchase and rent more land. In other words, increased scarcity of land induces land transactions through land rental and sale markets.

Parcel-level analysis

Finally, to test whether differences in land tenure institutions within households affect the adoption of agroforestry and management efficiency on agroforestry plots, we estimate the probability of tree planting, the determinants of yields (for cocoa in Ghana), and potential profits (for cinnamon in Sumatra), taking into account household-level unobservables using household fixed effects. Since the equations and estimation methods differ across the study sites, a more detailed discussion is provided subsequently.

Survey design and data

Our analysis includes a two-survey approach, one extensive and the other intensive. In the extensive survey, we collected community or village-level information over a large number of geographically dispersed communities. In the intensive survey, we collected more detailed household and individual-level data from a smaller number of communities selected from the extensive survey sample.

In both Ghana and Sumatra, we randomly selected sixty communities for the extensive survey, described in detail in Otsuka, Suyanto, and Tomich (1997) and Quisumbing *et al.* (1998). We collected community-level information on property rights institutions and land and forest resource management from a spatially diverse set of areas. We conducted a group interview in each community and obtained community-level information on the composition of ethnic groups, physical environment, modes of land acquisition, and rules of land rights under different land tenure systems. In order to obtain accurate information on the modes of land transfer and changes in land tenure over time, we implemented quick individual surveys of five households per village in Sumatra and seven households per village in Ghana.

The intensive survey data were used to examine the role of household and individual-level factors on land acquisition and the management of trees and crops. We conducted detailed household surveys in selected communities where different property rights institutions coexist. In both Sumatra and Ghana, we obtained detailed household and plot-level information on land rights, cropping patterns, and crop inputs and outputs (using a three-round household survey covering one crop year). In this chapter, we use both the extensive and intensive survey data for Sumatra, and only the extensive survey data for Ghana. The quick household survey data in Ghana are fairly detailed and can be substituted for the intensive household survey data.

Table 4.1. *Land use patterns in hectares, farm size, and man–land ratio, 1997, selected villages in Western Ghana*[a]

	Sample size (number of villages)	Bush-fallow cum forest area (ha)	Cocoa area per farm (ha)	Total farm size (ha)[b]			Man–land ratio[c]
				Mean	Minimum	Maximum	
Indigenous villages	36	5.50 (44.3)	4.99 (48.9)	11.98 (100.0)	0.76	139.44	1.16
Migrant villages	24	3.21 (37.1)	5.41 (59.1)	9.53 (100.0)	0.61	112.53	1.31

[a] Numbers in parentheses are the percentages of total farm area in cocoa and bush-fallow cum forest land.
[b] Total includes small areas used for other purposes.
[c] The average number of people per hectare of farm land.

Case studies of Western Ghana and West Sumatra

Western Ghana[7]

Study sites

We conducted the extensive survey in the three most active cocoa growing regions in Ghana: the Western, Brong Ahafo, and Sefwi Regions. These regions are under the customary land tenure system, with all land ultimately controlled by the village chief on behalf of the community, as in other cocoa growing areas of Ghana (Berry 1963). The majority of the people belong to the Akan ethnic group which practices (uterine) matrilineal inheritance, whereas a relatively small number of migrant villages are inhabited by largely patrilineal, non-Akan ethnic groups.[8] The area is characterized by undulating hills and cocoa (*Theobroma cacao*) is the dominant crop, grown mainly on mildly sloping parcels. While virgin forests have largely disappeared, annual crop fields and fallow areas under shifting cultivation, including secondary forests, coexist with cocoa fields. Table 4.1 summarizes the land use patterns, farm size, and man–land ratios in these extensive survey villages. Indigenous villages tend to have larger farm sizes, a lower man–land ratio, and a higher area devoted to bush-fallow land in each farm. Cocoa area per farm, however, is slightly lower than in migrant villages.

Both the mode of land transfers and land rights systems have evolved in Western Ghana. When virgin forests were abundant, forest areas were appropriated by individual members primarily for production of food crops. Relatively strong individual

[7] The Western Ghana case study presented in this chapter is based on the extensive survey of 60 villages, consisting of group interviews and a 'quick' survey of seven households randomly chosen from each village. Unless otherwise indicated, the data used for the Ghana case study come from the survey of seven households in each of the 60 villages.

[8] Some migrants also are of Akan ethnicity, but originate from nearby Akan areas.

Table 4.2. *Distribution of area by modes of acquisition in Western Ghana (%)*[a]

	Indigenous villages[b]	Migrant villages[b]
Allocated family land	22.4	8.5
Inherited family land	13.2	17.9
Appropriated village forest land	18.1	9.7
Purchased village forest land	0.4	12.4
Received as gift	33.0	25.8
Privately purchased	3.8	5.2
Acquired through past renting	1.0	3.3
Rented-in	6.6	15.5
Others	1.5	1.7

[a] Numbers pertain to percentages in areas.
[b] The differences in the proportion of land in indigenous villages and migrant villages are significant at the 0.05 level for all types of acquisition except Others.

land rights were granted in return for the substantial labor input required to clear forests. Traditionally, in the Akan matrilineal system, this type of land was either bequeathed to nephews or allocated to other male members of the extended family, leaving wives and children without clear rights to a man's property if he were to die intestate. More recently, the appropriated community land is increasingly being transferred directly to one's wife and children, and the family land is often given to one's children and wife with the consent of the family members. Such *inter vivos* transfers are termed 'gifts' in our study. Individual rights on such land are firmly established. Land rights have also been more clearly individualized among migrants, who have nuclear families or belong to patrilineal ethnic groups. This process was further strengthened in 1985 by the passing of the Intestate Succession Law (ISL), PNDC Law 111, which provides for the following division of the estate: three-sixteenths to the surviving spouse, nine-sixteenths to the surviving children, one-eighth to the surviving parent, and one-eighth in accordance to customary law. Thus the law allows children and wives to gain access to land previously denied under traditional law.[9] While it is tempting to attribute the high incidence of gifts to the ISL, such transfers have been observed long before the passage of the ISL (Hill 1963).

The distribution of land by mode of acquisition differs significantly between indigenous and migrant villages (Table 4.2). Allocated family land and appropriated village forest land account for a larger share in the indigenous villages compared to the migrant villages. More land in migrant villages has been acquired through purchase and rental agreements. The share of 'gifted' land to children and wives is also larger in indigenous villages compared to migrant villages, and the difference, while small, is statistically significant. In both migrant and indigenous villages, gifts also account

[9] Some authors (e.g., Asenso-Okyere, Atsu, and Obeng 1993) raise the caveat that this requires wives to be registered legally with the state, and that the provisions may not be applied in rural areas.

Table 4.3. *Index of land rights under different land tenure regimes in Western Ghana*[a]

	Indigenous village	Migrant village
Allocated family land		
Food-crop land from father	0.1	0.1
Food-crop land from family	0.5[b]	0.3[b]
Inherited family land		
Akan (matrilineal)	1.1	1.0
Non-Akan (patrilineal)	n.a.	3.3
Village forest land		
Appropriated by indigenes	3.0	3.4
Purchased by migrants	3.0[c]	3.9[c]
Tree-planted land transferred as gift		
From father	4.9	5.3

[a] Based on group interviews. The following six rights are considered: (1) plant or replant trees, (2) rent out, (3) pawn, (4) bequeath, (5) give, and (6) sell. The figures in this table show the average number of cases in which farmers have rights without approval from family members or village chief.
[b] *t*-test showed significant difference between means of indigenous villages and migrant villages at the 0.05 level.
[c] *t*-test showed significant difference between means of indigenous villages and migrant villages at the 0.10 level.

for a larger proportion of land than inherited land. Particularly in indigenous villages, the large share of gift land relative to inherited land reflects a shift to individualized property rights, reducing the matriclan's control over land. Indeed, Table 4.3, which shows an index of land rights, confirms that migrant villages have a larger share of land in categories with stronger individualized rights. We constructed the index as the sum of rights in six categories, namely, the right to: (1) plant or replant trees, (2) rent out land, (3) pawn, (4) bequeath, (5) give, and (6) sell without approval from family members or the village chief. The strongest land rights are observed in tree-planted land given as a gift. Slightly weaker rights are observed in village forest land purchased by migrants and land appropriated by migrants. Temporarily allocated family land in both indigenous and migrant villages is the weakest in terms of individual land rights. The differences between indigenous and migrant villages are significant in the case of allocated food crop land and village forest land purchased by migrants.

Village-level estimation

We hypothesize that the social and physical environment affect the proportion of areas under different land tenure regimes, proxied by the man–land ratio, the relative importance of the migrant population, access to physical and other infrastructure, and differences in ethnic groups across villages. To test this hypothesis, we estimated equation (1), with the proportions of land under (1) family ownership (i.e., allocated and inherited land), individualized ownership acquired by (2) gift, (3) forest clearance,

Table 4.4. *Determinants of proportions of areas under different land tenure institutions at the village level: Tobit regression*[a]

	Family land[b]	Gift	Village forest land	Acquired non-forest land[c]
Intercept	0.476***	0.197**	0.041	0.044
	(−3.856)	(1.989)	(0.324)	(0.505)
Man–land ratio	−0.070	0.183**	−0.009	−0.073
	(−0.710)	(2.332)	(−0.086)	(−1.045)
Proportion of migrant population	−0.001**	0.0003	−0.0003	0.001***
	(−2.468)	(0.623)	(−0.426)	(2.656)
Distance to town	−0.003*	−0.002	0.006***	−0.0001
	(−1.704)	(−1.399)	(2.985)	(−0.059)
Proportion of non-farm households	−0.002	0.002**	0.0002	−0.001
	(−1.458)	(2.422)	(0.204)	(−0.944)
School attendance ratio in 1984	0.348	−0.313	0.243	0.222
	(1.460)	(−1.638)	(0.974)	(1.334)
Wassa dummy	−0.065	−0.038	0.090	0.002
	(−1.138)	(−0.844)	(1.566)	(0.058)
Sefwi dummy	−0.096	0.030	0.084	−0.011
	(−1.545)	(0.608)	(1.342)	(−0.245)
Brong-Ahafo dummy	−0.147***	0.017	0.018	0.101**
	(−2.618)	(0.375)	(0.321)	(2.572)
p-value	0.01	0.04	0.02	0.0003
Number of observations	58	58	58	58

[a] Two-limit tobit estimates; ancillary parameter σ not reported. t-statistics in parentheses. *** indicates significance at 1% level, ** at 5% level, and * at 10% level; two-tailed tests.
[b] The sum of inherited and allocated family land areas.
[c] The sum of areas purchased, rented in, and acquired through past renting.

and (4) private purchase and renting, as the dependent variables. Since some categories were non-existent in some villages, we applied the two-limit Tobit estimation method with the results shown in Table 4.4.[10]

The coefficient of the man–land ratio is positive and highly significant only in the gift equation, which supports our hypothesis that population pressure induced institutional innovation towards individualized land tenure. As expected, the proportion of migrant population is negatively associated with the share of family land. Because migrants have less access to village forest land, they acquired cultivation rights mainly by renting-in land or sometimes purchasing land from indigenes (as is indicated by the positive coefficient of the proportion of migrant population in the acquired non-forest land equation).

[10] We did not include the indigenous village dummy since it is highly correlated with the proportion of migrants in the population ($r = -.70$).

Table 4.5. *Proportion of area planted to cocoa trees immediately before acquisition and in 1997, and average year of land acquisition by land tenure type in Western Ghana (mean values, except %)*

	Proportion of cocoa area			Average year of land acquisition
	Immediately before acquisition	1997	% change	
Acquired village forest land				
Indigenous villages	0.0	62.22	—	1975
Migrant villages	0.0	68.75	—	1968
Inherited family land				
Indigenous villages	28.04	35.94	101.5	1980
Migrant villages	40.21	53.34	332.6	1979
Allocated family land				
Indigenous villages	16.68	38.77	238.7	1983
Migrant villages	24.19	46.44	113.0	1990
Land received as gifts				
Indigenous villages	20.50	50.80	173.0	1982
Migrant villages	25.20	64.38	219.6	1983
Acquired land through past renting				
Indigenous villages	19.12	60.79	300.0	1987
Migrant villages	29.22	70.02	188.8	1975
Rented-in land				
Indigenous villages	2.59	46.87	1,362.0	1990
Migrant villages	2.22	55.39	555.4	1989
Privately purchased land				
Indigenous villages	3.60	48.87	782.2	1984
Migrant villages	3.83	62.42	885.4	1983

Other variables are insignificant except in two cases. First, distance to town has a positive effect on the proportion of forest land, which indicates that remaining forests are largely concentrated in areas quite remote from roads and urban centers. Second, the Brong-Ahafo dummy also has a negative effect on the proportion of family land and a positive effect on acquired nonforest land, suggesting that land tenure institutions have evolved towards market-based transactions in this region. This is not surprising since Brong-Ahafo was one of the earlier destinations of the westward geographical movement of the cocoa area from the Eastern Region (Hill 1963).

Do the type of land and its mode of acquisition then affect subsequent land use? Table 4.5 shows the proportion of area planted to cocoa trees immediately before land acquisition and in 1997, and the average year of acquisition. A large proportion of land classified as village forest land at the time of acquisition has been planted to cocoa. Large proportions of cocoa area (and larger increases from the area at the time of acquisition) are also observed on land purchased from nonrelatives and land acquired through renting. In the latter, this reflects a tenancy agreement in which tenants plant cocoa trees and receive a share of the land in return. Despite weak land rights, trees are often planted on allocated and inherited land. In these cases, the conversion of a large proportion of area to cocoa may reflect the use of tree planting as a means to strengthen tenure security. Surprisingly, the proportion of area planted to cocoa on land received as gifts is less than that on acquired village forest land and rental land in both indigenous villages and migrant villages. We speculate that receiving land as a gift provides sufficiently secure individual rights so that the plot holder has no additional incentive to plant cocoa to secure tenure security.

Household-level estimation

We now proceed to analyze households' land acquisition behavior. We estimate the recursive land acquisition model outlined in equations (2) to (4), in which, first, the area of forest land is expressed as a function of exogenous characteristics. These include the age of the household head, the year of marriage (a proxy for the start of own farming), years of schooling, a dummy for patrilineal household, a dummy for being a migrant to the village, distance to town, and regional dummies. Second, we examine the determinants of family allocated land as a function of the above exogenous variables, with the addition of forest area. Then, we treat both forest area and family land as given, and include them in the regression on nonforest land acquisition.

Since certain types of land are not observed in a number of sample households, and because unobservable characteristics of villages may affect land acquisition decisions, we applied Honoré's (1992) least absolute deviations Tobit estimation method with village fixed effects. The results are shown in Table 4.6. The first column shows the determinants of forest area acquisition by households. The age of the household head has a positive and highly significant effect, which indicates that cultivable primary forest lands have declined in recent years due to the clearance of primary forests on a first-come-first-served basis. The dummy for being born outside the village has a positive effect on acquired forest land, while the dummy for a patrilineal household has a negative effect on forest acquisition.[11] Patrilineal households, who are usually long-distance non-Akan migrants, have no rights to clear forests, unlike short-distance Akan migrants.

The next column displays the estimation results for the acquisition of family land including gifts. Contrary to our initial hypothesis that if communal land tenure institutions were designed to achieve equitable distribution of land, prior acquisition of forest land would decrease the amount of land allocated or given by the extended

[11] This result may appear inconsistent with the negative effect of the proportion of the migrant population on the share of acquired nonforest land reported in Table 4.4. The results in Table 4.6 suggest that the positive effect on forest clearance of being born in nearby indigenous villages is outweighed by the negative effect of patrilineal long-distance migrant households. The availability of forest land in the village is controlled for in the fixed-effects regressions.

Table 4.6. *Determinants of land acquisition at the household level: Tobit regression with village fixed effects*[a]

	Forest land	All family land[b]	Acquired nonforest land[c]
Forest land (current)	—	−0.08	−0.35*
		(−0.39)	(−1.79)
Family land (current)	—	—	−0.67*
			(−1.93)
Age of household head	9.19**	0.38	0.37
	(2.38)	(1.12)	(1.44)
Year of first marriage of household head	0.56	−0.24	−0.04
	(0.21)	(−0.63)	(−0.17)
Dummy for household head born outside of village	49.85**	−26.12*	9.34**
	(2.13)	(−1.59)	(2.12)
Years of schooling of head	−6.16	2.10***	0.56*
	(−1.62)	(3.07)	(1.91)
Dummy for patrilineal household	−90.54**	−10.21*	3.63
	(−2.16)	(−1.74)	(1.14)
Chi-square	18.1	31.1	32.5
p-value	0.2	0.0	0.0
Number of observations	386	386	386

[a] Least absolute deviations estimator. *t*-statistics in parentheses. *** indicates significance at 1% level, ** at 5% level, and * at 10% level; two-tailed tests.
[b] Family land includes allocation, inheritance, and gifts.
[c] The sum of areas purchased, rented in, and acquired through past renting.

family, the coefficient on previously acquired forest land is not significantly different from zero. Patrilineal households and those families with heads born outside the village also have smaller areas of family land since they do not inherit family land in the area of relocation. The coefficient of years of schooling is positive, which may be taken to imply that the amounts of schooling and land holdings of the extended family are positively correlated.

According to the last column, both forest and family lands have negative and significant effects on the acquisition of nonforest land. This indicates that households seek additional land through renting and purchase when land acquired through traditional methods is insufficient. In short, land scarcity stimulates land market transactions. Better-educated household heads are also able to acquire land through renting or purchase, probably because these require previous savings and managerial ability.

Parcel-level analysis

Finally, we attempt to assess the effects of land tenure institutions on management efficiency in terms of the proportion of area planted to cocoa in a parcel and cocoa yield per unit of cocoa planted area, using parcel-level data.[12] The proportion of cocoa planted area is supposed to measure the 'width' or extent of investment in trees, whereas the yield reflects the 'depth' of investment in management of cocoa cultivation. Note that if intensity of tree planting is low, the proportion of cocoa planted area may be large, even if cocoa yields are low.

Let us review Table 4.5, which exhibits the proportion of area planted to cocoa immediately before land acquisition and in 1997, by manner of land acquisition. Although the proportion of cocoa planted area tends to be higher in land with strong individual land rights than in land with weak land rights, the differences are not conspicuous. This observation indicates that incentives to invest in tree planting may not be simply determined by the strength of land rights or land tenure security but may also be affected by expected changes in land rights after tree planting. A good example is the case of *inter vivos* gifts; the right to transfer land as a gift to one's wife and children is granted by the extended family provided that trees are planted. Indeed, without considering the effect of tree planting on land rights, it is difficult to explain the non-negligible proportions of parcels planted to cocoa in inherited and allocated lands, which are characterized by weak individual land rights (see Table 4.3).

In general, the proportion of cocoa area is larger in migrant rather than indigenous villages, which may be due to greater individualization of land rights in non-Akan villages. The incidence of tree planting is very high in owned land acquired through past rental agreements, simply because tree planting is the required task under share rental arrangements. The proportion of tree planted area in currently rented-in parcels is lower, as tenants are currently engaged in tree planting. There is also a possibility that the opportunity to rent in land attracted migrants to plant cocoa trees.

Our maintained hypotheses are that cocoa tree planting is more profitable than shifting cultivation and that higher cocoa yields indicate higher production efficiency, both of which seem reasonable in view of the continued expansion of the cocoa area. We assume that land tenure institutions are predetermined for each household, but may differ within each household, depending on the mode of land acquisition. In order to control for possible correlation between land tenure variables and unobservable household characteristics, we applied the household-level fixed effects model for both the proportion of area planted to cocoa and cocoa yields.[13] For analyzing cocoa yield, we have 391 parcels of mature cocoa, for households with more than one mature cocoa parcel. We also estimate the percentage of area planted to cocoa using the same subsample of 391 parcels for comparability. In the latter, the dependent variable should

[12] We define a parcel as a contiguous area of land obtained through a single manner of acquisition at a point in time, and a field as a portion of the parcel used for a specific purpose, e.g., fallow, growing food crops, and growing cocoa.

[13] Since the proportion of area planted to mature cocoa is censored upwards at 100%, we applied a Tobit procedure with household dummy variables. We attempted to estimate this equation using the Honoré (1992) procedure but were not able to achieve convergence. We also estimated a random effects model for the cocoa yield function, but since the results are qualitatively similar, they are not reported here.

be interpreted as the percentage area planted to cocoa, conditional on mature cocoa being present in the parcel.[14]

The regressors in the proportion of area planted to cocoa and the cocoa yield regressions included ten land tenure dummies corresponding to the manner of land acquisition, with matrilineal inheritance as a base of comparison.[15] We also included current parcel characteristics, such as the distance from house to parcel, parcel size, years since acquisition and its squared term. In the cocoa planting function, years since acquisition and its square capture effects related to the timing of investment. We also control for characteristics of the parcel at the time of acquisition, including percentages of parcel covered by forest land and planted to cocoa before acquisition, and the real farm-gate cocoa price. It is expected that since virgin forest is more fertile than previously cultivated fallow land, the percentage of the parcel covered by forest may have a positive effect on tree planting.[16] We included cocoa prices at the time of acquisition to control for the possibility that the surge in cocoa prices in the 1980s stimulated a conversion of land to cocoa. In the cocoa yield function, we include the percentage of trees under five years and the percentage between five and twenty years to account for yield differences due to tree age. Traditional cocoa varieties only begin to bear fruit after five years. Since tree age may be correlated with the number of years since acquisition, we do not include the latter in the cocoa yield functions.

The estimation results are shown in Table 4.7. Parcel size is shown to have an extremely significant and negative effect on the proportion planted to cocoa, implying that an inverse correlation exists between parcel size and tree planting. This indicates that the land rental and sales markets are imperfect, because some portions of the parcel could have been rented for tree planting if the land rental market worked effectively (Hayami and Otsuka 1993). An alternative explanation could be that land quality differences across parcels, and risk aversion or safety-first behavior (not wanting to shift all land to cash crop because of risk in the food market) are responsible for the negative relationship between parcel size and the proportion planted to cocoa.

A more important finding is that the dummy for allocated family land has a positive and significant effect on tree planting. This is surprising, if current land tenure security alone is a critical determinant of investment in tree planting, because land rights are weakest for allocated family land (see Table 4.3). If trees are not planted, allocated family land may have to be returned to the extended family for use by other family members. If trees are planted, there is a possibility that the land parcel may be

[14] We also estimated the cocoa planting function using all parcels, for households with at least two parcels, but we report the results from the subsample with mature cocoa for comparability with the cocoa yield functions. It can also be argued that parcels with mature cocoa describe an equilibrium situation whereas those with only young trees are still subject to short-run adjustment processes. Parcels with mature cocoa may also have a mix of younger trees.

[15] The possibility that land tenure is endogenous with respect to household characteristics is controlled for using household dummies or the fixed effects procedure.

[16] Lopez (1997) found that biomass had a positive effect in his estimation of production functions using regional data from Western Ghana. While he attributes this effect to the positive production externality arising from the effect of biomass on protection from soil erosion and flooding, we consider it more plausible to interpret that the biomass is positively correlated with soil fertility.

Table 4.7. *Determinants of proportion planted to cocoa and cocoa production per hectare at the parcel level*

	Proportion planted to cocoa on plots with mature cocoa[a] (Tobit with household dummies)	Yield (production/ cocoa area) Household fixed effects[a]
Current parcel characteristics		
Distance to parcel	0.02	−17.79*
	(1.37)	(−2.00)
Parcel size (ha)	−0.03***	−3.25
	(−6.03)	(0.94)
Years since acquisition	0.01	—
	(1.15)	—
Years since acquisition squared	−0.00	—
	(−0.70)	—
Tree characteristics		
Amazonia dummy	—	29.86
		(0.49)
Hybrid dummy	—	−68.73
		(−0.89)
% of trees under 5 years	—	−0.27
		(−0.41)
% of trees 5 to 20 years	—	0.44
		(0.84)
Characteristics of parcel at acquisition		
% forest area at acquisition	0.04	43.06
	(0.53)	(0.74)
% cocoa area at acquisition	0.45***	−60.00
	(6.17)	(−1.08)
Real cocoa farm gate price at acquisition	0.00	—
	(0.29)	—
Land tenure dummies		
Dummy inherited and patrilineal	−0.24	−70.67
	(−0.47)	(−0.18)
Dummy allocated family land	0.20*	−165.09**
	(1.82)	(−2.06)
Dummy allocated family and patrilineal	−0.19	−74.35
	(−0.52)	(−0.31)
Dummy land received as gift	0.10	−100.78
	(1.03)	(−1.43)

Table 4.7. (*cont'd*)

	Proportion planted to cocoa on plots with mature cocoa[a] (Tobit with household dummies)	Yield (production/ cocoa area) Household fixed effects[a]
Land tenure dummies[b]		
Dummy gift and patrilineal inherited land	−0.18	33.84
	(1.37)	(0.25)
Dummy appropriated village forest land	0.18	−134.59
	(−0.94)	(−1.39)
Dummy purchased village forest land	0.20	−102.69
	(1.38)	(−0.91)
Dummy privately purchased land	0.25**	−156.11
	(1.96)	(−1.63)
Dummy rented-in land	0.20*	−174.04*
	(1.78)	(−1.95)
Dummy ownership through past renting	0.37***	−106.00
	(2.66)	(−1.02)
Constant	0.58**	415.28***
	(2.46)	(5.10)
p-value	0.00	
Breusch-Pagan Langrangian Multiplier Test (p-value)	—	35.1 (0.00)
Hausman Specification Test (p-value)	—	18.03 (0.45)
Number of observations	391	391

[a] Two-limit Tobit estimates; ancillary parameter σ not reported. *t*-statistics in parentheses.
*** indicates significance at 1% level, ** at 5% level, and * at 10% level; two-tailed tests.
[b] Base category is matrilineal inherited land.

transferred to the desired person as a gift. It seems that the expected strengthening of land rights associated with tree planting provides strong incentives to plant trees on allocated family land.

Dummies for land parcels with strongly individualized ownership, i.e., gift, appropriated village forest land, purchased village forest land, and privately purchased land, all have positive coefficients but only the dummy for privately purchased land is significant at the 5% level. Dummies for appropriated village land and purchased village land are positive but insignificant. Thus, although land tenure security may have a positive effect on tree planting, as argued by Besley (1995), its effect is not necessarily strong. Dummies for rented land and ownership through renting are positive and significant, reflecting the nature of the rental agreement whereby cocoa cultivation is required, and land ownership is eventually divided rather than sharing produce.

We also estimated cocoa yield functions with household fixed effects. In the estimation of cocoa yield functions, we included dummies for improved varieties of cocoa, i.e., *Amazonia* and hybrid, and proportions of trees younger than five years of age, which are immature, and between five and twenty years of age, which are highly productive. The estimation results of the cocoa yield function contrast markedly with those of tree planting. First of all, the dummy for allocated family land is negative and significant. Thus, tree planting density and subsequent management intensity of cocoa trees are lower in allocated family land, even though the proportion of tree planted area is larger. Such behavior is understandable if one plants trees in order to obtain permission to transfer land as a gift.

Second, the coefficient of the dummy variable for current renting under share tenancy is negative and significant. Contrary to the conjecture of Boadu (1992), share tenancy in Ghana's cocoa fields may be inefficient.[17] This finding is consistent with the finding of inverse correlation between parcel size and the proportion of area planted to trees, because it is not necessarily advantageous for a landowner to rent out a portion of a large parcel to a tenant if tenancy is inefficient.

Third, the coefficients of dummy variables representing gift, appropriated and purchased village forest land, and purchased private land are all negative, even though none of them is significant. If stronger land tenure security leads to much greater incentives to invest in management of trees, the coefficients of these dummy variables ought to be positive and significant. It may well be that once cocoa trees are planted, individual land rights are enhanced such that management incentives do not differ significantly among various land tenure institutions. This is consistent with the finding of Place and Hazell (1993) that land tenure security does not significantly affect crop yields in several Sub-Saharan African countries.

To sum up, the contrasting estimation results of cocoa tree planting and cocoa yield functions can be understood only if land rights are enhanced by tree planting, so that incentive structures are different for tree planting and management of trees.

West Sumatra

Study sites

For the extensive survey, we selected sixty villages randomly with probability proportional to village population from four districts in the West Sumatra and Jambi provinces along the buffer zone of the Kerinci Seblat National Park.[18] We classify study

[17] According to Hayami and Otsuka (1993), share tenancy in Asia, which is observed mainly in annual crop farming, is, in general, not significantly inefficient compared with owner-cultivation and fixed-rent tenancy. Under share tenancy in Ghana, the ownership of land, rather than the produce, is divided after tree planting is completed. Thus, yield under share tenancy may be low partly because some cocoa trees are immature, even though we attempted to control for the effects of tree age using age composition variables. A fixed-rent contract, which provides stronger work incentives, may not be preferred in the cocoa planting contract because future returns are too risky to be shouldered by the tenant alone.

[18] The village level results draw heavily on Otsuka, Suyanto, and Tomich (1997) and Suyanto and Otsuka (1998).

Table 4.8. *Land use patterns in hectares in 1995 and size of population in 1993 in selected villages in Sumatra*[a]

	Sample size	Exploited area in 1995 (ha)[a]			Total village area[b] (ha)	Primary forest area[c] (ha)	Population in 1993[b]	Population density in 1993[d] (persons/km^2)
		Paddy fields	Agro-forestry plots	Bush-fallow				
High Region	24	259 (31)	377 (45)	204 (24)	5,143	4,303	1,764	34
Middle Region	19	151 (19)	526 (66)	125 (16)	3,173	2,371	1,340	42
Low Region	17	102 (9)	594 (55)	385 (36)	6,735	5,654	772	11

[a] Based on community survey. Numbers in parentheses are proportions in exploited area in % terms.
[b] Based on Agricultural Census (Bureau of Statistics).
[c] Estimated by subtracting total exploited area from total village area.
[d] Population divided by village area.

sites into three regions depending on altitude. The High Region is located at an altitude of more than 1,000 meters above sea level, and the major tree crop is coffee (*Coffea canephora*), although the area planted to cinnamon has been increasing. Cinnamon (*Cinnanomum burmanii*) is the major tree crop in the Middle Region, whereas rubber (*Hevea braziliansis*) is the major tree crop in the Low Region.

Traditionally, inhabitants have relied upon wet rice cultivation and, hence, areas along streams and rivers are predominantly used as paddy fields. Paddy fields are surrounded by agroforestry plots, including both mature trees and newly planted trees intercropped with annuals, and shifting cultivation with bush-fallow. Natural forests typically are located in the mountainous terrain further away from village centers. The bush-fallow area originally was converted from primary forests and is planted with food crops periodically for a season or two followed by another fallow period.

Table 4.8 presents land use patterns and population statistics from selected villages in each of the three regions in 1995. Villages in the High Region have 31% of their land in paddy, in contrast to only 9% in the Low Region. Population density is highest in the Middle Region and lowest in the Low Region. Low population density in the Low Region can be explained by the paucity of paddy fields in this area. In contrast, the rich endowment of flat fertile area suitable for rice cultivation and the high profitability of cinnamon would explain the highest population density in the Middle Region. Bush-fallow area is smallest in the Middle Region and relatively abundant in the Low Region.

In Western Sumatra, the three major ethnic groups follow the matrilineal inheritance and matrilocal residence systems, even though the inheritance system has undergone substantial transformation over time (Errington 1984; Kahn 1980). Land property rights institutions and the mode of land transfers have evolved from the lineage or extended family ownership along matrilineal lines to joint and single family ownership. Traditionally, lineage land owned collectively by a group of matrilineal kin members was most common, particularly for paddy fields. No single member of the lineage has ownership rights and sale is strictly prohibited. Although formally the approval of the lineage or community head is required for clearing community-owned forests, approval is easily granted. Lineage land, however, occupies small areas in our sample villages at present.

Land under joint family ownership, which is inherited and owned jointly by daughters, is much more common than lineage ownership. The major difference from lineage land tenure is the ownership of land by a smaller number of family members. To prevent fragmentation of land beyond the minimum efficient size, cultivation of wet rice land is rotated among sisters' families. All types of decisions regarding land use, inheritance, renting, and pawning are made jointly by sisters and their husbands without intervention of other lineage members.

Joint family land tenure has developed in two ways. First, lineage members agree to divide lineage land into joint family land, usually at the time of inheritance. Second, daughters jointly inherit private land, which was acquired either by opening up forest land or by purchasing already exploited bush-fallow areas. Although the sale of lineage and family land has traditionally been prohibited, such land has actually been sold with the consent of group members. There have been cases in certain areas of the Middle Region, where sons, in addition to daughters, have jointly inherited land. Traditionally, sons participate in forest clearance and tree planting, but do not inherit. This new land tenure institution represents a break from the traditional rule of matrilineal inheritance.

Single family ownership, which has evolved from joint family ownership, is an emerging land tenure category. Similar to joint family ownership, daughters inherit land under single family ownership, but ownership rights are more individualized. More recently, inheritance by sons is also permitted, although daughters inherit areas larger than, or at least equal to, that of sons. Single family ownership could also have evolved from the inheritance of private land.

Through group interviews, we obtained estimates of the percentage of land under different land tenure institutions by type of land use. To reduce measurement errors associated with the finer classification of land tenure categories, we combine similar land tenure categories, such as single family ownership by daughters, and daughters and sons. Some trends can be observed in Table 4.9. First, the traditional system (joint ownership and small areas of lineage land) is dominant for paddy fields in the Middle and Low Regions, but accounts for only about one-fourth of bush-fallow and smaller portions of tree crop plots in all regions. Second, single family ownership is more important than joint ownership except for paddy fields. Third, private ownership tends to dominate in tree crop plots and accounts for a sizable portion of bush-fallow.

As in the case of Ghana, private ownership rights are granted to those who have cleared forest land, which requires a large amount of family labor. Those who have purchased land have even clearer individual land rights. If the matrilineal rule of inheritance to daughters is strictly followed, the acquired land ought to become joint family land in the next generation and lineage land after two generations. Yet area under joint family-cum-lineage ownership is small in all the regions, which indicates the erosion of the traditional matrilineal inheritance system.

Table 4.9. *Distribution of area under different land tenure regimes by land use type in Sumatra (%)*[a]

	Lineage ownership	Joint family ownership	Single family ownership	Private ownership I (purchase)	Private ownership II (clearance)
Paddy field					
High Region	2.2	9.0	75.7	7.9	4.1
Middle Region	10.4	63.9	6.3	5.5	7.8
Low Region	0.0	64.6	29.2	6.1	0.1
Tree plots					
High Region	3.1	5.2	41.8	10.4	37.1
Middle Region	4.7	1.5	61.7	13.5	18.5
Low Region	0.0	3.0	45.6	12.4	38.7
Bush-fallow area					
High Region	15.5	8.5	36.3	5.2	32.6
Middle Region	10.3	19.4	43.1	14.3	12.5
Low Region	22.5	3.1	41.7	5.7	27.0

[a] Based on community survey. Numbers in some lines do not add up to 100% because of small area of land under state ownership.

Primary forests are, in practice, characterized by open access and any member of the community can open the forest for cultivation. Tacitly, however, ownership of cleared land is subject to community regulation if it is fallowed for long periods. More often than not, lineage or family members claim use rights on such land, which originally belonged to the community. Since continuous cropping of annuals is infeasible due to quick fertility loss, trees must be planted to secure land rights. This practice is similar to that in Ghana. Again similar to Ghana, efforts to plant and manage trees confer strong individual land rights. This explains why joint family ownership is uncommon for tree crop areas.

In order to assess the strength of property rights under different land tenure institutions, we asked a group of knowledgeable farmers in each village whether the cultivating households possess rights to rent out under share tenancy, rent out under fixed-rent leasehold tenancy, pawn, and sell with and without approval of family and/or lineage leaders for the various tenure categories. The right to rent out under share tenancy is the weakest right followed closely by the right to rent out under leasehold tenancy (Hayami and Otsuka 1993), whereas the strongest right rests in the right to sell without approval. Except for the case of lineage-owned paddy fields, in which there is no individual right to sell at all, farmers' answers were either 'yes without approval' or 'yes with approval' (see Table 4.10). Since there is no difference in land rights between bush-fallow and tree plots for any tenure category, these two types of land are combined under the category of upland fields.

Individual land rights under lineage ownership are very weak, possessing at best the right to rent out under share tenancy. It is interesting to observe that individual land

Table 4.10. *Index of individual land rights under different land tenure regimes in Sumatra*[a]

	Lineage land	Joint family ownership	Single family ownership I (daughters)	Single family ownership II (daughters and sons)	Private ownership (purchased and cleared)
Paddy field					
High Region	0.5	0.8	1.6	3.2	3.6
Middle Region	0.8	2.2	2.0	2.8	3.9
Low Region	n.a.	2.7	2.0	n.a.	3.8
Upland field[b]					
High Region	0.0	0.6	1.6	2.0	3.1
Middle Region	0.8	0.9	1.9	2.9	3.8
Low Region	0.0	1.0	1.9	2.8	3.8

[a] Four rights are considered: rights to rent out under share tenancy, rent out under leasehold tenancy, pawn, and to sell. Numbers refer to the average number of rights without obtaining approval of the family and/or lineage members.
[b] Upland field refers to both agroforestry plots and bush-fallow.

rights for paddy fields under joint family ownership in the Middle and Low Regions are comparatively high, even greater than land rights under single family ownership by daughters in these two regions. It appears that individual land rights under joint family ownership have been strengthened by the deliberate agreement of the family members. Except for this somewhat anomalous phenomenon, land rights are stronger under single family ownership than joint family ownership, and within single family ownership, the rights are stronger in the case of ownership by daughters and sons. But even under single family ownership by daughters and sons, there is no right to sell without the approval of family members. The right to sell without approval is granted only to land acquired by clearing forest or by purchasing land. Particularly in the Middle and Low Regions, land rights in privately acquired land are close to perfect private ownership. Even in the High Region, where individuals' rights over cleared and purchased land are weaker, it does not seem too difficult to obtain approval from one's family members in order to sell land. The major difference between private ownership in Sumatra and in the western world is the lack of official registration, so that land cannot be used as collateral for loans from banks. However, land rights acquired by clearing forests tend to decline if they are fallowed, although it is difficult to quantify the extent of the decline.

Based on the data in Tables 4.9 and 4.10, it seems reasonable to hypothesize that land tenure institutions have evolved towards individualized tenure in order to enhance incentives to invest in commercial trees. Incentives to invest in tree planting and management are critically important, because large efforts are required for tree planting, pruning, weeding, and thinning. If secure individual ownership cannot be acquired, those who plant and grow trees may not be able to reap the future benefits

(Besley 1995). On the other hand, investment in traditional irrigation systems for paddy production requires a minimum of effort to maintain and repair simple, small-scale facilities. Thus, strong investment incentives are less of an issue for paddy fields. If population pressure is the driving force towards individualization of land tenure institutions, we would expect to observe a predominance of more individualized tenure on tree crop plots in areas where population density and population growth rates are high.

Village-level estimation

In order to identify the determinants of the choice of land tenure institutions at the village level (equation 1), we estimated functions explaining the proportion of land under lineage, joint and single family ownership, and the two types of private ownership (i.e., for purchased and cleared land) separately for paddy fields and tree crop plots, using a common set of explanatory variables. These included: population density, population growth rate, proportion of paddy area, proportion of ethnic minorities, traveling time to subdistrict town, walking time to forest, and regional dummies for the Middle and Low Regions. We estimated eight regression functions using the Tobit method and the results are shown in Table 4.11.

Our basic hypothesis that population pressure promotes the individualization of land tenure can be tested by examining whether higher population density and greater population growth rates are associated with greater incidence of private ownership and smaller incidence of lineage and joint-family ownership.[19] Consistent with our hypothesis, population density has a positive and significant effect on the incidence of private ownership through purchase in the case of paddy fields. Since all forest areas suitable for conversion to paddy cultivation have been exhausted, individualization took the form of replacing collective ownership by single family ownership and inducing market transactions in land. Note that the Middle and Low Region dummies have positive effects on the proportion of joint family ownership and negative effects on the proportion of single family ownership in the paddy field equations. These results are consistent with the observation from Table 4.10 that land rights for joint family tenure in the Middle and Low Regions were similar to or even stronger than land rights of single family ownership. According to the estimation results of the determinants of land tenure in agroforestry plots, higher population density reduced the incidence of single family ownership and stimulated forest clearance. Note that the Middle Region dummy has negative and significant coefficients in the joint family and cleared land

[19] We consider it legitimate to represent population pressure by past population density and the expected population growth rate, even though the expected value is replaced by the actual growth rate. We used the population growth rate from 1983 to 1993 as regressors, while the dependent variable pertains to 1995. Thus one can argue that past population growth rates, being lagged variables, are exogenous to the 1995 growth rate. Nevertheless, the statistical tests may still be biased to the extent that population variables are endogenous. Due to the paucity of data on exogenous variables and the similarity of population growth rates among the three regions (approximately 1% per year in each region, on the average), it was not feasible to apply the instrumental variables method. We believe, however, that the difference in land quality is well controlled for by regional dummies and the proportion of paddy area, since differences in land quality are primarily due to regional differences and favorable agricultural land is fully devoted to paddy fields without exception in our sites.

Table 4.11. *Tobit regression of proportion of village land area under different land tenure by land use type*[a]

	Paddy fields				Agroforestry plots			
	Joint family	Single family	Purchased	Cleared	Joint family	Single family	Purchased	Cleared
Intercept	21.29	75.29***	3.54	5.73***	−0.74	56.58***	7.44	27.74***
	(0.29)	(8.46)	(1.31)	(4.48)	(−0.06)	(7.09)	(1.46)	(3.41)
Population density	−0.20*	0.21*	0.11***	0.13	0.22	−0.47***	0.07	0.27*
	(−1.67)	(1.82)	(2.75)	(0.42)	(1.00)	(−3.13)	(0.70)	(1.80)
Population growth	0.39	−3.16	−0.32	4.07	−3.74	−4.88**	−2.45*	6.36***
	(0.19)	(−1.34)	(−0.41)	(1.13)	(−1.06)	(−2.23)	(−1.74)	(2.83)
% paddy area	0.28	−0.27	0.00	−7.73**	−1.45	2.11**	−0.85	−1.35**
	(0.47)	(−0.31)	(0.00)	(−2.29)	(−1.11)	(2.48)	(−1.52)	(−2.01)
% outsiders	−7.04***	−0.16	0.04	3.45***	0.47	−0.49	0.26	0.23
	(−4.22)	(−0.21)	(0.17)	(3.03)	(0.90)	(−1.32)	(1.08)	(0.56)
Travel time to town	−0.10	−0.07	0.02	−0.24	−0.14	−0.05	0.15**	−0.02
	(−0.91)	(−0.58)	(0.50)	(−1.41)	(−0.78)	(−0.56)	(2.56)	(−0.20)
Travel time to forest	0.11	0.37	−0.29	−1.10	−0.14	−0.47	1.15**	−1.73
	(0.17)	(0.37)	(−0.91)	(−0.35)	(−0.08)	(−0.53)	(2.09)	(−1.12)
Middle region	75.09***	−87.38***	−4.20	−7.76	−30.44*	29.90***	−0.77	−25.99***
	(8.79)	(−8.65)	(−1.43)	(−0.55)	(−1.89)	(3.61)	(−0.15)	(−3.03)
Low region	51.28***	−45.34***	0.85	−35.40*	−18.31	0.47	−2.03	8.19
	(6.39)	(−5.02)	(0.29)	(−1.85)	(−1.31)	(0.06)	(−0.39)	(0.96)
Log likelihood	−221.57	−204.45	−171.51	−67.40	−80.53	−257.83	−207.60	−232.10
Sample size	55	55	55	55	58	58	58	58

[a] Numbers in parentheses are *t*-statistics. *** indicates significance at the 1%, ** at the 5% level, and * at the 10% level; two-tailed tests.

regressions and a positive and significant coefficient in the single family land regression. These results indicate that in the regions where uncultivated forest land was available (i.e., the High and Low Regions), population pressure led to forest clearance, whereas in the region with limited forest land (i.e., the Middle Region), single family ownership was created at the expense of joint family ownership.

Population growth has a significant impact only on land tenure distribution in agroforestry plots, but not on tenure in paddy land. Similar to population density, higher population growth resulted in lower incidence of single family ownership and higher incidence of private ownership through clearance of forests. Counteracting the effect of the population variables is the negative effect of the proportion of paddy area on forest clearance. A larger per capita endowment of paddy fields, which produce more grain per unit of area than upland fields, lessens the population pressure on land.

The proportion of outsiders is associated negatively with the incidence of joint family ownership of paddy fields, suggesting that the inflow of outsiders helped undermine the traditional family ownership system of the matrilineal society.[20] Outsiders seem to have acquired paddy land in the past by clearing forest areas suitable for paddy cultivation, which is reflected in its positive coefficient in the cleared area regression for paddy fields. There is no evidence that outsiders actively purchase land from indigenous residents.

A major question is the relative speed by which primary forest and bush-fallow areas have been converted to commercial tree plots planted to rubber, cinnamon, and coffee under different land tenure institutions. If the major source of tree plots is primary forest, agroforestry development comes at the expense of the natural environment. On the other hand, if tree plots were primarily converted from bush-fallow, this development brings environmental benefits.

Household-level estimation

We now turn to household-level determinants of land acquisition. We estimated functions explaining the area of land acquired by forest clearance (deforestation) and by purchase. The explanatory variables in our regressions include the area of inherited land, which, in Sumatra, is determined by the parental generation and which is predicted relatively accurately by future heirs, the interaction of inherited land with two inheritance system dummies, with the base for comparison being inheritance by daughters, the percentage of trees planted at the time of acquisition of inherited land, age of household head, schooling of head, owned paddy area, the number of male and female workers between 16 and 60 years of age, and outsider household dummy for those who were migrants from Java or other areas in Sumatra.

Because certain types of land acquisitions do not exist for a number of sample households, and because unobservable village characteristics may affect land acquisition decisions, we applied the Tobit estimation method with village fixed-effects. The estimation results are shown in Table 4.12. The first column shows the determinants

[20] The proportion of outsiders, however, may be regarded as endogenous if they were attracted by the ease of obtaining paddy fields due to a more individualized ownership system.

Table 4.12. *Determinants of land acquisition and area planted to trees at the household level in Sumatra: Tobit regression with village fixed effects*[a]

	Forest clearance	Purchase	Tree planted area
Intercept	−2.99	−3.97	−0.54
	(−1.45)	(−1.53)	(−1.38)
Forest land	—	—	0.77***
	—	—	(25.67)
Inherited land[b]	−0.97***	−0.26	0.69***
	(−2.69)	(−0.65)	(8.63)
Inherited land x bilateral inheritance dummy	−0.12	1.42	−0.17
	(−0.12)	(1.62)	(−0.74)
Inherited land x patrilineal inheritance dummy	0.65	−0.16	0.19
	(1.18)	(−0.15)	(0.76)
Percentage of area planted to trees in inherited land	−0.01	−0.02**	—
	(−1.43)	(−2.00)	—
Purchased land	—	—	0.38***
	—	—	(5.43)
Age of head	0.05**	0.03	0.01
	(2.50)	(1.00)	(1.00)
Schooling of head	0.09	0.16*	0.03
	(1.13)	(1.78)	(1.50)
Own paddy area	0.97**	1.20**	0.19*
	(2.20)	(2.03)	(1.73)
Number of male workers	0.61*	0.42	0.16**
	(1.74)	(0.98)	(2.00)
Number of female workers	−0.26	0.10	−0.14**
	(−0.76)	(0.26)	(−2.00)
Outsider dummy	−12.46	−1.16	0.12
	(−0.03)	(−0.50)	(0.29)
Log likelihood	−305.19	−254.00	−223.97
Number of observations	273	273	231

[a] Two-limit Tobit estimates; ancillary parameter σ and village fixed effects not reported. t-statistics in parentheses. *** indicates significance at 1% level, ** at 5% level, and * at 10% level; two-tailed tests.
[b] Base category is inheritance by daughters; other inheritance categories are bilateral (by daughters and sons) and patrilineal (by sons only).

of acquired forest areas through forest clearance or deforestation. As we expected, inherited land, which is predetermined for the household, has a negative and significant effect on deforestation. This is consistent with the popular belief that increasing population pressure on limited land is a major cause for deforestation, to the extent that declining area of inherited land is due to an increase in the household size. Interaction terms of inherited land with two inheritance dummies, however, were not significant. From this result we conclude that incentives to invest in forest clearance under the traditional matrilineal inheritance system are as strong as those of the more recent bilateral and patrilineal inheritance systems. Owned paddy area has a positive and significant effect on deforestation, consistent with wealthier farmers hiring laborers to clear forests. The percentage of area planted to trees in inherited land is not significant, indicating that the development of profitable agroforestry does not deter deforestation. The age of the household head has a positive and significant effect on deforestation. This result is consistent with our hypotheses that the older the household head, the greater would be access to forest land in one's youth, hence, the larger would be acquired forest land area. A larger pool of male workers also promotes deforestation, since forest clearance is intensive in male labor.

The second column shows the estimation results of the determinants of purchased land. Owned paddy area and schooling of the household head both have positive and highly significant effects on purchased land, which indicates that wealthier and better-educated farmers tend to purchase larger upland areas. The percentage of area planted to trees on inherited land has a negative and significant effect. It may well be that the larger demand for labor in agroforestry deters the purchase of additional land.

In order to identify the determinants of the development of agroforests, we estimated a tree planting function in which area planted to trees is the dependent variable. The explanatory variables included the area of inherited land, interaction terms of inherited land with the two inheritance dummies, purchased land, age of household head, owned paddy area, the number of male and female workers of sixteen to sixty years of age, and the outsider dummy. Since some households have not planted trees, and because unobservable village characteristics may also affect tree planting decisions, we also applied the Tobit estimation method with village fixed-effects. The estimation results are also shown in Table 4.12.

Forest land and inherited land areas have positive and highly significant effects on the area planted to trees. Purchased land also has a positive but weaker effect, judging from its coefficient, which is significantly smaller than the coefficients of forest and inherited land. Thus, the incentive to plant trees in purchased land is lower, even though land rights on purchased land are very strong. It seems that, due to secure land rights, farmers are in no hurry to plant trees. In contrast, if land use is limited to food crops grown under shifting cultivation, individual rights acquired through forest clearance and inheritance tend to diminish over time. This explains why tree planting, which strengthens land rights, is more active on forest and inherited land.

The interaction terms of inheritance dummies (bilateral inheritance by daughters and sons, and patrilineal inheritance by sons only) do not have significant coefficients. It appears that the incentives to invest in tree planting are more likely and strongly affected by expected changes in land rights after tree planting than the level of land rights before tree planting. This is similar to our results for Western Ghana. Our result, however, is quite different from the findings of Besley (1995), who uses a data set from Western Ghana to show statistically that stronger land rights lead to a higher incidence of tree planting. We would argue that Besley's methodology of simply counting the number of rights (e.g., rights to rent out and sell) to measure the tenure security without considering the relative importance of each right leads to biased estimation.

The number of male workers has a positive and significant effect on tree planted areas, whereas the number of female workers has a negative and significant effect. These results are plausible, since the establishment of agroforest requires primarily male labor (Suyanto, Tomich, and Otsuka 1998; Barlow and Muharminto 1982). Finally, we found that more educated farmers tend to establish agroforest more actively.

Plot-level estimation

Finally, we examine whether plot differences in land tenure security affect the profitability of agroforestry.[21] We selected two typical cinnamon-growing villages in the Kerinci District of the Jambi Province and conducted a random sample survey of fifty households in each of the two contiguous villages with similar topographical, ecological, and socio-economic environments. We focus on the impact of different land tenure institutions on the profitability of cinnamon, controlling for household characteristics and unobservables.

Upland fields were divided into 155 young cinnamon fields with trees one to three years of age, 264 productive cinnamon fields with trees of age four to thirteen, and thirty-seven bush-fallow fields. A considerable number of cinnamon fields were intercropped with coffee, even though cinnamon trees occupied the major portion of the field. To simplify the analysis of profitability, we chose sixty-three young and 175 productive fields entirely planted to cinnamon for the detailed survey of production, input use, and cost. In this chapter, we focus on mature cinnamon fields. Cinnamon is harvested intermittently with a normal growth period of eight to ten years. During harvesting, all trees are felled and bark is removed. Coppices regrow after harvesting and this process can be repeated three times in most cases. Because of the declining rate of regrowth, trees are usually replanted after the fourth harvest. Minor output is 'produced' when branches are pruned, usually four years after planting or regrowth.

Farmers sell unharvested cinnamon trees to local traders, who offer prices to farmers based on their own assessment of the value of cinnamon. Taking advantage of this practice, we employed traders to assess the value of standing cinnamon trees in all productive sample fields. We define the sum of the estimated value of trees as 'potential value of output' and the potential value net of total non-land cost as 'potential profit.' We used both of these variables in our statistical analysis. We also measured the altitude and slope of plots to obtain information on land quality. Land quality may be affected not only by its physical characteristics but also by soil fertility, which is considered to be critically affected by the previous use of land (i.e., forest, cinnamon field, or bush-fallow). Thus, we also include indicators of previous land use in our sample plots. Although it is expected that previously forested land is more fertile, there were very few such cases in our sample due to the exhaustion of primary forests in Kerinci.

We estimated regressions of the potential value, total cost, and potential profit in cinnamon plots with household fixed effects for those households with more than one plot. In so doing, we control for household level unobservables, which could be

[21] This discussion draws heavily on Suyanto, Tomich, and Otsuka (1998).

correlated with differences in management efficiency across households. Results (not reported here) show that tree age dummies are highly significant due to the production and harvest cycle of cinnamon. Land tenure institutions, captured by the mode of acquisition dummies, do not seem to affect potential value. Total costs seem to be affected mostly by the life cycle of trees, with costs decreasing for trees between ten and thirteen years of age. Finally, potential profit is most significantly affected by the age profile of trees, though profit decreases at higher altitudes. This is consistent with the common perception of farmers that at higher altitudes trees grow less well and water content of the cinnamon bark tends to be higher. It is noteworthy that none of the land tenure variables is significant, which supports the hypothesis that customary land tenure institutions have been sufficiently individualized to provide tenure security comparable to that of private ownership. These results are consistent with earlier findings from the Ghana study, as well as those of Place and Hazell (1993), that land tenure institutions do not critically affect crop yields.

Summary and policy implications

We found a number of similar changes in land tenure institutions and similar management practices of forest, agroforest, and crop land in Western Ghana and West Sumatra. In Western Ghana, population pressure led to the widespread practice of gifts, whereas in West Sumatra, it increased the incidence of single family ownership or private ownership acquired through forest clearance. In both study sites, population pressure has led to the privatization of land rights on land converted and utilized for agriculture and agroforestry. Strong individual land rights are granted to cultivated land converted from forests, even though such rights are weakened when land is put into long fallow. Individual rights have been strengthened further through long-term investment, notably in tree planting. Thus, increased population pressure has reduced the acquisition of land through traditional mechanisms and increased the role of markets in land acquisition.

There does not seem to be any built-in mechanism under communal ownership to protect forest areas and forest resources. In both our study sites, although the village chief is the custodian of the communal forests, he generally allows villagers to clear forest for cultivation. Few woodlands and forests were conserved by traditional authorities due to the increasing demand for conversion from an increasing number of villagers and migrants. This demand arose partly because of poor markets for forest and food products, which meant that little could be earned from forest products, and they could not be easily traded for food. The clearance of primary forests on a first-come-first-served basis has led to the disappearance of cultivable primary forests over time. Moreover, the conventional rule of communal land tenure, which honors the ownership rights of cleared forest land, has created incentives for deforestation. Our case studies clearly show that those who clear forests are granted strong individual rights.

Nevertheless, communal land tenure institutions do not deter the development of agroforestry, irrespective of the levels of tenure security in these systems, because of the expected increase in land rights after tree planting. Commercial trees have been planted under the communal ownership system as widely and actively as under the private ownership system. This is because land rights have become highly individualized due to investment. Given that cultivators in hilly marginal areas tend to come from the poorest segments of society, it would be socially desirable to promote agroforestry systems since they reproduce many of the forest functions that provide positive environmental externalities, while providing income earning opportunities for the rural population.

Generally, communal land tenure systems distribute land relatively equitably across households. In land abundant situations, this was accomplished mainly through land clearing and inheritance acquisition methods. Similarly, the development of land rental markets through the privatization of communal systems has not led to land concentration, since renting is undertaken mainly by migrants and by households with poor access to inherited land. The effect of land sales markets tends to be regressive in Sumatra but progressive in Ghana. Ghana still has a relatively land abundant situation, evidenced by the division of land ownership rather than shares of produce in land rental agreements. Given the abundance of land relative to labor, land sales remain a way to distribute land from indigenes and earlier migrants to newcomers who are better endowed with labor or managerial ability. Sumatra is more similar to other labor-surplus countries in Asia with active labor markets and tenancy agreements involving sharing of output. In a relatively land scarce situation, it is not surprising that the land market is regressive. How far our findings can be generalized to other areas is an important question to be investigated in future work. Judging from the observation that similar evolutionary processes in land tenure institutions have taken place in Ghana and Sumatra, two areas characterized by vastly different social and cultural traditions and environments, our findings seem applicable to relatively diverse areas. Supportive evidence is also provided by recent studies of land tenure institutions in Malawi and Uganda by Place and Otsuka (2000*a*, *b*).

Finally, we discuss the policy implications emerging from our study. First, property rights institutions are largely favorable or evolving to provide incentives for efficient natural resource management. Indirect policies, such as the promotion of profitable agroforest opportunities and the encouragement of more efficient product markets, will be more effective in hastening this evolution than arbitrarily or prematurely imposed land titling schemes. While many titling programs have failed largely due to premature implementation, they have been found to be popular and sustainable in areas of high market and property rights development such as Central Kenya (Migot-Adholla *et al.* 1993). Land titling programs will become feasible once communal land tenure institutions become sufficiently individualized.

If implemented, titling programs must pay special attention to the gender issue. If men are traditionally owners of land, as in Western Ghana, land titling may strengthen their land rights at women's expense. To be fair, men and women should be equally qualified for acquiring land titles. Judging from the experience of Ghana, the promulgation of the Intestate Succession Law, which stipulates how property should be bequeathed to the spouse, children, and other family members, is likely to be an effective policy option, which would facilitate less gender-biased land inheritance systems in customary land areas. Transferring ownership of land to women, however, is unlikely to raise productivity if access to and use of other inputs remain unequal.

Second, given the existence of strong incentives to manage agroforestry plots on sloping lands under communal ownership, it is wise to develop and disseminate profitable agroforestry systems through the development of improved species of commercial trees, improving techniques for selecting and propagating useful indigenous tree germplasm, and providing proper incentives for germplasm delivery systems to develop. The establishment of profitable agroforestry systems will contribute significantly to the reduction of poverty by enhancing the efficiency of farming in marginal areas, as farmers in marginal areas are particularly poor. It will also contribute to the prevention of soil erosion and the creation of tree biomass, while helping to strengthen individual rights where they are weak.

Lastly, development of markets and rural infrastructure is critical to generate the degree of intensification required to enable rural people to increase their incomes without degrading the surrounding resource base. Given the strong influence of population pressure on deforestation, reducing population growth rates would help mitigate deforestation. Hand in hand with market development and policies aimed at reducing population growth, the development of nonfarm income opportunities would absorb increases in labor while increasing returns to human capital investment.

REFERENCES

Alchian, A.A. and Harold Demsetz. 1973. 'The Property Right Paradigm.' *Journal of Economic History* 16(1): 16–27.

Asenso-Okyere, W. Kwado, S.Y. Atsu, and Irene S. Obeng. 1993. 'Communal Property Resources in Ghana: Policies and Prospects.' Discussion Paper No. 27, Institute of Statistical, Social and Economic Research, University of Ghana, Legon.

Ault, David E. and Gilbert L. Rutman. 1979. 'The Development of Individual Rights to Property in Tribal Africa.' *Journal of Law and Economics* 22(April): 163–82.

Awusabo-Asare, Kofi. 1990. 'Matriliny and the new Intestate Succession Law of Ghana.' *Canadian Journal of African Studies* 24(1): 1–16.

Barlow, Colin and Muharminto. 1982. 'The Rubber Smallholder Economy.' *Bulletin of Indonesian Economic Studies* 18(1): 86–119.

Bassett, Thomas J. 1993. 'Introduction: The Land Question and Agricultural Transformation in Sub-Saharan Africa.' In *Land in African Agrarian Systems*, T.J. Bassett and D.E. Crummey (eds.). Madison, WI: University of Wisconsin Press.

Berry, Sara. 1963. *No Condition is Perfect: The Social Dynamics of Agrarian Change in Sub-Saharan Africa*. Madison, WI: University of Wisconsin Press.

Besley, Timothy. 1995. 'Property Rights and Investment Incentives.' *Journal of Political Economy* 103(October): 903–37.

Boadu, Fred. 1992. 'The Efficiency of Share Contracts in Ghana's Cocoa Industry.' *Journal of Development Studies* 29(October): 108–20.

Boserup, Ester. 1965. *The Conditions of Agricultural Growth: The Economics of Agrarian Change under Population Pressure.* London: George Allen and Unwin.

Bruce, John W. and Shem E. Migot-Adholla. 1993. *Searching for Land Tenure Security in Africa.* Dubuque, IA: Kendall/Hunt.

Demsetz, Harold. 1967. 'Toward a Theory of Property Rights.' *American Economic Review* 57(2): 347–59.

Errington, Frederick K. 1984. *Manners and Meaning in West Sumatra: The Social Context of Consciousness.* New Haven, CT: Yale University Press.

Feder, Gershon and David Feeny. 1993. 'The Theory of Land Tenure and Property Rights.' In *The Economics of Rural Organization: Theory, Practice, and Policy,* K. Hoff, A. Braverman, and J.E. Stiglitz (eds.). Oxford: Oxford University Press.

Feder, Gershon and Raymond Noronha. 1987. 'Land Rights Systems and Agricultural Development in Sub-Saharan Africa.' *World Bank Research Observer* 2(July): 143–69.

Gardner, Roy, Elinor Ostrom, and James Walker. 1990. 'The Nature of Common-Pool Resource Problems.' *Rationality and Society* 2: 335–58.

Hayami, Yujiro. 1997. *Development Economics: From the Poverty to the Wealth of Nations.* Oxford: Oxford University Press.

Hayami, Yujiro and Keijiro Otsuka. 1993. *The Economics of Contract Choice: An Agrarian Perspective.* Oxford: Clarendon Press.

Hayami, Yujiro and V.W. Ruttan. 1985. *Agricultural Development: An International Perspective.* Baltimore, MD: Johns Hopkins University Press.

Hill, Polly. 1963. *The Migrant Cocoa-Farmers of Southern Ghana: A Study in Rural Capitalism.* Cambridge: Cambridge University Press.

Honoré, Bo. 1992. 'Trimmed LAD and Least Squares Estimation of Truncated and Censored Regression Models with Fixed Effects.' *Econometrica* 60(May): 533–65.

Kahn, Joel S. 1980. *Minangkabau Social Foundations: Indonesian Peasants and the World Economy.* Cambridge: Cambridge University Press.

Lopez, Ramon. 1997. 'Environmental Externalities in Traditional Agriculture and the Impact of Trade Liberalization: The Case of Ghana.' *Journal of Development Economics* 53(1): 17–39.

Mendelsohn, Robert. 1994. 'Property Rights and Tropical Deforestation.' *Oxford Economic Papers* 46(5): 750–6.

Migot-Adholla, Shem E., George Benneh, Frank Place, and Steven Atsu. 1993. 'Land, Security of Tenure, and Productivity in Ghana.' In *Searching for Land Tenure Security in Africa,* John W. Bruce and Shem E. Migot-Adholla (eds.). Dubuque, IA: Kendall/Hunt Publishing Company.

Otsuka, Keijiro, S. Suyanto, and Thomas P. Tomich. 1997. 'Does Tenure Insecurity Discourage Tree Planting? Evolution of Customary Land Tenure and Agroforestry Management in Sumatra.' EPTD Discussion Paper No. 37, International Food Policy Research Institute, Washington DC.

Place, Frank and Peter Hazell. 1993. 'Productivity Effects of Indigenous Land Tenure Systems in Sub-Saharan Africa.' *American Journal of Agricultural Economics* 75(February): 10–19.

Place, Frank and Keijiro Otsuka. 2000*a*. 'Population, Land Tenure, and Natural Resource Management in Malawi.' *Journal of Environmental Economics and Management,* forthcoming.

—— 2000*b*. 'Population, Land Tenure, and Tree Resource Management in Uganda.' *Land Economics,* forthcoming.

Platteau, Jean-Philippe. 1996. 'The Evolutionary Theory of Land Rights as Applied to Sub-Saharan Africa: A Critical Assessment.' *Development and Change* 27(1): 29–86.

Quisumbing, Agnes R., Ellen Payongayong, J.B. Aidoo, and Keijiro Otsuka. 1998. 'Women's Land Rights in the Transition to Individualized Ownership: Implications for Tree Resource Management in Western Ghana.' Working paper, International Food Policy Research Institute, Washington DC.

Shepherd, Gill. 1991. 'The Communal Management of Forests in the Semi-Arid and Sub-Humid Regions of Africa.' *Development Policy Review* 19: 151–76.

Suyanto, S. and Keijiro Otsuka. 1998. 'From Deforestation to Development of Agroforests in Customary Land Tenure Areas of Sumatra.' Working paper, Tokyo Metropolitan University, Tokyo.

Suyanto, S., Thomas Tomich, and Keijiro Otsuka. 1998. 'Land Tenure and Farm Management Efficiency: The Case of Smallholder Rubber Production in Customary Land Areas of Sumatra.' Working paper, International Center for Agroforestry, Indonesia, and Tokyo Metropolitan University, Tokyo.

5

The Puzzle of Counterproductive Property Rights Reforms: A Conceptual Analysis

ELINOR OSTROM

Introduction

The last half-century has witnessed many efforts to improve the economic and ecological performance of developing countries through reforms of property-rights systems. Tragically, many of these reforms have not achieved their intended outcomes and some have instead generated counterproductive results.[1] Reform efforts need to be viewed as experiments that test the relevance or validity of the theory informing policy. Since many reforms of property-rights systems have been based on conventional theories of how property-rights systems affect economic development and the sustainability of natural resource systems, the multiple failures need to be viewed as evidence challenging the relevance or validity of conventional property-rights theory for the affected policy area. Currently accepted theories are based on idealized models of private property and government property.

In conventional theory, the concept of private property is conceptualized narrowly with a primary focus on the right to alienate property through sale or inheritance as *the* defining attribute of private property. The right of alienating property is thought to give a 'well-defined' property right. Individuals and firms with a clear and alienable title to a property are posited as being able to make the economically most efficient decision about how to manage properties with the characteristics of purely private goods. This is because the owner, or designated heir, is assured of reaping the long-term benefits that are generated through investments. If a property achieves a lower than feasible return, others who have the capacity to use it more efficiently will offer to buy the property through market transactions. Market institutions are the mechanisms that enable owners to realize financial returns on their past investments and to

Previous versions of this paper were presented at the UNU/WIDER project on 'Land Reform Revisited: Access to Land, Rural Poverty, and Public Action,' held in Helsinki, Finland, 30 May–1 June 1997 and in Santiago, Chile, 27–29 April 1998. Support from the Ford Foundation and the MacArthur Foundation is gratefully acknowledged. I am deeply appreciative of the useful comments made on earlier versions by Alain de Janvry, Klaus Deininger, Jean-Philippe Platteau and the other participants in these seminars, an anonymous referee, and the excellent editorial assistance provided by Patty Dalecki.

[1] The failure of state-led land reforms is discussed in de Janvry, Sadoulet, and Wolford, this volume, and reliance on titling by Carter and Salgado, this volume.

shift properties to those owners with the highest valued uses (see Brasselle, Gaspart, and Platteau 1998).

For goods and resources that are characterized as public goods, private property and market mechanisms are predicted to fail. Individuals will either overproduce negative externalities or underproduce positive externalities. The 'solution' to market failure in conventional theory is to turn to government ownership. National governments are posited as having superior powers and as having the means to use these powers to increase the productivity and efficiency of economies. Many natural resources in developing countries have been 'nationalized' so as to prevent the presumed perversities of leaving decisions about them to private individuals. The failure of these reform efforts has been well documented (for general reviews, see Wunsch and Olowu 1995; V. Ostrom, Feeny, and Picht 1993; Baland and Platteau 1996; Fairhead and Leach 1998). A third broad type of ownership—common property—has been treated ambiguously. When a group of individuals has held the rights to access, harvest, and manage a natural resource, but not the right to sell their interest in the resource, these rights have been treated as if they were without economic value.

Trying to achieve greater access to resources by poorer members of a society, while also creating property systems with incentives generating higher levels of efficiency, is a challenging goal. A similar challenge is reforming land-rights systems so that common-pool resources, such as forests and pastures, are harvested sustainably. Both are particularly difficult when the policy tools recommended by conventional theory are blunt and frequently produce more harm than good. A medicine cabinet with only two prescriptions in it—assign fully alienable rights for private goods or assign a resource to government ownership—is unlikely to generate successful reforms given the substantial ecological, economic, social, and institutional variety that occurs in most countries.

Consequently, the primary purpose of this chapter is conceptual. Before one can develop reform tools that are likely to provide access to resources to poorer members of society within the context of institutions that generate efficiency-enhancing incentives, and before one can reform property rights that lead to sustainable harvesting of common-pool resources, one needs a more precise conception of property-rights systems than exists in much of conventional theory. First, it is important to recognize that common-property regimes do involve real property rights and are not simply the same as open-access regimes. Section 2 examines some serious confusions about common property that have generated past misunderstandings and inadequate reform efforts.

Secondly, it is important to recognize that property consists of multiple bundles of rights and that the right to alienate a property right is a very important, but not the only, relevant right. Section 3 presents a more general concept of the bundles of property rights that are involved in any complex property-rights system. Section 4 addresses the question of 'who, what, when, where, and how' of a property system so as to broaden the points of intervention available to policymakers wishing to improve economic and ecological performance.

Third, it is important to recognize that common-property regimes are potentially efficient and more equitable regimes when utilized to cope with particular combinations of ecological characteristics. Further, many common-property systems evolve in conjunction with private-property systems so that a mixed property regime is created rather than a purely private- or a purely common-property system (Netting 1981; McKean 1992; McCarthy, de Janvry, and Sadoulet 1997). Thus, Section 5 focuses on the attributes of land that are conducive to the use of common-property institutions and the evolution of mixed property systems.

Fourth, in order to develop more effective reforms in the future, it is important to understand some aspects of the reforms of the past that did not work and Section 6 turns to this topic. The final section asks what has been learned that can be applied to future reform efforts.

Confusions that generate misunderstanding[2]

Common-property regimes are presumed to be inefficient for three reasons. One is rent dissipation, because no one presumably owns the products of a resource until they are captured, and everyone engages in an unproductive race to capture these products before others do (Gordon 1954; Scott 1955; Schaefer 1957; Clark 1976, 1980; Dasgupta and Heal 1979). The source of this inefficiency is overappropriation when there is no cooperation. The second reason is low productivity, because no one has an incentive to make investments to improve the condition of the resource (North 1990; Yang 1987). The source of this inefficiency is underprovision when there is an insufficient level of cooperation. The third reason is the high transaction and enforcement costs expected if communal owners were to try to devise rules to reduce the externalities of their mutual overuse (Demsetz 1967). This inefficiency stems from the presumed high cost of reaching agreement, if it can be achieved, as contrasted to a hypothetical, costless form of reaching optimal provision and appropriation levels.

The debate about the relative merits of private, common, and government property has been clouded by a troika of confusions that hinder scholarly communication. Different meanings are assigned to terms without clarifying how multiple aspects relate to one another. The source of confusion relates to the differences between (1) common-property and open-access regimes, (2) common-pool resources and common-property regimes, and (3) a resource system and the flow of resource units. All three sources of confusion reduce clarity in assigning meanings to terms and retard theoretical and empirical progress.

The confusion between common-property and open-access regimes

In a now classic article, Ciriacy-Wantrup and Bishop (1975) clearly demarked the difference between property regimes that are *open-access*, where no one has the legal right to exclude anyone from using a resource, from *common-property*, where the members of a clearly demarked group have a legal right to exclude nonmembers of that group from using a resource (see also Bromley 1991, 1992*a*, *b*). Open-access regimes (*res*

[2] This and the next several sections draw on E. Ostrom 2000.

nullius)—including the classic cases of the open seas and the atmosphere—have long been considered in legal doctrine as involving no limits on who is authorized to use a resource. If anyone can use a resource, no one has an incentive to conserve its use (appropriation) or to invest in improvements (provision). If such a resource generates highly valued products, then one can expect that the lack of rules regarding authorized use will lead to misuse and overconsumption. Some local grazing areas, inshore fisheries, and forests are effectively open-access resources, but many fewer than presumed in the literature.

Some open-access regimes lack effective rules defining property rights by default (Dales 1968). Either the resources affected by these open-access regimes are not contained within a nation-state or no entity has successfully laid claim to legitimate ownership. Other open-access regimes are the consequence of conscious public policies to guarantee the access of all citizens to the use of a resource within a political jurisdiction. The concept of *jus publicum* applies to their formal status, but effectively these resources are open-access. The state governments of Oregon and Washington intervened in the early twentieth century to prevent local salmon fishermen from devising rules that would have limited entry and established harvesting limits (Higgs 1982, 1996). Fishing unions along the U.S. coastal areas tried to organize inshore fisheries so as to limit entry and establish harvesting limits during the 1950s. If they had succeeded, they would have guaranteed their own long-term access to inshore fisheries and excluded new entrants from access. Even though their efforts could not have had a serious impact on prices due to the presence of an active international market for fish, the fishing unions were prosecuted by the U.S. Department of Justice and found in violation of the Sherman Antitrust Act (R. Johnson and Libecap 1982). Thus, U.S. inshore fisheries have effectively been open-access resources during much of the twentieth century as a result of governmental action to prevent local fishing groups from establishing forms of common-property regimes within those political jurisdictions. In more recent times, however, both the national and state governments have reversed their prior stands and have actively sought ways of creating forms of co-management in inshore fisheries (see Pinkerton 1992, 1994; Wilson 1995).

A third type of open-access regime results from the ineffective exclusion of nonowners by the entity assigned formal rights of ownership. Protecting borders and enforcing limits on harvesting are costly activities. The perceived costs for those assigned property rights do not always exceed the perceived benefits. Both private- and common-property regimes are known to have allowed their control over a resource to disintegrate so that the property effectively becomes an open-access regime (see de Janvry, Gordillo, and Sadoulet 1997; Becker and Gibson 2000).

The confusion between a resource system and a property regime

The problems resulting from confusing open-access regimes with common-property regimes are particularly difficult to overcome due to a second terminological problem. The term 'common-property resource' is frequently used to describe a type of economic good that is better referred to as a 'common-pool resource.' All common-pool resources share two attributes of importance for economic activities: (1) it is costly to exclude individuals from using the good either through physical barriers or legal instruments, and (2) the benefits consumed by one individual subtract from the benefits available to others (V. Ostrom and E. Ostrom 1977; E. Ostrom, Gardner, and Walker 1994). Recognizing a class of goods that share these two attributes enables scholars to identify the core theoretical problems facing all individuals or groups who wish to utilize such resources for an extended period of time. Using 'property' in the term used to refer to a type of good reinforces the impression that goods sharing these attributes tend everywhere to share the same property regime. This is definitely not the case.

Common-pool resources share with public goods the difficulty of developing physical or institutional means of excluding beneficiaries. Unless means are devised to keep nonauthorized users from benefiting, these users will receive benefits without any responsibilities to contribute to their provision. Once some users obtain benefits without bearing any costs, no one wants to be the sucker and pay the costs. Second, the products or resource units from common-pool resources share with private goods the attribute that one person's consumption subtracts from the quantity available to others. Thus, common-pool resources are subject to problems of congestion, overuse, and potential destruction unless harvesting or use limits are devised and enforced. Besides sharing these two attributes, particular common-pool resources differ on many other attributes that affect their economic usefulness including their size; shape; whether resource units are mobile (e.g., water) or stationary (e.g., trees); the presence of storage; the productivity of the resource; and the value, timing, and regularity of the resource units produced.

Common-pool resources may be owned by national, regional, or local governments; by communal groups; or by private individuals or corporations, or they may be used as open-access resources by whoever can gain access. Each of the broad types of property regimes has different sets of advantages and disadvantages, but at times may rely upon similar operational rules regarding access and use of a resource (Feeny *et al.* 1990). Examples exist of both successful and unsuccessful efforts to govern and manage common-pool resources by governments, communal groups, cooperatives, voluntary associations, and private individuals or firms (Bromley *et al.* 1992; Singh 1994; Singh and Ballabh 1996). Thus, as discussed below, there is no automatic association of common-pool resources with common-property regimes—*or, with any other particular type of property regime.* Further, one cannot make sweeping assertions based on solid theoretical or empirical grounds that there is only one type of property regime that is always the most efficient and sustainable form of property to be used in relation to common-pool resources.

The confusion between the resource and the flow of resource units

Common-pool resources are composed of resource systems and a flow of resource units or benefits from these systems (Blomquist and Ostrom 1985). The resource system (or alternatively, the stock or the facility) is what generates a flow of resource units or benefits over time. Examples of typical common-pool resource systems include lakes, rivers, irrigation systems, groundwater basins, forests, fishery stocks, and grazing areas.

Common-pool resources may also be human-made facilities that are constructed for joint use, such as mainframe computers and the Internet. The resource units or benefits from these common-pool resources include water, timber, medicinal plants, fish, fodder, central processing units, and connection time. The distinction between the resource and the resource unit is important when designing or evaluating property-rights regimes related to common-pool resources. If the production of resource units is relatively predictable and measurable, devising private-property rights to appropriate the *flow of resource units* may be feasible, sustainable, and efficient. Complementary rights and duties related to the resource system itself—which may not be divisible—are also needed, or investment in providing the system will be ignored while benefits are appropriated in an unsustainable manner. The design of private-, common-, and government-property systems to groundwater in Southern California illustrates how a successful system may involve aspects of multiple types of regimes (Blomquist 1992).

Property as bundles of rights

A property right is an enforceable authority to undertake particular actions in a specific domain (Commons 1968). Property rights define actions that individuals can take in relation to other individuals regarding some 'thing.' If one individual has a right, someone else has a commensurate duty to observe that right. Squatters do not possess property rights even though they may be users. No one else has a commensurate duty to protect squatters' continued use of a resource unless their adverse use eventually matures into a prescriptive right. If they gain prescriptive rights, they are no longer squatters. Schlager and Ostrom (1992) identify five property rights that are most relevant for the use of common-pool resources, including access, withdrawal, management, exclusion, and alienation. These are defined as:

1. access: the right to enter a defined physical area and enjoy nonsubtractive benefits (e.g., hike, canoe, sit in the sun);
2. withdrawal: the right to obtain resource units or products of a resource system (e.g., catch fish, divert water);
3. management: the right to regulate internal use patterns and transform the resource by making improvements;
4. exclusion: the right to determine who will have an access right, and how that right may be transferred;
5. alienation: the right to sell or lease management and exclusion rights (Schlager and Ostrom 1992).

In much of the economics literature, private property is defined as equivalent to alienation. Property-rights systems that do not contain the right of alienation are considered to be incomplete. Further, they are presumed to lead to inefficiency since property-rights holders cannot trade their interest in an improved resource system for other resources, nor can someone who has a more efficient use of a resource system purchase that system in whole or in part (Demsetz 1967). Consequently, it is assumed

Table 5.1. *Bundles of rights associated with positions*

	Owner	Proprietor	Authorized claimant	Authorized user	Authorized entrant
Access	X	X	X	X	X
Withdrawal	X	X	X	X	
Management	X	X	X		
Exclusion	X	X			
Alienation	X				

Source: E. Ostrom and Schlager (1996: 133).

that property-rights systems that include the right to alienation will be transferred to their highest valued use (for a different view, see Larson and Bromley 1990).

Instead of focusing on one right, it is more useful to define five classes of property-rights holders as shown in Table 5.1. In this view, individuals or collectivities may hold well-defined property rights that include or do not include all five of the rights defined above. This approach separates the question of whether a particular right is well defined from the question of the effect of having a particular set of rights.

'Authorized entrants' include most recreational users of national parks who purchase an operational right to enter and enjoy the natural beauty of the park, but are specifically forbidden to harvest a long list of subtractable resource units including most forest products. Those who have both entry and withdrawal use-right units are 'authorized users.' The presence or absence of constraints upon the timing, technology used, purpose of use, and quantity of resource units harvested are determined by operational rules devised by those holding the collective-choice rights (or authority) of management and exclusion. The operational rights of entry and use may be finely divided into quite specific 'tenure niches' (Bruce 1995) that vary by season, by use, by technology, and by space. Tenure niches may overlap when one set of users owns the right to harvest fruits from trees, another set of users owns the right to the timber in these trees, and the trees may be located on land owned by still others (Bruce, Fortmann, and Nhira 1993). Operational rules may allow authorized users to transfer access and withdrawal rights either temporarily through a rental agreement, or permanently when these rights are assigned or sold to others (see Adasiak 1979, for a description of the rights of authorized users of the Alaskan salmon and herring fisheries).

'Claimants' possess the operational rights of access and withdrawal plus a collective-choice right of managing a resource that includes decisions concerning the construction and maintenance of facilities and the authority to devise limits on withdrawal rights. The net fishers of Jambudwip, India, for example, annually regulate the positioning of nets so as to avoid interference, but do not have the right to determine who may fish along the coast (Raychaudhuri 1980). Farmers on large-scale government irrigation systems frequently devise rotation schemes for allocating water on a branch canal (Benjamin *et al.* 1994).

'Proprietors' hold the same rights as claimants with the addition of the right to determine who may access and harvest from a resource. Many property systems that are called 'common-property' regimes involve participants who are proprietors and have four of the above rights, but do not possess the right to sell their management and exclusion rights even though they most frequently have the right to bequeath it to members of their family (see Berkes 1989; Bromley *et al.* 1992; Martin 1979; McCay and Acheson 1987). Empirical studies have found that proprietors frequently have sufficient rights to make decisions that promote long-term investment and harvesting from a resource. In a series of studies of inshore fisheries, self-organized irrigation systems, forest user groups, and groundwater institutions, proprietors tended to develop strict boundary rules to exclude noncontributors; established authority rules to allocate withdrawal rights; devised methods for monitoring conformance; and used graduated sanctions against those who did not conform to these rules (Agrawal 1994; Blomquist 1992; Schlager 1994; Tang 1994; Lam 1998). In other words, *well-defined and secure property rights do not need to involve the right to alienation.*

Empirical studies of farmers who hold only proprietorship rights have also shown these to be more efficient than posited in theory. Place and Hazell (1993) conducted surveys in Ghana, Kenya, and Rwanda to ascertain if indigenous land-rights systems were a constraint on agricultural productivity. They found that having the rights of a proprietor as contrasted to a formal owner in these settings did not affect investment decisions and productivity. Other studies conducted in Africa also found that formal titling was not related to investment levels on a farm.[3] In peri-urban regions, however, where access to bank credit depends on formal title, a positive impact of formal titling systems has been found (Feder *et al.* 1988; Feder and Feeny 1991). After reviewing the extensive number of studies examining the impact of various efforts to increase the transferability rights of farmers through the extension of formal titles, and conducting their own carefully specified econometric study of land tenure rights in Burkina Faso, Brasselle, Gaspart, and Platteau (1998: 32) conclude that: 'In other words, basic use rights are apparently sufficient to induce farmers to make land-specific investments without necessitating the holding of many transfer rights.'

'Owners' possess the right of alienation—the right to transfer a good in any way the owner wishes that does not harm the physical attributes or uses of other owners—in addition to the bundle of rights held by a proprietor. An individual, a private corporation, a government, or a communal group may possess full ownership rights to any kind of good including a common-pool resource (Montias 1976; Dahl and Lindblom 1963).

The who, what, when, where, and how of property-rights systems

What should be obvious by now is that the world of property rights is far more complex than simply government, private, and common property. Further, how any of

[3] See Migot-Adholla *et al.* 1991; Carter, Wiebe, and Blarel 1994; Bruce and Migot-Adholla 1994; and the extensive citations in Brasselle, Gaspart, and Platteau 1998.

these property regimes operate in practice depends, to a large extent, on the types of relationships that participants have established among themselves (McCay and Jentoft 1998). Instead of using overly simplified notions of what are in practice highly complex, constitutive concepts, one really needs to answer the questions that we were all taught must be included in any complete story about some event or process. The 'what' of a property-rights system is the set of rights in the bundle held by any individual or group. Any property-rights owner may hold all five of the rights described in Section 3 or any subset of these rights.

The 'who' refers to the individual, or set of individuals, who hold a particular bundle of rights and the set of individuals who are expected to recognize these rights as legitimate. The set of rights-holders may be very well defined, as when rights are allocated to members of a clan or ethnic group, or residents of a village. Rights-holders may need to own some other asset to qualify (such as a fishing birth in order to fish in an inshore fishing grounds or private agricultural land in order to use a common pasture). If membership in the set of property-rights holders becomes fuzzy at the margins, through extensive in-migration of other cases, it is always possible for a set of well-defined property rights to erode.

The set of people who are expected to respect a property right is also an important 'who' question. In relatively stable communities, most relevant individuals can be expected to respect locally evolved property rights. Further, individuals can be expected to have multiple relationships with members of a group. Infringing on someone's right may have many negative future consequences in such a closely related group. But, not all people will respect locally evolved rights. Colonial powers have rarely fully recognized the property rights of the people they have conquered—particularly when the property-rights system itself was alien from the perspective of colonial administrators. When property-rights holders are interacting by force or willingly with an extended set of individuals who have little likelihood of recognizing and respecting locally evolved rights, moving to a system where formal titles are recorded may be an essential development. With formally recorded rights, those who infringe on rights may be challenged in an arena recognized by strangers as authoritative.

The 'how' question relates to the processes used to exercise rights. When a single individual owns a right, it is presumed that the individual will act so as to maximize expected returns. In times of considerable uncertainty about future events, this may prove difficult for even the most astute property-rights holder. When rights are held jointly, however, considerable problems can ensue in the processes of arriving at agreements concerning how to manage a resource. These problems are ignored in the conventional theory of the firm. The modern private corporation is treated as if it were a single decision maker. The opposite orientation has been taken toward local villages or groups who must engage in collective-choice activities. A frequent presumption is made that such groups cannot impose on themselves the kinds of restraints needed to manage property efficiently. Empirical evidence shows, however, that many such groups do craft decision-making rules that enable them to manage resources sustainably over long periods of time. It is, of course, the case that all types of organizations, including modern corporations, can and do fail. A growing literature is addressing the question of the conditions that enhance or detract from the probabilities of common-property regimes succeeding (Baland and Platteau 1996; E. Ostrom 1990, 1999; Gibson, McKean, and Ostrom 2000).

The 'where' of a property-rights system refers to the location where a particular right may be exercised. In some property regimes, a defined set of individuals is authorized to harvest and manage anything on or below the surface of the land. Much more complex systems do exist where the rights to one kind of product are held by one group while another product is 'owned' by someone else. Tenure niches can at times be quite intertwined. Further, mixed property systems are frequently interlinked (see below for a further discussion of mixed property-rights systems). The 'when' of a property-rights system relates to the expected length of time involved in holding any particular rights. Any of the rights described in Section 3, except alienation, may be 'rented' with a potential for increased efficiency due to the temporary transfer to a more efficient actor. Rental arrangements may be for a single season or in some settings they may be handed down across generations and represent very stable, long-term rights.

Given the complexity of property-rights systems as they have evolved in many locations, basing reforms on stylized versions of what officials and their advisors in a country's capital city think the property-rights system is in a far-away region related to a particular resource has often been the source of many reform efforts going awry. Effective reforms are based on substantial knowledge about the kinds of problems that people are facing, the conditions of the environment in which they live, and the social and institutional structures in which they interact.

If overharvesting of a forest, pasture, or other common-pool resource is the problem, one has to sort out whether it is a 'who,' a 'what,' or a 'how,' etc., problem. Is there a well-defined group who has access and use rights? Are these rights recognized by others? Providing arenas where these claims or counterclaims can be resolved will frequently be more effective than fabricating new property-rights systems *de novo*. What is the actual bundle of rights held by a group of individuals? Are they sufficient to provide assurance of reaping the benefits of investment? Are the benefits of harvesting large enough to justify costly efforts to monitor use and sanction nonconformers to jointly determined rules? Reforms aimed at increasing the assurance of or quantity of benefits achieved may be warranted if this is the source of the problem under analysis. How are decisions about governance and management being made? Providing training and effective extension services to increase the skills of local groups in managing valuable assets may be a more successful intervention than reforms related to the property-rights system itself. If reforms are to be successful, they need to address actual problems rather than hypothetical inadequacies of one type of property-rights regime compared to the idealized version of another regime.

While land is frequently thought of as the epitome of a pure private good—easy to exclude others from enjoying the fruits of one's labor—land used for pastures and forests is far more costly to fence and is frequently owned communally. Communal ownership of land has been an anathema for many. There may be, however, attributes of land that help to account for it being held as common rather than private property in some locations.

Attributes of common-pool resources conducive to the use of communal proprietorship or ownership

Where population density is low, land is abundant, and land generates a rich diversity of plant and animal products without much husbandry, the expected costs of establishing and defending boundaries to a parcel of land of any size may be greater than the expected benefits of enclosure (Demsetz 1967; Feeny 1993). Settlers moving into a new terrain characterized by high risk due to danger from others, from a harsh environment, or from lack of appropriate knowledge, may decide to develop one large, common parcel prior to any divisions into smaller parcels (Ellickson 1993). Once land becomes scarce, conflict over who has the rights to invest in improvements and reap the results of their efforts can lead individuals to want to enclose land through fencing or institutional means to protect their investments. There are tradeoffs in costs to be considered, however. The more land included within one enclosure, the lower the costs of defending all the boundaries, but the higher the costs of regulating the use of the enclosed parcel.

The decision to enclose need not be taken in one step from an open-access terrain to a series of private plots owned exclusively by single families (Field 1984, 1985, 1989; Ellickson 1993). The benefits of enclosing land depend on the scale of productive activity involved. For some agricultural activities, considerable benefits may be associated with smaller parcels fully owned by a family enterprise. For other activities, the benefits of parcelization may not be substantial. Moving all the way to private plots is an efficient move when the expected marginal returns from enclosing numerous plots exceed the expected marginal costs of fencing and defending a much more extended system of boundaries and the now reduced transaction costs of making decisions about use patterns (Nugent and Sanchez 1995).

In a classic study of the mixture of property-rights systems used for many centuries by Swiss peasants, Robert Netting (1976, 1981) observed that the same individuals fully divided their agricultural land into separate family-owned parcels, but that grazing lands located on the Alpine hillsides were organized into communal property systems. In these mountain valleys, the *same* individuals used different property-rights systems side-by-side for centuries. Each local community had considerable autonomy to change local rules, so the resulting mixed property-rights regime was not due to someone else imposing an inefficient set of rules on them. Netting argued that attributes of the resource affected which property-rights systems were most likely for diverse purposes. Netting identified five attributes that he considered to be most conducive to the development of communal property rights:

1. low value of production per unit of area;
2. high variance in the availability of resource units on any one parcel;
3. low returns from intensification of investment;
4. substantial economies of scale by utilizing a large area; and
5. high cost of division (fencing and enforcement of rights) (see also McCarthy, de Janvry, and Sadoulet 1997).

Steep land where rainfall is scattered may not be suitable for most agricultural purposes, but can be excellent land for pasture and forests if aggregated into sufficiently large parcels. By developing communal property rights to large parcels of such land, those who are members of the community are able to share environmental risks due to the unpredictability of rain-induced growth of grasses within any smaller region (Agrawal 2000). Further, herding and processing of milk products is subject to substantial economies of scale. If individual families develop means to share these reduced costs, all can save substantially. Building the appropriate roads, retaining walls, and processing facilities may also be done more economically if these efforts are shared.

While the Swiss peasants were able to devote these harsh lands to productive activities, they had to invest time and effort in the development of rules that would reduce the incentives to overgraze and would ensure that investments in shared infrastructure were maintained over time. In many Swiss villages, rights to common pasturage were distributed according to the number of cows that could be carried over the winter using hay supplies produced on the owners' private parcels. In all cases, the village determined who would be allowed to use; the specific access and withdrawal rights to be used; how investment and maintenance costs were to be shared; and how the annual returns from common processing activities were to be shared. Since each village devised their own rules, they were able to fit their rules to local circumstances using their time and place knowledge about the particular ecological characteristics of their alpine region and about the strategies used by villagers to make a living. Long-term residents kept their access to the mountain commons so long as they met their obligations and followed the rules set by the village. These systems were not, on the other hand, very open to new settlers gaining rights to the commons.

All of these systems included at least village proprietorship rights, but some Swiss villages developed full ownership rights by incorporating and authorizing the buying and selling of shares (usually with the approval of the village). Netting's findings are strongly supported by studies of mountain villages in Japan, where thousands of rural villages have held communal property rights to extensive forests and grazing areas located in the steep mountainous regions located above their private agricultural plots (McKean 1982, 1992). Similar systems have existed in Norway for centuries (Sandberg 1993; Örebech 1993) and in Mexico (McCarthy, de Janvry, and Sadoulet 1997; Alcorn and Toledo 1998).

The importance of sharing risk is stressed in other theoretical and empirical studies of communal proprietorships (Nugent and Sanchez 1993; Gupta 1986; Antilla and Torp 1996). When no physical or institutional mechanisms exist for sharing risk, communal property arrangements may enable individuals to adopt productive activities not feasible under individual property rights. A recent study has demonstrated that the variance in the productivity of land over space—due largely to the variance in rainfall from year to year—is strongly associated with the size of communally held parcels allocated to grazing in the Sudan (Nugent and Sanchez 1995). Ellickson (1993) compares the types of environmental and personal security risks faced by new settlers in New England, in Bermuda, and in Utah to explain the variance in the speed of converting jointly held land to individually held land in each of these settlements.

A consistent finding across many studies of communal property-rights systems is that these systems do not exist in isolation and are usually used in conjunction with individual ownership. In other words, rights-holders have dual property rights.[4] In most irrigation systems that are built and managed by the farmers themselves, for example, each farmer owns his or her own plot(s) while participating as a joint proprietor or owner in a communally organized irrigation system (Tang 1992; Sengupta 1991, 1993; Vincent 1995; Wade 1992; Coward 1980; Lam 1998). Water is allocated to individual participants using a variety of individually tailored rules, but those irrigation systems that have survived for long periods of time tend to allocate water and responsibilities for joint costs using a similar metric—frequently the amount of land owned by a farmer (E. Ostrom 1990, 1992). In other words, benefits are roughly proportional to the costs of investing and maintaining the system itself.[5]

Further, formally recognized communal systems are usually nested into a series of governance units that complement the organizational skills and knowledge of those involved in making collective-choice decisions in smaller units (O. Johnson 1972). Since the Middle Ages, most of the Alpine systems in both Switzerland and Italy have been nested in a series of self-governing communities that respectively governed villages, valleys, and federations of valleys (Merlo 1989). In modern times, cantonal authorities in Switzerland have assumed an added responsibility to make periodic, careful monitoring visits to each alp on a rotating basis and to provide professional assessments and recommendations to local villages, thereby greatly enhancing the quality of knowledge and information about the sustainability of these resources (Glaser 1987). Consequently national governments can make a substantial difference in the way local property-rights regimes operate in practice. Both private and common property require complementary activities of a national government to achieve efficient and sustainable outcomes. Among the essential governmental activities are providing large-scale public infrastructures, such as roads, and investments in scientific information that enable farmers to make their land more productive.

Reforms that do not work

Several chapters of this volume are devoted to an analysis of land reforms intended to increase the access of poor and landless people to agricultural land through large-scale redistributions of land. The intended beneficiaries of these reforms were the poor, but counterintentional outcomes frequently occurred. In their chapter, de Janvry, Sadoulet, and Wolford conclude: 'In summary, eighty years of land reform that started with the Mexican Revolution have deeply transformed the rural sector, but not to the advantage of the peasants and the landless' (Chapter 11, this volume). As analyzed in several chapters of this volume, many reasons exist for the lack of success, but a naive

[4] For an analysis of dual property rights, see de Janvry, McCarthy, and Sadoulet 1998; McCarthy, Sadoulet, and de Janvry 1998; and McCarthy, de Janvry, and Sadoulet 1997.

[5] See Design Principle 2 in E. Ostrom 1990: 90.

over-reliance on the presumed efficacy of private property by itself is one of them. Many of the land reforms of the last eighty years did not recognize the importance of the myriad of other institutional facilities—such as the availability of credit, good infrastructure, effective courts, strong local governments able to mobilize their own resources and respond to local needs, and user-managed pasture, forests, and riverine fisheries—for helping the poor and previously landless to become a successful and independent small-holder sector.

A second major land-reform effort had a somewhat different foundation. The conceptual confusion between common-property resources and open-access resources led many policymakers to urge that all common-pool resources in a particular sector, such as forests, should become national government property. It was thought that local users could not overcome the 'tragedy of the commons' they must face in trying to manage these resources. Common-property regimes controlling access and harvesting from local streams, forests, grazing areas, and inshore fisheries had actually evolved in many locations over long periods of time, but were rarely given formal status in the legal codes of newly independent countries.

As concern for the protection of natural resources mounted during the 1960s, many developing countries in Africa and Asia nationalized all land and water resources that had not yet been recorded as private property. The institutional arrangements that local users had devised to limit entry and use lost their legal standing, but the national governments lacked monetary resources and personnel to monitor the use of these resources effectively (Arnold, this volume). Thus, resources that had been under a *de facto* common-property regime enforced by local users were converted to a *de jure* government-property regime, but reverted to a *de facto* open-access regime. When resources that were previously controlled by local participants have been nationalized, state control has usually proved to be less effective and efficient than control by those directly affected, if not disastrous in its consequences (Hilton 1992; Curtis 1991; Panayotou and Ashton 1992; Ascher 1995). The harmful effects of nationalizing forests that had earlier been governed by local user groups have been well documented for Thailand (Feeny 1988), Niger (Thomson 1977; Thomson, Feeny, and Oakerson 1992), Nepal (Arnold and Campbell 1986; Messerschmidt 1986), and India (Gadgil and Iyer 1989; Jodha 1990, 1996). Similar results have occurred in regard to inshore fisheries taken over by state or national agencies from local control by the inshore fishermen themselves (Cordell and McKean 1992; Cruz 1986; Dasgupta 1982; Higgs 1996; Panayotou 1982; Pinkerton 1989).

A more recent effort has been to privatize some of these resources. Privatization has involved substantial distributional consequences. The individuals who are most likely to be aware of a potential division are those who are the best informed in a community and most likely to have more economic and political assets. Jodha (1990, 1996) documents the reduction in access to resources to poor farmers in India after many of the 'wastelands' were privatized. Full privatization of a commons is not, of course, the only time when distributional issues may be substantial. Efforts to further restrict entry to overutilized common-pool resources by communal groups (or by a national government in their name) frequently reduce the rights of those who already have the most marginal position in a community. Thus, those who come from a minority ethnic group or are nonpermanent residents of a local village (pastoralists, for example) are frequently the ones who lose access when efforts are made to further exclude users (see Baland and Platteau 1998).

What have we learned related to future reform efforts?

Many of the previous efforts to reform the structure of governance and property-rights systems in developing countries with the avowed aim of increasing the access of the poor to resources, or saving resources from overharvesting and destruction, have not succeeded. One reason for these failures—but not, of course, the only reason—has been an overly simplistic view of the institutional options available and the presumed ease of implementing policy reforms that will operate as panaceas to solve extremely difficult and complex problems.

In this chapter I have tried to clarify some of the previous misunderstandings related to common-property regimes and common-pool resources. Common-property regimes were confused for several decades of policy analysis with open-access regimes where no regulation of access, withdrawal, management, exclusion, or alienation occurs. While many common-property regimes do not confer individual rights of alienation onto users, they have been shown to be capable of achieving relatively high levels of efficiency when used for the management of local common-pool resources. The particular set of rights and how they are organized by common-property regimes varies dramatically from one setting to another, as does the performance of these systems. It is important, however, that common-property institutions be viewed as one of the institutional tools that individuals can use (frequently together with private property) to create incentives associated with efficiency and sustainability. Further, access to resources is generally more available to the poor in common-property regimes than in private regimes, holding other factors constant.

After years of reform that tried to eradicate common-property regimes, it is a strange irony that in some policy circles common-property regimes have become the new panacea. This is equally as dangerous as the earlier reliance on government or private property as a panacea. In the forestry sector, after years of recommending control of forests by powerful national agencies ('custodian forestry'), many policy analysts now recommend some form of devolution to the control of local users. Substantial evidence supports the claim that local users can organize to manage forest resources and do much better than distant, national ministries (Poffenberger 1990; Poffenberger and McGean 1996; Agrawal 1994). Simply declaring a change in national policy, however, and turning over large amounts of forested land to rapidly created 'user groups' may be another overly simplistic policy that will see its own failures in another decade or so.

In a recent briefing paper by the International Centre for Integrated Mountain Development (ICIMOD), for example, the following statement was made: 'Nepal has currently the most pioneering forestry legislation in the world. It was approved in 1993 and the rules gazetted in 1995. Approximately 350,000 hectares of forest have been handed over to 4,500 forestry user groups' (ICIMOD 1997). One would think that the comment would have been followed by a cautionary note that a rapid, wholesale transfer of forested land to a very large number of user groups within an extremely short period of time was a danger signal that a new policy was being implemented in a manner unlikely to succeed. While extensive research shows that Nepali villagers do have substantial capabilities for self-organization—especially in regard to irrigation[6]—simply giving them back the forested areas that were taken away from them forty years ago is no guarantee that most of these user groups will organize sufficiently that they will manage these lands sustainably and efficiently. By now, many of these lands are substantially degraded and will require costly investments. Fortunately, there are several different kinds of experiments going on right now in Nepal and some of these innovations are being monitored. Consequently, it will be possible in several years to understand which processes of implementing the massive turnover of forest lands to local users have been the most successful in helping forest users overcome the very high costs of initial organization and of making the investment needed to ensure the long-term sustainability of their recently returned and degraded forest lands.

Policy analysts need to move away from viewing any institutional arrangement as a panacea and learn how to analyze the attributes of a resource system and of the individuals using that system (Gibson, McKean, and Ostrom 2000). Sole reliance on the state, the market, or on common property to 'fix' any problem is unlikely to succeed. We need to offer the owners, proprietors, claimants, authorized users, and authorized entrants of a wide diversity of valuable resources a set of intellectual tools that they can use in crafting more robust local, regional, and national institutions and in learning how to cooperative effectively with one another so as to achieve higher long-term productivity. Real long-term gains are achieved by individuals who are motivated to work effectively together and are rewarded in the long-term for their efforts. Devising effective, autonomous, and honest court systems and multiple arenas where peaceful contestation can occur is as important as enabling problem-solving individuals to utilize a mixture of property-rights systems well matched to the situations they face.

REFERENCES

Adasiak, Allen. 1979. 'Alaska's Experience with Limited Entry.' *Journal of the Fisheries Research Board of Canada* 36(7): 770–82.

Agrawal, Arun. 1994. 'Rules, Rule Making, and Rule Breaking: Examining the Fit Between Rule Systems and Resource Use.' In *Rules, Games, and Common-Pool Resources*, Elinor Ostrom, Roy Gardner, and James M. Walker (eds.). Ann Arbor, MI: University of Michigan Press.

—— 2000. *Greener Pastures: Politics, Markets, and Community among a Migrant Pastoral People.* Durham, NC: Duke University Press, forthcoming.

[6] See the studies by Shivakoti *et al.* 1997; Lam 1998; Benjamin *et al.* 1994; and Shivakoti and Ostrom 2000.

Alcorn, Janis B. and Victor M. Toledo. 1998. 'Resilient Resource Management in Mexico's Forest Ecosystems: The Contribution of Property Rights.' In *Linking Social and Ecological Systems*, Fikret Berkes and Carl Folke (eds.). Cambridge: Cambridge University Press.

Antilla, Sten and Aivind Torp. 1996. 'Environmental Adjustment and Private Economic Strategies in Reindeer Pastoralism: Combining Game Theory with Participatory Action Theory.' Working paper, Mid-Sweden University.

Arnold, J.E.M. and J. Gabriel Campbell. 1986. 'Collective Management of Hill Forests in Nepal: The Community Forestry Development Project.' In *Proceedings of the Conference on Common Property Resource Management*, National Research Council. Washington DC: National Academy Press.

Ascher, William. 1995. *Communities and Sustainable Forestry in Developing Countries.* San Francisco, CA: ICS Press.

Baland, Jean-Marie and Jean-Philippe Platteau. 1996. *Halting Degradation of Natural Resources: Is There a Role for Rural Communities?* Oxford: Clarendon Press.

—— 1998. 'Wealth Inequality and Efficiency in the Commons, Part II: The Regulated Case.' *Oxford Economic Papers* 50(1): 1–22.

Becker, C. Dustin and Clark Gibson. 2000. 'The Lack of Institutional Supply: Why a Strong Local Community in Western Ecuador Fails to Protect its Forest.' In *People and Forests: Communities, Institutions, and the Governance of Forests*, Clark Gibson, Margaret A. McKean, and Elinor Ostrom (eds.). Cambridge, MA: MIT Press, forthcoming.

Benjamin, Paul, Wai Fung Lam, Elinor Ostrom, and Ganesh Shivakoti. 1994. 'Institutions, Incentives, and Irrigation in Nepal.' Decentralization: Finance & Management Project Report, Associates in Rural Development, Burlington, VT.

Berkes, Fikret (ed.). 1989. *Common Property Resources: Ecology and Community-Based Sustainable Development.* London: Belhaven.

Blomquist, William. 1992. *Dividing the Waters: Governing Groundwater in Southern California.* San Francisco, CA: ICS Press.

Blomquist, William and Elinor Ostrom. 1985. 'Institutional Capacity and the Resolution of a Commons Dilemma.' *Policy Studies Review* 5(2): 383–93.

Brasselle, Anne-Sophie, Fédéric Gaspart, and Jean-Phillipe Platteau. 1998. 'Land Tenure Security and Investment Incentives: Further Puzzling Evidence from Burkina Faso.' Working Paper on Development 201, CRED, University of Notre Dame de la Paix, Namur, Belgium.

Bromley, Daniel W. 1991. *Environment and Economy: Property Rights and Public Policy.* Cambridge, MA: Basil Blackwell.

—— 1992*a*. 'The Commons, Common Property, and Environmental Policy.' *Environmental and Resource Economics* 2(1): 1–17.

—— 1992*b*. 'The Commons, Property, and Common-Property Regimes.' *Making the Commons Work: Theory, Practice, and Policy*, Daniel Bromley *et al.* (eds.). San Francisco, CA: ICS Press.

Bromley, Daniel W., David Feeny, Margaret McKean, Pauline Peters, Jere Gilles, Ronald Oakerson, C. Ford Runge, and James Thomson (eds.). 1992. *Making the Commons Work: Theory, Practice, and Policy.* San Francisco, CA: ICS Press.

Bruce, John W. 1995. *Legal Bases for the Management of Land-Based Natural Resources as Common Property*, Forests, Trees and People Programme. Rome: FAO.

Bruce, John W. and Shem E. Migot-Adholla (eds.). 1994. *Searching for Land Tenure Security in Africa.* Dubuque, IA: Kendall/Hunt.

Bruce, John W., Louise Fortmann, and Calvin Nhira. 1993. 'Tenures in Transition, Tenures in Conflict: Examples from the Zimbabwe Social Forest.' *Rural Sociology* 58(4): 626–42.

Carter, Michael R., K.D. Wiebe, and B. Blarel. 1994. 'Tenure Security for Whom? Differential Effects of Land Policy in Kenya.' In *Searching for Land Tenure Security in Africa*, John W. Bruce and Shem E. Migot-Adholla (eds.). Dubuque, IA: Kendall/Hunt.

Ciriacy-Wantrup, Siegfried V. and Richard C. Bishop. 1975. '"Common Property" as a Concept in Natural Resource Policy.' *Natural Resources Journal* 15(4): 713–27.

Clark, Colin W. 1976. *Mathematical Bioeconomics: The Optimal Management of Renewable Resources.* New York: Wiley.

—— 1980. 'Restricted Access to Common-Property Fishery Resources: A Game Theoretic Analysis.' In *Dynamic Optimization and Mathematical Economics*, P.T. Liu (ed.). New York: Plenum Press.

Commons, John R. 1968. *Legal Foundations of Capitalism.* Madison, WI: University of Wisconsin Press.

Cordell, John C. and Margaret A. McKean. 1992. 'Sea Tenure in Bahia, Brazil.' In *Making the Commons Work: Theory, Practice, and Policy*, Daniel Bromley *et al.* (eds.). San Francisco, CA: ICS Press.

Coward, E. Walter, Jr. (ed.). 1980. *Irrigation and Agricultural Development in Asia: Perspectives from the Social Sciences.* Ithaca, NY: Cornell University Press.

Cruz, Wilfrido D. 1986. 'Overfishing and Conflict in a Traditional Fishery: San Miguel Bay, Philippines.' In *Proceedings of the Conference on Common Property Resource Management*, National Research Council. Washington DC: National Academy Press.

Curtis, Donald. 1991. *Beyond Government: Organizations for Common Benefit.* London: Macmillan.

Dahl, Robert A. and Charles E. Lindblom. 1963. *Politics, Economics and Welfare: Planning and Politico-Economic Systems Resolved into Basic Social Processes.* New York: Harper.

Dales, John H. 1968. *Pollution, Property, and Prices: An Essay in Policy-Making and Economics.* Toronto: University of Toronto Press.

Dasgupta, Partha. 1982. *The Control of Resources.* Cambridge, MA: Harvard University Press.

Dasgupta, Partha and Geoffrey M. Heal. 1979. *Economic Theory and Exhaustible Resources.* Garden City, NJ: J. Nisbet.

de Janvry, Alain, Gustavo Gordillo, and Elisabeth Sadoulet. 1997. *Mexico's Second Agrarian Reform: Household and Community Response, 1990–1994.* La Jolla, CA: University of California Center for U.S.-Mexican Studies.

de Janvry, Alain, Nancy McCarthy, and Elisabeth Sadoulet. 1998. 'Endogenous Provision and Appropriation in the Commons.' Paper presented at the Allied Social Science Association meeting, Chicago, IL, 2–5 January.

Demsetz, Harold. 1967. 'Toward a Theory of Property Rights.' *American Economic Review* 57(2): 347–59.

Ellickson, Robert C. 1993. 'Property in Land.' *Yale Law Journal* 102(6): 1315–1400.

Fairhead, James and Melissa Leach. 1998. *Reframing Deforestation: Global Analyses and Local Realities.* London: Routledge.

Feder, Gershon and David Feeny. 1991. 'Land Tenure and Property Rights: Theory and Implications for Development Policy.' *World Bank Economic Review* 5(1): 135–53.

Feder, Gershon, T. Onchan, Y. Chalamwong, and C. Hangladoran. 1988. *Land Policies and Form Productivity in Thailand.* Baltimore, MD: Johns Hopkins University Press.

Feeny, David. 1988. 'Agricultural Expansion and Forest Depletion in Thailand, 1900–1975.' In *World Deforestation in the Twentieth Century*, John F. Richards and Richard P. Tucker (eds.). Durham, NC: Duke University Press.

—— 1993. 'The Demand for and the Supply of Institutional Arrangements.' In *Rethinking Institutional Analysis and Development*, Vincent Ostrom, David Feeny, and Hartmut Picht (eds.). San Francisco, CA: ICS Press.

Feeny, David, Fikret Berkes, Bonnie J. McCay, and James M. Acheson. 1990. 'The Tragedy of the Commons: Twenty-Two Years Later.' *Human Ecology* 18(1): 1–19.

Field, Barry C. 1984. 'The Evolution of Individual Property Rights in Massachusetts Agriculture, 17th–19th Centuries.' *Northeastern Journal of Agricultural and Resource Economics* 14(2): 97–109.

—— 1985. 'The Optimal Commons.' *American Journal of Agricultural Economics* 67(2): 364–7.

—— 1989. 'The Evolution of Property Rights.' *Kyklos* 42(3): 319–45.

Gadgil, Madhav and Prema Iyer. 1989. 'On the Diversification of Common-Property Resource Use by Indian Society.' In *Common Property Resources: Ecology and Community-Based Sustainable Development*, Fikret Berkes (ed.). London: Belhaven Press.

Gibson, Clark, Margaret McKean, and Elinor Ostrom (eds.). 2000. *Keeping the Forest: Communities, Institutions, and the Governance of Forests.* Cambridge, MA: MIT Press, forthcoming.

Glaser (Picht), Christine. 1987. 'Common Property Regimes in Swiss Alpine Meadows.' Presented at the Conference on Advances in Comparative Institutional Analysis, Inter-University Center of Postgraduate Studies, Dubrovnik, Yugoslavia, 19–23 October.

Gordon, H. Scott. 1954. 'The Economic Theory of a Common-Property Resource: The Fishery.' *Journal of Political Economy* 62(2): 124–42.

Gupta, Anil K. 1986. 'Socioecology of Stress: Why Do Common Property Resource Management Projects Fail?' In *Proceedings of the Conference on Common Property Resource Management*, National Research Council. Washington DC: National Academy Press.

Higgs, Robert. 1982. 'Legally Induced Technical Regress in the Washington Salmon Fishery.' *Research in Economic History* 7: 55–86.

—— 1996. 'Legally Induced Technical Regress in the Washington Salmon Fishery.' In *Empirical Studies in Institutional Change*, Lee J. Alston, Thráinn Eggertsson, and Douglass C. North (eds.). New York: Cambridge University Press.

Hilton, Rita. 1992. 'Institutional Incentives for Resource Mobilization: An Analysis of Irrigation Schemes in Nepal.' *Journal of Theoretical Politics* 4(3): 283–308.

International Centre for Integrated Mountain Development (ICIMOD). 1997. 'Power, Equity, Gender, and Conflicts in Common Property Resources in the Hindu Kush-Himalayas.' *Issues in Mountain Development* (September).

Jodha, Narpat S. 1990. 'Depletion of Common Property Resources in India: Micro-level Evidence.' In *Rural Development and Population: Institutions and Policy*, G. McNicoll and M. Cain. Oxford: Oxford University Press.

—— 1996. 'Property Rights and Development.' In *Rights to Nature*, Susan S. Hanna, Carl Folke, and Karl-Göran Mäler (eds.). Washington DC: Island Press.

Johnson, Omotunde E.G. 1972. 'Economic Analysis: the Legal Framework and Land Tenure Systems.' *Journal of Law and Economics* 15(1): 259–76.

Johnson, Ronald N. and Gary D. Libecap. 1982. 'Contracting Problems and Regulation: The Case of the Fishery.' *American Economic Review* 72(5): 1005–22.

Lam, Wai Fung. 1998. *Governing Irrigation Systems in Nepal: Institutions, Infrastructure, and Collective Action.* Oakland, CA: ICS Press.

Larson, Bruce A. and Daniel W. Bromley. 1990. 'Property Rights, Externalities, and Resource Degradation: Locating the Tragedy.' *Journal of Development Economics* 33(2): 235–62.

Martin, Kent O. 1979. 'Play by the Rules or Don't Play at All: Space Division and Resource Allocation in a Rural Newfoundland Fishing Community.' In *North Atlantic Maritime Cultures: Anthropological Essays on Changing Adaptations*, Raoul Anderson (ed.). The Hague, Netherlands: Mouton.

McCarthy, Nancy, Alain de Janvry, and Elisabeth Sadoulet. 1997. 'Land Allocation under Dual Individual-Collective Use in Mexico.' Paper presented at the meeting of the UNU/WIDER Project on 'Land Reform Revisited: Access to Land, Rural Poverty, and Public Action,' Helsinki, Finland, 30–31 May.

McCarthy, Nancy, Elisabeth Sadoulet, and Alain de Janvry. 1998. 'Common Pool Resource Appropriation under Costly Cooperation.' Working paper, Department of Agricultural and Resource Economics, University of California, Berkeley, CA.

McCay, Bonnie J. and James M. Acheson (eds.). 1987. *The Question of the Commons: The Culture and Ecology of Communal Resources.* Tucson, AZ: University of Arizona Press.

McCay, Bonnie J. and Svein Jentoft. 1998. 'Market or Community Failure? Critical Perspectives on Common Property Research.' *Human Organization* 17(1): 21–9.

McKean, Margaret A. 1982. 'The Japanese Experience with Scarcity: Management of Traditional Common Lands.' *Environmental Review* 6(2): 63–88.

—— 1992. 'Management of Traditional Common Lands (*Iriaichi*) in Japan.' In *Making the Commons Work: Theory, Practice, and Policy*, Daniel Bromley *et al.* (eds.). San Francisco, CA: ICS Press.

Merlo, M. 1989. 'The Experience of the Village Communities in the North-Eastern Italian Alps.' In *Collective Forest Land Tenure and Rural Development in Italy*, M. Merlo, R. Morandini, A. Gabbrielli, and I. Novaco (eds.). Rome: FAO.

Messerschmidt, Donald A. 1986. 'People and Resources in Nepal: Customary Resource Management Systems of the Upper Kali Gandaki.' In *Proceedings of the Conference on Common Property Resource Management*, National Research Council. Washington DC: National Academy Press.

Migot-Adholla, Shem E., Peter Hazell, Benoit Blarel, and Frank Place. 1991. 'Indigenous Land Rights Systems in Sub-Saharan Africa: A Constraint on Productivity?' *World Bank Economic Review* 5(1): 155–75.

Montias, John Michael. 1976. *The Structure of Economic Systems.* New Haven, CT: Yale University Press.

Netting, Robert McCorkle. 1976. 'What Alpine Peasants Have in Common: Observations on Communal Tenure in a Swiss Village.' *Human Ecology* 4: 135–46.

—— 1981. *Balancing on an Alp: Ecological Change and Continuity in a Swiss Mountain Community*. New York: Cambridge University Press.

North, Douglass C. 1990. *Institutions, Institutional Change, and Economic Performance*. New York: Cambridge University Press.

Nugent, Jeffrey B. and Nicolas Sanchez. 1993. 'Tribes, Chiefs, and Transhumance: A Comparative Institutional Analysis.' *Economic Development and Cultural Change* 42(1): 87–113.

—— 1995. 'The Local Variability of Rainfall and Tribal Institutions: The Case of Sudan.' Presented to the Middle East Economic Association, Washington DC, 7 January.

Örebech, Peter. 1993. 'Common and Public Property Rights Regimes to Non-Private Resources. Some Legal Issues on Self-Governing Conservation Systems.' In *Common Property Regimes: Law and Management of Non-Private Resource*, Proceedings of the Conference, Volume 1, Erling Berge (ed.). Ås, Norway: Agricultural University of Norway.

Ostrom, Elinor. 1990. *Governing the Commons: The Evolution of Institutions for Collective Action.* New York: Cambridge University Press.

—— 1992. 'The Rudiments of a Theory of the Origins, Survival, and Performance of Common-Property Institutions.' In *Making the Commons Work: Theory, Practice, and Policy*, Daniel Bromley *et al.* (eds.). San Francisco, CA: ICS Press.

—— 1999. 'Social Capital: A Fad or a Fundamental Concept? In *Social Capital. A Multifaceted Perspective*, Partha Dasgupta and Ismail Serageldin (eds.). Washington DC: The World Bank.

—— 2000. 'Private and Common Property Rights.' *Encyclopedia of Law & Economics*, forthcoming.

Ostrom, Elinor and Edella Schlager. 1996. 'The Formation of Property Rights.' In *Rights to Nature*, Susan Hanna, Carl Folke, and Karl-Göran Mäler (eds.). Washington DC: Island Press.

Ostrom, Elinor, Roy Gardner, and James M. Walker. 1994. *Rules, Games, and Common-Pool Resources*. Ann Arbor, MI: University of Michigan Press.

Ostrom, Vincent and Elinor Ostrom. 1977. 'A Theory for Institutional Analysis of Common Pool Problems.' In *Managing the Commons*, Garrett Hardin and John Baden (eds.). San Francisco, CA: W.H. Freeman.

Ostrom, Vincent, David Feeny, and Hartmut Picht (eds.). 1993. *Rethinking Institutional Analysis and Development: Issues, Alternatives, and Choices*, 2nd edition. San Francisco, CA: ICS Press.

Panayotou, Theodore. 1982. 'Management Concepts for Small-Scale Fisheries: Economic and Social Aspects.' FAO Fisheries Technical Paper no. 228, FAO, Rome.

Panayotou, Theodore and Peter S. Ashton. 1992. *Not by Timber Alone: Economics and Ecology for Sustaining Tropical Forests*. Washington DC: Island Press.

Pinkerton, Evelyn (ed.). 1989. *Co-Operative Management of Local Fisheries: New Directions for Improved Management and Community Development*. Vancouver, Canada: University of British Columbia.

—— 1992. 'Conclusions: Where Do We Go From Here? The Future of Traditional Ecological Knowledge and Resource Management in Canadian Native Communities.' In *Traditional Ecological Knowledge and Environmental Assessment*, P. Boothroyd and B. Sadler (eds.). Ottawa: Canadian Environmental Assessment Research Council.

—— 1994. 'Local Fisheries Co-Management: A Review of International Experiences and Their Implications for Salmon Management in British Columbia.' *Canadian Journal of Fisheries and Aquatic Sciences* 51: 2363–78.

Place, Frank and Peter Hazell. 1993. 'Productivity Effects of Indigenous Land Tenure Systems in Sub-Saharan Africa.' *American Journal of Agricultural Economics* 75(1): 10–19.

Poffenberger, Mark. 1990. *Keepers of the Forest: Land Management Alternatives in Southeast Asia*. West Hartford, CT: Kumarian Press.

Poffenberger, Mark and B. McGran (ed.). 1996. *Village Voices, Forest Choices: Joint Forest Management in India*. New Delhi: Oxford University Press.

Raychaudhuri, Bikash. 1980. *The Moon and the Net: Study of a Transient Community of Fishermen at Jambudwip*. Calcutta: Government of India Press, Anthropological Survey of India.

Sandberg, Audun. 1993. 'The Analytical Importance of Property Rights to Northern Resources.' Colloquium presentation, Indiana University, Bloomington, Workshop in Political Theory and Policy Analysis, 27 September.

Schaefer, Milner. 1957. 'Some Considerations of Population Dynamics and Economics in Relation to the Management of the Commercial Marine Fisheries.' *Journal of the Fisheries Research Board of Canada* 14: 669–81.

Schlager, Edella. 1994. 'Fishers' Institutional Responses to Common-Pool Resource Dilemmas.' In *Rules, Games, and Common-Pool Resources*, Elinor Ostrom, Roy Gardner, and James M. Walker (eds.). Ann Arbor, MI: University of Michigan Press.

Schlager, Edella and Elinor Ostrom. 1992. 'Property Rights Regimes and Natural Resources: A Conceptual Analysis.' *Land Economics* 68(3): 249–62.

Scott, Anthony D. 1955. 'The Fishery: The Objectives of Sole Ownership.' *Journal of Political Economy* 63(2): 116–24.

Sengupta, Nirmal. 1991. *Managing Common Property: Irrigation in India and the Philippines*. New Delhi: Sage.

—— 1993. *User-Friendly Irrigation Designs*. New Delhi: Sage.

Shivakoti, Ganesh and Elinor Ostrom (eds.). 2000. *Improving Irrigation Governance and Management in Nepal*. Oakland, CA: ICS Press, forthcoming.

Shivakoti, Ganesh, George Varughese, Elinor Ostrom, Ashutosh Shukla, and Ganesh Thapa (eds.). 1997. *People and Participation in Sustainable Development: Understanding the Dynamics of Natural Resource Systems*. Proceedings of an international conference held at the Institute of Agriculture and Animal Science, Rampur, Chitwan, Nepal, 17–21 March 1996. Bloomington: Indiana University, Workshop in Political Theory and Policy Analysis; Rampur, Nepal: Tribhuvan University, Institute of Agriculture and Animal Science.

Singh, Katar. 1994. *Managing Common Pool Resources: Principles and Case Studies*. New Delhi: Oxford University Press.

Singh, Katar and Vishwa Ballabh. 1996. *Cooperative Management of Natural Resources*. New Delhi: Sage.

Tang, Shui Yan. 1992. *Institutions and Collective Action: Self-Governance in Irrigation*. San Francisco, CA: ICS Press.

—— 1994. 'Building Community Organizations: Credible Commitment and the New Institutional Economics.' *Human Systems Management* 13: 221–32.

Thomson, James T. 1977. 'Ecological Deterioration: Local-Level Rule-Making and Enforcement Problems in Niger.' In *Desertification: Environmental Degradation in and around Arid Lands*, Michael H. Glantz (ed.). Boulder, CO: Westview Press.

Thomson, James T., David Feeny, and Ronald J. Oakerson. 1992. 'Institutional Dynamics: The Evolution and Dissolution of Common-Property Resource Management.' In *Making the Commons Work: Theory, Practice, and Policy*, Daniel W. Bromley *et al.* (eds.). San Francisco, CA: ICS Press.

Vincent, Linden. 1995. *Hill Irrigation: Water and Development in Mountain Agriculture*. London: Overseas Development Institute.

Wade, Robert. 1992. 'Common-Property Resource Management in South Indian Villages.' In *Making the Commons Work: Theory, Practice, and Policy*, Daniel W. Bromley *et al.* (eds.). San Francisco, CA: ICS Press.

Wilson, James A. 1995. 'When are Common Property Institutions Efficient?' Working paper, Department of Agriculture and Resource Economics, University of Maine, Orono, ME.

Wunsch, James S. and Dele Olowu. 1995. *The Failure of the Centralized State: Institutions and Self-Governance in Africa*. San Francisco, CA: ICS Press.

Yang, Tai-Shuenn. 1987. 'Property Rights and Constitutional Order in Imperial China.' Ph.D. dissertation, Indiana University, Bloomington, IN.

6

Case Study. Property Rights: Access to Land and Forest Resources in Uganda

W.S. GOMBYA-SSEMBAJJWE, A.Y. BANANA, AND J. BAHATI

Introduction

Property rights influence the incentives and the behavior of individuals within a community with respect to rules that each and every person must observe in his/her interactions with other people (Hallowell 1943; Bromley 1992). Tenure consists of a bundle of rights that an individual has in a resource (Bruce 1989). It includes the terms and conditions under which resources are owned, accessed, managed, and transferred. Therefore, the rights that users have affect the incentives for sound use or misuse of resources. Consequently, tenure must be taken into account when planning strategies for natural resource management.

Uganda has a long history of a diverse set of laws and social systems governing access, management, and transfer of land. In the pre-colonial period, access, management, and transfer of land was granted or denied according to a clan's social norms/customary tenure. Whereas access to land depended essentially on membership (by birth, marriage, adoption, or co-option) to the clan, control was vested in the clan head or the committee of elders. The purpose of vesting the control in the clan leadership was threefold:

1. to guarantee security of tenure to all those who had access rights to the resource(s);
2. to ensure equity between and across generations; and
3. to determine specific land use patterns over clan land and prescribe conservation measures.

At the turn of this century, the British colonial administration introduced three new types of land tenure regimes: freehold, mailo (a modified form of freehold), and leasehold. At the same time, customary tenure was continued. The status quo was maintained until 1975, when the Land Reform Decree was promulgated. According to this decree individual freehold and mailo titles of land were reduced to leaseholds

This chapter is based on a study sponsored by UNU/WIDER Project on 'Land Reform Revisited: Access to Land, Rural Poverty, and Public Action,' carried out in Uganda in March 1998 by the authors. The authors are members of the teaching staff of the Department of Forestry, Makerere University, and Leaders of the Uganda Forestry Resources and Institutions Centre, at Makerere University.

of ninety-nine years. However, customary tenants on mailo and public land were legally recognized. In practice, a complex mixture of land tenure systems left by the colonial government continued to function throughout the country. We will briefly introduce the reader to the three major forms of land tenure in Uganda.

Customary tenure

Customary tenure represents the bulk of landholding in Uganda. An individual's access to and use of land is determined by the customary rules of the tribal or clan group to which the individual belongs. Access to and use of land under customary tenure is not static. The rules of access often change depending on the prevailing conditions. It is important to point out that customary tenure does not recognize individual ownership of land. However, it recognizes the various rights of the individual to possess and use land subject to the supervision by his clan or community leadership (Makubuya 1981).

Whereas the British colonial government attempted to alienate land from the people, only a small fraction of the available land was declared crown land. Since Uganda did not become a British colony, only a small percentage of the crown land was alienated to churches, schools, and individuals as freeholds (Ntambirweki 1998). Until the time of independence, access to most of the crown lands was according to the customary practices of the region in which they were located. After independence, crown lands were renamed public lands and continued to be in the domain of customary land tenure except in a few areas where the state had granted freeholds and leaseholds.

Customary tenure in Uganda enjoyed statutory protection under the Public Lands Act of 1969. It was legal for an individual to own land under customary tenure in rural lands not alienated in leasehold or freehold. Furthermore, the land commission had no power to grant a freehold or leasehold to any land occupied by customary tenure without the consent of the customary occupiers.

Mailo-land tenure

In 1900, the British government made an agreement with the Kabaka (king) of Buganda in which a new land tenure system, called the mailo-land, was introduced. The mailo-land tenure system is a modified form of freehold. Under this agreement, 19,600 square miles of land in the then Buganda Kingdom was divided among the royal family (626 square miles), notables (252 sq. miles), chiefs and individuals (8,000 sq. miles), missionary societies (92 sq. miles), Buganda administration (80 sq. miles), townships (50 sq. miles), central government forest reserves under Uganda government control (1,500 sq. miles), and 9,000 sq. miles were vested in the Queen of England as crown land. The word 'mailo' was derived from the square mile unit of measurement used in the allocation of land. Mailo-land tenure is similar to freehold in that a land title is issued, and the interest in land goes on in perpetuity (Marquardt 1994).

The Buganda Land Law of 1908 disallowed a mailo owner to transfer his land to a person not of the protectorate without the consent of the governor and the Buganda Legislature. Even with this restriction, a lively land market developed on the land thus allocated, allowing access to titled land for those having the means to purchase it. Individuals who were occupying the land under customary tenure at the time of the allotments became tenants of the new landowner. The original tenants (*Bakopi*) were allowed to stay on the land(s), while new ones were also encouraged to settle on the land(s) by the new landlords. Originally the land owners were satisfied in seeing a large number of *Bakopi* occupying their land. Later, it became advantageous to have a large number of *Bakopi* on one's land as they contributed labor for communal works (*Bulungi bwansi*) such as the roads for which the landlords had direct responsibilities, and to the payment of the newly introduced land tax.

The 1928 *Busuulu* and *Envujjo* Law fixed the rent and tribute payable to the mailo owner by a tenant and limited the freedom of the mailo owner to evict tenants. This guaranteed ample security of tenure to the tenants with respect to occupancy and inheritance. The *Busuulu* and *Envujjo* fees established in 1928 were, however, never revised until 1975, when they were abolished under the 1975 Land Decree. By this time, the fee had become of symbolic, rather than of economic value.

Since its introduction, mailo-land has been the subject of continual controversy and misunderstanding. With time, a deadlock over land rights evolved between the land owners who possessed *de jure* freehold rights over the land and their tenants who enjoyed *de facto* use rights (Nsibambi 1996).

Leasehold and freehold land tenure

Leasehold and freehold tenure are more formalized means of access to land especially by non-citizens and in urban centers. Freehold tenure is of limited extent, found mainly in former Ankole, Toro, Kigezi, and Bugisu districts. Both private lease and public statutory leases can be found in Uganda. A private lease is granted by an individual land owner to an individual or organization under terms agreed on by the respective parties. Statutory leases are provided for under the Public Lands Act of 1969.

Theoretically, the main advantage of a leasehold system is that it enables the government to control the use of land by imposing development conditions in leases. Those who fail to comply with the conditions may be deprived of their property rights and the land given to more serious developers. However, due to corruption in the civil service, people who fail to comply with the developmental requirements usually pay bribes to keep the lease.

The role of tenure in access to land

In Buganda, customary rules of tenure allowed a peasant to access portions of mailo-land through the *kibanja* (rented plots) from the landlords. Many Baganda and non-Baganda peasants were able to access land in this way. With the consent of the landlord, the *kibanja* owner could transfer his rights to a third party or through inheritance to his relatives. Due to the land market, which developed in Buganda after the introduction of the 1900 Buganda Agreement, the wealthy Baganda and non-Baganda were able to purchase titled lands from the original mailo landlords.

In Northern and Eastern Uganda, where most of the land is held under customary land tenure, land markets did not develop. Access to land in these two regions is determined by the prevailing customary rules. Only members of a clan have access to clan land. Access, use, and management of land closely follows common-property regime arrangements. In Western and Southwestern Uganda, landholding is primarily under customary tenure. However, a large number of wealthy farmers have been able to obtain statutory leaseholds provided for under the Public Lands Act of 1969.

Customary tenure restricts access to land by women to usufructuary rights only. The marginalization of women occupying land held under customary tenure is due to the fact that the land is inherited by the customary heir of the deceased, which is almost invariably a male member of the family. The 1995 Constitution attempts to address this problem by prohibiting cultures, customs, or traditions that are against the welfare and dignity of women. Parliament is in the process of establishing an equal opportunities commission for taking affirmative action in favor of groups marginalized on the basis of gender, age, and disability.

Recent developments

In recent years, the government of Uganda has taken interest in simplifying the nation's land tenure system to ease administration. It is generally acknowledged that the multiplicity of tenure systems has led to confusion and tenure insecurity. Confusion over *de jure* and *de facto* land-tenure rights has resulted in recognition of the need to regularize the tenure system. A general consensus for the need for a uniform tenure system has existed for some time. Whether that system is one of freehold, leasehold, or customary tenure has been the most difficult issue to resolve.

Following the consultation on Land Tenure Reform by the Makerere Institute of Social Research (MISR), in collaboration with the Land Tenure Center (LTC) at the University of Wisconsin, a draft Tenure and Control of Land Bill (1990) was submitted to cabinet. The salient features of the proposed bill were:

1. the repeal of the 1975 Land Reform Decree;
2. the introduction, with some exceptions, of freehold throughout the country;
3. all land in Uganda would be public land, vested in and administered by the Uganda Land Commission on behalf of the state until it was alienated in freehold;
4. restrictions to acquire land in Uganda would be imposed only on non-citizens;
5. the Land Registry would be decentralized to districts.

However, the government did not endorse the above recommendations. The government felt that it was critical to undertake a consultation exercise to solicit the views of the people, particularly those of the north and northeastern parts of the country where most of the land is held under customary tenure. Thus a second technical committee on land tenure reform policy was instituted in 1992 under the overall guidance of the Agricultural Policy Committee of the Bank of Uganda.

The committee identified the following issues as critical to the tenure reform process: uniformity of tenure, freehold tenure, urban land tenure, non-citizen ownership of land, and common-property resources. These formed the basis for discussion by the Constituency Assembly when debating the 1995 Constitution.

The 1995 Constitution of the Republic of Uganda vests the land in the citizens of Uganda. Instead of simplifying the land tenure system, the 1995 Constitution reaffirms the land tenure regimes that existed before the Land Reform Decree of 1975. For political reasons, the customary and mailo tenure could not be abolished. Although the mailo-land owners are the minority, they are often the elite and politically powerful. They are in a position to lobby and articulate their rights. On the other hand, a very large proportion of the peasant population in Uganda access land through the customary tenure arrangements. And yet these peasants are key producers in the agricultural sector, and they would be marginalized if customary tenure were abolished.

Although in the past, customary law has mostly been applicable as a reversionary law (i.e., in the absence of other laws), the 1995 Constitution recognizes customary tenure as one of the tenure regimes in the country. For the first time, it provides that the occupants of land under customary tenure should be issued certificates of ownership. What this implies is that customary ownership may be converted to freehold upon registration. Customary land tenure, therefore, has and continues to have great significance for access to land in Uganda.

The 1998 Land Act includes a provision that a lawful or bona fide[1] occupant of registered land shall enjoy security of occupancy on the land, shall be a statutory tenant of the registered owner, and shall pay a ground rent of Shs. 5,000 (approximately $5) every year, irrespective of the size of the land. It stipulates that where any group of persons holds land communally, the land may be held on behalf of the group by a trustee chosen by the group, according to the customs of such a community. This provision facilitates the registration of communal land.

The 1998 Land Act has been hotly debated and has generated a lot of controversy. The controversial issues include the legal recognition of bona fide occupants, the issue of certificates of occupancy to tenants, the conversion of tenancy on customary land to freehold, and the conversion of public land to customary land. The central government or a local government shall hold in trust for the people and protect natural lakes, rivers, ground water, natural ponds, natural streams, wetlands, forest reserves, national parks, and any other land reserved for ecological and tourism purposes for the common good of the citizens of Uganda.

The diverse set of laws and social systems governing access to land also determines the rights and responsibilities local communities have over common-pool resources such as forests, wetlands, and fisheries. Forest resources are governed by the 1964 Forest Act. Forest and tree tenure have been evolving since 1899, when the control of some of the forests in Uganda was vested in the colonial government.

[1] A bona fide occupant is defined as: (a) a person who occupied land which lawfully belonged to another person, but which the occupant occupied and utilized or developed, genuinely believing that no registered owner or agent of the registered owner was available from which the occupant could obtain consent to occupy, utilize, or develop the land; (b) a person who occupied and utilized or developed the land unchallenged by the registered owner or agent of the registered owner for twelve years or more; and (c) a person who has been settled on the land by the government or agent of the government which may include a local authority.

The evolution of forest and tree tenure in Uganda

In Buganda, the forested lands that were not allocated to individuals were declared forest reserves. Elsewhere in the country, the colonial government set aside sites as forest reserves as it so wished. Between 1899 and 1910, control of forests in Uganda was vested in the colonial government, through various agreements with native African authorities. These agreements made all forests and waste land the property of the Crown, subject to the natives being allowed to take produce for their domestic use.

Policies for the acquisition of forest land emphasized production and protection forestry. Consequently, the principal objectives of forestry policies included the provision of goods and services; maintenance and improvement of climatic and physical conditions of the country; and the need to conserve and regulate water supplies by the protection of water catchment areas. A report in 1929 stressed the role of forestry in climate and water regulation, and recommended much greater protection and major afforestation (Hamilton 1984). Based on this report and the significant advances in management and silviculture, which had been made by the Forest Department between 1900 and 1928, the 1929 Forest Policy was formulated. (This was the first forest policy produced in East Africa.)

The 1929 Forest Policy was periodically revised until 1948, when another forest policy was written. The key elements in the 1929 Forest Policy were:

1. to retain under forests or reafforest all areas of land, the retention of which under forest is considered necessary to climate or other indirect grounds;
2. to meet, with due regard to vested rights, such of the demands of the population of Uganda as cannot be met by individual or local administration efforts;
3. to advise individuals and local native administrations in all matters concerning arboriculture and forestry; and
4. insofar as it is consistent with the three preceding objectives, to manage the state forests of Uganda so that they will give the best financial returns on the capital invested (FD 1955).

In this policy the colonial government severely restricted the access of indigenous people to the forests reserved by the central government and the type of products they could harvest from those forests. However, the government encouraged local authorities to create local forest reserves that were to serve the interests of the local people. Legislation establishing forest reserves under district administrations was enacted in 1938 and 1947. These local government forest reserves were small, numerous, and gazetted to cater for local needs. The central government forest reserves were usually large and were supposed to serve national needs (Hamilton 1984). No mechanism was put in place, however, to manage and regulate the use of forest resources on private land. These could be cleared for agriculture depending on the prevailing economic opportunities.

The 1948 Forest Policy put emphasis on the protective services of the forests to preserve climatic and soil conditions suitable for agricultural production. It also encouraged local authorities and private enterprise to engage in sound forestry practice. Training of local foresters was also stepped up. In 1964, a Forest Act was enacted. The Act had several subsequent instruments. The most important, promulgated in 1967, centralized the administration of the formerly local forest reserves. This meant that the forest services, which had been run by district administrations, were absorbed into a centrally organized Forest Department. This was not based on an environmental or a forestry concern. Rather, it was part of a general political move towards centralization based on the belief that it would be more rational and efficient.

The 1971 Forest Policy emphasized the productive aspect of the forests as maximum economic returns from the forests were encouraged. This was to be achieved by ensuring efficient use of wood and wood products. However, the current forest policy established in 1987 again emphasized the protective aspects of forestry. Under this policy, nature forest reserves have been increased to 20% of the whole forest estate. In these areas, only non-extractive activities such as tourism and research are permitted. A further 30% is designated as buffer zones with strictly controlled extraction of non-timber forest products by the indigenous local population. On the remaining 50%, normal concessions for timber are allowed on a sustained-yield basis. Under this policy, access to forest resources by local communities has again been restricted.

It can be concluded, therefore, that the Ugandan forest policy has been characterized by a strong concentration of power over forest resources by the state, and a corresponding lack of ownership and local participation in forest and tree management by local communities. For example, most of the economic trees are reserved trees, and cannot be cut without the permission of the Forest Department, even if these trees are on private lands.

Prior to 1971, the forest policy in Uganda was strictly implemented by the Forest Department. Compliance to rules by the local people was very high because of the strict monitoring by the Forest Department. After 1971, however, the forest sector suffered alongside other sectors of the economy during the period of military dictatorship, which was characterized by budget constraints, civic unrest, and civil wars. During this period, there was no effective forest management. Forest resources on private, communal, and public land experienced an 'open access' exploitation and/or abandonment, and the Department lost control of some areas of the forest estate through agricultural encroachment.

Since 1986, however, law and order has gradually been restored by the National Resistance Movement (NRM) government. The Forest Department has been sufficiently funded to begin to rehabilitate the forest estate. Land that was lost through agricultural encroachment has been reclaimed. However, there are substantial unresolved problems.

Failure to recognize indigenous systems of forest management and indigenous rights to economically important tree species has led to:

1. loss of incentives by the local communities to protect trees;
2. discouragement of local people to engage in tree planting and reforestation projects; and
3. excessive reliance by the state on punitive measures to enforce the law.

In several countries, such forest policies have proven to be ineffective in solving and halting illegal access to forest lands and the rate of deforestation. The financial and human resources available to the forest departments are inadequate to carry out the task of policing forested areas without the participation of local communities. Most forest resources in Africa are scattered over large areas, which makes monitoring and rule enforcement by forest departments very costly, if not impossible.

Property-rights regimes and evidence of human disturbance to forests in Uganda

Without conducting extensive empirical research, it is impossible to ascertain whether formal property rights are effective. In other words, when formal property rights deny access to resources, are these rules followed in practice? And, are human disturbances higher in some kinds of property-rights regimes than in others? These are important questions to address before extensive policies are based entirely on formal categories of property regimes. If human disturbances are higher under some property regimes than others, policies attempting to achieve conservation goals may look good on paper but not in the field.

In order to address these issues, the Uganda International Forestry Resource and Institutions Center at Makerere University has joined an international network of scholars who are using an interdisciplinary set of research protocols that combine advanced methods in forest mensuration with recent techniques to assess the types of organization and rules-in-use operable in a particular location. The International Forestry Resources and Institutions (IFRI) research program is conducting research in Bolivia, Guatemala, Honduras, Kenya, India, Nepal, and Tanzania, as well as in Uganda (see E. Ostrom 2000). In this short chapter, we cannot address all of the questions that are central to our joint endeavor, but we will be able to provide a brief overview of our findings concerning the impact of property regimes on illegal access to forest resources.

We have studied both government-owned and privately owned forests that are all located within the same ecological region of Uganda. The tall grasslands and closed-canopy low-land forests that are located around Lake Victoria are similar enough that it is possible to compare conditions across different sites and attribute differences to demographic, institutional, and economic factors while holding ecological factors relatively constant.

As we have discussed above, government-owned forests in Uganda are principally of two types. The first type is reserved for natural protection and is not officially used for exploitation of timber. The second type of government-owned forest is managed for timber production. Potential users of both types of forests living in the area surrounding the forest do not have formal rights of access to harvest forest products from these forests. In particular, formal access rights to plant agricultural products, to harvest wood and make charcoal, or to produce timber or firewood for commercial sale are not authorized. In the forests managed for timber production, the Forest

Department decides when it wishes to harvest timber, and then contracts with commercial firms as a means of gaining income for the national government.

Private forests are also primarily of two types. The first type of private forest is owned by a single individual or family who then determines whether local residents may make claims on their traditional rights to use a forest. The second type is a communal forest where a local community makes major decisions concerning the access to a forest that individuals may or may not exercise. Some small communal forests are considered primarily religious forests and are reserved entirely for worship, and all harvesting activities are forbidden within their confines.

In the first set of studies, 16 forests located within 80 kilometers from Kampala were selected. Six forests were government-owned and eight forests were privately owned. Of the four communal forests, three were very small, sacred communal forests (Bukasa, Semalizi, and Mukasa), and the fourth (Magezigoomu) was a larger communal forest. The names of the other individual forests, and the subtype of government or private forest are shown in Table 6.1. In each of the larger forests, a random sample of thirty forest plots was taken and identified in the field, and an extensive battery of measures related to biodiversity, biomass, and regeneration rates was taken. After the measures were taken, the research team examined each plot and recorded whether there was objective evidence of specific types of human disturbances that are primarily illegal activities. There were four major types of human activities recorded: pitsawing (which is the dominant method for preparing timber for commercial sale), charcoal burning, harvesting of commercial firewood, and agricultural encroachment. A small number of other disturbances were coded as 'other.'

Table 6.1 presents the number of plots and the percentage of plots in each forest with evidence of human disturbance for all fourteen forests, as well as the specific type of disturbance observed. In some plots there was more than one type of disturbance recorded. The level of illegal human disturbance was lowest in one of the government nature reserves (Mpanga) and in all three of the small, communal sacred forests. At the other extreme, the remaining nature reserve and all four of the government forests managed for timber exploitation evidence high levels of illegal human disturbance—over 65% in all cases and reaching 100% in the case of the Mugomba government forest. The variance with private forests owned by individuals is relatively great, but two of the forests had less than 45% of the plots showing evidence of human disturbance. A chi square test indicates that there is a significant difference among the four types of forests ($p = .05$).

It appears from this data and from our observations in the field that even though local communities formally have no access to government forests, they do tend to use government forests more frequently than either neighboring private forests or communal sacred forests. One source of the difference is that government forests are unable to hire very many staff to patrol forest boundaries or enforce forest laws. Some of the owners of individually owned forests do hire forest guards and protect their forest lands extensively. Some of the private owners allow local neighbors traditional rights to harvest dead branches for firewood and various non-timber products of value to a local community. In these cases, neighboring users are also apt to monitor the boundaries

Table 6.1. *Types of human consumptive disturbances and their occurrence*

Type and name of forest	Size (ha)	Human disturbances		Type of human disturbance[a]					Number of sampled plots
		N[b]	%	PS	CB	CF	AE	Other	
Government nature									
Mpanga	453	2	7	0	0	0	0	2	30
Buttobuvuma	1,096	26	87	3	10	5	4	4	30
Government exploitation									
Mugomba	725	30	100	2	7	13	3	5	30
Lwamunda	4,696	20	67	13	3	4	1	4	30
Kizzikibi	520	28	93	16	2	3	0	7	30
Kyambogo	760	26	87	23	1	0	0	2	30
Private individual									
Mugalu	150	27	90	8	9	6	3	1	30
Namungo	40	13	43	3	1	1	7	1	30
Lukambagire	100	27	77	0	4	10	7	2	30
Najjakulya	50	13	43	10	1	0	1	1	30
Private communal									
Bukasa	0.5	0	0	0	0	0	0	0	3
Semalizi	0.5	0	0	0	0	0	0	0	5
Mukasa	1.0	0	0	0	0	0	0	0	8
Magezigoomu	20	20	67	10	3	1	2	4	30

[a] PS = pitsawing; CB = charcoal burning; CF = commercial firewood; AE = agricultural encroachment.
[b] Number of disturbances/number of plots. Some plots may have suffered more than one disturbance.

of the forest to ensure that others do not encroach on the forests (see Becker, Banana, and Gombya-Ssembajjwe 1995). While there has been some concern that communal sacred forests were slowly being eroded due to the change of values and increased population pressure, it does appear that at least the institutions related to the three small, sacred forests included in this study are still in place and effective.

In order to examine whether the distance of a forest from the major marketing center in Uganda—the capital city of Kampala—might be one factor affecting the conditions of forests being used for consumptive use, we compared those forests located within 30 km of Kampala with those that were located 30 to 80 km from Kampala. We did find that there were more occurrences of charcoal burning and agricultural encroachment in the forests nearer to Kampala than in those located further away. On the other hand, the frequency of pitsawing in forests further from Kampala was higher than in forests that were closer (p = .01). A possible explanation is that government exploitation of forests within 30 km has already resulted in the depletion of valuable timber species, and at present the major economic activities in these forests are charcoal burning and vegetable growing, even though these are forbidden activities.

Conclusions

There has been considerable change in the property-rights systems in use in Uganda during the past century, and there is a rich mixture of property-rights regimes that exist concurrently in the country. It appears, however, that formally designating forests as government property does not preclude extensive access of neighboring residents from surreptitiously engaging in various kinds of harvesting activities. Two of the private forests that were individually owned had a lower level of human disturbances than five out of six of the government forests, but the other two were heavily utilized. The conditions of these forests appeared to be determined by the conservation ethics of the owners and their willingness both to guard their forests and to extend traditional rights to harvest non-timber products to neighboring villagers. Thus, it takes considerably more than passing formal legislation to control access to resources via property-rights regimes.

REFERENCES

Becker, C.D., A.Y. Banana, and W.S. Gombya-Ssembajjwe. 1995. 'Early Detection of Tropical Forest Degradation: An IFRI Pilot Study in Uganda.' *Environmental Conservation* 22(1): 31–8.

Bromley, D.W. 1992. 'The Commons, Property, and Common-Property Regimes.' In *Making the Commons Work: Theory, Practices and Policy*, D.W. Bromley, D. Feeny, M. McKean, P. Peters, J. Gilles, R. Oakerson, C. Ford Runge, and J. Thompson (eds.). San Francisco, CA: ICS Press.

Bruce, J.W. 1989. 'Rapid Appraisal of Tree and Land Tenure.' Community Forestry Note 5, FAO, Rome.

Forest Department (Uganda). 1955. 'A History of the Uganda Forest Department, 1930–1950.' Entebbe, Uganda.

Hallowell, A.I. 1943. 'The Nature and Function of Property as a Social Institution.' *Journal of Legal and Political Sociology* 1: 115–38.

Hamilton, A.C. 1984. *Deforestation in Uganda*. Nairobi: Oxford University Press.

Makubuya, K. 1981. 'Land Law Reform and Development in Uganda.' In *Rural Rehabilitation and Development*, Apolo Nsibambi and J. Katorobo (eds.). Proceedings of the Conference on Rural Rehabilitation and Development, held at Makerere University, Kampala, Volume 1, 14–18 September.

Marquardt, M. 1994. 'Land Reform in the Making.' Paper presented at the workshop on 'Developing Uganda,' Lungby Land Brugsskole, Roskildi, Denmark, 2–5 June.

Ministry of Finance (Uganda). 1994. 'Background to the Budget, 1994/95.' Kampala, Uganda.

Nsibambi, A. 1996. 'Land Tenure Relations in Uganda, 1900–1995.' A paper presented at a sub-regional workshop, 'Land Tenure Issues in Natural Resources Management,' held at the Economic Commission for Africa (ECA), Addis Ababa, Ethiopia, 11–15 March.

Ntambirweki J. 1998. 'African Customary Law, Common Property and Emerging Environmental Law in Uganda.' In *Management of Common Property Resources in East Africa*, C. Gibson, A.Y. Banana, and J. Ntambirweki (eds.). Kampala: Ukinzi Enterprises Ltd., NRM Printary.

Ostrom, E. 1990. *Governing the Commons: The Evaluation of Institutions for Collective Action.* Cambridge: Cambridge University Press.

—— 2000. 'The International Forestry Resources and Institutions Research Program: A Methodology for Relating Human Incentives and Actions on Forest Cover and Biodiversity.' In *Forest Biodiversity in North, Central and South America and the Caribbean: Research and Monitoring, Man and the Biosphere Series*, F. Dallmeier and J.A. Comiskey (eds.), Volume 22. Camforth: UNESCO and the Parthenon Publishing Group, forthcoming.

Schlager, E. and E. Ostrom. 1993. 'Property Rights Regimes and Coastal Fisheries: An Empirical Analysis.' In *The Political Economy of Customs and Culture: Internal Solutions to the Commons Problem*, T.C. Anderson and R.T. Simmons (eds.). Lanham, MD: Rowman and Littlefield.

7

Devolution of Control of Common Pool Resources to Local Communities: Experiences in Forestry

J.E. MICHAEL ARNOLD

Introduction

Common pool resources (CPR) of forest products have been important in two main situations, which often overlap.[1] One is where rural households filled gaps in the material and income flows from their own resources by drawing on nearby areas of forest, woodland, or scrubland. The other is where forests and woodland formed part of larger livelihood systems in which land needed to be controlled by the users as a group—notably where the system is based on rotational agriculture, with periods of cultivation alternating with longer periods of forest fallow.

Over time, many common pool forest product resources, and the collective systems that controlled their management and use, have faced increasing pressures from growing populations and the effects of economic and political changes. Many have been greatly reduced and weakened, or have disappeared altogether. Nevertheless, land use practices that incorporate periods of forest or bush fallow, or that require access to off-farm forest or woodland resources, continue to be critical to the functioning of many rural farm household systems.

This chapter reviews information about experience with a number of systems involving a measure of local collective control over access to and management of forest and forest product resources. Nearly all the systems studied involve multiple forest products and multiple users, with the state usually being a major stakeholder and the owner of the underlying land. They are exercises in co- or joint management, rather than systems where control rests exclusively, or predominantly, with the local user group or community. Most are concerned with access to the resource rather than

The chapter is based on a larger review of information on managing forests as common property that was undertaken at the Overseas Development Institute for FAO (Arnold 1998), and draws on studies of seven case situations researched for that review. It has benefited from the advice of those who commented on that study during its preparation, and from useful comments on an earlier draft of this paper from members of the WIDER Project on Land Reform Revisited: Access to Land, Rural Poverty, and Public Action.

[1] In this chapter the term 'common pool resource' (CPR) is used to characterize a resource available for use by all, whether in unregulated ('open access') or regulated fashion. The term 'common property' (or 'common property regime') is used to denote situations in which a common pool resource is managed collectively, under rules that define membership of the group of users and which exclude others from access to the resource (McKean and Ostrom 1995).

the underlying land, and often with control just over flows of particular products from that resource.

The next section reviews the historical decline of forest CPRs, and of common property management regimes, and the recent revival of interest in this form of governance in some countries. The following section outlines the experience of a number of large contemporary state initiatives in Asia, based on analysis of documented information. The two subsequent sections examine local conditions and political economy issues influencing their success or lack of success.

Decline in availability of CPRs

Nearly everywhere forest CPRs have been massively reduced in modern times. Government appropriation, privatization and encroachment, and conversion to agriculture and grazing have been the main processes taking forest resources out of common use. Increasing pressures on what is left have frequently led to its progressive degradation.

One of the most pervasive factors has been expropriation of forests by governments as forest reserves or some other form of state property. In India, for instance, government started to lay legal claim over use of much of the forest estate, and to exercise these new powers, during the British colonial period. In the post-independence period, with the abolishment of the princely states and the expropriation of their forests, control by the central government was greatly extended. Many local people lost their rights of access to the forests during the process of forest reservation, and those 'rights' that were legally recognized at that time have tended to be progressively circumscribed, downgraded from 'rights' to 'privileges,' or extinguished by subsequent legislation and practices. By 1980, nearly 23% of India's total land area was under state management, while the rights of an estimated 300 million resource users have become increasingly unclear (Poffenberger and Singh 1996; Lindsay 1994).

Similar intrusions by the state occurred in other parts of Asia and in Africa. The huge expansion in the areas designated as state forests in some of the main countries of the Southeast Asia region in recent times also reflects increasing pressures to exercise physical control over upland areas for strategic reasons, the importance of such areas as a land bank for surplus lowland populations, or growing concerns about downstream damage resulting from overuse of upland areas (Peluso, Vandergeest, and Potter 1995; Lynch and Talbott 1995).

The impact of state intervention has often been intensified by failure to understand the functioning of the existing systems they were intervening in. A frequently cited instance was failure by colonial powers in Africa to recognize the role of fallow and common pool land, and to classify it as unoccupied and the property of the state (Shepherd 1992; Lawry 1989). There were similar failures of understanding when dealing with the sophisticated use and management systems in the forest areas in central India and in the Amazon basin (Davis and Wali 1993).

In addition, economic and demographic pressures have progressively increased the conversion of common property areas to agricultural use, and to individual control, in all regions. These shifts have often been encouraged by land re-allocation programs and practices, under policies that favored private ownership.

The impact of such pressures and changes can be illustrated from the results of Jodha's seminal study of village CPRs in the dry areas of India (Jodha 1986, 1990). In the twenty-one villages across seven states studied, it was found that the area of CPR land had been reduced by an average of 42% in the thirty years prior to 1980–82. Identifiable factors contributing to this huge reduction included: land reform in favor of expanded private land ownership, encroachment, expanded credit and subsidies for animals, more marketing links for common property related products (mainly milk, meat, wool, fuel, and various other bush and tree products), and the availability of technology (e.g., tractors) that enabled additional land to be brought under cultivation. The much-reduced remaining areas of village lands were typically heavily degraded and under open access usage, and the range, quality, and quantity of products collected had often been sharply reduced.

Decline in local governance

Combinations of these political, economic, and demographic changes have also severely reduced or undermined the systems of local collective governance under which use of many common property resources was historically controlled and managed. Thus, in the areas covered by Jodha's study, of the communities that in 1950 had exercised controls over CPR use, such as rotational grazing, seasonal restrictions, and watchmen, only 10% had such controls in 1980, while use of fines, taxes, and fees had ceased altogether (Jodha 1986).

The ostensible reason for the state claiming forest lands has usually been to ensure sustainable use for environmental and economic outputs. The potential value of forests as a source of rent to governments helps explain the reasons for breaking down existing management systems.

Governments have also tended to increase their control over local activities more generally, as they try to assert control over often diverse, fragmented, and dispersed populations. Inevitable conflicts with existing power structures and allegiances encourage measures to undermine and remove previously functioning local governance and management systems, and replace them with political and bureaucratic structures and regulations. This has not been confined to forestry, but has had a particular impact in this sector because the state usually has been unable to provide effective control over such large areas. Existing systems have consequently been undermined or suppressed, but have not been replaced by an effective alternative (Baland and Platteau 1996; Thomson 1992).

Traditional local systems of governance of forest and woodland resources are also eroded because of lack of clarity about the rights involved under overlapping and poorly reconciled systems of national and community land law and custom. Local courts and administrative units that have taken charge of conflict resolution generally do not understand indigenous tenure systems and make decisions based on other criteria. In order to avoid the high social transaction costs of organizing the management of small areas of forest in such difficult and adverse circumstances, people increasingly leave management of local tree resources to the forest department (Birgegård 1993; Shepherd 1992; Lawry 1989).

Contemporary approaches involving local management of CPRs

Despite this widespread erosion of the size and quality of CPRs, there are numerous instances where people do still rely on common pool resources to some extent. Even in the Indian villages that were studied by Jodha (1986), 84 to 100% of poor households still depended on village CPRs for fuel, fodder, and food items at the end of the period covered.

There has also been growing evidence, from a variety of different situations, of spontaneous indigenous efforts to strengthen remaining existing control systems, or to create new arrangements to bring resources under more effective local control (e.g., Pravongviengkham 1997; Richards 1997; Poffenberger 1996; Ganjanapan 1995; Thomson and Coulibaly 1995; Kant, N. Singh, and K. Singh 1991; Fisher 1989; Molnar 1981). Many of these appear to have their origins as responses to growing shortages of forest products and other forest outputs of value to the user community, or increased pressures from outside interests to use forest resources which are still important to the community (pressures that may be coming from the state as well as from loggers, neighboring communities, or other outsiders). Increasingly, such groups have been seeking more formal authorization for their activities, in order to strengthen their position in dealing with outsiders and the state.

Increased recognition of the continuing role of forest CPRs, and of such local initiatives at management, contributed to the revival of interest in local collective management, which is reflected in recent government and donor initiatives of the kind discussed in this chapter. However, the main stimulus underlying most of them, at least initially, has been recognition by governments that centralized management of forests in situations where local people also draw upon these resources simply does not work adequately.

The assessment that follows draws on the considerable body of work that has been undertaken in recent years to identify circumstances under which common property management is likely to be appropriate and successful, and when it is not (see Ostrom, Chapter 5, this volume). In particular, the paper explores the importance of four factors:

1. *characteristics of the resource*: appropriateness for management communally rather than privately or by the state; relevance to the needs of the user group; ease of management by the users; etc.
2. *characteristics of the community*: objectives of the members; impact of size of group and commonality of interest in the forest resource; leadership; etc.
3. *local institutional context*: local institutional capacity, authority, and effectiveness;
4. *macroeconomic context*: impact of market forces, etc.

In addition, the assessment explores the extent to which shifts in government attitudes have countered the earlier biases against management of forest resources as common property, and have created a sufficient and effective policy and regulatory environment.

Most of the cases reported on involve joint management between state and local user communities, rather than devolution of responsibility solely to the latter. The assessment therefore explores the role of the state in such arrangements, and the extent to which they reflect one or more of the following rationales for a preference for such arrangements:

1. It enables government (forest departments) to continue to exercise a strong regulatory role, which can be important where there are important externalities associated with the use of forests or forest lands (e.g., environmental values).
2. In state forests it both transfers some of the responsibility for and cost of forest protection to local user communities, and enables the forest department to retain control over components of the resource of direct value to the state (e.g., timber and forest land).
3. The forest department can act as arbitrator in disputes among groups with competing claims to be able to use the forests.
4. It can facilitate the provision of government support to user communities (e.g., investment, technical assistance, and strengthening local institutional capability).

Case studies

All the seven case studies discussed here involve some form of contractual arrangement between the state and local users, designed to improve management of the resource, and to increase the benefits from its use that flow to the latter. Five of the programs are on state forest lands. Three relate to joint management of forest resources, and the other two to use of forest land as well as the resource. In the two that involve communal or private land, the state intervened to define what form the changes in land use should take, and the conditions under which the new resources were to be managed. Therefore, between them, the cases cover three different types of relationships between state and user communities.

The cases have been selected as being among the largest, best documented, and most influential among government initiatives of this kind. All but one have their origins in the past thirty years, and reflect to some degree the trends and shifts in approach outlined in the first section.

This section relates the origins and evolution of each of the programs, and briefly describes its principal features, as background to the discussion of the reasons for success or lack of success that follows in the two following sections. To this end, each case study presentation covers the following points:

- background information on the resource and product situation;
- the stated objective of government in setting up the intervention, and the form it was designed to take;

- the form that local control and management was to take, and the benefits and incentives to local involvement;
- the magnitude of the program;
- perceived indicators of success, or lack of success, and the main issues that have arisen during implementation.

Woodlot resources on communal or private land

Two of the earliest instances of state intervention to increase the extent of local management of forest resources focused on creating collectively managed woodlots *outside* forests. They were located in areas of settled agriculture, where new and more accessible sources of forest products were needed in order to improve local supplies and reduce pressures on remaining natural forests.

Village forestry, Republic of Korea

The village forestry program of the Republic of Korea was initiated in the early 1970s in response to growing shortages of fuelwood and mounting problems of erosion, flooding, and downstream damage to agriculture as hillsides were stripped bare by harvesting for fuel and timber. The program is notable for the range and extent of prior planning and preparation that accompanied it, and because it dealt with private rather than public land.

As 73% of forest land was in private ownership, and many private landholdings were small, any move to improve the situation had to focus at the local level and be based on local involvement. New legislation and regulations were therefore enacted that required that forestry should be the main land use on lands with over 36 degree slope, and empowered the Office of Forestry to require landowners unable to reforest lands falling under this law to make that land available to Village Forest Associations (VFAs) to reforest on a cost-sharing basis. It thus created common property rights on private land (and in doing so implicitly redistributed benefits towards those in each community who had least land).

VFAs were established in all villages, with all households as members, building upon a tradition of forestry cooperatives, which were voluntary organizations operating in many areas to protect local forest resources with varying degrees of effectiveness. It also benefited from being part of the broader structure of the *Saemaeul Undong*, or New Community Movement, established in 1970 as a framework for collective self-help actions of all kinds, in response to village level changes that had included land reform that turned tenants into landowning farmers, a weakening of the clan structure that had earlier provided the basis for village cooperation, and the emergence of more modern and egalitarian forms of village government. At its height there were more than 20,000 VFAs, and by 1978 they had replanted more than one million hectares of denuded land.

VFA activities had access to subsidized credit, but members had to contribute their labor (with benefits being allocated proportionately). VFAs were grouped at county level into forestry associations (FAU), which in turn were members of a national federation (NFFAU), which was the mechanism through which the government channeled support and funding to the program. The rationale for establishing this network was that a non-governmental organization would be more effective than a government agency in working with villagers.

The program thus contained strong elements of both government pressure and incentives to get it started, but as its effectiveness became evident at the village level it acquired a momentum of its own. Factors that have been identified as having contributed to its success in mobilizing villagers to create their own village woodlots include: an incremental approach, identifying realistic village potentials at each stage; an orientation towards short-term results and income generation; financial and other assistance geared to self-help to avoid problems of village dependence on outside support; and formulation and application of strong, clear laws and regulations that empowered and provided authority to the VFAs. As a subsequent sharp decline in demand for fuelwood, due to large-scale rural-to-urban migration in the 1980s, and rapid increases in rural access to alternative fuels, made the program redundant in most rural locations before the woodlots reached harvest size, it is not possible to assess whether it would have also been successful in meeting the benefit expectations of those participating in it (Gregersen 1982).

Social forestry woodlots, India

In contrast to Korea, the woodlots established under Social Forestry projects in India were created mainly on village lands, and other uncultivated government lands available to villagers for communal use (e.g., revenue lands). The Social Forestry Program had its origins in a 1976 report of the National Commission of Agriculture, which recommended growing trees on lands accessible to village people in order to reduce the pressures on production forests caused by mounting rural demands for fuel, grazing, and other forest products.

The main focus was in the drier plain areas of the country where existing village CPRs had been subjected to the kind of degradation documented by Jodha (1986, 1990), and described earlier. The woodlots were to be established on non-arable communal land, to be managed collectively by the user community. Initiated in most states in the early 1980s, the program expanded very rapidly. The woodlots were usually established by the state forest departments, and the village lands to be planted were frequently transferred into the temporary control of that department for this purpose. Planning of the woodlot was intended to be in conjunction with the *panchayat* (the lowest level of political and administrative organization), or some other community level body, which was to take over responsibility for management in accordance with rules prescribed by the forest department and a management plan drawn up jointly with the latter. Benefits were to be split between the forest department and the community.

Forest department liaison with the communities was usually poor, and under its management the projects have created primarily tree stocks and wood products of commercial value, with few intermediate products such as fuelwood and grass that previously were harvested from the areas and used by villagers. They therefore had the effect of changing land use, and shifting benefit flows away from local subsistence users.

Though tens of thousands of woodlots have been established in this way, there has been reluctance on the part of the *panchayats* to assume control of them. This seems to reflect a number of factors: control carries financial responsibilities that villages and *panchayats* have difficulty meeting; woodlot management plans, village forest rules, etc., are often complex, unclear, and require skills and experience that *panchayats* do not possess; continued involvement of the forest department discourages local bodies from taking over and encourages them to opt for extending forest department management; and lack of local interest in the woodlots because of their small size (relative to local needs), difficulties in ensuring satisfactory distribution of benefits, and uncertainties about their status and access to the benefits. Villagers and *panchayat* bodies now appear to perceive the Social Forestry woodlots primarily as sources of communal income, rather than as sources of produce to meet village needs. The main benefit to the poor has usually been from the wage employment created.

Consequently, though successful in increasing the productivity of the sites used and generating a resource of considerable value to the communities, the interventions have not had the intended outcome of involving local users, strengthening local management capabilities, or creating alternative sources to meet their needs for forest products (Arnold and Stewart 1991; Chambers, Saxena, and Shah 1989; World Bank, USAID, and Government of India 1988).

Co-management of state forest resources

The high profile and achievements, or apparent achievements, of the Korea and India village woodlot programs heavily influenced other 'community forestry' approaches in the late 1970s and 1980s. There was a marked preference for creating new resources over management of existing forest stocks, and for locating these initiatives outside the forest, or on degraded sites in the forest. The three cases outlined below reflect an evolution from this initial strategy to a focus on collective management of forest resources. They are consequently concentrated in forested areas, many of which are in hilly or mountainous regions, where people often earlier had *de facto* use rights. These cases involve state forest land, on which forest departments have reversed the usual trend of increasing control over large tracts of degraded forests. Local control and authority was increased under agreements whereby villagers would get a much larger share of future produce, provided they managed the forests to meet agreed conservation and sustainability criteria. The state is therefore a direct stakeholder, through the forest department, as well as performing a regulatory role.

Joint forest management, India

In order to try and avoid some of the weaknesses and failures of the Social Forestry woodlot programs, the Joint Forest Management (JFM) programs in India moved collective forestry from *panchayat* and revenue lands to forest lands, on which competing claims should be less and forest departments would have a clearer remit. JFM built on a number of state or project-level initiatives of the 1970s and 1980s that had incorporated such a participatory strategy, with some apparent success. Of these, the one that had the most influence was a program of Village Protection Committees (VPCs) in the Southwest of the State of West Bengal.

The VPCs had their origin in a pilot project started by foresters in that state in the early 1970s, designed to encourage villagers to stop using forest land for fuelwood cutting and cattle grazing, in return for guaranteed employment. VPCs were created in an area where most of the land was previously a mixed forest dominated by sal (*Shorea robusta*) that had been substantially altered and degraded by heavy use. VPC members agreed to restrict fuelwood cutting and cattle grazing in forest areas, in return for employment in forestry work, and a substantially greater share of the eventual proceeds from the resource. The approach has been most successful in villages bordering extensive tracts of degraded forest land, where the forest-to-household ratio is relatively high, there is local forestry knowledge, and benefits accrue at a relatively early stage from the sale of non-timber forest products and improvements in the local environment (e.g., less erosion, improved water supplies).

Originally villages were chosen by the forest department, but the selection process has gradually given a greater voice to local *panchayats*. Since a second government order in 1990 opened membership to all, most if not all households usually belong to the VPC, which selects its own officials. Once they had been established in the first eleven villages, further VPCs have been organized and managed with no external financial or organizational assistance. By 1993, there were 2,350 VPCs, covering 350,000 hectares (ha) of forest (Saxena 1997; Malhotra 1995; Roy 1991; Malhotra and Poffenberger 1989).

Largely on the strength of the West Bengal experience, the government of India issued a circular to state governments in June 1990, recommending the adoption of Joint Forest Management on areas of state forest land. Its principal features (see Table 7.1) were to include: setting up a VPC, management plans established and monitored by the forest department, and local use to be confined to grass and non-timber forest products (and potentially a share of the income from the timber sold by the forest department). By 1995, fifteen states had adopted such collaborative programs involving local communities in the management and protection of forest lands in return for rights to use specified forest products. This huge program has attracted much attention, as a possible general model for local governance of forest resources in other countries as well as across India.

The principal problems that have arisen in implementation relate to how to create VPCs that are representative of the different categories of users within a community, to the relationship of VPCs to the forest department (which can dominate or unduly interfere in the workings of a VPC), to the functioning of VPCs (in particular as concerns their links with the *panchayat* system), to the adequacy of incentives for VPC members, and the distribution of benefits among different categories of user. Experience has also highlighted issues within forest departments—in particular as concerns conflicts with their conventional role of directly managing forests.

Some of the problems have arisen because of the speed and vigor with which JFM has been disseminated, and the difficulties in applying a single formula to a country with the ecological, economic, and cultural diversity of India. JFM is now coming to be seen more as a set of principles and a process rather than a preset formula, to be

Table 7.1. *Key features of the June 1990 Government of India circular 'Involvement of Village Communities and Voluntary Agencies in Regeneration of Degraded Forests'*

- JFM should involve an 'arrangement' between the village community (i.e., the 'beneficiaries'), NGOs, and the State Forest Department. The selected area of forest is to be managed in accordance with a working scheme approved by the state government, and prepared 'in consultation with the beneficiaries.' The working scheme is to cover such matters as steps for inducement of natural regeneration, seeding, soil conservation methods, fire protection, maintenance of boundaries, weeding, tending, thinning, etc.
- Beneficiaries should be entitled to usufructuary rights to such items as grass, loppings and minor forest products, in accordance with conditions set by the State. They may also be given a share of the proceeds from the sale of trees when they mature. They may also plant fruit trees 'that would fit in with the overall scheme of afforestation.'
- Only people willing to participate and organized in groups specifically for forest protection are to be made beneficiaries and thereby granted access and benefits. By way of example, the Circular mentions village panchayats or forest committees. However, whatever form it takes, the program is to be focused on communities or user-group subsets; the Circular is explicit that the access and benefits are not to be granted to individuals.
- Neither the beneficiaries or any NGO may acquire ownership or lease rights over the land in question. No grazing or agriculture is allowed on the site.
- Ideally, the selected site should be free from the claims of anyone who is not a beneficiary. In other words, sites that are burdened by rights, privileges, or concessions previously granted to anyone who is not part of the beneficiary group—say, someone from a distant village—is not preferable for JFM. In the alternative, the Circular says that for any given site, anyone who currently has a claim to forest produce should be given the opportunity to join the beneficiary group.
- The work of the beneficiaries is to be closely supervised by the forest department. If the work has been done in an unsatisfactory manner, 'the usufructuary benefits should be withdrawn without paying compensation to any one for any work that might have been done prior to it.'

Source: Lindsay 1994.

modified and adapted to local circumstances, but is still at a relatively early stage in this process. Progress has consequently been variable, with considerable achievement evident in some areas, but much less, and uncertain prospects for improvement, in others (Saxena 1997; Poffenberger and McGean 1996; Kurup 1996; Hobley 1996*a*; Femconsult 1995; Sarin 1993; Society for the Promotion of Wastelands Development (SPWD) 1992).

Van Panchayats, India

Although they attracted relatively little attention in the development of JFM, the Van (Forest) Panchayats in the hill areas of Uttar Pradesh in India constitute a co-management system that has been in existence for a much longer period. They were introduced in the 1920s by the civil administration after a prolonged period of intense agitation by villagers against a major expansion of British control over forest resources in the area. In order to resolve this dispute, a category of forest of little or no commercial importance was established to provide for local needs, to be managed by a village body (Van Panchayat) in accordance with a set of government regulations and legislation. The forest department retained control over timber and resin management in these areas but the village received any profit made from sale of these products.

The Van Panchayat body selects a leader from among its members, establishes management rules consistent with the authority established by the Forest Panchayat Act of 1931 (amended in 1976), establishes measures to ensure enforcement of these rules, and manages the disbursement of funds that accrue from forest activities. The collection of a tax, either at harvest or monthly, reinforces the legitimacy of the local institution, and provides the necessary funds at the village level (e.g., to pay forest guards). Where the level of annual use is kept to a reasonable level, natural regeneration has often led to significant improvements in the productivity of the resources they manage. (In many cases, however, the heavy demand for forest products has simply meant that harvesting has been shifted to other forest areas.)

Though many of these village bodies have ceased to function, new Van Panchayats continue to be formed. In 1995 it was reported that in the Kumaon region there were nearly 3,000 Van Panchayats controlling 35% of the forests. Factors for such success as has been achieved appear to include the following: confidence in government mechanisms for adjudicating boundary disputes and larger-scale external incursions; confidence in leadership of the Van Panchayat (e.g., open elections if there is no longer a traditional leadership); ability to support a guard system against encroachment and illegal felling; internal rules which ensure equitable distribution and compliance; and a rule-making mechanism which allows rules to be changed as needed (Agrawal and Goyal 1997; Agrawal 1994; Ballabh and Singh 1988; Tripathi 1987; Saxena 1987).

Hill community forestry, Nepal

The system of local management of forest areas that has evolved in the hill areas of Nepal differs from the Indian experience in that it has incorporated central features of indigenous local collective management systems that are widespread in these areas. Historically, forests were controlled under a variety of forms of tenure—some feudal, some in the name of the state, and some under communal forms of control. The overthrow of the feudal system in the 1950s led to the forests of feudal owners being brought under the control of the state, under the Private Forests Nationalization Act of 1957. Where local leadership was strong, more local groups appear to have taken steps to bring the forest areas they used under their own *de facto* control, in order to secure their access to them.

In 1978, the government passed legislation enabling substantial amounts of public forest land in the middle hills to be handed over to local communities to manage, in recognition of the practical difficulties of managing the country's dispersed forest resources through the forest department. Local management was to be achieved through the *panchayats*, which would enter into agreements with the government to manage local areas under agreed forest management plans. Subsequently, and following passage of the Decentralization Act in 1982, the government initiated a series of measures that moved the focus from the *panchayat* to the forest user group (FUG), with more authority and responsibility progressively devolving to these groups.

Much of the experimentation with new institutional formats has been formalized in a 1989 Master Plan for the Forestry Sector, with the user group approach given legal authority in the 1993 Forest Act. Ownership of the land remains with the state, but trees legally belong to FUGs, though the state reserves the right to take back possession of the community forest if the terms and conditions of handover are not met. Management control rests solely with the users of the resource, who now develop their own operational plans, set the prices at which the produce is sold, and determine how surplus income is spent.

The process of formalizing a largely self-governing system for managing local forest areas has thus proceeded further in Nepal than in most countries. Some reluctance and even resistance is still evident from some within the forestry establishment. Foresters also reportedly tend to be supportive of the tree planting activities of user groups, but more reluctant to endorse harvesting activities. In addition, lack of clear understanding of the rules governing user group activities is also evident, with conflicts over interpretation between the Forest Department and groups sometimes leading to the former disbanding a group. Such problems have led some to argue that the process of expanding FUG control may be proceeding too rapidly.

By June 1997, there were 6,000 user groups, managing 450,000 ha, with a further 6,000 waiting for formal registration. User groups are now coming together and forming larger network organizations. The largest network, the Federation of Community Forestry Users in Nepal (FECOFUN), with more than 1,000 user group members, is taking on a negotiating and mediating role, and the provision to members of some services previously provided by the Forest Department. However, some concerns have recently been expressed that there is a danger that the FUG system could become politicized, and used for purposes other than forest management and control (Shrestha and Britt 1997; Malla 1997; Campbell, Shrestha, and Euphart 1987; Arnold and Campbell 1986; Hobley 1996*a*; Srestha 1996; Gilmour and Fisher 1991; Fisher 1989; Molnar 1981).

Co-management on state forest lands

The last two cases are in countries where very substantial areas are classified as state forest land, but have large numbers of people practicing agriculture and other non-forestry activities. As a result, the resource has been widely degraded. In each case, the government has looked to a measure of local collective control as one way of stabilizing the land use situation, and maintaining under tree cover those parts of the area that should more appropriately stay as forest. In the first case this is being attempted through forms of zoning and resource sharing, in the second case the aim is to transfer control to communities with established rights in the area, and to provide them with the necessary support to then manage their resources.

Forest villages and community forestry, Thailand

During recent decades there has been a huge expansion in the areas designated as state forests (as was discussed in the first section of this paper). Large numbers of people already living in the areas thus found their activities increasingly curtailed, leading to growing conflict with the Royal Forestry Department (RFD). A continuing influx of hill people moving in from other parts of the region, and of lowland Thais seeking land to cultivate, has brought further pressure.

In the mid-1970s the government launched a number of initiatives to try and address these mounting problems. One authorized the RFD, and other government agencies, to set up Forest Villages. The objective was to regroup people already farming inside the forest into villages, in order to facilitate provision of infrastructure and services, stabilize the area under cultivation, and encourage reforestation. However, the incentives provided generally did not prove attractive to potential participants, and the mixture of local and migrant populations often created highly factionalized villages, making it difficult for village committees to command support from all sections of the community. The focus consequently increasingly shifted to another of the initiatives, the National Forest Land Allotment Project, which assigned rights to use forest land to individuals rather than communities. There has therefore been little success in creating new forms of collective management involving heterogeneous communities of recent migrants into forest areas.

At the same time, a major extension of the area classified as Protected Areas rather than Forest Reserves, had the effect of further restricting the position of long-resident indigenous hill communities that already practice collective forest management in these areas. Efforts to provide them with a more formal institutional basis for their forest management initiatives have been opposed by those who argue that this could put urban water supplies that originate in upland watersheds at risk. Nevertheless, by mid-1997, in response to countervailing arguments from those supporting their rights, a Community Forest Act had been drafted and had achieved a considerable measure of agreement. This would have given indigenous groups more tenurial security, but only limited rights of control—a compromise they were prepared to accept because of the protection the Bill would have provided against outside encroachers. Further progress of the Bill has been affected by the recent economic and political situation in the country, and the outcome of this initiative therefore remains unclear at present (Wittayapak 1996; Vandergeest 1996; Lynch and Talbott 1995; Ganjanapan 1995; Hirsch 1997; Poffenberger and McGean 1993; Pragtong and Thomas 1990).

Stewardship and ancestral domain certification, Philippines

Very large parts of the remaining forest in the Philippines, which have been extensively logged and settled in, overlap with territories of indigenous peoples. Since the late 1970s there has been increasing interest in community forestry as a means of meeting these issues. A number of different programs have been put in place to stabilize the situation by strengthening tenurial security and access to government services for long-term residents in the upland forest areas. The rationale has been that the presence of indigenous people practicing suitable forms of agroforestry helps protect against destructive land use due to indiscriminate logging and in-migration by lowlanders.

The largest forestry-related program has been the Integrated Social Forestry (ISF) Program initiated in 1982. This is based on the concept of 'stewardship,' granting exclusive rights to use and occupy land for twenty-five years, renewable for another twenty-five years, to individuals, associations, and indigenous communities. However, it became evident that stewardship agreements have the potential to provide only limited tenurial security. Ownership remains vested in the state, and agreements can be revoked by the Department of Environment and Natural Resource (DENR) if the latter considers that the community has failed to comply with the terms of its agreement.

There has consequently been growing interest among long-term occupants in forest areas in Certificates of Ancestral Domain Claims (CADC), which cannot be revoked by the government as they are based on a provision in the 1987 Philippine Constitution. By June 1997, 1.18 million hectares had been incorporated into CADCs awarded to seventy-nine indigenous groups.

This initiative is unusual in that it is intended to provide meaningful local autonomy. The program of delineating, assessing, and awarding CADCs is designed both to protect their tenure and ensure sustainable development of the forests in the certificated areas. Implementation has encountered problems—similar to those that plagued earlier initiatives—of overly bureaucratic procedures, disputes between and among those with claims on the areas (forestry and mining, immigrants and indigenous people, etc.), and organizational and leadership problems within the local groups. However, efforts continue to improve procedures and remove these operational issues (Sabban 1997; Hilario and Sabban 1997; Lynch and Talbott 1995; Sabban 1992; Plantilla 1991; Gibbs, Payuan, and del Castillo 1990; Borlagdan 1990).

Conditions for success

The present section discusses what can be deduced from the case studies, and from the literature on other experiences of co-management of forest resources, about the importance of the four following factors in explaining success, or lack of success, in such systems:

- characteristics of the resource;
- characteristics of the community;
- local institutional capacity;
- the macroeconomic context.

The adequacy of the performance of the different co-management arrangements reviewed is discussed in terms of both their efficiency in managing local forests, and the equity of the outcome (providing access to different categories of users, distribution of benefit among them, etc.).

Characteristics of the resource

Aspects of the location, composition, size, productivity, and product characteristics of a particular forest area can have a bearing on whether it is likely that it can be collectively or jointly managed. A basic characteristic related to these issues is whether the resource has definable boundaries and can be linked to a specific user group. It has been argued (Saxena 1997) that one reason joint management developed more easily and quickly in West Bengal than elsewhere, was because past land use practices had resulted in a dispersed forest resource which could not easily be managed by the forest department, while the topography allows each forest unit to be identified with one village, or a group of villages.

A resource is likely to be more efficiently managed collectively, rather than as individual woodlots, if there are economies of scale involved in its production. Multiple product resources also lend themselves to collective management because they can only be produced from a functioning forest ecosystem that usually cannot be parceled out as individual holdings.

The incentive for users to invest in collective management is likely to be greater if the resource is capable of meeting a substantial part of users' needs, and if these benefits can be obtained rapidly and regularly. Their small size relative to local needs proved to be one of the main disincentives underlying the failure of the Social Forestry woodlot projects in India—as did their focus on producing poles and timber rather than fuelwood, fodder and green mulch (Arnold and Stewart 1991). Similarly, a survey of indigenous user group systems in Nepal (Molnar 1981) found that these were not likely to be active if users felt their local resource was too poor or small to generate additional outputs commensurate with the efforts needed to protect and manage it. By the same token, situations involving forest that is producing already are likely to provide a greater incentive to local collective management than woodlots that will produce only after several years. In West Bengal, for example, the VPC program has been more successful in areas well endowed with sal forest, which regenerates rapidly and produces early returns from non-timber products, than in areas where returns had to be concentrated on slower growing plantations.

Consequently, the tendency in most of the programs reviewed to allocate degraded forest or scrubland for collective management, and the focus on encouraging users to plant new tree resources, has often weakened the incentive for users to participate. Thus, the fact that excluding richer and more productive areas of forest limits the potential benefits users can obtain, has been noted as a factor in the lack of commitment to forest management in JFM projects (Saxena *et al.* 1997; Hobley 1996*a*).

The ease with which the resource can be managed by the user group is also important. A study of management practices by indigenous forest user groups in the hill areas of Nepal (Arnold and Campbell 1986) showed that these were very conservative, focusing on restricting access or what could be harvested in ways that would avoid any risk of over-exploitation. This reflects the risks associated with running down a resource which takes so long to build up again, the limited knowledge that exists about yields and responses to intervention in multi-species forests, and the high costs of obtaining information on which to establish more intensive management and use practices. As has been noted in JFM projects (Saxena *et al.* 1997; Hobley 1996*a*), the task of developing systems that will enable user groups to sustainably manage their forest resources more productively, has not been helped by the tendency of supporting forest departments to develop management plans for local use that are based on conventional forestry practices, and that require considerable forestry skills.

Most functioning local collective systems in practice involve products such as fodder and fuel, which meet strong local needs, which can be produced easily and regularly, and which are also products that members of the user group can benefit from in an equitable manner. As was shown in the Social Forestry woodlot program in India, managing more complex, higher value, and higher cost resources, can introduce levels of complexity, financial obligations, and skills that groups may not wish to take on.

Characteristics of the community

Ability to collaborate effectively in the control and management of a local forest resource is clearly likely to be influenced by the objectives that members of the user community seek to pursue through such an activity, and the commonality of interests among them. Though user objectives are usually concerned with access to supplies of particular forest products, there can be other goals. Groups practicing indigenous management systems are often concerned, as in Orissa (India) and in north Thailand, with protecting and legitimizing their rights to the areas that they already occupy and use (Poffenberger 1996; Ganjanapan 1995). The primary interests of participants in many Social Forestry and JFM projects in India, on the other hand, appears to have been access to government benefits in the form of employment and income (Saxena *et al.* 1997; Arnold and Stewart 1991).

One of the main factors that can complicate governance of forest resources is the presence in a single location of more than one group of users, each with different interests and objectives. While some among multiple objectives for a forest area may be complementary, e.g., for different products, or for use at different times of the year, others may be more competitive or incompatible. In the areas studied by Jodha, for instance, the continued and often growing dependence of the poor on local CPRs conflicts with the interests of the wealthier in capturing CPR product flows for sale, and/or their interest in privatizing the land and putting it to private agricultural uses—conflicts that have contributed to the breakdown in local collective management in these villages (Jodha 1990). Many JFM projects have also encountered problems in accommodating the overlapping claims of different categories of user drawing on their forest areas. Problems have also arisen of people within communities who do not contribute to the work of forest management and forest work joining VPCs in order to be able to benefit from the income generated through the latter (Saxena 1997; Hobley 1996*a*; Sarin 1993).

There is considerable evidence that small uniform groups, with shared interests, do find it easier to establish and maintain collective management of local forest resources. For instance, these emerged as characteristics of surviving indigenous systems in the villages studied by Jodha (1990). Similarly, they were among the features identified by Sarin (1993) as facilitating successful establishment of JFM village institutions.

However, as Ostrom (this volume) has pointed out, although the task of dividing responsibilities and benefits may favor small and cohesive user groups, the task of managing and exercising control over the resource may call for a larger body that encompasses all those with a claim on the resource. Powers of negotiation with the state and of protecting boundaries are also likely to favor larger bodies (Ascher 1994). For example, a recent study of the Van Panchayats in Uttar Pradesh (India) has shown that moderately sized Van Panchayats are better able to protect their resource than small Van Panchayats, because they have greater resources to hire watchers, etc. (Agrawal and Goyal 1997).

Some forms of heterogeneity of interest and endowment among members of a user community may also be compatible with self-governance. One of the reasons collective management of forest resources in India is more prevalent in the hill areas, appears to be that both rich and poor households within villages depend on the forest for inputs of green manure, forest grazing and collected arboreal fodder, and fuel and timber. In contrast to the situation in plain areas outlined earlier (Jodha 1990), there is consequently a shared interest in how local common pool forest areas should be managed (Arnold and Stewart 1991). However, in general it is not clear whether differences in endowment or wealth create an incentive or impediment to collective regulation (Baland and Platteau 1996).

The importance of leadership within a community as a factor in enabling collective management has been stressed by many. Strong leadership has been identified as a factor associated with communities with functioning systems of indigenous collective management of local forests in Nepal (Molnar 1981). Trust in the Van Panchayat leaders, and in the process by which they were elected, has been identified as one of the factors associated with Van Panchayats that have survived in Uttar Pradesh (Ballabh and Singh 1988; Saxena 1987). Conversely, lack of trust in their leaders has proved to be one of the main constraints to progress with ancestral domain certification in the Philippines (Hilario and Sabban 1997).

Local institutional capacity

The presence of effective local institutions lies at the heart of any collective management system. In some situations, the authority to manage common pool forest resources has been entrusted to an existing local institution. Sometimes this will be a body or group dedicated to the task of forest management. More frequently, it will be a local body with general local administration responsibilities. However, the capacity of the latter to manage forests may be limited if, as is often the case, its boundaries and jurisdiction do not coincide with the boundaries of the forest to be managed, or it has no relevant experience in collective management of other local activities.

The extent to which the interests of those who run or control the organization coincide with the interests of the forest user group, or groups, is also often an issue. The elected *panchayat* bodies in India and Nepal proved to be unsatisfactory in this respect largely because of their predominantly political and bureaucratic agendas, and because they generally covered much larger areas and populations than the forest user group (Hobley 1996*a*). Another issue that has arisen is that an existing institution, reflecting social values from the earlier period when it came into existence, and long standing and entrenched patron–client relationships within a community, may not adequately reflect the current interests and concerns of all its present members. In particular, there can be continued widespread exclusion of, or failure to properly involve, women and other disadvantaged groups (Hobley 1996*b*; Sarin 1993).

Where suitable local institutions did not exist, programs to encourage and support local management of forests have usually tried to create them—e.g., the VPCs in India and the VFAs in Korea. The danger is that a new institution may not adequately reflect the reality of the situation, e.g., excluding some previous users of the CPR or leaving them worse off. An important step in refining the system of user group management in Nepal has been the recognition that there are different categories of users interested in a particular forest resource. These range from primary users who depend on the resource for all of their forest product needs, to secondary users who use it for a more limited purpose, to other interest groups such as collectors of medicinal products (Hobley 1996*a*).

Attempts to construct institutions to a particular formula can create groups that lack sufficient cohesion, so that they collapse or become dominated by particular interests or by the forest department (Hobley 1996*b*; Ascher 1994). The failure to create viable self-governing Forest Villages in Thailand was largely due to such conflicts among the disparate population groups that they attempted to bring together.

In recognition of the difficulties in creating effective new local organizations to manage forests, a recent study on the subject (Thomson and Freudenberger 1997) has stressed the importance of carefully weighing the potentials for basing a common property management intervention on existing institutions, even with the limitations these are likely to exhibit, against the problems of creating new institutions. Where it does prove necessary to set up separate village or user groups to manage local forest resources, or particular product flows, they will usually need to be recognized by, and affiliated with, the formal bodies of local government in order to get access to government resources, services, and authority. The involvement of higher level bodies can also be necessary for negotiations among different stakeholder groups when the forest is used for multiple products by more than one user group, and for conflict management.

Thus, as the Panchayati system becomes more firmly entrenched in India as the channel through which government resources flow to the community level, increasing attention is being given to how to link VPCs created under JFM to the related *panchayats*. Such linkages may often be achieved by 'nesting' the user group body in a larger local organization, such as the village leadership, a *panchayat* committee, or the District Council. Alternatively, user groups can join together to form larger and more influential organizations, as the VFAs in Korea did in the NFFAU (Gregersen 1982), and FUGs in Nepal through FECOFUN (Shrestha and Britt 1997). However, concerns have been voiced that such associations may unduly strengthen the position of those who provide leadership in the constituent user groups—who tend to be the village elites (Malla 1997).

Characteristics of the macroeconomic context

Most collective management of forest product resources has been primarily directed at meeting subsistence demand. Indeed, it has been argued that collective management is best suited to meeting subsistence demand, rather than production for the market

(Baland and Platteau 1996). Commercial demands on a common property system are likely to increase pressures from users both inside and outside the user group, attract the interest of privatizers and encroachers, increase conflicts between those users who can respond to market opportunities and those who cannot, and thereby undermine the mechanisms for exclusion and control (McElwee 1994; Jodha 1990; Runge 1986). Conversely, the added value that commercial demand might place on a resource may increase the incentive to conserve and manage it. In both of these scenarios more complex controls and institutional measures are likely to be needed in order to cope with the increased pressures.

In the main co-management cases, such as the Van Panchayats and JFM projects, the more complex, longer rotation, commercial components of the forest, such as timber, are generally handled by the forest department. However, the apportioning of the revenue has often resulted in village forestry bodies being awarded only small shares, and forest departments have often been slow to transfer these funds to them (Saxena 1997; Hobley 1996*a*). In some pilot projects, commercial components have been handled through contracts with the private sector, as in the Sukhomahri project in the Shivalik hills in northern India, where fodder grass for local self-use is protected collectively and distributed to all member households, while the rights to the commercially valuable bhabbar grass are auctioned to private contractors (Saxena 1997). In the Korea village woodlot case, separate cooperative organizations were created in order to handle marketing.

In some cases the intervention programs have themselves inadvertently aggravated, or created, the problems that commercial demand can bring. The Social Forestry Program in India invested in increasing the productivity of common pool land hitherto usable only for grazing and collection of biomass products, and created tree stocks on it. In doing so, prior uses have often been altered and the focus of control has shifted from the original subsistence users to those able to benefit from the opportunities to generate income that the new woodlots created (Arnold and Stewart 1991).

Changes in the economic conditions can alter the context of collective and co-management of forests in a number of other ways. As labor costs rise as more productive and convenient options become available, labor-intensive and often arduous forest product activities are likely to become less attractive and be abandoned. In parts of the middle hill areas of Nepal, where collective management of forests by FUGs has in the past been strong, there has recently been a big increase in the growing of tree stocks on farms as a source of forest products, and a related decrease in the harvest from locally managed forest areas. This has followed increasing out-migration to wage employment elsewhere, leading to withdrawal of marginal areas from cultivation (making farm land available for trees) and increasing the cost of collecting produce from more distant forest areas (Gilmour 1995).

Such shifts from forest to on-farm tree resources have been widely observed elsewhere as factor availability and cost patterns change (Arnold and Dewees 1995). Where this happens, the incentives to engage in collective control and management of a local common pool forest resource may consequently become weaker, because the viability or competitiveness of CPR products decline relative to supplies from other sources.

As the uses of many subsistence and low value forest products also decline as rural incomes rise, concern has been raised that the range of situations in which access to common pool forest resources is needed and appropriate could also decline—and that this needs to be taken into account in programs to extend collective control and management of forests (Byron and Arnold 1999).

Political economy of implementation and replication

As was discussed earlier, common property systems have long been subjected to pressures by governments wishing to increase their control over local activities and resources. Conflicts with existing power structures and allegiances encourage governments to take measures to undermine and remove previously functioning local governance and management systems, and replace them with political and bureaucratic structures and regulations (Thomson and Freudenberger 1997; Baland and Platteau 1996).

This constitutes one of the main constraints to achieving sustainable contemporary regimes of self-governance of forest resources. If the influence of such changes is not understood, and taken into account, there is a danger that interventions are put in place that try and sustain or create common property regimes and institutions that are not appropriate, or feasible, in a particular situation. That this danger has not been avoided has been evident in much of what is proposed in support of a greater role for common property regimes. As Campbell (1990) has pointed out, 'the arguments for increased community control of common property too often call for a wholesale change in the patterns of political life.'

In the rest of this section we look first at evidence that governments are, or are not, prepared and able to provide an appropriate policy basis for collective management of forest resources in some situations, and to back this with the necessary legal provisions. We then look at what the actual experiences reviewed earlier suggest about the effectiveness of such policy and strategic shifts; looking in particular at the factors that underlie the shift to devolution to co-management rather than self-governance systems in most of the cases. We also examine the performance of the forest departments and other government agencies responsible for delivering and supporting such change.

Policy changes in favor of local collective management

The recent upsurge in initiatives to increase local control and management of forest resources broadly coincides in time with the growth in strategies to bring about structural adjustment, and a reduction in the size and the role of government. It seems likely that the current interest in more local forest management is related to its relevance to the devolution and decentralization strategies through which these new priorities are being pursued in part. It is also more clearly linked to the higher priority attached to rural development, and to ensuring greater participation by rural stakeholders in decisions and actions affecting them.

In forestry the shift towards a greater involvement of rural users dates back to a major shift from exclusively industrial and conservation objectives that started in several countries in the late 1970s (FAO 1978; World Bank 1978). This was primarily triggered by recognition that existing forestry strategies and methods were failing to conserve essential aspects of the forest estate. The huge initiative in the 1970s by the South Korean government to encourage villages to create collective woodlots on their lands, was stimulated by the perception that this was needed in order to stop destructive use of hill forests that were protecting downstream agricultural lands. Hill community forestry in Nepal similarly had its origins in increasing concern about deforestation of watershed areas. In India, the Social Forestry initiatives arose from arguments by the 1976 National Commission on Agriculture that the country's remaining timber production forests needed to be protected against local users of fuelwood, etc. In the Philippines and Thailand there were growing concerns over the depletion of both the economic and environmental functions of the forest.

As has been previously documented, much of the earlier effort to respond to the conservation priority focused on trying to mobilize local users to collective activities that would move their production out of the forests, or that would re-create tree cover in critical areas. Subsequent moves to forms of co-management within forests reflected both perception of the flaws in the earlier approach, and growing acceptance of arguments that forestry needed to become more responsive to meeting local needs and concerns. In some initiatives, such as the Philippine ancestral domain certification programs, providing meaningful local autonomy has become a primary objective.

It would appear that in some countries one factor that has entered into government decisions to reduce their direct control over forests has been the declining economic importance of the forest sector at the national level. It has been argued that the 1978 decision by the government in Nepal to legislate to enable public forest land to be transferred to local communities reflected both a recognition that this dispersed resource could not be effectively controlled from the center, and also the declining importance of forests as a source of revenue to the central government (Malla 1997). In India, the 1988 Forest Policy radically changed the objectives for the forest sector, subordinating direct economic benefit to environmental stability and meeting subsistence needs, and stating that forests were not to be commercially exploited for industrial uses (Saxena 1997). Recent Supreme Court rulings that have severely restricted timber harvesting in natural forests have meant that JFM is assuming increased importance as a major form of forest management (Falconer, personal communication). In Thailand, on the other hand, where the direct value of the forests also declined sharply because of a logging ban, a shift towards greater emphasis on their environmental value has resulted in a stricter protective regime that has hampered the development of local management (Vandergeest 1996; Wittayapak 1996).

Legal base

At least in the particular countries reviewed, the policy environment has therefore usually shifted in ways that are more favorable to devolution of control to the local community level. But this has not always been accompanied by necessary legislation and regulations, or by measures to implement policy.

The programs in Korea, Nepal and the Philippines have benefited from having legislation specifically designed to support common property and self-governance systems. In each there are legislation and regulations that provide authority both to communities and government agencies that enable them to generate the necessary rules, regulations, and operational measures, and give them authority to implement and enforce them. In India, though individual states have often promulgated measures to support JFM, there is no national legislation. The 1988 Forest Policy, which provides the authority for the JFM initiatives, is a non-statutory and advisory statement issued by the government, not backed by law (Saxena 1997). That it has not been translated into legislation is said to be because there is a lack of a political constituency for legal change in this area at the national level (Vira 1997).

Lack of enabling legislation does not necessarily mean that programs to support local self-governance of forest resources cannot happen. Security of tenure can often be more important than type of tenure (Fisher 1995). In a number of Asian countries where legislation restricts what people can do in the forest, forest departments have arrived at extralegal arrangements with communities to enable them to continue to manage the forest areas from which they draw supplies (Fox 1996).

However, without a legal base, community-based rights can be challenged in terms of national law, and local groups can encounter difficulty in using the law to assert their rights (Seymour and Rutherford 1990). Without secure legal backing, local people are also left in a weak position in negotiating change with government and can be left exposed to risk by even the best intentioned initiatives introduced by the latter (Singh 1986). In Thailand, inability to arrive at agreement on community forestry legislation among the different political constituencies with interests in the management of forests has seriously impeded progress towards recognizing and empowering those with long standing *de facto* rights of control and use of areas of hill forest (Wittayapak 1996).

Such problems are often aggravated because the legal base is weak and confused. In most countries, Western tenure, and more recent systems designed to transfer control over land from local to the new political elites, co-exist with community systems, undermining the latter but seldom providing a satisfactory alternative because they are not enforced. This causes confusion because the legal status of land and forest resources becomes unclear (Bruce 1999). The existence of a dual or multiple legal system means that people can be faced with different fora for settling a dispute under the different legal systems. This complicates the task, at minimum causing lack of clarity and confusion to claimants. This has been particularly evident in Africa (Birgegård 1993; Shepherd 1992; Lawry 1989).

Policies of devolution of control in practice

One area of concern that has arisen relates to who benefits and who loses when governments decentralize responsibility for forest management to local levels. As was noted earlier, there is a danger in multiple user situations that formalizing rights of access and use may leave out or disadvantage some of those who previously had *de facto* use rights. For example, the Social Forestry programs in India were widely perceived as having adversely affected those who previously used the common lands on which the trees were planted for grazing, fodder, fuel, and other produce—generally the landless and poorer members of a community (Arnold and Stewart 1991).

A more widespread concern is the extent to which the state actually relinquishes power and responsibility through some of the community or village forestry programs. In most cases, forest departments have laid down tight rules for the operation of co-management arrangements, that effectively circumscribe the authority and freedom of the recipients to act (Ribot 1999, Hobley 1996*b*). This may have been in part to reduce the costs and burden of administration, or to ensure an even-handed approach to collaborating communities. But is has been widely perceived to reflect an intention by most governments to retain a large measure of control. It enables forest departments to create local partners that become their proxies, rather than representatives of local users able to challenge their actions when necessary (Hobley 1996*b*). People may acquiesce in such changes because there is a danger that devolution is pursued by forest departments primarily as a means of achieving better protection of the forest at low cost, rather than in terms of impacts on villagers' lives (Shepherd 1992).

Forest departments thus all too often remain as active, and frequently dominant, partners in local forest management. In this connection, concern has been expressed (e.g., Wily 1997) that in nearly all programs the state retains ownership of the land, and reserves the right to reverse the process of devolution of control over forest land to local groups. However, some of these concerns may be mistakenly equating rights of access and use with ownership. In most of the situations reviewed, communities have been seeking more secure and beneficial access to the forest resource, or to particular flows of products from the resource, not to the land. Also, *joint* management systems usually reflect the fact that the state has a continuing role, often both as a stakeholder in the use of the forest and as a regulator. For instance, forests frequently need to be managed *inter alia* to produce goods and services, such as watershed management, that are more logically the task of the state than local user groups.

Nevertheless, the concerns frequently expressed about the extent or nature of forest department involvement indicate that there is often an imbalance between state and local community in local level arrangements. In particular, it could be argued that a different and lesser involvement is required from forest departments in control and management of forest resources outside state forests. The widespread failure of Social Forestry woodlots on village lands in India seems to have been due in no small part to the fact that forest departments assumed such an intrusive and dominant role as to alienate the user communities, and undermine their incentive and capacity to take control (Arnold and Stewart 1991). A role of providing communities with the necessary authority, encouragement in creating needed institutional arrangements, and technical and financial support, as was the case in South Korea, could well have been more appropriate, and successful.

The lessons learned from these experiences also point to the need for more flexible, situation specific, application of co-management approaches. Preset formulaic rules are unlikely to match the needs of many of the groups to whom they are applied. Rules that cannot be altered by a group can freeze a constantly evolving relationship between people and the resource they draw upon at a particular point in time, preventing its adaptation to further change (Hirsch 1997). In most programs there is now progression towards more flexible rules, and to local adaptation. However, even in Nepal, where this has gone further than most, there remains considerable dispute and friction between FUGs and the forest department over the rules laid down and monitored by the latter (Srestha 1996).

Despite the criticisms of the continuing presence of forest department staff in user group institutions, there is growing evidence in many situations that groups recognize that they can act as a useful source of technical advice and a channel to government support services, and that they can also act as arbiters against internal or external expropriation. Where transfer of control to local bodies would otherwise lead to the resource falling into the hands of local elites or being sold to outsiders, a measure of continuing external monitoring or control may be desirable or necessary (Falconer, personal communication; Ribot 1999).

This can be important in the many situations where local institutions have broken down under market, demographic, and political pressures, and cannot be re-created easily. Under such circumstances, the low returns and high social cost associated with trying to control common resources may prove so unacceptable to users that they prefer to let the resource be managed by the forest department or some other arm of government. The question then arises, in the many situations in which social capital has been so seriously eroded as to make it difficult for users to organize effectively without support, as to whether it is the forest department that is best placed to provide this.

The issue of how to accommodate, and harmonize, the interests of other 'stakeholders' with interests in the management of the forests (commercial, biodiversity conservation, etc.) has also been attracting increasing attention. This has been reflected in recent searches for more 'pluralistic' approaches and mechanisms that are designed for conditions in which two or more groups, principals, sources of authority, etc., coexist. In essence, the new focus is pursuing three areas of improvement: a more acceptable balance between forest departments and other stakeholders; frameworks for negotiation, planning, and management that provide more equal participation by all; and methods of management, conflict resolution, and monitoring that can accommodate different objectives and measures of performance and adapt to them. Though some potential avenues have been identified, not enough successful experience of applying most of them has accumulated to allow conclusions to be drawn yet as to what might succeed (Anderson, Clément, and Crowder 1999).

Bureaucratic attitudes and practices

Co-management of forest resources with local user groups confronts forest departments with tasks that are radically different from those conventionally associated with management of state forests for timber and watershed protection. Recent studies have highlighted a number of issues that can arise as forest departments attempt to make this transition.

Forest departments are now generally responsive to the arguments that their traditional approach has failed to secure sustainable forest management, and is no longer appropriate to the demands currently being placed upon the forest sector. There is often considerable concern within departments that they become more successful, and be seen as being more relevant to current government (and donor) concerns (Vira 1999). But this may result in them moving in directions, such as the higher environmental and protection profile adopted by the forest department in Thailand, which makes co-management even more difficult (Wittayapak 1996).

Even where they do accept a greater degree of resource sharing in state forests as an objective, it can be difficult for forest departments in practice to give up the power, status, and control over budgetary and extra-budgetary resources and income that stem from their control over large areas of forest. Existing practices are usually well entrenched and strongly linked to the 'patronage systems and rent seeking behaviour, both within the service and with outsiders [that] are the real determinants of institutional performance' (Hobley 1996*b*: 23). The benefits of involvement in participatory forestry seldom appear to be as substantial or satisfactory, and there is not much evidence that the issue of providing those involved with career change options that compensate for this has received much attention.

The transition can be complicated by the fact that, in many countries, forest departments continue to be responsible for regulatory functions and direct management of large parts of the forest estate. Trying to combine this with transfer of control of parts of the forest estate to others creates understandable internal tensions and confusion. For instance, the comment has been made in relation to Nepal that: 'A major problem is that the organization which has been given the responsibility for devolving control of forests to local communities also represents the interests of those who have most to gain by maintaining control of forests themselves. The Forest Department is being asked to use its authority to give away its authority!' (Gilmour and Fisher 1991: 190).

Some of the problems encountered in co-management programs reflect the ambivalence, or lack of clarity about seemingly conflicting objectives, that this dual role can engender. It can lead, for instance, to reluctance to authorize indigenous local forest protection groups, because of a concern that this would enable them to encroach on the position of the forest department, as happened in Orissa (Poffenberger 1996). Restricting sales of particular forest products, in order to protect the position of the forest department as a producer, is likely to reduce local users' incentives to take responsibility for management of forest resources (Saxena *et al.* 1997). The distribution of benefits between forest departments and local users has similarly frequently been heavily biased in favor of the former (Saxena 1997). Poor communications with user groups can lead to misunderstandings over interpretation of rules, and unnecessary friction over incorrect assumed infractions (Srestha 1996).

A second problem area relates to the contrast in approaches appropriate to the traditional and new tasks foresters face. Public forests are most effectively managed by development and application of management models and techniques that can be applied uniformly over large areas. This encourages risk averse behavior that conforms to the norms associated with these standardized tasks. This contrasts strongly with the diversity of physical and social situations that participatory forestry represents. These factors put a premium on innovation, responsiveness, willingness to take risks, learning from experience, and flexibility—attributes unlikely to be nurtured in the highly structured bureaucracy of the usual forest department (Hobley 1996*b*).

It is also becoming clear that it is important to ensure that the institutional underpinnings of change are in place before initiating interventions. Though recognition of the importance of changes in attitudes and skills has led to a strong donor focus on training, this is unlikely to be productive unless it is preceded or accompanied by changes in the underlying culture and operating structures of forest departments (Hobley 1996*b*). Until this happens, field staff in particular, caught between the need to conform to the values of their service and being able to respond to the needs and aspirations of the communities whom they are expected to assist, run the risk of becoming severely overloaded (World Bank 1991; Campbell and Denholm 1993).

These difficulties encountered within forest departments help explain the problems that foresters have been encountering in responding appropriately to a role of supporting forest management by local user groups. Real progress is likely only when field staff feel involved and committed to the new approaches. This is likely to happen once their changed role and prospects are perceived to be as acceptable as the traditional forestry careers and benefits that they are losing. Encouragingly, there are signs in countries where the transition is relatively far advanced, such as India and Nepal, that such a change in attitudes and values is beginning to happen (Jeffery, Sundar, and Khanna 1998; Kurup 1996).

Intermediary institutions

The rigidities and constraints faced by many forest departments in making the transition to their new role has resulted in NGOs occupying an important position in many collective forest management programs. Operational NGOs can serve as intermediaries between state and users, can facilitate change at the village level and can act as trainers of government staff in community organizing skills. Other NGOs have taken on an advocacy role, seeking to influence policy. Experience in India has shown the need for clear understanding of the different roles on different NGOs, and of the interests each represents (Thin, Neeraj, and Gorada 1998).

In the Philippines and Thailand, NGOs have helped communities press their case for greater community rights, and in the former play an important part in helping them meet the requirements for ancestral domain certification. In the Philippines and India, NGOs play a prominent role in providing training and extension services, and producing guidelines and manuals that provide a framework for fieldworker activities. As has been described earlier, the program in Korea involved the creation of an umbrella NGO to perform the critical function of linking producer groups to the market and to government support services, and the FECOFUN federation in Nepal is taking on a somewhat similar function.

These intermediary organizations are generally encouraged by forest departments, as they can take on tasks that the latter find difficult or contentious, particularly where there has been a history of poor relations between people and the department. However, there is a danger that forest departments are sometimes delegating tasks to NGOs in order to 'avoid internal change' (Dove 1995). Concerns have also been raised that organizations such as FECOFUN in Nepal can become too closely associated with the forest department, or could become politicized (Shrestha and Britt 1997; Malla 1997).

Though evidence is accumulating that non-governmental institutions can be more effective than government bodies in helping communities and user groups develop a self-governing capacity and capability, not all NGO activity has been supportive of co-management. Not all are better equipped or skilled, or more appropriately motivated, than the government departments they seek to displace. There has been increased awareness that some NGOs are pursuing agendas for forest management (e.g., related to environmental issues) that are not necessarily congruent with the interests of the populations they work with. In addition, the confrontational positions adopted by some advocacy NGOs have sometimes hampered and curbed the development of viable joint management arrangements.

Conclusions

The role of local forest resources controlled by the user communities or groups has been much reduced over time, as demographic, economic, and political change make alternatives more appropriate or feasible. Nevertheless, over a wide range of situations there is still some reliance on common pool resources for local supplies of forest products. However, their management as common property is often constrained or discouraged by government policies that are directly or indirectly biased against local management of forest resources.

The recent growth in government programs that do devolve more control over forest resources to local communities in co-management with the state reflects a number of factors, prominent among which has been recognition by governments that control by the state was no longer effective in conserving and capturing forest values. In choosing ways to improve this situation, there has also been growing recognition that much local use of forest products draws upon forests as common pool resources, and of the vigor of spontaneous local collective management in many situations. The preference for co-management, rather than devolution of control solely to user communities, appears to be influenced *inter alia* by the interest of the state in continuing to exercise a considerable degree of involvement and control over forest resources and forest land. Co-management can also be a logical solution for communities when erosion of group social capital has weakened their capacity to manage their resource base unaided, and where the presence of multiple uses indicates the need for some form of pluralistic planning (Vira 1999).

The experience of some of the longer running and more flexible of the co-management initiatives has been encouraging. A substantial measure of local control has, in appropriate conditions, resulted in increases in product and other benefit flows to local users. There has also often been an improvement in the condition of the resource. Similar findings have emerged from some of the more robust indigenous local management regimes.

The fact that this can be reported for only some programs partly reflects the recent origin of many programs; most are still in a developmental phase. It often also reflects the fact that changes have sometimes been promoted ahead of the capacity to implement them. Heavy promotion of communal management, often at the urging of donors, has frequently imposed pressures on forestry bureaucracies that they have found difficult to absorb. Moves to introduce collective management as quickly and widely as possible have, on occasion, resulted in programs on a scale so large that centralized control and uniform patterns of intervention proved unavoidable, as happened with Social Forestry projects in India. The evolution from Social Forestry to Joint Forestry Management was similarly characterized by an initial framework that implicitly assumed that a single model would be appropriate everywhere.

It could be desirable if there is now a period of consolidation, moving from promotion to critical analysis, with more consideration of how best to address weaknesses and problems that have arisen. One is to better understand the circumstances under which local collective management is, and is not, likely to succeed, thereby avoiding initiatives in situations in which the policy framework, or demographic, economic, or resource characteristics, are not conducive to collective management. A second is the need to encourage a more flexible and responsive approach; one that is more situation specific and less formulaic. Another is to address the difficulties that forest departments have encountered. At the same time, the exaggerated expectations that co-management of forest resources has given rise to need to be corrected. It is important to recognize the limits to how much change can be achieved within the framework of forest-oriented programs, and to harmonize the latter with other community level government initiatives.

REFERENCES

Agrawal, A. 1994. 'Rules, Rule Making, and Rule Breaking: Examining the Fit between Rule Systems and Resource Use.' In *Rules, Games, and Common-Pool Resources*, E. Ostrom, R. Gardner, and J. Walker (eds.). Ann Arbor, MI: The University of Michigan Press.

Agrawal, A. and S. Goyal. 1997. 'Group Size and Collective Action.' Workshop in Political Theory and Policy Analysis, Indiana University, Bloomington, IN.

Anderson, J., J. Clément, and L.V. Crowder. 1999. 'Pluralism in Sustainable Forestry Development. An Overview of Concepts, Approaches and Future Steps.' In *Pluralism and Sustainable Forestry and Rural Development*. Rome: FAO.

Arnold, J.E.M. 1998. 'Managing Forests as Common Property.' FAO Forestry Paper 136, FAO, Rome.

Arnold, J.E.M. and J.G. Campbell. 1986. 'Collective Management of Hill Forests in Nepal: The Community Forestry Development Project.' In *Proceedings of the Conference on Common Property Management*. Washington DC: National Academy Press.

Arnold, J.E.M. and P.A. Dewees (eds.). 1995. *Tree Management in Farmer Strategies: Responses to Agricultural Intensification.* Oxford: Oxford University Press. [Also published as *Farms, Trees and Farmers: Responses to Agricultural Intensification*, 1997, London: Earthscan Publications.]

Arnold, J.E.M. and W.C. Stewart. 1991. 'Common Property Resource Management in India.' Tropical Forestry Paper 24, Oxford Forestry Institute, University of Oxford, Oxford.

Ascher, W. 1994. *Communities and Sustainable Forestry in Developing Countries.* San Francisco, CA: The International Center for Self-Governance (ICS).

Baland, J.-M. and J.-P. Platteau. 1996. *Halting Degradation of Natural Resources: Is there a Role for Rural Communities?* Oxford: Clarendon Press.

Ballabh, Vishwa and Katar Singh. 1988. 'Van (Forest) Panchayats in Uttar Pradesh Hills: A Critical Analysis.' Research Note, Institute for Rural Management, Anand, Gujurat.

Birgegård, L.-E. 1993. 'Natural Resource Tenure: A Review of Issues and Experiences with Emphasis on Sub-Sahara Africa.' Rural Development Studies No. 31, Swedish University of Agricultural Sciences, Uppsala.

Borlagdan, S.B. 1990. 'Community Organizing in Social Forestry.' In 'Voices From the Field,' Fifth Annual Social Forestry Writing Workshop, J. Fox, A. Flavelle, and N. Podger (eds.). Environment and Policy Institute, East West Center, Honolulu, HI.

Bruce, J.W. 1999. 'Legal Bases for the Management of Forest Resources as Common Property.' Community Forestry Note 14, FAO, Rome.

Byron, N. and M. Arnold. 1999. 'What Futures for the People of the Tropical Forests?' *World Development* 27(5): 789–805.

Campbell, J.G. 1990. 'Whose Land is This? Overlapping Tenure, Tenure Transitions, Tenure Options and Tenurial Technology in India's Common Property Resources.' Paper presented at the First Conference of the International Association for the Study of Common Property, Durham, NC, 27–30 September.

Campbell, J.G. and J. Denholm (eds.). 1993. *Inspirations in Community Forestry*, Report of the Seminar on Himalayan Community Forestry held in Kathmandu, Nepal, 1–4 June 1992. Kathmandu: International Center for Integrated Mountain Development (ICIMOD).

Campbell, J.G., R.J. Shrestha, and F. Euphart. 1987. 'Socioeconomic Factors in Traditional Forest Use and Management: Preliminary Results from a Study of Community Forest Management in Nepal.' *Banko Jankaari* 1(4): 45–54.

Chambers, R., N.C. Saxena, and T. Shah. 1989. *To the Hands of the Poor: Water and Trees.* New Delhi: Oxford and IBH Publishing.

Davis, S.H. and A. Wali. 1993. 'Indigenous Territories and Tropical Forest Management in Latin America.' Policy Research Working Papers Series 1100, Environmental Assessments and Programs, The World Bank, Washington DC.

Dove, M.R. 1995. 'The Theory of Social Forestry Intervention: The State of the Art in Asia.' *Agroforestry Systems* 30: 315–40.

Falconer, J. Personal Communication.

FAO (Food and Agriculture Organization). 1978. *Forestry for Local Community Development*, FAO Forestry Paper 7. Rome: FAO.

Femconsult. 1995. 'Study of the Incentives for Joint Forest Management.' Main Report prepared for The World Bank, Washington DC. [Femconsult is a consulting company based in The Hague, The Netherlands.]

Fisher, R.J. 1989. 'Indigenous Systems of Common Property Forest Management in Nepal.' Working Paper No. 18, Environment and Policy Institute, East West Center, Honolulu, HI.

—— 1995. 'Collaborative Management of Forests for Conservation and Development.' Issues in Conservation, International Union for the Conservation of Nature (IUCN), Gland, Switzerland.

Fox, J. 1996. Comments contributed to the FAO (FTPP) electronic conference on 'Addressing Natural Resource Conflicts through Community Forestry.'

Ganjanapan, A. 1995. 'Will Community Forest Law Strengthen Community Forestry in Thailand?' Mimeograph, Faculty of Social Sciences, Chiang Mai University, Thailand.

Gibbs, C., E. Payuan, and R. del Castillo. 1990. 'The Growth of the Philippine Social Forestry Program.' In *Keepers of the Forest: Land Management Alternatives in Southeast Asia*, M. Poffenberger (ed.). West Hartford, CT: Kumarian Press.

Gilmour, D.A. 1995. 'Rearranging Trees in the Landscape in the Middle Hills of Nepal.' In *Tree Management in Farmer Strategies: Responses to Agricultural Intensification*, J.E.M. Arnold and P.A. Dewees (eds.). Oxford: Oxford University Press.

Gilmour, D.A. and R.J. Fisher. 1991. *Villagers, Forests and Foresters: The Philosophy, Process and Practice of Community Forestry in Nepal*. Kathmandu: Sahayogi Press.

Gregersen, H.M. 1982. *Village Forestry Development in the Republic of Korea: A Case Study*. Rome: FAO.

Hilario, M.P. and M.V.M. Sabban. 1997. 'Delineation and Recognition of Ancestral Domain: Implementation Issues and Opportunities in Palawan.' Policy Research Brief 2.1, Participatory Uplands Management Program, De La Salle University, Manila.

Hirsch, P. 1997. 'Community Forestry Revisited: Messages from the Periphery.' Paper prepared for workshop 'Community Forestry at a Crossroads: Reflections and Future Directions in the Development of Community Forestry,' Regional Community Forest Training Center (RECOFTC), Bangkok, 17–19 July.

Hobley, M. 1996*a*. 'Participatory Forestry: The Process of Change in India and Nepal.' Rural Development Forestry Study Guide 3, Overseas Development Institute, London.

—— 1996*b*. 'Institutional Change within the Forest Sector: Centralized Decentralization.' Working Paper 92, Overseas Development Institute, London.

Jeffery, R., N. Sundar, and P. Khanna. 1998. 'Joint Forest Management: A Silent Revolution Amongst Forest Department Staff?' Paper presented at the Workshop on Participatory Natural Resource Management, Mansfield College, Oxford, 6–7 April.

Jodha, N.S. 1986. 'Common Property Resources and Rural Poor in Dry Regions of India.' *Economic and Political Weekly* 21(27): 1169–81.

—— 1990. 'Rural Common Property Resources: Contributions and Crisis.' *Economic and Political Weekly Quarterly Review of Agriculture* 25(26): 65–78.

Kant, S., N.M. Singh, and K.K. Singh. 1991. 'Community Based Forest Management Systems,' Case Studies from Orissa. ISO-Swedforest/Indian Institute of Forest Management/ Swedish International Development Authority (SIDA).

Kurup, V.S.P. (ed.). 1996. 'New Voices in Indian Forestry.' Society for Promotion of Wastelands Development, New Delhi.

Lawry, S.W. 1989. 'Tenure Policy and Natural Resource Management in Sahelian West Africa.' LTC Paper 130, Land Tenure Center, University of Wisconsin, Madison, WI.

Lindsay, J.M. 1994. 'Law and Community in the Management of India's State Forests.' Working paper, Lincoln Institute of Land Policy, Cambridge.

Lynch, O.J. and K. Talbott. 1995. *Balancing Acts: Community-Based Forest Management and National Law in Asia and the Pacific*. Washington DC: World Resources Institute.

Malhotra, K.C. 1995. 'Biodiversity Conservations and Community Development in Southwest Bengal.' In *Community Development and Conservation of Forest Biodiversity through Community Forestry*, H. Wood, M. Mcdaniel, and K. Warner (eds.). Bangkok: RECOFTC.

Malhotra, K.C. and M. Poffenberger (eds.). 1989. *Forest Regeneration through Community Protection: The West Bengal Experience.* New Delhi: Ford Foundation.

Malla, Y.M. 1997. '"Stakeholders'" Responses to Changes in Forest Policies.' Paper prepared for the FAO Workshop on Pluralism, Sustainable Forestry and Rural Development, Rome, 9–12 December.

McElwee, P.D. 1994. 'Common Property and Commercialisation: Developing Appropriate Tools for Analysis.' M.Sc. Dissertation, Oxford Forestry Institute, University of Oxford, Oxford.

McKean, M.A. and E. Ostrom. 1995. 'Common Property Regimes in the Forest: Just a Relic from the Past?' *Unasylva* 46(180): 3–15.

Molnar, A. 1981. 'The Dynamics of Traditional Systems of Forest Management: Implications for the Community Forestry Development and Training Project.' Report to The World Bank, Washington DC.

Ostrom, E. 1998. 'Some Organizing Thoughts on the Comparison of Private and Common Property Rights.' Paper prepared for the UNU/WIDER project on Land Reform Revisited: Access to Land, Rural Poverty and Public Action, Santiago, Chile, 26–29 April.

Peluso, N.L., P. Vandergeest, and L. Potter. 1995. 'Social Aspects of Forestry in Southeast Asia: A Review of Postwar Trends in the Scholarly Literature.' *Journal of Southeast Asian Studies* 26(1): 196–218.

Plantilla, J.R. 1991. 'Community Forest Management: Toward Strengthening the Certificate of Community Forest Stewardship.' In 'Voices From the Field,' Fourth Annual Social Forestry Writing Workshop, J. Fox, O. Lynch, M. Zimsky, and E. Moore (eds.). Environment and Policy Institute, East West Center, Honolulu, HI.

Poffenberger, M. 1996. 'Grassroots Forest Protection: Eastern Indian Experiences.' Asia Forest Network Number 7, Berkeley, CA.

Poffenberger, M. and B. McGean (eds.). 1993. 'Community Allies: Forest Co-Management in Thailand.' Asia Forest Network Report Number 2, Berkeley, CA.

—— 1996. *Village Voices, Forest Choices: Joint Forest Management in India.* Delhi: Oxford University Press.

Poffenberger, M. and Chatrapati Singh. 1996. 'Communities and the State: Re-establishing the Balance in Indian Forest Policy.' In *Village Voices, Forest Choices: Joint Forest Management in India*, M. Poffenberger and B. McGean (eds.). Delhi: Oxford University Press.

Pragtong, K. and D.E. Thomas. 1990. 'Evolving Management Systems in Thailand.' In *Keepers of the Forest: Land Management Alternatives in Southeast Asia*, M. Poffenberger (ed.). West Hartford, CT: Kumarian Press.

Pravongviengkham, P.P. 1997. 'Local Regulatory System in Support of Lao Swidden-Based Farm Economy.' Paper prepared for the workshop 'Community Forestry at a Crossroads: Reflections and Future Directions in the Development of Community Forestry,' RECOFTC, Bangkok, 17–19 July.

Ribot, J. 1999. 'Decentralisation, Participation and Accountability in Sahelian Forestry: Legal Instruments of Political-Administrative Control.' *Africa* 69(1): 23–65.

Richards, M. 1997. 'Common Property Resource Institutions and Forest Management in Latin America.' *Development and Change* 28(1): 95–117.

Roy, S.B. 1991. 'Forest Protection Committees in West Bengal: Emerging Policy Issues.' In 'Voices From the Field,' Fourth Annual Social Forestry Writing Workshop, J. Fox, O. Lynch, M. Zimsky, and E. Moore (eds.). Environment and Policy Institute, East West Center, Honolulu, HI.

Runge, C.F. 1986. 'Common Property and Collective Action in Economic Development.' In *Proceedings of the Conference on Common Property Management.* Washington DC: National Academy Press.

Sabban, M.V.M. 1992. 'Managing Decentralization in Social Forestry: A Review of Issues and Strategies in the Philippines.' In 'Voices From the Field,' Fifth Annual Social Forestry Writing Workshop, J. Fox, A. Flavelle, and N. Podger (eds.). Environment and Policy Institute, East West Center, Honolulu, HI.

—— 1997. 'Community Forestry and Decentralization Policies: Reflections on Experience from the Philippines.' Paper prepared for the workshop on Community Forestry at a Crossroads: Reflections and Future Directions in the Development of Community Forestry, RECOFTC, Bangkok, 17–19 July.

Sarin, M. 1993. 'From Conflict to Collaboration: Local Institutions in Joint Forest Management.' Joint Forest Management Working Paper No. 14, Society for Promotion of Wastelands Development (SPWD) and Ford Foundation, New Delhi.

Saxena, N.C. 1987. *Social Forestry in the Hill Districts of Uttar Pradesh.* Kathmandu: ICIMOD.

—— 1997. *The Saga of Participatory Forest Management in India*, CIFOR Special Publication. Bogor, Indonesia: CIFOR.

Saxena, N.C., M. Sarin, R.C.V. Dingh, and T. Shah. 1997. 'Western Ghats Forestry Project: Independent Study of Implementation Experience in Kanara Circle.' Report to UK Department for International Development (DFID), London.

Seymour, F.J. and D. Rutherford. 1990. 'Contractual Agreements in Asian Social Forestry Programs.' Paper prepared for the First Annual Meeting of the International Association for the Study of Common Property, Duke University, Durham, NC.

Shepherd, G. 1992. 'Managing Africa's Tropical Dry Forests: A Review of Indigenous Methods.' Agricultural Occasional Paper 14, Overseas Development Institute, London.

Shrestha, N.K. and C. Britt. 1997. 'Crafting Community Forestry: Networking and Federation-Building Experiences.' Paper prepared for the workshop on Community Forestry at a Crossroads: Reflections and Future Directions in the Development of Community Forestry, RECOFTC, Bangkok, 17–19 July.

Singh, C. 1986. *Common Property and Common Poverty: India's Forest, Forest Dwellers and the Law.* New York: Oxford University Press.

Society for Promotion of Wastelands Development (SPWD). 1992. 'Joint Forest Management: Concept and Opportunities.' Proceedings of the National Workshop at Surajkund, Society for Promotion of Wastelands Development, New Delhi, August.

Srestha, K.B. 1996. 'Nepal Madhyasthata Samuha: Community Forestry in Nepal—An Overview of Conflicts.' Discussion Paper Series No. MNR 96/2, ICIMOD, Kathmandu.

Thin, N., P. Neeraj, and P. Gorada. 1998. 'Muddles about the Middle: NGOs as Intermediaries in JFM.' Edinburgh Papers in South Asian Studies Number 12, Department of Social Anthropology, University of Edinburgh, Edinburgh.

Thomson, J.T. 1992. 'A Framework for Analyzing Institutional Incentives in Community Forestry.' Community Forestry Note 10, FAO, Rome.

Thomson, J.T. and C. Coulibaly. 1995. 'Common Property Forest Management Systems in Mali: Resistance and Vitality under Pressure.' *Unasylva* 46(180): 16–22.

Thomson, J.T. and K.S. Freudenberger. 1997. *Crafting Institutional Arrangements for Community Forestry*, Community Forestry Field Manual 7. Rome: FAO.

Tripathi, K.C. 1987. 'Local Institutions Involved in Forest Management: Panchayat Case Studies.' In *Peoples' Institutions for Forest and Fuelwood Development: A Report on Participatory Fuelwood Evaluations in India and Thailand*, R. Morse, C. Tingsabadh, N. Vergara, V. Vidyarthi (eds.). Honolulu, HI: East-West Center.

Vandergeest, P. 1996. 'Property Rights in Protected Areas: Obstacles to Community Involvement as a Solution in Thailand.' *Environmental Conservation* 23(3): 259–68.

Vira, B. 1997. 'Implementing Participatory Forest Management—Towards a Typology of Field-Level Interaction.' Voluntary paper prepared for the 11th World Forestry Congress, Antalya, Turkey, 13–22 October.

—— 1999. 'Analytical Tools for Assessing Institutional Pluralism.' In *Pluralism and Sustainable Forestry and Rural Development*. Rome: FAO.

Wily, L. 1997. *Finding the Right Institutional and Legal Framework for Community-Based Natural Forest Management: The Tanzanian Case*, CIFOR Special Publication. Bogor: CIFOR.

Wittayapak, C. 1996. 'Forestry Without Legal Bases: Thailand's Experience.' *Common Property Resource Digest* 38(June): 7–8.

(The) World Bank. 1978. 'Forestry.' Sector Policy Paper, The World Bank, Washington DC.

—— 1991. *Forestry Development: A Review of Bank Experience*. Washington DC: The World Bank.

(The) World Bank, USAID, and Government of India. 1988. 'National Social Forestry Project: Mid-term Review.' USAID, New Delhi.

8

Access to Land via Land Rental Markets

ELISABETH SADOULET, RINKU MURGAI, AND ALAIN DE JANVRY

Why do we care about land rental markets?

Whenever there are economies of scale in production or imperfect markets for the determinants of production, there exists an optimal operational farm size that may not correspond to current household land endowments. For instance, small family-operated farms can be more productive than larger farms in a context where labor supervision problems are important. In other contexts, the labor supervision advantage of small farmers can be outweighed by other market imperfections if, for instance, they are rationed out of the credit market. As a result, there is a role for efficiency enhancing land transfers from less to more productive households. While the land sales and land rental markets can both allow implementing these transfers, there are reasons to expect that the rental market is more effective, particularly for the poor. Indeed, we observe that tenancy is an institution of major importance in both less and more developed countries' agriculture.

Not only is the rental market more likely to allow transfers than the sales market, rental contracts can directly improve efficiency by compensating for market failures to which tenants are subjected. For instance, when land is rented on a sharecropping basis, the terms of the contract can help compensate for insurance market failures by sharing risk. When there are idiosyncratic market failures in factor inputs (such as labor supervision and managerial skills), a sharecropping contract in which the landlord and tenant each provide the non-tradable input in which they are better endowed can help circumvent the missing markets. When access to credit is limited to or easier for large landowners, a landlord could use the credit access that comes with land ownership to provide the tenant with working capital as part of the rental contract. Since the poor are particularly exposed to these market failures, access to land via land rental contracts can be quite effective for them.

Land rental markets also have welfare effects, even though rental is not a transfer of wealth. In the short run, there are welfare effects because access to land allows households to use idle assets that can only be valorized through access to land (such as captive family labor and unused managerial and supervisory skills), enables better use of indivisible assets, and helps households access resources for which the market is either

We are thankful for comments and suggestions received from Pranab Bardhan, Pierre Dubois, Michael Carter, Paul Gertler, Nora Lustig, and Keijiro Otsuka.

imperfect or missing. The land rental market, by allowing short-term adjustments to land holdings, provides an insurance substitute. In the long-run, access to land via tenancy may help the landless capitalize the returns to otherwise idle assets, accumulate wealth, and move up an 'agricultural ladder' toward land ownership.

For both efficiency and welfare reasons, it is consequently important to understand how land rental markets function. In this chapter, we analyze household participation in land rental markets, with a particular focus on the determinants of access to land for the landless and smallholders, and the conditions under which they gain this access. Our thesis is that policy interventions to improve the performance of land markets have been excessively oriented to land sales markets and land ownership (including the new thrust on 'market-assisted' land reform by international organizations, see Deininger, Chapter 13, this volume), while the role of land rental markets and idiosyncratic contracts has been generally neglected and their performance often suppressed by ill-advised policy interventions. Interest in land rental contracts, as reflected in the vast literature on contract choice (see a review in Hayami and Otsuka 1993), has been motivated by efficiency considerations more than by the potential role of these contracts as instruments for access to land by poor people. At the same time, we will show that the rising capital intensity of agriculture and the aging of the farm population make access to land via tenancy increasingly more difficult for the poor. This will lead us to discuss types of interventions that could help restore the role of land rentals as instruments to give the poor access to land, create short-run flexibility in adjusting operational farm size toward a changing optimum, and help tenants progress toward eventual land ownership.

The outline of this chapter is as follows. In the second section, we discuss reasons why land rental markets are likely to be more effective than land sales markets in providing access to land, particularly for the rural poor. In the third section, we develop a model to endogenously derive household participation in land rental markets in a context of labor and credit market failures, and transaction costs on land rental markets. The model provides hypotheses on the role of different household characteristics for access to land and optimal farm size under both fixed rent and sharecropping contracts. Based on these hypotheses, we draw implications on the impact of the agricultural transformation associated with the increasing capital and managerial intensity of agriculture, and changes in demographic structure on the ability of the landless to access land and progress toward land ownership (fourth section). These issues are examined empirically in the fifth section using agricultural census data and household survey data from Pakistan and Tunisia. We conclude with policy recommendations to preserve and enhance access to land for the rural poor via land rental markets.

Superiority of the rental market in providing access to land for the poor

If all markets were perfect, renting or buying land would be identical. Tenants would pay rent to landlords and buyers would pay equivalent amounts to banks as interest on loans. There are, however, reasons for landlords and tenants to prefer transacting land through the rental market instead of the sales market.

First, a significant impediment to the functioning of the land sales market is that land ownership generates benefits due to failures in other markets that raise the land price above the capitalized value of the farm profit stream (Binswanger, Deininger, and Feder 1995). These side benefits stem from the value of land as a good store of wealth (particularly in periods of inflation), as a secure source of self-employment, and from its use as collateral for agricultural credit. Land ownership, like any other asset that can be liquidated to cope with income shocks, also plays an important role as an insurance substitute, and unlike other assets, protects the owner against low nutritional outcomes by providing food security when food markets fail. Other factors and policy distortions that further increase the price of land are the future urban demand for construction, and the credit subsidies, tax advantages, and political capital conferred to large land owners. This poses problems to potential buyers, particularly the poor, either because the additional benefits of land ownership do not apply to them or because they lack the resources to purchase land at high prices. Small farmers that acquire a portion of a large landholding are unlikely to receive the corresponding benefits in terms of subsidies and tax breaks. A household that relies on a mortgage-based land purchase has to forgo the land's value as collateral to access working capital since the land it acquires is already fully mortgaged. Consequently, the stream of benefits generated tend to be lower than the price paid for land, making it difficult if not impossible for poor households to purchase land since the land needs to be paid for partly from household savings. These problems are exacerbated as the capital intensity of agriculture increases: buying land ties up the limited available equity, creating problems for the acquisition of working capital.

Second, high covariation in incomes in rural areas leads to a situation in which the conditions for transactions in the land sales market become quite unfavorable. In good years when savings are high and households wish to purchase land, there tend to be a plethora of buyers and few sellers, which results in high land prices. Conversely, during bad crop years when households need to sell land, prices tend to be low. This reduces participation to land markets by potential small buyers and pushes smallholders into distress sales.

Third, high transaction costs on land markets and larger transaction costs for sales from large to small farmers create thin and segmented markets. The result is that large farmers sell to large farmers, smallholders sell to large farmers under distress conditions, and the landless are largely excluded (Carter and Zimmerman 1998).

Fourth, adjustment of land holdings via the rental market provides more flexibility than the sales market. Households often require short-term adjustments to their operational farm size to accommodate life-cycle variations in resource allocation or transitory situations in the availability of family labor or in cash needs. Selling land with the intention of buying it back when needs turn around would obviously entail large transaction costs and the likely impossibility of retrieving the same plot of land later on, or one in a convenient geographical location. An interesting asymmetry has been observed in some Mexican *ejidos* in the behavior of households renting in and out plots of land. Renting out by resident landlords is often for one season only, in response to short-term cash needs or labor shortages, while the same tenants rent in plots year after year as they become available in order to sustain a sufficiently large operational area (Bouquet 1996). Analyzing this role of the tenancy market in accommodating short-term needs, in a study of an Indian village, Sharma and Drèze (1996) find that there is considerable mobility from year to year between different tenancy status groups, with some households participating in the market as landlords one season and as tenants the next. Reviewing a great variety of production arrangements in Africa, Robertson (1987) observes that land rental contracts give households the opportunity to extend their activity at a season's notice without alienating their property.

Fifth, households may prefer land rentals to purchases since the former come with an accompanying set of arrangements which enable tenants and landlords to overcome market failures that affect them. Tenancy, in particular share tenancy, helps circumvent problems of missing or imperfect markets in inputs such as family labor and draft animals by pooling together the resources of the landlord and tenant. Under sharecropping, the terms of the contract can also compensate for idiosyncratic market failures in credit, insurance, and management skills to which the poor are exposed.

Finally, land rentals may provide an entry point into an 'agricultural ladder' wherein households first accumulate wealth and farming ability as hired laborers, progress to bear more risk while benefiting from landlords' cost sharing and managerial inputs as sharecroppers, and then become fixed rent tenants for the final accumulation needed to access land in ownership (Reid 1977).

Taken together, these reasons suggest that land rental markets are likely to be relatively more effective than land sales markets in providing access to land, particularly for the poor. This of course does not mean that land ownership is not desirable and that it does not convey a set of extra benefits compared to access to land as a tenant (Deininger and Binswanger, Chapter 17, this volume). Most important among these benefits are the use of land as collateral and the privileges of wealth. Access to land via land rental is thus only a local first best alternative compared to land ownership when the other markets needed to make land markets work and to make use of land in ownership efficient fail, and when there are high transaction costs on the land sales markets. Redistributive land reform under these conditions is usually extremely costly and it places beneficiaries under conditions where the likelihood of failure is high (see for example Warriner 1969 and Dorner 1992).

In the following sections, we analyze theoretically and empirically the factors that determine who participates in land rental markets, focusing in particular on the conditions that determine which households are able to secure access to land through the rental market.

Theory of optimal farm size and land rental

In this section, we develop a model to endogenize household participation in land rental markets in a context where the following archetypical conditions hold:

- access to credit is wealth constrained, and land owned serves as collateral;
- there are moral hazards in hired labor requiring supervision of workers by household members;
- there are transaction costs in land rental markets, with effective rent paid higher than effective rent received;
- there are fixed set-up costs to enter into farming;
- farm households are heterogeneous in terms of labor, land, and fixed factor endowments.[1]

The optimal time allocation and operational farm size chosen by the household determines whether it participates in the land market as a landlord or as a tenant, or whether it chooses to rent land neither in nor out. The structure of the model follows closely the theoretical framework in Eswaran and Kotwal (1986).[2] We first consider the case of fixed rental contracts. We then see how the use of share rather than fixed rent contracts affects the household's participation in the land rental market by compensating for market failures in credit, insurance, and managerial skills.[3]

Consider a household that derives utility from income (earned in agricultural production and off-farm labor) and leisure. The household is endowed with land $\bar{A}$, labor $\bar{L}$, non-tradable inputs and fixed productive assets $\bar{Z}$, and liquid assets $\bar{M}$. Production of a single commodity q requires land A, family and/or hired labor that are perfect substitutes, fertilizer and other purchased inputs X with price p_x, and the fixed assets $\bar{Z}$ according to the production function $q(A, L^i + L^h, X, \bar{Z}; \alpha_q)$ where L^i and L^h are family and hired labor and α_q represents technological parameters in production. The household adjusts its operating area to A, by leasing in or leasing out land under a fixed rent or share contract. Time is allocated between working on-farm, L^i, working off-farm, L^o, and leisure (home time), L^l. The wage rate on the labor market is w, but the potential for moral hazard on the part of hired workers, L^h, makes their supervision imperative. We assume that the per unit cost of supervision is an increasing and strictly convex function of the number of workers hired. This raises the cost of hired labor to $w[1 + s(L^h; \alpha_s)]$, where w is the market wage and $s(\cdot)$ is a supervision function with parameter α_s and $s' > 0$.[4]

We assume that production entails fixed set-up costs, K_0.[5] Initial capital expenses and costs of production (net rental cost, net labor cost, and fertilizer cost) are incurred before the harvest income is realized, and therefore require working capital during the season. The amount of credit to which the household has access is typically determined by the assets it possesses—here the amount of land it owns (Binswanger and

[1] We consider the role of risk in the forthcoming section, *Other justifications for sharecropping*.

[2] Eswaran and Kotwal (1986) focus on the labor market participation decisions and the productivity effects of market failures in labor and credit. In this chapter, we are concerned with implications of these market failures for participation in land markets and operational farm scale.

[3] We do not analyze the interesting question of which contract type—fixed rent, sharecropping, or wage labor—persists in a particular environment in this chapter. See Eswaran and Kotwal (1985) and Hayami and Otsuka (1993) for detailed analyses of this issue.

[4] The usual assumption about convexity of the supervision function (see Eswaran and Kotwal 1986) is not needed because the presence of fixed factors in production is sufficient for the existence of a finite optimum farm size.

[5] These fixed costs will render unprofitable the cultivation of extremely small land areas.

Rosenzweig 1986). We assume that a household with owned landholding, $\bar{A}$, has available to it a maximum amount of credit, $M(\bar{A}; \alpha_M)$, where M is an increasing function of land ownership with parameter α_M.

Land rental market participation under fixed rent contracts

Under a fixed rent contract, the household can rent in or rent out land at an exogenous rate to be paid at the beginning of the season. Transactions costs in the land rental market, such as costs involved in finding plots of suitable size, location, and quality when renting in, and finding suitable tenants and establishing the terms of the contract when renting out, create a differential effective price between the rate for rental in r^i and out r^o of land, with $r^o < r^i$. The household's maximization problem is:

$$\underset{A^i, A^o, L^i, L^o, L^l, L^h, X}{Max} \quad pq(\bar{A} + A^i - A^o, L^i + L^h, X, \bar{Z}; \alpha_q) - p_x X$$
$$- w[L^h[1 + s(L^h; \alpha_s)] - L^o] + r^o A^o - r^i A^i - K_0 1(A > 0) + u(L^l)$$

s.t. $$L^o + L^i + L^l = \bar{L}, \text{ time constraint,}$$

$$p_x X + w[L^h[1 + s(L^h; \alpha_s)] - L^o] - r^o A^o + r^i A^i + K_0 1(A > 0) \leq \bar{M} + M(\bar{A}; \alpha_M),$$
$$\text{liquidity constraint,}$$
$$A^i, A^o, L^i, L^o, L^l, L^h, \text{ and } X \geq 0,$$

where $1(A > 0)$ is the indicator function equal to one when $A > 0$ and 0 otherwise.

The production function q and the utility function u are assumed to be increasing, strictly quasi-concave, and continuously differentiable in their arguments. In the absence of a credit constraint, there would exist an optimal farm size, $A^* = A^*(\bar{L}, \bar{Z}, p, p_x, w, r^o, r^i, \alpha_q, \alpha_s)$. However, the credit constraint prevents households from reaching this level of operation, and the optimal farm size also becomes a function of land ownership and initial liquidity. The solution of this constrained optimization problem can be formally written as:

$$Y = Y(\bar{A}, \bar{L}, \bar{Z}, \bar{M}, K_0, p, p_x, w, r^o, r^i, \alpha_q, \alpha_s, \alpha_M),$$

where Y is the vector of endogenous variables $\{A^i, A^o, L^i, L^o, L^l, L^h, X\}$.[6] Figure 8.1 illustrates the relationship between owned land $\bar{A}$ and operated land $A = \bar{A} + A^i - A^o$, at given family size $\bar{L}$, fixed assets $\bar{Z}$, and initial liquidity $\bar{M}$.[7] On the 45-degree line, operated farm size equals owned land, while deviations from this line imply renting land in or out.

[6] If rent were paid at the time of harvest (as observed in Sudan by Kevane 1996; and in Palanpur by Sharma and Drèze 1996), land rental income/expenditure would not affect the working capital constraint. In addition, if credit availability were unrelated to land ownership, operated area would not depend on owned land, and net area leased in would offset one to one additional area in ownership. This has been used as a test of well-functioning land market (Kevane 1996; Skoufias 1995).

[7] Without any proportional transaction costs on the land rental market, the operated area curve BCDEF would be continuous. There may also be fixed transaction costs in the land rental market that render unprofitable leasing in or leasing out small amounts of land (Skoufias 1995). This would lead to a friction model, setting rental to zero whenever the continuous model would have predicted small areas rented in or out.

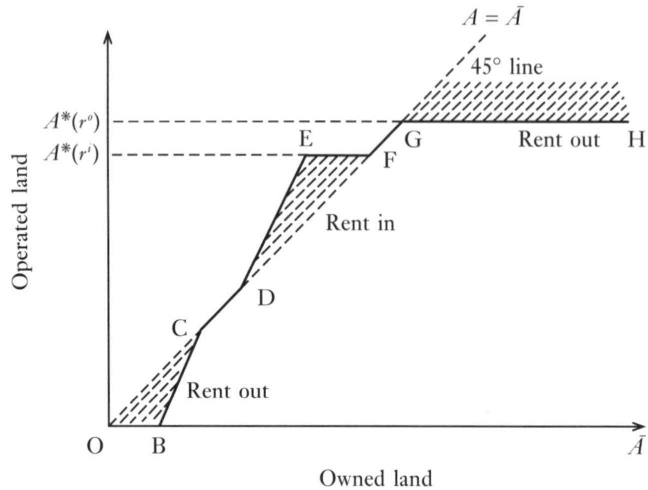

Figure 8.1. *Participation in the land rental market as a function of land ownership*

Small owners, with land ownership between O and B, cannot access the liquidity necessary to start cultivating on their own. They rent out all their land and hire their labor out. These households comprise a class of 'pure landlords' who rent out their land to other landless or landed households that have access to sufficient working capital. Once they own enough land to access the liquidity necessary to enter farming (the minimum amount of credit they need is lower than the fixed cost K_0 since part of the working capital is supplied by off-farm labor income and by their own liquidity endowment $\bar{M}$), households begin cultivating some of their own land, but the working capital constraint induces them to rent out the rest of their land (segment BCD). The vertical segment BC comes from the fact that start-up costs K_0 imply that there is a minimum viable size of operation at C. This is a class of 'cultivating landlords.' Due to the difference in the effective per-acre rental rate for renting in and renting out land, for a range of land ownership (segment DE), the household chooses to not participate in the rental market and remains a pure 'owner-operator.' For households with larger land holdings, renting in some land becomes possible and optimal, forming a class of 'owner-tenants.' These households rent in as much land as the liquidity constraint allows them (segment EF), until they reach the optimal farm size $A^*(r^i)$ at F. As farm size remains at this optimal level, rented land decreases down to the point where they are pure owner-operators again at the land rental rate r^i. Because there is a price band on the land rental market, the household remains in self-sufficiency in the range GH until the optimal farm size $A^*(r^o)$ is reached. Households that own more land than this optimal farm size rent out the surplus land (segment HI), reverting to the 'cultivating landlords' class.

The relationship between owned and operated land is conditional on exogenous household characteristics ($\bar{L}$, $\bar{M}$, $\bar{Z}$), on the technology of production (K_0, α_q), on best practices for labor supervision (α_s) and access to credit (α_M), on the transaction costs

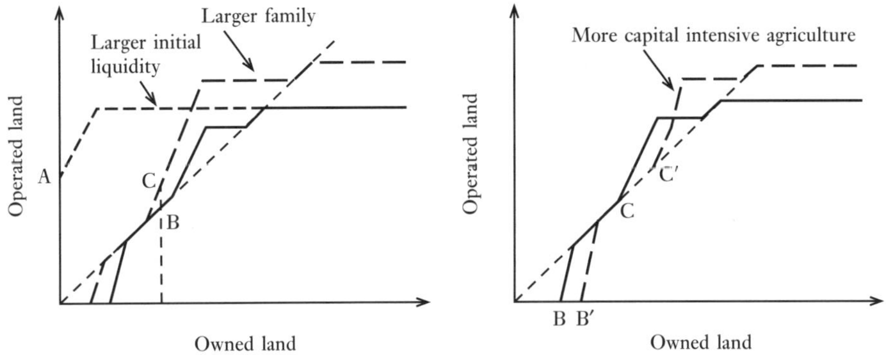

Figure 8.2. *Effect of family size, initial liquidity, and technology on participation in the land rental market*

on the land rental market (r^o, r^i), and on prevailing prices (p, p_x, w). We analyze here the role of some of these exogenous variables and parameters on land market transactions. With a larger *family size* $\bar{L}$ (Figure 8.2, left panel), wage income is higher and it generates the necessary liquidity to start production and to enter the rental market as a tenant at a lower level B' of land ownership. With a larger family size, the optimal farm size is also larger since supervision costs are less. Hence, cultivated area is greater in large households at every level of land ownership, except when there is self-sufficiency.

With sufficient *initial liquidity* $\bar{M}$, even landless households can start cultivating by renting in land.[8] Figure 8.2 (left panel) illustrates the case where a relatively wealthy landless household rents in and cultivates an area (at A) that is greater than the area operated by a landed household with poor liquidity that remains out of the market (at C) or by a household with a larger family that rents in some land.[9]

Households that own surplus *assets with imperfectly marketable services* $\bar{Z}$ relative to their land holdings will lease in land while households with excess land in relation to these factor endowments will lease out land. Some of the key factors with imperfect markets, other than credit and family labor, that have been emphasized in the literature include draft animals and managerial or technical skills that are not rewarded by the labor market (see Skoufias 1995, and citations therein). In the latter case, the better workers will self-select in taking rental contracts (Hallagan 1978). After the Civil War, the plantation system in the US shifted from slave labor to wage labor. However, the better skilled black workers could increase income by taking sharecropping contracts (Sutch and Ransom 1973).

[8] Sarap's (1998) study of rental markets in Orissa, India, provides empirical support for the role of liquidity. He finds that the landless in Orissa were unable to access land because they lacked sufficient working capital and cash to lease in land.

[9] For the impact of labor and credit market imperfections on the relationship between operational scale and farm productivity, with and without access to fixed rent tenancy, see Feder (1985).

Land owners with limited labor for supervision (absentee, old age, or high opportunity costs) or with limited *experience in supervision* (embodied in parameters α_s) will find it optimal to rent out land rather than farm it themselves (Eswaran and Kotwal 1985). Crops with complex hard-to-observe labor processes—e.g., vegetables in Tunisia, tobacco in the Dominican Republic, and strawberries in California (Wells 1996)—will be cultivated under tenancy since it provides access to the tenant's family labor and supervisory abilities.

How does the shift towards a more *capital-intensive agriculture* (embodied in parameters α_q) affect participation in the land rental market? The higher intensity in fertilizer use requires more working capital but the lower intensity in labor frees more family labor for the labor market. Whether the net of the two effects reduces or increases the optimal operated area depends on the relative importance of these two changes. Figure 8.2 (right panel) illustrates a case where the increase in fertilizer cost more than compensates for the decrease in labor cost. Some small landowners (between B and B') that could previously enter farming now opt to become agricultural workers rather than cultivate. Landed households (between C and C') that previously chose to augment their cultivated area by renting in land now exit from the rental market. And, for small landowners for whom the working capital constraint is stronger than the labor supervision constraint, operated area will be smaller than in labor-intensive agriculture. However, at the higher end of the land ownership spectrum, since labor cost is the limiting factor that defines optimal farm size, lower labor intensity and labor costs lead to larger farm sizes.

Land rental market participation under sharecropping contracts

In this section, we consider household participation in land rental markets under sharecropping contracts. We assume that a share contract entails payment of a fixed rent β (paid in advance) and a fraction $(1 - \alpha)$ of the output by the tenant to the landlord who contributes the same share for the purchase of material inputs, in this case fertilizer. α and β are parameters that are endogenously determined. In order to determine these parameters, first we examine the optimal decision of the tenant conditional on arbitrarily fixed values of α and β. Then we step back and have the landlord choose α, β, and the amount of land rented out in order to maximize his utility,[10] given the tenant's reaction function, and subject to the tenant being at no less than his reservation utility.[11]

The well-known Marshallian disincentive effect of sharecropping on the labor allocation decision creates different incentives for input use on the sharecropped and

[10] A sharecropping contract would induce the tenant to rent in land until its marginal productivity was down to zero, hence an infinite amount. To prevent this, we have the landlord decide on the amount of land the tenant can rent in.

[11] There are sharecropping models that assume that the terms of the contract are the outcome of bargaining between landlord and tenant (Bell 1989; Banerjee and Ghatak 1996). In the bargaining solution, the output share increases (and hence the inefficiency decreases) with the bargaining power of the tenant and is always greater than in the principal–agent framework that we use.

own plot. We therefore consider separately production on own land $q(\bar{A}, L1, X1; \alpha_q)$ and on sharecropped land $q(AS, L2, X2; \alpha_q)$, where AS represents the sharecropped area, and $L1$, $L2$, $X1$, and $X2$ are total labor and fertilizer on each land type, respectively.[12] Given the terms of the contract (α, β, AS), the tenant's optimization problem is:

$$\underset{\substack{L1,L2,X1,X2,\\ L^i,L^o,L^l,L^h}}{Max} \; U \equiv pq(\bar{A}, L1, X1; \alpha_q) + \alpha pq(AS, L2, X2; \alpha_q) - \beta - p_x(X1 + \alpha X2)$$
$$- w[L^h[1 + s(L^h; \alpha_s)] - L^o] - K_0 1(\bar{A} + AS > 0) + u(L^l)$$

s.t.
$$L^o + L^i + L^l = \bar{L}$$
$$L^h = L1 + L2 - L^i$$
$$p_x(X1 + \alpha X2) + w[L^h[1 + s(L^h; \alpha_s)] - L^o]$$
$$+ K_0 1(\bar{A} + AS > 0) + \beta \leq \bar{M} + M(\bar{A}; \alpha_M).$$

The solution of this constrained optimization problem can be formally written:

$$Y = Y(\bar{A}, \bar{L}, \bar{M}, K_0, p, p_x, w, \alpha_q, \alpha_s, \alpha_M, \alpha, \beta, AS), \tag{1}$$

where Y is the vector of endogenous variables $\{L1, L2, X1, X2, L^i, L^o, L^l, L^h\}$.

The landlord, as principal, takes into account the reaction function (1) of the tenant, and chooses α, β, and AS to maximize:

$$\underset{\alpha,\beta,AS}{Max} \; V \equiv (1 - \alpha)pq(AS, L2(\cdot), X2(\cdot); \alpha_q) - (1 - \alpha)p_x X2(\cdot) + \beta - rAS$$

s.t.
$$U \geq U_0$$

where $X2(\cdot)$ and $L2(\cdot)$are decided by the tenant according to (1), U_0 is the reservation utility of a potential tenant, and r is the opportunity cost of land for the landlord. The solution to this problem shows that the landlord chooses the amount of land AS and the share parameter α to maximize welfare, and sets the fixed payment β at the level that holds the tenant at (or barely above) his reservation utility (Stiglitz 1974). Hence, neither α nor AS depend on U_0 because there is no risk in the model:

$$AS = AS(\bar{A}, \bar{L}, \bar{M}, K_0, p, p_x, w, \alpha_q, \alpha_s, \alpha_M, r).$$

Under this specification, a tenant with a share contract requires less working capital than with a fixed rent contract since fertilizer costs are shared by the landlord and all rental payments are postponed to the end of the cropping season. As a result, a share contract considerably reduces the importance of the working capital constraint. The drawback of the sharecropping contract is the Marshallian disincentive on labor use since the tenant only captures a share of the return for on-farm labor while he has to pay its full cost. To reduce the Marshallian disincentive, the landlord will tend to increase the output (and fertilizer cost) share for those tenants who are less constrained by the liquidity requirements, while at the same time raising their fixed rent.

[12] We disregard here the role of fixed assets as the proper treatment of those that are not of a public good nature for the two plots is complex and not the focus of this section.

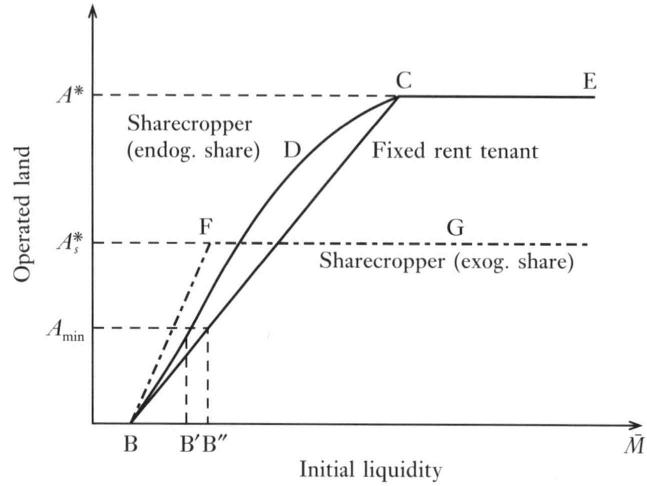

Figure 8.3. *Area operated by landless tenants, under sharecropping and fixed rent contracts*

In Figure 8.3 we compare the optimal operational scale for a landless household as a function of available initial liquidity $\bar{M}$ under fixed rent and sharecropping contracts. Tenants require a minimum amount of capital B to enter cultivation. As their access to capital increases, fixed rent tenants increase their farm size along BC until they reach the optimal farm size A^* dictated by increasing labor cost. Beyond this point, the working capital constraint does not bind and farm size remains at this optimal level (on segment CE). Sharecroppers who only support a fraction of the fertilizer costs operate larger farms (BDC).[13] Along this curve, as sharecroppers have better endowments of working capital, the share α offered by the landlord increases. When they reach the level C where the liquidity constraint is no longer binding, the optimal share is equal to one, i.e., the contract is *de facto* a fixed rent contract. This explains why the optimal farm size attained by sharecroppers is equal to the optimal farm size of fixed rent tenants. If, in addition, there are fixed transaction costs in renting land that make it unprofitable to rent/cultivate less than a minimum amount of land A_{min}, then sharecroppers will enter the land rental market at lower levels of liquidity than fixed rent tenants (B' compared to B'').

We also report in Figure 8.3 the case where the choice of the share payment is exogenously given, as is commonly found in many environments. Since the share cannot be adjusted in response to changing access to liquidity, the disincentive effects on labor persist regardless of the contract. Hence, the optimal farm size A_s^* chosen by the landlord for a pure sharecropper is smaller than that for a landless fixed rent tenant. When the working capital constraint is binding (segment BF), the landlord's optimal

[13] Sharecroppers *enter* cultivation at the same level of liquidity as fixed rent tenants because the minimum liquidity required to begin cultivation depends on the set-up costs which are the same under both contract types.

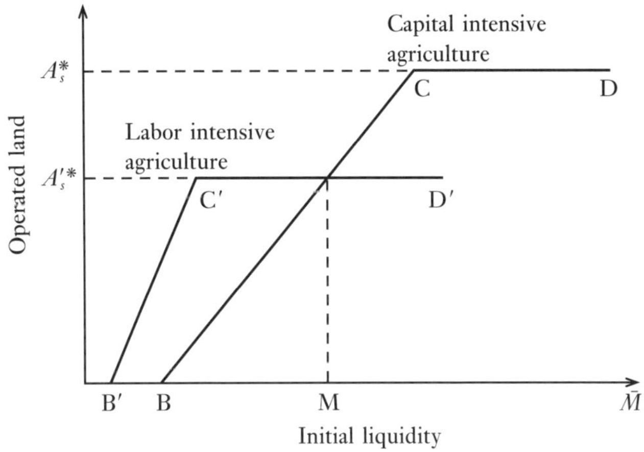

Figure 8.4. *Operated area as a function of capital intensity in agriculture*

decision is to give just enough land for the tenant to utilize all the available liquidity, but no more, so as not to exacerbate the distortion on factor use. However, the lower application of labor also leads to a lower use of fertilizer per hectare. The operated area for a credit constrained sharecropper is thus larger than when the landlord could adjust the share upwards: with a lower output share, the tenant pays a smaller share of fertilizer costs and the liquidity saving allows him to rent more land. The operated area for a credit constrained sharecropper is thus larger than when the landlord could adjust the share upwards.

Figure 8.4 illustrates how a shift from labor-intensive agriculture (with low fixed costs and a high share of labor in production) to more capital-intensive technologies (with higher fixed costs and a high share of fertilizer) affects access to land for the landless. We see that the increased importance of working capital in production makes it more difficult for the landless to access land. Entry into cultivation requires a greater endowment of liquid assets (B' rather than B), and for low levels of liquidity (below M), farm sizes are smaller than those operated in labor-intensive agriculture. However, with sharing of capital costs between landlords and tenants, and the lower intensity of labor use, large farm sizes can be operated when the liquidity constraint is relaxed ($A_s'^* > A_s^*$).

Other justifications for sharecropping

In the previous section, we emphasized the role of a sharecropping contract in relaxing the working capital constraint for tenants. Two other essential features of a share arrangement are the protection that it provides against risk and the direct participation of the landlord in management.

In the absence of access to good risk coping instruments (such as flexible credit, mutual insurance, and guaranteed employment schemes), risk averse landlords and tenants can opt for sharecropping contracts as a *source of insurance* (Stiglitz 1974; Otsuka and Hayami 1988).[14] When risk is an important consideration, as is the case with increasingly capital-intensive modern agriculture, a sharecropping contract is better than a fixed rent or wage contract as it allows risk to be shared between the landlord and the tenant. However, there is a trade-off between the insurance benefits of sharecropping (that require increasing the landlord's share to reduce the risk borne by the tenant) and the Marshallian disincentive in input use by the tenant (that requires lowering the landlord's share). As a result, landlords who have a choice of tenants would prefer to rent land to those households that are less risk averse (i.e., have more wealth) or that have access to sources of insurance such as secure off-farm incomes.[15]

Since sharecropping mitigates the impact of risk on the tenant, it also changes the optimal operational scale of the farm. The tenant's labor allocation between the labor market and on-farm work is a portfolio choice between a safe and a risky activity. Everything else equal, the tenant will allocate less labor to his farm activity the more risky agriculture is and the more risk averse he is. By providing some risk reduction, a share contract induces a higher level of labor use on-farm than a fixed rent contract. Higher labor use has to be balanced against the Marshallian disincentive, which reduces the incentive to apply labor on-farm. If risk, risk aversion, or the share of labor in production are high, sharecroppers apply more labor than fixed rent tenants. This suggests that under similar conditions of risk and risk aversion, the optimal farm size for sharecroppers is larger than for fixed rent tenants.

The role of sharecropping in mitigating the impact of risk is borne out in empirical studies. In Ghana, Boadu (1992) observes a greater incidence of sharecropping compared to fixed rent and wage contracts in regions with a higher coefficient of variation of cocoa yield. Similarly, tenants in France who are engaged in cultivation of labor-sensitive, risky crops such as grapes almost always choose to rent in land on a share basis. Schultz (1940) cites increasing farm income instability as a contributing factor to the shift to sharecropping contracts in the United States, while Dowell (cited in Otsuka and Hayami 1988) explains a gradual shift to fixed rent contracts by an increase in off-farm employment opportunities which likely reduced the level of income risk to which tenants were exposed. Not only does sharecropping reduce the tenant's exposure to risk, it can lead to higher expected incomes by helping tenants adopt more risky technologies (Shand and Kalirajan 1991).

Participation by both the landlord and the tenant in the *provision of non-tradable inputs* in which they are better endowed sets another justification for a sharecropping contract. Non-tradable inputs include cheap non-tradable labor, non-tradable farm capital (for example, bullocks which are highly labor intensive in maintenance and for which there are potential moral hazards in use), and supervisory and managerial skills. In the models elaborated in the previous sections, all these non-tradable inputs ($\bar{Z}$) are assumed

[14] Sharecropping is also chosen under risk to counteract the effect that a limited liability clause induces on a tenant's risk-taking behavior (Shetty 1988; Basu 1992).

[15] The terms of the contract for a tenant who is less risk averse or has external sources of income would entail a greater α and β. In the limit, the contract is *de facto* a fixed rent contract, as α equals 1 and β is the fixed rent.

to be provided by the tenant. However, while tenants are often better endowed with access to cheap labor and supervisory skills, landlords often have privileged access to market information and can better provide certain types of managerial skills. A share contract can be designed in which tenant and landlord each provide the inputs in which they are better endowed while both share the cost of the purchased inputs (Eswaran and Kotwal 1985). Unilateral provision of the non-tradable inputs by either tenant or landlord induces under-provision due to the Marshallian disincentive. However, the resulting inefficiency may be smaller than that created by market failure for these inputs under a wage or a fixed rent contract.

Sharecropping contracts may also be optimum when the tenant's effort is a source of degradation of the asset. If contracts are incomplete in the sense that they cannot be specified as contingent on land quality, because land quality is observable but not verifiable by third parties, the landlord must find an incentive to refrain a short-term tenant from abusing the asset. A sharecropping contract, by creating a Marshallian disincentive on effort, offers an instrument to achieve the goal of asset conservation. If the asset is at risk, the tenant's share will be raised, while his fixed payment will be lowered. Observations for the Philippines show that sharecropping contracts are preferred in contexts where the land can be easily degraded, while fixed rent contracts are chosen where land fertility is not an issue (Dubois 1999).

Whatever the advantages of sharecropping over a fixed rent contract, they have to be balanced with the negative effect on input use that results from the disincentive of sharing the product contribution of inputs which are not shared, the 'Marshallian inefficiency.' Empirical evidence suggests, however, that this inefficiency is on average not large: Shaban (1987) observes a 16% difference in yields between the owned and shared plots managed by a same household while Hayami and Otsuka (1993) calculate an average discrepancy in gross output per hectare of 17% across a large number of studies. In addition, there are many situations where the Marshallian inefficiency disappears or is mitigated by other incentives. It disappears when effort is contractible (Cheung 1969), when social norms reconcile individual and collective purposes, when safety-first considerations force poor tenants to work at maximum efficiency levels (Sadoulet, Fukui, and de Janvry 1994), when repeated tenancy contracts with gift exchange induce socially optimum levels of effort, and when interlinked transactions with the landlord induce the tenant to work hard in anticipation of deriving other benefits such as insurance (Sadoulet, de Janvry, and Fukui 1997). Sharecropping can also be used by landlords to compensate for excessive risk-taking behavior that limited liability on fixed rent payments implies when tenants have no wealth (Shetty 1988; Basu 1992). Finally, the efficiency of sharecropping can be raised by increasing the bargaining power of tenants through education, off-farm income opportunities, direct access to credit, and greater managerial abilities if it lowers the tenant's share toward fixed rent (Mookherjee 1997). We have also seen that relaxing the tenant's credit constraint allows the landlord to lower the tenant's optimum share toward fixed rent, decreasing the Marshallian inefficiency (see Laffont and Matoussi 1995). And, as the experience of Operation Barga in West Bengal demonstrates, increased security of tenancy can raise productivity (Banerjee and Ghatak 1996).

To summarize, in a context of market failures, land rental provides a means to access land and adjust farm size to household endowments in non-tradable assets. Under fixed rent contracts, landless households and small landowners who lack sufficient access to credit are unable to access land. Entry is more likely as their endowments of family labor, other non-tradable inputs such as draft animals, supervisory skills, and access to credit increase. Sharecropping contracts, by postponing rental payments to harvest time and sharing capital costs, reduce the liquidity needed to obtain access to land. By pooling risk and non-tradable inputs of tenants and landlords, sharecropping can also compensate for idiosyncratic market failures to which the poor are exposed, particularly for insurance and managerial skills. For these reasons, sharecropping allows the landless and small landowners to enter cultivation with smaller endowments of liquidity and non-tradable inputs and with higher levels of risk aversion, and to rent in larger plots of land than under fixed rent contracts.

Changing conditions of access to land for the landless

Sharecropping contracts have historically served as an entry into farming for the landless. A classical sequence is the 'agricultural ladder' in which a landless individual progresses from agricultural worker, to sharecropper, fixed rent tenant, and ultimately landowner. Upward progress on this ladder follows the accumulation of agricultural knowledge and capital (Binswanger, Deininger, and Feder 1995). Reid (1973) argues that tenancy played an important role for the vertical mobility of tenants after the abolition of slavery.[16]

However, the role of sharecropping as an entry device for the rural poor toward eventual land ownership seems to have declined over time, making entry into the agricultural ladder more difficult. In traditional agriculture, becoming a sharecropper was only possible for those privileged individuals who had control over non-tradable inputs not directly accessible by the landlord.[17] Because of these requirements, sharecroppers were typically sons of farmers or former permanent workers who had participated in the full agricultural cycle. Entry into sharecropping was, by contrast, difficult for landless seasonal workers since they only had partial knowledge of the farming cycle (Spillman 1919).

With increasing capital-intensity in agriculture, landlords look for tenants who can help share capital costs. We have seen that there are two reasons for this. One is that capital costs must be shared with the landlord to avoid a Marshallian disincentive on capital, and this becomes all the more important when capital costs are higher.

[16] Others have argued the opposite because black sharecroppers could not buy land due to racial discrimination, confining them to the permanent status of sharecroppers or fixed rent tenants (Sutch and Ransom 1973).

[17] These inputs include: (1) cheap non-tradable labor: plentiful family labor including women and children (Horowitz 1996), access to low cost community members (Lehmann 1986), or to illegal workers (illegal Mexican immigrants in California recruited by legal Mexican sharecroppers) (Wells 1996); (2) supervisory ability and some management experience; and (3) non-tradable farm capital such as bullocks.

The other is that greater access to liquidity allows to substitute capital for labor in production and to reduce the efficiency cost of the Marshallian disincentive on labor. Sharma and Drèze (1996) thus observe that the practice of cost sharing increases with the rising capital intensity of agriculture in Palanpur, India. For example, harvesting remains completely un-mechanized, and the costs of harvesting are borne solely by the tenant. Threshing, on the other hand, has become mechanized over time, and the costs are divided equally between the tenant and landlord.

As tenants need access to capital, for which they generally need to own land as collateral, there is a convergence in characteristics between landlord and tenant. This leads to a process of 'assortative matching' between landlord and tenant: they must have similar land endowments to have the same borrowing capacity. Landed tenants are also more able to contribute bullocks and farm capital. Tenancy status loses its role as an important factor in social stratification (Sharma and Drèze 1996). However, assortative matching implies increased social differentiation since the best landlords tend to choose to associate with the best tenants, and the landless who are comparatively disadvantaged are selected out of tenancy.

Finally, access to land for the landless through sharecropping becomes more difficult with aging of the farm population. As the absolute size of the agricultural population declines in the process of agricultural transformation (Dovring 1964), more landlords are old and absentee. These non-operating owners prefer fixed rent contracts to sharecropping since they cannot monitor their tenants. And, even if they choose to offer sharecropping contracts, non-operating landlords tend not to provide management services, implying that the tenants must have management experience. By raising the requirements on potential tenants, entry into sharecropping is further limited for the rural poor.

Empirical evidence on access to land via tenancy

Evidence from agricultural census data

A comparison of developed and developing countries indicates very different patterns of tenancy in the two groups (Figure 8.5). In the more developed countries, the graphs show that the percentage of farms with rented-in land (either by pure tenants or owner-tenants) increases with farm size, reaching very high percentages: 75% in the US and Belgium, 47% in Spain, and 35% in Italy. Hence, large farms rely on rentals more frequently than small farms to increase the size of their operated areas. In developing countries, the pattern is the exact opposite. In Brazil and the Philippines, small farmers use rentals more frequently (reaching 60% in Brazil and 51% in the Philippines) to increase the size of their operated areas. In Pakistan and Bangladesh, rentals are most frequent in intermediate size (5-hectare) farms. This supports the hypothesis that in regions with capital- and cash-intensive agriculture, land is leased in by large farmers while rentals in areas with traditional agriculture go to small farmers to help landlords access cheap labor through land rental contracts.

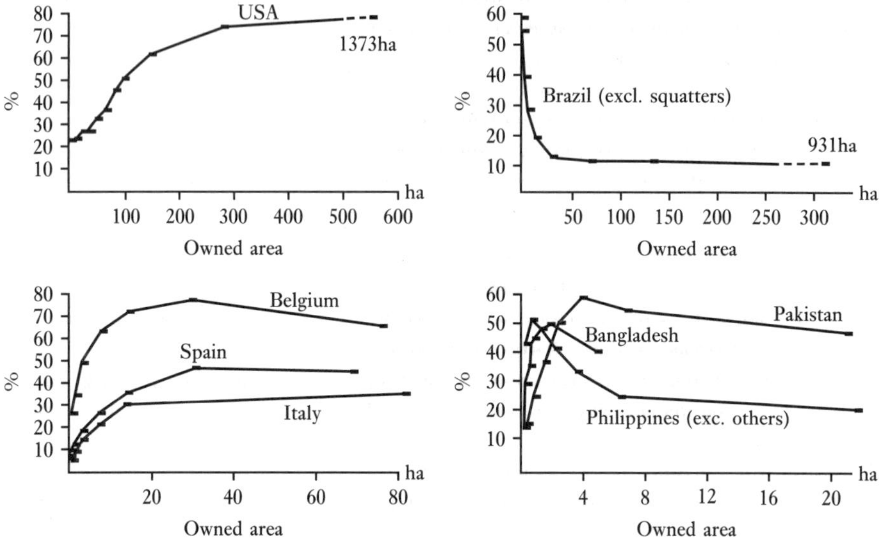

Figure 8.5. *Percentage of renters by farm size in ownership, 1980*

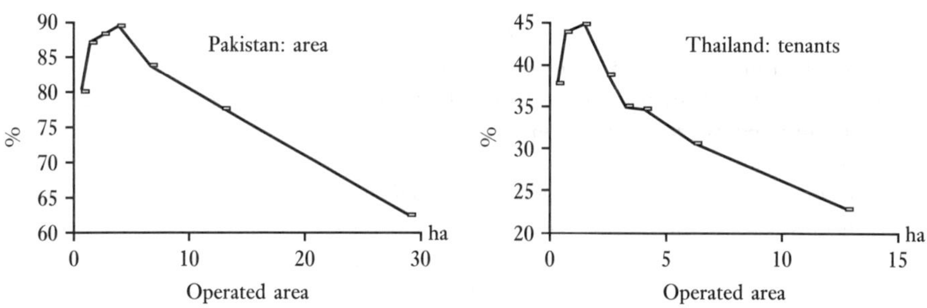

Figure 8.6. *Percentage of leased-in area in Pakistan and of leased-in farms in Thailand under share tenancy, 1980*

Among rental contracts, sharecropping is the dominant type in developing countries, and particularly on small farms (Figure 8.6). In Pakistan, on 4-hectare (ha) farms, 90% of the leased-in area is on a share basis. In Thailand, on 2-hectare farms, 45% of the leased-in farms are rented in on a share basis. Hence, fixed rent is a widely prevalent contract form in Thailand, but sharecropping nevertheless accounts for a very high percentage of land rented in. This supports the hypothesis that in areas typically characterized by widespread market failures for credit, insurance, and management skills, sharecropping tends to be the dominant contractual form since it can compensate for these idiosyncratic market failures.

Finally, it is interesting to analyze the evolution over time of tenancy in developing countries (Figure 8.7). We have established that access to land via rental should be particularly friendly to the rural poor. Yet, census data evidence a sharp decline in

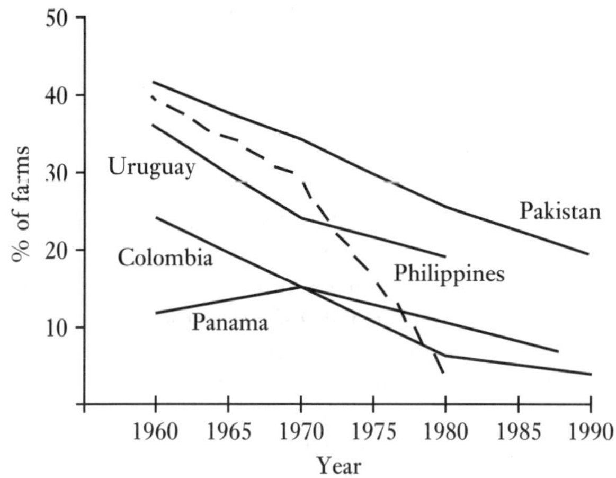

Figure 8.7. *Percentage of farms in pure tenancy, 1960–1990*

the percentage of farms under pure tenancy. This suggests that the role of tenancy to shift land toward cheap family labor may be on the decline, making it increasingly difficult for subsequent generations of landless to access land. It may also indicate that in many countries land rental markets have been atrophied by government intervention. If we are convinced of the importance of land rental for the rural poor, this should be cause for alarm and motivation for policy interventions to help this form of access to land regain importance.

Evidence from household survey data[18]

Evidence from Pakistan

The household survey data analyzed in this section were collected by the International Food Policy Research Institute in a series of twelve visits over a three-year period from the 1986 *kharif* (summer) season to the 1989 *rabi* (winter) season in rural Pakistan. There were six interviews during the first year and three in each of the other two years. The subset of data we use are from four districts: Attock and Faisalabad in Punjab province, Badin in Sind province, and Dir in the North-West Frontier province. We use a subsample of 694 households that derive at least a part of their income from agriculture or agriculture-related activities.[19]

Since many of the factors that potentially influence tenancy patterns (such as farming systems, degree of scarcity of factors, and capital intensity of agriculture) vary

[18] We are indebted to the International Food Policy Research Institute for the Pakistan data and to Jean-Louis Arcand for the Tunisia data used in this study.

[19] With the exception of Faisalabad, the districts chosen in the survey were among the poorest in the province. Villages in the districts were divided into three groups based on their access to local markets. Villages and households therein were selected randomly from these groups. A detailed description of the sample is provided in Alderman and Garcia (1993).

Table 8.1. *Classification of households by tenancy status, Pakistan*

	Landless			Landowning				
	Total number of households	Landless non-cultivators	Pure tenants[a]	Not leasing out		Leasing out		
				Pure owner-cultivators[b]	Owner-tenants[c]	Tenant-landlords[d]	Cultivating landlords[e]	Pure landlords[f]
Districts								
Faisalabad	129	30	17	44	21	1	7	9
Badin	234	16	96	45	32	11	24	10
Total sample	694	92	166	181	95	14	84	62
% of total	100	13	24	26	14	2	12	9

[a] Pure tenants are landless who rent in land.
[b] Pure owner-cultivators neither rent in nor rent out.
[c] Owner-tenants cultivate both their own land and rent in land.
[d] Tenant-landlords both rent in and rent out land.
[e] Cultivating landlords rent out part of their land.
[f] Pure landlords rent out all their land.

considerably across districts, we focus on a comparison of two districts: Faisalabad, which is the richest district in the sample, and Badin, which is the poorest. Faisalabad has good infrastructure and access to markets, and a diversified economy that derives a large share of its income from non-farm activities. Badin, on the other hand, is predominantly agricultural. The land ownership distribution is more equitable in Faisalabad than in Badin, with a smaller proportion of landless and large landowners in the former. The average land size owned in Faisalabad (about 5 acres) is much smaller than the average in Badin (about 9 acres).

The land rental market is very active in all districts (Table 8.1). A significant proportion of the households rent in (40%) or rent out (23%) land; very few households participate in the rental market as both landlords who rent out and tenants who rent in. Tenancy is important in terms of providing access to land for the landless. Over 64% of the landless are pure tenants who rent in land on a sharecropped or fixed rent basis, with relatively few households renting in on both share and fixed rent. Tenancy, by allowing households to adjust their operational holdings, is an institution of considerable importance for the landowning households. Nearly 60% of the landed households participate in the land rental market as landlords or tenants, with 25% renting in and 37% renting out. Owner-tenants are a large group (14%) who primarily rent in land on a sharecropped basis.

The patterns of participation differ both across and within land ownership classes. The tendency to lease out land is higher among large landowners, both in terms of the proportion of households that rent out land and the share of owned area that is rented out (Table 8.2). Interestingly, small and mid-sized landowners are also active in leasing out land, in some cases renting out as much as 19% of their owned land. In contrast, few large landowners rent in land, with an average share of operated land that is rented in at less than 5%. Within each land ownership class, there are some

Table 8.2. *Incidence of tenancy, by land ownership class, Pakistan*

Land ownership class (acres)	Proportion of households in the group (%)	Proportion of households renting in (%)	Proportion of households renting out (%)	Rented in area as a proportion of operated area (%)	Rented out area as a proportion of owned area (%)
Total sample					
0	37	64	0	100	0
0.1–3	22	39	20	34	18
3.1–5	7	31	21	22	19
5.1–10	14	20	31	11	24
10.1–20	9	8	60	6	41
above 20	10	12	71	4	47
Total	100	40	23	44	27

households that do not participate, either as landlords or as tenants. Importantly, 36% of the landless do not rent in any land and rely on non-farm income for the bulk of their earnings.

To explain differences in the patterns of participation across and within landownership classes, and within tenancy groups, we compare the characteristics of households in the different categories. The analysis is organized around a series of issues.

Who rents in and who rents out

There are some striking contrasts in the incidence and nature of tenancy in the two districts (Tables 8.3 and 8.4). First, even though rental markets are active in both districts, there is a lower incidence of tenancy in Faisalabad than in Badin. As seen in Table 8.1, in Faisalabad, the largest tenancy groups are pure owner-cultivators and landless non-cultivators (both non-participants in the rental market). In Badin, the largest tenancy group is the pure tenants, followed by approximately equal groups of pure owner-cultivators, landlords and owner-tenants. Second, relatively few (36%) of the landless in Faisalabad secure access to land. This is markedly different from Badin where over 85% of the landless rent in some land with a very small proportion of landless non-cultivators. Third, in Faisalabad, the landless that do cultivate are a small proportion of all operational area categories (except the smaller 0.1–3 acres class). In contrast, not only do a majority of the landless secure access to land in Badin, many become large cultivators. Fourth, approximately 50% of the landlords in Faisalabad rent out all their land. This is quite different from Badin where over 70% of the landlords rent out a part of their land, and they operate the remaining land.

The importance of labor in the production process in Badin, and that of capital and entrepreneurial resources in Faisalabad, may explain the preference for landed over landless tenants in the latter district. Two main reasons that determine the demand for different factors of production are the cropping pattern and the farming practices. First, the predominant crops grown in Badin are irrigated IRRI rice in the *kharif*

Table 8.3. *Incidence of tenancy, by land ownership class, Faisalabad and Badin*

Land ownership class (acres)	Proportion of households in the group (%)	Proportion of households renting in (%)	Proportion of households renting out (%)	Rented in area as a proportion of operated area (%)	Rented out area as a proportion of owned area (%)
Faisalabad					
0	36	36	0	100	0
0.1–3	19	56	0	41	0
3.1–5	13	18	12	12	12
5.1–10	21	15	33	8	27
10.1–20	5	0	29	0	29
above 20	5	17	67	2	37
Total	100	30	13	35	16
Badin					
0	48	86	0	100	0
0.1–3	10	71	4	52	4
3.1–5	5	64	18	46	18
5.1–10	11	36	20	23	16
10.1–20	12	11	46	8	29
above 20	15	21	71	8	43
Total	100	59	19	59	25

Table 8.4. *Transition matrices for land ownership and land operation class, Faisalabad and Badin*

	Land operation classes						
Faisalabad							
Land ownership classes (acres)	0	0.1–3	3.1–5	5.1–10	10.1–20	above 20	Total
0	30	6	2	6	3	0	47
0.1–3	0	13	2	5	4	1	25
3.1–5	2	0	12	2	1	0	17
5.1–10	4	2	2	17	1	1	27
10.1–20	2	0	0	0	5	0	7
above 20	1	0	0	0	2	3	6
Total	39	21	18	30	16	5	129
Badin							
Land ownership classes (acres)	0	0.1–3	3.1–5	5.1–10	10.1–20	above 20	Total
0	16	8	23	40	20	5	112
0.1–3	0	8	2	10	4	0	24
3.1–5	1	0	4	4	2	0	11
5.1–10	2	1	0	14	6	2	25
10.1–20	3	0	1	8	15	1	28
above 20	4	0	1	6	7	16	34
Total	26	17	31	82	54	24	234

Table 8.5. *Household characteristics, by tenancy status, Faisalabad and Badin*

District	Total	Pure tenants	Pure owner-cultivators	Owner-tenants	Landlords
Faisalabad					
Demographic characteristics					
Household size	8.1	9.1	7.5	9.1	7.3
Capital intensity					
Value of tools and machinery	5,375	2,424	6,721	10,016	4,999
Rs/acre spent on fertilizer	110	96	107	87	218
Rs/acre spent on pesticide	8.4	7.8	6.2	13.3	8.2
Badin					
Demographic characteristics					
Household size	8.4	7.9	9.0	8.4	9.9
Capital intensity					
Value of tools and machinery	1,453	366	739	1,739	4,798
Rs/acre spent on fertilizer	69	27	83	51	186
Rs/acre spent on pesticide	1.3	0.3	2.0	0.8	3.5

Note: value of tools and machinery includes flour mills and saw mills, threshers, cane crushers, ploughs, levellers, sprayers, fodder cutters, electric saws and drills, and other implements.

season and barley in the *rabi* season. One-third of the villages in Faisalabad have farming systems dominated by the cotton-wheat rotation, and sugarcane (a perennial crop) is important in some areas. Rice and barley cultivation is far more labor-intensive than both wheat and cotton. Second, households have adopted modern farming practices in Faisalabad, involving much higher use of non-labor inputs and managerial skills. As Table 8.5 shows, households in Faisalabad own more agricultural tools and machinery, and spend relatively more on modern inputs such as fertilizers and pesticides.

Further support for this hypothesis comes from the asset ownership of the different tenancy groups. The distance between landlords and pure tenants in terms of ownership of tools and machinery is much lower in Faisalabad than in Badin. Further, owner-tenants and pure owner-cultivators as a group own more of this fixed capital than the group of landlords. This is clearly not the case in Badin (Table 8.5).

Who rents to whom, and the emergence of assortative matching between landlord and tenant characteristics as the capital intensity of agriculture rises, can also be seen by comparing the Gini coefficients of land owned and land rented in Badin and Faisalabad. In Badin, the Gini of land owned is 0.74 while that of land operated is 0.47. Hence, when agriculture is labor intensive, the land rental market serves to redistribute land toward the landless, equalizing land distribution. In Faisalabad, by contrast, the Gini for land owned is 0.69 and that for land operated is 0.64, showing no significant decline. Hence, when agriculture is capital intensive, landlords rent to other landlords, seeking tenants who can match capital contributions and entrepreneurial skills. In this case, the land rental market does not equalize land distribution.

In summary, in Faisalabad we see a congruence in the preference for capital-endowed and entrepreneurial tenants, the predominance of owner-cultivators, relatively much greater prevalence of fixed rent contracts, and a lower incidence of tenancy than in Badin. Further, a significantly smaller share of the landless lease land in Faisalabad than in Badin. Jointly, these factors lend support to the hypothesis that with increasing capital intensity in agriculture, the role of tenancy in shifting land towards cheap family labor may be on the decline.

Differential landlord participation across contracts

Differences in access to land for the landless may also be explained by qualitative differences in landowners between the two districts. In Badin, the average age of the household head for landlords and tenants is forty-five years and forty-one years, respectively. In contrast, in Faisalabad both landlords and tenants tend to be older (fifty years and fifty-two years, respectively). In this district, 47% of the pure tenancy contracts are either fixed rent or mixed (both fixed and share), while 98% of the pure tenancy contracts in Badin are share contracts. In 61% of the sharecropping cases, managerial decisions (in particular, the decision on which crops to plant) are made by the landlord in Badin. Landlords participate significantly less in Faisalabad, with only 6% making the planting decision. These characteristics indicate that landlords in Faisalabad are older, there is lower farm participation (higher absenteeism), and many landlords prefer to rent out on fixed rather than share rent in the advanced district. These factors raise the requirements of tenants who need to be able to bear the costs of cultivation, bear all the risk in farming and have entrepreneurial or management skills. Jointly, these requirements make it more difficult for the landless to access land.

Short-term flexibility and long-term mobility

The panel data were collected over twelve rounds in a period of three years. However, because recall information was also obtained, movements across tenancy categories are available over eight seasons and four years. We can consequently analyze how each household moved across tenancy categories over a four-year interval to disentangle flexibility from mobility and assess which households were best able to use the land market for each of these two purposes.

Over this period of time, 35% of the households changed tenancy status at least once. This proportion is much greater in Faisalabad (44%) than in Badin (35%). During the period, 16% of the households changed tenancy status at least twice (24% in Faisalabad and 14% in Badin). Hence, flexibility in accessing land and potential mobility are quite high, and greater in more advanced Faisalabad.

Table 8.6 shows the percentage of households in each tenancy group that remained within the same status (i.e., had only one tenancy spell) over the entire four-year period. There are marked differences in the degree of mobility in the groups. There is much greater instability (flexibility or mobility) among the group of owner-cultivators with only 44% remaining stable in this tenancy category through the period. This

Table 8.6. *Stability across tenancy categories, four-year period*

Tenancy category	All regions		Faisalabad		Badin	
	Percentage distribution of households in first round	Percentage who remained stable	Percentage distribution of households in first round	Percentage who remained stable	Percentage distribution of households in first round	Percentage who remained stable
Landless	13	70	23	66	6	33
Pure tenants	24	79	14	61	42	83
Owner-cultivators	26	44	34	39	19	36
Owner-tenants	14	64	16	71	14	53
Landlords[a]	23	72	13	59	19	78
All categories	100	65	100	56	100	65

[a] Landlords includes both cultivating landlords and pure landlords.

Table 8.7. *Transitions among tenancy status for households with two tenancy spells*

Initial tenancy status	Terminal tenancy status			
	Landless	Pure tenant	Ownership	Total
Landless	—	13	3	16
Pure tenant	13	—	13	26
Ownership[a]	2	2	86	90

[a] Ownership includes owner-cultivators, owner-tenants, and landlords; 86 is the number of observed transitions among these categories.

observation is true for both districts (39% in Faisalabad and 36% in Badin). By contrast, greatest stability is found among pure tenants with 79% still in that category four years later. Stability of pure tenants is particularly striking in Badin with 83% remaining in this group that comprises a substantial 42% of all households in the district.

If we analyze patterns of movements for households who had two tenancy spells (i.e., changed tenancy category once over the period analyzed), we can characterize the origins and destination of changes (Table 8.7). These changes do not allow a distinction between movements that correspond to long-term mobility versus short-term flexibility since the spells are incomplete (i.e., unbounded).

Among pure tenants who change tenancy status, there is an equal 50% chance of moving up to the ownership category (most move to be an owner-tenant) and a 50% chance of returning to the landless status. In contrast, for households who own land (owners and landlords), most of the movements are restricted to renting land in and out within that category, with very little likelihood of falling back to the status of pure tenants or landless. Hence, there is some evidence of an agricultural ladder, even over such a short period of time. We should recall, however, that 79% of pure tenants do

Table 8.8. *Flexibility and mobility over three and more tenancy spells (based on 145 households)*

Initial tenancy status	Frequency distribution initial status (%)	% of households who returned to initial status (flexibility)	Intermediate status (% of initial status)					
			Landless	Pure tenants	Owner-cultivators	Owner-tenants	Landlords	Total
Landless	9	92	—	75	8	8	8	100
Pure tenants	8	58	100	—	0	0	0	100
Owner-cultivators	17	63	0	0	—	80	20	100
Owner-tenants	41	85	2	0	39	—	59	100
Landlords[a]	25	89	0	0	6	94	—	100
All categories	100	81	7	8	20	37	29	100

[a] Landlords includes both cultivating landlords and pure landlords.

not change tenancy status (see Table 8.6). Hence, a 50% chance of moving toward land ownership among those households that change status is only a 10% chance for all households within the pure tenant group. Upward mobility is thus fairly restricted, but again the period analyzed is quite short.

If we analyze transitions among households that had three or more tenancy spells during the period (i.e., changed tenancy status at least twice), as a first step, we can separate flexibility from mobility by using households who returned to the same tenancy category two moves apart to characterize flexibility. The remaining households that did not return to the same category may be engaged in transitions that lead to a longer-term process of mobility. However, since some of these households may return to the initial status at a later stage, this approach likely overestimates the extent of mobility during the period.

Table 8.8 shows that 81% of the households with three or more spells returned to their original tenancy status after one spell in an intermediate status. This suggests that the land market is used to provide considerable short-term flexibility to access land and adjust operational farm size. Short-term flexibility is greatest for the landless, followed by landlords, and owner-tenants. For the landless, 75% of those who moved flexibly into the land market got in and out of pure tenancy. For the landlords, 94% temporarily stopped renting out land before returning to this status. Owner-tenants both temporarily stopped renting in (80%) and rented out some of their land (20%). It is among pure tenants that there is more mobility with 42% using the land market without returning to their initial tenancy status. Owner-tenants are also mobile, with 37% moving away from tenancy to pure owner-cultivator or landlord status.

The average duration of an intermediate spell for all households with three or more spells was fairly short, at 1.8 seasons. It was shortest for the landless, lasting only 1.1 seasons. Hence, there is very rapid movement out of landlessness for those who used the land rental market. The middle spell was longest for landlords who rent out for 2.2 seasons before moving to a different status or returning to their previous status. For landlords, the land rental market hence also shows fluidity in allowing them to

Table 8.9. *Characteristics of landless households, by land operation class, Badin*

	Total	Land operation class			
		0	0.1–5	5.1–10	above 10
Number of households	112	16	31	40	25
Demographic characteristics					
Household size	7.5	5.6	7	7.4	9.7
Number of adult males	2.1	1.4	1.8	2.2	2.9
Number of adult females	1.9	1.5	2	1.8	2.4
Average education in household	1.4	1.7	1.3	1.4	1.2
Age of household head	40.6	38.5	36.6	42.3	44.1
Asset positions					
Value of tools and machinery (Rs)	349	172	323	261	584
Per capita income	17,782	14,311	14,842	16,794	24,230

rent out but return to owner-operation or owner-tenancy over a relatively short period of time.

We thus conclude with the observation that the land rental market shows a great deal of activity and allows considerable flexibility in changing tenancy status. It is used by the landless to move in and out of land rental (mainly sharecropping) as well as by the landed to rent land in and out. There is also evidence of some upward mobility, with a fraction of the landless moving into land ownership with no return to landlessness, supporting the notion that the land rental market can indeed provide an intermediate step toward land ownership.

Who among the landless are excluded

To examine the diversity in the degree of access obtained by the class of landless households in Badin, Table 8.9 compares their characteristics by land operation class. Households that are unable to secure access to land or are able to rent in small amounts of land have smaller labor endowments (particularly in terms of the number of adult males) and younger household heads. Interestingly, households that rent between 5 and 10 acres of land do not have larger capital endowments than small operators. Jointly, these patterns once again suggest that the primary motive of leasing out land in Badin is to obtain labor for cultivation. As a result, those households that have fewer able, working males are unable to enter the agricultural ladder.[20]

Evidence from Tunisia

This analysis is based on two surveys of agricultural households in a Tunisian village conducted in 1986 by Laffont and Matoussi (see Laffont and Matoussi 1995) and in

[20] A similar analysis for Faisalabad is not possible due to the small number of pure tenants.

1993 by Arcand and Ethier (see Arcand and Ethier 1995; Ai, Arcand, and Ethier 1997). Pooling the two years gives 191 households, cultivating 554 plots. The village is situated in a relatively rich area of intensive agriculture, with irrigation on 88% of the plots. High value crops dominate, with 42.5% of the plots in onions, vegetables, tomatoes, and melons, 24.6% in cereals, 10.5% in fodder, 9.6% in olive and fruit trees, and 8.5% in potatoes. 26.2% of the plots are in tenancy (10.5% in sharecropping and 15.7% in fixed rent contracts), occupying 32.6% of the area (15.1% in sharecropping and 17.5% in fixed rent).

We only report here information on the performance of the land rental market that is not already provided by analysis of the Pakistan data. Two features are of interest to characterize the role of tenancy in getting access to land. One is the role of the landlords in providing non-tradable services to their tenants. The other is the assortative matching between landlord and tenant characteristics.

Differential landlord participation across landless and landed tenants

As expected, landlords who rent out under fixed rent contracts neither supervise nor participate in the production process on their tenant's farm. 78% of them never visit their tenants, and another 10% visit only once or twice a season. In contrast, 44% of the landlords visit their sharecroppers at least twice a week.

While there is no difference in the frequency of visits to landless and landed tenants, there are significant differences in landlord involvement in production between these two categories of tenants. Landlords of landed tenants do not participate in production decisions, but in the case of landless tenants, 33% of them directly take some responsibility for plowing, transportation, or even are reported to have the final say regarding management of the plot. Landlords also contribute a lower share of the labor costs but a higher share of all the other costs (notably irrigation, plowing, and transportation) with landless tenants compared to landed tenants.

This contrast suggests that the nature of sharecropping is markedly different in the cases of landless and landed tenants. For contracts with the landless, sharecropping provides the landlord with a secure access to the tenant's family labor while the tenant gains access to the capital and management capability of the landlords. Share contracts with landed tenants, on the other hand, have much less participation by the landlord in terms of both managerial input and cost sharing. The idiosyncratic nature of sharecropping contracts is thus an important facilitator for the landless in accessing land.

Assortative matching between landlords and tenants

A particular feature of the Tunisian surveys is the identification of the landlord of each rented-in parcel, which allows a comparison of landlord and tenant characteristics. The hypothesis advanced earlier is that in an area which relies on labor-intensive traditional farming techniques, land is rented in by large households that are labor-rich but possibly with poor capital endowments. There is thus a complementarity between landlords' and tenants' asset endowments. However, as agriculture intensifies in its use of expensive, non-labor inputs, tenants need to be better off in terms of access to liquidity and capital endowments. One consequently expects a positive correlation

Table 8.10. *Matching of landlords and tenants, Tunisia (correlation between landlord and tenant characteristics)*

	All crops	Capital intensity of crops	
		Low	High
Household characteristics			
Age of household head	−0.52	−0.68	−0.20
Asset position			
Value of machinery	0.24	0.36	0.18
Value of livestock	0.07	−0.10	0.30
Land ownership	0.29	−0.02	0.40
Initial wealth	0.47	0.23	0.66

between the asset endowments of landlords and tenants in this village of cash-demanding, modern agriculture. As seen in Table 8.10, we indeed find a positive correlation between the endowment position of the landlords and tenants: 0.24 for machinery, 0.29 for land asset, 0.47 for wealth, and 0.44 for non-agricultural income. However, there is interestingly a negative correlation between their ages, indicating that older farmers tend to rent out their land to younger tenants.

Even though the survey is done in a region of intensive agriculture, we can separate more cash-demanding crops (potatoes, garden vegetables, melons, and other fruits and vegetables) from less cash-intensive crops (cereals, fodder, onions, tomatoes, beet roots, and fruit trees). Table 8.10 shows that the correlation between assets of landlords and tenants is substantially higher for the more intensive crops, except for machinery that is used more in field crops. These patterns support the hypothesis of assortative matching in the asset position of landlords and tenants and suggest that poor landless tenants will face increasing difficulties in accessing land via tenancy as agriculture becomes more capital-intensive, unless they can find sufficient access to credit and agricultural capital on their own account.

Regulating tenancy contracts

There has been a long history of government interventions in land rental markets. Interventions have been motivated by the desire to improve tenants' security by protecting them from arbitrary evictions and to reduce the monopoly power of rich landlords over poor tenants by controlling the level of rents. In many countries, sharecropping has simply been denounced as exploitative or archaic and banned outright. Interventions have sometimes been successful in redistributing income in favor of tenants, like in the Philippines, Kerala, and West Bengal (Operation Barga). However, interventions have generally created nefarious effects on most tenants. Landlords have responded by evicting tenants, shifting to second-best contracts, increasing owner-cultivation, and adopting labor extensive practices (such as livestock) and labor-saving innovations. The remaining tenants have suffered from neglect of investment by landlords and dismantling of the accompanying contractual arrangements that are extremely important to help tenants overcome market failures that affect them but not landlords. Short-term gains for the beneficiaries have thus generally evolved into long-term losses. Alternatively, landlords go around legal restrictions by confining sharecropping to kin and close friends, forcing them to choose from a restricted pool of candidates. These restrictions reduce the supply of tenancy contracts for other households, particularly the next generation of potential tenants. As a consequence, government interventions in tenancy markets have systematically been denounced by economists as inefficient and inequitable (Binswanger, Deininger, and Feder 1995). Since contracts are largely bilateral arrangements, a hands-off attitude by government has been the implied alternative.

While the record of government intervention in rental markets on balance supports this position, there are opportunities for interventions that hold promise to achieve greater efficiency and sustainable redistributive gains in favor of tenants. If rental markets have important roles to play in permitting access to land for the landless and smallholders, and if tenancy contracts are sources of efficiency gains in the second-best context where they occur, there exists a set of government interventions that can help enhance the roles fulfilled by tenancy contracts. Some desirable interventions are the following:

Titling

Well-defined property rights, clear ownership titles, and reliable conflict resolution mechanisms reduce the fears of landowners that their land will be taken from them if they rent out. Otherwise, landlords will refrain from renting out as they fear not being able to recuperate their land or they will shift to short-term contracts that are sub-optimal. Olson-Lanjouw and Levy (1997) thus observe that female-only households with uncertain (urban) property rights face greater difficulty in leasing land since they are less able to claim their property back from tenants compared to households with adult males. Hence, there are bilateral gains from clear and secure titles. Regularizing titles and enforcing property rights are hence fundamental to unleash efficient land rental markets. Assessing the benefits of titling programs should thus not be confined to their (often disappointing) impact on access to credit and capital formation (see Feder *et al.* 1988), but also on activating land rental markets.

The process of titling, like the individualization of common property resources (see Ostrom, Platteau and Baland, and Arnold in this volume), can, however, lead to expropriation of the weaker groups. Binswanger, Deininger, and Feder (1995) thus caution that titling can, in practice, lead to greater concentration of land and to the dispossession of groups that have enjoyed land rights under the traditional system. Wealthier and better-connected individuals can use their information and lobbying advantages to claim land over less informed and less well-connected individuals. Therefore, titling should be systematic rather than on individual demand, accompanied by broad publicity campaigns, and it should call upon participation of the community to arbitrate conflicts, as was done for example for the titling of *ejido* lands in Mexico under the PROCEDE program.

Enabling legislation to negotiate and enforce well-defined contracts

Agriculture is by nature a long-term activity. Land improvements take time to achieve and damages to the land often have long-lasting effects. Hence, the commodity that is exchanged is not just land, but land in certain conditions for a certain time. A well-defined tenancy contract should thus specify the length of the lease, and include contingent clauses in case of premature contract termination and provisions for compensation for the residual value of improvements and/or damages done to the asset. This is not the same as saying that tenancy needs to be secure, but only that, whatever the agreed upon terms of the lease, it can be enforced so that the tenant does not feel threatened about being expelled at any time and has incentives to invest in maintaining and improving the quality of the land, while the landlord does not fear losing his property rights to long-term tenants or seeing the quality of his land being abused by the tenant.

Increasing the bargaining power of tenants in sharecropping contracts and increasing their ability to shift to fixed rent contracts

Increasing the bargaining power of tenants can lead to more equitable contractual arrangements and may also increase efficiency (Banerjee and Ghatak 1996). There are several policy instruments that can be used for this purpose: (1) provide a legal structure for registering and enforcing contracts; (2) increase the fall-back option of tenants by improving their access to credit, risk coping instruments, education, and off-farm employment opportunities; and (3) remove policy distortions and overvalued exchange rates that favor capital-intensive agriculture and assortative matching with wealthier tenants.

Organize rural development programs specifically tailored to the needs of tenants

Operation Barga (OB) in West Bengal gives a good example of the conditions under which intervention in the land rental market can create both efficiency and welfare gains (U. Saha and M. Saha, this volume). OB succeeded in registering 1.5 million sharecroppers with minimal expropriations due to strong political commitment by the Left Front government that assumed power in 1977, active support of local governments, and effective grassroots participation to supervise the process. The program offered long-term security of tenure to tenants by giving them hereditary rights. Tenants' share was raised to 75% of output, which induced landlords to reduce their participation in the provision of purchased inputs and non-tradable services. To compensate for this loss, which exposes tenants to market failures that were previously compensated through contractual arrangements with landlords, the government launched a major rural development initiative to provide tenants with direct access to credit, technical assistance, lower transaction costs in accessing markets, and public investments in irrigation and infrastructure. Banerjee and Ghatak (1996) observed that the tenancy reforms were sources of major gains in crop productivity, achieving more gains than investments in irrigation. While the conditions that insured the success of OB are clearly very demanding and difficult to replicate, they also indicate that large-scale interventions in tenancy markets are not necessarily doomed to failure.

Concluding remarks

Land rental markets provide a means to access land, flexibly adjust farm size, and initiate upward mobility toward eventual land ownership by scaling up the agricultural ladder. Land rental markets are likely to be more friendly to the poor than land sales markets in helping them access land. Compared to land purchases, land rentals do not suffer from the impact of overpricing of land in large farms for smallholders, do not require large cash down payments and access to long-term credit, and do not entail high transaction costs in titling and in subdividing land to accommodate short-term adjustments in operated farm size. This role of land rentals in allowing access to land for the landless and flexible adjustments in the operational farm size for the landed is evident in both Pakistan and Tunisia. The empirical evidence, however, points to distinctly different patterns of access to land in the regions considered. In Pakistan's poor district, Badin, where farming practices are still traditional and largely unmechanized, land is primarily rented in by the landless on a share basis. In contrast, Faisalabad has made the transition to capital-intensive, modern agriculture, leading to an increasing prevalence of fixed rent contracts and a far lower incidence of share tenancy, particularly among the landless. At a more aggregate level as well, census data show that there is a reversal from land being rented in by small farmers in LDCs to land being rented in by large farmers in MDCs.

Besides providing access to land, tenancy contracts can also help households make more efficient use of land by mitigating market failures. Under sharecropping, the terms of the contract can be designed to compensate for idiosyncratic market failures to which poor tenants are exposed, particularly for credit, insurance, and managerial skills. In Tunisia, for instance, landlords participate more in management and cost sharing with the landless than landed tenants. This should explain why sharecropping is widely prevalent in LDCs, and particularly on smaller farms.

We have seen that capital-intensification of agriculture reduces the potential of the land rental markets in providing access to land for the poor and the landless. The logic of cash-demanding and capital-intensive agriculture is such that it creates incentives for landlords to rent in land to capture economies of scale or to rent land out to tenants that have a comparative advantage in access to credit and other farm assets. These requirements are naturally harder for the landless to meet and, as a result, lead to assortative matching on capital endowments. In Tunisia, assortative matching increases with more capital-intensive crops. In Pakistan, there is a lower difference in the ownership of tools and machinery between tenant and landlord in Faisalabad compared to Badin.

Access to land for the poor via share tenancy also worsens with increasing aging and absenteeism (urbanization) of the landlord class. Older and absentee landlords in Faisalabad rent out land on fixed rent, and participate less in management and capital contributions. Thus, tenants increasingly must have the capacity to bear higher risks, to control the cash required for rent and input payments, and to provide the necessary managerial skills themselves.

In conclusion, the evidence suggests that as agriculture becomes more capital intensive and the landlord class older and more urbanized, use of land rental markets for gaining access to land, adjusting farm sizes, and providing upward mobility toward eventual land ownership becomes more difficult for the poor. To maintain and promote land rental markets that are effective for poverty reduction, policy interventions are needed that increase the direct access to capital and the management abilities of landless and small land owners, increase security of continuous access to land, and offer compensations for the residual value of investments in the case of dismissal.

REFERENCES

Ai, Chunrong, Jean-Louis Arcand, and Francois Ethier. 1997. 'De l'efficacité allocative des contrats agricoles: Cheung avait-il raison?' *Revue d'Économie du Développement* 0(2): 103–27.

Alderman, Harold and Marito Garcia. 1993. 'Poverty, Household Food Security, and Nutrition in Rural Pakistan.' Research Report 96, International Food Policy Research Institute, Washington DC.

Arcand, Jean-Louis and Francois Ethier. 1995. 'Description of the Variables.' Working paper, Project Paradi, University of Montreal, Montreal, Quebec.

Banerjee, Abhijit V. and Maitreesh Ghatak. 1996. 'Empowerment and Efficiency: The Economics of Tenancy Reform.' Working paper, Department of Economics, Massachusetts Institute of Technology (MIT), Cambridge, MA.

Basu, Kaushik. 1992. 'Limited Liability and the Existence of Share Tenancy.' *Journal of Development Economics* 38(1): 203–20.

Bell, Clive. 1989. 'A Comparison of Principal-Agent and Bargaining Solutions: The Case of Tenancy Contracts.' In *The Economic Theory of Agrarian Institutions* (Chapter 4), Pranab Bardhan (ed.). Oxford: Clarendon Press.

Binswanger, Hans and Mark Rosenzweig. 1986. 'Behavioral and Material Determinants of Production Relations in Agriculture.' *Journal of Development Studies* 22(3): 503–39.

Binswanger, Hans, Klaus Deininger, and Gershon Feder. 1995. 'Power, Distortions, Revolt, and Reform in Agricultural Land Relations.' In *Handbook of Development Economics*, Vol. 3B, J. Behrman and T.N. Srinivasan (eds.). Amsterdam: North-Holland.

Boadu, Fred. 1992. 'The Efficiency of Share Contracts in Ghana's Cocoa Industry.' *Journal of Development Studies* 29(1): 108–20.

Bouquet, Emmanuelle. 1996. 'La Tierra Ejidal en México: Mercancia u Objeto Social?' *Estudios Agrarios* 5: 79–104.

Carter, Michael and Fred Zimmerman. 1998. 'The Dynamic Costs and Persistence of Inequality in an Agrarian Economy.' Agricultural Economics Staff Paper, The University of Wisconsin, Madison, WI.

Cheung, Steven. 1969. *The Theory of Share Tenancy*. Chicago, IL: University of Chicago Press.

Dorner, Peter. 1992. *Latin American Land Reforms in Theory and Practice: A Retrospective Analysis*. Madison, WI: The University of Wisconsin Press.

Dovring, Folke. 1964. 'The Share of Agriculture in a Growing Population.' In *Agriculture in Economic Development*, K. Eicher and L. Witt (eds.). New York: McGraw-Hill.

Dubois, Pierre. 1999. 'Contrats Agricoles, Risque et Marchés Incomplets.' Doctoral dissertation in economics, Ecole des Hautes Etudes en Sciences Sociales, Paris.

Eswaran, Mukesh and Ashok Kotwal. 1985. 'A Theory of Contractual Structure in Agriculture.' *American Economic Review* 75(3): 352–67.

—— 1986. 'Access to Capital and Agrarian Production Organization.' *Economic Journal* 96(382): 482–98.

Feder, Gershon. 1985. 'The Relation Between Farm Size and Farm Productivity: The Role of Family Labor, Supervision and Credit Constraints.' *Journal of Development Economics* 18(2/3): 297–313.

Feder, Gershon, Tongroj Onchan, Yongyuth Chalamwong, and Chira Hongladarom. 1988. *Land Policies and Farm Productivity in Thailand.* Baltimore, MD: The Johns Hopkins University Press.

Hallagan, William. 1978. 'Self-selection by Contractual Choice and the Theory of Sharecropping.' *Bell Journal of Economics* 9(2): 344–54.

Hayami, Yujiro and Keijiro Otsuka. 1993. *The Economics of Contract Choice.* Oxford: Clarendon Press.

Horowitz, Andrew W. 1996. 'Wage-Homestead Tenancies: Technological Dualism and Tenant Household Size.' *Land Economics* 72(3): 370–80.

Kevane, Michael. 1996. 'Agrarian Structure and Agrarian Practice: Typology and Application to Western Sudan.' *American Journal of Agricultural Economics* 78(1): 236–45.

Laffont, Jean-Jacques and Mohamed S. Matoussi. 1995. 'Moral Hazard, Financial Constraints, and Sharecropping in El Oulja.' *Review of Economic Studies* 62(3): 381–99.

Lehmann, David. 1986. 'Sharecropping and the Capitalist Transition in Agriculture: Some Evidence from the Highlands of Ecuador.' *Journal of Development Economics* 23(2): 333–54.

Mookherjee, Dilip. 1997. 'Informational Rents and Property Rights in Land.' In *Property Rights, Incentives, and Welfare*, J. Roemer (ed.). London: Macmillan Press.

Olson-Lanjouw, Jean. 1998. 'Information and the Operation of Markets: Test Based on a General Equilibrium Model of Land Leasing in India.' Working paper, Department of Economics, Yale University, New Haven, CT.

Olson-Lanjouw, Jean and Philip Levy. 1997. 'Untitled: A Study of Formal and Informal Property Rights in Urban Ecuador.' Working paper, Department of Economics, Yale University, New Haven, CT.

Otsuka, Keijiro and Yujiro Hayami. 1988. 'Theories of Share Tenancy: A Critical Survey.' *Economic Development and Cultural Change* 37(1): 31–68.

Otsuka, Keijiro, Hiroyuki Chuma, and Yujiro Hayami. 1992. 'Land and Labor Contracts in Agrarian Economies: Theories and Facts.' *Journal of Economic Literature* 30: 1965–2018.

Reid, Joseph. 1973. 'Sharecropping as an Understandable Market Response: The Post-Bellum South.' *Journal of Economic History* 33(1): 106–30.

—— 1977. 'The Theory of Share Tenancy Revisited—Again.' *Journal of Political Economy* 85(2): 403–8.

Robertson, A.F. 1987. *The Dynamics of Productive Relationships—African Share Contracts in Comparative Perspective.* Cambridge: Cambridge University Press.

Sadoulet, Elisabeth, Alain de Janvry, and Seiichi Fukui. 1997. 'The Meaning of Kinship in Sharecropping Contracts.' *American Journal of Agricultural Economics* 79(2): 394–406.

Sadoulet, Elisabeth, Seiichi Fukui, and Alain de Janvry. 1994. 'Efficient Share Tenancy Contracts Under Risk: The Case of Three Rice-Growing Villages in Thailand.' *Journal of Development Economics* 45(2): 225–43.

Sarap, Kailas. 1998. 'On the Operation of the Land Market in Backward Agriculture: Evidence from a Village in Orissa, Eastern India.' *The Journal of Peasant Studies* 25(2): 102–30.
Schultz, Theodore. 1940. 'Capital Rationing, Uncertainty, and Farm-Tenancy Reform.' *Journal of Political Economy* 48(3): 309–24.
Shaban, Radwan A. 1987. 'Testing between Competing Models of Sharecropping.' *Journal of Political Economy* 95(5): 893–920.
Shand, Richard T. and K.P. Kalirajan. 1991. 'Agricultural Modernization and the Distribution of Benefits: Some Evidence from Malaysia.' *Journal of Development Studies* 27(2): 277–92.
Sharma, Naresh and Jean Drèze. 1996. 'Sharecropping in a North Indian Village.' *Journal of Development Studies* 33(1): 1–39.
Shetty, Sudhir. 1988. 'Limited Liability, Wealth Differences and Tenancy Contracts in Agrarian Economies.' *Journal of Development Economics* 29(1): 1–22.
Skoufias, Emmanuel. 1995. 'Household Resources, Transactions Costs, and Adjustment Through Land Tenancy.' *Land Economics* 71(1): 42–56.
Spillman, W.J. 1919. 'The Agricultural Ladder.' *American Economic Review* 9(1): 170–79.
Stiglitz, Joseph. 1974. 'Incentives and Risk Sharing in Sharecropping.' *Review of Economic Studies* 41(2): 219–55.
Sutch, Richard and Roger Ransom. 1973. 'The Ex-Slave in the Post-Bellum South: A Study of the Economic Impact of Racism in a Market Environment.' *Journal of Economic History* 33(1): 131–48.
Warriner, Doreen. 1969. *Land Reform in Principle and Practice*. Oxford: Clarendon Press.
Wells, Miriam J. 1996. *Strawberry Fields: Politics, Class, and Work in California Agriculture*. Ithaca, NY: Cornell University Press.

9

Case Study. Regulating the Sharecropping System: Operation Barga

UDAY SHANKAR SAHA AND MANDIRA SAHA

Introduction

In 1978, the West Bengal government initiated 'Operation Barga' (OB), a comprehensive program designed to reform the sharecropping system that was widespread throughout the state. In terms of area, West Bengal is one of the smaller states in India but it is the most populous state with 68 million people; 72% live in rural areas on 6.3 million fragmented landholdings. According to the 1991 census, the average land holding size is only 0.9 hectares (ha). By 1978, sharecropping was widespread in the region, characterizing 20–25% of all farms (Government of West Bengal (GOWB) 1991, 1995). The institution was, in most cases, highly exploitative of the poorer laborers (Byres 1983; Dasgupta 1984*a*, *b*). Since 1978, however, OB has been successful in registering 1.48 million sharecroppers with the state, controlling rents, and conferring hereditary rights to tenants.

In order to assess the overall impact of OB, the authors conducted a rapid appraisal study, which covered 80 sharecroppers from six villages under four Panchayats (the local system of government). The selected areas were differentiated by their comparative level of agricultural development: Area I was less developed and Area II was more developed. This differentiation was chosen to highlight the differential regional effect of OB. The results of this rapid appraisal show that OB created substantial benefits for a majority of the sampled sharecroppers.

There has been much debate as to whether rents can be controlled, particularly from a long-term perspective. OB offers a case study to answer this question. We begin by

The opinions of the authors are personal and not necessarily those of the organizations to which they are affiliated. The authors are very thankful to Professors Alain de Janvry and Elisabeth Sadoulet for their guidance, critical comments, and full support in preparation of this chapter. The authors would also like to thank Drs. Emery Roe, Rinku Murgai, Xue Jun Wang, Avijit Banerjee, A.B. Khan, and Y. Nishigaki for comments, review, and help in the preparation of this chapter; and to the Honorable Ministers, Dr. Surya Kanta Mishra, for Land Reform and Revenue, Mr. Partha Dey, for Health, and Mr. Razzak Molla for Horticulture, and Sundarban Development, Government of West Bengal for sharing their valuable experiences and cooperation while carrying out the field study. The authors are also grateful for the opportunities provided by WIDER, UN University. Dr. Uday Shankar Saha gratefully acknowledges and thanks the National Bank for Agriculture and Rural Development, India for awarding him a post-doctoral scholarship and the University of California, Berkeley where he carried out his research.

outlining the history of OB and show that the program was effectively complemented by an array of state-initiated rural development projects that will also be described. We then assess the impact of both OB and the rural development projects and conclude with the lessons that can be derived from the analysis.

Historical perspectives

Although sharecropping has been practiced since ancient times in India, the institution was widely expanded during the British period (Hunter 1876; Kosambi 1970), and the number of non-cultivating landowners also grew rapidly (Dasgupta 1984*a*). These non-cultivating landowners, along with large cultivators, have used the sharecropping institution as a means of accessing cheap labor, which has inspired several agrarian movements.

One of the most vibrant movements, the Tebhaga Movement of 1946–47, demanded —without success—that the sharecroppers receive a fair two-thirds share of their agricultural production (Chowdhury 1993). The sharecropping system varied widely across different areas, crops, and seasons, depending on the bargaining power of the sharecroppers (O'Malley 1910; O'Malley and Chakravarti 1909; Colebrooke 1804, cited in Dasgupta 1984*b*). Because the sharecroppers generally had little bargaining power, the landlords were able to increase their own share by manipulating loans, making threats, harassing the sharecroppers physically, and frequently evicting them (Pal 1995). A detailed study by Cooper (1988) argues that the relationship between sharecroppers and landlords was no better than that between a servant and a master.[1]

The problems of sharecroppers were not addressed during British colonial rule. Legislation such as the Bengal Tenancy Act of 1885 (amended in 1929) only served to help the landlords. Ironically, at the end of the period of British colonial rule, a commission was set up to assess the institution of sharecropping. The report, known as the Floud Commission Report (1940), made several recommendations that would have been beneficial for sharecroppers, but were never implemented (Government of Bengal 1940; GOWB 1979).

After Independence, the new government made various attempts to respond to the Tebhaga Movement and to the inequities of the sharecropping system. In 1950, the Bargadar Act was proposed and subsequently incorporated in the West Bengal Land Reform Act (WBLR) of 1955 as a separate chapter.[2] Although the share of production for sharecroppers was theoretically raised to 60% (without cost sharing by the

[1] The economic malpractice of sharecropping included rent distribution in favor of the landlord, illegal shares going to supervisors, hereditary indebtedness, etc. The different instruments used for non-economic exploitation were landlord strictures for social behaviors and living style in the society, and exploitation of women (wives, daughters, and daughters-in-law) in the sharecropper families for the satisfaction of the landlord and his family members (Cooper 1988).

[2] The recorded sharecropper (popularly known as a 'Bargadar') has been defined under Section 2(2) of the WBLR Act as a person who cultivates the land of another person on condition of delivering a share of produce of such land to that person under the system generally known as adhi, barga, or bhag (Shukla 1996; T. Saha 1996).

landlord), the Act was seldom carried through in practice. Further, an amendment to the WBLR was legislated in 1970 by an ordinance from the President of India and enacted in 1972. This amendment promised revolutionary advances in favor of sharecroppers such as share increases from 60 to 75% without input-cost sharing and 50% with cost sharing, hereditary rights for cultivation, redefinition of self-cultivation, issuance of a crop-share receipt by the landlord, and provisions for the legal means of evicting sharecroppers (Dasgupta 1984*b*; T. Ghosh 1986; T. Saha 1996). These revolutionary steps were also never carried out in practice.

Operation Barga

The left-front government that assumed power in West Bengal in 1977 inherited a rural situation characterized by agricultural stagnation, widespread impoverishment, and social tensions around the issue of land reform. The government decided that proper implementation of the West Bengal Land Reform Act would be an immediate priority in order to provide justice to the long-standing demands of sharecroppers and to reactivate agricultural production in the state (Dasgupta 1984*b*; Chowdhury 1993). A comprehensive and integrated program was designed with the participation of government officials, sharecroppers, local people, elected representatives, and landlords. Workshops were organized at the state level with the purpose of formulating a detailed program called Operation Barga that was put into place on 5 July 1978 (T. Ghosh 1986). By 1984, OB had successfully registered more than a million sharecroppers (GOWB 1985*a*) and, by 1997, 1.48 million sharecroppers (covering 74% of the estimated 2 million sharecroppers) had been registered (see also GOWB 1997).[3]

In very simplistic terms, OB is a program to register those who cultivate land owned by others according to agreed-upon rental terms. However, in a broader perspective, OB is an intervention that seeks to provide production stability by giving legal rights to sharecroppers for cultivation, facilitating the provision of credit, ensuring higher incentives for efforts, and restoring vitality to the agricultural sector by stimulating production and ultimately bringing prosperity to the rural society. Elaborate mechanisms were adopted to create widespread awareness among the people, mobilize political support, and prepare the local administration so that the program could be implemented successfully (GOWB 1978*a*, *b*).

A major obstacle that OB had to overcome was the difficulty sharecroppers had in proving their tenancy agreements. To solve this problem, new legislation was created that placed the burden of proof on the landowners and made issuance of a receipt for crop share mandatory. Non-issuance of such a receipt was treated as a criminal offense. When sharecroppers were identified and issued temporary certificates, they received legal rights which cannot be encroached upon by landowners, and remain unaffected by sale or transfer of the land. The certificates, which are legally inheritable, can be

[3] The recorded population may in fact be as high as 98.7% if the number of recordable sharecroppers is 1.5 million as estimated by Bandopadhayay and Krishnaji (1982).

used as collateral for obtaining bank credit. The sharecropper, however, can be lawfully evicted if he fails to cultivate the land, uses it for non-agricultural purposes, or fails to tender due share of produce to the landowner (T. Saha 1996).

The identification, verification, and registration of sharecroppers were carried out in meetings where free discussions were held. More than 8,000 evening meetings were organized with the interested parties: Panchayats, voluntary agencies, members of the legislature and senior officers, members of peasant organizations, and often the Commissioner of Land Reform and Revenue Directorate (T. Ghosh 1986).[4] Block-level committees were set up to supervise implementation of the program and to resolve all related issues through local deliberations. In conjunction, district and state-level monitoring workshops were organized at regular intervals in order to assess OB's progress, get feedback, and invite suggestions from grassroots participants. At various points, key officials decided the course of action. The Minister for Land Reform and Revenue and the Ministers in charge of the respective districts, for example, were personally involved in overseeing the implementation of the program and interacted frequently with both sharecroppers and landowners. The success of OB was facilitated, in particular, by the stewardship and personal involvement of a senior Cabinet Minister for Land Reforms and Revenue who had long experience with land-related matters and close associations with grassroots agrarian struggles such as the Tebhaga Movement.

While OB was effective in providing secure land titles to sharecroppers, it was complemented with a broad integrated rural development program in order to encourage higher agricultural productivity and improve welfare. One of the most important elements of this program was the involvement of the newly established local democratic institutions in the form of the three-tier Panchayat system, which is the culmination of decentralized planning in West Bengal. The program also implemented several economic development projects in the OB regions. Programs such as Food for Work (FfW), the Integrated Tribal Development Project, the Integrated Rural Development Program, and other programs aimed at overall agricultural development were intended to assist sharecroppers in building their asset position, offer insurance through employment opportunities for generating income during lean periods, and provide a free supply of mini-kits to producers that included high quality seeds, fertilizers, and pesticides. According to Lieten (1992), the FfW (called the National Rural Employment Program since 1980) and the Rural Employment Guarantee Program introduced in 1983, were not only meant to rescue the rural poor from starvation, but were also intended to create an environment in which small sharecroppers and landless laborers could organize themselves. The organization of these groups has been instrumental in implementing OB.

This case study, therefore, is intended to study the effect of both OB and the government-initiated rural development programs. The methodology utilized in

[4] Due to the weakness and ignorance of the sharecroppers and to make the program a success, the implementation of OB needed to involve panchayat members, peasant organizations, locals, and the political forces (but carefully avoided politicizing the program) in order to create awareness, convince and mobilize the sharecroppers, and also to provide moral support as facilitators. Police forces were kept alert for maintaining peace.

the study included questionnaires for a sample of both recorded and unrecorded sharecroppers and for landlords; interviews with ministers, peasant organizations, academicians, and government officials; and comparisons of the authors' observations with results from other studies.

An evaluation of OB

Tenure security

Of the eighty sharecroppers included in the study, only nine had not been registered through OB.[5] Approximately 60% of the sharecroppers who registered did so because they felt threatened by the landlords and the remaining 40% registered in spite of having a good relationship with the landlords because they desired greater freedom of action (27%) or were afraid that their land holdings would be jeopardized by inheritance in the landlord's family (13%). The main reason given for not registering was good personal relations with the landlord.

One of the greatest concerns in implementing OB was that the program would lead to an increased rate of evictions, as landlords would choose to exit the sharecropping relationship rather than comply with the new regulations. In the case study area, we observed no evidence of increased evictions due to OB (see also Socio Economic Research Institute (SERI) 1981; Bandyopadhyaya and Krishnaji 1982; J. Ghosh 1990; Pal 1995). In one case, a title change occurred but the sharecropper continued to possess full freedom of cultivation and received additional help from the landlord (Lieten 1992). A recent study by Banerjee and Ghatak (1996) similarly observed a very low rate of eviction (4% of 344 respondents) across several different districts. Our study also indicated that in some cases a change of title occurred where, for example, the recorded sharecropper purchased the land from the landlord at a 'compromise price,' or the sharecropper received compensation for agreeing to allow a landlord to sell the land because of a family emergency (see also Chaudhuri and Pal 1993). Although the eviction record is encouraging, there was one case of a landlord refusing to file a return with the government. In their study, Chaudhuri and Pal (1993) also recorded six instances of non-compliance. Non-compliance constitutes an indirect form of harassment by the landlords. We may therefore conclude that because of the way OB was implemented, landlords could not use eviction as a means of evading the new rule.

Provision of credit

Credit or input support to the sharecroppers were the main tools used by the landlords for extracting more rent from the tenants and for exploiting them and their families

[5] It is interesting to note that it was difficult to find unrecorded sharecroppers in the sample area; the percentage of recorded sharecroppers was as high as 88.8%, which matches the recording of 86.7% reported by Chaudhuri and Pal (1993). These percentages are higher than the estimated overall achievements. It is, however, not the intention of the authors to draw conclusions regarding a possibly higher effective success rate based on this small sample.

Table 9.1. *Access to credit*

Principal source	Pre-Operation Barga (OB) (% respondents)	Post-Operation Barga (OB) (% respondents)
Banks	13.7	82.5
Landlords	53.8	6.2
Moneylenders	23.8	3.8
Relatives	8.7	7.5
Total	100.0	100.0

Source: survey in two districts of West Bengal, 1998.

(Cooper 1988). Most sharecroppers depended on landlords not only for such support for cultivation but also for family expenses. With this background, the government decided right from the beginning of the program to act as a facilitator to ensure institutional credit flow to this vulnerable group so as to bring them out of the clutches of landlords. Therefore, one of the most important effects of legalized tenure has been to give sharecroppers the possibility of accessing institutional credit using their sharecropping certificates as collateral (see also Bandyopadhyaya and Krishnaji 1982; Kohli 1987; Chaudhuri and Pal 1993; Banerjee and Ghatak 1996). Credit had traditionally been one of the most oppressive aspects of the landlord–sharecropper relationship. The government has been active in facilitating access to credit for the beneficiaries of OB (GOWB 1979*b*). Participation targets were set in consultation with the state and private banks, and the process is closely monitored by the government (T. Ghosh 1986). This new lending system was responsible for giving access to approximately 370,000 sharecroppers in 1983 and 304,000 sharecroppers in 1984, a significant increase from the mere 59,000 sharecroppers who received loans in 1979–80 (GOWB 1985*a*). As can be seen from Table 9.1, after Operation Barga, 82.5% of the respondents (sixty-three of whom were registered and three of whom were not) were able to obtain credit from banks for cultivation purposes. This is a substantial improvement from the pre-OB when only 13.7% of the sharecroppers in the study had access to bank credit. It is also an improvement over the early years of OB. In 1981, R. Ghosh reported that only 130,000 sharecroppers and assignees of land vested with the government had received bank loans during 1979–80. This is still, however, an improvement over the number of sharecroppers who were able to obtain bank loans before OB: between 1972 and 1978, a mere 79,000 farmers had received loans. The number of sharecroppers accessing institutionalized credit has, therefore, definitely increased relative to the pre-OB period (see also Bhaumik 1993). The credit relationship also changed somewhat for unrecorded sharecroppers: of those interviewed, three out of nine were able to acquire bank loans by using their own cultivated land as security.

Although many of the recorded sharecroppers are obtaining credit through banks, it is clear that not all sharecroppers have been accommodated, and it is probable that not all will be in the near future. It would be very difficult for bankers—private or public—to reach all the sharecroppers; many of them remain outside the bank credit network because the transaction costs involved in lending are too high for small landholders. For a greater number of sharecroppers to receive institutional credit, it would be necessary to create a different lending mechanism and policy with lower transaction costs.

Distributional relationship

In addition to registering sharecroppers with the local government, OB has made it mandatory for landlords to issue a formal, legal receipt listing the quantity and quality of goods received from sharecroppers. If the landowner fails to issue a receipt, 100% of the crop legally belongs to the sharecropper. Our study reveals only one instance in which this occurred: the landlord did not issue a receipt for his share of the crop, so his share was deposited at the district land reform office which, in turn, issued a receipt of the share to the sharecropper as per legal stipulation. It has been observed that acceptance of the crop share regulations has been increasing steadily. This is a result of two decades of learning about the system in which all actors have realized that protecting the rights of both sharecropper and landlord is a priority of the state government.

The registration of crop share has had an important impact on the relative distribution of production. There are various types of rental systems prevalent in West Bengal, such as crop share (with different proportions), fixed crop share, fixed money rent, and others. During the 1960s and 1970s, those sharecroppers participating in crop-share agreements, which represented a majority, were legally eligible for 50% or less of total production (National Commission on Agriculture 1976; Rudra 1975, 1981). The crop share pattern, however, varied widely from season to season, crop to crop, and area to area, and average distributions ranged from 33 to 67.67% (Pal 1995) with some sharecroppers receiving as little as 20% (case study). Our study revealed that both crop share and fixed rent were being practiced in the selected areas, although the former was by far the predominant system with 96% of the respondents during pre-OB and 89% during post-OB. Although a minority of the sharecropping contracts was based on fixed rents (11% of the sample), the system does appear to be on the rise in relation to the pre-OB period (from about 4 to 11%). The decision to change contract form is decided at the local level in-group meetings, and occasionally in court. Although the shift towards fixed rent contracts is marginal, it is noteworthy as an indicator of leasing trends.

Prior to the implementation of OB, it was observed that 49% of the sharecroppers in West Bengal received less than the legally stipulated 50% of production (see Table 9.2). Since OB was implemented, the percentage of production going to the sharecroppers in the survey regions has increased from 50% to approximately 75% (Table 9.2; see also Bhaumik 1993; Chaudhuri and Pal 1993; Sengupta 1993). Out of seventy-one sharecroppers (90% of whom were recorded and 10% unrecorded), 94% received a crop share that was 50% or more of total production. It is significant to note that all the recorded sharecroppers received shares of 50% or more, and 69% of

Table 9.2. *Distribution of tenants' crop shares*

% share	Pre-OB (% respondents)	Post-OB (% respondents)		
		(Recorded)	(Unrecorded)	Total
20	7.8	—	—	—
33	22.1	—	2.8	2.8
40	19.5	—	1.4	1.4
50	46.7	8.5	5.7	14.2
60	3.9	4.2	—	4.2
67	—	7.0	—	7.0
75	—	69.0	—	69.0
100	—	1.4	—	1.4
Total	100.0	90.1	9.9	100.0

Source: survey in two districts of West Bengal, 1998.

them received the legally stipulated share of 75% of the produce. This signifies a substantial improvement after OB when compared with the 49.4% of sharecroppers who received a crop share ranging from 20 to 40% only prior to implementation of OB (46.7% got 50%) (Table 9.2). Other studies have also shown that the size of the producer's share has increased: from 33 to 50% before OB to more than 50% following OB (see SERI 1981; Bandyopadhyaya and Krishnaji 1982; T. Ghosh 1986; Kohli 1987; J. Ghosh 1990; Banerjee and Ghatak 1996). These studies show that the recorded sharecroppers obtained a share of more than 50% (the majority of them got 75%) while most of the unrecorded sharecroppers received a 50% share or less, and thus conclude that there was more improvement in rent distribution for the recorded than for the unrecorded sharecroppers.

However, there are still some recorded sharecroppers who have not been able to claim the legally stipulated share. We conclude that this may not be uncommon and it depends on factors such as location and character of the parties to the contract. Detailed investigation may reveal that these sharecroppers have other obligations toward their landlord such as payment for input support and consumption loan repayment that accounts for their inability to claim the full legal share of their production.

Cost sharing

In order to understand why there are large variations in crop sharing, it is necessary to analyze the interdependent nature of rural factor markets in West Bengal. In the case study, we found that cost sharing was widespread in the 1960s with almost 65% of the sharecroppers relying on landlord assistance (Bardhan and Rudra 1978). After OB, only one of the recorded and four of the unrecorded sharecroppers (totaling 6%

of the sample) in the study received inputs from the landlord, while a majority of the unrecorded sharecroppers received either loans or inputs (see also Chaudhuri and Pal 1993; Sengupta 1993). The sharecroppers who no longer received cost-sharing support after implementation of OB, particularly the recorded sharecroppers, were those who obtained a 75% share of crop production. These correlations confirm the previous observation that the government needs to provide rural development services such as access to credit as a complement to rent control to replace the loss of cost sharing and of inter-linked transactions with landlords.

Agricultural productivity

Following the implementation of OB, a spectacular increase in agricultural production was experienced in the state of West Bengal (A. Saha and Swaminathan 1994). Between 1969–70 and 1981–82, agricultural production grew at an annual compound rate of 0.6% in West Bengal, while the national average was 2.2%. Between 1981–82 and 1994–95, however, the production in West Bengal grew at a rate of 6.3%, which was the highest growth rate experienced in any of the seventeen major states in India. The average national growth rate during that period was only 3.1%. Our study revealed that in the two case study areas, productivity increased for both kharif and rabi rice crops relative to the pre-OB period. The intensity of land use has also increased following implementation of OB as people diversified production to include cash crops such as potatoes, oilseeds, and vegetables.

In Area I, the yield of kharif rice increased by 229% for the recorded sharecroppers and by 120% for non-recorded sharecroppers (see Table 9.3). The yield of rabi rice in Area I has also increased by 240% and 138% for recorded and unrecorded sharecroppers, respectively. In Area II, kharif and rabi rice yields were found to have increased by 170 and 192%, respectively, for recorded sharecroppers, and by 138 and 125%, respectively, for unrecorded sharecroppers. The data show that yields obtained by the unrecorded sharecroppers were greater than those obtained by the recorded sharecroppers prior to implementation of OB (Table 9.3). After OB, however, the situation was reversed

Table 9.3. *Productivity of rice cultivation (in kg/ha)*

Area	Season	Recorded sharecropper (pre-OB)	Unrecorded sharecropper (pre-OB)	Recorded sharecropper (post-OB)	Unrecorded sharecropper (post-OB)
I	Kharif	700	1,000	1,600	1,200
I	Rabi	1,000	1,300	2,400	1,800
II	Kharif	1,000	1,300	1,700	1,800
II	Rabi	1,300	1,600	2,500	2,000

Source: survey in two districts of West Bengal, 1998.

for both crops in both regions, with the exception of kharif rice in Area II. Similar observations were recorded by Pal (1995) in a study conducted in the Birbhum district. It is interesting to note that the yield increases were higher in Area I than in Area II, indicating that there was more room for improvement via better management in the less developed region and suggesting also that the recorded sharecroppers had a greater incentive to manage their land productively.

According to both the data collected and the general impressions derived from visiting the case study areas, the recorded sharecroppers paid greater attention to their land which involved increasing the intensity of their labor in order to increase crop yields. The increase in labor intensity was not matched by an increase in input use, although input use is on the rise as well. The recorded sharecroppers have in some cases obtained comparatively higher yields than the landowners (SERI 1981). Basu and Roy (1982) demonstrated that the legalized system of share tenancy was responsible for a higher use of variable factors such as labor, which led to higher agricultural yields. According to Chattopadhyay and Associates (1984) there was an increase in production following OB because the recorded sharecroppers have greatly intensified the use of their cultivable land. The authors, however, observed that some sharecroppers did not believe that productivity had increased since implementation of OB. Kohli (1987) concluded from a study of three districts that the crop productivity of sharecroppers had increased in 70% of the cases since registration. Chaudhuri and Pal (1993) reported that the recorded sharecroppers obtained a higher yield of kharif (Aman) paddy as compared to the unrecorded sharecroppers. While 28% of the recorded sharecroppers obtained more than 935 kg of kharif paddy per acre, only 20% of the non-recorded sharecroppers were able to obtain the same yield level. It is striking that there was very little difference between the percentage of recorded sharecroppers who obtained more than 935 kg of kharif paddy per acre, and the percentage of landowning cultivators who achieved the same level of high yield (28.6%). Banerjee and Ghatak (1996) observed that the West Bengal tenancy reforms have done more to increase crop productivity for both kharif rice (Aman rice by 102%) and Rabi rice (Boro rice by 84%) than have irrigation facilities. Their study concluded that OB has been beneficial in improving the production of the recorded sharecroppers and in increasing the overall agricultural output of the state.

Fixed assets

Draught animals and ploughs are the most crucial production assets for tenants. It is noteworthy, therefore, that as per the study of Pal (1995), while only 372 households had draught animals before OB, the number has now increased to 545 households, and the percentage of households that possess draught animals rose from 44.6% of the sampled sharecroppers (pre-OB) to 65.3% after OB. According to Banerjee and Ghatak (1996), the recorded sharecroppers possessed more assets, such as ploughs, draught animals, carts, pump-sets, and other assets for household use than the unrecorded sharecroppers.

Technology adoption and land use

Cropping intensity

A significant increase in cropping intensity has occurred in both case study areas, particularly in Area I where 90% of the recorded sharecroppers and 70% of the unrecorded sharecroppers now practice double cropping, as opposed to a total of 10% who practiced double cropping prior to OB. It is estimated that cropping intensity in Area I increased from the level of about 110% to around 210% for recorded sharecroppers and from about 110% to about 180% for unrecorded sharecroppers after OB. In Area II, the percentage of sharecroppers practicing double cropping increased from 80 to 100% for recorded sharecroppers. In addition, the percentage of sharecroppers practicing multiple cropping increased from about 30% during pre-OB to 70% for the recorded sharecroppers, and 40% for the unrecorded sharecroppers after OB. Increases in overall levels of cropping intensity were observed for all, but increases for unrecorded sharecroppers were marginal compared to recorded sharecroppers.

Irrigation

Both case study areas witnessed a substantial increase in the use of irrigation after implementation of OB. In Area I, the percentage of sharecroppers with irrigated land increased from 10 to 50%, while in Area II, the percentage increased from a range of 30–40% in pre-OB to 70–90% for recorded sharecroppers, and 60–80% for unrecorded sharecroppers in post-OB. Irrigation facilities were created primarily by the state. Minor irrigation facilities were, however, created by individual farmers.

Input use

The level of input use increased significantly in both case study areas, although there was very little difference observed between the recorded and unrecorded sharecroppers in the use of HYV seeds, manure, and chemical fertilizers. In fact, the unrecorded sharecroppers were found to use marginally more inputs than the recorded sharecroppers in both Areas I and II. The increase in the use of manure was the most dramatic: whereas manure was used by only about 50% of the sharecroppers prior to OB, it is now used by 100% in both case study areas. Chemical fertilizer use had increased from 10 to 60% in Area I, and from 40 to 100% in Area II for both recorded and unrecorded sharecroppers. The percentage of sharecroppers using HYV seeds has also increased from 5% in Area I to a range of 30–50% for recorded sharecroppers, and 40–50% for unrecorded sharecroppers. The same has increased in Area II from 30% to a range of 60–80% for recorded sharecroppers, and 50–90% for unrecorded sharecroppers. The significant increases in input use suggest that the state's rural development programs have played a key role in providing better access to factor markets for all sharecroppers, recorded or unrecorded.

The recorded sharecroppers were found to be using inputs without assistance from the landlords. They were able to access inputs by using bank credit with their tenure certificates, and by the previously mentioned government-provided agriculture and rural development kits. The main reasons landlords were not assisting sharecroppers were because approximately 80% were absentee (Kohli 1987), and also because many of the landlords chose not to cooperate in order to signal their non-acceptance of the state's land tenure reforms, with an expectation of changing the system. Although the lack of support from landlords may be seen as a drawback of OB, output effects show that the state's efforts in promoting rural development have more than compensated for the landlords' withdrawal (see also Kohli 1987). However, landlords have in due course realized the priority accorded by the state government to land reforms and agricultural and rural development because they have seen the beneficial aspect of reforms, which have helped to increase productivity, and, as a result, many landlords in the study area have gradually started accepting the reforms.

Lessons from OB

We may conclude in view of the above analysis that the 'Operation Barga' program has achieved its basic objectives by registering sharecroppers and providing them with tenure security for cultivation as a hereditary right, drastically reducing evictions and other such threats. OB has also helped to facilitate the recorded sharecroppers in accessing bank credit. As a result, the recorded sharecroppers have now become much more independent and are able to stand on their own in several matters related to production decisions. It is significant that OB has helped to enhance crop production for an extended time period, which has allowed the state to achieve higher agricultural growth for the last fifteen years or more (GOWB 1995; CMIE 1997).

An analysis of OB offers several suggestions for rural development interventions that aim to reform land rental markets. The first lesson is that the state has been involved in a way that complemented the legal implications of tenure reform. OB would not have been successful in increasing rural development or agricultural productivity without state-led efforts to provide sharecroppers with access to production inputs such as irrigation, HYV seeds, fertilizers, etc. The second lesson is that the registration of sharecroppers appears to have broken many of the inter-linkages between sharecroppers and landlords that require that rural markets be 'improved' so that transactions are not biased against small producers. In other words, while the state cannot be responsible for providing all the necessary production inputs, it is necessary for the state to ensure that markets and institutions are operating sufficiently well for tenants.

In theory, there could potentially be two areas of concern that may remain in relation to the continued implementation of OB: (1) new entrants may be blocked because current sharecroppers will be difficult to dislodge, and (2) agricultural productivity may fall due to lack of landlord participation, particularly to long-term investments in the quality of the land.

Regarding the blockage of new entrants, tenure security is compatible with the preservation of a minimal land market given that OB was complemented with regulations that provided for the removal of sharecroppers in the event of cultivation negligence, lack of management, failure to provide the legal share to the landlord, etc. There are also legal provisions for landlords to sell land on the basis of consent of and agreement with the sharecroppers as per legal stipulation.

Regarding the potential decline in agricultural productivity, the information provided by the case study and other reviewed research suggests a high correlation between OB and production improvement including investment in irrigation and fixed assets. There is no reason why such improvement should not continue, as long as the government remains vigilant in monitoring the regulations of reform, rural development programs, and the operation of rural markets and institutions.

A final issue of concern is that it is not clear from this analysis whether a program like OB could be successfully implemented in other Indian states or in other countries. One of the most important factors contributing to the success of OB was the coming to power of the Left Front led by the Communist Party of India (Marxist) in West Bengal in 1977. The reforms of the sharecropping system were effective because the program received long-term government support in a variety of ways such as: safeguarding the sharecroppers' interests, promoting participation at the grassroots level, creating incentives for production activities, developing new credit facilities, mitigating eviction threats, and above all, changing the general attitude of the administration. It is the collective efforts of all those concerned that have helped to successfully implement the reform program. One of the important lessons of this collaboration is that comprehensive programs such as OB will be difficult to implement without full state support.

This state support has made it possible for sharecroppers to increase their involvement in production decisions and land management. Credit, government support, and assistance in the form of input mini-kits have helped in minimizing the role of landlords in management and input provision for agricultural productivity improvement. Therefore, less participation by landlords did not affect the agricultural productivity.

It is very important to mention that the program has been successful also because of the decentralized governance through the three-tier Panchayati system, which was first democratically elected in 1978 and then re-elected every five years. The Panchayat system has greatly facilitated the mobilization of people's support and the implementation of programs for agricultural and rural development (see also Lieten 1994, 1996). The success of OB is a result of the efforts of an integrated program that involves multi-institutional efforts, participation by the majority of sharecroppers, and a strict monitoring of the whole program on a priority basis. Therefore, it seems evident that a program of this nature can only be effectively implemented in other parts of India and in other countries, if it is accompanied by a similar state-sponsored approach to the implementation of a comprehensive and integrated program of rural development, with grassroots level involvement, legislative mechanisms that are enforced, and a program implementation that is closely monitored (see also Appu 1996 and Sobhan 1993), conditions which may be different, but not impossible to replicate.

REFERENCES

Appu, P.S. 1996. *Land Reforms in India: A Survey of Policy, Legislation and Implementation*. New Delhi: Vikas Publishing House Pvt. Ltd.

Bandyopadhyaya, N. 1981. '"Operation Barga" and Land Reforms Perspective in West Bengal.' *Economic and Political Weekly* 16(25/26): A38–42.

Bandyopadhyaya, N. and N. Krishnaji. 1982. 'A Study on Evaluation of Land Reform Measures in West Bengal.' A report prepared for the International Labor Organization by the Center for Studies in Social Sciences, Calcutta.

Banerjee, A.V. and M. Ghatak. 1996. 'Empowerment and Efficiency: The Economics of Tenancy Reform.' Working paper, Massachusetts Institute of Technology (MIT) and Harvard University, Cambridge, MA.

Bardhan, P. and A. Rudra. 1978. 'Inter-linkage of Land, Labor and Credit Relations: An Analysis of Village Survey Data in Eastern India.' *Economic and Political Weekly* 13(6/7): 367–86.

Basu, K. and P. Roy. 1982. 'Share, Size and Subsistence: Revisiting some old Controversies of Tenancy.' *Economic and Political Weekly* 17(30): 1196–2000.

Bhaumik, S.K. 1993. *Tenancy Relations and Agrarian Development: A Study of West Bengal.* New Delhi: Sage Publications.

Byres, T.J. (ed.). 1983. *Sharecropping and Sharecropper.* London: Frank Cass & Co.

Center for Monitoring Indian Economy (CMIE). 1997. Economic Intelligence Service, Agriculture, India.

Chattopadyaya, B. and Associates. 1984. 'Tenancy Reforms, the Power Structure and the Role of Administration. An Evaluation of Operation Barga.' *Cressida Transactions* 3(2): 1–75.

Chaudhuri, M. and S.S. Pal. 1993. 'Present Status of Land Reform: A Case Study in a Village.' In *Proceedings of National Workshop on the Socio-Economic Impact of Land Reforms*, K.P. Shandilya and S.S. Pal (eds.). Calcutta: Viswa Bharati, Santiniketan, and Board of Revenue, Government of West Bengal.

Chowdhury, B.K. 1993. 'Land Reforms in West Bengal and its Impact on Rural Economy.' In *Proceedings of National Workshop on the Socio-Economic Impact of Land Reforms*, K.P. Shandilya and S.S. Pal (eds.). Calcutta: Viswa Bharati, Santiniketan, and Board of Revenue, Government of West Bengal.

Colebrooke, H.T. 1804. 'Remarks on the Husbandry and Internal Commerce of Bengal, Calcutta.' Government Report. [Cited in Dasgupta, B. 1984*a*.]

Cooper, A. 1988. *Sharecropping and Sharecroppers' Struggle in Bengal—1930–1950.* Calcutta: K.P. Bagchi and Co.

Dasgupta, B. 1984*a*. 'Sharecropping in West Bengal During Colonial Period.' *Economic and Political Weekly* 19(13): A2–8.

—— 1984*b*. 'Sharecropping in West Bengal—From Independence to Operation Barga.' *Economic & Political Weekly* 19(26): A85–96.

Ghosh, J.K. 1990. 'The Changing Agrarian Scene under the Impact of Land Reforms Program: A Case Study of Operation Barga Program in West Bengal.' In *Economy of West Bengal: Problems and Prospects*, A. Raychaudhury and D. Sarkar (eds.). Calcutta: Allied Publishers Ltd.

Ghosh, R. 1981. 'Agrarian Program of Left Front Government.' *Economic and Political Weekly* 16(25/26): A49–55.

Ghosh, T.K. 1986. *Operation Barga and Land Reforms.* Delhi: B.R. Publishing Corporation.

Government of Bengal (GOB). 1940. 'Report of the Land Revenue Commission of Bengal.' (Chairman: F.L.C. Floud), Vols. I–VI, Alipur Bengal Government Press, Calcutta.

Government of West Bengal (GOWB) 1978*a*. 'Directorate of Land Reform and Revenue, Proceedings of Reorientation Camp on Land Reform at Narayangarh P.S., District Midnapur.' Government publication, Midnapur.

—— 1978*b*. 'A Few Operational Decisions.' In Proceedings on Workshop on Land Reforms, Board of Revenue, Calcutta, 23–24 June.

—— 1979*a*. 'From Tebhaga to Operation Barga.' Board of Revenue, Calcutta. (In Bengali language.)
—— 1979*b*. 'Credit Delivery Project for Sharecroppers and Assignees of Government (vested) Land from the Banking Institutions.' Government publication, Calcutta. (In Bengali language.)
—— 1985*a*. 'Statistical Handbook on Bargadars of West Bengal.' Directorate of Land Records and Surveys, Calcutta.
—— 1985*b*. 'Seventh Workshop on Land Reform—Field Problems, Suggested Actions and Government Decisions.' Calcutta, 4–5 August.
—— 1989. 'Statistical Abstract of West Bengal, 1978–89.' Bureau of Applied Economics & Statistics, Calcutta.
—— 1991. 'Agricultural Census, West Bengal, 1990–91.' Government report, Calcutta.
—— 1995. 'Estimates of Area and Production of Principal Crops in West Bengal, 1994–95.' Directorate of Agriculture, Calcutta.
—— 1997. 'Monthly Statistical Report on Land Reform in West Bengal.' Directorate of Land Records and Surveys, Calcutta.
Hunter, W.W. 1876. 'A Statistical Account of Bengal: The Census of Bengal in 1872.' Government publication. [Cited in Dasgupta 1984*a*.]
Kohli, A. 1987. *State of Poverty in India*. Cambridge: Cambridge University Press.
Kosambi, D.D. 1970. *The Culture and Civilization of Ancient India in Historical Outline*. Delhi: Vikash Publishing House.
Lieten, G.K. 1992. *Continuity and Change in Rural West Bengal*. New Delhi: Sage Publications.
—— 1994. 'For a new Debate on West Bengal.' *Economic and Political Weekly* 29(29): 1835–8.
—— 1996. *Development, Devolution and Democracy: Village Discourse in West Bengal*. New Delhi: Sage Publications.
National Commission on Agriculture (NCA). 1976. *Land Reforms*. Chapter XV, Appendix 67. New Delhi: Ministry of Agriculture, Government of India.
O'Malley, L.S.S.O. 1910. *District Gazetter, Chittagong, Bankura, Midnapur, Darjeeling, Jalpaiguri*, Government publication. Calcutta: Bengal Secretariat Book Depot.
O'Malley, L.S.S.O. and M. Chakravarti. 1909. *District Gazetteer, Howrah*, Government publication. Calcutta: Bengal Secretariat Book Depot.
Pal, S.S. 1993. 'A Discussion on the Character of the Share Cropping Institution. A Case Study in the District of Birbhum, West Bengal.' In *Proceedings of National Workshop on the Socio-Economic Impact of Land Reforms*, K.P. Shandilya and S.S. Pal (eds.). Calcutta: Viswa Bharati, Santiniketan, and Board of Revenue, Government of West Bengal.
—— 1995. 'Impact of Tenancy Reforms on Production and Income Distribution. A Case Study of Operation Barga in West Bengal Report.' Study initiated in 1985, final report published 1995 as Policy Paper I, National Center for Agricultural Economics and Policy Research (ICAR), New Delhi.
Rudra, A. 1975. 'Sharecropping Arrangements in West Bengal.' *Economic and Political Weekly* 10(27): A58–63.
—— 1981. 'One Step Forward, Two Steps Backward.' *Economic and Political Weekly* 16(13): A61–68.
Saha, T.N. 1996. *The West Bengal Land Reforms Act, 1955*, 8th edition. Calcutta: Eastern Law House.
Saha, A. and M. Swaminathan. 1994. 'Agricultural Growth in West Bengal in the 1980s. A Disaggregation by Districts and Crops.' *Economic and Political Weekly* 24(13): A2–11.
Sengupta, S. 1993. 'Land Reforms in West Bengal, Rural Poverty Performance and Perspective.' In *Proceedings of National Workshop on the Socio-Economic Impact of Land Reforms*,

K.P. Shandilya and S.S. Pal (eds.). Calcutta: Viswa Bharati, Santiniketan, and Board of Revenue, Government of West Bengal.

Socio Economic Research Institute (SERI). 1981. 'Study on the Impact of Operation Barga.' Report, Calcutta.

Sobhan, R. 1993. *Agrarian Reform and Social Transformation: Preconditions for Development.* London: Zed Books.

Shukla, T.N. 1996. *West Bengal Land Reforms Act, 1955.* Calcutta: Kamal Law House.

10

Land Market Liberalization and the Agrarian Question in Latin America

MICHAEL R. CARTER AND RAMÓN SALGADO

Land policy and the search for a 'post-Washington Consensus'

The search for what Joseph Stiglitz (1998) calls a 'post-Washington Consensus' is emblematic of the renewed priority given to economic development policies that explicitly redress poverty and inequality. At one level, the continuing development of the micro- and macroeconomic theory of the economic costs of inequality has renewed attention to poverty and inequality.[1] At another and more fundamental level, this renewed attention reflects the reality of post-liberalization growth in Latin America that has done little to eradicate stubbornly long-lived economic inequalities, especially in the rural sector (see Carter and Coles 1998 and de Janvry and Sadoulet 1996). While agrarian structure no longer corresponds to the stark dualism of the traditional latifundia/minifundia structure (Kay 1995), the evolving land access of the rural poor (the 'agrarian question') remains an economically vital, often politically explosive issue (see de Janvry, Sadoulet, and Wolford, this volume).

Despite the renewed prominence of these issues, the traditional policy instrument of state-mandated redistributive land reform is decidedly off the agenda in most Latin American countries. Contemporary land policy is primarily comprised of two instruments: (1) land titling, including the assignment of individual, marketable land titles to the beneficiaries of earlier redistributive reforms; and (2) negotiated or market-assisted land reform (see Deininger, this volume). Both instruments can be theoretically argued to address rural inequality and answer the agrarian question in favor of improved land access for the rural poor. Whether or not they do so in practice depends critically on

The conceptual framework presented here draws on work carried out with Fred Zimmerman and supported in part by a grant from the John D. and Catherine T. MacArthur Foundation. The work on Paraguay results from the efforts of Diana Fletschner and especially Pedro Olinto. The Paraguay work was supported by a grant from the World Bank. The work on Chile reflects the efforts of Dina Mesbah and was also supported by the MacArthur Foundation. The authors thank all these individuals and institutions, while of course absolving them for responsibility for the interpretations put forward below. Finally we would like to thank the participants in the Helsinki and Santiago WIDER workshops who contributed a number of extremely useful comments, especially Klaus Deininger, Agnes Quisumbing, and Marcel Fafchamps.

[1] Bardhan, Bowles, and Gintis (1998) summarize the microeconomic literature that has grown from the economics of imperfect information, while the more macroeconomic literature has emerged from the endogenous growth literature (e.g., Persson and Tabellini 1994). Specifically on land, see Besley and Burgess (1998).

the way liberalized land market functions in the actually existing world of imperfect rural markets. Are smallholders—including the now individualized beneficiaries of earlier reforms—competitive in Latin America's liberalized agricultural economies? If not, then land titling and other efforts to improve tenure security and facilitate land transactions may simply move smallholders out, and negotiated land reform may prove to be an elaborate subsidy scheme that slowly decapitalizes its beneficiaries.

Not surprisingly, there are strongly divergent opinions concerning the function of the land market. The goal of this chapter is to evaluate the functioning of liberalized land markets, first by carefully considering the theory of smallholder land market competitiveness, and then by examining the recent experience of three Latin American economies. The remainder of this chapter is organized as follows. Section 2 summarizes and modestly extends the relevant theoretical literature. (The reader who wants to skip over the theoretical details can refer to the summary that concludes Section 2.) Section 3 then builds on that theoretical analysis and econometrically estimates the functioning of both the land purchase and rental markets in Paraguay. The rental market appears to function as an avenue of land access for poor households, while the sales market seems to be leading to greater land ownership concentration. While lacking the same sort of data used to test the theoretical model in Section 2, Sections 4 and 5 use other sorts of evidence to explore the functioning of the land market in Chile and Honduras. Both countries have seen the individualization of property rights in their reform sectors, as well as programs designed to replace either customary or legally uncertain tenure with legally complete and fully marketable property rights. In both countries, the impact of the former appears to have been larger than the impact of the latter, and in neither country is there evidence suggesting that the reforms have enhanced the land access of landless and near-landless households. Section 6 concludes the paper by drawing together its implications for policy in a post-Washington Consensus era.

Class competitiveness in the land market

Market transactions require that there be individuals willing to both buy and sell at a single price. In other words, market transactions require agent heterogeneity. This chapter discusses four types of agent heterogeneity that are crucial to shaping the distributional impacts of land markets:

- differential endowments of conventional productive factors, land and labor;
- differential skill, or technical efficiency;
- differential access to capital; and
- differential dynamic risk bearing capacity.

Drawing on the theory of rural markets, this section develops a number of propositions about the impacts that these forms of agent heterogeneity will have on land market behavior. This section will also explore the possible effects of land titling on the land market competitiveness of different strata or classes of producers.

The shadow price of land in the presence of class and idiosyncratic heterogeneity

The model sketched out in this section (which is a modest modification of the production period model in Carter and Zimmerman 1999) captures both class and idiosyncratic sources of heterogeneity. Idiosyncratic heterogeneity refers to differences that are individually specific and not correlated with wealth, whereas class heterogeneity refers to differences that are systematically related to an agent's physical wealth or endowment position. The model itself belongs to a broad class of models that have explored the impact of imperfect markets on resource allocation in the agrarian economy (e.g., Feder 1985; Eswaran and Kotwal 1986; Kevane 1996).

Given endowments of land (T^0), labor (L^0), and money (M^0), we assume that each agent attempts to maximize household income defined as:

$$\pi \equiv \{p_c Q - wL^d - FP_f - 1[z + iB]\} + \{w\phi(L^S)\} + [iS], \tag{1}$$

where the first term in curly brackets gives the net income from agricultural production, the second term gives labor market earnings, and the third gives returns to money invested in a bank over the production cycle. Note that i is the interest rate that for simplicity is assumed to be the same on both savings and borrowings. Agricultural output is produced with a constant returns to scale technology,

$$Q = \tau f(F, T^0, L), \tag{2}$$

where F measures inputs purchased at a price P_f, T is the land stock, and L is labor measured in quality-adjusted, efficiency units, and $0 \leq \tau \leq 1$ is an index of technical efficiency. Efficiency labor is produced according to the following technology:

$$L = L^h + \gamma(T, L^h)L^d, \tag{3}$$

where L^h is family labor devoted to home on-farm production, and the function $\gamma(\ )$ gives the amount of efficiency labor extracted from an input L^d of hired labor. The employment function, $\phi(L^S)$ gives days employed as a function of days of labor supplied to the off-farm job market. We assume that $\phi(L^S) \rightarrow L^S$ as $L^S \rightarrow 0$, and that $0 < \phi' < 1$ to capture the notion that employment becomes increasingly difficult to obtain as increased desire to sell labor forces one to search for employment in the slack season. Note that this specification can be seen as a less extreme form of Chayanov's assumption that off-farm sales of labor are impossible (Chayanov 1925; Sen 1966).

Maximization of (1) is further constrained by an *ex ante* working capital constraint:

$$wL^d + P_f F + P_c R_0 \leq M^0 - S + w\phi(L^S) + 1[B - z], \tag{4}$$

which simply says that the agent needs sufficient cash on hand to finance cash costs of production plus family subsistence over the production cycle season ($P_c R_0$). Working capital can be obtained from money endowments that are not saved in a bank ($M^0 - S$), from contemporaneous off-farm wage earnings, and from the net proceeds of any loans taken out by the household, $1[B - z]$, where B is the gross loan amount, z is a fixed transaction cost and 1 is an indicator taking the value of one if B is positive. Finally, each agent faces a borrowing ceiling tied to the amount of land owned,

$$B \leq \beta T, \tag{5}$$

and the following miscellaneous non-negativity restrictions:

$$(L_0 - L^h - L^h), S, L^d, B \geq 0. \tag{6}$$

The agent's objective is thus to maximize (1) subject to (2)–(6) and we denote the optimum value function corresponding to this problem as $\pi^*(T^0, M^0, \tau)$ to emphasize its dependence on wealth and idiosyncratic skill endowments.

This income maximization problem gives prominence to the intrinsic (asymmetric information-based) capital and labor market imperfections that have been extensively discussed in the context of developing country agriculture. The working capital constraint (3) makes the specification of the rules of access to capital of primary importance. While some would argue that because of asymmetric information, small farmers are completely rationed out of credit markets (e.g., see Eswaran and Kotwal 1986 and Carter 1988), we more conservatively assume that all agents have equal access to credit at a given market rate of interest. Borrowers do, however, face a fixed transactions cost, z, that is associated with the cash and opportunity costs of loan application, investigation, and approval. The fixity of z makes small loans unattractive for all agents (rich or poor). Note that because of these transaction costs and the consequent reluctance of some agents to borrow, the shadow price of the working capital constraint (3)—which we denote as μ—will endogenously vary over the endowment space even though there is a parametrically given market rate of interest.

The second feature of the production problem is that output depends on inputs of labor effort, not just labor time. The non-contractability of labor effort in spatially disperse, biologically based production process has a long history in agricultural economics (e.g., see Brewster 1950), and we follow Bowles (1985) in specifying labor extraction technologies (2) that transform labor power or time into labor effort. Family labor may be used for supervision, but consistent with the findings of Frisvold (1994), the efficacy of family labor supervision diminishes as farm size grows and family labor becomes spread too thinly over a large area. Specifically we assume that $\gamma(T, L^h) < 1$ for all values, that $\partial\gamma/\partial T \leq 0$ and that $\partial^2\gamma/\partial T^2 \geq 0$ such that beyond some farm size, γ flattens out.[2]

As with the shadow price of capital, the effect of this labor market specification is to make the effective or shadow price of labor endogenous to the individual's choices and, ultimately, their endowments. The end result is an analogue to the Chayanovian world in which the opportunity cost of labor is subjectively (or endogenously) determined. While the more recent literature on household models tends to characterize an endogenous shadow price of labor as reflecting a non-separability between consumption and production decisions (e.g., see Singh, Squire, and Strauss 1986), it results here, as in those household models, from the fact that labor markets are thin or otherwise imperfect.

[2] This assumption is meant to simply account for the switch to a hierarchical supervision model that would be anticipated to occur as the efficacy of informal, family labor supervision diminishes with operational farm size (see Carter and Zimmerman 1998 for a more complete specification).

One way to explore these countervailing market failures and aggregate their cross-cutting economic impacts on the land market is to examine their impact on the shadow price of land assuming self-cultivation:

$$r = \partial\pi^*(T, M, \iota)/\partial T. \tag{7}$$

If we capitalize an infinite stream of the income increments given in (7), we arrive at a possible measure of the shadow asset of price of land that we will refer to as the net present production value (NPPV) of land:

$$\rho = \sum_{t=1}^{\infty}[r(T^0, M^0, \tau)]/(1 + \mu(T, M))^t, \tag{8}$$

where the discount rate, μ, is the shadow price of the capital constraint given in expression (3) above. Note that this expression will not in general be independent of relative factor prices and technology, as these two things effectively shape how costly any particular market failure is. To keep matters simple, we will assume that market prices and technologies persist indefinitely into the future so that Δ does not change over time.

The Chayanovian base case and peasant hyper-competitiveness in the land market

Using the model just developed, this section explores the operation of the land market under a simplifying base case scenario in which the shadow price of capital defined by the working capital constraint (expression 3 above) simply equals the market interest rate 'i' for all individuals. Under this scenario, maximization of (1) departs from a standard, perfect markets profit maximization problem only in terms of the labor market imperfections described above.

The top panel of Figure 10.1 displays the qualitative nature of the relationship between the shadow land valuation measure (expression 7 above) and the land–labor endowment ratio, T^0/L^0. The solid, base case line in the figure is drawn conditional on average technical efficiency or skill endowment, $\bar{\tau}$, and is of course conditioned on the assumption that the shadow price of capital equals the market rate, $\mu = i$. This case exhibits what might be termed 'peasant hyper-competitiveness' in the sense that those units with the lowest relative land endowments have the highest shadow price for land. The shadow price curve flattens out as shown given the assumption above that beyond some point, the efficiency of labor extraction bottoms out at some constant rate.

Given a market rental rate for land, p_r, (and assuming, for the moment, that there are no transaction costs), the lower panel in Figure 10.1 displays the desired land transactions as a function of the endowment ratio. Let Δ^* denote desired land transactions. A production unit with endowment ratio $\bar{t}$ would have a shadow rental rate exactly equal to the market rate and would have no incentives to make any transactions. Units with endowment ratios below $\bar{t}$ would tend to rent land in until their operational land–labor ratio equaled $\bar{t}$, while those with more abundant land endowment would rent land out.

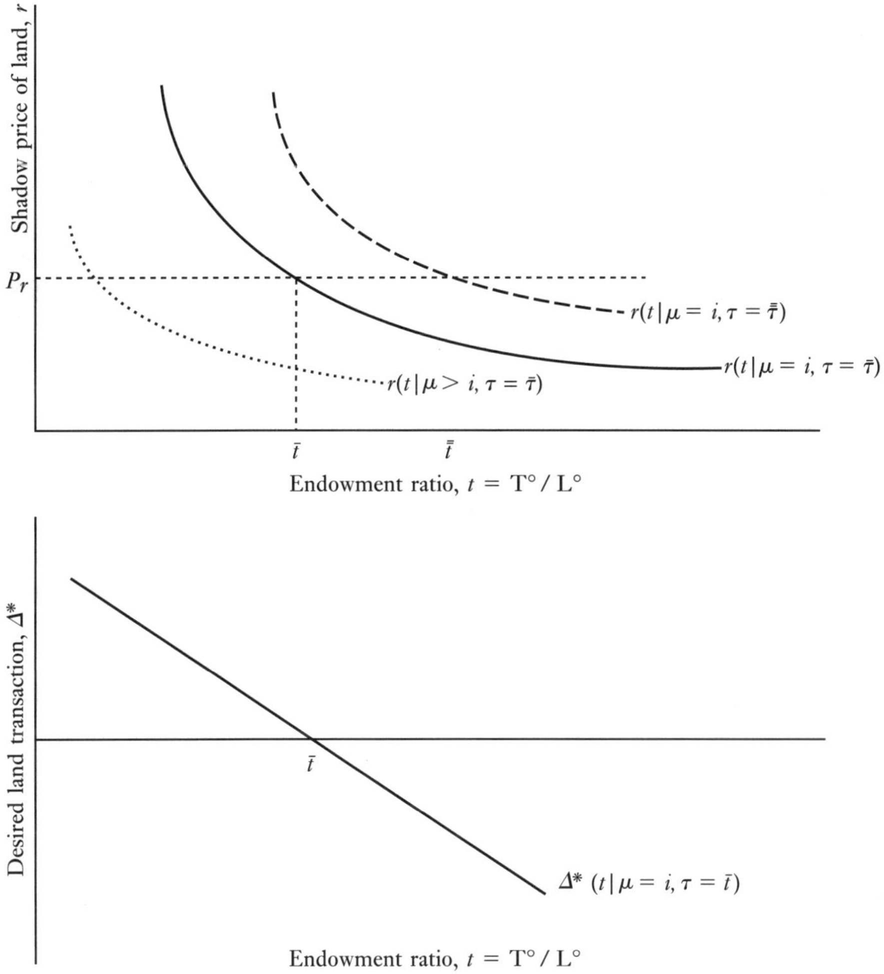

Figure 10.1. *Agent heterogeneity and the land*

As shown by the dashed line in Figure 10.1, the net present production value of land under self-cultivation (expression 8 above) would exactly mirror the shadow price r in this base case scenario where the shadow price of working capital is assumed to equal the market rate for all agents. If there were no land rental market at all, and the market price of purchasing land was p_t, then agents would face incentives to use the land sales market to expand or contract their land holdings to $\bar{t}$. If there were a land rental market, then the incremental annual income an agent could get from owning additional land would never fall below the rental rate. If the land market were perfect (in the sense that its operation was uninhibited by transaction costs, credit constraints, and agency problems associated with share contracts), then the mapping between endowment ratio and the net present value of land would be the same for all agents. In the intermediate case in which rental markets exist but are imperfect, then the ownership value of land under self-cultivation would be higher then rental return, at least for agents with small enough endowments. In this more realistic case, the mapping from endowments to ρ would continue to mirror that shown in Figure 10.1. We will refer to the mapping between endowment ratio and the shadow price of land as the 'class competitiveness regime.'

Now consider what happens to the shadow rental rate and desired transactions for units that enjoy a higher level of technical efficiency or skill, $\bar{\bar{\tau}} > \bar{\tau}$. Other things equal, the shadow price of land for these units would lie above that for units of average technical efficiency, as shown by the dashed line in the top panel of Figure 10.1. Given a market rental rate of p_r, the higher efficiency units would want to expand or contract their operational farm size until their land–labor endowment ratio matched $\bar{\bar{t}}$. If there were no land rental markets, then the NPPV asset value of land would mirror the shadow rental value curve, and high efficiency units would have incentive to expand through the land purchase market up to farm size $\bar{\bar{t}}$.

To summarize, in this Chayanovian base case, the class competitiveness regime favors low wealth, peasant producers. In addition, technically more efficient agents are also competitively favored in the land market.

Countervailing capital constraints and land market competitiveness

The base case scenario in the prior section assumed that all units faced a shadow price of capital equal to the market rate of interest. Other things equal, capital-constrained units with a shadow price of capital in excess of the market interest ($\mu > i$) will be described by a shadow rental rate curve similar to the dotted line in Figure 10.1 and they would tend to an operational farm size such as $\bar{t}^{cc}$. The decrease in the shadow price of land results of course from the inability of capital constrained agents to produce with the same factor intensities as unconstrained agents.[3] The shadow price of land curve for technically more efficient, but capital-constrained producers (i.e., those with $\tau = \bar{\bar{\tau}}$ and $\mu > i$) would lie somewhere between the dotted and dashed lines. While it is not possible without additional assumptions or information to say anything more about the relative competitiveness of different types of producers, note that it would be possible for a technically efficient, low wealth producer to have a shadow price of land below that of a less efficient, but better capitalized and better endowed unit. Moreover, since the net present production value of land, ρ, is found by discounting a stream of single period shadow prices at the rate μ, capital constraints doubly dampen competitiveness in the land purchase market.[4]

[3] The first order conditions that describe optimal factor allocation for the maximization problem given above equate the marginal value product of each input to its effective factor cost marked up by the shadow price of capital. For example, the first order condition for fertilizer is: $p_c \partial Q/\partial F = p_f(1 + \mu)$. Units with higher shadow prices of capital will thus use less labor and fertilizer per hectare than capital unconstrained units.

[4] Discounting future income at a rate other than μ would be economically irrational as it would imply a different rate of return on farm intensification versus farm extensification.

Unlike the Chayanovian base case in which low land wealth assured competitiveness, in this more general model, the competitive survival of the 'poor but efficient' is not guaranteed in the sense that better endowed and less efficient producers, but capital unconstrained producers, may have higher shadow prices of land. Indeed, since the net present production value of land, ρ, is found by discounting a stream of single period shadow prices, any differences between short-term shadow prices will be magnified by differences in the shadow price of capital used as the discount rate in (8).

Land as an asset and the dynamics of accumulation

While informative about the core income factors that shape the willingness to pay for land, the net present value approach to land valuation used so far overlooks both risk and intertemporal considerations (the trade off between current and future consumption) which influence a household's willingness to pay for land. These additional considerations create two opposing forces, one increasing the relative valuation of land by poor households, and the other diminishing it.

In simplest terms, the addition of dynamics to the land valuation problem gives the household one more degree of freedom by permitting it to trade off current consumption for future assets. Resource-poor households may have a greater incentive to forgo current consumption and accumulate assets because these assets carry what might be termed a strategic value beyond increased future income. The strategic value lays in the extent to which additional accumulation of assets permits households to (eventually) circumvent market failures (for example, credit rationing) that constrain their income.

Carter and Zimmerman (1999) explore the impact of these dynamic considerations in a theoretical model that allows households to allocate income earned in each production period between consumption and accumulation of the stocks of two assets, liquid savings, and land. One accumulation strategy for capital-rationed, resource-poor households is to suppress current consumption, accumulate liquid savings in order to better capitalize their production process, and work around the countervailing capital market failure which limits their land valuation according to the simple net present value criterion. Numerical simulation of this model shows that there is indeed a tendency for the economy to eventually move toward a more egalitarian distribution. However, the process is slow, and there are likely other dynamic factors that inhibit this redistribution of wealth.

Risk is one of those dynamic factors. In multiple asset models, such as Carter and Zimmerman's, risk can differentially affect portfolio choice according to a household's initial wealth level. Resource-poor households may allocate a disproportionately large share of their wealth to safer, liquid savings, while wealthier households may acquire more entrepreneurial portfolios (Rosenzweig and Binswanger 1993; Murdoch 1995). Indeed, it can be shown that households value discount land, based on the severity of their risk aversion and risk exposure.

Zimmerman and Carter (1999) derive asset accumulation trajectories from the simulation of a dynamic stochastic general equilibrium model similar in structure to the non-stochastic model described above. Each individual in this economy receives a common, or covariate, shock each period (e.g., weather), as well as an individual, or idiosyncratic, shock. Each period, individuals allocate their wealth between consumption, productive assets, and safe savings. Savings are assumed to be in-kind (grain store), and the productive asset (land) will generate an expected positive, but risky, rate of return. The asset price is endogenous to supply and demand each period. Households maximize an infinite stream of (expected) utility with rational expectations on price distributions.

In the Zimmerman and Carter model, the economy bifurcates toward two stable asset positions: wealthier households accumulate land, assembling a riskier, but higher returning portfolio, while poorer households shy away from land accumulation and accumulate in-kind savings.[5] Central to the operation of this model is the covariance between the land price and the common, or covariate, shock. Resource-poor households are driven toward safe but low-yielding portfolios not just because of production risk, but also because endogenous land price movements make it hard to use the land to smooth consumption (for example, when the weather is bad, land prices tend to be low, and when the weather is good, land prices tend to be high). If they instead tried to smooth consumption using land assets, poor households would find that distress sales, coupled with those covariate land price swings, would render their asset position indefensible over time. Market-based land sales in this model actually lead the economy to a position of lower aggregate productivity. However, perhaps the important point of this theoretical analysis is that risk and land prices are both affected by the severity of covariate risk and the breadth of the market in which land can be sold. Together these considerations suggest that poor households' willingness to pay for land, as an asset, and their land market competitiveness, may be less than that suggested by the simpler net present value criterion.

Land titling and land market competitiveness

As described in Section 1 above, land titling is one of the primary instruments in contemporary Latin American land policy. This section explores its possible impacts on peasant competitiveness and the land market.

When an agent holds land under an insecure form of tenure, the shadow price of land (in the net present value terms introduced in equation (1) above) can be written as:

$$\rho = \sum_{t=1}^{\infty}[(1-\phi)^t r(T^0, M^0, \phi)]/(1+\mu)^t, \tag{9}$$

where the new term, $0 < \phi < 1$, is the single-period probability that the household will be dispossessed of its land. Assuming that this probability is constant over time, $(1-\phi)t$ gives the probability that the household will still be in possession of its land at the end of period t. As t increases, $(1-\phi)t$ decreases, reflecting the uncertainty-based discounting of future earnings, and hence an undervaluation of land as reflected

[5] The results presume the existence of a subsistence minimum, below which consumption is presumed to irrevocably damage future utility possibilities.

in a lower ρ. To the extent that this tenure insecurity depresses fixed capital investment in land, incremental earnings from land, $r(T^0, M^0, \phi)$, will be depressed, further eroding the shadow price of land.

Tenure insecurity may not be identical for all individuals. To the extent that less well-off individuals are politically weaker and more vulnerable to land loss, tenure insecurity may disproportionately reduce their competitiveness in the land market relative to wealthier and politically better-connected individuals. Under this circumstance, a program of land titling that equalizes tenure security for all individuals may actually bolster the land market competitiveness of landless and near-landless people.

Tenure insecurity may also make the land market thin and inactive. Current land occupants may (uniquely) enjoy relatively great security, while other individuals—potential buyers—may not. In this case, transactions will be discouraged, as everyone except the current occupant will heavily discount earnings, making it less likely that a mutually beneficial transaction can take place. Similarly, such asymmetric tenure security may apply to distinct groups of individuals. Individuals resident in the same community (and social situation) as a current landholder may enjoy a similar amount of tenure insecurity. Outsiders, however, may not. Property rights reform (e.g., land titling) that secures the land rights of all agents might thus be expected to activate the land market.[6] Exactly how an activated land market works of course depends ultimately on the underlying class competitiveness regime.

Finally, land titling may have a credit supply effect. To the extent that (1) insecurity rests most heavily on smaller scale producers, and (2) titling suffices to boost credit supply, then land titling may help boost the competitiveness of small landless and near landless households by helping them get on to the unconstrained reservation price and land demand curves shown in Figure 10.1. However, to the extent that credit markets remain biased against low wealth agents irrespective of the legal collateralizability of their land (see Barham *et al.* 1995), then land titling may have no or even perverse effects upon the relative land market competitiveness of small farm households.

Summary of the theoretical model and hypotheses to be tested

A single period model drawn from the literature on agrarian markets suggests that other things equal, a household's desired land purchases are decreasing in its land–labor

[6] Even when land rights are well defined and marketable, there are two categories of transaction costs that potentially affect the ability of resource-poor households to participate in land markets. Conventional fixed costs may make small transactions prohibitively expensive and weigh heavily against the land market participation of landless and near-landless people. In addition, bargaining and subdivision or agglomeration costs—which are related to the degree of heterogeneity between trading partners—may discourage what might be termed inter-class transactions in which the poor buy from the rich or the rich from the poor. If sufficiently severe, these costs may segment the land market such that the market for a small piece of land is really a different market than that for a large piece of land. Stringer and Lambert (1989) and Lambert and Stanfield (1990) present evidence of segmentation for Guatemala and Ecuador, respectively. Such land market segmentation would obviously pose a barrier to inter-class land transfers, including those which are potentially efficiency enhancing and poverty reducing. Presuming that resource-poor households would purchase land in small lots, their competitive advantage in the land market would have to be strong enough to overcome any systematic net price differentials generated by these various transaction costs.

endowment and increasing in its technical efficiency. However, other things are often not equal, especially between households of different wealth levels. In particular, capital constraints have the capacity to blunt the competitive advantage of low wealth or technically efficient producers. Moreover these effects are magnified in the land asset market, as compared to the land rental market. Finally, dynamic models show us that intertemporal and portfolio considerations have an ambiguous effect on the relative land market competitiveness of the land poor. However, as risk increases the competitiveness dampening effects of credit constraints are likely to be enhanced. Ultimately, whether or not low wealth, peasant producers are competitive is an empirical question whose answer is likely to vary across agro-ecological environments. Finally, while there is reason to expect that land titling programs may bolster the relative competitiveness of small-scale producers and accelerate land market activity, transaction costs may continue to discriminate against small-purchasers, and inter-class transactions between rich and poor may be difficult. In short, from a theoretical perspective there can be no easy presumption that liberalized land markets will suffice to resolve the agrarian question in favor of the landless and near landless households.

A microeconometric analysis of the land market in Paraguay

In contrast to the cases of Honduras and Chile to be discussed below, Paraguay has not recently experienced any major reform or redistribution of agrarian property rights. Colonization projects, primarily launched in the 1960s and 1970s, assigned legally secure, but initially unmarketable property rights to their beneficiaries. Those rights became fully marketable once the individual had paid off his or her colonization debt. More generally, however, rural Paraguay has been typified by a wide variety of tenure regimes, including significant informal squatting that developed given the country's historically long period of land abundance. From an analytical perspective, Paraguay thus gives us an (uncontrolled) experiment that we can use to explore the operation of the land market and the impact of land titling upon it.

In order to study these questions, this chapter draws upon the panel data utilized by Carter and Olinto (1996) to study the impact of land titling on investment demand and credit supply. As detailed in that earlier study, the data emerged from a stratified, multi-stage random sample of 300 producer households distributed across three distinctive regions of rural Paraguay: the traditional core 'minifundia' zone of Paraguarí; the colonization zone of San Pedro; and the department of Itapúa, located in the frontier region with Brazil which has seen both significant immigration and agro-export growth. The producer households were first interviewed in 1991, and again in 1994. Whenever possible, households which exited farming between 1991 and 1994 were replaced by successor units which were found in 1994 to be cultivating at least some portion of the land resources of the exiting household. Both interviews collected full production and income information as well as a detailed accounting of the modes of land access and land transactions.

Table 10.1. *Characteristics of land sales and rental market participants*

	Rental market			Sales market		
	Rented-in 1991	Non-participants 1991	Rented-out 1991	Net buyers 1991–94	Non-participants 1991–94	Net sellers 1991–94
Number of households	72	159	48	20	217	42
1991 net rental	16.48	0.00	−4.56	6.17	3.24	3.36
1991–94 mean net purchases	0.38	−0.22	−2.29	18.49	0.00	−11.60
Mean-owned land	13.65	32.85	43.71	88.76	26.45	18.83
(median)	(0.88)	(10.0)	(20.0)	(12.75)	(10.0)	(10.0)
Mean family labor force	3.19	3.70	4.02	3.75	3.68	3.31
(median)	(2.75)	(3.0)	(4.0)	(3.75)	(3.0)	(2.50)
Mean endowment ratio	5.20	10.12	11.77	19.13	8.81	6.07
(median)	(0.29)	(3.42)	(6.31)	(2.89)	(2.88)	(5.0)
Mean-operated land (1991)	31.14	32.85	43.80	95.43	30.73	23.60
(median)	(6.0)	(10.0)	(20.0)	(12.75)	(10.0)	(10.0)
Mean age of HH head	44.65	49.64	57.88	46.00	50.57	47.43
Mean credit constraint	0.74	0.56	0.39	0.51	0.57	0.66
Probability (median)	(1.0)	(0.53)	(0.33)	(0.55)	(0.60)	(0.84)
Median technical efficiency	0.84	0.82	0.85	0.87	0.84	0.83

A descriptive statistical portrait of the operation of the land market

In order to get an initial feel for the operation of the land market in rural Paraguay, Table 10.1 presents descriptive indicators for the household production units that were included in the initial 1991 survey stratified according to their position in the land rental and sales markets. For each production unit it is possible to calculate both owned[7] and operated area for 1991, with the difference between the two being net rentals for 1991. In addition, using the 1994 data, each household can be classified based on whether it increased, decreased, or did not change its land ownership between 1991 and 1994. The full data required for the analysis were available for only 279 of the 300 units covered in the original survey.[8]

The descriptive statistics in Table 10.1 give some idea about the relationship between changing land access and various household characteristics that the discussion in Section 2 suggests may create heterogeneous land valuation. In terms of the land rental market, the descriptive statistics reported in Table 10.1 suggest that households exhibiting high owned land to labor endowment ratios are indeed more likely to rent

[7] Here 'owned' is used loosely to mean that the household either owns the plot with legally recognized title or is a squatter on the plot, meaning that other agents (the state or private individuals) could contest that individual's rights to the plot.

[8] There was some attrition from the sample between 1991 and 1994. Farm units that exited were, when possible, replaced by a successor farm unit, which was found to be using at least one of the plots or parcels of land cultivated by the 1991 unit.

land out. While the mean (median) endowment ratio of the group of households renting land in is 5.2 (0.29) hectares per family worker, for households renting land out, the figure is 10.12 (3.43). Therefore, those who rent land in tend to be relatively land scarce, while those who rent it out are relatively land abundant. The mean endowment ratios do follow the pattern suggested in the conceptual discussion in the previous section. Older farmers also appear more likely to rent out land. The average age of the heads of the households renting land out is 58, while for those renting land in, the average age is 45. At this level, there are no apparent differences in the technical efficiency among those who rent land in versus those who do not.[9]

Farmers renting land out also seem to enjoy better access to formal credit. The mean (median) of the estimated credit constraint probabilities for households renting land in is 0.74 (1.0), for households renting land out it is 0.39 (0.33). These credit constraint probabilities derive from the disequilibrium credit market model that Carter and Olinto (1997) estimate using unobserved switching regression methods for this Paraguayan panel data set. Having estimated the notional demand (D^*_{it}) for and supply (S^*_{it}) of formal credit, Carter and Olinto are able to calculate the probability that a particular household k in period t is credit rationed at the observed market rate of interest:

$$\Pr[D^*_{kt} - S^*_{kt} \geq 0 \mid Q_{kt}, \phi_{kt}, X_{kt}, Z_{kt}], \tag{10}$$

where the conditioning variables are observed borrowing (Q_{kt}), household endowments that influence demand (X_{kt}) and supply (Z_{kt}) of credit, and the percent of own land that is titled (ϕ_{kt}). It is these estimated probabilities that are used to derive the descriptive statistics in Table 10.1. Because these probabilities are also important to the estimation and interpretation of the econometric model of the land market below, Figure 10.2 portrays the estimated pattern of credit constraints.[10] As a function of the household land–labor endowment ratio, Figure 10.2 portrays the estimated probability of being credit constrained when the owned land is both titled (the solid line) and untitled (the dashed line). As can be seen, land title has no impact on credit constraints for households with fewer than 2 hectares of land per family worker, and even for households with up to 5 hectares of titled land per family worker, the estimated probability of being credit-constrained still exceeds 50%. We thus see that although land titling has the potential to level access to capital, and thus to serve as an instrument to enhance small farm land market competitiveness (see the discussion above), it does not seem to function in this fashion in the case of rural Paraguay.

Table 10.2 also gives descriptive statistics for households based on their position in the land sales market. While the mean of the land–endowment ratio for net buyers is three times larger than the mean for net sellers (respectively, 19.13 and 6.07 hectares per family worker), the median is smaller (2.89 and 5.00 hectares respectively). This

[9] The measures of relative technical efficiency were generously provided by Diana Fletschner. The details on the computation of these non-parametric measures of relative technical efficiency can be found in Fletschner (1995).

[10] Figure 10.2 is drawn for a household with a median labor endowment of three workers.

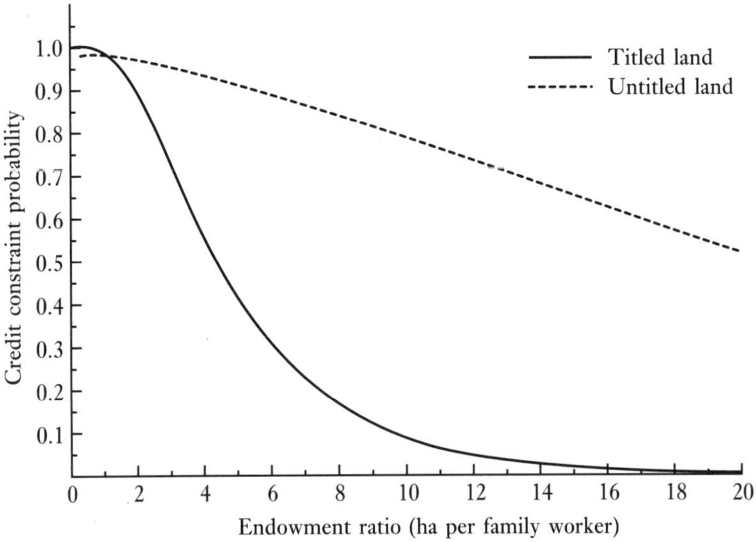

Figure 10.2. *Wealth-differentiated credit supply effect of land titles*

may indicate that while net sellers belong to a more homogeneous class of farmers, there are probably two types of buyers: (1) labor abundant farmers, who exhibit a high willingness to pay for land because of their competitive advantage in the labor market; and (2) land rich farmers, for whom better access to formal credit may put them in a better financial position to acquire land from possibly financially distressed farmers. The statistics on total owned land somewhat confirm this distinctive heterogeneity between buyers and sellers. While the median owned areas are similar across buyers, sellers, and non-participants (12.75, 10, and 10 hectares, respectively), the mean owned size for buyers (88.76 hectares) is substantially larger than for sellers (18.83 hectares) and non-participants (26.45 hectares).

Matching the predictions of the theoretical model above, net buyers of land also appear to enjoy a better access to institutional credit. The mean (median) of the estimated probabilities of being credit-constrained is larger for sellers than it is for buyers. The descriptive statistics again reveal little apparent impact of technical efficiency differences, nor does age appear to be much of a factor distinguishing land sellers from land purchasers at the descriptive level.

Econometric estimates of the land market

The theoretical model presented above suggests the following switching regressions specification:

$$\Delta_k^* = \begin{cases} \beta^c x_k^c + \epsilon_k^c & \text{if } \mu_k > i; \\ \beta^u x_k^u + \epsilon_k^u & \text{otherwise,} \end{cases} \tag{11}$$

where Δ_k^* is household k's desired net purchase of land over the 1991 to 1994 period of the panel; and where the regression switches depending on whether or not the household is constrained in the formal credit market ($\mu_k > i$) and the superscript β^c refers to parameters and variables for the capital-constrained case and the superscript β^u for the unconstrained case. Included in the vector, x_k, of explanatory variables are measures of the factors (other than capital constraints) hypothesized above to influence land valuation, including a measure of technical efficiency (derived from non-parametric, data envelopment techniques), the household's land–labor endowment ratio, age of household head (included to adjust the land–labor ratio for the presumably lower effective labor supply of older people). Note that we have no measure of risk-bearing capacity or desired portfolio holdings, although we expect them to be correlated with both endowment wealth and credit constraints.

Econometrically, the impact of the fixed transaction costs discussed above would be to censor the regression relationship. Following the econometrics of so-called 'friction models' (e.g., see Madalla 1983), and letting Δ_k denote the actual, or censored net-purchase, the switching regression system (10) above can be rewritten as:

$$\Delta_k = \begin{cases} \Delta_k^* & \text{if } \Delta_k^* < -\alpha^j \Rightarrow \epsilon_k^j < (\alpha^j + \beta^j x_k^j) \\ 0 & \text{if } -\alpha < \Delta_k^* < \alpha^j \Rightarrow -(\alpha^j + \beta^j x_k^j) < \epsilon_k^j < (\alpha^j - \beta^j x_k^j) \\ \Delta_k^* & \text{if } \Delta_k^* > \alpha^j \Rightarrow \epsilon_k^j > (\alpha^j - \beta^j x_k^j) \end{cases} \qquad (12)$$

where $j = c$, u indexes the credit and unconstrained regimes.

Carter, Olinto, and Fletschner (1997) estimate the endogenous switching regression specification in (12) using the estimated credit constraint probabilities in a two-stage procedure. Figures 10.3 and 10.4 present the most important results from that estimation. Figure 10.3 displays the estimated relationships between the probability that a household rents in land as a function of its land–labor endowment ratio. That is, it estimates the probability that

$$\Pr[\epsilon_k^c > (\alpha^c - \beta^c x_k^c)]. \qquad (13)$$

The complementary probability is divided between the events that either the household rents out land, or that they do not participate at all in the land rental market (given transaction costs that discourage small adjustments). The non-participation probability is in fact quite large for all endowment ratios. The probability estimates in the top panel are conditional estimates in the sense that they condition on, or control for, the credit constraint regime.

Consistent with the predictions of the Chayanovian base case, the probabilities for both credit-constrained and unconstrained regimes are decreasing in the land–labor endowment. Somewhat surprisingly, the predicted probabilities are higher for the credit-constrained case for farm units with a land–labor ratio below 5 hectares per worker (or about 15 physical hectares for a household with a median endowment of three family workers). Perhaps these units are in fact using rental relationships to access capital that otherwise would not be available to them. Note also that predicted rental probability decreases very little as the endowment ratio increases for households in the

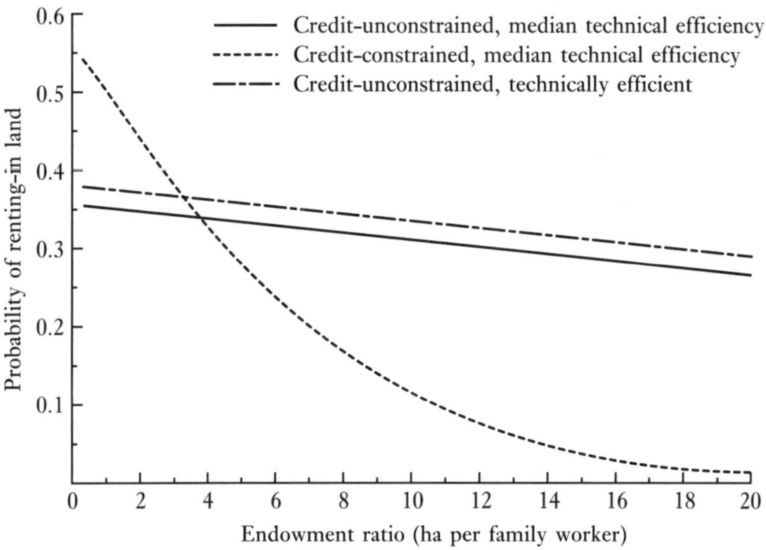

Figure 10.3. *Land rental market*

unconstrained regime. Finally, note that the rental probability increases with estimated technical efficiency in the credit-unconstrained case, as predicted. In the credit-constrained case, the estimated impact of technical efficiency is both numerically small and statistically insignificant.

Figure 10.4 shows unconditional land purchase probabilities as a function of the land–labor endowment. These probabilities are unconditional in that they weigh together the conditional probabilities for the credit-constrained and unconstrained regimes by the probability that a household of the indicated endowment level is in the indicated regime. As shown in Figure 10.2 above, households with endowment ratios below 5 hectares per family worker are estimated to more likely be in the credit-constrained regime. These unconditional estimates thus give insight into the actual sorts of structural incentives that there are for land purchase by farms of different sizes. In addition, the figure has been constructed on the assumptions that all households hold full, marketable title to their land. The figure can thus be read as an indicator of the operation of the land market following a full land titling program.

In sharp contrast to the land rental market estimates, we see that the estimated land purchase probability increases sharply with land–labor endowment.[11] Technically efficient producers with relatively large land endowments are estimated to enjoy a (statistically significant) boost of 10 percentage points in the probability that they will purchase land (as compared to an otherwise identical household with the median level of technical efficiency of 80%). In contrast, the 'poor but efficient' producer (who is also most likely credit-constrained) is estimated to have no chance of participating in the land market as a buyer. In short, these estimates indicate that the land purchase

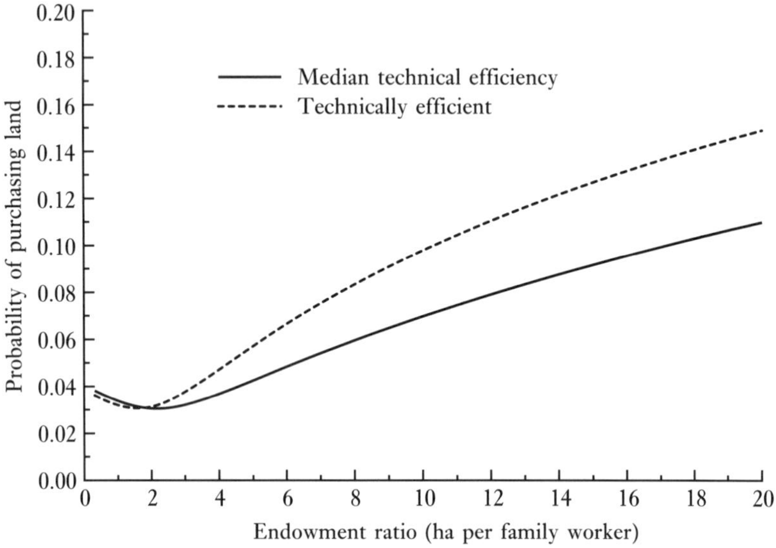

Figure 10.4. *Land sales market, unconditional probabilities*

market is not a realm in which landless and near-landless households are likely to be competitive.

In addition to its deleterious impact on factor allocation and hence on the shadow value of land defined in equations (7) and (8) above, there are two other effects of borrowing constraints that might be contributing to these results: a transaction costs effect and a portfolio effect. While the transaction costs effect influences households' ability to buy land in the increments that they can self-finance, the portfolio effect influences their dynamic willingness to pay for land. In Paraguay, there is no credit for land purchases for most households—including rich ones. A household's inability to meet its working capital needs (which is what the credit constraint indicator variable measures) is surely correlated with its ability to finance land purchases. Moreover, transaction costs discourage the purchase of land in tiny incremental amounts. It might be the case that a household desiring to increase its land holdings by 10 hectares would not be able to do so by purchasing small amounts, say 1 hectare for the next ten years. Instead, the household must save enough to purchase chunks of 5 hectares. That is, because land cannot be purchased in small incremental amounts, households need first to accumulate enough liquid wealth in order to become able to bid for a given parcel of land. And yet it is precisely a scarcity of liquidity that the credit constraint variable signals.

[11] The estimated effect of an incremental increase in the land–labor endowment ratio on the probability of a household participating in the land sales market as a buyer, evaluated at the median values of the explanatory variables, is 0.22, which is significantly different from zero at the 5% level of significance (the Wald statistic for the restriction $\partial\Delta_i^*/\partial(T_i/N_i) = 0$ is 5.41). For the households in the credit-constrained regime, the estimated effect of T_i/N_i on Δ_i^* is slightly negative, but not significantly different from zero at any of the conventional levels.

In addition, a portfolio effect could be caused by the precautionary behavior of credit-constrained households. Households identified as credit-constrained econometrically may in fact perceive themselves as having difficulty in accessing institutional credit in the future. Therefore, depending on the magnitude of the effect that land wealth has on access to institutional credit, constrained households may prefer to hold more liquid portfolios, with less land and more livestock and/or grains. Thus, this portfolio effect—highly correlated with current working capital constraints—is caused by the household's expectation of facing borrowing constraints in a future in which income is uncertain.

In summary, while this section's results give evidence that land rental markets are a medium of land access for land-scarce households, they also show that there is little hope that the land purchase market can work in favor of small-scale producers, even in the wake of property rights reform that provided legally clear and marketable title to all land owners. Capital and financial market constraints appear to lie at the heart of this result. In particular, the failure of land titles to bolster the formal capital access of smallholders appears to be a key breakdown in the linkage between land titling and improved land access of the less well off. In short, land titling appears to be an insufficient instrument to bolster the competitiveness of the poor and turn the land market into an arena in which the agrarian question is resolved in favor of peasant land access. The concluding section of this paper will return to some of the policy implications of these observations.

The Honduran Agrarian Modernization Law and its impact on the land market and peasant land access

Similar to other countries in the Latin American region, Honduras has entered what de Janvry, Sadoulet, and Wolford (this volume) call a Phase III land policy that looks to the land market to secure peasant access in the wake of measures designed to individualize land ownership, establish legal tenure security, and increase the marketability of land. In addition to land titling efforts that began in earnest in the mid-1980s, the Honduran National Congress set the stage for this Phase III in March of 1992 when it adopted the 'Modernization and Development of the Agrarian Sector Law.' Among the most controversial components of this law were its provisions relating to land tenure that:

- eliminated the prospect of future redistributive expropriation of large farms;
- allowed land reform beneficiaries to lease or sell their land;
- permitted land reform beneficiaries to enter into co-investment projects with private businesses.

Those favoring the Agrarian Modernization Law argued that the agrarian reform had run its course (and probably was never very effective), and that continuing the threat of further expropriation only caused uncertainty in the rural area that limited investment.[12]

[12] For a review of the various viewpoints on the agrarian modernization debate, see Sandoval Corea (1992) and the other papers included in that issue of *Puntos de Vista*.

From this perspective, a dynamic land market was needed to increase investments, production, and job opportunities in the Honduran agrarian economy; and to consolidate an agro-export sector.

Opponents of the Agrarian Modernization Law agreed that the agrarian reform process was going nowhere in the late 1980s and that there was a need to modernize it. From their perspective, 'modernization' should include a re-conversion of the peasants' enterprises, which would include better use of the land, technological development, and business methods to consolidate peasants' cooperatives. These opponents also doubted that a more dynamic land market would do anything more than increase land ownership concentration and expand the gap between the rich and poor, differences which the agrarian reform intends to abolish (Sandoval Corea 1992). From this perspective, further expropriation appeared as the only avenue toward enhanced land access for the peasantry.

The Agrarian Modernization Law was to have been accompanied by a land bank and a rural credit fund. However, while approved legally, these ancillary measures have yet to be implemented (Moreno 1994). While the measures approving the land bank and the rural credit fund were approved in 1993, as of the end of 1997, neither had taken effect either due to lack of financial resources, the slow and complex bureaucracy of the legal system that exists in the country, and/or simply because of a lack of political will to carry them out (Suazo 1996). The result is that Honduras has entered Phase III in a fairly *laissez faire* spirit. The remainder of this section will discuss in turn the available evidence concerning the impact of both land titling and the Agrarian Modernization Law on land markets and peasant land access.

Impact of land titling on the development of the land markets

There has always been a market where transactions for the purchase and sale, leasing, inheritance, and donations of land are carried out in Honduras. This market presents three basic working characteristics: it is segmented, it is a means of accruing land, and it is quite informal (Salgado *et al.* 1994). The latter is the most important one since, in land transactions, informal means are predominant because they are based more on the usage and local customs than on legal rules.

Historically in Honduras, there have been government and municipal lands that peasants have held without legal rights of ownership. One might expect that the prevalence of such lands would have restricted the development of the land markets. When such land is sold, at best the seller can provide a title of eminent domain or a private purchase-sale contract where what has been sold are the improvements made to the land but not the land itself which continues being the sole property of the government (Salgado *et al.* 1994). These informal documents are rarely accepted by the state and private banks to grant loans but are so accepted among the peasants in the purchase-sale transactions of properties.

While governments in Honduras have granted formal land titles to land occupants throughout the post-independence period (Perez Brignoli 1973), systematic data collection on the practice did not begin until 1982 when the government of Honduras and USAID launched a land-titling project geared to small and medium independent farmers. The life of the agreement was of five years (1983–87) and included seven of the eighteen departments of Honduras. The project was subsequently expanded until 1990 and one more department was included.

Initially, the main objective of the project consisted in granting titles of property to the small and medium coffee producers who held government or municipal land not bigger than 50 hectares. Later, the project was expanded to include farmers with other types of crops. As a result of the approval of the Agrarian Modernization Law in 1992, land lots of up to 200 hectares were also granted titles. The initial AID/Government of Honduras agreement ended in 1990 and the project, from that day on, became a permanent titling office of the National Agrarian Institute (INA). This office continues receiving funds from international institutions. This financial support has allowed the INA to expand their titling plans to eight more departments, thus increasing its influence to seventeen of the eighteen departments in the country. INA statistics show that since 1982, nearly 95,000 property titles have been granted, covering some 843,000 hectares.

In terms of quantifying achievements, as of June 1997, a total of 94,608 land titles have been granted with a land extension of 842,740.57 hectares. Since the project began in 1982 there has been a drastic increase in the number of titles as well as the quantity of legalized hectares. However, evidence concerning the impact of the land-titling project on investment is mixed. Stanfield *et al.* (1990) find that obtaining a land title does little in terms of enhancing access to credit, a result similar to that reported for Paraguay above. Even in those cases where farmers reported having credit, they observe that this has not had a positive impact and that, definitively, title has not motivated the farmers (as was expected) to increase their production and to carry out improvements on their parcels. Larsen (1993) finds a similar lack of impact of titles on productivity and investment.

In contrast to these studies, Lopez (1996), using a different econometric methodology, identifies a positive association between titles, investment, and agricultural productivity. While the collective ambiguity of these studies is frustrating, it may reflect the difficulty of identifying the impact of titling *per se* given that titles were frequently handed over as part of a package that included credit and technical assistance for coffee and other higher valued crops.

Regarding the impact of titling on the land market, a study done by Coles (1989), five years after the titling project began, compared farmers who had received titles in Santa Barbara (the first department in Honduras targeted by the titling project) with farmers in Ocotepeque, a department that was excluded from the project. Coles found that in Santa Barbara, 15.8% of the people interviewed had newly purchased their land during the 1983 to 1988 period. However, Coles found a similar turnover rate in Ocotepeque. As a result, Coles concludes that titling did nothing to make the land market more dynamic in Santa Barbara, and that land transactions followed the same pattern of previous decades, and are within the normal historical parameters.

Stanfield *et al.* (1990*b*) reach a similar conclusion based on their analysis of empirical data from the departments of Santa Barbara and Comayagua. In Santa Barbara (where land titling took place), after five years, 16.6% of the land parcels had changed ownership. In the control group, which had no titled land, 22.3% of parcels changed hands. They find similar results for Comayagua: 5.7% of titled land parcels changed owners, whereas 14.3% of the control group of untitled parcels changed hands over the same period.

Slightly higher transfer rates are found by Larsen (1993) in her study of Santa Barbara. Unfortunately, neither Larsen's nor the other studies were able to properly control for the amount of transactions induced by old age or other life cycle phenomena. Larsen does find that that those small farmers who live in poverty are the ones more inclined to sell their land parcels (Larsen 1993).

To summarize, while the empirical evidence is weak, it seems relatively safe to conclude that while there is indeed a fairly active land market in the independent farmers sector, its development seems to be rather independent of titling as land transactions seem no more likely in areas with titling than in those without. Obviously these are preliminary results dealing with only two of the thirteen departments where the project of land titling is currently in operation. It might also be of interest to know whether land titles facilitate particular sorts of transaction—especially those between strangers or those that occur for reasons other than standard life cycle turnover reasons. Further studies of the remaining departments with characteristics different from those of Santa Barbara and Comayagua such as types of soil, crops, and access to different means of transportation and communication among other things, will allow us to have a more solid conclusion on the impact titling has had on the land market.

Leasing, sales, and joint ventures in the reform sector following the Agrarian Modernization Law

Agrarian reform in Honduras always separated the affectation, the adjudication, and the final titling of land brought into the agrarian reform. Normally, agrarian reform beneficiaries were not given legal right of ownership titles. Instead, they were granted a temporary title that allowed them to work the land without being the definitive owners. Titling was seen as the last step of the process after a reasonable period of time had elapsed and a selection of those beneficiaries who wanted to remain in the agrarian cooperatives as future owners, and those who preferred to abandon the land and become rural or urban employees.

Out of a total of 2,884 agrarian reform beneficiary groups that existed in 1995, only 965 (34%) had legal rights of ownership land titles, while the rest still had only provisional, and unmarketable, titles of ownership. The negative impact of this situation on the land market was both known and seen as desirable by the former head of the INA, Rigoberto Sandoval Corea, who stated that when there is an ongoing process of agrarian reform the existence of a land market cannot be justified because it simply fosters land concentration.

The first revision to this no land-sales policy occurred in May of 1990 when the National Congress and the INA, inspired by the emerging neoliberal ideas, agreed to the selling of the Farmers Associate Enterprise of Isletas to the transnational Standard

Fruit Company. As described above, the marketability of agrarian reform land was later generalized with the 1992 Agrarian Modernization Law. This law decreed that those groups which benefited from the agrarian reform and which had received their legal rights of ownership titles are empowered to sell their land. Properties larger than 100 hectares that are sold are subject to a tax of 20% that is to be used to finance the land fund and the rural credit funds. This law and the further opening of the land market in the reformed sector has been supported by AID, the World Bank, and the Inter-American Development Bank, as well as by the Federation of Ranchers and Farmers of Honduras, and the Honduran Council of Private Enterprises (COHEP). These institutions and organizations perceive the titling of land as a means to free peasants from government intervention and send them into market conditions, which are considered by these institutions as the best place to improve national production, and living conditions of the farmers (Banco Mundial 1995).

Despite the enthusiastic promotion of land marketability by these groups, peasant organizations saw land titling as the preamble to the destruction of the reformed sector and to the farmer organizations themselves. In response to the fact that a great number of agrarian reform enterprises were selling their land, the National Congress partially re-regulated land sales by reform enterprises in mid-1994. Under the new regulations, beneficiary groups can sell their lands only with the prior approval of INA. In addition, the tax levy was raised to 30%, plus all prior condemnations of debts made by the government to the beneficiary groups had to be repaid (*La Gaceta* 1994). Following these changes, peasant organizations that had opposed the land tenure provisions of the Agrarian Modernization Law adopted a more pragmatic attitude, if for no other reason than they found it impossible to oppose the penetration of the neoliberal model to the countryside. Both the Coordinating Council of Peasant Organizations (COCOCH) and the National Council of Peasants (CNC) eventually accepted the titling process promoted by the INA (Salgado 1996*a*). As of mid-1997, a total of 1,197 final land titles had been issued in the reform sector enterprises, covering 159,908 hectares nationwide. According to INA figures, nearly all these titles were granted following the approval of the Agrarian Modernization Law.

Titling and other provisions of the Agrarian Modernization Law opened the way to three types of arrangements: outright land sales, land leases, and co-investment or joint ventures between reform enterprises and agri-businesses. Table 10.2 gives a regional breakdown for each of these arrangements. While there have been many studies of land sales by reform enterprises (e.g., Ruben and Funez 1993; Chavez 1993; Salgado *et al.* 1994), the most complete is the 1994 Instituto Nacional Agrario study. As reported in Table 10.2, this study shows that of a total of 2,783 peasant enterprises nationwide, 257 (9.3%) had either sold their land totally or partially. Of a total of 426,257 hectares of granted land, the groups had sold 31,187 (or 7.3% of the total).

The regional pattern of these sales is informative. According to the data, the Bajo Aguan, Litoral Atlantico, and the South regions are where the largest numbers of groups that have sold their land are registered, as well as the largest amount of hectares. This does not happen casually, as these are the regions that have become important areas for agricultural investment on products such as bananas, citrus, African palm, cattle,

Table 10.2. *Post-agrarian modernization law transactions in the reform sector*

Region	Total number of reform groups		Land sales		Leasing and joint ventures		
	Number	Hectares	Number	Hectares	Hectares	Number of groups leasing out land	Number of groups in co-investment projects
South	351	42,888	60	2,681	1,355	37	7
Olancho	221	16,198	2	43	494	10	10
Comayagua	299	64,330	14	829	233	0	5
Atlantic Coast	133	12,730	51	3,800	2,000	0	16
Aguan	182	97,985	70	23,434	n.a.	n.a.	n.a.
Norte	974	123,309	37	n.a.	n.a.	n.a.	n.a.
F. Morazon	127	20,337	12	280	n.a.	n.a.	n.a.
Danli	120	20,214	11	118	n.a.	n.a.	n.a.
Occidente	356	28,265	0	0	n.a.	n.a.	n.a.
Total	2,683	426,257	257	31,187	4,802	47	38

Source: sales information elaborated based on Instituto Nacional Agrario (1994). Lease and other information from Cruz and Muñoz (1997).

melons, watermelons, and shrimp, all of them marked for export. The predominance of sales in these more dynamic regions suggests that many reform beneficiaries were simply unable to compete in the new, higher valued activities.

Besides land sales, the land market in the reformed sector has become more dynamic through new legalized means such as leasing and co-investment. The agrarian reform law originally prohibited leasing and co-investment is a new way introduced by the Modernization Law to allow businessmen and peasants to form a partnership and to better use the land. Research carried out in four regions where leasing and co-investment have occurred reveals a pattern similar to that for land sales. Such arrangements are most common in export areas, especially in the southern region where such contracts are for sugar cane (31 contracts) and melons (the remaining 13 contracts). The welfare impacts of these contracts on beneficiaries have not been extensively studied. Newspapers report examples of both positive and negative effects, with the former happening when peasant beneficiaries find themselves deeply indebted to the joint venture operator, with future land sales to cancel the debt likely. In other instances, beneficiaries report significant gains from the improved technical and managerial access made possible by joint venture and other leasing arrangements.

Finally, it is interesting to note that in contrast to the impact of land titling in the non-reform sector (where there is scant evidence of real impacts on either productivity or the land market), the impact of titling and the Agrarian Modernization Law in the reform sector seem much more pronounced as partial land sales, leasing, and co-investment projects have all increased. Clearly, these phenomena are most visible in regions where there are lands producing for agroindustries or for export such as the Aguan Valley, Sico, Sula, Choluteca, or in regions with a strong potential in the production of basic grains such as Olancho.

Poor farmers' access to land through the market

Access to land in Honduras historically has occurred through two mechanisms. First, the national government and local municipalities have granted land to independent producers and peasant cooperatives. Second, land has been accessed through a formal land market where farmers use purchase-sale mechanisms, inheritance, or leasing. While INA does not have statistics on grants made to independent farmers, between 1962 and 1964, the state granted a total of 426,257 hectares to a total of 2,683 agrarian cooperatives (INA 1994).

However, the approval of the Agrarian Modernization Law eliminated this second mechanism of land access, leaving only the market.[13] Land acquisition through the market has not, however, proven easy. Prices have gone up in the last few years, and fertile land is scarce. The tendency observed is that the great land owners acquire the fertile land from small and medium farmers but small farmers do not have any possibility of buying land from the large land owners who do not sell or lease. A similar conclusion follows from Childress (1996), who calculates the shadow value of land for various strata of producers based on econometric estimates of an income function similar to that implied by the model in Section 2 above. In Childress' estimation, capital and other constraints limit the participation of smallholders in some of the more remunerative agro-export activities and thereby limit their ability to effectively utilize the land market as a device to maintain or increase their access to land.

The land market in Chile following redistribution and property rights reform[14]

Chile in the last half century has experienced an array of land redistribution and property rights reform policies, including land redistribution, the later 'regularization' and individualization of redistributed rights, and the reform of land rights held under various customary and informal tenure forms. Over the latter part of this period, Chile's agricultural economy has also become one of the fastest growing sectors in the region, if not the world. This section reviews evidence on the land market impacts, giving special prominence to the micro studies of Mesbah (forthcoming) and Scott (1996) that focus specifically on the land access impacts of these various reforms.

In the face of stagnating agricultural growth in the mid-1960s, the Frei administration (1964–70) embarked Chile on one of the most ambitious land reform programs in Latin America. The agrarian reform, extended and intensified by the Allende administration (1970–73), expropriated 43% of agricultural land measured in quality-adjusted terms. The land reform was abruptly curtailed by a military coup in 1973 and 30% of reform-sector land was returned to former owners. The military allocated

[13] As mentioned above, the new law foresaw the formation of a land bank to assist the peasantry in accessing land. Though enacted in 1993, the Land Fund (FONTIER) has yet to begin operation due to lack of funds, though there is a preliminary study that describes its functioning (Strasma *et al.* 1993).

[14] This section draws heavily on Carter, Barham, and Mesbah (1996).

most of the remaining land in the reform sector to individual beneficiaries as private parcels. Upon the completion of the process of parcelization in 1979, 48,000 families had received plots of land averaging 10 BIH ('basic irrigated hectares')[15] in size. At the same time, legislation introduced in 1979 and 1984 sought to abolish other forms of collective property rights that existed in the communities of the indigenous Mapuche people and in other sections of the country where forms of communal tenure had evolved over the nineteenth and twentieth centuries for complex historical reasons. As reviewed by Scott (1996), these latter reforms were intended to lead to consolidated individual holdings with sharper investment incentives that could form the basis for more rapid agrarian growth.

From 1973 onwards, the military also implemented a sequence of liberal, market-oriented agricultural policies, seeking to insert Chile more firmly into the international market. Agricultural and forestry exports were heavily promoted. As a result, total area under fruit cultivation nearly tripled in the period 1974–90, and the current dollar value of the agro-forestry exports in 1990 was more than ten times as large as that of 1974, garnering widespread admiration for the Chilean export model.

It is evident that the land transactions were a critical ingredient in the above story. As Vogelgesang (1998) remarks, it is hard to imagine that the transformation and growth of the Chilean agrarian economy could have occurred without an active land market. In an effort to obtain a sharper picture of the operation of that market, we turn to two recent surveys that draw on pre-land reform sample frames. In 1965, the Chilean land reform research institute, ICIRA, surveyed 110 large estates in the Central Valley. In the early 1990s, Mesbah then selected a sample of thirteen of these estates and created a listing of the 207 successor smaller-scale farming units that existed on the land of these thirteen former estates following the tenure regularization and parcelizations of the Pinochet government *circa* 1976. She then gathered farm level data on the successor units which are located in two regionally distinct economic environments: one where the production of fruit for export has been booming (the province of Cachapoal, in the northern Central Valley, which has about 25% of the land under fruit cultivation nationwide), and one where the production of traditional domestic market crops is still dominant (the province of Ñuble in the southern Central Valley).

In 1968, ICIRA undertook a nationwide survey of smallholders. In 1986, Scott resurveyed these approximately 200 farm units that were spread across ten communities from northern to southern Chile. The resulting panel data is the base for his comprehensive 1996 manuscript.

The land market in the former large estate area of the Central Valley

The number of parcel sales in the brief period since 1973 has been staggering, especially since in other countries—pre-1975 Chile included—agricultural land markets are

[15] The 'basic irrigated hectare' is a quality-adjusted land measurement unit. It may take as many as 40 physical hectares of poor quality land to equal 1 BIH.

fairly inactive. ICIRA's 1979 study indicated that about 15% of the land reform assignees had sold their land as early as June 1978. Rough estimates suggest that at least 30% of the *parcelas* had been sold by December 1979 (Jarvis 1989) and about 40% by the end of 1986 (Gomez and Echenique 1988). A recent study on *parcelero* land sales estimates that at the national level, 57% of the original 48,000 beneficiaries have sold their land (Echenique and Rolando 1991).

The data on 207 farms collected by Mesbah show that sales by *parceleros* have been more prevalent in the northern Central Valley where production for export crops have been the most profitable (the so-called *fruticola* or fruit-growing zone). Land sales have been less common in areas more suited to the production of traditional crops (the *policultura* or mixed-cropping zone). Using the 1977–91 sales data for the sample of 207 *parcelas*, the disparity in total parcels sold between the predominantly fruit-growing region (54.4%) and the region where fruit production has not yet made such an inroad (45.2%) is significant. Moreover, for the fruit-growing region, the percentage of *parcelas* sold by 1991 increases to 65.3% after excluding the parcels of land located in a more isolated *comuna* where fruit production has only recently become established.

Further evidence on the structural effects of these transactions can be obtained from identifying the extent and patterns of mobility that lead to the dominance of one category of producers over others. Carter, Barham, and Mesbah (1996) use the Mesbah data to construct transition matrices that record the movement of households between different land-size categories between 1977 and 1990. The picture presented by these transition matrices appears somewhat ambiguous at first glance. On the one hand, all households in the top categories (> 40 BIH) in 1977 belonged to those same categories in 1990. In fact, in both regions, several large landlords accumulated land over this period. On the other hand, we observe signs of considerable upward mobility for households in the lowest categories. In both regions, a number of new farming units had been formed by 1990 by households that had no land in 1977. While this observation seems to signal an upward mobility for the landless, closer examination of the background of individual entries in the tables reveals that the new entrants were practically all-new actors in the rural economy with substantial non-agricultural sources of income. These well-financed new individuals—often professionals—have successfully accumulated land at the expense of *parcelero* smallholders.

In fact, the mobility tables reveal a high degree of de-accumulation for land reform *parceleros*. Among households belonging to the 8–12 BIH category that included the majority of *parceleros*, 44% in the mixed-cropping region and only 40% in the fruit-growing region still remained in that category by 1990. Nearly all the other units in these initial size categories diminished in size over the time period. In the southern Central Valley, 35% of households in the 8–12 BIH category in 1977, and 46% in the northern Central Valley, were landless by 1990. In sum, the mobility tables reveal very little upward mobility by *parcelero* households.

This stark and rapid restructuring following the parcelization of the 1970s has led a number of observers (Jarvis 1989; Cox, de Zepeda, and Rojas 1990; and Ortega 1988) to comment on the exclusionary nature of Chile's agro-export growth experience.[16] Other studies on fruit producers, for both the fruit-growing region and the region where the production of traditional crops dominate, reveal low adoption rates of export crops by small-scale farmers (Centro de Informacion de Recursos Naturales—CIREN—1990, 1991). In the fruit-growing region where the province of Cachapoal is located, farms in the 0–5 hectares (ha) size category represent 57% of all agricultural units, but only 16% of fruit growers. Meanwhile, farms greater than 20 ha represent 14% of the agricultural units in the region, but comprise 43% of fruit growers. In the VIII Region, which includes the province of Ñuble, 47.5% of farm units are in the 0–5 ha farm size category, but represent only 15% of fruit producers. Meanwhile, less than 25% of farm units are greater than 20 ha but they represent 62% of fruit producers. In both regions, adoption of fruit crops is clearly dominated by larger growers.[17]

The limited extent of export-crop adoption by smallholders can be explained by the specific characteristics of fruit production, which in an environment of information and wealth-constrained markets, create a bias against smaller production units. Shifting production to fruit plantations is a long-term process that requires large, sunk capital investments with no returns over a long gestation period. Fruit cultivation and export also require standardized production and packaging, necessitating large quantities of working capital and access to additional investment funds. In Chile, exporter credit was available for such production but most smallholders and *parceleros* could not borrow. Smallholders also lacked the human capital attributes such as technical expertise in fruit production or the entrepreneurial ability and familiarity with institutions such as banks and export firms involved in export production (Jarvis 1989). Moreover, smallholders were constrained by agro-export firms' reluctance to commonly contract with small-scale fruit growers, because of the transaction costs involved in working with multiple small producers. The absence of well-organized marketing and processing cooperatives further limited small farmers' participation in the export boom.

Not only were small farmers and *parceleros* generally unable to participate in the export boom, but also the production of the traditional crops they most commonly produced for the domestic market became increasingly less profitable from 1973 until the severe economic and agricultural crisis of 1982–83. Meanwhile, the fruit boom created a strong demand for high-quality *parcelero* land on the part of individuals with sufficient financial resources—including easier access to credit—to participate in the boom. 'Squeezed economically, on the one hand, and offered high prices for land, on the other, many *parceleros* chose to sell out' (Jarvis 1989: 242).

[16] However, such direct exclusionary effects on land use and access of the rural resource-poor in the northern Central Valley may be offset by positive indirect effects from increased employment. Preliminary evidence from the production data gathered in the fruit-growing region reveals that smaller farms are more labor intensive than larger operational units for a given crop; yet, because the direction of induced structural change has also shifted patterns of land use into more labor-intensive crops, the overall impact of the agro-exports boom appears to have increased labor absorption.

[17] In the absence of a new agricultural census, the information on distribution of agricultural properties in the two regions under study is based on agricultural tax rolls for 1989.

The land market in smallholder communities, 1968–1986

Similar to the Carter, Barham, and Mesbah (1996) study, Scott (1996) employs transition matrices to study the operation of the land market in his sample area over the 1968–86 period. After accounting for demographic rhythms of retirement and the formation of new farming household units, Scott finds little evidence of structural change in his *minifundista* farming communities. Moreover, despite the strong debate that surrounded the property rights reform and land titling measures of 1979 and 1983, Scott finds that their impacts were quite modest in his study communities, despite the controversy that originally surrounded the adoption of the property rights reform measures. The contrast between the rapid restructuring that took place in the liberalized reform sector, and the quietude of the traditional smallholder, offers an interesting parallel with Honduras. As discussed in the prior section, there is little consistent evidence that land titling either dynamized the land market or had major investment effects. In contrast, market activity (sales, leases, and joint venture schemes) in the agrarian reform sector was much more pronounced and visible.

Can land markets be enabled for the rural poor? Policy instruments, options and open questions

Policy interest in agricultural property rights and land markets remains high, especially in Latin America (see Inter-American Development Bank 1998). As Vogelgesang (1998) emphasizes, there are various tasks that one might expect or hope the land market to carry out. In an effort to rethink agrarian reform, this chapter has focused squarely on distributional issues, asking whether and when property rights reform and the land market can be enabled to serve as instruments of redistribution, enhancing the land access of well-off rural people. In other words, how do land markets fit into a 'post-Washington Consensus' rural poverty policy?

The theory of the land market presented here suggests that while low-wealth households are likely to enjoy a 'Chayanovian' competitive edge in the land market, there are countervailing forces that potentially blunt this advantage. These countervailing forces are likely to be strongest in the land sales market where capital access, risk, and portfolio considerations are likely to weigh most heavily against the peasantry.

Panel data econometric estimates from Paraguay confirm these theoretical suspicions. The land rental market appears to work, at least modestly, to enhance the land access of land-scarce, labor-abundant households. The land purchase market, however, works in quite the opposite direction. Evidence on Honduras and Chile in the wake of property rights reform measures in those countries similarly show that in some, but not all, instances, land markets have not been enabled to permit the less well-off to successfully accumulate within them. In the language of Carter and Barham (1996), the land market does not appear to present a level playing field to the least well-off. Whether property rights reform itself is sufficient actually to activate a land market that otherwise would be inactive is not, however, something that the available evidence permits us to judge adequately.

What, then, might be done to enable the peasant sector to utilize the land market more effectively? Carter and Barham (1996) suggest that the array of available policy instruments can be divided into those that attempt to answer this question by operating directly on the land market (e.g., land banks, long-term mortgage finance) and those that operate on the fundamental competitiveness problems of the peasantry (e.g., by leveling access to working capital or technology, or by addressing some of the problems such as asset price risk that distort dynamic portfolio choice, as Zimmerman and Carter 1997 explore). These are, of course, not mutually exclusive policy approaches, and indeed are more likely to be complementary than competitive. Determining which elements need to go into the policy mix requires, first and foremost, getting a handle on what we have here called the class competitiveness regime, understood as the mapping between wealth endowments and willingness to pay for land. As Carter and Galeano (1995) show, with that information, it is possible to analyze which policy mixes are likely to work and enable the poor to accumulate in the land market. While not a trivial exercise, such analysis and context-specific policy may indeed be the most effective way to locate a contemporary answer to the problem of land reform and resolve the agrarian question in favor of landless and near-landless households.

REFERENCES

Banco Mundial. 1995. 'Honduras, Memorandum Económico y Evaluación de la Pobreza.' Oficina Regional para América Latina y el Caribe, Marzo.

Bardhan, P., S. Bowles, and H. Gintis. 1998. 'Wealth Inequality, Wealth Constraints and Economic Performance.' In *Handbook of Income Distribution*, A. Atkinson and F. Bourguignon (eds.). Amsterdam: North Holland.

Barham, B., M.R. Carter, and Wayne Sigelko. 1995. 'Agro-Export Production and Peasant Land Access: Examining the Dynamics Between Adoption and Accumulation.' *Journal of Development Economics* 46(1): 85–107.

Binswanger, H., G. Feder, and K. Deininger. 1996. 'Power, Distortions and Reform in Agricultural Land Relations.' In *Handbook of Development Economics, Volume 3*, J. Behrman and T.N. Srinivasan (eds.). Amsterdam: North Holland.

Bowles, Samuel. 1985. 'Hobbesian, Walrasian and Marxian Theories of the Labor Market.' *American Economic Review* 75(1): 16–36.

Brandao, A. and R. Lopez. 1993. 'Land Tenure Insecurity and Small Farm Productivity in Honduras and Paraguay.' Working paper, The World Bank, Washington DC.

Brewster, John. 1950. 'The Machine Process in Agriculture and Industry.' *Journal of Farm Economics* 32(1): 69–81.

Carter, M. 1988. 'Equilibrium Credit Rationing in LDC Agricultural Credit Markets.' *Journal of Development Economics* 28(1): 83–103.

Carter, M. and B. Barham. 1996. 'Level Playing Fields and Laissez Faire: Post-Liberal Development Strategy in Inegalitarian Agrarian Economies.' *World Development* 24(7): 1133–50.

Carter, M. and A. Coles. 1998. 'Inequality Reducing Growth in Agriculture: Towards a Market Friendly Policy Agenda.' In *Beyond Tradeoffs: Market Reform and Equitable Growth in Latin*

America, N. Birdsall, C. Graham, and R. Sabot (eds.). Washington DC: Inter-American Development Bank/Brookings Institution Press.

Carter, M.R. and Luis Galeano. 1995. 'Campesino, Tierra y Mercado.' Centro Paraguayo de Estudios Sociologicos, Asuncion, Paraguay.

Carter, M. and D. Mesbah. 1993. 'Can Land Market Reform Mitigate the Exclusionary Aspects of Rapid Agro-Export Growth?' *World Development* 21(7): 1085–1100.

Carter, M. and P. Olinto. 1996. 'Getting Institutions Right for Whom? The Wealth Differentiated Impacts of Land Titling on Agricultural Investment and Productivity in Paraguay.' Working paper, University of Wisconsin, Madison, WI.

—— 1997. 'Wealth, Property Rights and Credit Rationing: Simulated Maximum Likelihood Estimates of a Disequilibrium Credit Market.' Working paper, University of Wisconsin, Madison, WI.

Carter, M. and E. Zegarra. 1995. 'Reshaping Class Competitiveness and the Trajectory of Agrarian Growth with Well Sequenced Policy Reform.' Working Paper No. 379, University of Wisconsin, Madison, WI.

—— 1996. 'Land Markets and the Persistence of Rural Poverty in Latin America: Post-Liberalization Policy Options.' Paper submitted to A. Valdes and R. Lopez, *Rural Poverty in Latin America.* [Currently under review for possible publication by The World Bank.]

Carter, M.R. and F. Zimmerman. 1999. 'The Dynamic Costs and Persistence of Inequality in an Agrarian Economy.' Staff Paper 416 (revised), Department of Agricultural and Applied Economics, University of Wisconsin, Madison, WI.

Carter, M.R., B. Barham, and D. Mesbah. 1996. 'Agro-Export Booms and the Rural Poor in Chile, Paraguay and Guatemala.' *Latin American Research Review* 31(1): 33–65.

Carter, M., P. Olinto, and D. Fletschner. 1997. 'Do the Poor but Efficient Survive in the Land Market? Capital Access and Land Accumulation in Paraguay.' Paper presented to the MacArthur Workshop on the Economic Costs of Inequality, MIT, Cambridge, MA.

Chávez, Héctor. 1993. 'Apuntes Sobre la Venta de Cooperativas de La Reforma Agraria.' Working paper, Tegucigalpa, Honduras.

Chayanov, A.V. 1925 [1966]. *The Theory of the Peasant Farm Organization.* Homewood, IL: Irwin.

Childress, M. 1996. 'Land Tenure, Credit Access and Agricultural Productivity in Honduras.' Ph.D. Dissertation, University of Wisconsin, Madison, WI.

CIREN (Centro de Informacion de Recursos Naturales). 1990. *Catastro Fruticola Nacional, VI Region, Actualizacion 1990.* Santiago: CIREN-CORFO.

—— 1991. *Catastro Fruticola Nacional, VIII Region, Actualizacion 1991.* Santiago: CIREN-CORFO.

Coles, Alexander. 1989. 'Transacciones de Parcelas y el Proyecto de Titulación de Tierras en Honduras.' Working paper, Land Tenure Center, University of Wisconsin, Madison, WI.

Cox, Maximiliano, A. Nino de Zepeda, and A. Rojas. 1990. 'Politica Agraria en Chile: Del Crecimiento Excluyente al Desarrollo Equitativo.' Centro de Estudios para America Latina Sobre Desarrollo Rural, Pobreza y Alimentación, Santiago, Chile.

Cruz, Juan Ramón and G. Milton Munoz. 1997. 'Situación Actual de la Coinversión y el Arrendamiento de Tierras en Grupos del Sector Reformado de Cuatro Regiones de Honduras.' PRODEPAH, Tegucigalpa, Honduras.

de Janvry, A. and E. Sadoulet. 1996. 'Growth, Inequality and Poverty in Latin America: A Causal Analysis, 1970–1994.' Working paper, Department of Agricultural and Resource Economics, University of California, Berkeley, CA.

Echenique, J. and N. Rolando. 1991. *Tierras de Parceleros: ¿Donde Están?* Santiago, Chile: Agraria.

Eswaran, M. and A. Kotwal. 1986. 'Access to Capital and Agrarian Production Organization.' *Economic Journal* 96(2): 482–98.

Feder, Gershon. 1985. 'The Relation Between Farm Size and Farm Productivity: The Role of Family Labor, Supervision and Credit Constraints.' *Journal of Development Economics* 18(2): 297–313.

Feder, Gershon and N. Akihiko. 1996. The Benefits of Land Titling and Registration: Economic and Social Perspectives.' Working paper, The World Bank, Washington DC.

Feder, Gershon and David Feeney. 1993. 'The Theory of Land Tenure and Property Rights.' In *The Economics of Rural Organization: Theory, Practice and Policy*, K. Hoff, A. Braverman, and J.E. Stiglitz (eds.). Oxford: Oxford University Press.

Feder, Gershon, T. Oncham, Y. Chalamwong, and C. Hongladaron. 1988. *Land Policies and Farm Productivity in Thailand.* Baltimore, MD: Johns Hopkins University Press.

Fletschner, Diana. 1995. 'Efficiency of Small Landholders in Eastern Paraguay: A Non-Parametric Approach.' M.S. Thesis, Department of Agricultural and Applied Economics, University of Wisconsin, Madison, WI.

Frisvold, George. 1994. 'Does Supervision Matter? Some Hypothesis Tests Using Indian Farm-Level Data.' *Journal of Development Economics* 43(1): 217–38.

Gomez, S. and J. Echenique. 1988. 'La Agricultura Chilena: Las Dos Caras de la Modernizacion.' Working paper, Facultad Latinoamericana de Ciencias Sociales and Agraria, Santiago, Chile.

Instituto Nacional Agrario (INA). 1994. 'Encuesta Nacional Sobre Las Ventas de Tierra de las Cooperativas Agrarias del Sector Reformado.' Working paper, Tegucigalpa, Honduras.

Inter-American Development Bank. 1998. *Perspectivas Sobre Mercados de Tierras en América Latina.* Washington DC: Inter-American Development Bank.

Jarvis, L. 1989. 'The Unraveling of Chile's Agrarian Reform, 1973–1986.' In *Searching for Agrarian Reform in Latin America*, W. Thiesenhusen (ed.). Boston, MA: Unwin Hyman.

Jiménez, Pedro, Héctor Chávez, and Jolyne Melmed-Sanjak. 1994. 'Análisis del Mercado de Tierra Según el Registro de la Propiedad.' Working paper, PRODEPAH, Tegucigalpa, Honduras.

Kay, Cristobal. 1995. 'Rural Development Issues in Contemporary Latin America.' In *Structural Adjustment and the Agricultural Sector in Latin America*, John Weeks (ed.). New York: St. Martin's Press.

Kevane, Michael. 1996. 'Agrarian Structure and Agricultural Practice: Typology and Application to Western Sudan.' *American Journal of Agricultural Economics* 78(1): 236–45.

La Gaceta. 1994. 'Diario Oficial de la Republica de Honduras.' 8 June.

Lambert, V. and D. Stanfield. 1990. 'Case Studies of Rural Land Markets in Ecuador.' Working paper, Land Tenure Center, University of Wisconsin, Madison, WI.

Lanjouw, J. 1995. 'Information and the Operation of Markets: Tests Based on a General Equilibrium Model of Land Leasing In India.' Working paper, Department of Economics, Yale University, New Haven, CT.

Larsen, Janell. 1993. 'Land Titling Project in Honduras.' Working paper, Tegucigalpa, Honduras.

López, Ramón. 1996. 'Land Tenure Insecurity and Farm Productivity in Honduras.' Working paper, The World Bank, Washington DC.

Madalla, G.S. 1983. *Limited-Dependent and Qualitative Variables in Econometrics.* Cambridge: Cambridge University Press.

Mesbah, D. Forthcoming. 'Agrarian Change in Chile.' Unpublished Ph.D. dissertation, Oxford University, Oxford.

Moreno, D. Alonso. 1994. 'Ajuste Estructural y Modernización Agrícola en Honduras: Una Visión Crítica.' Ediciones Zamorano, Tegucigalpa, Honduras.

Murdoch, Jonathan. 1995. 'Income Smoothing and Consumption Smoothing.' *Journal of Economic Perspectives* 9(5): 103–14.

Nesmand, E. and M. Seligson. 1988. 'Land Titling in Honduras: An Impact Study in the Santa Barbara Region.' Working paper, Land Tenure Center, University of Wisconsin, Madison, WI.

Ortega, Emiliano. 1988. 'Transformaciones Agrarias y Campesinado: De la Participación a la Exclusión.' Corporación de Investigación para Latinoamerica, Santiago, Chile.

Perez Brignoli, Hector. 1973. 'La Reforma Liberal en Honduras.' Editorial Nuevo Continente, Tegucigalpa, Honduras.

Persson, T. and G. Tabellini. 1994. 'Is Inequality Harmful for Growth?' *American Economic Review* 84(3): 600–21.

Platteau, J.-P. 1996. 'The Evolutionary Theory of Land Rights as Applied to Sub-Saharan Africa: A Critical Assessment.' *Development and Change* 27(1): 29–86.

Rosenzweig, Mark and Hans Binswanger. 1993. 'Wealth, Weather, Risk and the Composition of Agricultural Investment.' *Economic Journal* 103(416): 56–78.

Ruben, Raúl and Francisco Funez. 1993. 'La Compra y Venta de Tierras de la Reforma Agraria.' Editorial Guaymuras, Tegucigalpa, Honduras.

Sadoulet, E., A. de Janvry, and C. Benjamin. 1998. 'Household Behavior with Imperfect Labor Markets.' *Industrial Relations* 37(1): 85–108.

Salgado, Ramón. 1996*a*. 'Subdesarrollo y Sector Agrícola.' Working paper, Tegucigalpa, Honduras.

—— 1996*b*. 'La Tenencia de la Tierra en Honduras, El Agro Hondureño y su Futuro.' Editorial Guaymuras, Tegucigalpa, Honduras.

Salgado, Ramón, Pedro Jimenez, Hector Chavez, Hugo Noe-Pino, Jolyne Melmed-Sanjak, Ana Lucia Restrepo, and Andy Thorpe. 1994. 'El Mercado de Tierras en Honduras.' Centro de Documentación de Honduras, Poscae-Wisconsin, Tegucigalpa, Honduras.

Sandoval Corea, Rigoberto. 1992. 'La Ley para la Modernización y el Desarrollo del Sector Agrícola y sus Efectos en el Proceso Agrario.' *Puntos de Vista* 5, CEDOH-UNAH, Tegucigalpa, Honduras.

Scott, Christopher D. 1985. 'El Ascenso de la Mediana Produccion en la Agricultura Latinoamericano.' Working paper, Food and Agricultural Organization (FAO) of the UN, Rome.

—— 1996. 'Peasantry, Property and Poverty: State, Market and Economic Institutions among the Rural Poor in Chile.' Draft manuscript, London School of Economics, London.

Sen, A.K. 1966. 'Peasants and Dualism with and without Surplus Labor.' *Journal of Political Economy* 74(5): 425–50.

Singh, I., L. Squire, and J. Strauss. 1986. *Agricultural Household Models*. Baltimore, MD: Johns Hopkins Press.

Stanfield, David. 1989. 'La Tierra Vista como un Recurso Económico: El Mercado de Tierras y las Fincas Familiares.' Working paper, Land Tenure Center, University of Wisconsin, Madison, WI.

Stanfield, David, Edgar Nesman, Mitchell Seligson, and Alexander Coles. 1990. 'The Honduras Land Titling and Registration Experience.' Working paper, Land Tenure Center, University of Wisconsin, Madison, WI.

Stiglitz, Joseph. 1998. 'More Instruments and Broader Goals: Moving Toward the Post-Washington Consensus.' 1998 WIDER Annual Lecture, Helsinki.

Strasma, John, Ricardo Arias, Magdalena Garcia, Daniel P. Meza, René Soler, and Rafael Umaña. 1993. 'Estudio del Diseño Conceptual de un Fondo de Tierras en Honduras.' Report prepared for the Honduras Government and El Proyecto de Análisis de Políticas Agrícolas para Honduras (APAH), Tegucigalpa, Honduras, 9 March.

Stringer, R. and V. Lambert. 1989. 'A Profile of Land Markets in Guatemala.' Working paper, Land Tenure Center, University of Wisconsin, Madison, WI.

Suazo, Javier. 1996. 'La Política Agraria en Honduras Durante los 90's.' CEDOH, Tegucigalpa, Honduras.

Vogelgesang, Frank. 1998. 'Tierra, Mercado y Estado.' In *Perpsectivas sobre Mercados de Tierras en América Latina*. Washington DC: Inter-American Development Bank.

Zimmerman, F. and M.R. Carter. 1999. 'Asset Smoothing, Consumption Smoothing and the Reproduction of Inequality under Risk and Subsistence Constraints.' Staff Paper 402 (revised), Department of Agricultural and Applied Economics, University of Wisconsin, Madison, WI.

—— Forthcoming. 'A Dynamic Option Value for Institutional Change: Marketable Property Rights in the Sahel.' *American Journal of Agricultural Economics*.

11

The Changing Role of the State in Latin American Land Reforms

ALAIN DE JANVRY, ELISABETH SADOULET, AND WENDY WOLFORD

The agrarian question revisited

Over the last eighty years, virtually all Latin American governments have used the power of the state to alter access to land for specific categories of households in regions where there is population pressure on the land and to redefine land rights for those with access.[1] Extensive land reforms were part of the outcome of revolutions in Mexico (1917), Bolivia (1952), and Nicaragua (1979). Authoritarian governments imposed land reforms in Peru (1969–75) and Ecuador (1964). Democratically elected governments also pursued land reforms in Chile (1964–73), Colombia (1961–), Guatemala (1952–54), Honduras (1973–), El Salvador (1980–), and the Dominican Republic (1961–). Even in Brazil, where settlement of frontier lands was substituted for land reform until 1985, new initiatives have been taken to promote redistribution.

A historical overview of land reform in Latin America, which can be divided into three phases, helps explain why eighty years of reforms have not been more effective in solving the problems of lack of access to land for many rural households and in reducing the very high inequality in land distribution. In the first phase, some of the land in large traditional estates was expropriated, principally to the benefit of the former permanent workers of these estates. These beneficiaries were usually granted property rights as members of collective farms and *ejido* communities but were rarely offered the infrastructural and institutional support required to make them efficient producers.[2] In the second phase, initiated in Chile in 1973 with the military coup, and extended throughout Latin America in the early 1980s in the context of adjustment policies, lands in collectives and *ejido* communities were transformed into individually titled farms. At the same time, some of the reform sector lands were restituted to previous owners.

[1] Regions of Latin America with population pressure on the land are Mexico and Central America, the Caribbean countries, the high Andean countries, and Brazil (North-East). Land reform is not a major issue in land-abundant countries such as Argentina, Uruguay, and Paraguay. Countries with open frontiers have engaged in settlement programs, but we do not include this form of access to land as part of land reform.

[2] On the collective farms, production was collective while, in the *ejidos* and *asentamientos*, production was on individually usufructed plots with centralized management of access to the market, supportive organizations, and public services.

Table 11.1. *Growth and poverty in Latin America, 1970–95*[a]

Economic performance	1970–80	1980–90	1990–95
Average annual growth rate GDP (%)	3.6	2.1	2.8
Average annual growth rate value added in agriculture (%)	6.7	1.3	3.1
Poverty	**1980**	**1990**	**1994**
Number of poor (million)			
Urban	49.6	81.4	86.1
Rural	49.6	48.8	43.0
Poverty headcount ratio (%)			
Urban	29	36	33
Rural	55	57	52

[a] Data for Brazil, Chile, Colombia, Costa Rica, Honduras, Mexico, Panama, Peru, and Venezuela.

Sources: economic performance: IADB, Inter-American Development Bank (1996); poverty: ECLAC, Economic Commission for Latin America and the Caribbean (1997).

In the process, individually titled beneficiaries were exposed to the rigors of market competition and to new options on the land market.

In spite of this long history of land reform, land remains extremely unequally distributed and this skewed distribution is associated with much misuse of the land from a social standpoint. At one extreme of the distribution of land, 26% of the total number of farms control 90% of the total arable land, and in these farms land is frequently extensively used, and in some cases, completely idle. At the other extreme, the 50% smallest farms only control 2% of the land, and land in these farms is generally very intensively used leading to resource depletion.

Rural poverty, which is closely associated with landlessness and insufficient access to land, also remains extensive. In nine countries with comparable data that account for nearly 80% of the Latin American population (Table 11.1), 52% of the rural households were in poverty in 1990–95 as compared to 33% of the urban households. While there are success stories like Brazil, Chile, Panama, and Venezuela where the number of rural poor declined, driving down the continental aggregate, it increased in the other countries.

Inefficiencies due to inequality in access to land, persistent rural poverty, and environmental pressures are reopening the case for land reform as a fundamental aspect of the agrarian question. Structural adjustment forces agriculture to be competitive under the same terms as the other sectors of the economy. With more widespread organization of the rural poor, the decentralization of governance, and greater democratic representation, rural poverty is increasingly difficult to ignore. In several countries, rural poverty is a source of violence and a destabilizing factor for economic recoveries (*The Economist* 1996). Market integration and globalization redefine the rules of competitiveness for smallholders, threatening them with elimination if they fail to compete, while the agricultural sector initiates a recovery from the depths of the debt crisis (see data on the growth rate of value added in agriculture in Table 11.1). Rural poverty also intensifies urban migration, contributing significantly to the sharp rise in urban poverty, with the number of urban poor doubling over the last fourteen years (Table 11.1). Environmental pressures are associated with insufficient access to land and ill-defined property rights, inducing land degradation in small plots and expansion of agricultural frontiers onto fragile lands and tropical forests.

As Latin American countries emerge from the second phase of land reform, two critically important issues regarding land reform remain unanswered. Resolution of these issues will determine the future social structure of Latin American agriculture, in particular whether or not a viable rural middle class will emerge from the land reforms. These two issues, which define the agenda for the third phase of land reform, are (1) access to land for the landless and minifundists, and (2) competitiveness of titled beneficiaries in the reform sector.

Access to land for the landless and minifundists

With increasing labor market integration and de-centralization of non-agricultural activities toward rural areas, there are now more options to escape rural poverty without the need for access to land compared to when land reform started. However, access to land remains a fundamental component of the solution to rural poverty in circumstances where there is extensive rural unemployment, inability to migrate due to low skills and lack of migration capital, and indigenous populations that have limited non-farm options due to discrimination outside the community and strong attachment to homelands. The FAO (1988) estimated that 66% of the rural poor in Latin America are smallholders, 30% landless rural households, and 4% indigenous populations. Of the 66% smallholders, one-third are minifundists with insufficient access to land to escape poverty. Hence, including indigenous populations among the minifundists, a total of 56% of the rural poor lack access to land, making them potential candidates for land reform. This implies that land reform needs to be expanded to include new clientele, namely the landless and minifundists who were generally discriminated against in favor of the permanent workers of traditional estates during the first phase of land reform. Pressures to satisfy the demands of these rural poor is often voiced by violence and land invasions, and we will show that grassroots initiatives play an important role in driving this process.

Competitiveness of titled beneficiaries in the reform sector

Prior to the second phase of land reform, beneficiaries were largely placed under the tutelage of the state and specialized parastatal agencies to manage production. Following decollectivization and structural adjustment, their survival now depends on competitiveness in a market environment that has been increasingly globalized. Whether they will succeed or not depends on the ability of the state and civil society to complete the reforms with effective rural development programs consistent with the new macro-policy context, the new rules of market competitiveness, the new forms of governance, and the new set of rural institutions that emerged from structural adjustment. We will see that grassroots initiatives are also important in helping reform sector beneficiaries achieve competitiveness.

The current third phase of land reform thus provides significant space to grassroots initiatives. To identify their potential in solving the two issues mentioned above, we proceed as follows. In the following section, we analyze the first two phases of land reform to identify who received access to land and under what conditions, with the goal of assessing the competitiveness and the economic viability of the beneficiaries. In Section 3, we analyze three approaches to land reform still in progress: state-led land reform in Nicaragua and El Salvador; land market-assisted land reforms in Guatemala, Colombia, and Brazil; and grassroots-initiated land reform through the role of the Rural Landless Workers' Movement (MST) in Brazil. In Section 4, we analyze emerging approaches to rural development and assess their potential to secure the competitiveness of land reform beneficiaries. Finally, in Section 5, we outline a set of policy principles aimed at enhancing the likelihood of successful outcomes during this last phase of land reforms in Latin America.

Paths of state-led land reform

The first two phases of land reform took place at different times in different countries, but they were experienced at some point by most countries with population pressure on the land. In the first phase, a reform sector was created based on expropriations of traditional estates. In the second phase, individual land rights were granted to beneficiaries. In what follows, we retrace these two phases.

Phase I: expropriations and threats of expropriations

The objectives pursued through land reform in Latin America cannot be understood by looking at the reform sector alone (de Janvry 1981). To the contrary, one of the most important objectives—the creation of a thriving, private agricultural sector based on large or mid-sized farms—was achieved in the non-reform sector, using the reform sector as an instrument for this purpose. In fact, the reform sector was rarely looked at as a solution to agricultural stagnation. The actual role of the reform sector was varied. It served as an incentive for private owners to modernize in order to escape expropriation, as a political buffer to shelter investment in the private commercial sector, as a means of defusing political tensions by co-opting the most organized sector of agricultural workers, as a counter-insurgency strategy where there was armed rebellion and guerrilla warfare, and as a reservoir of semiproletarian labor for commercial agriculture. Where popular pressure for reform was high, the size of the reform sector was eventually very large, giving access to land to 52% of the rural households in Mexico and 75% in Bolivia (see Table 11.2). Where pressures were low, such as in Ecuador and Colombia, the size of the reform sector was small, giving access to only 10% and 4% of rural households, respectively.

Table 11.2. *Data for Phases I and II of land reform, selected countries*

	Phase I		Phase II	
	Agrarian reform legislation	% of farm families benefited	Agrarian reform legislation	% of collective lands parcelized
Mexico	1917	52	1992	72[a]
Bolivia	1952	75	—	—
Colombia	1961	4	1994	reform continues
Chile	1962	20	1973	41 (28 restituted; 20 sold)
Nicaragua	1963	15–20	1990	90
Brazil	1964	<1	n.a.	grassroots initiatives
Ecuador	1964	10	—	—
Peru	1964	25–30	1981	75
El Salvador	1980	22	1991	100[b]

[a] This figure refers to the percentage of *ejidos* participating in PROCEDE, a program to parcelize *ejido* lands.
[b] This is an estimated figure. The Salvadoran government promised, in May 1996, to forgo 70% of the debt held by former reform beneficiaries, which is expected to act as an incentive for privatization (Deere and León 1997).

Sources: agrarian reform legislation, Phase I: Grindle (1981); farm families benefited: Grindle (1981); Dorner (1992); Thiesenhusen (1995); agrarian reform legislation, Phase II: Deere and León (1997); de Janvry (1993); Thiesenhusen (1995).

Starting the analysis of these reforms with the traditional estates, the state-led land reforms re-allocated these lands towards other classes of farms following four different paths (see Figure 11.1).

Non-reform sector

Path 1.1.

The threat that land would be expropriated if it were not utilized according to certain productivity standards was used to induce defensive modernization (de Janvry and Sadoulet 1989). To encourage modernization, landowners were given a generous span of time to adjust productivity levels, as well as access to subsidized credit and new technological options. This path was followed where landlords had considerable political power, popular pressures were low, and urban industrialists needed to get agriculture moving in support of import substitution policies. It was implemented in Colombia (1961), Ecuador (1964), Chile under Alessandri (1962–67), Peru under Belaunde (1963–68), Brazil (1964), Honduras (1973), and Venezuela (1960). For the scheme to work, threats of expropriation had to be sufficiently credible. With threats credible, the size of the reform sector needed to achieve this goal was eventually minimal.

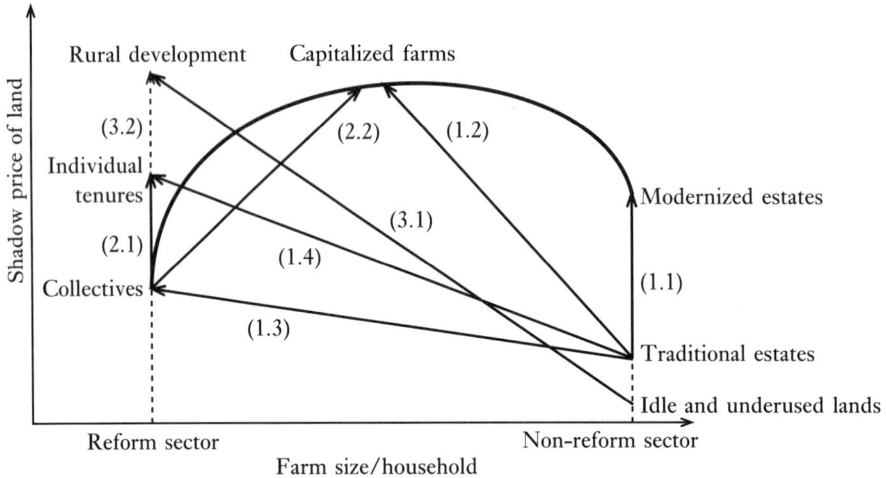

Figure 11.1. *Land reform phases in Latin America*

Phase I of land reform

(1.1) Non-reform sector under threats of expropriation (conservative modernization): modernized estates. Venezuela (1960), Colombia (1961), Chile (1962–67), Peru (1963–68), Ecuador (1964), Brazil (1964), Honduras (1973).

(1.2) Non-reform sector under land ceilings (reserves, voluntary divisions): capitalized farms. Mexico (1917–92), Bolivia (1952), Chile (1967–73), Peru (1970–80), Honduras (1973), Nicaragua (1979), El Salvador (1980).

(1.3) Reform sector organized in *ejidos*, collectives, and state farms: Mexico, Chile, Peru, Honduras, Nicaragua, El Salvador, Dominican Republic.

(1.4) Reform sector distributed as individual tenures: Guatemala (1952–54), Dominican Republic, Honduras, El Salvador.

Phase II of land reform

(2.1) Reform sector: individual titling of collective lands: Chile (1973), Peru (1980), Nicaragua (1990), El Salvador (1991), Mexico (1992), Honduras (1992).

(2.2) Non-reform sector via restitutions and distress sales of beneficiaries: Chile (1973–).

Phase III of land reform

(3.1) Reform sector: access to land for the landless and minifundists. Land market-based land reform: Guatemala, Colombia, Brazil. Grassroots-initiated land reform: MST Brazil.

(3.2) Reform sector: rural development for individual beneficiaries of land reform.

Path 1.2.

Where there was serious revolutionary pressure (Mexico, Bolivia, Nicaragua, El Salvador), or where urban interests wanted to accelerate the process of modernization and also expand the size of the domestic market for their industrial goods (Chile, Peru, Honduras), expropriations were implemented by imposing a ceiling on land ownership.[3] This ceiling was in general quite generous, set at 80 hectares (ha) of irrigated land in Chile, between 100 and 200 ha of irrigated land in Mexico, the so-called 'small

[3] Note that many countries, like Honduras, used both land ceilings and land productivity as criteria for land expropriation.

properties,' 50 ha of irrigated land on the coast of Peru, and 500 ha of rainfed land during Phase I in El Salvador, and 245 ha in Phase II. Owners were allowed to keep a land reserve according to the maximum legal size. Time was also given for owners to escape expropriation by dividing their estates into farms that satisfied the legislated maximum and passing excess land onto kin and name bearers. The best lands with the most secure access to water and available farm equipment were concentrated in this sector of capitalized farms.

Reform sector

Path 1.3.

Along this path, lands expropriated from under-used or over-sized estates were principally assigned to the former workers of the estates (Thiesenhusen 1995). Because these lands were originally in large, centralized estates, production in the reform sector was organized into labor cooperatives, *ejidos*, or state farms, at least as a transitory stage toward eventual parcelization. In all cases, centralized management was important. This form of tenure allowed the government to postpone investments in infrastructure that would have been needed to establish family farms. Instead, it focused on training former estate workers who had hands-on farming experience (since many of them had been paid in land under rent-in-labor-services contracts) (Schejtman 1971), but little managerial experience in relating to markets, banks, and public agencies.[4]

In Mexico, by 1992, the ejido sector included half of the nation's agricultural land, and some 52% of the farm households had been organized into 29,000 *ejidos* and indigenous communities. In this case, access to land went beyond former workers of estates since the constitution allowed for restitution of land to expropriated communities, and formation of new *ejidos* based on expropriations to accommodate demands by organized landless households (Gordillo 1997). In Chile, by 1973, 76,000 permanent farm workers had been organized into collective farms. Families were allocated individual subsistence plots, but most of the land was cultivated collectively. In Peru, by 1980, one-third of the rural households had been given access to half of the country's agriculture and forest lands in agricultural production cooperatives (CAPs) and peasant communities. In Honduras, one-third of the land reform beneficiaries were in associative enterprises. In El Salvador, the 1980 land reform organized the former permanent workers of expropriated estates into production cooperatives. In Nicaragua, 48% of the farmland was expropriated with 14% transformed into production cooperatives and 12% in state farms. In Colombia, expropriations were extremely modest. In twenty-five years of land reform that started in 1961, only 35,000 households had been given access to land, representing less than 4% of the target population. As in the other countries, beneficiaries were usually organized in associative enterprises.

[4] Carter and Mesbah (1993) offer a more idealistic interpretation for the choice of a collectivist as opposed to a distributist approach: policymakers' prejudices against peasant production and fallacious beliefs in the superiority of large farm agriculture.

In general, those who benefited from the reforms along this path were the resident workers of the traditional estates who fiercely resisted the incorporation of landless workers (particularly in Chile and El Salvador), largely because they wished to secure future access to land for their own descendants (Thiesenhusen 1995). Hence, the reforms excluded the poorest households, namely the landless farm workers and the very large segment of independent minifundists. It created instead a lower middle class of accommodated farm households while having minimal benefits for the rural poor.

Path 1.4.

Along this path, which was followed only in a few cases, land was distributed in individual tenures. This was the case under the Arbenz government in Guatemala (1952), an extensively redistributive reform that was reversed in 1954. In Bolivia, the workers of traditional estates independently appropriated the land in individual parcels (Furtado 1976). In the Dominican Republic, lands in large rice estates with centralized irrigation systems were transformed into *asentamientos*, but other lands were allocated as family farms (Meyer 1989). In Peru, 20% of the land reform beneficiaries were assigned individual farms. In Honduras, two-thirds of the beneficiaries were outside the cooperative sector, but it benefited only 9% of the rural households. In El Salvador, in Phase III of the reform, tenants on properties of less than 100 ha were given access to subsidized credit to buy 7-hectare plots over a thirty-year period.

In many situations, beneficiaries with both collective and individual tenures received bad quality and marginal lands that had been de-capitalized in the process of expropriation. Once in place, beneficiaries were, as a rule, forgotten by policy makers more concerned about catering to the commercial agricultural sector and to urban import substitution industrialization than to productivity in the reform sector. Beneficiaries were left without sufficient access to the credit, technical assistance, modern inputs, or education that were necessary to enable them to keep up with the private sector. In Mexico, a successful initial phase of vigorous output expansion in the reform sector based on large-scale public irrigation projects was not sustained, in part due to severe government control over beneficiaries' decision making. Public authorities, more interested in monopolizing rural votes than in promoting production, stifled individual innovations and prevented adaptation to local circumstances (Gordillo 1997). In Bolivia, services such as credit, marketing, and extension bypassed the land reform sector in favor of commercial agriculture. Agricultural output fell following land distribution (Furtado 1976). Inadequate market integration combined with demographic pressures increasingly transformed the reform sector beneficiaries into semi-proletarian households actively involved in rural labor markets and seasonal migration.

Phase II: individualization of tenures

Following the military coup in Chile (1973) and the implementation of adjustment policies introduced in response to the debt crisis (starting in 1982) throughout Latin America, policy emphasis turned to the promotion of market forces and reduction of the role of the state (Williamson 1990). Lands that were held in collectives were parcelized into individual tenures, some were restituted to former owners, and many public lands were auctioned. In countries where the land reform was still on-going, it was officially brought to an end (Peru, 1991; Mexico, 1992; Honduras, 1992). The termination of reform meant that those who had never gained access to land during Phase I would now have to do so through other channels such as rentals, land purchases, or illegal squatting. In most situations, the reform sector had become highly inefficient and the objectives of parcelization during Phase II were to promote efficiency by creating individual incentives to effort and fluid land markets. The collective stage, that had usually been intended to be transitory, had been prolonged by neglect for the reform sector once political goals had been achieved or by ideological shifts enshrining collectivization. The drive to dismantle collectives and activate land markets in the hope of providing the more efficient entrepreneurs with access to land was one of the salient features in this phase of reforms.

Path 2.1. Individual titling

As stated above, in all countries, collectives (production cooperatives and *ejidos*) had been transformed into generally inefficient operations by the time decollectivization occurred. Comparing the two alternative forms of tenure—associative and individual—the balance sheet in favor of decollectivization was as follows:

Gains from decollectivization

- Improve resource management by eliminating incentives to free ride on labor effort (under-provision) and on resource extraction if rival (over-appropriation) (a particular problem of collectives).
- Remove inefficient controls of centralized management over individual decision-making (a particular problem of *ejidos*).

Losses from decollectivization

- Loss of economies of scale in production, for instance, in the use of infrastructure (tubewells, buildings), equipment (heavy machinery), and division of labor (managerial skills).
- Loss of insurance that had been achieved via geographical scale and institutionalized output or income sharing.
- Loss of advantages in reducing transaction costs on product, input, credit, and insurance markets.
- Loss of lobbying capacity in accessing public goods and services and in influencing policy.

Once the option to parcelize was offered, it usually spread very rapidly among beneficiaries concerned with securing their privileges, suggesting that the inefficiencies due to moral hazards in labor effort and centralized management outweighed the benefits of collectivization. In Chile, 36,500 of the 76,000 reform sector beneficiaries were selected to receive titles to farms that averaged 10 ha of irrigated land, accounting for 41% of the expropriated area (Jarvis 1985). Beneficiaries were selected for their political record, rather than for their demonstration of entrepreneurship.

In Peru, upon returning to power in 1980, Belaunde initiated parcelization of the CAPs on the coast, giving plots of 4 to 6 ha to members (Deere and León 1997). In the Sierra, lands in production cooperatives were partially distributed among individual cooperative members, and partially transferred to adjacent peasant communities. Progress initially was slow. By 1990, only 15% of the land reform beneficiaries had been granted titles, although they received 53% of the reform sector land. However, a major effort was made starting in 1996 to develop a modern land registration system and title all properties, accelerating parcelization. Only peasant communities were to remain in common property, with usufruct rights allocated to individual households by the community itself.

In Mexico, the 1992 amendment to the constitution of 1917 opened the door to individual titling of land in the *ejidos*, and the freedom to sell and rent these lands. Privatization of individual plots has proceeded in two steps. First, certificates are issued by PROCEDE, allowing *ejidatarios* to rent their land and sell it to other *ejidatarios*. Second, full titles can be issued with the right to sell to outsiders if approved by a two-thirds majority vote of the *ejido* assembly. By 31 December 1996, 72% of the *ejidos* had participated in PROCEDE, but full titles had been issued to only a few households. As this occurred in the context of a serious profitability crisis for agriculture and de-institutionalization of support for smallholders (particularly credit and technical assistance), many *ejidatarios* have opted for renting their lands to non-*ejidatario* entrepreneurs with better access to capital and technology. Slow progress toward full titling is due to high legal costs (whereas certification was free), low value of the land in much of the *ejido* sector, fear of loss of the land due to outstanding bad debts, and concerns over loss of access to government privileges if the *ejido* disappears.

In Honduras, land titling started in 1992. Cooperative members received shares that they were allowed to sell. In addition, cooperatives were allowed to sell land, initiating a rapid process of internal disintegration. Land titling was also initiated on public lands, doubling the number of beneficiaries by allocation of these lands.

In El Salvador, cooperatives created under Phase I of the reform were given the option of parcelization in 1991. In Nicaragua, the process of tenure individualization started with the 1990 elections that removed the Sandinistas from power. The new government proceeded to restitute lands that had been illegally expropriated, to give individual titles to members of production cooperatives, and to privatize state farms. By 1994, 90% of the land formerly in cooperatives had been parcelized and cooperatives had sold an important share of their lands in response to the profitability crisis in agriculture associated with the withdrawal of state support. 80% of the state farms had been privatized, with land generally returned to private owners or sometimes acquired by their workers. Anxious to protect their newly acquired property rights, the beneficiaries of land reform now constitute a conservative block that was instrumental in defeating the Sandinistas' bid to return to power in 1996 even though they originally owed them their access to land.

Path 2.2. Restitutions and sales of reform sector lands

Complementary to the titling of land reform beneficiaries, lands that had been expropriated have frequently been restituted to former owners or auctioned off to non-beneficiaries. This has helped consolidate the formation of a sector of medium-sized, capitalized farms. In Chile, 3,806 of the 5,800 estates that had been expropriated were partially or totally returned to their former owners as these expropriations were declared to have occurred illegally. A total of 30% of the reform sector land was thus returned (Jarvis 1989). The process of private appropriation of reform sector land was opened to agronomists, former administrators of collectives, public sector employees, and urban professionals. In the end, 20% of the land was sold to these private and institutional investors. Only some 50% of the land was allocated to former land reform beneficiaries. In the face of adverse macroeconomic conditions, high debts to pay for the land, and lack of a supportive rural development program, this sector rapidly fell apart. An estimated half of the beneficiaries sold their land to commercial farmers who used this opportunity to consolidate medium-sized tenures. All in all, it is likely that not more than 5% of the Chilean peasantry gained and retained access to land through the land reform.

The legacy of land reform: toward a Phase III?

In summary, eighty years of land reform that started with the Mexican revolution have deeply transformed the rural sector, but not to the advantage of the minifundists and the landless. Traditional estates with permanent workers partly paid in access to internal land plots have disappeared. Under the pressure of population growth and the need for optimal scale economies, modernized estates have gradually been divided through inheritances and the land market. As a result, the old latifundio-minifundio dualism has been transformed into a more complex and heterogeneous agrarian structure (Kay 1995). A thriving group of mid-sized capitalized farms has emerged in the non-reform sector. By design, they were the main beneficiaries of the land reform and now provide the engines of supply response to the recent economic reforms aimed at inducing new investments in agriculture. These winners do not have their origins in the peasantry or the reform sector. They originated in the breakup of the traditional estates and in the consolidation of land (including lands formerly in the reform sector) by landowners, urban professionals, and agroindustrialists through the land market. Parcelized farms in the reform sector do open the possibility of a successful, independent smallholder sector, a historical novelty for most of Latin America. Whether this sector will survive and create a thriving rural middle class is one of the great challenges of today's agrarian question. The minifundio sector has experienced the least change, as it did not benefit from the land reforms. Due to demographic pressures and environmental degradation, households in this sector are increasingly dependent on off-farm sources of income, mainly derived from the rural and urban labor markets and international migration. Finally, the landless remain the great forgotten group in land reform and rural policy. Except in Chile, where rapid growth of the fruits sector has pushed real wages upwards, rural workers are increasingly participating in precarious seasonal and migratory employment.

The agrarian question has thus been redefined, but important issues remain unresolved. While there have been very significant efficiency gains in the medium-sized farms, land is still highly unequally distributed with some lands under-used and others overworked. The minifundists and landless farm workers are the main reservoirs of poverty, particularly extreme poverty, in the national population. They suffer from structural poverty and long-term social exclusion. The indigenous population and female heads of household are among the poorest with the fewest opportunities for vertical mobility (Deere and León 1997). In several countries, rural violence remains as serious a problem as it was when the Punta del Este Charter (1961) mobilized the Latin American governments in support of land reform. Environmental degradation has introduced a further dimension to the agrarian question as degradation is tied to the problems of inequities in access to the land and ill-defined property rights.

The legacy of land reform thus points to two great challenges in this third phase: providing channels of access to land for the landless and minifundists, and achieving sustained competitiveness for the beneficiaries of the land reforms. We address these two issues in what follows.

Access to land for the landless and minifundists

Both the pressures of, and the new avenues available for, implementing land reform have contributed to the search for fresh initiatives to redistribute land. They can be grouped into three categories: state-led, market-assisted, and grassroots-initiated.

State-led land reforms: Nicaragua and El Salvador

Although the general trend in Latin America has been towards the search for market responses to redistribution, state-led land reforms continue in Nicaragua and El Salvador where the end of protracted civil wars has provided the opportunity to resolve the countries' land tenure disputes.

In Nicaragua, election of the Chamorro government in 1990 spelled the end of the Sandinista agrarian reform although not the end of disputes over land rights. There were two components of land reform that continued to concern the state: access to land for ex-soldiers, former contras, and landless squatters; and confirmation of 40% of the titles awarded by the Sandinista government that continue to be insecure or actively contested. In order to accomplish the first mandate, the government privatized a number of state farms totaling 305,000 hectares, of which 31% was returned to the previous owners, 17% given to ex-soldiers, 20% given to demobilized members of the civilian militias, and 32% given to workers of the state farms (Hendrix 1995). The terms of receipt were very favorable as the land was distributed without cost to beneficiaries, while the original owners were ordered to pay for any improvements that had been made to the land that they received. The United Nations Development Program (UNDP) provided US $3.6 million for the creation of an assistance program that would increase the technical competence of the 18,934 new land reform beneficiaries. The second component of reform, the insecurity of, and dispute over, land titles are much more complex and remains a volatile issue today. In 1990, the government legalized all the titles that had been given to small farmers (less than 100 m^2).

By the end of 1994, the government paid 60% of the property claims filed totaling approximately US $171 million in indemnity bonds. In 1995, the government agreed to resolve further title disputes that would be paid for by privatizing the state telecommunications firm. Those who had received medium-sized plots (between 100 and 200 m^2) were given five to ten years to purchase the property and those with large properties (over 200 m^2) were given two years. These legislative attempts have not significantly reduced land disputes—between 1990 and 1995, titles were issued for only 110 collective farms (1,545 families) and 23,928 individual farms (Hendrix 1995), and, in 1997, government passed yet another bill intended to clarify titles on the 170,000 properties that were distributed under the Sandinista agrarian reform. The large owners who disagreed with the settlement were given the option of taking the case to court and, if they received a favorable ruling, the government had fifteen years to compensate them for approximately 60% of the market value of the land. It is unclear whether this legislation will have the desired effect but, in the meantime, peasants without land have been settled on the frontier, increasing the amount of forest land that is being converted to pasture (Thiesenhusen 1995). In 1996, the target number of beneficiaries was reduced to 94% of the original total and by March 1996, 18,934 beneficiaries had received land, approximately 40% of the original goal.

In El Salvador, land reform has remained active in accordance with the 1992 Peace Accords that promised access to land for the 14% of the national population displaced by the war, including 7,500 FMLN ex-combatants, 15,000 army soldiers, and 25,000 squatters who occupied land in the war zone. In all, the accords laid out three phases during which 47,500 beneficiaries would receive 165,350 hectares of land (Seligson 1995) that would solve the problem of land for 75,000 adults, although it would still leave 300,000 with little or no land (Acevedo, Barry, and Rosa 1995). Although no farms below 245 hectares were legally subject to expropriation after 1986, the government intended to buy private land for redistribution as well as commandeering unused lands within existing cooperatives (Deere and León 1997). Although the land issue was one of the highest priorities for the Salvadoran government following the Peace Accords, redistribution has been extremely slow: by mid-1995, less than 50% of the target population had received land (Wood and Segovia 1995). As a result, the National Land Bank that was created in 1991 with US $7.75 million from USAID in order to facilitate land transactions between large sellers and small buyers, may prove to be a more important source of land transfers. Potential beneficiaries of the National Land Bank have thirty years to pay the market rate for the land with a four-year grace period and a 6% annual interest rate (Deere and León 1997).

Land market-assisted land reforms: Guatemala, Colombia, and Brazil

A number of governments have turned to intervening in the land sales markets to help the rural poor gain access to land (see Deininger in this volume). Operating on their own, land sales markets are notably thin, segmented, and exclusionary of the poor (see Carter and Salgado in this volume). Indeed, land markets have failed to autonomously allocate land to smallholders in spite of the presumed inverse relation between total factor productivity and farm size created by moral hazards in the use of hired labor. Special interventions are consequently needed if the rural poor are to participate in these markets. The basic principle of market-assisted land reforms is that transfers are voluntary, based on identification of desirable lands by beneficiaries, and negotiations between buyer and seller that are mediated by government. Land reform is targeted in regions with enough excess supply of land relative to the program of land purchases to avoid triggering an increase in land prices. The role of land reform agencies (Fondo Fideicomisos de Tierras in Guatemala, INCORA in Colombia, INCRA in Brazil) is to help determine the right price for the purchase; provide a subsidy to the transaction (70% of the price in Colombia with a ceiling of approximately US $21,000 per beneficiary; $11,000 per household in Brazil in loan for the purchase of land and grant for investments; and a flat US $1,600 subsidy in Guatemala); help local governments develop a land reform plan; assist beneficiaries develop productive projects before land is acquired; promote competitiveness of beneficiaries through training, technical assistance, and access to credit and markets; and activate the land market through land registries, long-term credit, and market information. Implementation is decentralized to local governments and participatory of organized groups and non-governmental organizations (NGOs), for instance for the selection of beneficiaries from among the rural poor. Many of the services provided to beneficiaries in support of competitiveness are delivered by the private sector in response to demands by the communities funded by fungible matching grants. Hence, the approach carefully complements access to land with rural development programs in support of competitiveness of beneficiaries. Efforts are also made to complement it with policy reforms that remove the credit, tax, and livestock subsidies that favor large farmers and raise land prices for small buyers.

In Colombia, where the option of modernizing peasant farms through an extensive program of Integrated Rural Development had been preferred to land reform (see de Janvry and Sadoulet 1993), continuing violence and appropriation of large tracts of land by drug traffickers has induced government to open a new phase of market-assisted land reform with the Agrarian Law of 1994. INCORA, the land reform agency, can also buy or expropriate lands and transfer them to beneficiaries with the same 70% subsidy. By 1996, most of the transactions had occurred through this latter mechanism. The total number of transfers for 1995 (4,172) was only slightly higher than the annual average in previous years (3,673) (Deere and León 1997). In December of 1996, Law 333 provided vast, if uncertain, means for the expropriation and redistribution of huge tracts of land acquired illegally by drug traffickers. Whether the government will have the political power to pursue this radical approach remains to be seen.

While highly promising, these experiments are still in progress and in need of careful monitoring. The market-assisted approach is expensive and funds have been slow to come, particularly in Guatemala. The current economic situation throughout Latin America, however, creates a favorable political context for the approach. With structural adjustment and the elimination of discriminatory subsidies to large farmers, land prices in large farms have fallen sharply. To boost the demand for land and find a way out of agriculture, landlords are in favor of governments promoting market-assisted land reforms. The approach thus attempts to capitalize on this political opportunity to reduce rural poverty via increased access to land and to raise efficiency by facilitating access to uncapitalized lands (which are cheaper to acquire by willing buyers) to family farmers.

Grassroots-initiated land reform

The third type of land reform present in Latin America today is characterized by the heavy involvement of grassroots organizations (GROs). One of the most important GROs currently involved in the struggle for access to land is the Movement of Rural Landless Workers (MST) in Brazil (see Wolford in this volume). In the fifteen years since its inception, the MST has helped to establish over 1,100 land reform settlements by mobilizing approximately 145,000 families to occupy underused land and pressuring the government to negotiate for title to the property. Underused land, defined as that which violates a constitutional clause establishing the social functions of land, is estimated to total as much as 44% of the country's arable land (Instituto Brasileiro de Geografia e Estatistica 1991). The MST is of particular interest because it organizes civil society through local and global-level interventions that address both the issues of access to land and the provision of long-term services to secure the economic competitiveness of beneficiaries. This is analyzed in detail by Deininger and Binswanger (this volume).

The MST is clearly the result of a particular historical context, and it would be impossible to replicate it entirely elsewhere. It capitalizes, in particular, on the explicit legal contradiction that exists between constitutional law that imposes social functions to land ownership, and civil law that recognizes the inalienable right of ownership. Making the first prevail over the second to gain access to land requires considerable political power, mass movements, and often recourse to violence to dramatize events. It is consequently a road of access to land that is increasingly difficult to implement (while remaining open in other countries such as Honduras and the Dominican Republic) and in conflict with the need to secure property rights in order to attract capital-intensive investments in the modernization and diversification of agriculture.

Competitiveness of the land reform beneficiaries

The Latin American agrarian structure has been altered in recent years by a number of factors that have operated to create a significant class of independent smallholders. The most important of these factors are: the parcelization of collectives throughout Latin America and the titling of *ejido* lands into individual tenures in Mexico; continuing state-led land reforms in Nicaragua and El Salvador; new initiatives with market-assisted land reform in Guatemala, Colombia, and Brazil; and grassroots-initiated efforts at achieving access to land for the landless and minifundists in Brazil. The ultimate achievement of land reform policy would be to enable these smallholders to become competitive in the context of liberalized markets and a sharply reduced role of the state. The introduction of land markets would allow better farmers to replace older or less skilled farmers, inducing a slow process of social differentiation. This process would gradually transfer the land toward the most competitive farm sizes and the better farmers. However, for this to happen both efficiently and fairly, those who sell should not be doing this because they are differentially exposed to market failures and farm-specific policy distortions that prevent them from being competitive, even if potentially good managers.

Post reform differentiation

Once tenure has been individualized and the rules of competitiveness (however distorted against smallholders) are let to play, the reform sector beneficiaries can follow three alternative adjustment paths:

Path 1. Failure to be competitive, land sales leading to land reconcentration, proletarianization of former beneficiaries, and migration.
Path 2. Involution into largely self-sufficient peasant farming operations, complemented with seasonal participation in labor markets and migration, leading to semi-proletarianization and functional dualism (de Janvry 1981).
Path 3. Successful, stable, capitalized, and modernized smallholders.

Given heterogeneity of the land reform beneficiaries, these paths generally coexist within the reform sector of any given country, but with different relative weights. For instance, *ejidos* in Mexico have widely divergent resource endowments, some with high potential for modernization and production for global markets, allowing them to follow Path 3, others with little prospects other than subsistence production, confining them to Path 2, and yet others with good resource endowments but no ability to compete with other farm entrepreneurs, throwing them into Path 1. Evidence from past experiences of decollectivization tends to support occurrence of the first and second paths, with little incidence of the third.

Path 1. Land sales and reconcentration
The archetypal occurrence of this path is Chile. Parcelized land reform beneficiaries were poorly prepared to participate in the fruit and vegetable export booms that followed decollectivization. Beneficiaries generally possessed low levels of technical knowledge and education, lacked management experience, and had very limited access to credit and modern inputs (Carter 1991). In addition, parcelization occurred in an unfavorable market context as trade liberalization and real exchange rate appreciation induced a serious profitability crisis in traditional crops. Strapped with high debts to pay for the lands transferred to them, many beneficiaries went bankrupt and were forced to offer their lands for sale. At the same time, the profitable options that were emerging carried high risks due to the need for heavy capital investments, long maturation periods, and the use of sophisticated technologies and marketing systems. Land reform beneficiaries were not in a position to enter into these activities, in part because their lands were already heavily mortgaged and in part for lack of a comprehensive rural development program to assist them. Half of the beneficiaries sold out. Of the lands that were sold, Echenique and Rolando (1991) estimate that:

- 67% was acquired by larger farmers who consolidated land in capitalized medium-sized farms. In the better-endowed areas with potential for fruit production, 70% of the land reform beneficiaries sold their lands.
- 21% was sold to other smallholders.
- 5% was sold to minifundist or landless households.

Exposure to the forces of competition, in an institutional context highly biased against the land reform beneficiaries, led to the liquidation of much of the achievements of the long legacy of state-led land reform. Instead of creating a class of smallholders, the reform helped consolidate a class of modernized capitalized farms that did not originate in the peasantry.

Path 2. Involution into production for home consumption and semi-proletarianization
The two features that precipitated the downfall of land reform beneficiaries in Chile (heavy debt burdens associated with access to the land that acted as a push factor, and highly profitable options in agricultural investment that increased the demand for land by entrepreneurs more competitive than them) were not present in the rest of Latin America. There, the land market was incipient and options outside farming were more limited.

In Peru, Carter and Alvarez (1989) observe that decollectivization did create an incentive effect on labor effort. Beneficiaries worked more hours on their own land than they had worked on the collective. However, this effort was partially in substitution for labor formerly hired by the collective, and partially in substitution for the declining use of machine power. Hence, net output effects did not materialize. The effort to organize service cooperatives to assist individual farms in reducing transaction costs and sharing machinery failed. The land reform thus culminated in what Carter and Alvarez called 'disorganized decollectivization.' Most beneficiaries lost access to credit (33% had access in 1986) in spite of the possession of land titles as collateral, due to the high costs to banks of loaning to individual smallholders. Beneficiaries also lost access to technical assistance and to economies of scale in the purchase of inputs and the use of machinery. An outcome of this was an increased use of manual and animal power and a shift to peasant farming systems with greater presence of subsistence food crops.

The effects of 'disorganized decollectivization' were uneven, as some beneficiaries were able to take advantage of institutional innovations to overcome market failures. Contract farming with merchants or processors provided access to credit and technical assistance. Sharecropping contracts emerged where a beneficiary contributed land and labor and a partner provided capital, technical assistance, and management expertise. Some market sales transferred lands to these more successful farmers. Sales were, however, incipient for several reasons. Land titling and registration remained uncertain. Credit for the purchase of land was not available. And the subsistence option complemented with part-time labor market participation provided a resistance strategy that helped poorer beneficiaries retain their lands.

Early responses to individual titling in Mexico have followed the same path as in Peru (de Janvry, Gordillo, and Sadoulet 1997). There, the transition occurred in the context of a serious agricultural profitability crisis coupled with the de-institutionalization of state support to the *ejido* sector. Most beneficiaries lost access to credit, technical assistance, modern inputs, and crop insurance. In response to the greater freedom to define individual strategies, to the low profitability of new investment, and to the lack of access to state support, many *ejidatarios* switched to traditional peasant farming systems. Use of manual and animal traction substituted for mechanical power, intercropping expanded, extraction from common property resources increased, and migration accelerated. With land titles not yet fully marketable, land rentals rose. Again, responses were uneven due to heterogeneity of the *ejido* population. Some *ejidatarios* with better land endowments were successful in modernizing and diversifying their crops, initiating a process of differentiation across *ejidatarios*. In addition to better land endowments, the determinants of success included: greater availability of family labor, higher educational levels, better access to credit and technical assistance, and membership in producers' organizations (see de Janvry, Sadoulet, and Gordillo 1995).

Rural development for smallholder competitiveness: toward Path 3?

Existence of an inverse relation between total factor productivity and farm size has been the fundamental economic argument to justify a redistributive land reform that creates both efficiency and equity gains. This inverse relation derives from the moral hazard disadvantage for larger farms in using hired labor while small farms use self-motivated family labor. There are, in addition, transaction costs on labor markets that make working at home cheaper than using hired labor. As agriculture becomes more capitalized, this advantage of smallholders tends to be erased by disadvantages on financial markets. Lopez and Valdés (1997) thus do not find evidence of an inverse relation in the five countries they studied (Chile, Colombia, Paraguay, El Salvador, and Honduras). This reversal of the inverse relation is fundamentally due to government, market, and institutional failures that discriminate in favor of large farmers. This stresses once more the fundamental thesis of this chapter: that access to land as a poverty reduction strategy requires joint efforts to create access to land for the rural poor and to set up rural development initiatives to secure their competitiveness relative to large farmers.

The context in which land reform beneficiaries are seeking to achieve competitiveness is very different from the context of the 1970s when efforts at integrated rural development took place throughout Latin America. Today's context is characterized by the globalization of market forces, a policy context that is less discriminatory against agriculture, a sharply reduced role for public subsidies due to budgetary restrictions, large institutional gaps for services accessible to smallholders previously delivered by government agencies, new forms of governance with greater decentralization toward municipalities, more democratic representation, an increasing role of NGOs and GROs in providing new institutional alternatives, the rapid spread of contract farming with agroindustry and exporting firms, and the penetration of a private sector delivering services to farmers with effective demand. Attempts to define and implement a renewed effort for rural development that would boost the competitiveness of smallholders remain incipient and dispersed. In Mexico, for instance, the government's rural development program, *Alianza para el Campo*, only reached some 13% of the *ejidatarios* in 1997. In Nicaragua, only 13% of smallholders (many of whom are land reform beneficiaries) had access to credit and technical assistance in that same year (Davis, Carletto, and Sil 1997).

Even if incipient and dispersed, recent approaches to rural development have introduced a set of interventions that contain fundamental shared principles, consistent with the context described above. This new approach has been analyzed in particular by Echeverria (1997), the World Bank (1997), and de Janvry, Murgai, and Sadoulet (2000). These interventions are backed by significant advances in the theory of rural economics. In particular, the New Institutional Economics has opened novel avenues to understand the behavior of households, communities, and agrarian institutions, and the theories of endogenous growth provide better understanding of the dynamics of regional development.

The main common elements of these interventions are that they:

1. Take advantage of greater *decentralization* of governance and of progress toward improved managerial capacity and financial autonomy of municipal governments, which gives smallholders more direct access to policy makers in the definition and implementation of policy and public goods.
2. Promote the *organization* of households in GROs and the mediation by NGOs of relations between these organizations, market forces, and government programs.
3. Seek greater and more broad-based *participation* of organized stakeholders and communities in the definition of priorities for public investment and the allocation of public revenues (Romero 1996). Participation allows greater focus on heterogeneity of the rural population. This is important as household income strategies typically contain varied mixes of farm and off-farm activities (labor market, non-agricultural employment, microenterprises, migration), affording a wide range of roads out of poverty that are differentially suited to different categories of households (Reardon, Cruz, and Berdegue 1998).
4. Achieve higher *mobilization* of resources both locally through the taxation of real assets and the collection of license fees, and via transfers to the region. A matching grant approach is frequently followed to pay the cost of local and community-level public goods (infrastructure, health, education) and projects. This demand-led approach allows a better matching up of local desires with project definition, but not necessarily a better targeting of the poor within the community since targeting is delegated to the forces of the community's political economy that may be more prone to capture by the interests of the elite than central governments.
5. Seek to achieve efficiency gains through the widespread *devolution* of management of common property resources and local public services to user groups, for example irrigation systems, social forestry, and artesanal fisheries.
6. Make progress in the reconstruction of *institutions* able to mitigate market and government failures and to complement opportunities offered by the market and the state, particularly in the field of rural financial services supporting credit and savings (Otero and Rhyne 1994).

7. Take advantage of increased political pressures to deal with *environmental* issues, which offer opportunities for resource transfers in support of rural development initiatives that promote conservation and sustainability, and deliver environmental services.

8. Respond to international and domestic pressures to promote *gender* and *indigenous* populations' welfare. The main front of action consists in reducing the government's own biases toward gender and ethnicity, for instance in the allocation of public goods and the legal definition of inheritance rights.

9. Promote new institutional arrangements to *administer* rural development on a territorial basis. The decentralization of governance, participatory rural development, and civil society-based institutional reconstruction have called for administrative designs for rural development programs that differ markedly from the centralized and sectorally based approach to integrated rural development followed in the 1970s. A typical approach is one where funds are channeled to a Local Economic Development Agency (LEDA) that includes representatives of local government, deconcentrated public agencies, the private sector, NGOs, and community organizations (Romero 1996). These agencies receive requests for project funding from organized groups in the community. Assistance for the formulation of these projects can be given by NGOs or by private firms if communities receive vouchers from the LEDA to defray the cost of these services. The LEDA then competitively allocates loans, subsidies, and technical assistance to the best projects according to predefined criteria reflected in formula matching. Although this demand-led pattern of development appears promising, it must confront in its design ways to reduce corruption and to create incentives for targeting poor households within the recipient communities.

10. Make efforts to improve the *coordination* among local agencies and between local and national agencies involved in rural development (Manor 1997).

There are a number of programs in progress in Colombia, Bolivia, Chile, Brazil, and Mexico that incorporate components of this new approach. These programs are often still in their formative stages and much work is left to be done to experiment with both the approach and its application in order to fit it to heterogeneous contexts. Yet, the following examples from Colombia, Bolivia, Chile, and Brazil illustrate the thrust of the new approach.

Although integrated rural development (DRI) projects stressing local participation and governance have been present in Colombia since 1976, the current phase of DRI takes an original approach characterized by the creation of Municipal Councils for Rural Development (CMDRs) (del Valle 1994). Of the 1,074 municipalities in Colombia, CMDRs have been established in 925 in order to incorporate the rural poor in community decision-making (FAO 1997). Although it is difficult to quantitatively measure the success of the CMDRs, one study has found that government decentralization in Colombia is positively correlated with high rates of property tax collection, suggesting that citizens have demonstrated their approval of such decentralization and integration by 'voting with their feet' (Bernall 1997, cited in Piriou-Sall 1997). Another key program in the current phase of decentralized rural development is the Integrated Rural

Development Fund (Fondo DRI) which co-finances projects that are self-selected by local communities. Fondo DRI's funding policy deliberately targets low-income rural families in poorer municipalities to support projects that would not be attractive to private investors but have large, positive spillover effects for the community as a whole. In 1993, Fondo DRI financed approximately 1,600 projects, totaling US $38 million, which was partly provided by the World Bank and the Inter-American Development Bank (Parker 1995). NGOs and GROs have also been invited onto local planning committees concerned with the re-organization of Colombia's agricultural technology transfer program which has been the province of local municipalities since 1987 (Bebbington and Farrington 1993). Although the decentralization of governance and inclusion of previously marginalized populations has injected necessary finances and authority into local areas, there are considerable difficulties because many of the communities were not prepared for the increased responsibilities (del Valle 1994). The presence of guerrilla activity in 569 of the 1,074 municipalities has also impaired the efficacy of the CMDRs.

In Bolivia, decentralization has occurred at a rapid pace since the Popular Participation Law (LPP) of 1994 devolved a number of decision-making duties to the municipal level. Although the decentralization was heavily criticized by civil groups and local peasant organizations who feared reduced public support, the creation of community 'vigilance committees' that oversee the proper and transparent execution of local government mandates, has been a successful means of incorporating commonly excluded groups into the government process. The previously excluded communities were often marginalized because they did not exist as legal bodies under Bolivian law, having been formed before the creation of the state. As a result, prior to the decentralization of government and incorporation of local communities, a mere 22% of the Bolivian population was responsible for electing state bodies. This practice ended with the LPP: between April 1994 and December 1996, 12,321 community-based organizations (of peasants, indigenous people, etc.) have been recognized as juridical bodies with full citizenship rights (Cossio 1997).

In Chile, recent rural development initiatives that emphasize local participation and state decentralization are characterized by the Solidarity and Social Inversion Fund (FOSIS), created in 1990 as a means of promoting rural development through the mediation of self-selected NGOs and local service organizations. Between 1991 and 1994, FOSIS funded more than 5,200 rural and urban development projects totaling US $100 million of which approximately 70% were mediated by NGOs and local service organizations (Gacitua 1994). The National Institute for Agricultural Development (INDAP) has also encouraged local organizations to compete for contracts to implement agricultural extension projects (Bebbington and Farrington 1993). As a result of the emphasis on non-governmental actors, the presence of local organizations in the Chilean countryside has increased rapidly—a recent study identified over 85 different organizations tied to rural development (Amtmann 1994).

The Brazilian case suggests a similar experience with decentralization although analysts have argued insistently that, while decentralization has increased the autonomy and decision-making capacity of rural areas in the Northeast, the state needs to continue providing technical assistance because most target areas are chronically underserved by private service providers (Van Zyl and Parker 1997; Ostrom 1996). Parker (1995) describes a new approach to participatory rural development in Northeastern Brazil where community support programs generate and approve project proposals that are submitted to state technical units for approval. This participatory approach outperformed the previous top-down approach because it reached more beneficiaries per comparable project, and was between 15 and 75% cheaper per beneficiary (Van Zyl and Parker 1997).

Conclusions

We have argued in this chapter that the eighty-year legacy of state-led land reforms has left two major tasks incomplete: (1) providing access to the land for the rural poor, particularly the landless and minifundists, in situations where other routes out of poverty are socially more costly, and (2) securing the competitiveness of land reform beneficiaries on their individualized parcels. We have explored how new approaches to land reform and to rural development that rely heavily on the role of land markets, decentralized governance, and participation of beneficiaries through GROs and NGOs show promise in completing these tasks.

Unless the two unfinished tasks of land reform are given priority by governments and development agencies, the end product of a long history of land reforms will fall short of its true potential in creating a sustainable, capitalized smallholder sector. We have seen that promising initiatives are in progress with market-assisted and grassroots-initiated land reform and with decentralized/participatory rural development, but that these initiatives are precarious, dispersed, and still poorly understood. Unless they are successfully adapted and implemented for the broad constituency of rural poor and land reform beneficiaries, liberalization of the land market will simply marginalize the rural poor from access to land and precipitate the sale of land or the involution into self-sufficiency of land reform beneficiaries. The consequences will be continued rural violence, high incidence of extreme poverty, accelerated urban migration, and failure to capitalize on the labor productivity advantages of smallholders. Successfully completing the two unfinished tasks of land reform should thus have a high priority in the Latin American countries' rural policy agendas.

REFERENCES

Acevedo, Carlos, Deborah Barry, and Herman Rosa. 1995. 'El Salvador's Agricultural Sector: Macroeconomic Policy, Agrarian Change and the Environment.' *World Development* 23(12): 2153–72.

Amtmann, Carlos A. 1994. 'Descentralización y Participacion Comunitaria: Potencialidades, Limitaciones y Desafios Para el Desarrollo Rural.' In *El Desarrollo Rural en America Latina*

Hacia el Siglo XXI (Tomo-I Ponencias), Memorias Del Seminario Taller-Internacional. Colombia: Pontificia Universidad Javeriana.

Bebbington, Anthony and John Farrington. 1993. 'Governments, NGOs and Agricultural Development: Perspectives on Changing Inter-Organizational Relationships.' *The Journal of Development Studies* 29(2): 199–219.

Bernall, Fernando. 1997. 'Colombia: Rural Decentralization, Local Government Performance and its Determinants.' Working paper, The World Bank, Washington DC.

Carter, Michael. 1991. '"Experiments" in Agrarian Class Formation and Structural Evolution: Agricultural Decollectivization in Peru and Chile.' Working paper, Department of Agricultural Economics, University of Wisconsin, Madison, WI.

Carter, Michael and Elena Alvarez. 1989. 'Changing Paths: The Decollectivization of Agrarian Reform Agriculture in Coastal Peru.' In *Searching for Agrarian Reform in Latin America*, William Thiesenhusen (ed.). Boston, MA: Unwin Hyman.

Carter, Michael and Dina Mesbah. 1993. 'State-Mandated and Market-Mediated Land Reform in Latin America.' In *Including the Poor,* Michael Lipton and Jacques van der Gaag (eds.). Washington DC: The World Bank.

Cossio, Ivan. 1997. *Bolivia: Descentralizacion, Participacion Popular y Desarrollo Rural.* Rome: FAO.

Davis, Benjamin, Calogero Carletto, and Jaya Sil. 1997. *Los Hogares Agropecuarios en Nicaragua: Un Análisis de Tipología.* Rome: FAO.

de Janvry, Alain. 1981. *The Agrarian Question and Reformism in Latin America.* Baltimore, MD: Johns Hopkins University Press.

de Janvry, Alain and Elisabeth Sadoulet. 1989. 'A Study in Resistance to Institutional Change: The Lost Game of Latin American Land Reform.' *World Development* 17(9): 1397–1409.

—— 1993. 'Path-Dependent Policy Reforms: From Land Reform to Rural Development in Colombia.' In *The Economics of Rural Organization: Theory, Practice, and Policy*, K. Hoff, A. Braverman, and J. Stiglitz (eds.). Oxford: Oxford University Press.

de Janvry, Alain, Gustavo Gordillo, and Elisabeth Sadoulet. 1997. *Mexico's Second Agrarian Reform: Household and Community Responses.* La Jolla, CA: University of California Center for US-Mexican Studies.

de Janvry, Alain, Rinku Murgai, and Elisabeth Sadoulet. 2000. 'Rural Development and Rural Policy.' In *Handbook of Agricultural and Resource Economics*, B. Gardner and G. Rausser (eds.). Amsterdam: Elsevier Science, forthcoming.

de Janvry, Alain, Elisabeth Sadoulet, and Gustavo Gordillo. 1995. 'NAFTA and Mexico's Maize Producers.' *World Development* 23(8): 1349–62.

Deere, Carmen Diana and Magdalena León. 1997. 'Women and Land Rights in the Latin American Neo-Liberal Counter-Reforms.' Working Paper 264, Michigan State University, East Lansing, MI.

Del Valle, Vargas Ricardo. 1994. 'El Desarollo Rural en Colombia Hacia el Siglo XXI.' In *El Desarrollo Rural en America Latina Hacia el Siglo XXI (Tomo-I Ponencias)*, Memorias Del Seminario Taller-Internacional. Colombia: Pontificia Universidad Javeriana.

Dorner, Peter. 1992. *Latin American Land Reforms in Theory and Practice: A Retrospective Analysis.* Madison, WI: The University of Wisconsin Press.

Echenique, Jorge and N. Rolando. 1991. *Tierras de Parceleros. ¿Donde Estan?* Santiago, Chile: Agraria.

Echeverría, Ruben. 1997. *Elementos Estrategicos Para la Reducción de la Pobreza Rural en America Latina y el Caribe.* Washington DC: Inter-American Development Bank.

Economic Commission for Latin America and the Caribbean (ECLAC). 1997. *Social Panorama of Latin America, 1996.* Santiago, Chile: ECLAC.

Economist (*The*). 1996. 'Backlash in Latin America: Gestures Against Reform.' 30 November.

Food and Agriculture Organization of the United Nations (FAO). 1988. *Potencialidades de Desarrollo Agrícola y Rural en América Latina y el Caribe.* Rome: FAO.

—— 1997. 'La Municipalización del Desarrollo Rural en America Latina: Situación Actual y Perspectivas.' Balance del Seminario Internacional, 'El Espaco Municipal: Nuevos Desafios y Possibilidades Para el Desarrollo Rural con Participacion Cuidadana,' Cochabamba, Bolivia.

Furtado, Celso. 1976. *Economic Development of Latin America.* New York: Cambridge University Press.

Gacitua, Miguel Diaz. 1994. 'Chile: Programas Rurales de Fondo de Solidaridad e Inversion Social. Lecciones y Experiencias en un Escenario de Apertura y Competitividad Economica.' In *El Desarrollo Rural en America Latina Hacia el Siglo XXI (Tomo-II-Experiencias)*, Memorias Del Seminario Taller-Internacional. Colombia: Pontificia Universidad Javeriana.

Gordillo, Gustavo. 1997. 'Between Political Control and Efficiency Gains: The Evolution of Agrarian Property Rights in Mexico.' Paper presented at the International Agricultural Economics Association Conference, Sacramento, CA, August.

Grindle, M. 1986. *State and Countryside: Development Policy and Agrarian Politics in Latin America.* Baltimore, MD: Johns Hopkins University Press.

Hendrix, Steven. 1995. 'Insecurity of Land Tenure in Nicaragua.' Research Paper No. 120, Land Tenure Center, University of Wisconsin, Madison, WI.

Instituto Brasileiro de Geografia e Estatistica. 1991. *Censo Demografico de 1991.* Brasilia, DF: Brazilian Government.

Inter-American Development Bank (IADB). 1996. *Economic and Social Progress in Latin America, 1996 Report.* Washington DC: IADB.

Jarvis, Lovell. 1985. *Chilean Agriculture under Military Rule: From Reform to Reaction, 1973–1980.* Berkeley: Institute of International Relations, University of California at Berkeley.

—— 1989. 'The Unravelling of Chile's Agrarian Reform.' In *Searching for Agrarian Reform in Latin America*, William Thiesenhusen (ed.). Boston, MA: Unwin Hyman.

Kay, Cristóbal. 1995. 'Rural Development and Agrarian Issues in Contemporary Latin America.' In *Structural Adjustment and the Agricultural Sector in Latin America and the Caribbean*, John Weeks (ed.). New York: St. Martin's Press.

López, Ramon and Alberto Valdés. 1997. *Rural Poverty in Latin America: Analytics, New Empirical Evidence, and Policy.* Washington DC: The World Bank.

Manor, James. 1997. *The Political Economy of Decentralization.* Rome: FAO.

Meyer, Carrie. 1989. 'Agrarian Reform in the Dominican Republic: An Associative Solution to the Collective/Individual Dilemma.' *World Development* 17(8): 1255–67.

North, Douglas. 1990. *Institutions, Institutional Change, and Economic Performance.* Cambridge: Cambridge University Press.

Ostrom, Elinor. 1996. 'Crossing the Great Divide: Co-production, Synergy and Development.' *World Development* 24(6): 1073–85.

Otero, Maria and Elisabeth Rhyne. 1994. *The New World of Microenterprise Finance.* West Harford, CT: Kumarian Press.

Parker, Andrew N. 1995. 'Decentralization: The Way Forward for Rural Development?' Policy Research Working Paper 1475, Agriculture and Natural Resources Department, The World Bank, Washington DC.

Piriou-Sall, Suzanne. 1997. 'Decentralization and Rural Development: A Review of the Evidence.' Draft prepared for the World Bank, Washington DC.

Reardon, Thomas, María Elena Cruz, and Julio Berdegué. 1998. 'Los Pobres en el Desarrollo del Empleo Rural No-Agricola en América Latina: Paradojas y Desafíos.' RIMISP (Red Internacional de Metodologia de Investigación de Sistemas de Producción), Santiago, Chile.

Romero, Leonardo. 1996. 'Local Development Funds: Promoting Decentralized, Participatory Planning and Financing.' Working paper, Policy Series, United Nations Capital Development Fund, New York.

Schejtman, Alejandro. 1971. *El Inquilino de Chile Central.* Santiago, Chile: Instituto de Capacitación e Investigación en Reforma Agraria.

Seligson, Mitchell. 1995. 'Thirty Years of Transformation in the Agrarian Structure of El Salvador.' *Latin American Research Review* 30(3): 43–73.

Thiesenhusen, William. 1995. *Broken Promises: Agrarian Reform and the Latin American Campesino.* Boulder, CO: Westview Press.

Valdés, Alberto. 1996. 'Surveillance of Agriculture Price and Trade Policy in Latin America During Major Policy Reforms.' World Bank Discussion Paper No. 349, The World Bank, Washington DC.

Van Zyl, Johan and Andrew Parker. 1997. 'Assessing the Performance of Local Governments: Rural Municipalities in Northeast Brazil.' Draft for the World Bank, Washington DC.

Williamson, John. 1990. *Latin American Adjustment: How Much Has Happened*? Washington DC: Institute for International Economics.

Wood, E. and A. Segovia. 1995. 'Macroeconomic Policy and the Salvadoran Peace Accords.' *World Development* 23(12): 2079–99.

World Bank (The). 1997. *Rural Development: From Vision to Action*, ESSD Studies and Monographs Series No. 12. Washington DC: The World Bank.

12

Case Study. Grassroots-Initiated Land Reform in Brazil: The Rural Landless Workers' Movement

WENDY WOLFORD

Ironically, the drive to provide land for the poorest rural groups is taking place in one of the Latin American countries that to this date has made the least progress with state-led land reform: Brazil. As opposed to previous attempts in the 1960s, however, the initiative now comes not from the government but from small communities of squatters that have been organized nationally by one of the largest grassroots organization in Brazil's history, the Rural Landless Workers' Movement (MST). In the fifteen years since its inception, MST has helped to establish over 1,000 land reform settlements by mobilizing approximately 145,000 families to occupy 'unproductive' land and pressuring the government to negotiate for title to the property.[1] According to one observer: 'MST is the most dynamic, best organized and effective social movement in Brazil today' (Petras 1997). In relation to the issue of access to land for the landless, one of the most unusual and potentially valuable lessons to be learned from MST's experience is the importance of the social networks that link MST settlements nationwide, providing global support to local initiatives.[2] In what follows, we outline how MST's 'civil society' approach uses local and global-level interventions in order to win access to land for the landless and to provide long-term services that potentially further the sustainability and competitiveness of the settlements.

The people and the process

Over the past fifteen years, MST has successfully reintroduced the campaign for agrarian reform in Brazil by exploiting a constitutional clause that land has a social function to fulfill. Introduced in 1964, the most recent Constitution upholds the social responsibility of land use, declaring unproductive properties to be eligible for expropriation and

[1] Although these figures are substantial, it is estimated that there are approximately 10.6 million people with insufficient or no land (Brasilia 1985, cited in Hall 1991).

[2] The networks in this study are divided into two types: formal and informal. The formal networks are structured by MST activists known as 'militants' who travel between settlements with information from the regional MST offices concerning political issues (e.g., mobilization for political demonstrations) and economic issues (e.g., market opportunities). The informal networks consist of the settlers who receive this information and discuss it in a number of different arenas (e.g., group meetings, classrooms, and soccer events).

Table 12.1. *Owners of the 46 biggest estates by economic group*

Group	Land (million ha)	Area utilized (million ha)	Area utilized (%)
Financial	22.13	3.79	17.2
Industrial	10.99	1.99	18.1
Agricultural	6.28	0.91	14.4
Total	39.40	6.70	17.0

re-distribution. Unproductive land is constitutionally defined as that which violates either the 'degree of utilization' or the 'degree of efficiency' established by the federal government.[3] According to the latest agricultural census, approximately 44% of the country's arable land—both public and private—is legally unproductive, 80% of which is in the hands of large estates; and it is this land that the movement occupies with intent to settle.[4] There are a number of reasons why holding unproductive land is financially attractive. Landowners have traditionally received artificially low tax rates and access to government subsidies, and used land ownership as shelters of wealth during high inflation periods (Pinto 1995).[5] As can be seen from Table 12.1, the forty-six largest estates in the country utilize only 17% of their land (see Chiavenato 1996).

The contradictory nature of the Brazilian legal system complicates the process by which property claims are disputed and defended. While the two main legal instruments in the country—the Federal Constitution and the Civil Code—both uphold the sanctity of private property, the former stipulates that private ownership will only be recognized if the property in question is fulfilling its 'social function' (Strozake 1998). The idea that property has a responsibility to society is stated strongly in Article 5, Section 23 of the 1988 Constitution, and is described in Article 186 as the use of property in a rational way such that the land's resources contribute to the well being of both owners and workers. MST's method of occupying unproductive land—land that is not fulfilling its social function—has highlighted these difficulties existing within the legal system. Because individual judges are responsible for choosing which legal body will be utilized in any particular court case, landowner and landless alike have recourse to a certain legitimacy, creating a stalemate that is often resolved only by a

[3] The 'degree of land utilization' required for an area to be considered productive was set at 80% of the total arable land. The 'degree of efficiency and exploitation' has been determined for all individual products and varies according to region.

[4] Most of the unproductive land is kept as unimproved pasture, which accounts for 33% of all farmland in Brazil (Thiesenhusen 1995).

[5] Land is subject to an artificially low tax rate through undervaluation and provides a tax umbrella because agricultural income is taxed less heavily than industrial income. In 1964, the Tax on Rural Land (ITR) was created to provide a progressive tax scheme for financing agrarian reform. Instead, the practice of allowing landowners to value their own land has resulted in a regressive tax system that is exacerbated by the reluctance of large landowners to pay. In 1975, the value of land for establishments over 10,000 hectares was 42 Cr$ while the value for minifundia was 901 Cr$/ha. (Pinto 1995). In 1990, 66% of rural establishments paid their ITR, but this only amounted to 34% of the projected total, indicating that those who did not pay were the larger farms.

fait accompli or force (Silva 1997). Even in situations where the Federal Constitution is applied, the considerable ambiguity regarding the definition of 'social responsibility' attenuates the law's effectiveness (Palmeira and Leite 1998). Further, there is concern that with the recent fall in land prices, landowners have actively sought expropriation under the Constitution with the intent of securing inflated land prices from the Federal agrarian reform agency, INCRA (Fernandes 1998).

MST began in 1984 as a coalition of three grassroots squatters' groups in the southernmost Brazilian state of Rio Grande do Sul. The First National MST Congress, held in 1985 and attended by 400 people, formally established the short-term goal of securing land for landless workers and the long-term goal of creating a more just and equitable society. Since 1985, a National Congress has been held every six years in order to reformulate long-term goals and is attended by representatives from every affiliated encampment and settlement. National and state governing bodies are elected every two years and a National Coordinating Board made up of 100 people consistently formulates short-term policy guidelines. MST is supported by funds generated internally, by volunteer activity, and by external contributions from charitable organizations such as Christian Aid.[6] Movement activists known as 'militants' (both self-selected and recruited) attend MST workshops to learn about the history of the struggle for land, about MST's national program, and about how to mobilize popular recruits and support. The militants then travel nationwide throughout the peripheries of urban areas talking to people during religious events, at charitable institutions such as soup kitchens, and at labor union meetings, etc. The militants' intention is to gather a group large enough to carry out an occupation on land that has been determined by the movement as legally unproductive. The militants and new members plan the occupation, usually entering the property late at night and erecting temporary barracks out of heavy plastic and wood. Post hoc word of the occupation spreads quickly and the members rarely wait long before being visited by either representatives of the landowner or government officials. Each occupation group selects representatives who will negotiate with the government for title to the land. Although the negotiations, which involve proving that the land is unproductive, determining the method of appropriation, and planning for settlement, may last between six months and six years, the occupants usually begin planting agricultural crops immediately.

The political process behind the negotiations is complex. There are four potential outcomes of an occupation. First, the property holders or the police can simply expel the occupants preemptively by force. This outcome has been made more likely due to the passing of decree No. 2250 (11 June 1997) disqualifying any territory from expropriation if it is already occupied by squatters.[7] Second, the federal government

[6] In 1995, MST ran an operating budget of US $901,519, 62% of which was generated through international donations and 29% through internal or national income generating activities. Member contributions totaled 66% of this latter category and revenue from the sale of publications, videos, etc. totaled 32% (figures cited in de Kadt 1997).

[7] The government has in the past been more tolerant of squatters (Grindle 1986). It is not clear what effect this new legislation will have on MST. Thus far, it has not slowed down the rate of occupation nor has it prevented government officials from negotiating with squatters.

can determine that the land was actually productive and the occupants have no claim.[8] Third, the government can legitimize the need for land but relocate the squatters to an alternative site, usually on public land. Fourth, the government can recognize the claim, estimate a fair value for the land, and serve the owner with notice, at which time the owner has 150 days to respond and either agree to the settlement or file a legal complaint. In practice, this process of establishing an appropriate value is protracted because the government representatives are usually open to bargaining, even though they are constitutionally empowered to impose a figure according to certain guidelines.

If the government and the landowner agree upon a price to be paid in agrarian debt bonds (TDA) or in cash,[9] then the government divides the land into individual parcels that are given to the occupants and possibly other selected beneficiaries.[10] Although it is unclear what can be attributed to MST activities, data gathered on settlements nationwide indicates that 90% of the beneficiaries believed their welfare has been improved due to the land reform. On average, the settlers were able to increase their capital by 206% in relation to when they entered the settlements and were earning an average monthly income that was 3.7 times the national minimum wage (FAO 1992) as compared to 3.4 for the national average (male) and 2.1 (female) (Instituto Brasileiro de Geografia e Estatistica 1991, cited in de Kadt 1997). The failure rate on settlements during the period 1985–91 was estimated at 22%, although MST argues that on settlements affiliated with the movement the failure rate was closer to 10%.

Insights from MST's experiences

As outlined in Table 12.2, there are three time periods to consider when assessing the role that MST plays in fighting for agrarian reform: (1) the mobilization period, (2) the occupation and negotiation period, and (3) the long-term consolidation period that follows titling. There are also two levels of operation: the local and the global. While it may be too early to argue that MST is capable of securing the long-term viability of the settlers, the movement has increased access to land for the landless in Brazil and, as such, deserves to be taken into consideration during this third phase of reform. Although the specificity of this land reform and the high level of attendant rural violence make it neither directly possible nor desirable to simply replicate the experience of MST across Latin America, the way in which the movement utilizes local and

[8] It is the jurisdiction of the Federal Government, and the president in particular, to authorize a 'social' expropriation although local and state governments often involve themselves in occupations by lending or denying support and delivering or withholding provisions.

[9] In 1992, the 'Land Program' legislated the purchase of lands for the fulfillment of their social purchase, an instrument that has been used more extensively by FHC than by any previous president. The TDAs, however, could usually be held as highly liquid assets leaving little distinction between TDAs and cash (Hall 1991).

[10] The size of the parcels is determined according to the quantity of land in each region deemed necessary to support a single family of four (known as a rural module). According to a study undertaken in 1996, the average farm size on the settlements was 27.5 hectares (Vox Populi 1996*a*, *b*).

Table 12.2. *Roles of MST in assisting access to land*

Periods	Levels of intervention	
	Local	Global
Mobilization	• Self-selection of beneficiaries • Identification of unproductive land for settlement site • Resource transfers	• Access to religious networks
Occupation	• Organization, monitoring, and mobilization • Provision of basic services • Creation of social capital	• Pressure on government • Dissemination of information to the public • Negotiation with government • Mobilization of resources outside the community
Consolidation	• Organization of support services • Access to technical and local-market information	• Pressure for continued reform and services • Creation of a national network • Access to international resources

global-level interventions is instructive for any country characterized by high levels of rural poverty, a gap between state mandate and state means, and access to organized local populations.

Mobilization period: local interventions

Self-selection of beneficiaries

As explained previously in the paper, an important concern is who the potential beneficiaries of this third phase of reform are in light of the exclusionary character of earlier reforms. Although this is a difficult question to answer empirically, according to official MST guidelines, members are required to have had a background in agricultural work and be landless at the time of occupation. This definition of membership is supported by the way the movement operates which is more likely to generate support from landless and nearly landless workers than from middle-level tenants as members are forced to occupy unused land and establish a home there. There is evidence that MST monitors for inappropriate claims to land and takes action against individuals identified as not belonging. At the same time, the negative public image of individuals who join the movement acts as a deterrent against freeloaders. Given the limited information that most governments in Latin America have on the rural and urban poor, access to local information such as can be self-provided by community groups is important in determining who is eligible for land and under what conditions.

Determination of unproductive land
In order to plan an occupation, MST militants work collectively or with local agronomists to select a legally 'unproductive' area for occupation. The local knowledge and effort employed in determining the productivity of potential settlement sites—as well as their applicability for the location of settlement households in terms of the available infrastructure, land fertility, location of water, etc.—de-centralizes the act of gathering information and can be considered a service that MST provides to the state. This de-centralization could be replicated in other countries if the criteria for expropriation were legally established and representatives of any national or local-level organization authorized to gather information regarding those criteria.

Resource transfers
Although it is unclear whether MST successfully privileges landless agricultural workers, the movement does facilitate the participation of the poorest rural and urban classes by mobilizing resources that the poorest people might have otherwise lacked. In the northern region of Rio de Janeiro, for example, an occupation that was to take place some distance from the nearest city would have excluded those who could not find transportation if the militants involved had not secured extra funds by asking bus drivers and others to provide rides (*Jornal Sem Terra* 1997). The importance of mutual assistance suggests that the grassroots nature of participation should be encouraged wherever possible.

Mobilization period: global interventions

Access to religious networks
The Catholic Church has been involved with the struggle for land in rural Brazil for over 30 years. In the 1960s, support for the peasantry and indigenous people became part of the Church's official mandate and priority was given to the establishment of Ecclesiastical Base Communities (CEBs) that were to serve as links between the clergy and laity. Although individual church officials hold very different opinions on MST, the movement is generally able to access church meetings held by the progressive ecclesiastic majority, where the movement can recruit members with the ideological sanction of organized religion (see Houtzager 1997: 85–106). In this way, organized religion can provide both a physical arena as well as moral legitimacy to grassroots mobilization efforts.

Occupation period: local interventions

Organization, monitoring, and mobilization
During the occupation period, the members self-*organize* on the occupation site, thereby contributing to a lower attrition rate on occupation sites than would otherwise occur. The members meet regularly to discuss difficulties and any issues considered important. One of the most important things to be decided and organized collectively in the

early days of an occupation is how and where the members are to begin planting food crops. Planting food crops is important both for subsistence reasons and because, according to the Federal Constitution, crops belong to the person who planted them, even if the land does not. The members of the group also self-*monitor* in the sense that MST establishes certain rules of conduct to maintain 'order' on the occupation sites. Drinking is discouraged through peer supervision, disorderly behavior is frowned upon, and intra-community violence is supposed to be avoided at all costs. Finally, the members of the community are self-*mobilizing* in the sense that there is a constant attempt to build morale and keep members focused on the goal of independent land ownership. As mentioned above, the importance of mutual assistance suggests that the grassroots nature of participation should be facilitated wherever possible.

Provision of basic services

During the occupation period, MST members also organize themselves in order to provide basic social services. A 24-hour guard is established that is in charge of protecting the community from intruders, as well as maintaining internal order. A temporary school is built and classes are held daily for the children and for any adults who cannot read and write. A rudimentary pharmacy is also constructed, usually simply housing the medical supplies provided to the members by outside communities. These are services that could not be effectively provided by individuals and have historically rarely been provided by governments.

Creation of social capital

Organization, monitoring, mobilization, and the provision of basic services are facilitated by the creation of solidarity during the occupation period. Although the MST members are extremely heterogeneous, ties are created by emphasizing the group's common plight through the construction of a group 'background' as well as a group future. The common background is traced back over 100 years to the rebellion and massacre of 5,000 peasants at Canudos in the Northeast of Brazil. The common class heritage is framed as one of rural proletarianization in the face of increasingly powerful capital and foreign interests. The common future is characterized as one of social justice (land to those who work it) and harmony (the creation of a socialist state). Various techniques are employed to construct these ties, such as group memorization of motivational songs, impassioned speeches delivered by militants, etc. Although the particular techniques used by MST are site-specific, the importance of creating effective group ties for enhancing solidarity among reform beneficiaries is instructive. Group solidarity facilitates mutual assistance and collaboration in the provision of services, etc.

Occupation period: global interventions

Pressure on government

During the mobilization period, MST performs its most visible role in effectively organizing the often-sensationalized occupations. Since its inception in 1984, MST's membership and activities have increased steadily. Today, the movement has an estimated 500,000 members who carried out 518 occupations between 1990 and 1996.[11] Although government officials and landowners consistently argue that MST's tactics are unnecessary in light of every administration's stated willingness to carry out agrarian reform, the figures indicate that over half of the settlements in Brazil received land as a direct result of social pressure (Vox Populi 1996*a*, *b*). This suggests that the mobilization of the rural and urban poor in the pursuit of land reform is a fundamental determinant of success.

Dissemination of information to the public

MST performs an important role in accessing media channels and informing the public about the details of an occupation in order to gain their support and generate further pressure on government. MST's activities have received substantial media coverage, both national and international, which has created a widespread awareness of the landless' plight and the possibilities for redistribution. The 'intellectual leaders' of the movement are interviewed regularly in the national newspapers and on television. MST also operates its own newspaper, *O Jornal Sem Terra*, which carries information about recent occupations, the progress of affiliated settlements, and various legal negotiations to approximately 3,500 people. Informed popular support is an important means of creating a critical mass of social pressure for reform.

Negotiations with government

The process by which the outcome of an occupation is negotiated is extremely complex and involves regular recourse to the legal system. The members of an occupation generally select one or two representatives to meet with the government and these representatives are sometimes joined by official MST lawyers or offered legal services by NGOs such as Amnesty International.[12] The value of such representation for the poor suggests that productive alliances can be encouraged between NGOs that provide legal support and grassroots organizations.

Mobilization of resources outside the community

An occupation can last anywhere from six months to six years and the most pressing issue during that time is how the group will feed itself. Although members typically possess some personal resources, which are complemented by the immediate planting of food crops on the occupation site, this is rarely sufficient. The members, therefore, depend on MST's high degree of organization and institutionalization (in that it is an easily recognizable, well-organized, national, official group) which allows the movement to seek aid from local churches, neighboring communities, and even from the municipal government if the latter is sympathetic to the members' situation. In other

[11] The rate of occupation has increased steadily in recent years. Between 1990 and 1994, the average number of occupations per year was 50. In 1995, it jumped to 93, and in 1996 to 176.

[12] The MST has one official lawyer whom the movement supported during law school in exchange for his services. There are other lawyers who regularly work with the movement, although they did not come from the settlements.

words, a high degree of organization at the global level is an important source of external resources for local communities.

Consolidation period: local interventions

Organization of support services

MST provides a number of social and economic services that promote the settlers' welfare and competitiveness as smallholders. This 'co-production' of public services between civil society and the state has recently generated considerable interest as it offers a democratic, 'cost-effective' means of compensating for the decline in the direct provision of social services by government. One of the most important services that MST provides is education. In 1996, MST operated 600 elementary schools and twenty schools at the fifth through eighth grade level that serviced 35,000 children with the help of 1,400 teachers (MST/CONCRAB 1996).[13] The provision of these goods by local groups such as the MST is relatively cost-effective given their access to detailed information regarding local conditions and personalities.

Access to technical and local-market information

One area in which MST performs an important economic function is in the generation of agricultural and agro-industrial production information (e.g., information regarding crop suitability, production techniques such as fertilizer and pesticide application, and possibilities for irrigation installation) via the movement's own agronomists or through mediated exchanges between the settlers, academics, and professional agronomists. According to MST figures (MST/CONCRAB 1996), approximately 3,000 people have received some sort of agronomic education provided by the movement. Two hundred and fifty settlers have been certified at MST schools as technical experts while thirty more have been sent on to higher education outside of the movement. These people have their education funded by MST and are subsequently expected to travel between settlements assisting production efforts. The exchanges between university groups and the settlers also increase the settlers' access to market information, encouraging the production of crops and commodities that have a higher market value such as cotton. This transfer of market and environmental information is cost-effective because it is generated directly by, and for, the target population.

Establishment period: global interventions

Pressure on government for continued reform and services

Aside from the land occupations, MST also organizes general demonstrations in favor of land reform, nationwide marches, and occupations of important political offices which have the effect of mobilizing popular awareness and support as well as lobbying the

[13] In 1995, MST received the Itau-UNICEF Award for superior 'Education and Participation' in a national competition of social projects (MST/CONCRAB 1996).

government for specific services (Torrens 1994). The movement has successfully increased the settlers' access to credit and other government services such as education by organizing demonstrations intended to lobby local officials and mobilize the support of the surrounding population. On 8 June 1997, for example, approximately 600 Sem Terra occupied the offices of the Secretary of Agriculture in São Paulo to demand the release of smallholder credit (*Jornal Sem Terra* 1997).

Creation of national network

An important component of MST's organization is the creation of networks between the settlements that provide a continuous flow of information, people, and resources nationwide. In a seminal article on network analysis, Granovetter (1973) argued that 'weak,' distant ties provided greater access to economic information than strong, intimate ties (see also Burt 1992). Although the affection implied by a strong tie was likely to be greater than in a weak tie, the latter would have access to information that individuals and their close friends did not. MST militants create these weak links by traveling between the settlements, providing information regarding MST's demonstrations and other political activities, and encouraging settlers to attend regional and national meetings. In this way, MST creates an ongoing reserve of political pressure that can be activated when there is general or 'national' need as well as a reserve of economic resources that acts as a safety net for settlements that encounter emergency situations and as a reservoir of group information. The creation of a national network between reform recipients is one of the most valuable lessons provided by MST and perhaps the least difficult to replicate in other countries.

Access to international resources

At the consolidation stage of a settlement, international resources have often been secured from donors such as the Institute for International Cooperation and Development (IICD), which is located in Massachusetts. Through IICD, teams of volunteers are sent down to settlements where they perform various services, such as housing construction, at the request of the movement. IICD also donates money and solicits charitable donations from other US sources. International organizations contribute generously to the movement's activities. In 1995, 62% of MST's operating budget came from donations and only 29% came from internal or national income generating activities (de Kadt 1997). If the government in Brazil, and in other countries, can ally with grassroots social movements who have access to international resources, then the governments will also benefit from the external aid.

REFERENCES

Burt, R. 1992. *Structural Holes: The Social Structure of Competition.* Cambridge, MA: Harvard University Press.

Chiavenato, J. 1996. *Violencia no Campo: O Latifundio e a Reforma Agraria.* São Paulo, SP: Editora Moderna.

de Kadt, E. 1997. *NGOs and Institutional Development: The Dutch Co-Financing Programme in Brazil*. The Hague: DGIS/Bilance, Icco and Novib.

Food and Agriculture Organization (FAO)/Ministério da Agricultura e Reforma Agrária (MARA). 1992. *Os Indicadores Socio-Economicos Nos Assentamentos*. São Paulo, SP: FAO.

Fernandes, Bernardo M. 1998. 'Gênese e Desenvolvimento do MST.' MST, São Paulo.

Granovetter, Mark. 1973. 'The Strength of Weak Ties.' *American Journal of Sociology* 78(6): 1360–80.

Grindle, M. 1986. *State and Countryside: Development Policy and Agrarian Politics in Latin America*. Baltimore, MD: Johns Hopkins University Press.

Hall, A. 1991. 'Land Tenure and Land Reform in Brazil.' In *Agrarian Reform and Grassroots Development: Ten Case Studies*, Roy L. Prosterman, Mary N. Temple, and Timothy M. Hanstad (eds.). Boulder, CO: Lynne Reiner Publishers.

Houtzager, Peter. 1997. 'Caught Between Church and State: Popular Movements in the Brazilian Countryside 1964–1989.' Ph.D. Dissertation, University of California, Berkeley, CA.

Instituto Brasileiro de Geografia e Estatistica (IBGE). 1991. *Censo Demografico de 1991*. Brasilia, DF: Brazilian Government.

Jornal Sem Terra. 1997. 'São Paulo: Movimento dos Trabalhadores Rurais Sem Terra.' July Issue.

Leite, S. 1996. 'Assentamentos Rurais no Brasil: Impactos, Dimensoes e Significados.' Unpublished paper, Universidade Federal Rural do Rio de Janeiro.

Lopes, E. 1995. 'Organizacao de Producao e Resultados Economicos dos Assentamentos de Reforma Agraria de Sergipe.' *Reforma Agraria* 25(2): 70–86.

MST/CONCRAB. 1996. *Quatro Anos Organizando a Cooperacao*. São Paulo, SP: MST Publications.

Palmeira, Moacir and Sérgio Leite. 1998. 'Debates Economicos, Processos Sociais e Lutas Politicas.' In *Política e Reforma Agrária*, Luiz Flávio Carvalho Costa and Raimundo Santos (eds.). Rio de Janeiro: Editora MAUAD.

Petras, J. 1997. 'Latin America: The Resurgence of the Left.' *New Left Review* 223: 17–47.

Pinto, L. 1995. 'Reflexoes Sobre a Politica Agraria Brasileira no Periodo de 1964–1994,' *Reforma Agraria* 25(1): 65–93.

Silva, Ligia Osorio. 1997. 'As Leis Agrárias e o Latifúndio Improductivo.' *São Paulo em Perspectiva* 11(2): 15–26.

Strozake, Juvelino. 1998. *A Lei e As Ocupacões da Terras*. São Paulo: MST.

Thiesenhusen, William. 1995. *Broken Promises: Agrarian Reform and the Latin American Campesino*. Boulder, CO: Westview Press.

Torrens, J. 1994. 'O Processo de Construcao das Linhas Politicas do Movimento dos Trabalhadores Rurais Sem Terra.' In *Assentamentos Rurais: Uma Visao Multidisciplinar*, Leonilde Medeiros, Maria Valéria Barbosa, Mariana P. Franco, Neide Esterci and Sérgio Leite (eds.). São Paulo: Universidade Estadual de São Paulo (UNESP).

Vox Populi. 1996*a*. Popular summary of 1996b. June.

—— 1996*b*. *Relatorio de Pesquisa de Opiniao Publica e Caracterizacao Socio Economica em Projetos de Assentamento do INCRA no pais*. Belo Horizonte, Minas Gerais: Vox Populi Press.

13

Negotiated Land Reform as One Way of Land Access: Experiences from Colombia, Brazil, and South Africa

KLAUS DEININGER

Introduction

A large body of research has demonstrated the existence of a robustly negative relationship between farm size and productivity due to the supervision cost associated with employing hired labor. This implies that redistribution of land from wage-operated large farms to family-operated smaller ones can increase productivity (Binswanger, Deininger, and Feder 1995). In addition, access to assets in general, and land ownership in particular, can improve credit access and help smooth consumption intertemporally. By enabling the poor to undertake indivisible productive investments (or by preventing them from irreversibly depleting their asset-base), measures to improve the distribution of assets could lead to higher aggregate growth, thus improving both equity and efficiency (see Bardhan, Bowles, and Gintis 2000 for references). Cross-country regressions and micro-level evidence support the potential poverty-reducing and growth-enhancing impact of a better distribution of productive assets.

This apparent potential notwithstanding, land reform has in many instances fallen short of expectations and remains a hotly debated issue in a number of countries (e.g., Zimbabwe, Malawi, South Africa, Guatemala, El Salvador, Brazil, Colombia), some of which are spending considerable amounts of resources for this purpose. A mechanism to provide an efficiency- and equity-enhancing redistribution of assets that would increase overall investment at a cost that is comparable to other types of government interventions would be very desirable.

This chapter describes initial experience with a new type of *negotiated* land reform that relies on voluntary land transfers based on negotiation between buyers and sellers, with government establishing the necessary framework and making available a land

I would like to thank Hans Binswanger, Juliana Bottia, Alain de Janvry, Gershon Feder, Gustavo Gordillo de Anda, Adriana Herrera, John Heath, Nick Krafft, Marcos Lins, Michael Lipton, Anibal Llano, Absalon Machado, Indran Naidoo, Pedro Olinto, Manuel Rojas, Elisabeth Sadoulet, Edson Teofilo, Dina Umali-Deininger, Hernando Urbina, Martien van Nieuwkoop, Stefan Oehrlein, two anonymous reviewers, and seminar participants in Helsinki, Santiago, Bogota, the University of Sussex, and Washington, for valuable insights and discussions. The opinions expressed in this chapter are those of the author and do not necessarily represent the views of the World Bank, its Board of Directors, or the countries they represent.

purchase grant to eligible beneficiaries. Section 2 discusses the land reform experience in general, thus providing the historical background and conceptual basis for the subsequent argument. Section 3 is devoted to a more detailed description of negotiated land reform in Colombia, covering the reasons for choosing a negotiated approach, its principles, and its implementation in a number of pilot *municipios*. Section 4 compares the mechanisms utilized to those adopted in Brazil and South Africa and briefly highlights some of the implications for monitoring the new approach. Section 5 concludes.

The historical experience with land reform

While land reform has long been the subject of policy debate, the motivation for addressing land issues has shifted considerably over time. Initial discussions were largely motivated by political considerations, supported by the notion of the inverse farm-size productivity relationship. This notion had received empirical support from cross-sectional studies across states (Kutcher and Scandizzo 1981), countries (Berry and Cline 1979), or individual farms (Barraclough 1970).[1] More recent contributions have emphasized the importance of asset ownership in situations characterized by incomplete contracting (Bardhan, Bowles, and Gintis 2000), elaborating on models such as Dasgupta and Ray (1986, 1987) and Moene (1992). The reasoning is that, in situations characterized by credit rationing, individuals may not be able to undertake indivisible investments in human capital (schooling) or productive assets (wells, bullocks, or perennials with a long gestation period) that need to be financed through credit. This has been formalized in a number of theoretical models where lack of collateral keeps individuals in 'poverty traps,' unable to undertake highly profitable indivisible investments (Galor and Zeira 1993; Eckstein and Zilcha 1994; Aghion, Caroli, and Garcia-Peñalosa 1999).[2]

Under such circumstances the poor would fail to get out of poverty not because they are inherently less productive or lack the necessary skills, but because informational imperfections preclude them from access to credit markets. As a consequence, they never get the opportunity to utilize or fully develop their abilities. If this is true, a one-off redistribution to low-wealth groups could strictly dominate other policy instruments (Hoff and Lyon 1994). In particular, in the medium to long term, it will be more effective and less costly than continuing redistribution of income (e.g., through social programs) that would be associated with strong disincentive effects (Banerjee and Newman 1993; Mookherjee 1997).

Support for the importance of asset (and income) distribution for economic outcomes is provided by cross-country regressions that indicate the presence of a significant negative impact of the initial *asset* distribution on subsequent economic growth (Birdsall and Londoño 1997). This growth-reducing impact is particularly severe for

[1] One of the first studies to provide both a theoretical model and an empirical investigation of the potential impact of land reform is Rosenzweig (1978).

[2] Empirical evidence supports some of these conclusions (Jalan and Ravallion 1997; Fafchamps and Pender 1997).

the poor (Deininger and Squire 1998). Indeed, overall inequality seems to have an important impact on society's ability to effectively and quickly respond to exogenous shocks (Rodrik 1998), the level of crime (Fajnzylber *et al.* 1998), and the degree to which special interest groups are able to appropriate rents—with implications for overall productive efficiency (Banerjee *et al.* 1997).

Although inequality may significantly affect economic performance, historical examples for major changes of inequality within a country are rare (Li, Squire, and Zou 1998). More specifically, the success of land reform was critically dependent on the form of production into which it was introduced. In *landlord estates* where tenants already cultivated the land and all that was required was a reassignment of property rights, land reform was relatively straightforward and associated with significant productivity increases and the emergence of stable systems of production.[3] The main reason is that the organization of production remained the same family farm system, and beneficiaries already had the skills and implements necessary to cultivate their fields. Organizational requirements of conducting such land reforms were minimal—making them comparable to the 'stroke of a pen' reforms familiar from the literature on macroeconomic reform. Indeed, since the end of World War II, landlord estates in Bolivia, large areas of China, Eastern India, Ethiopia, Iran, Japan, Korea, and Taiwan have been transferred to tenants in the course of successful land reforms.[4]

By contrast, land reform in *haciendas*, i.e., systems where tenants had a small houseplot for subsistence but worked the majority of the time on the landlord's home farm, has been very difficult, up to the point where the 'game of Latin American Land Reform' was declared to be lost (de Janvry and Sadoulet 1989). In the large majority of cases large landowners responded to the threat of land reform with large-scale evictions long before governments were able to effectively implement laws aimed at tenant protection or land reform. They either resumed extensive livestock production and ranching or, aided by significant credit subsidies, started highly mechanized self-cultivation (Binswanger, Deininger, and Feder 1995). This reduced tenant welfare, depopulated farms, and created further difficulties for redistributive land reform. The experience with land reform in these environments points towards three specific difficulties.

First, the transfer from large to small farmers requires a change in the pattern of production, construction of complementary infrastructure, subdivision of the farm, and settlement of additional beneficiaries over and above the workers who have already been living on the farm.[5] Farms acquired for purposes of land reform have generally not

[3] While more in-depth study would be desirable, there is agreement in the literature that such reforms have been associated with significant increases in output and/or productivity (Callison 1983; Koo 1968; King 1977; Lieten 1996; Besley and Burgess 1998; Dorner and Thiesenhusen 1990; Otsuka 1991).

[4] Conceptually, one would expect productivity gains from improved work and investment incentives in the post-reform regime. Where security of tenure had already been high before the reform, where cash rather than share-rent contracts had prevailed, and where landlords had provided tenants with access to markets for credit, inputs, and outputs, static efficiency gains from land reforms may be modest and the bulk of reform benefits should come through enhanced investment incentives (and credit access on better terms) associated with land ownership.

[5] In many cases where large farms were distributed exclusively to the resident labor force (e.g., in Peru, Nicaragua, Honduras, and Cuba), the resulting units were too large to be able to reap the benefits from utilization of family labor. Production on reformed farms was often characterized by labor problems and productivity increases failed to materialize.

been farmed at full capacity, are run down or decapitalized, or highly mechanized. In all of these cases, failure to bring in additional beneficiaries, to provide resources for simple works (cleaning of pastures, fencing, construction of basic infrastructure, etc.) during the startup phase, and to ensure the availability of productive assets and technical assistance to go with the land have often contributed to the failure of reform efforts.[6]

Second, land reform beneficiaries, even if they are workers of the former farm, are rarely accustomed to making independent entrepreneurial decisions, a constraint that is particularly important if (as in many of the cases described above) realization of the potential benefits from land reform requires significant modifications in the farm's cropping pattern. Programs that are limited to the mere transfer of land, without training and technical assistance, have made it difficult for beneficiaries to quickly reach an equilibrium characterized by high levels of productivity and savings and, to the degree that beneficiaries were not able to get access to these, may have resulted in a permanent decrease in agricultural productivity.

Third, in rural environments with multiple market imperfections, providing beneficiaries with access to land but not with access to markets for output and credit may fail to make them better off than before. This will be the case particularly if landlords had provided their labor tenants with inputs, credit, or market outlets before the reform.[7] Land markets will therefore have to be viewed in the context of the operation of other factor markets.

In past attempts to effect the redistribution of land to the poor, these generic land reform difficulties were often exacerbated by implementation-related issues. Instead of aiming to increase productivity and reduce poverty, the main goal of many land reforms in the past has been to calm social unrest and allay political pressures by peasant organizations.[8] Such reforms had often been initiated in response to political pressure (or to divert attention from other problems) rather than as part of a long-term rural development strategy.[9] The resulting reform measures were generally designed ad hoc, bore little relation to actual needs on the ground, and commitment to them faltered once social emergencies had subsided. Furthermore, attention often focused

[6] The only exception is where already well-established plantations were redistributed to the former workers, a case that is very costly and characterized by relatively low social benefits (Adriano, Hayami, and Quisumbing 1990).

[7] In Ireland, in the early 20th century, a large-scale 'negotiated' land reform transferred 9.3 million acres (about half of the agricultural land available) from landowners to tenants, with very limited impact on productivity. One reason is that land reform—which was enacted on top of earlier legislation—did little to alter the structure of production or increase investment incentives. At the same time land reform led to a *worsening* of access to credit, by limiting the ability of new landowners to mortgage land while at the same time cutting off informal credit they had earlier obtained from the landlord (Guinnane and Miller 1997). Severely restricted access to credit, together with insecure property rights have also led to widespread selling of land by former land reform beneficiaries in Nicaragua—often at prices way below the productive value of the land (Jonakin 1996). Lack of access to other markets has been identified as a key obstacle to the initiation and success of independent small farming operations in Eastern Europe (Brooks and Lerman 1994).

[8] This is consistent with an interpretation of land reform as a piecemeal strategy by the rich to avoid the imminent threat of revolt—with backtracking as soon as the threat weakens as modeled by Horowitz (1993).

[9] Even where there was a genuine commitment to breaking the power of landed élites, agrarian reforms were generally designed by urban intellectuals with little idea of the realities of agricultural production and suspicion against small-scale cultivators' ability to increase productivity (Barraclough 1970).

on the politically vocal and well-connected peasants rather than rural dwellers with the best ability to make productive use of the land, or the most deserving on poverty grounds.[10]

The costs of carrying out land reform were often increased by the continued existence of implicit and explicit distortions that drove land prices above the capitalized value of agricultural profits and made it attractive for land reform beneficiaries to sell out to large farmers, thus contributing to reconcentration of holdings.[11] Also, instead of aiming to create conditions that would improve the functioning of land rental and sales markets to complement state-led reform efforts, governments have often completely outlawed or severely restricted the operation of land rental (and to a lesser degree sales) markets. This has eliminated an important opportunity for landless individuals to acquire farming experience, made the progress of land reform totally dependent on bureaucratic efforts, and complicated the task of targeting assistance to the poor. This complete reliance on government spawned complex regulations and cumbersome bureaucratic requirements to implement land reform that stretched available administrative capacity (Lipton 1974) and resulted in highly centralized processes of implementation. Government bureaucracies at the central level—justified by the need to provide technical assistance and other support services to beneficiaries—proved expensive and, unable to utilize information from the local level, often also quite ineffective.

Negotiated land reform in Columbia

Background

The traditional process

In Colombia, land reform has been a long-standing concern to correct an extremely inequitable distribution of land, to increase the productivity and environmental sustainability of agricultural production, and to reduce widespread rural violence. Maldistribution of land in rural areas, while dating back to the *encomiendas* given out following the Spanish conquest, has been reinforced and exacerbated in more recent times by a number of policy related factors.[12] These include:

[10] The importance of political factors is also evident from a number of Eastern European countries where political constraints generally led to a relatively 'inefficient' way of implementing land reform—through physical restitution of plots rather than compensation of former owners through fungible cash payments (Swinnen 1997).

[11] Despite attempts to limit beneficiary desertion through legal restrictions, anecdotal evidence points towards a large amount of land sales by reform beneficiaries in Nicaragua, Colombia, and El Salvador. In a recent Census of Brazilian land reform settlements, only about 60% of land reform beneficiaries were found tilling their land.

[12] Market imperfections that are common in rural areas of developing countries can lead to concentration of land in the hands of larger producers (e.g., Carter and Mesbah 1993). However, credit market imperfections alone—without policy interventions—cannot explain the heavy *underutilization* of land in Colombia where 75% of potential cropland is currently under pasture—it would presumably be more profitable for large landowners to rent their land to share tenants rather than using it for extensive cattle ranching or leaving it completely fallow.

1. Tax incentives for agriculture that implied that rich individuals acquired land in order to offset taxes on nonagricultural enterprises.
2. Legal impediments to the smooth functioning of the land rental and sales markets. Share tenancy was either directly outlawed or, when this was lifted, discouraged by the fact that tenants would receive property rights to whatever land improvements they had made, making it in principle impossible to terminate their leases.
3. Credit and interest rate subsidies plus disproportionate protection of the livestock subsector provided incentives for agricultural cultivation with very low labor intensity (World Bank 1996).
4. The use of land to launder money that had been acquired by drug lords.

These factors have profound implications for factor use, employment generation, and welfare in rural areas. First, while small farmers were often driven off their traditional lands to eke out a living in marginal and environmentally fragile areas, much of the best agricultural land (75% of the land suitable for crop production) was devoted to extensive livestock grazing or not farmed at all due to violence (Heath and Binswanger 1996). This suggests that there are indeed large tracts of unutilized or underutilized land which could be subjected to land reform in order to increase agricultural productivity—a notion in line with available empirical evidence.[13]

Second, rather than making use of labor, economic growth has been labor-saving. Since the 1950s, the rate of growth of rural employment has been significantly lower than aggregate economic growth, which is surprising even by the standard of other Latin American countries (Mision Social 1990). This appears to have increased peasants' inclination to support, or at least live with exceptionally high levels of rural violence that increasingly constitute a drag on the whole economy (estimates in the Colombian press put the losses associated with rural violence at about 15% of GDP). The government sees the reduction of rural violence as an important goal of land reform.

Third, structural adjustment made the lack of adaptability in the large farm sector particularly blatant. Elimination of credit subsidies caught large mechanized farms that cultivated mainly traditional crops with minimal labor inputs in a debt-trap that made them unable to adjust to the new environment and take advantage of the opportunities for exports of nontraditional and more labor-intensive crops. Unable to respond to the loss of agricultural protection in a productive way, the large farm sector resorted to large-scale lobbying. Establishment of a dynamic small farm sector would, it was hoped, enable Colombia to capitalize on its agro-ecological diversity and significantly increase its exports of traditional and nontraditional crops.

None of these concerns is new. In the 1950s, a World Bank mission identified the maldistribution of productive resources, especially land, as one of the root causes of

[13] Balcazar (1990) summarizes the existing literature in three points, namely (1) small farms farm more intensively than large farms, as measured by value of output per unit area; (2) between 1973–76 and 1988 average physical yields on small farms have increased by about 82% (this seems to be an unweighted average across different types of crops), whereas those on large farms have remained stagnant; (3) regional as well as commodity-specific studies do not find any systematic relationship between farm size and adoption of new technology or improvements in productivity.

economic stagnation. In 1961, the government established the National Land Reform Institute (*Instituto Nacional Colombiano de Reforma Agraria* or INCORA), to bring about a more equitable distribution of assets in the rural economy. However, even though considerable amounts of resources were spent on land reform (INCORA's average annual budget in the late 1980s was about US $140 million), most was spent on a large bureaucracy,[14] and almost thirty-five years of operations had produced little visible effect on the ground. INCORA appeared to be more effective in regularizing spontaneous settlement on the frontier than in converting the landless into successful agricultural entrepreneurs in areas that were previously cultivated by large owners. Even where land reform did distribute land, lack of capital forced many beneficiaries to abandon full-time agriculture and rent out part or all of their land, often to the old landlord. In the aggregate, between the 1960s and 1990, the Gini coefficient of the operational land distribution fell by only 3 percentage points, from 0.87 to 0.84.

Law 160 (1994)

Not unrelated to the loss of INCORA's traditional source of finance—a share of duties on agricultural imports that was eliminated with agricultural trade liberalization—a law was passed in 1994 that would allow for a more decentralized and demand-driven process. However, despite favorable preconditions, and the government's expressed determination to distribute one million hectares within four years, the land reform program had a disappointingly slow start.[15] Before describing the new implementation arrangements that emerged to improve on this, it is worthwhile to consider the main reasons for this lackluster performance and the measures taken to address this issue.

To overcome the 'fundamental financing problem of the poor' (Binswanger and Elgin 1988; Carter and Mesbah 1993), i.e., the fact that fully mortgage-based financing of land purchases by the poor is infeasible, the Colombian Land Reform Law provides for a land purchase grant. The grant amounts to 70% of the negotiated land purchase price, up to a maximum that was based on historical land reform allocations.[16] However, the grant was restricted to the purchases of *land* and could not be used to

[14] In the early 1990s the administrative costs of transferring land were very high, amounting to about 50% of the total land reform budget or about $15,000 per beneficiary.

[15] This failure to proceed more swiftly with implementation of the negotiated model of land reform was not due to resource constraints but rather institutional rigidities and resistance. In fact, resources available for market-assisted land reform were accumulated until the end of the year and then disbursed in a rushed process that bore little relationship to the regulations of the law, using the argument that it would be better to spend the resources imperfectly than losing them.

[16] For historical reasons, the grant was set to be 70% of the purchase price of the land. The remaining 30% of the land purchase price, plus any additional startup investment, has to be obtained from other sources—either the farm household's own resources or a regular loan from a financial institution at market rates, i.e., without any specific subsidy for land reform beneficiaries. It was hoped that by sharing the risk, financial intermediaries would provide additional assurance of the economic viability of land reform enterprises. While the high level of subsidy received strong political support from large landowners, experience thus far indicates that beneficiaries would be better served by a more modest grant that can be used for either land purchase or investments related to the startup of the new enterprise, i.e., that the 70% is too high.

undertake complementary investments. This created incentives for collusion between sellers and buyers to overstate land prices, divide the surplus between them, and let the government foot the bill.[17] The resulting incentive structure was strongly biased in favor of the transfer of developed agricultural land close to infrastructure and already well endowed with the necessary complementary investment. This tended to reduce land reform to a mere redistribution of existing assets rather than the creation of new ones, by targeting underutilized lands and helping beneficiaries to undertake significant investments. To deal with these issues, it was clarified that the goal of market-assisted land reform is the establishment of viable productive projects (*proyectos productivos*), rather than the mere transfer of land. A mechanism was devised to facilitate use of grant funds to finance nonland investments, thus overcoming the bias inherent in previous legal provisions.[18]

A second issue was that, to create viable agricultural enterprises, rather than a 'rural proletariat,' a target income from full-time agriculture (equivalent to a minimum farm size of about 15 hectares) was legally required. This neglected the potential of the poor—especially those in proximity to urban areas—to derive income from a variety of sources and left little room either for the exit of unsuccessful beneficiaries, or the gradual expansion of the holdings of successful ones through rental or purchase of additional land. It also demonstrated little awareness of the requirements, in terms of human capital, other assets, and experience with financial and marketing institutions, associated with operating a 15-hectare farm.[19] As a result, the law was in danger of concentrating large amounts of subsidies on a well-connected 'agrarian bourgeoisie' while leaving the majority of potential beneficiaries uncovered.[20] To overcome this shortcoming, the target income was reduced by one-third and, rather than being based on general averages, is to be assessed based on a project-specific plan elaborated by beneficiaries that includes income from non-agricultural sources.

[17] Landlords have in many instances overstated the price of land, and—by covering the complete land value with the 70% grant—have obtained a subsidy element of 100%. Consequently, in 1996 the price of land acquired through 'direct intervention' by INCORA (under a residual budget) was lower than the price of land acquired by beneficiaries through 'negotiated' land reform in the open market, leading to widespread dissatisfaction and calls for the return to the interventionist paradigm.

[18] Given that this regulation creates another layer of bureaucracy, transaction costs, and uncertainty about approval (or scope for politically motivated interventions), it would have been more desirable to change the underlying legal framework than develop ad hoc solutions.

[19] The concentration of benefits may be expedient from a political point of view—especially if the benefits can be appropriated by about 10–15% of the peasantry that is politically well organized and that closely collaborates with INCORA. However, comparison with European standards can put the farm size issue in perspective. In 1990 (the latest year for which these statistics are available), average farm size in the EU (including former East Germany) was (at 14.8 hectares) slightly below the Colombian 'minimum size' of 15 hectares. Average farm sizes in Greece and Italy are only 4 and 5.6 hectares, respectively, and even in the Netherlands and Germany, the average size of well-established farms was only 16 hectares (Eurostat 1995).

[20] The categorical prohibition of rental of land reform land (included in the 1994 law) is unlikely to be enforceable, and may even be counterproductive in that it would discourage successful reform beneficiaries from intensification on part of their land and renting out the other part while preventing unsuccessful reform beneficiaries from exiting.

Finally, even though the law provides for an exemplary and elaborate institutional structure[21] to facilitate an encompassing process of reform, the fact that there was little incentive for local leaders to actually establish the necessary structures implied that it was difficult to make the model operational and ensure effective beneficiary participation. Lack of dissemination of the law prevented a truly democratic process at the local level. Continued subsidization of INCORA drove out private service providers[22] and 'success' continued to be defined in terms of transferring land and exhausting budgets rather than in establishing viable rural enterprises. To change this, a shift of responsibility for approval from INCORA's headquarters to regional offices had to be accompanied by transferring resources directly to local communities and by clarifying that, among others, existence and functioning of a municipal council was a precondition for *municipios* to become eligible for land reform funds.

Implementation

While the first two years of program implementation highlighted critical shortcomings, they provided little insight in how to actually implement such a program. In this section we use the experience from five pilot *municipios,* selected to reflect the heterogeneity of the country,[23] to illustrate four key elements for implementation, namely:

1. Making land reform a program 'owned' by the local government, thus achieving better integration of land reform with existing municipal development priorities or investments, and at the same time greatly reducing transaction costs.
2. Requiring the elaboration of productive projects that provide the basis for a more programmatic approach to beneficiary training, negotiation of land prices, and an economic evaluation of the expected benefits and costs of land reform.
3. Establishing a decentralized and 'hands on' program of beneficiary training that would act as a means of pre-selecting beneficiaries (based on their willingness to participate), help them to overcome their structural difficulties, ensure greater 'ownership,' and ultimately economic sustainability of projects.

[21] The institutional structure is exemplary from a conceptual point of view, comprising (1) decentralized decision-making characterized by maximum local participation expressed through the pre-eminent role of the local councils; (2) private sector involvement in bringing together potential buyers, provision of complementary credit, and technical assistance to continue during the first two years of production on the land received; and the (3) limitation of INCORA to a regulatory role preventing misuse of funds, ensuring that regulatory requirements are met, and coordinating the different government agencies involved.

[22] Private real estate agents, who were supposed to act as information brokers in making potential buyers and sellers aware of market demands, found it difficult to compete with comparable INCORA services which were offered free of charge. In addition, INCORA's continued involvement in the decision-making process —including its ability to manipulate political levers—put the institution in a position to virtually guarantee a 'successful' outcome.

[23] These *municipios* are San Benito Abad in Sucre, Riveria in Huila, Fuente de Oro in Meta, Montelibano in Cordoba, and Puertowilches in Santander. While continued guerrilla activity throughout Colombia undoubtedly affects the scope for implementing land reform, acceptance of and support for the process at the local level has virtually eliminated guerrilla-related disruptions.

4. Insisting on a transparent and public process of project approval, and linking the needed mechanisms of accountability directly to a process of monitoring and evaluation that links to the municipal land reform plan, aims to quickly detect deviations from targets and the reasons for them, and forms the basis for an in-depth impact assessment of the land reform process at a later stage.

The expectation is that the steps taken by local governments to improve infrastructure and functioning of other factor markets, together with the land-reform specific measures (described in detail below), would improve potential beneficiaries' capacity to negotiate and make productive use of land, and at the same time, reduce the gap between the net present value of agricultural profits and land prices. This, in turn, would reduce the size of the land purchase grant required per person, thus making it possible to use a given amount of grant money to attend to a larger number of beneficiaries.

Local-level participation

A key document in the pilot *municipios* has been a municipal land reform plan. This plan, elaborated in a decentralized fashion, contains information about demand and supply of land for land reform purposes, and a characterization of the institutional environment and responsibilities for land reform. Following a systematic procedure to establish a municipal plan is expected to have three main benefits.

The first is to *identify potential demand* for this type of land reform. This includes steps such as: increase awareness among the beneficiary population and help target the most needy; establish a transparent process that can ground land reform firmly within the context of other local development initiatives; identify the potential demand for land reform; and develop realistic expectations about the extent to which land reform can contribute to the solution of existing problems.

A second benefit is to *identify potential supply* and to generate the basis for reasonably competitive land markets by ensuring that supply of land (at reasonable prices and in areas suitable for small farmer cultivation) exceeds demand. A final issue is the establishment—at the local level—of the *institutional infrastructure* needed for effective implementation of land reform. To ensure sustainability of land reform projects, it has proven to be critical to identify non-governmental organizations (NGOs) that are able to provide continuing technical assistance, and financial institutions that are in a position to extend and effectively supervise credit to land reform beneficiaries. These elements, together with information on the contributions expected from different participants (beneficiaries, central government, local institutions), make it much easier for local authorities to elaborate a coordinated program of land reform that is in line with the specific needs and opportunities, including the fiscal capacity, of the *municipio*.

Dissemination and beneficiary selection

Under the process followed before initiation of the pilots, selection of beneficiaries was often arbitrary and ad hoc. Despite the regulations of the new law, INCORA continued to select beneficiaries on a case by case basis once a given farm had been put up for sale and central approval for the release of the necessary land purchase funds had been obtained. In these cases, to be able to disburse funds quickly, sales of farms were often quite secretive, despite the existence (on paper) of a needs-based qualification system. The selection committees that were established included workers of the existing farm who were generally careful not to admit too many contenders from outside.[24]

To ensure participation beyond the membership of well-established *campesino* organizations and a transparent and more competitive market for land, this approach has, in the pilot *municipios*, been replaced by a procedure that aims to create the basis for land transactions through a more competitive market. To identify potential demand, a systematic information campaign to disseminate the law, with subsequent inscription of potential land reform beneficiaries (*aspirantes*) in a registry to be maintained by INCORA, is conducted throughout the *municipio*. A questionnaire provides basic information on beneficiaries' educational level, their agricultural experience (if any), their income sources, and their access to other types of government services such as education or health. Based on this, a pre-qualification, essentially a means test based on assets, is conducted.

Experience indicates that enabling potential beneficiaries to register at public offices and police stations in outlying villages has considerably broadened the outreach of the program. Contrary to the procedures followed earlier by INCORA, the information supplied is checked for consistency, resulting in the elimination of a large number of non-qualified applications. The names of rejected and accepted *aspirantes* (with reasons for rejection) are posted publicly. The publicity of the selection process seems to have increased accountability, and facilitated a better understanding of the scope and limitations of land reform by local authorities and potential beneficiaries. In all of the pilot *municipios*, alternative programs have been initiated to (temporarily or permanently) take care of the specific needs of groups who will not be able to benefit from land reform in the immediate future. These programs include chicken hatcheries and other microenterprises for female household heads, construction of rural roads under seasonal food for work schemes, as well as reforestation of environmentally fragile zones.

In addition to generating awareness for the program, its potential target group, and the characteristics of demand, the process of beneficiary selection also provides a basis for local authorities to integrate land reform into a broader program of capacity building and social assistance at the municipal level. This could contribute to the resolution of at least some aspects of the potential conflict between the dual objectives of equity and efficiency that is to some extent unavoidable if land reform is to make a long-term sustainable contribution to poverty reduction.

Institutional preconditions for a land market

The availability of large amounts of unutilized or underutilized land in large holdings implies that, in a reasonably fluid land market there would be plenty of supply to enable

[24] While one would expect that the transfer of large and relatively extensively cultivated farms would provide an opportunity for accommodating additional workers, the opposite often happened in practice, due to the unwillingness of existing workers to reduce their share and the associated incentives to exaggerate the amount of land needed to establish a productive unit. This tendency to expel laborers is well known from the theory of cooperatives.

potential beneficiaries to choose the most suitable lands and negotiate to obtain a competitive price. In practice, however, land markets have been thin, highly segmented, characterized by high transaction costs, and often pushed into informality (FAO 1994). Credit market imperfections, lack of market information by potential sellers, and the lack of farm models suited to the specific needs and factor endowments of small agricultural producers, have prevented such an outcome and contributed to the fact that beneficiaries under the old-style reform program often acquired marginal lands at highly exaggerated prices without making productive use of it.[25]

In the pilot *municipios*, a procedure similar to the identification of demand for land is being followed on the supply side as well. The first step is to determine ecologically suitable zones and, based on cadastral information, establish an inventory of the land according to size classification that could be used to identify target areas for agrarian reform. Areas where land reform would result in environmental hazards, where soil fertility is insufficient, or where the existing ownership structure is already characterized by small to medium-sized holdings, are thus eliminated *a priori*. This gives beneficiaries a better idea of where to focus their efforts, helps to set realistic goals, and puts into perspective the potential contribution of land reform for solving the social problems of a given *municipio*. It increases not only awareness of the scope for land reform as compared to other options aiming at overall development of the *municipio* (and the degree to which the success of land reform will depend on such complementary measures), but also forces local governments to think about potential levers (from land taxes to land price information systems and training to increase the productive capacity of potential beneficiaries) that they can utilize to achieve a process of 'integrated land market development.'[26] Experience from the pilots indicates that land that had traditionally been offered to INCORA for land reform was often of marginal quality and hardly suitable for land reform while some of the best land continued to lie idle or underutilized. Specific measures to resolve this issue have included:

- increasing sellers' awareness of the scope and potential for alternative forms, such as land rental, which increases efficiency and could temporarily or permanently provide potential beneficiaries with access to land, and may serve as a springboard for the landless to acquire the information and agricultural experience necessary to put together a productive project;
- encouraging more effective collection of existing municipal land taxes—a strategy in line with the central government's desire to increase the revenue base of local governments and to gradually reduce the need for central transfers;

[25] As highlighted earlier, even under the new land reform law, rationing was largely by non-price means—including outright corruption—and the main challenge for landowners willing to sell was to obtain clearance from the regional and central INCORA offices regarding the availability of funds to purchase their land, which was seen as the precondition for proceeding with negotiations.

[26] In principle the decentralized implementation mechanism, if coupled with competitive allocation of funds across *municipios*, should eliminate the scope for spending scarce resources on *municipios* where land reform is not economically feasible and outmigration is the most cost-effective form of satisfying demands for land. Due to the limited extent of the pilot, no such cases have, as of yet, been encountered.

- more effective and systematic dissemination of information not only among potential buyers but also any sellers of land, specifically information on the mechanisms of market-assisted land reform and the modalities of payment under this program.

There is justified concern that a program that provides targeted support to land purchases may contribute to an increase in land prices, and therefore benefit former landowners rather than the poor farmers who receive the land. To deal with this, it has been decided that, to be eligible for land reform benefits, *municipios* need to provide evidence (using actual sale inscriptions/offers by landowners) that existing land supply is at least three times the amount of land to be transacted under the land reform program.

Creating conditions for continued cultivation

Experience suggests that, in the absence of technical support during the startup phase and without access to markets for finance and outputs, the sustainability of newly initiated land reform settlements will be limited. The municipal plan thus contains a list of qualified providers of technical assistance from which potential beneficiaries can choose one to use the part of the land purchase grant that is earmarked for technical assistance. In addition, it aims to identify financial institutions that would be willing to lend to land reform beneficiaries. The rationale for this is simple. It is likely to be futile to initiate a large process of land reform in a *municipio* where neither credit nor product markets are accessible to potential beneficiaries, or where capacity to provide technical assistance is grossly inadequate. While identifying financial intermediaries who would in principle be willing to lend to land reform beneficiaries does not imply that every application will automatically be approved, it can help both parties to be clearer about the rules of the game from the beginning and, in addition, significantly reduce the search cost to be incurred by individual beneficiaries.

Productive projects

To help beneficiaries assess the requirements, opportunities, and risks they will face as independent farmers more realistically, elaboration of model farm projects has proven to be critical. While these models are necessarily abstract and therefore not directly applicable to the circumstances of specific beneficiaries or farms, they enable beneficiaries and technical assistance providers to be more specific about key factors such as marketing channels, input supplies, working capital requirements, etc. that need to be made more concrete during the subsequent process.

Under the approach followed by INCORA, where agricultural productivity received little if any consideration, beneficiaries generally elaborated their 'productive projects' *after* getting access to the land, with little systematic guidance and no discretion in the use of the technical assistance funds which were administered by INCORA (often with 'beneficiaries' receiving no benefits at all). Without a clear understanding of the economic potential of the farms to be established, expected returns, and alternative options (within or outside the land reform program), beneficiaries' ability to engage in substantive bargaining was greatly diminished. It was only natural that INCORA took the lead in 'negotiating' with the landlord;[27] a type of negotiation which ordinarily amounted to a mere formality and generally resulted in acceptance of the price set by an 'independent' valuer who was contracted by the landlord and paid in proportion to the assessed farm value.

The pilot experience has indicated that, unless beneficiaries have a clear idea of productive opportunities consistent with their abilities *before* they formulate productive projects that form the basis for 'shopping' for land, it is very difficult to break this deadlock. To this end, agricultural professionals that are contracted through beneficiary representatives help establish crop budgets for a range of options actually practiced in the *municipio* and conduct training courses and meetings to disseminate them. Aggregation of these into farm plans involving more intensive land use and sustainable income to beneficiaries provides the basis for the formulation of 'productive projects' by individual beneficiaries. Only after potential beneficiaries have understood the model budgets, including their requirements and economic implications, do they proceed to a pre-selection of farms they might like to visit.

Thus, instead of being regarded as a tedious necessity to obtaining access to complementary credit (as under the old program), farm plans under the pilot program acquired significant importance in a number of aspects. First, from a substantive point of view the farm models that have been established thus far do constitute a break with the past in that the main goal is to provide full employment of the family's labor force throughout the year. Second, farm plans are characterized by a focus on high value crops rather than traditional bulk commodities, greater diversification of crop production, and an important livestock component. Third, all plans include a significant 'garden plot,' setting aside about one hectare for domestic consumption needs (including chickens, one pig, and a cow) and intensive cultivation of vegetables or fruits, the surplus of which is to be sold in the market. In the process of shifting emphasis towards these goals, the importance of land area has declined significantly—in many cases the land area is between 30% and 50% of what had been the standard under earlier land reform programs. In addition to this, farm plans also serve as a first step towards the identification and prioritization of investment needs, and provide a justification for guiding the allocation of public funds to the most productive use.

Training and approval process

Negotiated land reform requires beneficiaries to take considerable initiative and perform tasks such as group formation, selection of a viable farm model, adaptation of this general model to the conditions of a specific farm, identification of the productive value of at least a number of farms available for sale, negotiation of a purchase price with the farm owner, arrangement for credit to finance the land and capital requirements that are not covered by the purchase grant, formulation of a strategy to establish needed on-farm infrastructure, and eventually cope with the challenges and risks

[27] This perception is illustrated by the fact that official records for the land transferred in 1996 indicate that in all cases where no credit from Caja Agraria was needed (because the seller advanced the 30% complementary credit to the buyer), a farm plan or productive project was 'not required.'

associated with sustaining an economically viable farm enterprise. Given their limited endowments and experience, potential beneficiaries are generally unable to go through the steps required in a 'negotiated' type of land reform without assistance. In fact, while most of the beneficiaries pre-selected in the pilot had some kind of agricultural experience, almost one-quarter was illiterate and 70% had five years or less of formal education. While many were in a great rush to receive land, their ability to negotiate or manage resources was clearly limited. Furthermore, even though many beneficiaries came in pre-existing groups, these groups were often based on coincidence more than on similarity of interest. The capacity of these groups to resolve internal conflicts or to devise effective strategies to achieve common goals was low or non-existent. Problems that will inevitably arise in jointly establishing and sustaining an agricultural enterprise would probably have led to the paralysis or breakup of many of these groups.[28]

To remedy this, and thus increase the scope for land reform to lead to productivity-enhancing outcomes, an in-depth training program for pre-selected *aspirantes* was developed.[29] This program, which is financed from INCORA's administrative budget, aims to cover not only abstract principles but to enable beneficiaries to formulate a viable farm plan. The 'theory' part includes topics that range from group dynamics and negotiation to economic analysis, farm management, and budgeting. Simultaneously, or as soon as beneficiaries have tentatively formed groups and decided for certain crop combinations, this is translated into practice in the context of visits to farms that have been offered for sale, calculation of the potential of these farms to generate revenue, the implications for the price that can be paid, the needed startup investments to allow productive use of the farm, and the way in which these can be effected in practice by the beneficiary group.

Contrary to widespread fears, lack of local capacity has not been a problem in developing these training programs. Local universities, NGOs, farmers' organizations, and government institutions (including INCORA) are enthusiastic to utilize synergies in providing such support in the expectation that they will follow the projects at least through the establishment phase. While the costs of this component are not negligible (about US $1,800 per beneficiary), this is not only less than one-third of what was spent by INCORA under the old process but can be more than justified in terms of the outcomes achieved in negotiations. Prices paid for comparable farms under the pilot were 30–40% lower than what had been paid in the previous year under INCORA's program.[30] Furthermore, while under the INCORA process some beneficiaries cancelled

[28] Indeed one of the surprising insights from the pilot was that virtually all of the groups that had initially existed were disbanded and replaced by new ones that were based more on commonality of interest (e.g., in specific production systems) or complementarity in experience.

[29] The number of pre-selected *aspirantes* is about double the number of those that could be accommodated as beneficiaries with given budgets to allow for attrition and to ensure that potential beneficiaries do indeed compete in trying to put together the most viable farm projects.

[30] These price differences are not due to quality factors. In one case, a farm neighboring (and almost identical) to one that had been acquired in 1996 by INCORA (supposedly under the market-assisted program) was acquired under the pilot with a price saving of about 40%—money that beneficiaries used to pay for complementary investments and working capital. In other cases, discounts of similar magnitude were obtained on the 'official valuations' that had been commissioned by the landowners.

technical assistance contracts that had existed under the previous owner, pilot beneficiaries are keenly aware of the importance of continuing technical support, and provisions to pay for this service out of farm revenues are made in all of the respective farm budgets.

A review of unsuccessful land reform cases had indicated two main reasons for failure. One was the absence of a fully funded plan to undertake the investments needed to convert the large farm into an enterprise suitable for small farmer cultivation, and the lack of funds to carry beneficiaries through to the first harvest. To deal with this, the training phase is utilized to develop, together with beneficiaries, a detailed plan (with monitorable indicators) for the on-farm investments needed to convert the farm into a smallholder enterprise. The ability to obtain partial funding for the startup activities undertaken during this phase has proven to be critical for the project's success.

The second problem was related to lack of access to credit and output markets. Under the pilot, agreements have been reached with a number of cooperative banks already active in rural areas to lend to land reform beneficiaries and thus compete with the government-owned bank that has traditionally provided financing to land reform beneficiaries. The preferred arrangement bears similarity to contract farming whereby the bank works closely with the providers of technical assistance (ensuring that the farm business established by beneficiaries would indeed generate the desired revenues and help farmers market produce). This enables them to supervise the use of the credit more closely, to ensure that enterprises are indeed developing their productive potential, and to deduct loan repayments at the source, rather than relying on unrealistic expectations of foreclosure. Problems of inter-institutional coordination (essentially the inability of the institutions who have traditionally administered these funds to work with non-governmental institutions) have prevented extending this model to all of the pilot *municipios*. However, beneficiaries from all the pilot *municipios* are unequivocal in their preference for dealing with a predictable private sector institution rather than with an unpredictable bureaucracy that is directly or indirectly dependent on government.[31]

All of the pilot *municipios* decide about the approval (and funding) of specific productive projects in public sessions of the municipal council—generally with record attendance. In these sessions beneficiaries have to present and defend their project, thus not only indicating that they understand the critical issues, but also providing an example to guide other candidates for the land purchase grant, and thus setting the stage for a transformation of the image of land reform in more general terms. In addition to generating positive feedback loops—beneficiaries who were selected in last year's

[31] Indeed, obtaining financing for the projects elaborated by beneficiaries in the pilot *municipios* developed into one of the main obstacles for smooth implementation. Even though all projects had been thoroughly evaluated and approved at the local level (including visits by bank representatives), it took the government-owned Caja Agraria between four and five months to obtain central approval from Bogota. This severely damaged the goodwill of landlords who wanted to sell and jeopardized beneficiaries' ability to proceed with their plans in a timely fashion, and was often combined with dictating of changes to the projects that were incompatible with beneficiaries' preferences or needs. In view of this, all the parties (including beneficiaries) involved in the pilot agree that the pilot experience can be successfully transformed into a broader national program only if the monopoly of Caja Agraria is broken and private sector institutions finance land reform projects. This would, of course, imply that they assume some of the associated risks.

Table 13.1. *Comparison between different processes of market-assisted land reform*

	Municipios		Regular INCORA
	Pilot	Non-pilot	
Primary channel of information on the program (%)			
INCORA or Caja Agraria	0.00*	25.00	41.74
Municipality/UMATA	47.06*	0.00	3.48
Preparation and land use			
Analyzed general situation in *municipio* (%)	90.20*	58.33	65.22
Considered farms in other *municipios* (%)	21.57	8.33	18.26
Number of farms visited before making a purchase decision	4.53*	1.08	0.90
Number of households per project	27.47	17.96	18.71
Beneficiaries concerned about deficiencies in (%)			
Institutional presence	47.06	66.67	60.87
Training	50.98*	83.33	60.00
Technical assistance	43.14*	91.67	62.61
Legal assistance	39.22*	70.83	57.39
Group was formed (%)			
Before the training process	39.22*	70.83	49.57
During the training process	60.78*	12.50	25.22
Use of property is collective (%)	100.00*	62.50	24.35
Total area of project (ha)	246.82	265.04	309.62
Area per household (ha)	8.99*	14.76	16.55
Negotiation and financing			
Price of land (US $/ha)	1,456.29	1,705.96	1,946.65
Cost of land per family (US $)	13,084.00*	25,177.00	32,222.00
Satisfied with (%)			
Support by the relevant institutions	50.98	41.67	30.44
Beneficiaries' participation in decision-making	49.02*	29.17	33.91
Beneficiaries' access to information	68.63*	20.83	20.00
Total time required for project implementation (months)	12.49*	18.68	22.08
General satisfaction with (%)			
The agrarian reform process	80.39*	58.33	57.39
The supply of land	49.02	45.83	62.61
Land prices	45.10	29.17	48.70
Support programs accompanying land reform	66.67*	33.33	33.91

* indicates that values for the pilot are significantly different from those in the other two columns.

INCORA land reform projects have already demanded access to similar technical assistance—this also establishes the basis for community-based monitoring and social control to ensure that beneficiaries' performance does actually live up to expectations.

Impact

Table 13.1 presents evidence based on a 1997 household survey that included a sample of about 220 land reform beneficiaries, fifty from the pilot and 170 from implementation of Law 160 under INCORA—thirty of them located in the same *municipios* and 140 in a random sample of *municipios*. Three issues are noteworthy.

First, compared to the implementation of Law 160 through INCORA, the pilot is characterized by greater municipal ownership as indicated by the fact that almost half of the beneficiaries mention the local government (or its technical assistance arm, the

UMATA) as the primary source of information on the program. This is important in view of the limited awareness of the program as indicated by the household survey—only about 20% of those interested know about the land reform process and only 7% are actually registered in INCORA's lists.

Second, the training component appears to be of importance in inducing a greater number of beneficiaries (90% as compared to around 60% earlier) to analyze the economic situation of the *municipio*, to visit several farms (4.5 as compared to barely one earlier) before making a purchase decision, to establish groups based on similarity of productive interests, and to go for projects that require less land per family (8.99 as compared to 15–16 hectares). These achievements notwithstanding, the share of beneficiaries who consider buying farms in other *municipios* is still low and the fact that all of the properties are initially farmed collectively suggests the issue of the transition phase should be given careful thought and monitoring.

Finally, the process adopted is perceived to be faster and more satisfactory by beneficiaries—notwithstanding the fact that land prices and supply of land are still problems, as indicated by the high costs (US $13,000) per beneficiary family.

Probit analysis of the characteristics of people who express interest in land reform based on a nationally representative household survey (results not reported) indicates that such demand comes from comparatively illiterate landless workers (*jornaleros*) with few non-land assets but large families. If the process of beneficiary selection can be made to respond to actual demand, land reform could therefore target a segment of the population that has proven to be difficult to reach by other programs, a conclusion that receives statistical support. Although based on relatively few observations, analysis of the targeting criteria implicit in INCORA and pilot approaches suggests that the pilot does better in selecting individuals with low levels of assets and could have some multiplier effect. Further analysis of the targeting of land reform under the new model, and a comparison to costs and benefits of other government programs, will be required to assess to what degree the pilot process succeeds in targeting the poor and how such land reform compares to other measures aimed at poverty reduction.

A study of the actual productive performance of the pilot projects in the middle of 1999 (Forero 1999) demonstrates that, despite numerous institutional problems, formerly landless cultivators are able to establish highly productive agriculture and that results are much superior to those from INCORA's simultaneous implementation of the Law 160 approach. Pilot projects are reported to be superior in virtually all aspects to those established simultaneously under INCORA's approach. In all the *municipios* studied, participants from the pilot are the only land reform beneficiaries who have repaid their loans and therefore continue to be able to access commercial and supplier credit for their production. This notwithstanding, there are a number of critical issues which, if unattended, may jeopardize the scope for replicating and/or scaling up this experience.

First, there is clear evidence that the complicated legal arrangements that were designed to soften the law's restriction on the use of the grant to land only without actually having to change the law proved ineffective. Beneficiaries suffer from lack of funds for investment, leading to the perverse situation that their farms consist of very small areas of perennials or vegetables where productivity often exceeds expectations, together with large tracts of land that continue to be farmed under the original pattern (often pasture)—which in many cases generate less revenue than is necessary to service interests on the debt (30% of the land value) incurred to purchase the land. Changing the program structure so as to avoid this pattern and instead allow beneficiaries to purchase and make investments in high-value crops on a much smaller area (about 2–3 hectares) sufficiently large to fully occupy their family labor could greatly increase the economic return and reduce the fiscal cost of the program.

Second, the failure to institute measures (e.g., effective collection of the existing land tax) that would increase supply of land, together with the lack of an effective link between the land price and the productive value of the project makes it impossible for beneficiaries to use the value of land under current production as the basis for their bargaining. This is exacerbated by the continuing dominant role of INCORA (which, during the 1994–97 period purchased land for about 10,000 beneficiaries per year, in contrast to about 200 under the pilot) and the fact that, under pressure to lose its budget, INCORA continues to purchase land at prices that bear little relationship to its current productive potential and that are substantially higher than what had been paid under compulsory acquisition before Law 160 came into force. As a result, virtually all the surplus continues to be transferred to former landowners and the projects formulated are (as noted above) often not even in line with beneficiaries' aspirations.

Third, while the activity of the CMDRs, in particular the process surrounding the formulation of the municipal land reform plan, was perceived to be an extremely positive aspect of the pilot program, improvements are possible with respect to the institutional structure to resolve conflicts, the integration of land reform in the broader context of local development, and the economic evaluation of individual projects.

1. Especially in backward *municipios* with feudal social relationships (which are the ones where land reform is most needed and has the highest potential), the authority of the CMDR and the ability of beneficiaries to challenge established power-structures was contingent on an outside authority (in this case the project unit) imposing strict standards of accountability in the use of project funds and providing access to legal assistance. Greater emphasis on the associated social aspects, including the establishment of sustainable institutions and mechanisms to resolve conflicts, ensure rule of law, and represent beneficiaries' interests, is an important pre-condition for sustainable land reform that needs to receive adequate attention.
2. There is considerable scope for putting land reform into the broader context of local development, especially in two respects. First, setting a certain time horizon for the resolution of land issues within a community and considering other mechanisms of providing poor people with land ownership could increase the effectiveness and appeal of a program at the local level. In at least one of the pilot communities, a program to resolve conflicts and provide small-scale cultivators with secure land rights would have had great benefits, while in others, helping tenants to make the transition to land ownership may be an effective strategy. Second, the pilot experience demonstrates that, to be able to effectively represent beneficiary interests, it will be useful to

define the institutional structure and source of funding of the CMDR in more detail and to provide technical assistance for its members where needed.

3. Not surprisingly, the quality of municipal land reform plans showed great variations across *municipios*, an issue that can only be addressed through an iterative process that builds on past experience and exchange across municipalities. One recurring concern was beneficiaries' dissatisfaction with the collective form of production imposed on them and their desire to individualize as soon as possible.

Regarding the overall nature of the program, the experience suggests that, unless the government can muster the political support needed to make the necessary modifications in the law and the way in which it is being implemented, truly negotiated land reform at prices that reflect the productive value of the land will remain at best a marginal phenomenon. Law 160 will be in danger of being used to protect existing power structures and, in the process, artificially prop up land prices.[32] If, on the other hand, the necessary changes and measures to increase land supply can be taken, the pilot experience and the lessons learned provide a good basis to create structures at the local level, improve beneficiaries' social, economic, and productive capacity, and thus implement a land reform process to benefit the poor. While INCORA has officially taken over the decentralized pilot methodology as its model of choice, it is important to be aware of the fact that—especially without the legal changes described above and the creation of accountable local institutions—it will be difficult to follow the credit repayment pattern achieved in the pilot instead of INCORA's own unimpressive record in implementing Law 160 during the 1994–97 period.[33]

Negotiated land reform in other countries

In addition to Colombia, Brazil and South Africa have, under different conditions, recently initiated programs of negotiated land reform. With an institutional background very similar to that of Colombia (presence of land reform legislation and a central land reform institute dating from the early 1960s), negotiated land reform in Brazil has been driven by the initiative of individual states. The purpose of the Brazilian interventions is to establish cheaper, more agile policy alternatives to centralized land reform in an environment where the issue of land reform is high up on the political agenda and potential beneficiaries have at least some idea of what to do with the land.

By contrast, negotiated land reform in South Africa has been adopted in the context of the national reconstruction program, in an environment in which productive small-scale agriculture was eradicated almost a century ago. This implies that, in its present form, the program bears many similarities to an urban settlement project and greater effort is required to establish the decentralized infrastructure necessary to implement

[32] A more in-depth investigation of the political economy of Law 160 is beyond the scope of this paper.

[33] While precise information on the extent of bad debts is unavailable, conversations with officials from Caja Agraria and FINAGRO suggest that there are few, if any, beneficiaries of the INCORA program in these years who are not in default (a view that is supported by Hoellinger 1999).

land reform, to provide complementary services such as marketing and technical assistance, and to increase beneficiaries' agricultural and entrepreneurial capacity.

Brazil

With a land distribution among the most unequal in the world, Brazil's situation is similar to Colombia's in a number of respects. There is a very large and vocal political demand for land reform; a recent FAO study estimates the number of families who are potential candidates for land reform at 2.5 million. A land reform institute (INCRA) was established in 1969, distributing 10 million hectares to 200,000 families and colonizing about 14 million hectares for about 75,000 beneficiary families since then. Land reform has recently acquired considerable political importance; a federal Minister for Agrarian Reform was appointed in 1996 and the land reform budget tripled from US $0.4 billion in 1994 to $1.3 billion in 1995 with a further increase to $2.6 billion proposed in 1997.

The large majority of these federal funds will be spent according to the old process, which has been costly (about $30,000 per beneficiary) and bureaucratically cumbersome. However, state governments in the Northeast have been moving ahead and have set up a decentralized market assisted pilot scheme (Cedula da Terra).[34] This scheme (supported by a 90-million dollar external loan) aims to speed up the land reform process, reduce costs, and provide the basis for a model that could eventually be expanded to cover the whole nation.[35]

Program characteristics and incentive structure

The main differences from the old mechanism are the following (see also Table 13.2):

1. Rather than relying on a lengthy process of expropriation, land is selected by community groups on a willing seller–willing buyer basis. This is expected to reduce the price of land from currently US $11,000 to $3,000, mainly by avoiding the need to pay for expensive land improvements that are of little use for small-scale agriculture. Funds for the land purchase are extended to beneficiaries as a pro forma

[34] The steps involved in the process of expropriation, which is applicable to land that is utilized at less than 80%, are as follows. First there is a visit by an INCRA mission to assess the value of land and improvements, followed by expropriation through presidential decree and confirmation of expropriation through a federal court (*emissao de posse*) in a process that takes about a year. Once this is accomplished, landowners are compensated with *Titulos da Reforma Agraria* (with a real interest rate of 6%; bearing a discount of 25–40% in the market); anecdotal evidence of excessive compensation abounds. The necessary infrastructure investment is then included in the subsequent year's INCRA budget (it takes 1–2 years for the infrastructure to be established) and INCRA announces that the land is available, selecting beneficiaries based on agricultural skills, although in practice all cases are limited to regularization of existing squatter settlements. Once selected, beneficiaries are eligible for credit from PROCERA (max US $7,500; average US $4,500), a special program for land reform beneficiaries administered through INCRA (with an effective subsidy of about 70%).

[35] The emphasis on land reform by the federal government and the initiation of alternative approaches by state governors (essentially in the hope of being able to demonstrate that they are able to deal with the problem more effectively) is certainly not unrelated to the political strength of the landless movement (*Movimiento sem Terra*, MST).

Table 13.2. *Comparison of mechanisms to implement market-assisted land reform in Colombia, Brazil, and South Africa*

	Colombia		Brazil		South Africa
	INCORA	Market assisted	*INCRA*	Market assisted	Pilots
Land selection	• Selection by *INCORA* de facto based on political pressure. • Cost of $18,000–22,000 per family.	• By beneficiaries, with means to increase transparency and provide technical assistance.	• Purchase or expropriation. Average cost of $11,600 per family. • Mainly legalization of occupied lands.	• Negotiated by community. • Willing seller (including banks), willing buyer. • Expected cost $3,000 per beneficiary.	• Community initiative.
Land financing	• 70% of land value (up to $22,000) as grant (20% cash; 50% bonds). • 30% through *Caja Agraria* credit (lengthy delays).	• Commercial bank administers grant resources and provides additional credit for land purchase and working capital.	• TDAs for unimproved land and cash for improvements and crops. • Beneficiaries in theory expected to pay back • Not enforced.	• Loan to approved beneficiaries from a commercial bank (considerable subsidy element).	• Maximum grant of R 15,000 for land purchase. • Separate planning grant.
Beneficiary selection	• Point scheme for social need and agricultural experience. • In practice, ad hoc selection based on individual farms.	• Comprehensive registration and pre-selection based on social criteria. Final selection based on productive projects.	• Through INCRA based on examination of agricultural knowledge. • In practice almost all are regularized squatters.	• Self-selection of beneficiaries. • Clearance of price and title by State Land Institute. • Decentralized approval. • Occupied lands ineligible.	• Self-selection of beneficiaries subject to maximum income criterion (< R 1,500 per month).
Farming project definition	• Perceived to be necessary only for obtaining a bank loan.	• Key issue for selection; different forms of technical assistance available. • Farm models available at municipal level.	• No specific arrangements.	• Up to 8% of project value available for technical assistance in project preparation and implementation. • Farm models elaborated at state level.	• Provincial plan is a precondition but few specific guidelines provided and no farm models are elaborated.
Other financing	• Credit for land and working capital is the big bottleneck causing implementation delays.	• Independent financial institutions to provide integrated credit for the whole project.	• Credit of up to $1,150 (average $610) for food and housing and $7,500 (average $4,500) for working capital. 70% subsidy element. • Minimal cost recovery.	• Access to PROCERA credit like other land reform beneficiaries.	• Responsibility of beneficiaries.
Off-farm investments	• Complex set of interinstitutional coordination with little results up to now.	• Identified and costed in municipal land reform plan.	• Provided by INCRA ($3,200 in 1994, now up to $8,000); almost all for roads.	• Grant of $4,000 per beneficiary; disbursed directly to community.	• Services and to some extent infrastructure are provincial responsibility. • Coordination with the center is still weak.

credit that has to be repaid upon *emancipacion*, an official declaration that the farmer is now able to farm independently, that is combined with the transfer of the title.[36]

2. Instead of compensating landlords with highly discounted government bonds, they are paid cash. This provides a strong incentive for landowners—including many banks that hold title to large tracts of land as a collateral for non-performing loans—to sell land-to-land reform beneficiaries.
3. Government's role is reduced to providing assurance that there are no problems with the land titles, and ensuring that the price negotiated between community groups and landlords is within acceptable boundaries. Projects are approved at the state level.
4. Technical assistance is provided on a strictly demand driven basis; beneficiaries can use part of the community grant made available under a World Bank loan to contract private providers; CONTAG (Federation of Rural Workers) participates in the state councils and assists with information dissemination and land purchase negotiations.
5. The only commonality between pilots and the nationwide land reform process is the fact that beneficiaries under the new process have access to a subsidized loan under a special program (PROCERA) for land reform beneficiaries.

While the broad principles are similar to those in Colombia, the process is considerably more flexible and agile. The main points of difference are the following:

1. Since grant financing is provided for complementary and community-level infrastructure rather than land itself, beneficiaries who expect to repay their land purchase loan have an incentive to bid down the price for land as much as possible. This creates an incentive to focus on lands that are currently underutilized, thus reducing the expected purchase price and directing land reform to areas where the social gains from the intervention are maximized.
2. The process of beneficiary selection is less formal and bureaucratic than in Colombia, relying on an infrastructure of existing community associations to conduct information campaigns. Community control facilitates greater flexibility in project execution but also creates a danger that, without mechanisms for supervision and *ex post* accountability, landowners select former workers as beneficiaries and a minority of politically vocal and well represented monopolizes a large part of program benefits.
3. As long as beneficiary organizations exist that can assist farmers in preparing projects and in the initial stages of establishment, the solution chosen—where technical assistance can be financed, on a voluntary basis, through the community grant—is appropriate. However, evaluation of the initial projects should examine whether this prevents beneficiaries from shifting to higher value crops and a shift in production patterns.
4. Given the high subsidy element (about 70%) in the working capital credit provided to beneficiaries, availability of government funds for this credit may easily become

[36] Not surprisingly, the number of land reform properties that have been emancipated is minuscule.

a binding constraint for program implementation. In addition, the longer-term economic viability of land reform beneficiaries will depend critically on their ability to gain access to alternative sources of working capital and marketing channels. This, together with the question to what degree beneficiaries do actually expect to repay even working capital credits, could become one of the critical issues for the long-term success of land reform.

Evidence

Given the political importance of land reform and the limited knowledge of both the most appropriate mechanisms to implement this reform as well as the magnitude of the productivity and poverty-impact, the government has established the Central Institute for Agrarian Studies to: (1) encourage discussion between all parts of civil society, academics, and politicians on land reform issues; (2) carry out a thorough and careful monitoring and evaluation of the land reform process either directly or through local institutions; (3) make the data collected in this process available to national and international researchers, thus acting as a hub in a broader network of countries and researchers interested in negotiated land reform.[37]

In contrast to Colombia, where the size of the pilot is marginal, the Brazilian program has made rapid progress—about 10,000 households have benefited since the project was started and negotiations for a follow-up project at a national scale (Banco da Terra) are under way. Given the rapid pace of implementation, monitoring has taken somewhat of a back seat. Community and individual interviews in 104 (out of a total of 223) projects undertaken in late 1998 and early 1999 draw a number of conclusions (Buainain *et al.* 1999).

First, although evidence on actual productive performance is limited due to the recent drought in Northeast Brazil, farm models built to reflect actual conditions of the beneficiary population suggest that, except in highly drought-prone areas where additional insurance may be needed, land reform offers poor people an opportunity to sustainably improve their livelihood and escape poverty. Although the program does not yet reach out to the poorest segments of society, it is targeted to the 'non-marginal poor' (Bunainain *et al.* 1999). Land prices are, with an average of about US $5,500 per beneficiary household, slightly above original expectations but significantly lower than in alternative programs.

Second, great differences continue to persist in the degree of institutional development and community involvement across communities and projects. Efforts to involve all players at the local level, possibly in a more coordinated and formalized way, could help to improve performance in at least three respects:

1. They could help to guarantee a minimum level of accountability and transparency, thus allowing existing suspicions to be dispelled that, at present, the demand-driven nature of the program allows local politicians and landowners to hijack the program and utilize it to their own advantage (Navarro 1999).

[37] The websites at www.nead.gov.br and www.dataterra.br provide a rich set of materials and activities.

2. It would set in motion a process to build beneficiary capacity to facilitate more conscious selection of the land to be acquired, the productive structure to be adopted, and the complementary investments to be undertaken. At the same time it would help improve beneficiaries' awareness of the project rules the lack of which may seriously compromise the longer-term sustainability of the whole program.[38]
3. It would help improve the technical quality of the projects, their ability to draw on existing structures for marketing, credit, and technical assistance, and to learn from the experience of other settlements. Establishment of demonstration projects at the local level in partnership with social movements (including the MST) would be the best way of demonstrating the viability of the approach.

Finally, even though there is a vociferous public debate on the merits of different approaches to land reform, the opportunity to use survey data to directly compare INCRA and Cedula da Terra, thereby channeling the dispute into a more constructive direction, lies still unutilized.

South Africa

While South Africa shares with Brazil and Colombia a highly unequal land distribution, policies that neglected the land rights of the nonwhite population have systematically exacerbated these inequalities. The Native Lands Act of 1912 prohibited the establishment of new farming operations, sharecropping, or cash rentals by blacks outside of the reserves, which made up only 7.7% of the country's area. Inside the reserves an artificial form of 'traditional' tenure with maximum holding sizes and restrictions on land transactions was imposed. Subsequent policies of 'black spot removal' transferred the large majority of black farmers who had legitimately owned land outside the reserves into the homelands where tenure restrictions, high population density, and lack of capital and market access made commercial agriculture virtually impossible. Labor laws that discriminated against blacks in favor of white workers and generous capital subsidies contributed to successive evictions of large parts of the black population from white farms, where they had been employed as labor tenants and farm workers (Binswanger and Deininger 1993).

Program structure

While the Native Lands Act was repealed in 1993, the momentous task of a comprehensive reversal of these policies and their consequences was left to the government

[38] The preliminary evaluation indicates that more than half of the associations (52%) interviewed chose the first-best property they could find, with little economic evaluation or negotiation, and that complementary investments appeared dispersed with little apparent economic rationale. In fact, in about a quarter of the cases, the negotiation was conducted directly between the landlord and the government or 'politicians,' and in another 25%, government or state organizations were involved. Even after probing, 90% of beneficiaries did not know the interest they had to pay on the loan and about one-third indicated that they had received the land for free, without any credit—figures that did not improve much in interviews with the presidents of the beneficiary associations (Bunainain *et al.* 1999).

that entered power following the 1994 elections. In attempting to do so, this government had to contend not only with the extremely unequal land distribution (the average amount held per person was 1.3 hectares by blacks compared to 1,570 hectares by whites) but also the lack of any local government structure, widespread absence of administrative capacity, a highly indebted large farm sector, and fear that redistribution would wreak havoc with agricultural productivity and jeopardize national food security. The government decided to adopt a land reform policy that would redress the injustices of apartheid, foster national reconciliation and stability, underpin economic growth, improve household welfare, and alleviate poverty (Government of South Africa 1996). The three central components of this policy are as follows:

1. *Restitution*. Legal processes have been put in place to compensate (in cash or kind) individuals who had been victims of forced removals after 1913. All Restitution cases are dealt with through the Land Claims Court and Commission, established in 1994 to which claims have to be submitted within three years (i.e., by the end of 1997). Even if the legal process can be completed in a speedy manner, the inability of the vast majority of the population to furnish written evidence makes this option feasible for only a small part of the population.
2. *Land tenure reform*. This component seeks to improve tenure security of all South Africans by recognizing individual as well as communal ownership rights to land, giving people the right to make decisions about their own tenure system, adjudicating disputes, reforming tenancy laws, and attempting to end discrimination against women in land allocation and holding. It is intended to create the administrative infrastructure that will provide hitherto disadvantaged groups with access to land under a wide array of arrangements that are in line with agro-ecological endowments and community characteristics. It is hoped that this will provide the regulatory environment for a land rental market by transferring land to more productive users, redressing the inefficiencies of the apartheid system.
3. *Redistribution*. As the main component of the government's land reform policy, redistribution aims to complement the market by providing land for productive and residential purposes to a large number of rural blacks who were dispossessed during apartheid and who are interested in obtaining land. It aims to do so by providing a one-time Settlement/Land Acquisition Grant of R15,000 (US $3,300), the amount of which is equivalent to the National Housing Subsidy available in urban areas to eligible beneficiaries, defined as anyone with a monthly salary below R1,500. The choice of negotiated land reform rather than expropriation (which, as in Colombia, can still be used as an instrument of last resort) was based on the need to maintain public confidence in the land market, and more generally to affirm the government's respect for individual property rights. It also reflects the recognition that, in other countries, expropriation has failed to provide rapid access to land for a large number of people and instead degenerated into lengthy political maneuvering and rent seeking. The number of potential land reform beneficiaries is considerable; estimates indicate that there are about 200,000 labor tenants and 1 million farm workers, and as many as 7–8 million blacks in the reserves.

Program implementation and initial experience

The fact that the large majority of the rural population has never seen a successful and productive small farm, and that many of the land reform beneficiaries themselves seem to believe that efficient agricultural production is possible only on large farms, gives capacity building particular importance. The South African government is well aware of these issues and has set up a number of pilots in different provinces to accumulate experience and improve the execution of land reform. These projects are now gathering momentum and have provided a number of valuable lessons, many of which are currently being integrated into government policies.

1. The almost complete fungibility of the land purchase grant represents an important advantage over the Brazilian and Colombian models. It prevents individuals without comparative advantage in farming from becoming land reform beneficiaries just to secure the government subsidy, while at the same time eliminating the possibility that land reform will inflate land prices. However, the absence of any effective beneficiary contribution has resulted in the formation of unwieldy organizational structures (the average 'Community Trust' established under the program comprises about 200 households) that are geared more towards acquisition of land than successful operation of an agricultural enterprise.[39]
2. While it is the government's goal to execute land reform with maximum local participation, the lack of an institutional structure has, up to now, made effective decentralization and beneficiary participation difficult. This has resulted in huge demands being placed on the Department of Land Affairs (DLA) staff and at the same time considerably slowed down the process (the projected time for DLA to process a project is about fourteen months, and often more time is required). Progress has been made in addressing this issue, real involvement of local players is likely to require some devolution of decision-making authority (at present each land designation has to be signed by the Minister himself) and a shift towards *ex post* control. This, of course, is contingent on appropriate information systems being in place.
3. Beneficiaries' access to complementary services and infrastructure has been problematic—a situation that was exacerbated because responsibility for these services rests outside DLA, the agency responsible for land reform execution.[40] These shortcomings can be addressed by empowering emerging local governments to play a stronger role in coordinating the different institutions involved at the local level. In addition, more systematically incorporating the private sector (banks and other financial institutions, as well as current land owners) in the formulation and evaluation of farm plans,

[39] In the meantime, DLA has virtually eliminated these large projects.

[40] Based on a case study of one of the provincial land reform pilots in KwaZulu Natal, Cross *et al.* (1996) report four main shortcomings, namely: (1) a complete lack of interinstitutional coordination (e.g., concerning access to water resources); (2) underestimation of the time and energy required for legal issues such as adjudication between conflicting land claims; (3) political tensions between ANC and IFP (at the national and provincial level, respectively) which prevent the effective delivery of services other than land to the beneficiaries, and (4) a tendency to interfere by local chiefs who perceive land reform mainly as a means to enhance their own power which depends on the number of people they are able to accommodate rather than the productive success of the programs that are established.

the provision of technical assistance, as well as marketing and input supply, could effectively address the current problems of 'aftercare.'

4. While there is strong emphasis on elaboration of land use and business plans by beneficiaries, many of these plans have been elaborated by entities that do not have responsibility for the long-term economic success of the project and do not contain arrangements for technical assistance in the project's establishment phase. The experience from land reform in Latin America illustrates that, in the absence of a clear plan that is available before accessing the land, there is a danger that beneficiaries will eat up whatever capital stock was transferred with the farm and subsequently revert to survival farming. This neglect of the productivity aspect of land reform, often exacerbated by unwieldy group sizes and lack of coordination among different institutions, could seriously threaten the poverty-reducing potential of this intervention, in addition to having negative environmental consequences (Cross *et al.* 1996).[41]

A survey of 1,168 randomly selected beneficiaries in eighty-seven (out of the about 200 existing) land reform projects conducted in the second half of 1999 allows one to complement the case study evidence with more systematic evidence on targeting, inter-provincial differences, and characteristics of successful projects which could help in possible program redesign (Deininger *et al.* 1999).

Regarding the first aspect one notes that the program is targeted towards households with low income, with low levels of education, high level of family labor endowment, but also with some productive assets (e.g., livestock). Female-headed households have a higher probability of participating in land reform projects, rejecting the hypothesis that these households are discriminated against.

Across provinces, the existence of large inter-regional differences in key parameters such as project size, economic viability, access to complementary credit, and socio-economic characteristics is noteworthy.[42] To the degree that these characteristics correspond more to the prevailing socio-economic structure than the local economic potential (and beneficiaries' aspirations), this would suggest that the program is still very much supply-driven and, as a consequence, has not yet succeeded in harnessing the full benefits of decentralization.

The survey also suggests that, even though most of the projects were established very recently and an unknown number of 'livelihood projects' may be directed towards non-economic objectives, about 20% of the projects are generating respectable economic returns. The data also indicate that economically successful projects share a number of characteristics.

[41] 'NGOs and pilot structures are . . . beginning to be afraid that they would not be able to do more than provide land redistribution beneficiaries with the minimum of land and secure tenure and that this alone would amount to just dumping them—equivalent to the apartheid practice of dumping removals victims in the middle of the field with no shelter and no way to make a living' (Cross *et al.* 1996: 166).

[42] For example, the average project in Northern Province and Eastern Cape includes 80 and 96 beneficiaries, respectively, compared to a national average of 25. Also, not a single one of the 13 projects sampled in KwaZulu Natal makes a profit.

Regarding the social structure, successful projects are characterized by greater ownership in the sense that they require beneficiaries to make a regular cash contribution. This is facilitated by generally smaller group sizes, a factor the importance of which is by now commonly recognized. Concerning productive aspects, it is of interest that successful projects are (1) more likely to be run by a manager than by a common property association or a trust; (2) much more likely to have access to group credit; (3) characterized by much higher awareness of the decision-making structure on the part of beneficiaries—which again is likely to increase voice, ownership, and sense of participation. While none of these findings can be interpreted in the sense of establishing causality, it is interesting to observe that it is possible to reject the hypotheses that successful projects achieve high rates of return because they 'pick' beneficiaries with higher levels of observable endowments (education, assets, etc.). As all of the indicators of economically successful projects in South Africa appear to be consistent with the design factors of a viable program of negotiated land reform discussed earlier, exploring in somewhat more detail the scope to which these indicators can serve to pre-select economically viable projects might be of some interest.

Conclusion

While a final judgement on whether or not negotiated land reform can rise to the challenges that administrative land reform has failed to solve will have to await availability of appropriate data,[43] the experience from the three countries provides valuable lessons that can guide attempts to implement programs of land reform. It suggests that: (1) land reform through negotiation can only succeed if measures are taken to make the market for land sales and rental more transparent and fluid; (2) productive projects are a core element of market-assisted land reform that is designed to establish economically viable and productive projects at a socially justifiable cost rather than to transfer assets; (3) the only way to achieve effective coordination of the various entities involved in this process is through demand-driven and decentralized implementation; and (4) the long run success of land reform is likely to depend critically on getting the private sector involved in implementation, and the ability to utilize the land purchase grant to 'crowd in' private money.

Making land markets more transparent and fluid. While there is broad agreement that selection of land and beneficiaries should be demand-driven and effected at the local level, the problem is that the conditions for local land markets to function, such as information on land prices as well as beneficiaries' ability to assess the value of a piece of land or the potential productive returns of its more intensive cultivation, are often limited. Three mutually reinforcing strategies to deal with this constraint are: (1) the provision of technical assistance at the community level, including assessment of the adequacy of the land price at the point of transaction; (2) co-financing of the land

[43] Data for such an exercise will hopefully be supplied by the monitoring systems that are established in all of the countries described.

purchase through a private financial intermediary which, because it shares in the risk of default, will have an incentive to assess the economic feasibility of the proposed farming project; and (3) a 'market information system' to provide prices for plots transacted in the market—both with and without use of a land purchase grant.

Negotiated land reform is a complement, rather than a substitute for other forms of gaining access to land, especially land rental. In this sense, land rental should be understood as a means for beneficiaries to accumulate experience and start-up capital thus reducing the size of the land purchase grant required under a model of negotiated land reform. This has to replace an understanding whereby renting out might cause owners to lose their land or renting in may cause tenants to become ineligible for a land purchase grant. Up to now none of the models considered here have contemplated in depth the potential benefits of inter-regional migration, and ways to encourage such migration to reduce the cost of a land reform program and at the same time enhance its impact on productivity.

Focusing on productive projects. Productive projects are likely to be the key to market-assisted land reform because (1) they are the only objective criterion to put an upper bound on the price that can be expected to be paid; (2) they provide a necessary basis for financial intermediaries to evaluate and eventually support such projects; and (3) they require beneficiaries to familiarize themselves with the realities they are likely to confront as independent farmers, and in the process provide them with greater clarity on their own aspirations as well as the potential—and the limitations—of land reform to contribute to the attainment of these goals. In contrast to previous plans that were imposed from the top with little awareness of local constraints, these plans aim to create the basis for a more transparent market at the local level and are the starting point rather than a substitute for more active beneficiary involvement.

Decentralizing implementation. Experience with centralized land reform has revealed it as a slow—and costly—alternative to decentralized negotiation. In Colombia, the whole pilot, from the first dissemination efforts to project approval by a technical committee and local financial intermediaries, was completed within seven months[44]—with landlords being the most eager party to see it advance. Prices paid under the decentralized approach were below the cost of land that had been paid earlier and beneficiaries see a major benefit from training and detailed project planning in their ability to negotiate independently with landowners, in addition to the fact that they have a clear idea of how to proceed once they receive the land. Similar figures are available from Brazil where the presence of community-organizations allowed even speedier implementation. Even in South Africa, where the absence of local institutions at the start of the program made a relatively centralized mode of implementation necessary, the rapid emergence of local governments has already facilitated significant steps toward greater decentralization and advances in program implementation.

[44] Following approval of productive projects at the local level, centralized institutions (INCORA and Caja Agraria) engaged in endless soul-searching and tried to reject projects because they were 'too far from infrastructure' (even though construction of bridges or rehabilitation of roads were part of the farm development plan), or otherwise not suited for smallholder cultivation. Even though in the end all of the projects were approved, this did much to undermine the credibility of the process with sellers.

Maximizing private sector involvement. Two lessons have become evident about the financing of land reform. First, restricting a land reform grant to a specific part of the land reform package to the exclusion of others (as was originally the case in Colombia) is likely to be counterproductive; a flat grant that can be used for all types of expenditures (as in South Africa) is clearly preferable. Second, without effective beneficiary contribution and assured access to financial markets as a part of the land reform package, it will be difficult for beneficiaries to develop financially sustainable operations. There seems scope for exploring possibilities of combining this with mechanisms aimed at sustainable savings generation. Given the high transaction costs of providing credit in rural areas and the increased need for monitoring when most clients lack previous exposure to credit, it is important that this issue be given sufficient attention. This relies heavily on the formulation of economically viable and technically feasible productive projects. Getting participants—government bureaucrats and NGOs as well as potential beneficiaries—to realistically assess the potential as well as the dangers inherent in negotiated land reform is critical.

Such a focus on 'integrated land market development' that aims to develop land markets jointly with markets for other factors may offer potential not only in situations such as the ones described here where land is distributed very inequitably. It may also help countries (e.g., Nicaragua, Honduras, El Salvador) where large land reforms have not had the desired productivity impact to realize the productive potential of the reform sector and provide a model for 'fair' dispute resolution in situations (e.g., Uganda) where overlapping claims and long-standing disputes over land ownership have severely affected the productivity of land use. Ultimately, negotiated land reform aims to provide a catalytic input that would help beneficiaries improve their human capital endowments, change from passive objects into subjects of the development process, and convert a one-time subsidy into a permanent improvement of their livelihood.

REFERENCES

Adriano, L.S., Y. Hayami, and M.A.R. Quisumbing. 1990. *Toward an Alternative Land Reform Paradigm: A Philippine Perspective.* Manila: Ateneo de Manila University Press.

Aghion, Philippe, Eve Caroli, and Cecilia Garcia-Peñalosa. 1999 'Inequality and Economic Growth: The Perspective of the New Growth Theories.' *Journal of Economic Literature* 37(4): 1615–60.

Balcazar, Alvaro. 1990. 'Tamano de Finca, Dinamica Tecnologia y Rendimientos Agricolas.' *Coyuntura Agropecuaria* 7(3): 107–25.

Banerjee, Abhijit V. and Maitreesh Ghatak. 1996. 'Empowerment and Efficiency: The Economics of Tenancy Reform.' Working paper, Department of Economics, Massachusetts Institute of Technology, Cambridge, MA.

Banerjee, Abhijit V. and Andrew F. Newman. 1993. 'Occupational Choice and the Process of Development.' *Journal of Political Economy* 101(2): 274–98.

Banerjee, Abhijit, Dilip Mookherjee, Kaivan Munshi, and Debraj Ray. 1997. 'Inequality, Control Rights and Rent Seeking: A Theoretical and Empirical Analysis of Sugar Cooperatives in Maharashtrai.' Working paper, Boston University, Boston, MA.

Bardhan, Pranab, Samuel Bowles, and Herbert Gintis. 2000. 'Wealth Inequality, Wealth Constraints and Economic Performance.' In *Handbook on Income Distribution*, Anthony Atkinson and François Bourguignon (eds.), forthcoming.

Barraclough, S.L. 1970. 'Agricultural Policy And Land Reform.' *Journal of Political Economy* 78(4): 906–47.

Berry, R.A. and W.R. Cline. 1979. *Agrarian Structure and Productivity in Developing Countries.* Geneva: International Labour Organization (ILO).

Besley, T. and R. Burgess. 1998. 'Land Reform, Poverty Reduction, and Growth: Evidence from India.' Working paper, Department of Economics, London School of Economics.

Binswanger, Hans P. and M. Elgin. 1988. 'What are the Prospects for Land Reform?' In *Agriculture and Governments in an Interdependent World,* A. Maunder and A. Valdes (eds.). Proceedings of the Twentieth International Conference of Agricultural Economists, Buenos Aires.

Binswanger, Hans P. and Klaus Deininger. 1993. 'South African Land Policy: The Legacy of History and Current Options.' *World Development* 21(9): 1451–75.

Binswanger, Hans P., Klaus Deininger, and Gershon Feder. 1995. 'Power, Distortions, Revolt and Reform in Agricultural Land Relations.' In *Handbook of Development Economics,* Volume 3B, J. Behrman and T.N. Srinivasan (eds.). Amsterdam: Elsevier Science North Holland.

Birdsall, Nancy and Juan Luis Londoño. 1997. 'Asset Inequality Matters: An Assessment of the World Bank's Approach to Poverty Reduction.' *American Economic Review* 87(2): 32–7.

Brooks, K. and Zvi Lerman. 1994. 'Land Reform and Farm Restructuring in Russia.' World Bank Discussion Paper 223, The World Bank, Washington DC.

Buainain, Antônio Márcio, José Maria da Silveira, Hildo Meireles Souza, and Marcelo M. Magalhães. 1999. 'Community-Based Land Reform Implementation in Brazil: A New Way of Reaching Out to the Marginalized?' Paper presented at the GDN Launch Workshop, Bonn, 5–8 December (www.gdnet.org).

Callison, C.S. 1983. *Land to the Tiller in the Mekong Delta: Economic, Social and Political Effects of Land Reform in Four Villages of South Vietnam.* Lanham, MD: University Press of America.

Carter, Michael R. and Dina Mesbah. 1993. 'Can Land Market Reform Mitigate the Exclusionary Aspects of Rapid Agro-Export Growth?' *World Development* 21(7): 1085–1100.

Cross, C., T. Mngadi, S. Sibanda, and V. Jama. 1996. 'Making a Living under Land Reform: Weighing up the Chances in KwaZulu-Natal.' In *Land, Labour and Livelihoods in Rural South Africa: Volume II: KwaZulu-Natal and Northern Province*, Michael Lipton, F. Ellis, and Merle Lipton (eds.). University of Natal, Durban, South Africa: Indicator Press.

Dasgupta, P. and D. Ray. 1986. 'Inequality as a Determinant of Malnutrition and Unemployment: Theory.' *Economic Journal* 96(384): 1011–34.

—— 1987. 'Inequality as a Determinant of Malnutrition and Unemployment: Policy.' *Economic Journal* 97(385): 177–88.

de Janvry, A. and E. Sadoulet. 1989. 'A Study in Resistance to Institutional Change: The Lost Game of Latin American Land Reform.' *World Development* 17(9): 1397–1407.

Deininger, Klaus and Lyn Squire. 1998. 'New Ways of Looking at Old Issues: Inequality and Growth.' *Journal of Development Economics* 57(2): 257–85.

Deininger, Klaus, Julian May, Johan v. Zyl, Benjamin Roberts, and Indran Naidoo. 1999. 'Implementing Market-Friendly Land Redistribution in South Africa: Lessons from the First Five Years.' Paper presented at the GDN Launch Workshop, Bonn, 5–8 December 1999 (www.gdnet.org).

Dorner, P. and W.C. Thiesenhusen. 1990. 'Selected Land Reforms in East and Southeast Asia: Their Origins and Impacts.' *Asian Pacific Economic Literature* 4(1): 69–95.

Eckstein, Zvi and Itzhak Zilcha. 1994. 'The Effects of Compulsory Schooling on Growth Income Distribution and Welfare.' *Journal of Public Economics* 54(3): 339–59.

Eurostat. 1995. 'SPEL Data for EU Agriculture.' Office des Publications Officielles des Communautés Européennes, Luxembourg.

Fafchamps, Marcel and John Pender. 1997. 'Precautionary Saving, Credit Constraints, and Irreversible Investment: Theory and Evidence from Semi-Arid India.' *Journal of Business and Economic Statistics* 15(2): 180–94.

Fajnzylber, P., D. Lederman, and N. Loayza. 1998. 'What Causes Violent Crime?' Working paper, World Bank, Washington DC.

Forero, Roberto. 1999. 'Evaluacion de proyectos piloto de reforma agraria en Colombia, Informe fina.' Report, Bogota, Colombia.

Food and Agriculture Organization (FAO). 1994. 'Mercado de Tierras en Columbia.' Report, FAO, Rome, Italy.

Galor, Oded and Joseph Zeira. 1993. 'Income Distribution and Macroeconomics.' *Review of Economic Studies* 60(1): 35–52.

Government of South Africa. 1996. 'Our Land.' Green Paper on South African Land Policy, Head Office, Department of Land Affairs.

Guinnane, Timothy W. and Ronald I. Miller. 1997. 'The Limits to Land Reform: The Land Acts in Ireland, 1870–1909.' *Economic Development and Cultural Change* 45(3): 591–612.

Heath, John and Hans P. Binswanger. 1996. 'Natural Resource Degradation Effects of Poverty and Population Growth are Largely Policy-Induced: The Case of Columbia.' *Environment and Development Economics* 1(1): 65–84.

Hoellinger, Frank. 1999. 'Del Mercado de Tierras al Mercado de Reforma Agraria.' In *El Mercado de Tierras en Colombia. Una alternativa viable?* A. Machador and R. Suarez (coordinadores). 1999. Bogota, Columbia: Tercer Mundo en coordinacion con el CEGA y el IICA: 137–96.

Hoff, Karla and Andrew B. Lyon. 1994. 'Non-Leaky Buckets: Optimal Redistributive Taxation and Agency Costs.' NBER Working Paper Series No. 4652, National Bureau of Economic Research, Cambridge, MA.

Horowitz, Andrew W. 1993. 'Time Paths of Land Reform: A Theoretical Model of Reform Dynamics.' *The American Economic Review* 83(4): 1003–10.

Jalan, Jyotsna and Martin Ravallion. 1997. 'Are the Poor Less Well Insured? Evidence on Vulnerability to Income Risk in Rural China.' Report, The World Bank, Washington DC.

Jonakin, Jon. 1996. 'The Impact of Structural Adjustment and Property Rights Conflicts on Nicaraguan Agrarian Reform Beneficiaries.' *World Development* 24(7): 1179–91.

King, R. 1977. *Land Reform: A World Survey*. London: G. Bell and Sons.

Koo, A.Y.C. 1968. *Land Reform and Economic Development: A Case Study of Taiwan*. New York: Praeger.

Kutcher, G.P. and P.L. Scandizzo. 1981. *The Agricultural Economy of Northeast Brazil.* Washington DC: World Bank.

Li, H., L. Squire, and H.F. Zou. 1998. 'Explaining International and Intertemporal Variations in Income Inequality.' *Economic Journal* 108(446): 26–43.

Lieten, G.K. 1996. 'Land Reforms at Centre Stage: The Evidence on West Bengal.' *Development and Change* 27(1): 111–30.

Lipton, Michael. 1974. 'Towards a Theory of Land Reform.' In *Peasants, Landlords and Governments: Agrarian Reform in the Third World*, D. Lehman (ed.). New York: Holmes & Meyer.

Machado, Absalon and Ruth Suarez (coordinadores). 1999. '*El Mercado de Tierras en Colombia. Una alternativa viable?*' Bogotá, Colombia: Tercer Mundo en coordinacion con el CEGA y el IICA.

Mision Social. 1990. 'El Desarrollo Agropecuario en Colombia, Tomo 1.' Ministerio de Agricultura, Departamento Nacional de Planeacion, Bogotá, Colombia.

Moene, K.O. 1992. 'Poverty and Landownership.' *American Economic Review* 82(1): 52–64.

Mookherjee, Dilip. 1997. 'Informational Rents and Property Rights in Land.' In *Property Rights, Incentives & Welfare*, J. Roemer (ed.). London: Macmillan Press.

Otsuka, K. 1991. 'Determinants and Consequences of Land Reform Implementation in the Philippines.' *Journal of Development Economics* 35(2): 339–55.

Reydon, Bastian Philip and Pedro Ramos. 1996. 'Mercado y Politicas de Tierras.' Instituto de Economia, Universidade Estadual de Campinas (UNICAMP/IE), Campinas.

Rodrik, Dani. 1998. 'Where Did All the Growth Go? External Shocks, Social Conflict, and Growth Collapses.' Working paper, Harvard University, Cambridge, MA.

Rosenzweig, Mark R. 1978. 'Rural Wages, Labor Supply and Land Reform: A Theoretical and Empirical Analysis.' *American Economic Review* 68(5): 847–61.

Swinnen, Johan F.M. 1997. 'Does Compensation for Disruptions Stimulate Reforms? The Case of Agrarian Reform in Central and Eastern Europe.' *European Review of Agricultural Economics* 24(2) 249–66.

World Bank. 1996. *Review of Colombia's Agricultural and Rural Development Strategy*. Washington DC: World Bank.

14

Transition from Collective Farms to Individual Tenures in Central and Eastern Europe

JOHAN F.M. SWINNEN

Introduction

In all Central and Eastern European Countries (CEECs) land reform was a key part of the overall agrarian reforms that began in the early 1990s; it was an important precondition for the restructuring of state and collective farms. (This chapter makes reference to the Central European countries (CECs) which include Albania, Bulgaria, Czech Republic, Hungary, Poland, Romania, Slovakia, and Slovenia; and the former Soviet Union countries (FSU) which include the Baltics, Russia, and Ukraine. All of these countries (CECs and FSU) are referred to as the Central and Eastern European Countries.) Various land reform procedures have been chosen to transfer land property rights from the state or from collective farms to private agents.[1] For example, land has been restituted to its former—that is, pre-collectivization—owners in most Central European countries (CECs) and in the Baltics, while ownership shares have been distributed to state and collective farm workers in Ukraine and Russia. In some Central Asian countries, private land ownership is still prohibited.

In all CEECs the reforms have induced an increase in individual tenures. However, the extent of the shift from collective and state farms to individual farms differs tremendously among CEECs and between regions and farming specializations within CEECs. For example, in 1995 the share of total agricultural land (TAL) used by individual farms was less than 20% in Slovakia, Russia, and Ukraine, and over 80% in Latvia, Armenia, and Albania.

This chapter presents a comparative analysis of land reform and the transition from collective to individual tenures in CEECs. The chapter first discusses land reforms

This chapter presents insights based on research financially supported by UNU/WIDER, the Foundation for Scientific Research (FWO) and the European Commission. Erik Mathijs has contributed extensively to the research and insights presented in this chapter. I also thank Karen Macours, Hamish Gow, Azeta Cungu, Jason Hartell, Stefan Bojnec, and Marvin Jackson for research collaboration, and Alain de Janvry, Elinor Ostrom, Zvi Lerman, Alexander Sarris, Marian Rizov, Sophia Davidova, Allan Buckwell, Konrad Hagedorn, Csaba Csaki, and many others for discussions and comments on the issues discussed in the paper. The views expressed here do not necessarily reflect those of the European Commission.

[1] I follow Barzel's (1989) definition of property rights of individuals over assets, including the rights, or the powers, to consume, to obtain income from, and to alienate these assets. Legal rights, as a rule, enhance economic rights, but the former are neither necessary nor sufficient for the existence of the latter.

and agricultural privatization, its causes and implications for efficiency and equity. Then it analyzes the impact of these reforms, and of other factors, on the shift from collective farming to individual farms. The last section describes the different patterns of transition and complementary institutional reforms.

Agricultural privatization and land reform

Pre-transition property rights and production organization

The widespread collectivization of agriculture started in 1928 in the former Soviet Union (FSU) and in 1948 in Central European countries and the Baltics. The objective of collectivization was first to pool peasant farms into large-scale collective farms, and then, to nationalize the land and convert these collectives into even larger state farms or agro-industrial complexes. However, collectivization was implemented differently in each country, reflecting different stages of state control, and thus resulted in a mixture of property rights regimes (Mathijs 1997) including:

- state-owned land used by state farms: land that was completely nationalized and the state held both legal and economic rights;
- state-owned land used by collective farms: land that was nationalized; the state held the legal rights, while the collective farm held (some of) the economic rights. All land cultivated by collective farms in Albania and the FSU was state-owned;
- collectively owned land used by collective farms: the collective held both legal and economic rights. Two-thirds of collective farmland in Hungary was collectively owned because members who left or the heirs of members who had died were forced to sell their land to the collectives;
- privately owned land used by collective farms: individuals retained legal rights on collective farmland in most Central European countries. However, the collective farm or the state held most economic rights, the extent of which differed between CEECs. For example, since 1968 Hungarian collective farms were given much more autonomy in decision-making than in other CEECs;
- privately owned land used by private farms: members and employees of collective and state farms were allowed to cultivate some gardens and household plots privately. The share of these private farms in total agricultural land (TAL) varies between 2% in the FSU and 15% in Romania. The only exceptions were Poland and former Yugoslavia, where collectivization either failed or was never initiated and where about 80% of TAL was cultivated by individual family farms.

Originally, farm workers in *collective farms* (kolkhozes) were remunerated at the end of the year as a return on their inputs, based on the performance of the collective farm. Collective farms enjoyed somewhat more autonomy than *state farms* (sovkhozes) in their decisions. In state farms all assets, including land, were owned by the state and farm workers were like employees in any other (industrial) firm, receiving fixed wages and social security benefits. However, gradually collective farm workers received the same social benefits as state farm workers. By the 1980s, workers in both state farms and

Table 14.1. *Most important land reform procedures in Central and Eastern European countries (CEECs)**

	Collective farmland		State farmland[a]	
	Procedure	% of TAL[†]	Procedure	% of TAL
Albania	Distribution (physical)	76	Distribution (physical)[b]	24
Bulgaria	Restitution	72	Miscellaneous[d]	9
Czech Republic	Restitution	61	Sale (leasing)[c]	25
East Germany	Restitution	82	Sale (leasing)[c]	7
Hungary	Restitution + distribution (phys.) + sale for compensation bonds[f]	70	Sale for compensation bonds + sale (leasing)[c]	12
Latvia	Restitution	57	Restitution	38
Lithuania	Restitution	62	Restitution	30
Poland	—	4	Sale (leasing)[c]	19
Romania	Restitution + distribution (phys.)	58	Undecided[e] + Restitution	28
Russia	Distribution in shares[g,h]	40	Distribution in shares[g]	58
Slovakia	Restitution	71	Sale (leasing)[c]	15
Slovenia	—	0	Restitution	17
Ukraine	Distribution in shares[g]	n.a.	Distribution in shares[g]	n.a.

* Special procedures for marginal amounts of land are not included in the table.
[†] Total agricultural land.
[a] Excluding research farms which are not privatized.
[b] Farm workers received vouchers in newly established joint ventures. However, as most of these joint ventures failed, farm workers received first user rights and eventually full property rights.
[c] Land is leased to individuals or entities pending sale.
[d] In Bulgaria the distinction between state and collective farms is more complicated than in other CEECs because of the creation and later abolition of the so-called Agro-Industrial Complexes. Part of the land classified under 'state farmland' is restituted because it was initially collective farmland and has a similar status; another part will not be privatized, and another part is the land on which large pig and poultry enterprises are built and which will be privatized separately.
[e] The Romanian government has not decided how to privatize the state farms, including the land, on two-thirds of state farmland.
[f] Each of the land reform procedures applies to approximately one-third of the collective farmland.
[g] Distribution of collective and state farmland equally per capita among collective farm members or state farm employees in the form of paper shares or certificates. Outsiders who are not entitled to land shares can receive land for private farming from a special state reserve established for this purpose (15–20% of TAL).
[h] Private ownership is prohibited in 10 ethnic republics of the Russian Federation.

cooperatives had a high degree of job and wage security, little responsibility for financial performance of the farm, and little incentive to improve productivity. Both types of farms were protected from bankruptcy by a soft budget constraint (Brooks *et al.* 1991).

Post-communist agricultural privatization and land reforms

Restitution of farmland to former owners is the most important process of land reform (in terms of share of total agricultural land) in the CEECs (Table 14.1). Typically, the reform laws specify that former owners be restituted the land in historical boundaries, if possible. Otherwise they receive property rights to a plot of land of comparable size and quality. With the exception of Poland and Albania, an important share of farmland

Table 14.2. *Legal attitudes to land ownership and land transactions in the Former Soviet Union (FSU) countries*

	Private ownership	Transactions
Armenia	Yes: all land	Buy and sell, mortgage (law of 1991)
Azerbaidjan	No	—
Belarus	Yes: household plots (June 1993)	Buy and sell allowed Use rights non-transferable
Georgia	Yes: all land	Buy and sell allowed only in Feb. 1996 law
Kazakhstan	Yes: only household plots (decree)	Buy and sell, mortgage Use rights: permanent and tradable
Kyrgyzstan	No	Use rights secure to 99 years and tradable
Moldova	Yes: all land	Moratorium until 2001
Russia	Yes: all land (No in 10 ethnic republics)	Buy and sell, mortgage (moratorium lifted by 1994 presidential decree)
Tadjikistan	No	—
Turkmenistan	Yes: potentially all farm land (constitution)	Prohibited to sell, exchange, give as a gift; leasing allowed Use rights non-transferable
Ukraine	Yes: all land	Moratorium on buy and sell; no mortgage
Uzbekistan	No: lifetime inheritable possession	Prohibited to sell, exchange, give as a gift, mortgage

Source: Lerman (1997).

is restituted to its former owners in all CECs. And even in Albania collective farmland property rights have been restituted to former owners in some mountainous regions.

In the FSU land is restituted to former owners in the Baltic countries only. Russia and Ukraine distribute land in two forms. The most important form is the distribution of collective and state farmland equally per capita among collective farm members or state farm employees in the form of paper shares or certificates. Outsiders who are not entitled to land shares can receive land for private farming from a special state reserve established for this purpose (15–20% of TAL).

Land reforms differ widely in other FSU countries (see Table 14.2). For example, private ownership of land has not been recognized in Kyrgyzstan and Uzbekistan, while in Belarus and Kazakhstan only private ownership of household plots is allowed. Nevertheless, user rights were made secure and marketable in Kazakhstan and Kyrgyzstan. In Georgia the buying and selling of land has only been allowed since 1996; in Turkmenistan it is still not (Lerman 1997).

There is an important difference in land reform procedures between collective farmland and state farmland in CECs, but not in the FSU countries. In the latter, collective and state farmland are treated the same in the reforms. In CECs, *collective farmland* is mostly restituted to former owners. The main exceptions to restitution of collective farmland are in Hungary and in Albania. In Hungary, one-third of collective farm land is auctioned for compensation bonds, and another one-third is distributed among farm workers. Albania distributes its collective farm land among rural households. In the majority of CECs, *state farmland* is leased, pending sale of the land. The main exceptions are the restitution of state farmland in Slovenia, and the distribution to farm workers in Albania.

Whereas land has mostly been restituted in kind, this has not been the general rule for other assets. Non-land assets have been restituted in some countries, but in many cases were privatized using vouchers that could be turned into capital shares in the new cooperative farm or used for purchasing non-land assets for private use. The distribution of those vouchers was the subject of much debate. In general, the principle was that members (or their heirs) who had contributed land, labor, or other assets to the cooperative over the forty-five years of its existence should receive some share of the remaining assets. To implement this required an inventory of the cooperative's assets, their value, and a formula to determine the shares of each contributor. Both aspects posed great difficulties.

Factors affecting privatization and land reform policy choices

Four historical-institutional factors have influenced the choice of privatization and land reform policies in CEECs: (1) the post-collectivization asset ownership status; (2) the ethnicity of the pre-collectivization asset ownership; (3) the equality of pre-collectivization asset distribution; and (4) the length of Communist rule (Swinnen 1999).

Legal asset ownership

All agricultural assets, which were still legally privately owned in 1989, have been restituted in all CEECs. The principle that agricultural assets, which were formally still privately owned, are restituted to their formal owners explains several observations.

- Differences among CEECs: where land is not restituted to former owners (such as Albania, FSU, and Poland), the land was state-owned.
- Differences within CEECs: where part of the land is restituted (e.g., Hungary), the difference is due to legal ownership.
- State farm land, unlike collective farm land, is often not restituted, as it was mostly state-owned.
- In several CEECs, the basis for land restitution is the ownership distribution of land reforms implemented under Communist-dominated governments following World War II, determining the 1989 legal ownership.
- Differences between land and non-land assets.

Ethnicity

The privatization policy choice affects the distribution of asset ownership between ethnic groups. A general observation is that agricultural assets are not restituted to former owners who are, or have become, foreigners. The choice of the privatization process also affects the distribution of (agricultural) assets between ethnic groups within the country. Intuitively, one would expect that this motivation would lead to the choice of a privatization policy that transfers property rights mostly to the ethnic majority for the same reason that foreigners do not receive land. This occurred in the Baltics where restitution of land was chosen to allocate assets to native citizens in the presence of large ethnic minorities (Rabinowicz 1997). However, this is not always the case because it depends on the influence of ethnic minorities on the political economic equilibrium. An example of a privatization policy which benefits ethnic minorities is found in Bulgaria where the allocation of a high share of non-land assets to 'labor contributions' partly placated the Turkish ethnic minority who were largely employed in agriculture and not eligible for much land, although they were an important political force (Davidova and Buckwell 1994).

Equality of pre-collectivization asset ownership

Equality of pre-collectivization asset ownership determines the potential conflict between the objectives of 'equity' and 'historical justice.' Theory suggests both positive and negative effects of an egalitarian pre-collectivization land distribution on the likelihood that restitution will be chosen as privatization policy. Empirical observations suggest that when social equity conflicted with historical justice, equity prevailed in the government's choice. For example, with more than half of the Albanian population active in agriculture and a highly unequal pre-reform land distribution, land restitution would have transferred most of the fertile land into the hands of a small group of families, leaving the bulk of rural households without land. Instead, the government decided to distribute the land to rural households because the prime importance of the land issue for the large number of rural voters was more important (politically) than the large vested interests and lower collective action costs of fewer former landlords.

Length of Communist rule

The most straightforward effect of the historical legacy of the land ownership is the lack of *demand* for land restitution in large parts of the FSU. Lerman (1997) states that nearly a century of Communism has washed away all traces of former land ownership and that very little tradition of private land ownership remains in most of the FSU. Voices for restitution or some form of compensation to former owners were raised only in the Baltics, in Western Ukraine, Moldova, and Western Belarus. In those areas, collectivization was imposed only after World War II. However, in the rest of the FSU, there was hardly any demand for restitution of land. Besides the impact on farm disruptions (see further), this lack of tradition of private ownership and demand for land restitution may also have contributed to the choice of share distribution, rather than distribution-in-kind, of land in Russia and the Ukraine.

Land reform, property rights, and access to land

Procedures and property rights

Property rights are fully restored if all rights (user, income, and alienation rights) are given to the owners. Not all land reform schemes fulfill these criteria. For example, land reform in Latvia started during the Soviet period with the creation of private farms on a usufruct basis. Farmers were not allowed to sell this land. In addition, not all of these farmers were former owners, so they received someone else's land. When the next Latvian government decided to restitute agricultural land to former owners, conflicting claims on land were frequent, as were conflicts between land claims and privatization of farm enterprises. Such conflicts increase the discretion of local administrations. Furthermore, the conflicting claims, court procedures, and inherent uncertainty impede the progress in privatization and reduce production (Rabinowicz 1997).

Another example of incomplete property rights is 'restitution in comparable boundaries.' While they have chosen to restitute land, many CEEC governments have included specifications in the land law that allow the return of a 'comparable' piece of land (instead of the original plot with its 'historical boundaries'). This process transfers the rights to derive income from, but not the right to sell or to withdraw an asset on which the legal ownership rights apply. Such programs allow for an individual to take out an 'equivalent' piece of land when s/he chooses to retrieve the land from the (reformed) collective farm. However, there are transaction costs in the process of being assigned an 'equivalent' or 'comparable' plot of land, as the plot has to be assigned by the management of the reformed farm. Although the claimant can go to court if s/he disagrees with the assignment and 'restitution in comparable boundaries' is often applied because of technical reasons, it affects the distribution of bargaining power between collective farm management and the claimant. In any case, in the presence of transaction costs, *a priori* property rights that are restituted are incomplete in this process.

The distribution of land in shares in Russia and Ukraine resulted (even more) in imperfect property rights. The distribution of land shares does not imply physical allocation of land plots corresponding to the shares. Despite the allocation of land shares to the members, the land remains in joint cultivation pending further restructuring decisions by the 'share-owners.' A share-owner who wishes to establish an independent farming operation (individually or with a group of co-workers) in principle is entitled to receive from the collective farm a physical plot of land corresponding to the land share. Obviously, this process implies potentially large transaction costs resulting in imperfect property rights.

These limitations on property rights are reinforced with limitations or moratoria on buying, selling, and mortgaging the land. Ukraine has a moratorium on buying and selling, and does not allow land to be used for collateral. A 1994 presidential decree lifted such a moratorium in Russia, but much uncertainty remains with a pending land law which is supposed to define the final regulations (Lerman 1997). In Belarus and Kazakhstan, private ownership is limited to household plots and hence to a small share of total agricultural land. Table 14.2 summarizes the legal attitudes regarding ownership of land in all FSU countries as of 1996, and shows how property rights are incomplete in those countries except in Armenia and Georgia.

In several CEECs, recent amendments to the privatization and land reform laws limit the restitution of full property rights to former owners. The most striking examples of such measures are the introduction of the 'good landlord' and 'co-ownership' rules in Slovenia which allocate part of the decision-making rights on the use of the agricultural land under restitution to the state farms, which are currently using the land, as long as the state farms behave as 'good landlords.' Similar legal initiatives that allocate part of the effective property rights to the users of the land (the former state and collective farms) have been introduced in other CEECs (such as Bulgaria), often as a result of the return to power of ex-Communist parties.

Implementation and property rights

The most radical reform policies on paper may result in little effective change in property rights unless they are well implemented, which is influenced by: (a) technical factors and transaction costs in the reform implementation; (b) the extent to which interest groups can influence the reform implementation; and (c) the detailed regulations for implementation, in turn affected by the political influence of interest groups and political coalitions. Hayami (1991) argues that (1) using simple, transparent, and uniform rules, and (2) limiting the scope for discretionary government involvement in implementation are two key variables in a successful land reform. Little progress was achieved in some reform programs because the rules were unclear, insufficient incentives for change were provided by a little-committed government, and further blocked by collective farm management.[2]

The reform implementation depends critically on the institutional design of the reforms and on transaction costs. While the government has control over the choice (the design) of the policy, it has less control over the implementation (Swinnen 1997*b*). The problems include:

- Technical problems. Trying to value assets, to assess the validity of land and asset claims, to assign land parcels to claimants, or to develop voucher schemes and auctions has proven a very difficult process.
- Reform implementation requires shifting powers to the relevant local institutions, which may create principal–agent problems in the presence of imperfect information. Those institutions are often influenced by local preferences and biased towards

[2] In some cases governments have intentionally slowed down and hindered the land reform implementation. Both de Janvry (1981) and Hayami (1991) argue that one of the most important factors in explaining worldwide land reform failures is that the ruling class, which opposes reforms, will concede to reform pressures only for the sake of legitimizing their dominance (i.e., de Janvry's 'Conservative Model'). When political crises occur, the ruling order will 'allow' land reforms to take place because the likelihood of remaining in power without some reform has declined with the chance that a lack of reform will increase the potential of a revolution. By allowing limited reforms, it is hoped that the pressure for more substantial reforms is reduced. Hence, in this perspective, land reform programs are expected to be as limited as possible while achieving their political purpose. A typical way of achieving such an objective is to deliberately choose a reform process with complex rules and insufficient means to execute it.

management and employee interests, who are closely involved in the decision-making and the activities of the institutions. The potential for the existing management to manipulate the reform implementation and resulting property rights distribution depends strongly on the transaction costs for the various partners (legal owners, potential users) in a potential exchange of the assets.

- Timing and government credibility. The privatization and transformation processes require much time, even when all parties support the reforms. Therefore, there exists a real chance that before the reforms are finished, or even well under way, the government is replaced by another which may be less supportive of the reforms. While the new government may not choose to change the privatization process, it may very well introduce a number of regulations and policies that have an important impact on the speed and the extent of the reform implementation. As a consequence, local administrations and executing institutions may feel less inclined to follow government regulations that they privately oppose, because enforcement procedures may not come into effect if the government is replaced.

Therefore, governments in favor of radical reforms have tried to restrict the ability of collective farm members and managers to influence the implementation. An example of this is from Bulgaria. The 1991 Land Law passed by the ex-Communist government did not include detailed specifications about how to implement the law. Much leeway was given to local government and collective farm management. After the 1991 elections, the new reformist government amended the law. Liquidation councils, chaired by outsiders, were installed to oversee the strict implementation of the liquidation of the collectives. Not surprisingly, the role and the composition of these institutions were changed when the ex-Communists came back to power (Swinnen 1997*a*). The 1991 Sajudis government in Lithuania also removed the existing management from its controlling positions and created new institutions, the Municipal Agrarian Reform Services, chaired by outsiders. As in Bulgaria, the re-elected ex-Communist government changed the role and the composition of these institutions in 1993 (Rabinowicz 1997).

Post-reform access to land

Both so-called 'historical justice' (i.e., restoration of property rights to pre-collectivization owners) and 'equity' (i.e., egalitarian land ownership or access) have been key factors in the political discussions and have strongly affected the choice of policies.[3] From the above discussion it is clear that access to land during and after transition for different groups (former owners, collective farm workers, rural households, etc.) differs among CEECs. Access to land for certain groups depends on the choice of the land reform procedure, on the reform implementation, but also on the pre-reform land distribution, the current economic structure, and on the development of leasing and land sales markets.

[3] The design of transformation policies also has distributional implications. It will, for example, influence the ability of current management to remain in charge of the transformed cooperative farm. It will also affect the chances for current employees to remain employed or to become private individual farmers. Transformation policies will therefore influence the distribution of future income streams and economic rents.

For example, land distribution primarily benefits people active in agriculture, while restitution to former owners may transfer an important share of the land to non-farmers. However, the impact that this has on access to land for various groups also depends on:

- The implementation of the reforms (see above).
- The pre-collectivization land ownership distribution. The pre-collectivization land distribution was rather egalitarian, in Bulgaria for example, due to previous land reforms. In contrast, land ownership was more concentrated in Bohemia (Czech Republic) or Albania. Hence, land restitution would have had very different equity effects in these countries.
- The structure of agriculture and the economy at large at the time of Communist take-over, as well as the speed of structural transformation of the society during the Communist period. Negative equity effects from land restitution are more important in countries with a large present employment in agriculture which had a very skewed land distribution in the pre-Communist period, such as Albania, with 50% of people employed in agriculture, low incomes, and large food security problems, compared to the Czech Republic where incomes are considerably higher and less than 5% of people are active in agriculture.
- Whether potential farmers can lease or purchase land from the new owners. Land sales have been legally restricted in many CEECs. Leasing is widespread, especially with informal contracts. Formal contracting is conditional on the necessary legislation and government regulations, which are not yet available in several CEECs.

Efficiency implications

Efficiency arguments in reform discussions can refer to various issues, such as timing of reforms (e.g., gradual versus big-bang), distortions caused by the process of privatization (restitution versus vouchers or sales), and various outcomes of the process (e.g., allocative efficiency[4] and the impacts on production organizations).[5] Here I discuss efficiency aspects of the nature and distribution of property rights induced by the land reforms.

The nature of the property rights

The nature of the property rights that result from land reform have important efficiency implications (Baland and Platteau 1996; Ostrom 1999).[6] For example, land reform in Russia and Ukraine (and several other FSU countries) has resulted in the

[4] Furthermore, Schumpeter (1942), Hayek (1945), and, more recently, North (1990) and Williamson (1991) argue that allocative efficiency is less important than efficiency in change and adaptation. There is no *a priori* reason why both should coincide in institutional choice; in fact a trade-off may exist (Williamson 1991).

[5] For example, many experts argued that restitution of land in historical boundaries is an inefficient land reform procedure because it was assumed to cause disruptions of the farms with strong ownership fragmentation and allocation of land property rights to people not active in agriculture—a view disputed by Mathijs and Swinnen (1998*a*). Here inefficiency does not refer to the nature of land ownership but to its impact on the farm structure.

[6] For related discussions on the role of private ownership for market economies, see Vickers and Yarrow (1991), and for the effective conduct of stabilization policy, see Hillman (1992) and Hinds (1991).

transfer of incomplete property rights. The distribution of land shares in Russia and Ukraine awards much leeway to old management and local institutions, opens the way for rent seeking, and prevents efficiency gains by restricting competition for land use, land exchange and/or the shift to individual tenures. This is in sharp contrast to the distribution of land in physical boundaries in Albania that has established clear and strong individual property rights on land. Although, as explained in a previous section, the restitution of land in comparable boundaries transfers *a priori* incomplete property rights to individuals, the implementation seems to have created much stronger and clearer land property rights in CEECs such as the Czech Republic, Slovakia, and Hungary than the land reform in Russia and Ukraine. The difference in resulting property rights has had a significant impact on growth in agricultural productivity (Macours and Swinnen 1998).

The distribution of the property rights

The distribution of land ownership does not influence efficient land use when markets are perfect and transaction costs are zero. However, in general, land sales markets tend to work imperfectly due to imperfections in other markets such as the credit market (Binswanger, Deininger, and Feder 1995; Sadoulet, Murgai, and de Janvry, this volume; Platteau 1992). These imperfections are reinforced in transition countries. The larger the market imperfections, the more important it is that the reform transfers the land to the most efficient users.

The reform procedure that does this most effectively depends on market imperfections and on characteristics of the agricultural economy (Mathijs and Swinnen 1998*b*). For example, allocating land to the most efficient users can be done in auctions or, with imperfect credit markets, in voucher-based auctions. However, taking into account the implementation costs of auctions, the best policy might be to lease the land (i.e., auctioning user rights), pending sales, when agriculture's share in employment is small and technology advanced. However, when agriculture's share in employment is large and technology less advanced, equal distribution of land in physical boundaries may be preferable to voucher auctions because the implementation costs of distribution are lower than a voucher-based auction, while resulting in a relatively similar distribution of property rights.

In addition, such land distribution contributes to equity, which may have additional positive efficiency effects, especially under conditions of a large farming population, a low level of technology, and income and food insecurity. If land were unequally distributed, most farmers would not own the land they cultivate. They would have to rent the land or work as wage earners. Both options have important disadvantages (Stiglitz 1993).[7] Land rental contracts either force the landless farmer to bear all or some of the risks, while wage contracts provide poor work incentives. With sharecropping arrangements the farmer still has to bear considerable risk, while his work incentives

[7] Stiglitz (1993) argues that, in general, the more equally distributed property rights are, the better society's incentive structure is likely to be, because, while incentive problems arise both in the capital market and in the labor market, the labor incentive problem is more important, and unequal wealth (land) distribution induces inefficient labor contracts.

are attenuated. This argument is especially relevant in countries where agriculture is still a large share of the economy and where land reform has a strong effect on total wealth distribution.[8]

Empirically we observe that, taking into account the political constraints as outlined above, these efficiency arguments seem to have affected the choice of land reform policies. Most CECs privatized land that was not to be restituted for political-institutional reasons (between 15 and 25% of TAL) by selling or leasing it (pending sales). However, land use rights were not allocated through auctions, but through the provision of short-term leases for a fixed rent. More specifically, in the Czech Republic, Eastern Germany, Hungary, Poland, and Slovakia, state farmland was transferred to a Land Fund managed by the state, and subsequently leased to individual farmers or farm organizations, pending sales.[9] Only a very small percentage of state farm land was actually sold in auctions (or by tender). For example, in Poland, less than 5% of the land in the Land Fund had been sold and 60% was being leased, while the rest was state-managed or in the process of being sold or leased by the end of September 1995 (Organization for Economic Cooperation and Development (OECD) 1996).

In Hungary, collectively owned land was either distributed to collective farm workers and employees or auctioned in exchange for vouchers. These vouchers were allocated to compensate former owners for their lost property. They could also use the vouchers to buy an apartment or a lifetime bond. Although in theory the use of voucher-based auctions should be an efficient policy, some of the key conditions for an optimal mechanism were not fulfilled because first, there was collusion among bidders, such that most land was sold for the reserve price, which was set too low; and, second, in an economy characterized by high inflation and uncertainty, a lifetime bond did not prove to be a credible alternative for the security of land ownership, so that all the beneficiaries wanted to buy land with their vouchers (Mathijs and Mészáros 1997).[10]

In contrast, in Albania and Romania, characterized by low farm technology and a high share of agriculture in total employment, land was distributed. In Albania, where all land was state-owned, land was distributed on an equal per capita basis among the rural population.[11] In Romania limits were imposed on restitution and part of the land was distributed to farm workers.

[8] Land ownership inequality may also have negative implications on economic growth as it fuels social discontent and political unrest. Socio-political instability may reduce economic growth in two ways. First, socio-political instability increases entrepreneurial uncertainty, which may result in low investment and capital flight, and hence reduce growth (Alesina and Perotti 1992; Perotti 1994). Second, if the governing coalition is insecure, its continuation may depend on the dispensation of patronage, which could drain the economy of its productive potential (Binswanger and Deininger 1995). These arguments are contrary to the older view that inequality of income increases economic growth because people with higher incomes will save relatively more. An unequal income distribution hence increases investment (Kaldor 1956).

[9] In Eastern Germany the Gattermann proposal to privatize land through auctions encountered much opposition and was not accepted (Hagedorn 1997).

[10] In terms of auction design problems, the reservation utility was not high enough to ensure incentive-compatibility of the auction scheme (Mathijs and Swinnen 1998*b*; Vickrey 1961; McAfee and McMillan 1987).

[11] However, the pressure to change land reform policies, from former owners whose land was not restituted, has created uncertainty of property rights. The uncertain nature of the property rights limits transactions of and investments in land (see attached case study).

In many cases where governments restituted land to former owners for historical-legal reasons, they have implemented additional measures to restrict the transfer of property rights from the people using the land to the former owners. Examples are the increase of (opportunity) costs for submitting land claims, giving former collectives more rights and decision authority on the use of assets under privatization, and limiting new owners' rights in transferring and using assets. These policy adjustments had both distributional and efficiency consequences. For example, a regulation such as the seven-year moratorium on the withdrawal of land from reformed collective farms in Slovakia prevented the disruption of a highly mechanized and capital-intensive production system. At the same time, it reduced access to land for people wanting to start an individual farm and it distributed rents from them and the new owners to the current management and farm workers. A different example is the limit that was set on the amount of land that could be restituted to former owners in Romania. By distributing the remainder to farm workers, the government wanted to rectify the spontaneous privatization of land at the beginning of reform (Jackson 1997). Such a policy restricts the rights of former owners, but at the same time improves access to land for a large rural population active in agriculture (36.3% of total employment in 1994).

Land leasing

With ownership on much agricultural land transferred to individuals not active in agriculture, exchange of land is important. Sales markets of land are unlikely to provide an efficient solution to the demand for land exchange in CEECs. As argued above, land sales markets generally work imperfectly. In transition countries land sales are further restricted or absent due to missing legislation, or the unwillingness of many owners to part with their newly acquired land. In FSU countries all land sales remain a controversial issue, while in CECs land sales to foreigners are very controversial, blocking land market legislation.

Land leasing is a widespread phenomenon in Western market economies (Swinnen 1998) and is extensively used by highly efficient farms in Europe and the United States. The main benefits of land ownership vis-à-vis land renting are 'the privileges of wealth' and improved access to credit with the use of land as collateral (Sadoulet, Murgai, and de Janvry, this volume). However, recent studies on land use and investment incentives in Asia and Africa indicate that secure land-use rights are sufficient conditions for efficient land use and optimal investments by farmers (Brasselle, Gaspart, and Platteau 1998; Feder and Feeny 1991; Rozelle, Li, and Brandt 1998). Further, in developed market economies the importance of land as collateral to get access to credit is limited with the availability of other assets and various institutional arrangements to secure loan repayment.

Therefore a key policy focus should be on land leasing, and on how to regulate and enforce leasing contracts such that they provide sufficient security to tenants for making the necessary investments and sufficient incentives for land owners to lease their land to the best user.

Farm restructuring

Observations on farm restructuring

A wide variety of farm organizations, such as producer cooperatives, joint stock companies, limited liability companies, partnerships, and individual farms have emerged in CEECs. Often it is not fully clear what the various names, such as 'joint stock companies' and 'private cooperatives,' mean. Table 14.3 distinguishes between five production structures depending on ownership and use of assets.

- *Public or state farms* which are entirely owned by the state. They have not yet been privatized or will not be privatized because, as in the West, they remain active in public research.
- *Cooperatives* are characterized by joint ownership and joint operation of the means of production. They range on average from 475 hectares in Romania to 1,461 hectares in Eastern Germany.
- *Companies* include all kinds of enterprise structures (limited liability companies, legal entities, etc.) owned by shareholders. Their average size ranges from 281 hectares in Bulgaria to 823 hectares in Eastern Germany.
- *Partnerships* are characterized by joint operation and ownership, but at a smaller scale than companies or cooperatives. Moreover, partners are often family members. They are medium-sized farms of 100 to 500 hectares.
- *Individual farms* are farms managed by a single individual or household. These farms typically include both family farms and household plots, and are generally characterized by their small scale: from 1 to 50 hectares. In Eastern Germany, only the 'single proprietorships' are classified as individual farms.

In Romania individual farms occupied 61% of TAL, and in Albania, by the mid-1990s, virtually all of the land (95%) was used by small private farmers. In Slovenia, as in Poland, the large majority of land was already used by individual farms under the Communist period. However, the break-up of large-scale agricultural production units into individually operated 'farms' is considerably less in the other CEECs, where large-scale farms still dominated by 1994. Cooperatives, partnerships, and companies used more than two-thirds of TAL in Eastern Germany, the Czech Republic, Slovakia, Hungary, and Bulgaria. In the Czech Republic, Slovakia, and former East Germany, most restituted land was leased to transformed cooperatives or to state farms.

Table 14.4 presents calculations of a farm individualization index (FII)—based on the percentage of agricultural land used by individual farms but corrected for the initial situation—for eighteen CEECs (Mathijs and Swinnen 1998*a*). The FII is low in countries where large-scale successor organizations to the former state and collective farms still dominate, such as Slovakia (5%), Hungary (13%), and the Czech Republic (20%). The FII is highest in Albania (95%) and Latvia (80%) where a massive break-up of the collective farms resulted in a domination of small-scale production units. Within the CEECs there also exists a wide variation in the importance of individual farming of different regions and agricultural subsectors.

Table 14.3. *Farm structures in Central Europe in 1994 based on agricultural land*

	Albania	Bulgaria[a]	Czech Republic	East Germany	Hungary	Romania	Slovakia	Slovenia
State farms number	13	1,009	239	—	36	550	262	n.a.
area in 1,000 ha	n.a.	328	199	—	[b]	2,051	444	85
average size in ha	150–200	325	498	—	n.a.	3,729	1,695	n.a.
% of total area	n.a.	7.0	2.8	—	[b]	15.5	20.3	10.9
Cooperatives number	—	2,373	1,468	1,336	2,048	3,970	961	—
area in 1,000 ha	—	2,260[d]	2,043	1,952	2,306	1,780	1,531	—
average size in ha	—	953	1,392	1,461	1,126	446	1,563	—
% of total area	—	48.2	47.7	35.9	37.7	13.4	69.9	—
Companies number	—	142	1,461	1,563	3,311	—	219	—
area in 1,000 ha	—	40	876	1,286	1,164[b]	—	101	—
average size in ha	—	281	600	823	n.a.	—	459	—
% of total area	—	0.9	20.5	23.7	19.0[b]	—	4.6	—
Partnerships number	—	—	47	2,379	2,369	13,741	—	—
area in 1,000 ha	—	—	15	1,116	[b]	1,537	—	—
average size in ha	—	—	310	469	n.a.	112	—	—
% of total area	—	—	0.3	20.5	[b]	11.6	—	—
Individual farms number	490,000	2,010,961	60,666	22,505	1,203,000	3,579,234	7,759	n.a.
area in 1,000 ha	n.a.	2,059	872	1,082	2,652[c]	7,905	115	697
average size in ha	1.05	1.0	14	48	n.a.	2.21	15	n.a.
% of total area	n.a.	43.9	20.4	19.9	43.3[c]	59.6	5.3	89.1

[a] Arable land.
[b] 'State farms' and 'partnerships' are included in 'companies.'
[c] 'Other' is included in 'individual farms.'
[d] Including organizations under liquidation.

Source: Swinnen, Buckwell, and Mathijs (1997).

Table 14.4. *Farm individualization index (FII), 1995*[a]

Country	FII	Country	FII
Albania	94.2	Kyrgyzstan	23.2
Armenia	81.8	Latvia[b]	80.2
Belarus	15.2	Lithuania[b]	60.4
Bulgaria	45.4	Romania	55.2
Czech Republic	22.1	Russia	12.1
Estonia[b]	37.5	Slovakia[b]	3.1
Georgia	21.2	Turkmenistan	7.1
Hungary	17.3	Ukraine	14.1
Kazakhstan	0.0	Uzbekistan	13.1

[a] The FII is calculated by dividing the difference between the share of individual farms in total agricultural land in 1995 (IND95) and in 1989 (IND89) by 100 minus the share of individual farms in total agricultural land in 1989: FII = (IND95 − IND89) / (100 − IND89) × 100. For all Former Soviet Union (FSU) countries except the Baltic countries, an initial share of individual farms equal to 1% is assumed.
[b] 1994.

Source: Mathijs and Swinnen (1998*a*).

While the break-up of state and collective farms into individual farms clearly causes fragmentation in some cases (e.g., Albania), this is not the case in general. In most of the CEECs individual farms cover 100 hectares and more. The Latvian case in particular shows that a high FII (80%) does not necessarily imply a high degree of fragmentation: only 23% of TAL is cultivated by farms smaller than 5 hectares. Most of the land is farmed by farms between 5 and 100 hectares. (See Table 14.5. In general, the data underestimate the average size of part-time and—even more—of full-time individual farms because available statistics often do not distinguish between household plots, part-time farms, and full-time, individual farms.)

The most important factor explaining fragmentation is the size of the rural work force. A high share of agriculture in employment implies a strong demand for small household plots, thus contributing to the fragmentation of land. Figure 14.1 shows an almost perfect linear correlation (regression $R^2 = 0.92$) between the share in TAL of farms less than 5 ha as a measure for fragmentation, and the share of agriculture in the economy. Additional factors have apparently stimulated the start-up of larger individual farms. Finally, since the mid 1990s the share of individual farms increased further in all CEECs, while the share of especially cooperative farms continued to decline.

Factors affecting farm restructuring

Farm restructuring depends on the pre-reform farm structure, on the *design* of the privatization and transformation policies (itself influenced by political economy factors), on the *implementation* of the policies, and on a series of additional factors, including the economic environment, affecting the *outcome* of the reform process.

Table 14.5. *Degree of fragmentation of agricultural production based on land use data*[a]

Country	Share of individual farms in TAL[b] (%)	Share of farms smaller than 5 ha in TAL (%)	Share of farms larger than 5 ha in TAL (%)
Albania	94	95	—
Bulgaria	44	30	14
Czech Republic	20	1	n.a.
East Germany	20	n.a.	15
Estonia	40	25	19
Hungary	22	12	10
Latvia	81	23	58
Lithuania	64	33	31
Romania	61	45	16
Slovak Republic	5	2	3

[a] Total agricultural land, 1994.
[b] Own estimate based on the 1994 survey of small farmers.

Sources: Swinnen, Buckwell, and Mathijs (1997); Organization for Economic Cooperation and Development, OECD (1996).

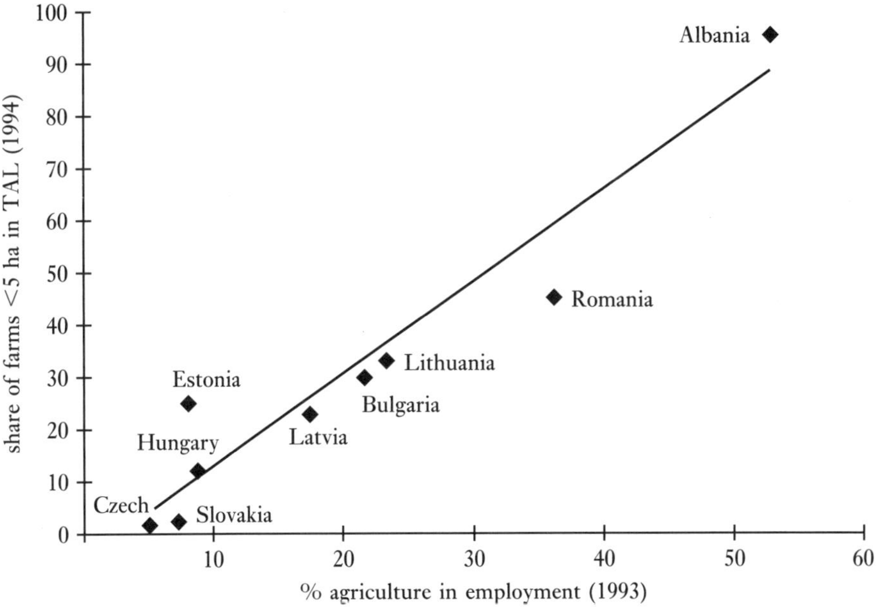

Figure 14.1. *Relationship between the share of farms smaller than 5 hectares and the share of agriculture in total employment*

Note: the curve on the graph is based on a least squares regression.

Source: Mathijs and Swinnen (1998*a*).

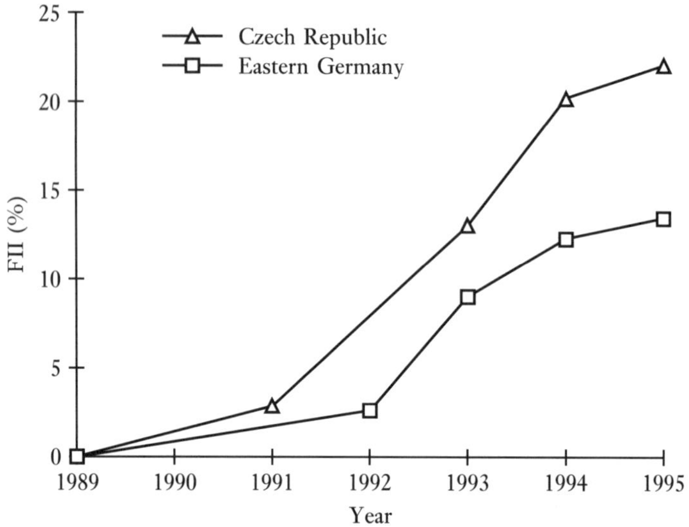

Figure 14.2. *Farm individualization index (FII) for Eastern Germany and the Czech Republic, 1989–1995*

Source: Mathijs and Swinnen (1998*a*).

1. Transition-related risk and adverse terms of trade have negatively affected the creation of individual farms.

Risk has a negative impact on the shift to individual tenures if the collective farm is better at coping with risk than the individual farm, e.g., by risk pooling. This is more likely to be the case in the beginning of transition than in a situation with better functioning markets and developed institutions (Mathijs and Swinnen 1998*a*). The same reasoning applies for institutional access to credit, accumulated social capital, influence with policy makers, etc. However, for all these factors the benefit of staying in the collective framework is not necessarily positive. For example, banks may be unwilling to lend to debt-ridden collective farms with unclear property rights on assets. Similarly, the influence with policy makers depends strongly on the political preferences of the governing parties. Reform-minded politicians may be more inclined to support individual farms than collective farms.[12]

Available evidence is, in general, consistent with the hypotheses that high transition risk and falling terms of trade have reduced the shift to individual tenures at the start of transition. The FII remained low in the 1989–92 period, characterized by high price variability and strong declines in terms of trade. Afterwards, the FII increased, as reflected in Figure 14.2. However, other factors have also played a role, such as the fact that most privatization and transformation legislation was only passed in parliaments in 1991 and 1992 in most CEECs.

[12] Preliminary evidence indeed suggests that government support, *ceteris paribus*, is higher in sectors with more small-scale family farms (Swinnen 1996).

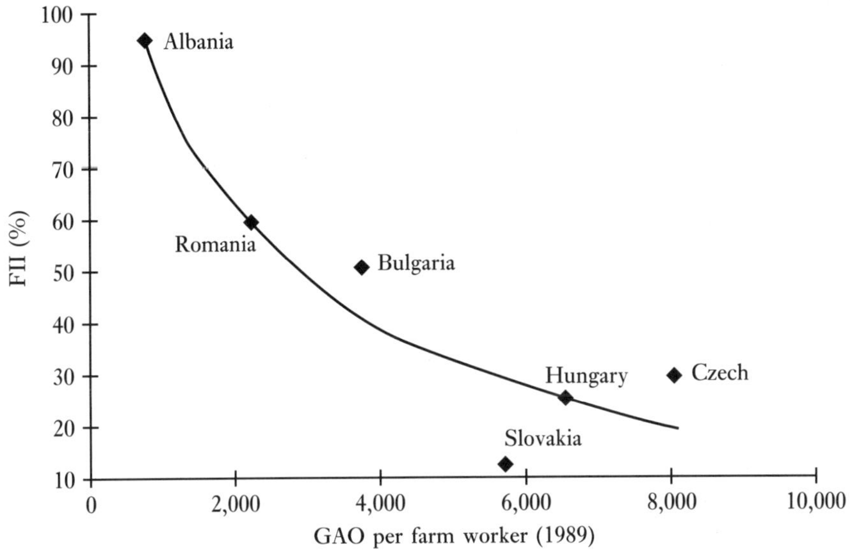

Figure 14.3. *Relationship between FII in 1995 and initial collective farm productivity in 1989 for six CEECs*

Source: Mathijs and Swinnen (1998*a*).

2. The break-up of collective farms is strongest for the least productive farms and the most labor-intensive farms.

Figure 14.3 shows how the FII is negatively correlated with gross agricultural output (GAO) per farm worker in 1989 (as a proxy for average collective farm productivity) for six CEECs. Countries with low productivity on collective farms, such as Albania, have a significantly higher degree of decollectivization than those where collective farm productivity was higher, such as Hungary. Furthermore, especially in those countries where productivity on collective farms is too low to provide for the basic needs of members, the members will leave. The issue of relative productivity is thus related to consumption risk, or more generally, food security, reflected in the share of the budget spent on food. In countries characterized by a large share of the budget spent on food, food security is more critical. This factor appears to be important for countries such as Albania and Romania, where extremely low productivity of collective farms, in combination with government policy favoring state farms and taxing collective farms, caused very low incomes on the collective farms. In the case of Albania, where about 70% of income is spent on food, the situation was so extreme that food shortages and hunger resulted, causing a massive break-up of the collective farms after 1991.

Regional (within country) differences in decollectivization are also correlated with productivity differences and scale economies in production. Decollectivization is found to be significantly lower in plains where crop production with scale economies is the main activity. For example, data from Hungary and Romania show a strong negative correlation between the percentage of plains in a region and the share of individual farms.

3. The emergence of individual farms is reduced by the costs of leaving the cooperative farms. These 'exit costs' are affected by the procedures for withdrawing assets from the cooperative farms and the ownership of the assets. These factors, in turn, are influenced by the privatization and transformation regulations.

The method of privatization and land reform will in this way affect the emergence of individual farms. For example, in the case where many former owners are no longer active in agriculture, restitution of assets to former owners induces a conservation of the collective farm structure compared to a privatization procedure that allocates assets to the collective farm members, such as distribution, because collective farm managers have lower transaction costs than (potential) individual farmers in contracting with new owners. Similarly, share distribution and the resulting imperfect land property rights for individuals are key obstacles for the growth of individual tenures in Russia and Ukraine.

Transformation regulations can also hamper the break-up of collective farms by making it more difficult for individuals to withdraw their assets. For example, Slovenia introduced co-ownership of land between private individuals and state farms. In Bulgaria, amendments to the original land law include the institution of an extended administrative procedure, the possibility of reviewing the restitution process, and several restrictions to sales of land. In Hungary members can leave their cooperative after its transformation but they cannot withdraw their land or non-land assets. They receive a compensation that is only a fraction of the real value of the assets. In Slovakia, cooperatives can issue vouchers instead of restituting assets to former owners, but these vouchers cannot be traded for seven years.

Table 14.6 presents various indicators of reform legislation in CEECs. The shift to individual tenures is stronger where (1) more of the land was distributed to farm workers instead of restitution to former owners, (2) the share of agriculture in employment is high,[13] and (3) exit costs are low. It is remarkable to see how the two countries at the extremes of the spectrum are exactly opposite in these three factors. Albania, where FII is highest, distributed all the land to farm workers, and has a high share of agriculture in employment and low exit costs. Slovakia, where FII is lowest, restituted land to former owners, and has a low share of agriculture in employment and high exit costs.

[13] The share of agriculture in total employment for CEECs is positively related with FII because, first, the share of agriculture in total employment is typically negatively correlated with the level of development and the use of technology in agriculture. A country with a high share of agriculture in employment is typically less developed and uses inferior technology compared to a country with a low share of agriculture where there was a substitution of labor by capital as a result of the technological progress. Second, a high share of agriculture in total employment is an indication that relatively few people have left agriculture. Recent World Bank surveys suggest that the overwhelming majority of individual farmers are former cooperative members or employees of state farms (Csaki and Lerman 1996). Since in general outsiders lack the appropriate skills to start up a private farm, the number of farm workers is a good reflection of the number of people actually interested in individual farming.

Table 14.6. *Various indicators of land reform and transformation regulations*

	Share of total agricultural land (%)			Share of agriculture in total employment (1994)	Man/land ratio (workers/ 10 ha)	Exit costs due to government regulations[a]
	Privatized land by		State-owned land (1994)			
	Restitution	Distribution				
Albania	—	93	3	53	6.8	1
Bulgaria	81	—	7	22	1.1	2
Czech Republic	79	—	13	5	0.6	2
East Germany	82	—	8	n.a.	n.a.	2
Estonia	74	22	—	8	0.6	2
Hungary	62	19	5	9	0.6	3
Latvia	64	30	2	17	0.9	1
Lithuania	96	21	1	23	1.1	2
Romania	43–58	15–30	13	36	2.4	2
Slovakia	74	—	20	7	0.7	3

[a] Own estimate of exit costs induced by farm transformation regulations (1 = low, 2 = medium, 3 = high).

Source: Mathijs and Swinnen (1998*a*).

Additional factors have stimulated decollectivization in the Baltic countries and especially in Latvia. Becoming independent from Russia has been a key political strategy, affecting their reform policies. Collective farms were partly seen as a segment of a system imposed on them by the Russian occupation. Decollectivization was thus part of their independence strategy (Rabinowicz 1997). These additional factors have apparently stimulated the start-up of larger individual farms. Farms larger than 5 hectares have emerged more strongly in the Baltics and especially in Latvia than in CEECs with a similar agricultural share in employment. One explanation is that land ownership in 1945 was less fragmented and more egalitarian than in many other countries. Another important factor is the active Latvian restitution and decollectivization policy, which was inspired by nationalistic motivations. Restitution of land allocated property rights exclusively to native Latvians in a country with a very high share (46%) of ethnic non-Latvians (mostly post-1945 Russian immigrants). Further, the Latvian reform regulations specify that individual farms be given the highest priority in land allocation. The lowest priority is given to reforming collective farms (quite unlike many other CEECs, where collective farms receive preferential treatment).

Efficiency effects

Are individual farms more efficient than transformed state and collective enterprises, such as private cooperatives or joint stock companies ('large-scale successor organizations' or LSOs)? In *theory*, two factors have an important, and opposite, effect on the relative efficiency of these various organizations in agricultural production: labor transaction costs and scale economies. First, LSOs are expected to display lower levels of technical efficiency than family farms because of their inherent problems in solving principal–agent problems in labor contracting related to the difficulties of linking effort in production to income (Schmitt 1993; Pollak 1985). Metering effort in production is particularly stringent in agriculture because of its biological and sequential nature and spatial dimensions (Brewster 1950; Binswanger and Rosenzweig 1986). Family farms are more efficient in this regard because family members maximize family welfare rather than individual welfare and hence face no incentive to free ride, so that the costs of monitoring and controlling labor effort are lower (Carter 1984).

Second, scale economies would favor the largest organizations. However, many studies suggest that there are no increasing returns to farm size in production beyond what can be captured by the family farm, both in developing (Berry and Cline 1979; Hayami and Ruttan 1985) and in developed countries (Kislev and Peterson 1991; Peterson 1997). Advantages of cooperation and economies of scale do exist in output marketing, input purchasing, credit and information provision, and risk management. In many countries these scale economies are captured by marketing and credit cooperatives. However, in a transition economy where such cooperatives are typically absent, these 'intrinsic' scale advantages may provide important advantages to LSOs and may offset their transaction cost disadvantages, at least during the transition period (Carter 1987; Machnes and Schnytzer 1993; Deininger 1995). Moreover, some argue that state and collective farms performed poorly not because of their intrinsic problems, but because of extrinsic problems, such as bureaucratic controls and extractive external environments (Johnson 1983; Putterman 1985). This result would imply that LSOs would be able to survive and compete as production organizations even after the transition is over.

The first empirical analyses of differences in efficiency between different farm organizations after the 1989 reforms in CEECs yield mixed results.[14] Using data from former East Germany, Mathijs and Swinnen (2000) argue that new partnerships, using on average 500 hectares and five workers, and large individual farms are the most efficient farm organizations as they combine maximum scale efficiencies with low labor supervision costs. We also find that the efficiency differences between LSOs and partnerships and family farms have declined during transition, suggesting that hard budget constraints and independent management have induced significant efficiency gains in LSOs.[15] Our analyses of farm-level data of Czech and Slovak farms indicate similar results (see case study attached). The calculated efficiency indicators are lowest for the

[14] Pre-1989 comparisons of small-scale family farms and large-scale collective (or state) farms in Poland and Yugoslavia also yield mixed results. Boyd (1987*a*, *b*) and Brada and King (1993) argue that there is no difference in technical efficiency between state farms and private farms and conclude that 'it is the environment of socialized agriculture rather than the socialized nature of farms that leads to the poor performance of the agricultural sector in Eastern Europe and the former Soviet Union' (Brada and King 1993: 54). Hofler and Payne (1993) disagree based on their Yugoslavia study.

[15] In 1995 individual farms occupied 21% of total agricultural land, partnerships 22%, and LSOs 57% (34% cooperatives and 23% companies) (Beckmann and Hagedorn 1997). Partnerships were mostly established as new enterprises. They typically result from the collaboration of only a few people (five labor units on average) that in many cases are family related. Their average size is 500 ha of land.

largest LSOs and the smallest family farms. However, between these two extremes there exists a wide range of farm sizes and different governance structures where relatively little difference in efficiency can be observed. Still, the calculations also suggest that the cooperative farms are the least efficient, a result consistent with the continuing decline of the share of cooperative farms in land use over the past decade (see above).

However, after reviewing several survey-based analyses of FSU farms, Lerman (1998) concludes that the quantitative data on the relative performance of the various farm structures are inconclusive. Furthermore, Sedik, Trueblood, and Arnade (1997) measure a decline in overall farm efficiency during transition in Russia. Unlike in some CEECs where improved LSO management has followed effective organizational reforms and the introduction of hard budget constraints, Lerman and Csaki (1997), and Sedik (1996, 1997) report that, despite some downsizing in restructured farms, internal reorganization has not produced deep results in countries such as Russia and Ukraine, and that the collective framework has preserved most of its traditional functions. According to recent surveys in the Ukraine and Russia, about half the employees of farm enterprises report that no real change has taken place so far in the 'reorganized' farms. These surveys confirm intuitive insights that changes in large farms have been mostly superficial. Also, most managers report that their farm enterprise continues to be committed to a lifetime employment policy for its members, and they do not acknowledge disguised unemployment on their farms. The only real change appears in the abolition of outside imposition of production plans. However, because of informal dependency between large farms and local authorities, production plans continue to be influenced by (local) authorities.[16]

Transition to individual tenures, land reform, and productivity growth

In contrast to the small efficiency differences between farms within CEECs, differences between CEECs in terms of changes in aggregate productivity of agriculture are large (Macours and Swinnen 1998). While agricultural labor productivity (ALP) has fallen between 1989 and 1994 in most CEECs, it has increased around 40% in the Czech Republic, Slovakia, and Hungary (CSH). This increase in ALP coincided with restitution of land to former owners, a consolidation of large-scale farm structures, and

[16] There is no pervasive intervention in the production plans of farm enterprises, except in the case of strategic commodities, such as cotton in Turkmenistan and Uzbekistan. Farms are allowed considerable independence in their production and marketing decisions. Yet old habits die hard, and there is a strong informal chain of dependency and ongoing consultation between managers and the district bureaucracy. Managers cannot ignore the goals and objectives of district authorities, and, in this sense, they are not free to adjust their product mix completely in response to market signals. One of the most glaring examples is the relatively slow decrease of livestock production in farm enterprises; although livestock has been unprofitable in recent years, and the new private farmers indeed have changed their orientation to emphasize crop production, managers of large farms cannot afford to ignore the traditional insistence of district authorities on maintaining the herd as 'a source of milk for our school children' (Lerman 1997).

a strong decline in output and, even more, in labor input. In contrast, in Russia and Ukraine, ALP declined with around 35% over the same period, although the shift to individual farms was equally limited. Outside CSH, labor productivity increased only in Slovenia and Albania (10–20%), countries with very different adjustment patterns from CSH. In Albania agricultural labor input remained constant, while land was distributed to rural households and a dramatic shift to individual tenures occurred. In Slovenia (and Poland) land reform and farm restructuring was less dramatic. In Romania and Bulgaria, where land was restituted as in CSH and the shift to individual farms was moderate, ALP declined by 10% to 40%. Here, agriculture played a role as an employment buffer with low performance in the rest of the economy.

This suggests that there is no simple relationship between the choice of land reform, the shift to individual tenures, and productivity growth. Instead, the optimal reform and adjustment path differs among CEECs because it depends on the structure and the technology of the agricultural system and on the overall economic development. Some hypotheses on the impact of land reform and the transition to individual tenures on productivity growth are as follows.

First, a condition for growth is that land reform allocates strong and clear property rights on land to individuals (restitution and physical distribution in CECs versus share distribution in Russia and Ukraine). Furthermore, the *nature* of the property rights is more important than the *distribution* of the property rights, even in transition countries. In fact, ALP growth is strongest in those countries where an important share of the land is allocated to individuals not active in agriculture.

Second, the impact of the shift to individual tenures depends on the factor input and technology of the farms. In capital-intensive production systems, such as CSH, the costs from disrupting the capital stock and breaking up the large-scale technology may outweigh the benefits from improved supervision and labor effort on individual farms. In contrast, in labor-intensive farming, such as Albania, the incentive problems are likely to outweigh costs of technology disruption with the break-up of collectives.[17] Therefore, in labor-intensive production systems, productivity growth is more likely to come from the shift to individual farms, while in capital-intensive systems, important productivity improvements may come from improved LSO management. However, the latter requires effective organizational reforms, including the introduction of hard budget constraints. In those CEECs where LSOs seem to operate relatively efficiently they have undergone substantial effective restructuring, including both management reform and operation adjustments.

Third, land reform and farm restructuring need to be complemented by other institutional reforms to improve access to land, credit, technology, and information. The role of land leasing was already discussed above. Another important contracting problem in transition agriculture is credit. Only part of this is due to the shift to individual tenures. Credit constraints have been severe for all farms. Finance and credit problems result, among other problems, from the reform of the banking sector and

[17] Furthermore, terms of trade and output have declined less strongly in Albania than in other CEECs. As such, Albania's transition pattern is similar to that of China and Vietnam (Macours and Swinnen 1998).

the transition problems of enforcement mechanisms to ensure loan repayments (Swinnen and Gow 1999).[18]

The rural finance situation is improving in some CEECs due primarily to two factors: (1) improved profitability in agriculture since 1995, and (2) the emergence of institutional innovations, such as credit cooperatives, leasing, and various forms of contracting between farms and the up- and downstream sectors. The contracts can take various forms, e.g., leasing of equipment, forward contracting of output deliveries in return for inputs and working capital, producer loan guarantees backed by processing companies with delivery contracts, the provision of commodity loans to contracted farms by processors and input suppliers, warehouse receipts, etc. All of these contractual arrangements somehow address the loan collateral problem, and the credibility of future cash flows for loan repayment, and play an important role in improving access to credit for farms.

Foreign direct investment (FDI) in up- and downstream sectors has also contributed to solving credit and contract enforcement problems at the farm level. In some cases FDI has induced dramatic increases in productivity as it simultaneously tends to solve problems of access to credit, information, management advice, and technology (Gow and Swinnen 1998). Further, once one company successfully introduces such institutional innovations, there is an important spillover effect to other enterprises and even other sectors.

In conclusion, complementary institutional reforms are necessary to solve contracting problems in the agro-food chain and thereby, access to credit, information, technology, land, etc., for farms are requirements for sustainable productivity growth. The form of the institutional solutions—such as the role of leasing or of cooperatives for purchasing inputs, credit supply, and marketing—will differ for the large-scale farms in CSH, the small fragmented holdings in Albania and Romania, and the part-time family farms in Poland and Slovenia. Not surprisingly, in those CEECs where ALP has increased most, complementary institutional reforms and innovations, such as leasing of land and equipment, forward contracting, etc., and also the inflow of FDI, have progressed most.

REFERENCES

Alchian, Armen A. and Harold Demsetz. 1972. 'Production, Information Costs and Economic Organization.' *American Economic Review* 62(5): 777–95.

Alesina, Alberto and Roberto Perotti. 1992. 'Income Distribution, Political Instability, and Investment.' IPR Paper 53, Institute for Policy Reform, Washington DC.

[18] Agricultural and rural credit and risk markets in the most advanced countries work imperfectly, largely due to imperfect and costly information (Stiglitz 1993). In addition to these 'normal' imperfections, a series of specific, transition-related problems have further constrained the financing of the Central and Eastern European agricultural economy since 1989. These transition-specific problems have to do with the role of credit in the economic system, the institutional reforms occurring within the financial system, the declining profitability in agriculture, accumulated debts, high inflation, risk and uncertainty, and collateral problems (Calomiris 1993).

Baland, J.-M. and J.-P. Platteau. 1996. *Halting Degradation of Natural Resources—Is There a Role for Rural Communities?* Oxford: Clarendon Press.

Barzel, Y. 1989. *Economic Analysis of Property Rights.* Cambridge: Cambridge University Press.

Beckmann, Volker and Konrad Hagedorn. 1997. 'Decollectivisation and Privatisation Policies and Resulting Structural Changes of Agriculture in Eastern Germany.' In *Agricultural Privatisation, Land Reform and Farm Restructuring in Central and Eastern Europe*, Johan F.M. Swinnen, Allan Buckwell, and Erik Mathijs (eds.). Aldershot: Ashgate.

Berry, R. Albert and William R. Cline. 1979. *Agrarian Structure and Production in Developing Countries.* Baltimore, MD: Johns Hopkins University Press.

Binswanger, Hans P. and Klaus Deininger. 1997. 'Explaining Agricultural and Agrarian Policies in Developing Countries.' *Journal of Economic Literature* 35(4): 1958–2005.

Binswanger, Hans P. and Mark R. Rosenzweig. 1986. 'Behavioural and Material Determinants of Production Relations in Agriculture.' *Journal of Development Studies* 22(3): 503–39.

Binswanger, Hans P., Klaus Deininger, and Gershon Feder. 1995. 'Power, Distortions, Revolt and Reform in Agricultural Land Relations.' In *Handbook of Development Economics,* Vol. 3B, J. Behrman and T.N. Shrinivasan (eds.). Amsterdam: North-Holland.

Boyd, Michael L. 1987*a*. 'The Performance of Private and Cooperative Socialist Organization: Postwar Yugoslav Agriculture.' *Review of Economics and Statistics* 69(2): 205–14.

—— 1987*b*. 'The Performance of Private and Socialist Agriculture in Poland: The Effects of Policy and Organization.' *Journal of Comparative Economics* 12(1): 61–73.

Brada, Joseph C. and Arthur E. King. 1993. 'Is Private Farming More Efficient than Socialized Agriculture?' *Economica* 60(237): 41–56.

Brasselle, A.-S., F. Gaspart, and J.-P. Platteau. 1998. 'Land Tenure Security and Investment Incentives: Further Puzzling Evidence from Burkina Faso.' CRED Cahiers de Recherche, Faculty of Economics, FUNDP, Namur, Belgium.

Brewster, John M. 1950. 'The Machine Process in Agriculture and Industry.' *Journal of Farm Economics* 32(1): 69–81.

Brooks, K.M., J.L. Guasch, A. Braverman, and C. Csaki. 1991. 'Agriculture and the Transition to the Market.' *Journal of Economic Perspectives* 5(4): 149–61.

Calomiris, C.W. 1993. 'Agricultural Capital Markets.' In *The Agricultural Transition in Central and Eastern Europe and the Former USSR*, A. Braverman, K.M. Brooks, and C. Csaki (eds.). Washington DC: The World Bank.

Carter, Michael R. 1984. 'Resource Allocation and Use Under Collective Rights and Labor Management in Peruvian Coastal Agriculture.' *Economic Journal* 94(376): 826–46.

—— 1987. 'Risk Sharing and Incentives in the Decollectivization of Agriculture.' *Oxford Economic Papers* 39(3): 577–95.

Csaki, C. and Z. Lerman. 1996. 'Agricultural Transformation in Central and Eastern Europe and the Former USSR: Issues of Land Reform and Farm Restructuring.' Plenary Paper presented at the 8th Congress of the European Association of Agricultural Economists, *Redefining the Roles for European Agriculture*, Edinburgh, 3–7 September.

Cungu, A. and J. Swinnen. 1999. 'Albania's Radical Agrarian Reform.' *Economic Development and Cultural Change* 47(3): 605–19.

Davidova, S. and A. Buckwell. 1994. 'Agriculture Reform.' In *Privatization of Agriculture in New Market Economies: Lessons from Bulgaria*, A. Schmitz, K. Moulton, A. Buckwell, and S. Davidova (eds.). Boston, MA: Kluwer Academic Publishers.

de Janvry, A. 1981. 'The Role of Land Reform in Economic Development: Policies and Politics.' *American Journal of Agricultural Economics* 63(2): 384–92.

Deininger, Klaus. 1995. 'Collective Agricultural Production: A Solution For Transition Economies?' *World Development* 23(8): 1317–34.

Feder, G. and D. Feeny. 1991. 'Land Tenure and Property Rights: Theory and Implications for Development Policy.' *The World Bank Economic Review* 5(1): 135–53.

Gow, H. and J. Swinnen. 1998. 'Agribusiness Restructuring, Foreign Direct Investment, and Hold-Up Problems in Agricultural Transition.' *European Review of Agricultural Economics* 25(2): 331–50.

Hagedorn, K. 1997. 'The Politics and Policies of Privatization of Nationalized Land in Eastern Germany.' In *Political Economy of Agrarian Reform in Central and Eastern Europe*, Johan F.M. Swinnen (ed.). Aldershot: Avebury.

Hart, O. 1995. *Firms, Contracts and Financial Structure*. Oxford: Oxford University Press.

Hayami, Y. 1991. 'Land Reform.' In *Politics and Policymaking in Developing Countries. Perspectives on the New Political Economy*, G. Meier (ed.). San Francisco, CA: ICS Press.

Hayami, Yujiro and Vernon W. Ruttan. 1985. *Agricultural Development: An International Perspective*. Baltimore, MD: Johns Hopkins University Press.

Hayek, F. 1945. 'The Use of Knowledge in Society.' *American Economic Review* 35(4): 519–30.

Hillman, Arye L. 1992. 'Progress with Privatization.' *Journal of Comparative Economics* 16(4): 733–49.

Hinds, M. 1991. 'Incentives and Ownership in Socialist Countries in Transition.' In *Markets and Politicians: Politicized Economic Choice*, A.L. Hillman (ed.). Boston, MA: Kluwer.

Hofler, Richard A. and James E. Payne. 1993. 'Efficiency in Social versus Private Agricultural Production: The Case of Yugoslavia.' *Review of Economics and Statistics* 73(1): 153–7.

Jackson, M. 1997. 'Political Economy of Agricultural Reform in Romania.' In *Political Economy of Agrarian Reform in Central and Eastern Europe*, J. Swinnen (ed.). Avebury: Aldershot.

Johnson, D. Gale. 1983. 'Policies and Performance in Soviet Agriculture.' In *Prospects for Soviet Agriculture in the 1980s*, D. Johnson, D. Gale, and Karen M. Brooks (eds.). Bloomington, IN: Indiana University Press.

Kaldor, Nicholas. 1956. 'Alternative Theories of Distribution.' *Review of Economic Studies* 23(2): 83–100.

Kislev, Yaov and Willis Peterson. 1991. 'Economies of Scale in Agriculture: A Reexamination of the Evidence.' Staff Papers Series, Staff Paper P91–43, Department of Agricultural and Applied Economics, University of Minnesota, St. Paul, MN.

Klein, B., R.G. Crawford, and A.A. Alchian. 1978. 'Vertical Integration, Appropriable Rents, and the Competitive Contracting Process.' *Journal of Law and Economics* 21(2): 297–326.

Lerman, Z. 1997. 'Experience with Land Reform and Farm Restructuring in the Former Soviet Union.' In *Agricultural Privatization, Land Reform and Farm Restructuring in Central and Eastern Europe*, J. Swinnen, A. Buckwell, and E. Mathijs (eds.). Aldershot: Ashgate.

—— 1998. 'Does Land Reform Matter? Some Experiences from the Former Soviet Union.' *European Review of Agricultural Economics* 25(3): 307–30.

Lerman, Z. and C. Csaki. 1997. 'Land Reform in Ukraine: The First Five Years.' World Bank Discussion Paper 371, The World Bank, Washington DC.

Machnes, Yaffa and Adi Schnytzer. 1993. 'Risk and the Collective Farm in Transition.' In *Agricultural Cooperatives in Transition*, Csaba Csaki and Yaov Kislev (eds.). Boulder, CO: Westview Press.

Macours, K. and J. Swinnen. 1998. 'Patterns of Agrarian Transition: Comparing Central and Eastern Europe, the former Soviet Union, and East Asia.' Policy Research Group Working Paper, Department of Agricultural Economics, Katholieke Universiteit, Leuven, Belgium.

Macours, K. and J. Swinnen. 2000. 'Causes of Output Decline in Central and East European Agriculture.' *Journal of Comparative Economics*. forthcoming.

Mathijs, Erik. 1997. 'An Historical Overview of Central and Eastern European Land Reform.' In *Political Economy of Agrarian Reform in Central and Eastern Europe*, Johan F.M. Swinnen (ed.). Aldershot: Avebury.

Mathijs, Erik and Sándor Mészáros. 1997. 'Privatisation and Restructuring of Hungarian Agriculture.' In *Agricultural Privatisation, Land Reform and Farm Restructuring in Central and Eastern Europe*, Johan F.M. Swinnen, Allan Buckwell, and Erik Mathijs (eds.). Aldershot: Ashgate.

Mathijs, E. and J. Swinnen. 1998*a*. 'The Economics of Agricultural Decollectivization in East Central Europe and the Former Soviet Union.' *Economic Development and Cultural Change* 47(1): 1–26.

—— 1998*b*. 'The Efficiency of Land Reforms in East Central Europe and the Former Soviet Union.' Policy Research Group Working Paper, Department of Agricultural Economics, Katholieke Universiteit, Leuven, Belgium.

—— 2000. 'Production Organization and Efficiency During Transition: An Empirical Analysis of East German Agriculture.' *Review of Economics and Statistics*, forthcoming.

McAfee, R. Preston and John McMillan. 1987. 'Auctions and Bidding.' *Journal of Economic Literature* 25(2): 699–738.

North, D. 1990. *Institutions, Institutional Change and Economic Performance*. Cambridge: Cambridge University Press.

Organization for Economic Cooperation and Development (OECD). 1996. *Agricultural Policies, Markets and Trade in Transition Economies, Monitoring and Evaluation 1996*. Paris: Center for Co-operation with the Economies in Transition, OECD.

Ostrom, E. 1998. 'Efficiency, Sustainability, and Access Under Alternative Property Rights Regimes.' Paper presented at the WIDER/UNU/FAO seminar on Access to Land, Rural Poverty and Public Action, in Santiago de Chile, 27–29 April.

Perotti, Roberto. 1994. 'Income Distribution and Investment.' *European Economic Review* 38(3–4): 827–35.

Peterson, Willis L. 1997. 'Are Large Farms More Efficient?' Staff Papers Series, Staff Paper P97–2, Department of Applied Economics, College of Agricultural, Food, and Environmental Sciences, University of Minnesota, St. Paul, MN.

Platteau, J.-P. 1992. 'Land Reform and Structural Adjustment in Sub-Saharan Africa.' Economic and Social Development Paper 107, FAO, Rome.

Pollak, Robert A. 1985. 'A Transaction Cost Approach to Families and Households.' *Journal of Economic Literature* 23(2): 581–608.

Putterman, Louis. 1985. 'Extrinsic versus Intrinsic Problems of Agricultural Cooperation: Anti-incentivism in Tanzania and China.' *Journal of Development Studies* 21(2): 175–204.

Rabinowicz, E. 1997. 'Political Economy of Agricultural Privatization in the Baltic Countries.' In *Political Economy of Agrarian Reform in Central and Eastern Europe*, J. Swinnen (ed.). Aldershot: Ashgate.

Rozelle, S., G. Li, and L. Brandt. 1998. 'Land Rights, Farmer Investment Incentives, and Agricultural Production in China.' Paper presented at the WIDER/UNU/FAO seminar on Access to Land, Rural Poverty and Public Action, in Santiago de Chile, 27–29 April.

Schmitt, Günther. 1991. 'Why is the Agriculture of Advanced Western Countries Still Organized by Family Farms? Will this Continue to be so in the Future?' *European Review of Agricultural Economics* 18(3): 443–58.

—— 1993. 'Why Collectivization of Agriculture in Socialist Countries Has Failed: A Transaction Cost Approach.' In *Agricultural Cooperatives in Transition*, Csaba Csaki and Yaov Kislev (eds.). Boulder, CO: Westview Press.

Schumpeter, J. 1942. *Capitalism, Socialism and Democracy*. New York: Harper & Bros.

Sedik, D. 1996. 'Agricultural Policies Mitigate Production Declines but Have Considerable Costs for the Countryside.' United States Department of Agriculture, Economic Research Service (USDA/ERS) *NIS and the Baltics Situation and Outlook Series*, WRS 96–1, 4–8 May.

—— 1997. 'Status of Agricultural Reforms in the NIS/B Countries in 1997.' USDA/ERS *NIS and the Baltics Situation and Outlook Series*, WRS 97–1, 4–9 May.

Sedik, D., M.A. Trueblood, and C. Arnade. 1998. 'Agricultural Enterprise Restructuring and Land Reform in Russia, 1991–1995: An Efficiency Analysis.' Working paper, USDA/ERS, Washington DC.

Stiglitz, Joseph E. 1993. 'Incentives, Organizational Structures, and Contractual Choice in the Reform of Socialist Agriculture.' In *The Agricultural Transition in Central and European Europe and the Former USSR*, Avishay Braverman, Karen Brooks, and Csaba Csaki (eds.). Washington DC: The World Bank.

Swinnen, J. 1996. 'Endogenous Price and Trade Policy Developments in Central European Agriculture.' *European Review of Agricultural Economics* 23(2): 133–60.

—— 1997*a*. 'On Liquidation Councils, Flying Troikas and Orsov Cooperatives: The Political Economy of Agricultural Reform in Bulgaria.' In *Political Economy of Agrarian Reform in Central and Eastern Europe*, J. Swinnen (ed.). Aldershot: Ashgate.

—— 1997*b*. 'Does Compensation for Disruptions Stimulate Reforms? The Case of Agrarian Reform in Central and Eastern Europe.' *European Review of Agricultural Economics* 24(2): 249–66.

—— 1998. 'Land Leasing in Western Europe: A Historical Perspective.' Policy Research Group Working Paper, Katholieke Universiteit, Leuven, Belgium.

—— 1999. 'Political Economy of Land Reform Choices in Central and Eastern Europe.' *Economics of Transition*. 7(3): 637–64.

Swinnen, J. and H. Gow. 1999. 'Agricultural Credit Problems and Policies During the Transition to a Market Economy in Central and Eastern Europe.' *Food Policy* 21(1): 21–47.

Swinnen, J., A. Buckwell, and E. Mathijs (eds.). 1997. *Agricultural Privatization, Land Reform and Farm Restructuring in Central and Eastern Europe*. Aldershot: Ashgate.

Vickers, J. and G. Yarrow. 1991. 'Economic Perspectives on Privatization.' *Journal of Economic Perspectives* 5(2): 111–32.

Vickrey, William. 1961. 'Counterspeculation, Auctions, and Competitive Sealed Tenders.' *Journal of Finance* 16(1): 8–37.

Williamson, O. 1985. *The Economic Institutions of Capitalism*. New York: Free Press.

—— 1991. 'Economic Institutions: Spontaneous and Intentional Governance.' *Journal of Law, Economics and Organization* 7(0): 159–87.

Preface to Chapters 15 and 16

The two case studies that follow report on the transition from collective to individual tenures in Albania (Azeta Cungu) and in the Czech Republic (Tomas Doucha and Erik Mathijs). They present two very different cases of land reform and decollectivization in Central and Eastern Europe. The countries differ strongly in the initial conditions (e.g., their economic structure), in the land reform they have chosen, and in the resulting impact on individual tenures and the productivity changes in agriculture (as summarized in the table below).

Structure and policies of the countries in the case studies in 1995

	Share of agriculture in total employment (%)	Agricultural labor intensity (person/ha)	Land reform procedure	Share of total land used by individual tenures (%)
Albania	53.0	0.63	Distribution to rural households	94
Czech Republic	4.7	0.12	Restitution to former owners	22

15

Case Study. The Dramatic Rise of Individual Farming in Albania: Causes and Effects

AZETA CUNGU AND JOHAN F.M. SWINNEN

Introduction

The agrarian reform was a very important part of the overall economic reforms in Albania because of the relative importance of agriculture in total GDP and the large farming population. The reform distributed land and most other assets to farm workers and resulted in a complete decollectivization of collective farms and a radical shift to private ownership of land. The individual family farm is the main form of farm organization that has emerged.

The distribution policy, and the following radical decollectivization that took place, made the Albanian case different from reforms in other Central and Eastern European countries (CEECs) where land was mostly restituted to former owners and large-scale farming still occupies an important share of land.

The reform in Albania was followed by strong growth in the agricultural output for several consecutive years (Figure 15.1). This was mainly due to better labor incentives and improved resource allocation following privatization and liberalization measures.

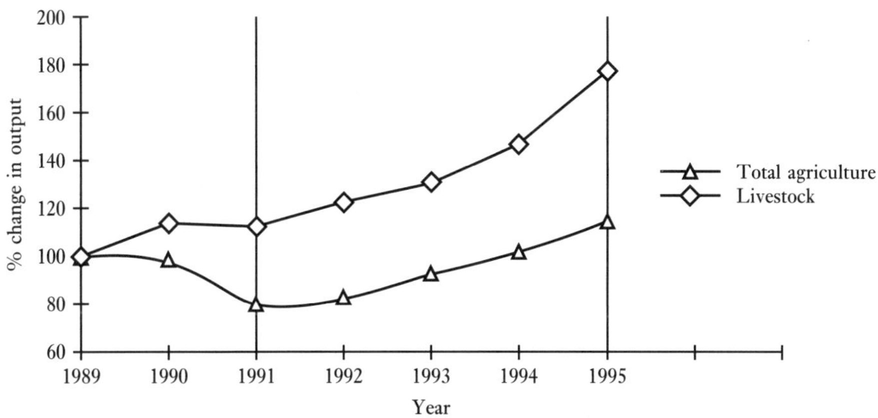

Figure 15.1. *Output changes in Albania, 1989–1995*

Despite recent economic growth, however, rural poverty, especially in the Northeastern part of the country, still remains widespread. Moreover, in recent years, there has been a slow-down in growth rates which can be explained by the main shortcomings of the reform: the high fragmentation of holdings which emerged from the reform, uncertain and incomplete property rights over the newly distributed land, missing markets for land, and restricted access to agricultural credit.

This chapter presents an overview of the process and determinants of the land reform and agricultural privatization policies. Other sections in the chapter examine the farm structures that emerged, the causes for the rise of individual farming, and the differences between the collective and state farms in the privatization process. The chapter further examines the impact of the reform on: (a) effective property rights in agriculture, (b) the efficiency of asset use, (c) agricultural production, (d) labor use, and (e) rural poverty.

Land reform and agricultural privatization

The land reform in Albania started spontaneously at the beginning of 1991 when farm workers began to break up the collective farms and distribute land and other assets among themselves. A formal framework was established by the Land Law (July 1991) and the August 1991 law, 'On the Sanctioning and Protection of Private Property, Free Initiative, and Independent Private Activities, and Privatization,' which declared agriculture open to private activity.[1]

The reform of the Agricultural Production Cooperatives

According to the Land Law, in Agricultural Production Cooperatives (APCs), land was to be distributed for free to member families on an equal per capita basis, proportional to the total area of land available in the APC. Other rural residents permanently employed in the non-agricultural sector were only eligible to land equivalent to half the size allocated to cooperative members. Land Distribution Councils (LDCs) were created to organize and implement the distribution process at national, district, and village levels. LDCs were expected to correct the improper possession of assets that occurred when villagers spontaneously broke up the collectives.

In APCs composed of several villages, the land was first to be broken up among villages on the basis of their per capita size, and the distribution was to be done in such a way as to put all farmers more or less on an equal footing. Further, the shares to each rural family were to be calculated taking account of their per capita composition. A number of additional legal acts provided for the distribution of the other APC assets to farm workers, including livestock, orchards, fruit trees, draught animals, implements, etc., once all APC debts were paid off.[2]

[1] For a detailed discussion of the process and the legal framework see Cungu and Swinnen (1997*a*).

[2] Initially, APC debts were charged to members in proportion to the area of land they had received. Later, the state decided to write off part of the remaining APC debts to ease the decollectivization process.

In principle, 'land distribution' meant conceding property rights to the rural population or, in other cases, the right to use the distributed land.[3] In terms of effective rights, however, only user rights were initially reallocated since, even where ownership rights were officially granted, the newly acquired land could not be leased or sold.

The only exception to the equal distribution rule was in mountain areas of the country where land was restituted to ex-owners in their old boundaries. The functions of the formal village LDCs were, for this purpose, performed by the so-called 'Councils of the Elderly' composed of old village people known for their 'fairness and wisdom.'[4] The proposals of the Councils of the Elderly were accepted, as it seemed to be very much the will of the villagers themselves. However, a handful of families who joined the villages during the socialist period were excluded from the process, unlike elsewhere in the country where the reforms tried to accommodate for the inclusion of all of the rural population in the privatization process.

The main reasons for this difference were that in the mountainous areas: (a) the collectivization process began later than other parts of the country, making it easier to recognize old boundaries; (b) the pre-collectivization land distribution was much less concentrated than in the plains, creating fewer conflicts and equity problems; and (c) the mountainous areas are still strongly guided by the deeply rooted 'Code of Leke Dukagjini' (the moral code of the Albanian mountains), which considers an individual's private property, including the right to inheritance, as sacred.

The reform of the State Farms

State Farms (SFs) created by merging collectives were split into their component APCs and then privatized according to the Land Law. In SFs based on large expropriated estates or where the state financed important investments such as land improvements, the state retained land ownership with user rights granted to former workers. Beneficiaries were given a formal 'user rights' certificate for an indefinite period of time and without charges. Elsewhere they were granted the possession of the land without such a certificate (Stanfield and Jazo 1995). The remainder, which was considered to be the best agricultural land in the country, was pooled into joint ventures with foreign capital. When these joint ventures failed (and many of them did), the land was given to workers for cultivation whereas the actual ownership remained initially with the state. In 1995, new legislation stipulated the free transfer of 'user rights' to 'full ownership rights.' Full ownership rights were also given on ex-joint venture land once disputes over the termination of these lands had been cleared. In the dismantled SFs, non-land assets were either directly sold to workers or otherwise auctioned. In either case, the farm workers of the farm received preferential treatment.

[3] User rights were allocated for land distributed to rural residents employed in the non-agricultural sector, and for land within the village residential boundaries.

[4] Government regulation did provide some room for a *de jure* accommodation of this by specifying that the 'quantity, quality and location of land for distribution are decided by the village councils which are to be democratically elected by the village members.'

Compensation for former owners

The pre-1945 land ownership was unequally distributed, especially the ownership of the best land which was concentrated in a few families. In 1945, the Communist regime, which took power after World War II, initiated a radical land reform that confiscated anything above 5 hectares (ha) of land and distributed it to landless families or those who only possessed tiny plots. Soon after this, collectivization was initiated. This resulted in the establishment of state ownership over all land in 1976.

The 1991 Land Law did not recognize pre-collectivization land-ownership rights. Opposition to this process was strongest from pre-1945 owners.[5] In early 1993, pressure from pre-1945 owners increased; they organized and formed the 'Property with Justice Movement,' which gave them more effective representation in political parties. In April 1994, this resulted in a law providing financial compensation for the loss of pre-1945 property rights. However, former owners rejected the idea of financial compensation and demanded full, physical restitution of property rights. The continued opposition of former owners, in combination with the large technical difficulties in implementing compensation, increased pressure on the government. As a compromise, in July 1995, ex-owners were compensated with seaside and tourist site properties.

An explanation of the choice of the land reform

Albania's choice of distribution reform was very different from land reforms in other CEECs (Swinnen 1997). In Cungu and Swinnen (1999), we argue that a combination of factors have affected the political calculations behind the reform government's decisions on land reform which contribute to the explanation of why Albania, in contrast to the CEECs, has chosen land distribution over restitution. A crucial factor is that in Albania all land was state-owned pre-reform; other factors include the difficult income situation of collective farm workers, the concentrated pre-collectivization land ownership, and the predominantly agrarian economy of Albania.

A key difference with other Central European countries, where land remained formally in private hands throughout the collectivization period, was that in Albania agricultural land was formally state-owned on the eve of the 1991 reforms. With land in state ownership, the Albanian government had more options than the other central European governments, because all CEECs (former Soviet Union countries not included) restituted assets that were still privately owned by former owners (Swinnen 1997).

Another factor has to do with the relative roles and influence of the interest groups involved, i.e., the farm workers, the nomenclature, pre-1945 and 1946–1948 owners. Farm workers were the main group to demand land distribution. Three other interest groups opposed this choice. First, the rural nomenclature, i.e., former collective farm managers and Communist leaders, opposed both distribution and/or restitution since these would imply loss of their economic and political power. In fact, in 1991 the reform

[5] There was less opposition from those who acquired land from the Communist inspired reform during 1946–48. See next section for an explanation of this.

was initiated by farm workers who started breaking up the collectives. After March 1992, with a right-wing majority in the Parliament, policies were aimed at complete dismantling of pre-reform structures to destroy the basis for Communist support in rural areas.

Second, former owners who received land during the Communist reforms in 1946–48 were much less opposed to distribution than the pre-1945 owners. Why? The first reason is that restitution based on the 1948 ownership situation would have very similar results as the redistribution option. Most 1948 owners were to receive land under the current distribution program because the structure of the APCs in terms of member families did not change much over the years due to restrictions in labor mobility. Moreover, in most cases, the area of land assigned to families under the land distribution program was larger than what they would have received under restitution. This is partly due to increases in the arable land area and improvements in land quality resulting from state investments, and partly because restituted land would have to be divided among heirs (the Albanian population had tripled since 1945). Second, for the small landowners, the marginal costs of lobbying and costs of submitting valid claims per hectare of land to be restituted (or compensated for) were high compared to the expected additional benefits. A third reason might have been that the 1946–48 land reform was seen as a Communist action and a first step towards collectivization.

These three reasons also explain the much more vigorous opposition of the pre-1945 owners to land distribution. They had much more to gain from restitution in comparison to what they would receive under the distribution program in addition to the costs of lobbying and submitting restitution claims. They also felt they were the legitimate owners of the land, which was violently expropriated by the Communists.

The argument of political organization costs predicts that former owners would be much more influential on decision-making than farm workers because their group has all the characteristics reducing transaction costs of political organization (Olson 1965). Why then did the reformers in government choose land distribution over restitution? Why were the pre-1945 owners less influential than the peasants in determining the reform choice?

The most important explanation has to do with the effects of the reform and the low-income level of farm workers. Because of the large impact on marginal welfare and on income security the land reform choice was very influential in determining peasants' political reactions. A vast number of people (50% of the labor force, and 65% of Albania's population) all benefited at least to some extent from land distribution, and many of them would have reacted vehemently against restitution to pre-1945 owners. In comparison, only a very small portion of the population would benefit from restitution to pre-1945 owners. Thus, the important marginal benefit effect of reforms for the many peasants strongly offsets the 'land dilution effect.' In combination with the vast numbers difference, this more than offsets the concentration and organizational cost advantages of the pre-1945 owners.

Clearly, the political motivation for distribution is strongly related to equity concerns. In fact, social equity considerations would motivate the government to choose land distribution as it clearly causes a much more equitable asset distribution in Albanian society. Most people were strongly opposed to the restoration of a feudal structure in the best agricultural areas through restitution to the heirs of a handful of families. Finally, as we will explain in Section 5, in Albania, land distribution was also preferable to land restitution for efficiency reasons.

The radical shift to individual tenures

The emerged structures

The large pre-transition agricultural structures have been almost completely abolished. In 1996 small-scale farmers in individual production units were farming more than 95% of the arable area. The farm structure which has emerged is highly fragmented: 490,000 new private farms use 1.9 million parcels, ranging from 1–10 parcels per farm with an average of about 3.3 separately located parcels per family farm. The average farm size is 1.05 ha ranging between 1.29 hectares in valleys and foothills to 0.55 hectares in the mountains (Grace 1996; International Fertilizer Development Center 1994). In an environment of underdeveloped market institutions, fragmentation and the associated high transaction costs have contributed to the creation of predominantly subsistence farming in many regions of the country, especially in upland and hilly areas.

Predominantly, small farm activities combine crop and animal production to ensure adequate household consumption although the pattern of the activities varies according to climatic conditions, availability of resources, and land quality. Small farms typically use family labor and are managed jointly by family members.

Causes of the radical shift to individual farming

While spontaneous privatization has occurred to some extent in virtually all CEECs, the extent to which this spontaneous process has led to a complete break-up of the collective farms in Albania is unique. In most CEECs, most farm workers remained with the cooperative-under-transformation during the early years of transition (Swinnen and Mathijs 1997). Two factors played a key role in causing the radical shift to individual tenures: the extreme inefficiencies in Albania's APCs (reflected in their low incomes) and the labor intensity of the production systems.

Albania had the lowest per capita income in Europe and APCs incomes were even lower than average incomes. Moreover, the virtual collapse of the agricultural sector between 1989 and 1991 (Figure 15.1) worsened the economic crisis in the country, especially in rural areas, to the point where it induced a radical reaction from the farm workers in an environment of reduced social control and political instability. The fact that a complete break-up of APCs resulted despite all problems associated with credit supply and lack of machinery—which in many other CEECs discouraged individuals from leaving the cooperative—reflects farm workers' expectations of poor benefits from remaining in the APC framework compared to the alternative (i.e., small individual farms). It also reflects the fact that in a labor-intensive production system the gains in efficiency from individual farming are larger and the disruption costs smaller.

Differences between APCs and SFs

The privatization of SFs was done through different procedures and also more gradually than the APCs. Why was that? To understand the rationale behind this, one has to bear in mind that the APCs' status and organization under central planning was different from that of the SFs. At least in theory, in APCs the means of production were collectively owned, except for the land which was state property after 1976. Land used by APCs was previously privately owned by peasants and then pooled into the collectives which were created all over the country including the mountainous areas. The produce was shared between members, while a special quota went to the state and surpluses were sold in cities.

Unlike the APCs, SFs were operated like any other state enterprise. Everything was state-owned and workers (mostly urban residents) were government employees. Their benefits (guaranteed state salaries) were higher than those of APC members. The state invested heavily in SFs by providing special facilities, including greenhouses, high quality inputs, irrigation water, and agricultural machinery. Moreover, SFs were created on big estates confiscated from the church or from the pre-Communist state and were often on the best land in the country.

While APCs were privatized (and decollectivized) quickly, the privatization of SFs started later and proceeded slower. The reasons were:

1. there was relatively less pressure from state farm workers to privatize the farms and distribute the land because of their relatively better situation and benefits;
2. in most cases there were no former owners demanding land restitution;
3. the privatization of state farms was technically more complicated because more land improvements and investments, including non-land asset constructions, had occurred over the past forty years; and
4. given the break-up of the APCs and the fragmentation of land, the government hoped to preserve SFs as large production structures to attract foreign investment.

The impact of the reform

In this section we discuss further how the reforms have affected: (a) effective land property rights, (b) efficiency of land use and agricultural production, and (c) rural welfare and labor adjustments.

Impact on effective property rights

Three main factors have influenced the effectiveness of the distribution of land property rights: (a) pressure from pre-1945 landowners and their growing political power; (b) delays in the process of assigning land titles; and (c) restrictions on sales. These factors have contributed to uncertainties over property rights in agriculture.

First, although the legal bases for the compensation of former landowners exist, no steps have so far been taken for the implementation of the process. Moreover, experience shows that whenever political pressure from former owners intensifies, the government responds with increasingly favorable deals. Therefore, unless the problem of compensating ex-agricultural landowners is settled, uncertainty over the rights on the distributed assets will remain.

Second, the redistribution process was initiated with the physical distribution of the property and carried out separately from the formal distribution of rights. The latter process lagged behind the physical distribution and many farmers were farming without an official ownership title.

Third, land transactions remain restricted despite the approval of laws for land renting (June 1993) and land markets (July 1995). Although the Land Market Law provides for sales, it prohibits any transactions until all land has been appropriately registered. The registration process, while under way, is not expected to be complete before 2001.

New initiatives are to be launched for establishing clear property rights in agriculture. A key element is the removal of remaining obstacles for the development of land markets. This includes decisive steps towards compensating ex-owners, faster land registration, and the designing of special procedures for the sale of individual holdings (Government of Albania 1997).

Efficiency effects of the reforms

Efficiency considerations have to do with: (a) the costs of reform implementation, (b) potential disruptions caused by the reforms, and (c) the effect of the resulting asset distribution and its effect on economic performance. We argue that the positive incentive and allocation effects of the land reform and the shift to individual tenures have strongly offset the disruption implications during transition. However, in the longer run, land fragmentation is likely to hamper growth and development. This is likely to persist as long as land, labor, and credit market imperfections remain important.

Transition period

First, the implementation costs of land distribution are considerably lower than for alternative land privatization processes. Distribution is technically easier to implement than restitution to former owners, especially in the absence of adequate land maps indicating old property boundaries.

Second, under the conditions of virtual collapse in agriculture and widespread spontaneous privatization, it was important to act quickly and to ensure some continuation of production by allocating land to those who were actually farming it.

Third, in an agricultural production system that is characterized by imperfect factor markets, low technology, and labor-intensive production, such as in Albania, land distribution probably also ensures the most efficient distribution of property rights (Mathijs and Swinnen 1998). With imperfect capital and land markets, the optimal land reform strategy must allocate a maximum share of the land to those with a comparative advantage in agricultural production. Assuming that these are part of the current users because of human capital investments, this implies that the optimal land reform strategy would allocate land to (some of) the current users. With low scale effects because of labor intensive technology and high labor transaction costs, equal distribution of land among current users is likely to be as efficient as any alternative policy in creating the most efficient initial asset distribution, especially if one includes organization and transaction costs of alternative reform processes, such as auctions.

Further, Stiglitz (1993) argues that equally distributed property rights have the potential to increase the efficiency of the agricultural sector, by providing better incentives to labor and better access to credit for farmers who own land. This argument is especially relevant for Albania where agriculture is still a large share of the economy and where land reform has a strong effect on wealth distribution.

A negative effect of land distribution is its contribution to fragmentation of ownership and its impact on production structures. However, with declining scale economies in Albanian agriculture (Hatziprokopiou and Karagiannis 1996) due to low technology production and increasing labor transaction costs, the potential negative impact of the break-up of collective farms is relatively limited, at least in the short run.

This is consistent with the observation of strong growth in farm output after the reforms, suggesting that any negative effects during transition have been offset by improved labor effort and resource allocation following price liberalization and privatization (Figure 15.1). With an average annual increase of 10% for several consecutive years since the reform, growth in the overall agricultural output in Albania constitutes by far the largest among all CEECs.

Improved incentives through privatization and restructuring have been an important but not necessarily only source of growth. Other factors might have played a role, such as a potential early improvement in the terms of trade for farming suggested in Macours and Swinnen (1998). Insufficient data are available at this moment to allow an analysis of how much growth can be attributed to various sources.

Allocative adjustments are notably reflected in the dramatic increase in livestock production (Figure 15.1). A shift in relative prices seems to have been important (Macours and Swinnen 1998). Additional factors include: (a) concerns about meeting family consumption needs in a predominantly subsistence-oriented agriculture, and increased demand for marketed livestock products;[6] (b) the low capital requirements of livestock production at a time when finance is scarce; (c) marketing advantages compared to crops (Christensen 1995); (d) a return to traditional patterns of doing agriculture and the associated know-how; and (e) geographical and soil conditions which in many regions are more suitable for livestock production.

Institutional constraints and implications for long-run growth

In years 1996 and 1997 agriculture only grew by 4 and 2%, respectively, the lowest levels since the initiation of the reforms (Ministry for Economic Development and

[6] Grace (1996) finds that livestock products are the principal source of gross cash income to farmers in the coastal and hilly regions and the principal source of subsistence for farmers in the upland zones.

Cooperation 1997).[7] This slowdown in recent growth rates might be due to the main shortcomings of the reform, i.e., fragmentation, incomplete markets for land and finance, and uncertain property rights.

The reform of the banking system, restricted macro-economic policy, overall uncertainty, and the absence of collateral due to non-functioning markets for land have put a major constraint on credit supplies to agriculture. Available financial resources have mostly been shifted to other faster and higher-return and less risky sectors such as services.

The main inflow of finance into the rural areas comes from foreign aid and remittances from migrants.[8] Agriculture received the bulk of the country's aid allocations because of: (a) the difficult food situation in Albania prior to reform; (b) the big share of agriculture in the economy; and (c) the incidence of poverty which is highest among the rural population.

In addition, in the absence of clear legal and policy solutions, some attempts to deal with constraints from market imperfections have emerged with mixed success. For example, some Private Farmers Associations (PFAs)[9] were formed by the need to overcome the problems of fragmentation, restricted access to inputs and finance, and the need to bargain with the up- and downstream sectors. Such structures, however, have yet to prove effective, especially since Albanian farmers have shown little interest in group activities.

Summarizing, sustained growth in the agricultural sector will largely depend on how fast and with what success the current drawbacks of the reform will be dealt with to allow for land consolidation, private investment, and the rapid introduction of new technology.

Finally, even with perfect markets and property rights, a substantial and quick consolidation of holdings is unlikely to happen as long as access to credit and employment possibilities outside of agriculture are limited. The rate of consolidation will also depend on improvements in overall living standards in rural areas because poor farmers are less likely to give up their land as it represents security for their families.

Implications for labor use and rural poverty

With the reforms, the overall household welfare and food security have improved compared to the situation between 1989 and 1991. However, the concern over food security is a key reason the reforms have not caused an important outflow of agricultural labor, despite overemployment. With land distribution providing access to land for all rural households, and low labor opportunity costs, rural households have chosen subsistence farming, reducing labor outflows. Available data show a small but steady decline of

[7] It is argued that the 1997 political instability in Albania had little effect on the agricultural production.
[8] The reader is referred to the next section, for a discussion of the remittance payments from emigrants.
[9] See Cungu and Swinnen (1997*b*) for a discussion of the main features of the PFAs in Albania.

agricultural employment after 1991 (Christensen 1995),[10] although the relative share of employment in agriculture increased during transition as unemployment in the rest of the economy soared up (International Monetary Fund 1994). Out-migration from mountainous to more fertile regions has occurred mainly due to unfavorable land conditions, a very low ratio of land per capita, and limited off-farm opportunities in mountainous areas.

A certain amount of substitution of labor for other factors of production as well as farm inputs seems to have occurred during transition. First, with missing land markets and very restricted credit, labor has become the most abundant but also the cheapest factor of production for many farmers. Second, both disruptions in input supply chains and increases in the relative prices of farm inputs might have contributed to further substitution.[11] This last point is supported by observations from a number of studies (International Fertilizer Development Center 1994; Ministry of Agriculture and Food 1995; Christensen 1995).

Despite recent economic growth, rural poverty has not disappeared and seems to have increased since 1993, at least in relative terms. There are big disparities between regions and seasonal variations in the levels of living. Poverty is deeply rooted in the Northeast where arable land is marginalized. Incomes in those regions were only 75% of the country average in 1993, and this gap is believed to have gone up since then.

Poverty is especially problematic for households with: (a) the smallest plots and in less fertile areas, and (b) little access to off-farm incomes. An estimated quarter of the rural population lives on a farm that is too small to provide even a modest level of subsistence from farming alone. With low initial endowment (small plots) and poor access to credit, farmers cannot raise the initial capital required to produce at a level required to generate more adequate farm incomes.

The poorest of rural people are unable to meet their annual staple food requirements and must depend on subsidized wheat or flour in the winter months and public cash transfers (The World Bank 1997).

With little land and no credit, poor households cannot purchase critical inputs essential for higher yields and thus larger marketed surplus. Christensen (1995) finds that, due to high prices, current fertilizer use is extremely low regardless of returns to its use being quite high even with the current input/output prices. With little initial endowment (small plots) and restricted access to credit, farmers cannot raise the initial capital required to produce at a more efficient level to generate more adequate farm incomes. Moreover, poor households cannot purchase critical inputs essential for higher yields and thus larger marketed surplus.

[10] In fact, unemployment in rural areas grew with the reform. In an FAO study, about 6% of the rural population in the area surveyed became unemployed because of the disappearance of services associated with the APCs and SFs, the collapse of the manufacturing sector, and reduced labor demand following its privatization, and from a 'general lack of investment' (FAO/AUT 1995). The observed agricultural output growth after the reform can be mostly attributed to increases in labor productivity rather than evolution in employment. Thus, agriculture did not fill the rural unemployment gap.

[11] This remains hypothetical since data on the evolution of wages and input prices are not available at present.

Off-farm income comes mainly from wages for non-agricultural employment, pensions for public services, targeted transfers to the poor, and unemployment benefits. Rural pensioners (150,000 people) fell below urban subsistence levels from the second half of 1992 onwards because of the collapse of the rural social security system after the privatization of APCs. Unemployment transfers and social welfare payments for those below the minimum subsistence level are extremely low, and only reach about 35% of the poor (The World Bank 1997). In any case, benefits to recipients have declined in recent years due to budgetary cuts and inflation erosion.

The most important factor in alleviating poverty has been migration to neighboring countries, such as Greece and Italy. This has reduced pressure in rural job markets and has become an important source of rural household income. Surveys show that remittances made up 87% of rural households' off-farm incomes in the region of Korca, which is known for the large numbers of emigrants to Greece (Food and Agriculture Organization of the United Nations and Agricultural University of Tirana 1995). Initially, the very poor regions benefited less from migration, but recently a much larger migration flow has emerged from these regions.

Conclusions

Agricultural reforms in Albania consisted of an equal per capita distribution of land to rural households and the complete break-up of the former structures of production. These key features of the Albanian reform were in contrast to other CEECs where restitution was the commonly chosen privatization policy, and decollectivization was modest in the first years.

The structure of institutions and of the economy, the historical and legal status of the assets under privatization, and farm productivity have all played a role in determining the reform policies. Reforms have resulted in a more efficient use of unit labor and land, at least in the short run, which is consistent with the observations of strong recovery following the reform. However, sustained future growth is constrained by highly fragmented holdings, uncertain property rights on the recently acquired land, and difficult access to credit. Underdeveloped contract markets and the lack of adequate access to extension services put additional strains to further growth.

Finally, despite strong economic growth and important overseas remittances, the rural poverty incidence is fueled by the small size of the emerged farms and fragmentation, the overall economic uncertainty, and limited off-farm opportunities.

REFERENCES

Christensen, G. 1995. 'Policy Issues for the Agricultural Sector in Albania.' Report commissioned by the FAO, Rome, Italy and Tirana, Albania.

Cungu, A. and J. Swinnen. 1997*a*. 'Agricultural Privatization and Decollectivization in Albania: A Political Economy Perspective.' In *Political Economy of Agrarian Reform in Central and Eastern Europe*, J. Swinnen (ed.). Aldershot: Ashgate.

—— 1997*b*. 'Agricultural Privatization, Land Reform and Farm Restructuring in Albania.' In *Agricultural Privatization, Land Reform and Farm Restructuring in Central and Eastern Europe*, J. Swinnen, A. Buckwell, and Erik Mathijs (eds.). Aldershot: Ashgate.

—— 1999. 'Albania's Radical Agrarian Reform.' *Economic Development and Cultural Change* 47(3): 605–19.

Food and Agriculture Organization of the United Nations/Agricultural University of Tirana (FAO/AUT). 1995. 'Rural Employment Problems in Albania.' Unpublished report by FAO/AUT, Rome-Tirana.

Government of Albania. 1997. 'Albania—Post Conflict Rehabilitation: A Framework of Economic Policies 1997–2000.' Tirana, Albania.

Grace, C. 1996. 'The Hill and Mountain Farmers of Albania.' USAID, Tirana, Albania.

Hatziprokopiou, M. and G. Karagiannis. 1996. 'Production Structure, Technical Change, and Productivity Growth in Albanian Agriculture.' *Journal of Comparative Economics* 22: 295–310.

International Fertilizer Development Center (IFDC). 1994. 'Agricultural Production in Albania, Socio-Economic Survey, 1993–1994.' International Fertilizer Development Center and USAID, Tirana, Albania.

International Monetary Fund (IMF). 1994. 'Albania—Recent Economic Developments.' Washington DC-Tirana, Albania.

Macours, K. and J. Swinnen. 1998. 'Patterns of Agrarian Transition.' PRG Working Paper Series, Department of Agricultural Economics, Katholieke Universiteit, Leuven, Belgium.

Mathijs, E. and J. Swinnen. 1998. 'The Economics of Agricultural Decollectivisation in East Central Europe and the Former Soviet Union.' *Economic Development and Cultural Change* 47(1): 1–26.

Ministry of Agriculture and Food, Government of Albania. 1995. '1994 Special Agricultural Survey.' Tirana, Albania.

Ministry for Economic Development and Cooperation, Government of Albania. 1997. Data provided by the Macroeconomics Department, Ministry for Economic Development and Cooperation, Tirana, Albania.

Olson, M. 1965. *The Logic of the Collective Action: Public Goods and the Theory of Groups.* Cambridge, MA: Harvard University Press.

Stanfield, D. and A. Jazo. 1995. 'Privatization of Immovable Property and the Creation of Land Marker Institutions in Albania.' Paper presented at the 1995 ACSM/ASPRS Convention in Charlotte, NC, 27 February–2 March.

Stiglitz, J. 1993. 'Incentives, Organizational Structures, and Contractual Choice in the Reform of Socialist Agriculture.' In *The Agricultural Transition in Central and European Europe and the Former USSR*, Avishay Braverman, Karen Brooks, and Csaba Csaki (eds.). Washington DC: The World Bank.

Swinnen, J. 1997. 'The Choice of Privatization and Decollectivization Policies in Central and Eastern European Agriculture: Observations and Political Economy Hypotheses.' In *Political Economy of Agrarian Reform in Central and Eastern Europe*, J. Swinnen (ed.). Aldershot: Ashgate.

Swinnen, J. and E. Mathijs. 1997. 'Agricultural Privatisation, Land Reform and Farm Restructuring in Central and Eastern Europe: A Comparative Analysis.' In *Agricultural Privatisation, Land Reform and Farm Restructuring in Central and Eastern Europe*, J. Swinnen, A. Buckwell, and E. Mathijs (eds.). Aldershot: Ashgate.

The World Bank. 1997. 'Albania—Agriculture Sector Assessment.' World Bank Draft Report, Washington DC-Tirana, Albania.

16

Case Study. Post-Communist Land Reform and Changes in Tenure in the Czech Republic

TOMÁŠ DOUCHA, ERIK MATHIJS, AND JOHAN F.M. SWINNEN

Introduction

During Communism, Czech agriculture was organized in large-scale state and collective farms. In 1989—the last year of Communist rule—174 state farms covered 29.2% of total agricultural land (TAL), cultivating on average 6,261 hectares (ha) and employing on average 735 workers. The 1,024 collective farms occupied 70.4% of TAL. They cultivated on average 2,561 ha and employed on average 394 people. Private agriculture was marginal, accounting for only 0.4% of TAL. It was organized in 3,205 small individual farms, cultivating on average 4 ha with 0.6 labor units per farm. Many were operated on a part-time basis.

The ownership of farm assets differed in these three farm types:

- All of the assets in state farms were state-owned: most of the land they used was nationalized before 1948, the start of Communism.
- Non-land assets of collective farms were collectively owned by the members. The land in the collective farms was still formally privately owned by members. However, the owners lost the effective property rights, i.e., rights to decide what to do with the land and were not paid a rent. The collective farm management changed boundaries and designation of parcels without the consent of the formal owners.
- All the assets in private farms were privately owned.

Given these property right categories, post-Communist agricultural reform included:

- The restoration of effective land property rights to individual owners, a process commonly known as *restitution*.[1]
- The *transformation* of collective farms into private businesses and the settlement of property rights to their non-land assets.
- The *privatization* of the state farms, that is, privatizing non-land assets and non-restituted land.

[1] Restitution applies to the land to which owners lost their effective property rights to the collective farms or to the state during Communism, that is, between 1948 and 1990.

The legislative framework for these three main processes was provided by a set of laws passed by the Czechoslovak parliament (which was formed following the first free elections in June 1990) as will be discussed in Section 2. Section 3 reviews the changes in land tenure and the access of land as a result of these laws. Section 4 assesses the implications of these changes on the productivity of Czech agriculture and of different farm types.

Post-Communist property rights reforms[2]

The legislative and institutional framework

Several laws regulate the use of and access to land in the Czech Republic. First, the Land Law settles the property rights of land. The Business Code and Civic Code define the general conditions on exchange of goods and services. The Land Consolidation Law and the Cadastral Law regulate the registration of land titles and the consolidation of fragmented plots and the construction of new infrastructure. Finally, the Environment Protection Law and Land Protection Law oversee the environmental protection of land. However, specific legislation dealing with land leasing, land sales, and the use of land as collateral for loans is still missing. This is a major impediment to the optimal allocation of land. For example, under these conditions, banks do not provide loans on purchases of land.

Within this legislative framework, several institutions were created to facilitate access to land and to regulate its use. The Land Fund administers the land that is still in the hands of the state (about 25% of the total Czech agricultural area). The Land Authority controls transfers of land (e.g., in the framework of restitution) and land consolidation projects. The Cadastral Authority ensures registration of land ownership, including the mapping of parcels. District State Authorities and the Environment Inspection Agency control environment-related issues, including the protection of land. Local governments can influence the land use in their cadastres, as they are authorized to penalize users or owners who do not take proper care of their land. They can also provide development plans for their municipalities and organize land consolidations in their cadastres in co-operation with the District Land Authorities.

Land restitution

The restitution rules of farm assets to which owners lost their property rights during Communism were laid down in several restitution acts of which the Land Law (Act 229/1991) was the most important (passed by Parliament in May 1991). Czech (or Slovak) individuals with permanent residence in Czechoslovakia could claim back the property they (or their predecessors) lost between 25 February 1948 and 1 January

[2] This section is based on Organization for Economic Cooperation and Development (1995), Lindemans (1997), and Ratinger and Rabinowicz (1997).

1990. In most cases, the original property could not be restituted; claimants could receive cash compensation up to CZK 10,000 dollars for non-land assets and receive land plots of equivalent size and quality.[3] The state or collective farm that had been using the land had to approve the legitimacy of the claim and was obliged to give back the land only if the claimant was registered as a farmer or if the claimant had passed on the property rights to another farmer or farm organization.

The restitution of land led to a very fragmented distribution of land property rights: approximately 3 million hectares were restituted to 3 million owners, such that the average size of land ownership is 1 hectare. Only a small share (500,000 or 17% in 1991, and 240,000 or 8% in 1995) of the more than 3 million landowners is active in agriculture.

Land restitution is difficult, particularly the exact identification of boundaries and the provision of physical access to the parcels. During Communism, land consolidation resulted in large fields, often hundreds of hectares in size. In the process, boundaries and the majority of other ownership marks, including points of orientation in the fields, were abolished. As a result, there are persistent problems with identifying the exact boundaries of land parcels in the cadastres.

The state (through the District Land Authorities) covers all expenditures linked with the identification of land boundaries in cadastres for landowners who have decided to reclaim their land. However, when plots are located in the middle of extremely large fields, the physical access to the restituted pieces of land is a problem. According to the present legislation, the collective and state farms that are obliged to give back the land must allocate the land in a way that makes it physically accessible to the restituents. If it is not possible (e.g., for operational reasons or when the land was built on), the farms are obliged to give other pieces of land in the same cadastre of the same size and quality. Despite fears of difficulties and disputes in identifying land of the same size and quality in the given cadastre, the problem does not seem to have materialized significantly.

Previous land consolidation efforts resulted not only in the removal of boundaries, but also of farm field roads. Subsequently constructed field roads alongside the peripheries of large fields belonged to the assets of the collective and state farms. During the reform, they have been transferred to the successor farms, following the Transformation Laws. The reconstruction of the field road networks and other infrastructure are provided under the current land consolidation programs. Despite annual state spending of more than CZK 1 billion dollars (about US $30 million) annually through the District Land Authorities, land consolidation will take several years to be completed.

Privatization of collective farms' non-land assets

The Transformation Law (Act 42/1992) prescribed that the net asset value of all non-land assets be calculated by subtracting from total assets: all debts, the value of

[3] Boundaries could have been changed, buildings erected, roads constructed, etc.

holdings in joint agricultural companies, investment liabilities, provision for outstanding property restitution, and original collectivized assets. Based on this value, the assets were converted into shares. During one month, 25% of these shares were offered for sale to the collective farm members and owners of restituted assets, but only a few of them could afford to buy shares as no special credit schemes were provided. The remaining shares were distributed proportionally to the original contributors by the following rule: 50% in proportion to land, 30% in proportion to original non-land assets, and 20% in proportion to the numbers of years worked on the collective farm.

The distribution of shares had to be approved by an assembly consisting of all eligible persons. New shareholders could withdraw property within 90 days if they intended to use it for farming. The shareholders who become a member (partner) of a new business entity have the right to withdraw assets or receive compensation in cash at the nominal value of the share in accordance with the internal rules governing the new entity, which are in turn subject to the Commercial Code. The settlement of property withdrawal of shareholders who did not become a member (partner) of the new business entity could be delayed up to seven years (until the end of 1999). It is estimated that the value of the assets that cooperatives owe to non-members amounts to about one-third of the cooperatives' total asset value.

Privatization of state farms

Around 25% of the state farm land was restituted. The remainder (767,675 ha in 1994) has been transferred to the Land Fund, a state-controlled institution managing the land and the property that cannot be separated from the land as long as it has not been privatized (Act 569/1991). Most of the land managed by the Land Fund has been leased both to individual farmers and farm organizations pending privatization. The law on the privatization of state land has been discussed in parliament for a long time. The discussions continue on whether the land designated for privatization (about 500,000 ha, i.e., 12% of the total Czech agricultural area) could be purchased only by physical entities (the governmental proposal), or both by physical and legal entities (the proposal of several members of parliament). The decision can significantly impact the structure of tenure and the development of rural areas. For the time being, there is only a general consensus that foreigners are not allowed to buy land.

In principle, state farms could be privatized in the same framework as large-scale industrial privatization (including the voucher method, Act 92/1992). However, only a few state farms were privatized by large-scale voucher privatization. Most state farms' non-land assets have been privatized through sales both to individual farmers and farm companies. New owners were allowed to pay the government in instalments over a long period. Because of most farmers' current financial position, they are not (and in the near future will not be) able to meet payments for the privatized non-land assets, and are very unlikely to be able to purchase the land they currently use. This raises the question of whether the restructuring of the present debts of farms and even the restructuring of farms (including the liquidation of farms) should precede the process of land privatization.

Table 16.1. *Changes in land tenure from 1989 to 1995 in the Czech Republic*

	Number	Total land (1,000 ha)	% leased	Total labor (000 labor units)	Average land use (ha)	Average labor input (labor units)	Share in total land (%)
State farms							
1989	174	1,089	—	128	6,261	734.9	29.2
1995	87	53	—	10	607	112.8	1.3
Collective farms							
1989	1,024	2,622	—	403	2,561	393.7	70.4
1995	—	—	—	—	—	—	—
Cooperatives							
1989	—	—	—	—	—	—	—
1995	1,266	1,832	96	128	1,447	101.3	46.7
Companies							
1989	—	—	—	—	—	—	—
1995	1,573	1,071	95	82	681	51.9	27.3
Partnerships							
1989	—	—	—	—	—	—	—
1995	33	14	95	0.4	409	12.5	0.3
Individual farms							
1989	3,205	13	—	2	4	0.6	0.3
1995	66,201	956	62	41	14	0.6	24.3
Total							
1989	4,403	3,725	—	533	846	121	100.0
1995	69,160	3,925	—	261	57	4	100.0

Source: Ministry of Agriculture and Central Statistical Office.

Changes in land tenure and access to land

Changes in land tenure

Table 16.1 shows that joint stock and limited liability companies cultivated 27.3% of total agricultural land (TAL) in 1995. Cooperatives cultivated 46.7%. Together, these large-scale successor organizations (LSOs) to the collective and state farms still cultivated most Czech agricultural land (74% of TAL) in 1995. Land use by individual farms has increased since 1989 from 0.3% to 24.3% in 1995 (see Figure 16.1). The average size of individual farms has increased from 4 to 14 ha. However, employment has remained unchanged at an average of 0.6 labor units per farm because a significant number of the individual farms are operated on a part-time basis.

All collective farms have been either transformed into a production cooperative or a joint stock company, or have been liquidated. It is impossible to attribute what share of collective farms has been transformed into companies and cooperatives. However, all cooperatives are with certainty successor organizations to the collective farms. They are about half the size of their predecessors (1,447 compared to 2,561 ha).

State farms have virtually disappeared between 1989 and 1995 (from 29 to 1% of TAL). Most of them have been transformed into several joint stock companies and

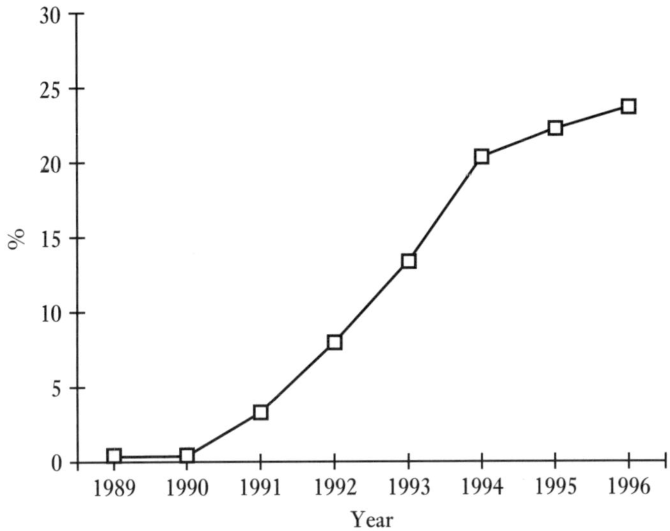

Figure 16.1. *Evolution of the share of individual farms in total agricultural land, 1989–1996*

Table 16.2. *Size distribution of land withdrawn from collective and state farms, 1994*

	Area in 000 ha	%	Cumulative %
Withdrawn land			
Under 2 hectares	89	12.7	12.7
2–5	100	14.3	27.0
5–20	345	49.3	76.3
20–50	94	13.4	89.6
Over 50 hectares	73	10.4	100.0
Total	70	100.0	

Source: Ratinger and Rabinowicz (1997).

they lease land from the state. The average size of joint stock companies is much smaller than the former state farms (681 ha compared to 6,261 ha). The companies are relatively more specialized in intensive animal production.

Most of the restituted land was not withdrawn from LSOs for individual use: by 1994 only 700,034 hectares (18% of TAL) had been withdrawn from LSOs, most of it in farms smaller than 20 hectares (76.3%) (see Table 16.2). The large majority of the land was left in the successor organizations that lease it from the (new) owners: 89% of the land used by the former collective farms was transferred to new cooperatives between 1992 and 1993. As a result of the high incidence of absentee landownership, all types of farms have to lease most of the land they cultivate. In 1995, individual farmers leased 62% of the land they cultivated, while corporate or cooperative farms leased 95–96%.

The high incidence of absentee land ownership does not seem to have significant negative effects on agricultural productivity. Long-term rental contracts prevail and the average rental prices are very low (CZK 400–700 per ha). In 1997, total rents (including other financial payments and payments in kind) represented about 1.5% of total production value.

It is remarkable that individual farms are considerably less important in the Czech Republic than in other CEECs such as Bulgaria (44%), Romania (54%), or Albania (95%), (and considerably less than many had expected *ex ante*). In the next section we discuss which factors have caused this result.

Constraints on the shift to individual tenures

A collective farm member will leave the collective farm if the expected utility from leaving is larger than the expected utility from staying in the collective farm (Carter 1987; Machnes and Schnytzer 1993). Mathijs and Swinnen (1998) show how the break-up of large-scale structures into individual farms in CEECs is a function of the differences in expected income between LSOs and individual farming, net of 'exit costs.' Exit costs are defined as the costs involved in leaving the collective farm and setting up a new individual farm. Factors that affect the expected profitability of individual farming compared to collective farming include the relative productivity of individual and collective farming and the economic and institutional environment (e.g., terms of trade, risk). Exit costs for collective farm members are determined primarily by land reform, privatization, and decollectivization regulations.

The reason why the shift to individual tenures in the Czech Republic is low compared to other CEECs is because the productivity of LSOs is relatively high; they are more capital intensive; and the opportunity costs of labor are higher—all vis-à-vis other CEECs. Exit costs in Czech agriculture are higher due to transformation legislation favoring LSO farming and land restitution, all complicating the withdrawal of assets for individual use (Mathijs and Swinnen 1998).

For example, by restituting land to former owners and distributing non-land assets to collective farm workers (including pensioners) in shares, reform legislation has resulted in a mismatch of land and non-land assets. Insiders who are not former owners of land only own business shares in the LSO they are (or used to be) members of. These insiders have to turn to the market to acquire land for individual use where they face considerable transaction costs. These transaction costs are higher for these individuals than for the LSOs, as the latter typically play an important role in privatization implementation, have better access to information, and possibly also to resources available for dealing with transaction costs. (Prior to 1999, outsiders could not withdraw non-land assets from the LSO, nor cash in or trade the business shares they received.)

Furthermore, LSOs in the Czech Republic (and also in Hungary and Slovakia) have been successful in improving their labor productivity because of massive labor shedding (see Figure 16.2). The reason for this is (again vis-à-vis other CEECs) the relative independence of Czech LSO managers in making labor decisions, but especially the high opportunity costs of farm labor because of low unemployment (3%) and relatively

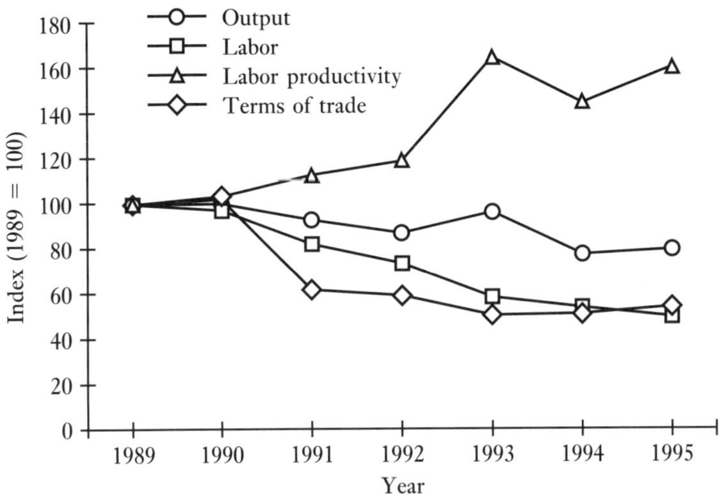

Figure 16.2. *Changes in agricultural output, labor, labor productivity, and terms of trade, 1989–1995*

generous welfare schemes (Macours and Swinnen 1997*b*). Out of all workers that left agriculture since 1989, about 50% retired, 45% started working outside of agriculture (75% in urban and 25% in rural areas), and 5% were unemployed.

In addition, about one-third of the officially registered decline in agricultural labor use was due to the separation of non-agricultural activities (e.g., repair and construction services, industrial production) from the collective farm. This factor was especially important in the period of initial farm restructuring (1990–92). Since then, the continued decline in agricultural workers was due to retirement and migration to other jobs. Hence, by 1997, each factor (non-agricultural activities, retirement, other jobs) accounted for approximately one-third of the total reduction of farm labor.

Future developments

Figure 16.1 shows how the increase in individual tenures has slowed since 1994. Does this imply that the current situation will be a long-run equilibrium? Not necessarily. Whether important shifts toward individual tenures can be expected will depend on two key factors: the settlement of the LSOs' old debts, and the demands from shareholders who want to cash in their business shares. The LSOs are lobbying the government to extend the deadline; if LSOs are released from these obligations, there is a good chance that they will survive in the medium term. But if the government decides to impose hard budget constraints and insists on paying shareholders who want to cash in their shares from 1999 onwards, productivity of LSOs will decrease and members will withdraw their land and start up individual farms. In addition, the future sale of state farmland (12% of TAL) will improve the access to land for many individuals who want to start an individual farm.

Implications of changes in land tenure on productivity

Aggregate productivity

Czech agricultural output has declined around 20% between 1989 and 1994. Since 1994, agricultural output has stabilized (see Figure 16.2). A key cause was the change in terms of trade that declined sharply in 1991 following the liberalization of output and input prices.

Using a production function and supply response framework, Macours and Swinnen (1997*a*) calculated for Albania, Bulgaria, the Czech Republic, Hungary, Poland, Romania, Slovakia, and Slovenia that the deterioration of the agricultural terms of trade explains on average 40 to 45% of the change in crop output. Weather conditions explain 10 to 20% of the output decline, whereas transition uncertainty accounts for 10 to 15%. The structural reforms influenced production in two ways: the shift of production to individual tenures caused on average a productivity increase due to improved labor effort, but the disruptions of the production structures due to the reforms caused a (temporary) negative effect. Overall, privatization had a strong negative effect on output mainly as a result of labor outflow from agriculture.

Strong labor outflow is especially important in the Czech Republic (as well as in Slovakia and Hungary). With very little change in land use, the factor mix in agriculture changed strongly: the labor to land ratio declined from about 14 labor units per 100 hectares to about 7 (see Figure 16.3). Importantly, as labor input has declined much stronger than output, aggregate labor productivity has increased substantially between 1989 and 1995 (see Figure 16.2).

Productivity differences between farms

In analyzing the efficiency of different farm organizations, it is convenient to make a distinction between 'scale efficiency' and 'technical efficiency.' A farm is *technically efficient* if it produces on the boundary of the production possibilities set, that is, it maximizes output with given inputs and after having chosen technology. This boundary is defined as the best practice observed (Färe, Grosskopf, and Lovell 1985). Two sets of constraints on technical efficiency can be distinguished. First, some enterprise structures (e.g., cooperatives) may display low technical efficiency because of *internal* constraints. For example, the workforce may not have enough incentives to provide maximum effort. The governance structure in such enterprises does not prevent farm workers from shirking (Carter 1984, 1987; Lin 1988). Self-enforcing contracts can be set up to solve this problem (Lin 1990). Second, technical inefficiency may result from *external* constraints, e.g., imposed upon their farms by government (restrictions, obligations) or the up- and downstream industries (delayed payments, buyers' or suppliers' monopoly).

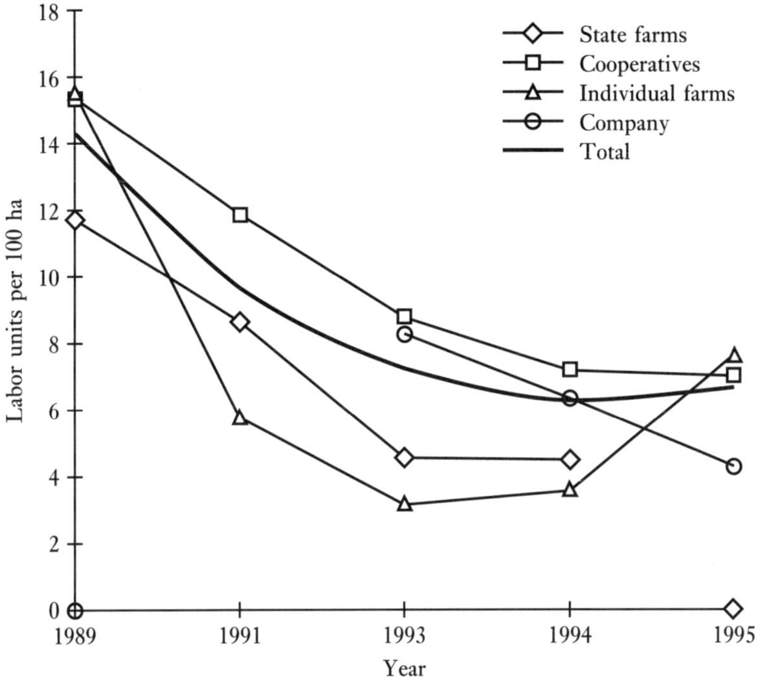

Figure 16.3. *Man/land ratio (labor units per 100 ha), 1989–1995*

Scale (in)efficiency refers to the deviation from the minimum of the long-run average-cost curve (Chavas and Aliber 1993). Farms may be technically efficient, but scale inefficient. This may be due to a lack of access to credit and inputs or because farms are not maximizing profits. Earlier evidence from Slovenia (Piesse, Thirtle, and Turk 1996) and Eastern Germany (Mathijs and Swinnen 1997) suggest a trade-off between technical and scale efficiency. These studies found that individual farms display higher technical efficiency, but lower scale efficiency than their corporate or cooperative counterparts.

Mathijs *et al.* (1998) used accounts from a panel of farms collected by the Research Institute of Agricultural Economics (VÚZE) to calculate technical and scale efficiency in Czech agriculture. The database contains data for 1996 on output, labor, land, and capital for about 900 farms. After cleaning the data and excluding farms with less than 70% of their revenues originating from agricultural production, 27 joint stock companies, 102 production cooperatives, and 109 individual farms were retained for analysis.

Output is calculated by valuing physical production at national average prices to control for price differences between farms. Crop products produced for own consumption in animal production were excluded to avoid double counting. Labor units were recalculated on the basis of 2,150 working hours per worker per year. Land is total agricultural land in hectares. (Quality adjustments were available, but did not change the results significantly.) Capital represents the total value of assets reported on the balance sheet.

Table 16.3. *Non-parametric efficiency measures per production specialization*

	Number	Total efficiency	Technical efficiency	Scale efficiency
Animal production				
Company	—	—	—	—
Cooperative	6	67.5	92.0	73.4*
Individual farm	24	79.1	86.8	91.1
Crop production				
Company	4	62.1	83.5	74.4
Cooperative	2	46.3**	59.5**	77.8
Individual farm	49	64.4	81.0	79.5
Mixed production				
Company	23	57.6	58.3***	98.8***
Cooperative	90	58.6	59.6***	98.3***
Individual farm	29	56.0	85.4	65.6

Note: statistical significance of pair-wise differences with individual farms as reference point is given at the 1%***, 5%**, and 10%* level.

Source: Mathijs *et al.* (1998).

Mathijs *et al.* (1998) calculated radial measures of efficiency for each farm by assuming a deterministic production frontier characterized by a piece-wise linear technology and strong disposability of outputs and inputs. Efficiency is measured relative to this frontier, which joins the best-practice farms within the data set considered.[4] Calculations were made both based on the whole data set (a single frontier) and per production sector (a frontier for each specialization). Farms were categorized in the following specializations: crop production, animal production, and mixed production (combination of crops and animal production), based on the share of crops or animal products in total sales.

Different farm types are compared controlling for production specialization, that is, a frontier is calculated for each production specialization separately, and comparisons are made within a specialization. Table 16.3 shows how the results differ between the production specializations:

- In crop farming, there is little difference between companies and individual farms. However, cooperatives display considerably lower levels of technical efficiency than individual farms (−21%) and companies (−24%). Scale efficiency does not differ much between farm types.

[4] This technique is also referred to as Data Envelopment Analysis (DEA). See Farrell (1957), Charnes, Cooper, and Rhodes (1978), Banker, Charnes, and Cooper (1984), Färe, Grosskopf, and Lovell (1985), and Chavas and Aliber (1993) for the theoretical background on DEA and Piesse, Thirtle, and Turk (1996) and Mathijs and Swinnen (1997) for empirical applications on Central European farms.

- In animal farming, technical efficiency does not differ much between individual farms and cooperatives. However, total efficiency is 12% higher in individual farms than in cooperatives. Somewhat surprisingly, the analysis suggests that this is mainly due to scale (dis)economies.
- In mixed farming, which includes most LSOs, there is a clear trade-off for individual farms between higher technical efficiency (17 and 18% higher than companies and cooperatives) and lower scale efficiency (23% lower than companies and cooperatives). As a result, there are hardly any differences in total efficiency between the farm types. Contrary to crop farming, there is hardly any difference in (technical and scale) efficiency between cooperatives and companies.

To conclude, individual farms display higher levels of technical efficiency than cooperatives in crop and mixed farming. They do not in animal farming. Moreover, companies display comparable levels of technical efficiency in mixed farming to cooperatives, but are clearly more efficient in crop farming. The scale inefficiency of individual farms can only be confirmed for mixed farming. Individual animal farms are even more scale efficient than cooperatives. A more disaggregated analysis of scale efficiency reveals that there is a big difference between small and large individual farms. These differences give rise to an L-shaped average cost-curve. Hence, the lower scale efficiency of individual farms is mostly relevant for the smallest individual farms. Larger individual farms are able to combine scale efficiency and technical efficiency.

Conclusions

The shift from collective to individual tenure following the democratic changes in 1990 has been modest in Czech agriculture compared to other Central and Eastern European countries: only about a quarter of total agricultural land was cultivated by individual farms in 1995. This lack of 'decollectivization' can be explained in part by the lack of incentives for individuals to start up an individual farm: technology is advanced and requires considerable capital investment, while the transition imposes constraints on individual farmers to deal with high uncertainty, disadvantageous terms of trade, and missing markets.

In addition to these adverse conditions, the reform legislation regulating the privatization of state property, and the transformation of the old collective and state farms has created high transaction costs for individuals to access land and other farm assets. Individuals wishing to start up an individual farm face significant transaction costs when they want to withdraw land and non-land assets from the large-scale successor farms of the state and collective farms. Land and non-land assets are locked-in this way in the large-scale successor farms. In addition, most farms have to lease land, adding to the tenure uncertainty of both collective and individual tenures.

The reduced access of individual farmers to land and non-land assets is translated into lower levels of scale efficiency compared to large-scale companies and cooperatives. This is especially the case for the smallest farms. However, individual tenures are technically more efficient than collective tenures.

REFERENCES

Banker, R.D., A. Charnes, and W.W. Cooper. 1984. 'Some Models for Estimating Technical and Scale Efficiency in Data Envelopment Analysis.' *Management Science* 30(9): 1078–92.

Brooks, K. and M. Meurs. 1994. 'Romanian Land Reform: 1991–1993.' *Comparative Economic Studies* 32(2): 17–32.

Carter, M.R. 1984. 'Resource Allocation and Use Under Collective Rights and Labor Management in Peruvian Coastal Agriculture.' *Economic Journal* 94(376): 826–46.

—— 1987. 'Risk Sharing and Incentives in the Decollectivization of Agriculture.' *Oxford Economic Papers* 39(3): 577–95.

Charnes, A., W.W. Cooper, and E. Rhodes. 1978. 'Measuring the Efficiency of Decision Making Units.' *European Journal of Operations Research* 2(6): 429–44.

Chavas, J.-P. and M. Aliber. 1993. 'An Analysis of Economic Efficiency in Agriculture: A Nonparametric Approach.' *Journal of Agricultural and Resource Economics* 18(1): 1–16.

Deininger, K. 1995. 'Collective Agricultural Production: A Solution For Transition Economies?' *World Development* 23(8): 1317–34.

Doucha, T. and A. Jurica. 1997. 'Farm Structure and Farm Managers in the Transition Period: The Case of the Czech Republic.' Working paper, Research Institute of Agricultural Economics (VÚZE), Prague.

Färe, R., S. Grosskopf, and C.A.K. Lovell. 1985. *The Measurement of Efficiency in Production.* Boston, MA: Kluwer-Nijhoff.

Farrell, Michael J. 1957. 'The Measurement of Productive Efficiency.' *Journal of the Royal Statistical Society* 120(3): 253–82.

Gow, H.R. and J.F.M. Swinnen. 1998. 'Up- and Downstream Restructuring, Hold-Ups and Foreign Direct Investment in Transition Agriculture.' *European Review of Agricultural Economics* 25(3): 331–50.

Lin, J.Y. 1988. 'The Household Responsibility System in China's Agricultural Reform: A Theoretical and Empirical Study.' *Economic Development and Cultural Change* 36(3): S199–S224.

—— 1990. 'Collectivization and China's Agricultural Crisis in 1959–1961.' *Journal of Political Economy* 98(6): 1228–52.

Lindemans, I. 1997. 'Process and Politics of Agricultural Privatization in the Czech and Slovak Republics.' In *Political Economy of Agrarian Reform in Central and Eastern Europe*, J.F.M. Swinnen (ed.). Ashgate: Aldershot.

Lyons, R., G. Rausser, and L. Simon. 1994. 'Disruption and Continuity in Bulgaria's Agrarian Reform.' In *Privatization of Agriculture in New Market Economies: Lessons from Bulgaria*, A. Schmitz, K. Moulton, A. Buckwell and S. Davidova (eds.). Norwell, MA: Kluwer Academic Publishers.

Machnes, Y. and A. Schnytzer. 1993. 'Risk and the Collective Farm in Transition.' In *Agricultural Cooperatives in Transition*, C. Csaki and Y. Kislev (eds.). Boulder, CO: Westview Press.

Macours, K. and J.F.M. Swinnen. 1997*a*. 'Causes of Output Decline in Economic Transition: The Case of Central and Eastern European Agriculture.' Policy Research Group Working Paper No. 11, Department of Agricultural Economics, Katholieke Universiteit, Leuven, Belgium.

—— 1997*b*. 'Agricultural Labour Adjustments during Transition in Central and Eastern Europe.' Policy Research Group Working Paper No. 13, Department of Agricultural Economics, Katholieke Universiteit, Leuven, Belgium.

Mathijs, E. and J.F.M. Swinnen. 1997. 'Production Organization and Efficiency During Transition: The Case of East German Agriculture.' Policy Research Group Working Paper No. 7, Department of Agricultural Economics, Katholieke Universiteit, Leuven, Belgium.

—— 1998. 'The Economics of Agricultural Decollectivization in East Central Europe and the Former Soviet Union.' *Economic Development and Cultural Change* 47(41): 1–26.

Mathijs, E., T. Doucha, L. Dries, and Johan F.M. Swinnen. 1998. 'Production Organization and Efficiency of Czech Agriculture.' Policy Research Group Working Paper No. 14, Department of Agricultural Economics, Katholieke Universiteit, Leuven, Belgium.

Office of Economic Development (OECD). 1995. *Review of Agricultural Policies: The Czech Republic*. Paris: OECD.

Piesse, J., C. Thirtle, and J. Turk. 1996. 'Efficiency and Ownership in Slovene Dairying: A Comparison of Econometric and Programming Techniques.' *Journal of Comparative Economics* 22(1): 1–22.

Ratinger, T. and E. Rabinowicz. 1997. 'Changes in Farming Structures in the Czech Republic as a Result of Land Reform and Privatisation.' In *Agricultural Privatisation, Land Reform and Farm Restructuring in Central and Eastern Europe*, J.F.M. Swinnen, A. Buckwell, and E. Mathijs (eds.). Aldershot: Ashgate.

Swinnen, J.F.M. 1995. 'Agricultural Credit Problems during the Transition to a Market Economy in Central and Eastern Europe.' In *Agro-Food Sector Policy in OECD Countries and the Russian Federation*, OECD Centre for Co-operation with the Economies in Transition. Paris: OECD.

—— 1997. 'Does Compensation for Disruptions Stimulate Reforms? The Case of Agrarian Reform in Central and Eastern Europe.' *European Review of Agricultural Economics* 24(2): 249–66.

17

The Evolution of the World Bank's Land Policy

KLAUS DEININGER AND HANS BINSWANGER

Introduction

In rural areas of most developing countries, land is not only the primary means for generating a livelihood but often also the vehicle to accumulate wealth and transfer it between generations. Due to the key role land plays in rural life, the ways in which access to this resource are regulated, land rights are assigned, and conflicts around land ownership are resolved have broad implications beyond the sphere of agricultural production. These factors (among others) affect: (1) the ability of households to produce for their subsistence and generate marketable surplus; (2) the social and economic status of households (and often their collective identity); (3) their incentive to exert non-contractible effort, make investments, and use scarce natural resources in a sustainable manner; and (4) their ability to self-insure and/or access financial markets. It is thus not surprising that the institutional, policy, and regulatory framework that governs ownership rights to land and the way in which they are distributed is deeply engrained in the institutional fabric of societies, with far-reaching implications for overall economic development.

Land rights and the administrative infrastructure needed to facilitate the smooth operation of land markets are important public goods. However, instead of helping to establish an environment where markets can cheaply allocate land to more efficient users, throughout history governments have taken measures that have distorted the operation of land as well as other factor markets, over and above the difficulties posed by material conditions in rural areas. This has not only reduced static efficiency but also, by reducing the scope for the accumulation of human and physical capital, negatively affected overall growth in rural areas. It has made it more difficult for rural financial markets to emerge and has diminished the opportunities for the poor to use such markets as a means to accumulate physical and human capital. As countries have undertaken adjustment policies to restore macro-economic balance, they have discovered that, where property rights are non-existent or ill-defined, or where assets are distributed in a way

We would like to thank Alain de Janvry, Gustavo Gordillo de Anda, Michael Carter, Pedro Olinto, Shem Migot-Adholla, and participants at a WIDER workshop in Santiago for very detailed comments. The opinions expressed in this chapter are our own and do not necessarily reflect those of the World Bank, its Executive Directors, or the countries they represent.

that marginalizes large parts of the population, 'getting prices right' alone is not enough for rural factor markets to function properly. To address this issue and provide the basis for a sustained reduction in rural poverty, a second generation of more structural reforms will be needed.

In undertaking such structural reforms, it is natural to look for guidance in historical experience and precedent. Indeed, the World Bank (Bank) has long been aware of the importance of land issues for sustainable poverty reduction and economic development. To guide its policy in this area, in 1975 it issued a 'Land Reform Policy Paper' (LRPP). This chapter reviews the LRPP's recommendations, the analytical foundations on which they were built, and the lessons learned from their implementation. The goal is to provide a state-of-the-art picture of the World Bank's policy in dealing with land issues that can serve as a guideline for assessing the adequacy of Bank interventions in the future.

The key principles enunciated in 1975 were: the desirability of owner-operated family farms, both on efficiency and equity grounds; the need to promote markets to facilitate efficiency-enhancing transfers to better and more efficient users; and the desirability of an egalitarian asset distribution and redistributive land reform. These conceptual foundations remain as valid today as they were more than twenty years ago. However, sweeping changes in the international environment, among them, the collapse of Communism and the end of the cold war, and the broad move towards liberalization of agricultural trade, have considerably changed the way in which these principles are implemented in practice.

First, the Bank discovered that the past approach of initiating narrow interventions in individual areas (such as titling) to establish the basis for a broader policy dialogue did not reach this objective. It was gradually replaced by a strategy that aims to base land market interventions on a broad and encompassing policy dialogue and consensus in the client country. In countries where land issues have in the past been the cause of wars, revolutions, and civil strife, reaching such a consensus requires time and a sustained dialogue on key policy issues between government, NGOs, and civil society at large. Initiating such a process, ensuring its integration into a broader framework of rural development interventions, and strengthening the capacity of key players has become a critical component of the Bank's 'land policy.'

Second, the political sensitivity of land issues, and the need to adapt implementation to location-specific conditions, often requires that the viability of proposed approaches be demonstrated on a small scale before policy makers are willing to adopt them on a broader basis. In response to this need, Bank projects in the area of land are, in many cases, preceded by extensive pilots in diverse regions to benefit from the feedback by local stakeholders and to ensure that the approach is suitable and implementable under local conditions. As decentralized implementation is contingent on the availability of the necessary capacity, these pilots are generally demand-driven and combined with capacity-building efforts at the local level.

Finally, a significant research effort—much of it supported by the Bank—has helped to clarify and better understand key issues associated with land tenure and land rights, and has led to significant changes in the World Bank's policy recommendations:

- Instead of recommending abandonment of communal tenure systems in favor of freehold title and subdivision of the commons (as in the LRPP), the Bank now recognizes that communal tenure systems are often a more cost-effective solution than formal title and that, in situations where this is the case, efforts to reduce the cost of cooperation, improve accountability, and facilitate evolution of communal systems in response to local needs may be necessary.
- In addition to clarifying the preconditions for titling to be economically viable, research has shown that in situations where credit markets are imperfect, the benefits from titling programs can easily favor the better off, implying a need for greater attention to the functioning of other factor markets and the equity impact of titling programs.
- Instead of expecting the liberalization of land sales markets to lead to instantaneous transfers of land to more efficient producers, it is now understood that under (credit) market imperfections common in rural areas or in the presence of policy distortions, land sales markets may not increase efficiency or equity, and a more integrated approach to the development of rural factor markets is needed.
- The LRPP's support for redistributive land reform on both efficiency and equity grounds has been vindicated by a growing literature on the importance of asset ownership for human and physical capital formation and economic growth. Empirical experience on the potential and shortcomings of this approach is, however, still limited and should be generated, in a learning process, jointly with the countries currently implementing such reforms.

This chapter is structured as follows: Section 2 highlights how land policies relate to the Bank's main goals of economic growth and poverty reduction; Section 3 examines the analytical basis underlying the LRPP's main conclusions and how this held up to evidence that became available more recently; Section 4 focuses on how these principles might be implemented in an actual setting, and the implications for modifying the LRPP's recommendations; and Section 5 concludes by outlining challenges facing future operations and research.

The rationale for the Bank's interest in land issues

Land issues are of critical importance for the World Bank's dual objective of fostering economic growth and sustainably reducing poverty. It has long been recognized that a framework of secure, transparent, and enforceable property rights is a critical precondition for investment and economic growth. In addition, access to land allows the poor to make more productive use of family labor, to smooth consumption, and in many cases to access credit markets. The importance of land *distribution* for growth as well as poverty reduction is confirmed by aggregate cross-country regressions.

Security of property rights as the basis for sustainable growth and economic development

Property rights that provide longer-term tenure security will increase the demand for long-term investment and thereby establish the basis for an increase in the capital stock. For example in Ghana, having more secure tenure to a certain plot increases the probability that individuals will plant trees, and undertake a wide range of other investments such as drainage, irrigation, mulching, etc. (Besley 1995). The need for a 'minimum' level of tenure security (which need not necessarily be a formal title) to facilitate improvements clearly emerges from Burkina Faso (Brasselle, Gaspart, and Platteau 1997) and Niger (Gavian and Fafchamps 1996). Similarly, in China, higher tenure security increases investment (Yao 1996) and the same farmers apply more manure and labor, and obtain significantly higher yields on plots to which they have more securely defined property rights (Rozelle, Guo, and Brandt 1996). In India, where tenure security was already high, possession of title did not do much to increase investment. Nonetheless, it was associated with a 15% increase in land values (Pender and Kerr 1994). Individual property rights, even if they are only of a temporary nature, will increase individuals' incentives to work hard, as is illustrated by the tremendous productivity increases associated with the transition from collective to individual (*usufruct*) rights, e.g., in China (McMillan, Whalley, and Zhu 1989; Lin 1992).

Secure land ownership is likely to increase the supply of credit from the formal credit system, in addition to augmenting demand for investment, thus making an important contribution to the evolution of financial markets in more general terms. Because of its immobility and virtual indestructibility, land is an ideal collateral with secure, clearly defined, and easily transferable ownership rights. Formal title to land would therefore not only increase an individual's incentive to undertake land-related investments but also would reduce the cost of credit needed for such investments. The importance of this 'credit supply effect' is supported by evidence from Thailand where title-owners' better access to credit enabled them to invest more, resulting in titled land having significantly higher market values and higher productivity per unit than untitled land (Feder, Onchan, and Raparta 1988). Similar findings are reported from Brazil (Alston, Eggertson, and North 1996), Honduras (Lopez 1997), and Paraguay (Carter and Olinto 1996) using panel data. In line with the above, title was found to have little impact on farm investment or farm income where no formal credit markets were available (Atwood 1990; Carter and Wiebe 1990; Migot-Adholla *et al.* 1991).

Due to the immobility of land, land markets are normally highly localized. As a consequence, the ability to transfer land between users may be of limited importance in the early stages of development when there is little heterogeneity of skills across the population, and where inter-regional migration and non-agricultural opportunities are limited. However, the importance and value of being able to transfer use—or ownership—rights to land does increase with economic development, specialization, and better functioning of other markets. Secure ownership rights to land will therefore enhance allocative efficiency in the economy, a hypothesis that is indeed confirmed by data from China (Yao 1996).

Lack of enforceable—though not always *individual*—property rights is a key factor in many cases of unsustainable use and natural resource degradation. The breakdown of communities' ability to coordinate was shown to be at the root of environmental degradation in Mexico (Key *et al.* 1998; McCarthy, de Janvry, and Sadoulet 1998). While privatization of property rights is clearly not a magic solution (Andre and Platteau 1996), helping communities to develop structures that overcome these problems and establish effective property right regimes can enhance the sustainability of resource use, prevent environmental degradation, and promote the overall efficiency of land use (Baland and Platteau 1996).

Land as a fundamental asset for the poor

Property rights are not only of relevance for economic growth in general but they are of particular importance to the poor, for a number of reasons. First, lack of property rights does in many cases exclude the poor from equally sharing in economic opportunities (de Soto 1989). A more egalitarian distribution of land ownership would not only increase their welfare but also aggregate production (Mookherjee 1997; Bardhan, Bowles, and Gintis 1998) to the degree that it enhances the bargaining power of potential tenants, as compared to the landlord and tenant in an environment where effort is not enforceable.

A second way in which land ownership would affect poverty is through credit-financed investment. The underlying idea is that lack of collateral precludes individuals from making indivisible investments (in schooling, bullocks, wells, or perennials) that would have to be financed out of credit. In this case, even though the investments would be profitable both socially and individually, and credit-unconstrained individuals would easily be able to undertake them (Galor and Zeira 1993; Eckstein and Zilcha 1994), poor people who do not have access to assets might be caught in 'poverty traps.' They would then fail to get out of poverty not because they are unproductive or lack skills, but because, due to credit market imperfections, they never get the opportunity to utilize their innate ability. Indeed, emerging empirical evidence suggests that such poverty traps may indeed exist (Jalan and Ravallion 1997; Fafchamps and Pender 1997).

A third mechanism is that, in settings where credit and product markets are incomplete, access to land has a large impact on nutritional welfare (larger than the redistribution of output or income generated from the same land) because land ownership does fulfill an important function as an insurance substitute and an efficient source of self-employment. Evidence from China suggests that households' access to land acts as an *ex ante* lump sum transfer, provides effective insurance against low nutritional outcomes, and is much more efficient and incentive-compatible than an *ex post* redistribution. Land is distributed largely independently of economic status. Even though households within any given village are only moderately insured against idiosyncratic income shocks, there is almost complete insurance against malnutrition (Burgess 1997). This insurance benefit seems to be at the root of customs such as the biblical law to periodically redistribute land, to leave spaces for communal grazing, or to provide the poor with the possibility of collecting leftovers. Many of these survive up to this day in communal tenure systems.

While cross-country regressions are not able to distinguish which of the specific channels (bargaining, investment, or insurance) is at work, they do provide support for the importance of asset (and income) distribution on economic outcomes and the welfare of the poor in particular. Such regressions indicate the presence of a significant negative impact of the initial *asset* distribution on subsequent economic growth (Birdsall and Londoño 1997). This growth-reducing impact is particularly severe for the poor (Deininger and Squire 1998). Indeed, overall inequality seems to have an important impact on societies' ability to effectively and quickly respond to exogenous shocks (Rodrik 1998), the level of crime (Fajnzylber, Lederman, and Loayza 1998), and the degree to which special interest groups are able to appropriate rents in the political arena—with implications for overall productive efficiency (Banerjee *et al.* 1997).

Secure property rights as a key public good

Clarification of property rights and the establishment of a system for efficient conflict resolution can prevent wasteful 'overinvestment' by individuals in staking out and defending their property rights, increase investment due to higher tenure security, and provide the basis for land markets to bring about a larger number of efficiency-enhancing transactions. Property rights are a public good and, in the absence of public enforcement and the sanctioning of property rights, individuals will overinvest in protective measures to claim and secure such property rights (Malik and Schwab 1991). The privately 'optimal' amount of spending by individuals on means of protection will be inefficient from a social point of view (Feder and Feeny 1991; de Meza and Gould 1992). This is of particular importance if the ways in which such ownership rights are claimed or secured are associated with negative environmental externalities, as is the case in many frontier situations. In many of these, unsustainable practices are followed, not because of their inherent profitability, but because of legal stipulations (proper use clause) or the inability to enforce them (Binswanger 1991).

Even where publicly sanctioned property rights exist, they are often not well defined or enforced. This situation not only causes societies to forgo economic benefits and dissipate valuable resources in disputes, but also undermines the basis for the development of an efficient financial sector. In countries where post-conflict settlement is a critical issue (e.g., South Africa, Nicaragua, El Salvador, Mozambique, Angola, Uganda, Vietnam, Laos, and Cambodia), the clarification of ownership rights and the establishment of institutions that facilitate effective and low-cost dispute resolution are key elements of structural reforms.

In addition to the two channels discussed above, written records of land ownership allow the verification of ownership status at low cost, thus reducing the scope for asymmetric information about ownership and the quality of land, and making land sales and rentals cheaper to implement. This reduction of transaction costs would increase the liquidity of the land market and could bring the number of efficiency-enhancing transactions closer to the optimum, i.e., helping to transfer more land from less productive to more productive individuals.

The conceptual basis of the Bank's land policy

The conceptual basis for the Bank's land policy—in 1975 as well as today—is based on three key elements, namely (1) the desirability of smallholder agriculture from an equity as well as an efficiency perspective; (2) the desire to facilitate efficiency-enhancing transfers of land to better users through land sales and rental markets; and (3) the desirability (but also the difficulty) of land reform.

Efficiency of owner-operated family farms

A fundamental principle enunciated in the LRPP is that owner-operated smallholder farms are desirable from an equity as well as an efficiency perspective. The reason is that there are few, if any, economies of scale in agricultural production, but that hired labor (in contrast to family labor) requires costly supervision. These advantages can, however, be offset by credit market disadvantages which may arise due to the high transaction costs associated with providing credit to small producers.

Economies of scale can arise from the presence of indivisible factors of production which would lead to an initial portion of declining average costs with farm size. In agricultural production, such indivisibility arises with respect to machinery, management, and marketing. Machinery, such as tractors for plowing, is clearly an indivisible input. However, the farm size at which a pair of bullocks or a small tractor can be fully utilized is small (Jodha 1984), implying that indivisibilities associated with machinery alone rarely increase optimal farm size beyond the level at which, with existing technology, family labor is fully utilized. Even where they would, rental markets can partially overcome this indivisibility.[1] This is in line with the finding that, both in developing and developed country agriculture, the optimal size of a farm—in environments where other markets function reasonably well—generally does not exceed the scale at which family labor is fully occupied (utilizing seasonal hired labor for specific tasks). A large number of empirical studies (Olson-Lanjouw 1995 for India; Feder *et al.* 1989 and Burgess 1997 for China; Chavas and Cox 1994 for the US) are indeed unable to reject the hypothesis of constant returns to scale in agricultural production.

While agricultural production is characterized by absence of economies of scale with the exception of a few specialized cases (e.g., intensive broiler production), economies of scale do exist in processing and marketing of many agricultural products. This is, however, not of importance for the size of farming operations as long as products are storable and competitive markets for outputs and inputs do exist. Only where markets do not exist and in the case of a few 'plantation crops' such as sugarcane, bananas, or tea does the need for immediate large-scale processing or marketing transmit economies of scale from the processing stage to production. To reap the economies of scale associated with the former, production of these crops is generally organized on a scale that corresponds to the optimum scale of the processing factory. Even in this case, the supervision advantages of owner-operators have in many cases motivated large processors to contract production out to smallholders under outgrower or contract farming schemes, often providing credit in kind as well as technical assistance (Glover 1990).

[1] Farm management and supervisory skills are of importance not only because farmers with better management skill will operate larger farm units, but also because they will generally want to obtain a remuneration for their management input, comparable to what could be obtained in other sectors of the economy. This leads farm operators to substitute capital for labor as non-agricultural wage rates increase (Kislev and Peterson 1982). Such an increase in farm size over time does not necessarily indicate the presence of increasing returns to scale.

Constant returns to scale would imply that the size of agricultural operations has little impact on economic efficiency. By contrast, the need to supervise hired labor would confer a productivity advantage on owner-operated farm units. The fundamental reason for family-operated farms to have an efficiency advantage is the presence of agency costs (Jensen and Meckling 1976), which result from the need to manage wage labor and enforce effort on large-scale operations. The cost of supervision is particularly large in agricultural production due to spatial dispersion of the production process and the need to constantly adjust to micro-variations of the natural environment. It has therefore long been recognized that supervisory capacity is an important determinant of the mode of operation of large tracts of land (Feder 1985; Eswaran and Kotwal 1985). The fact that family members are residual claimants to profits and thus have higher incentives to provide effort than hired labor, that they share in the risk, and that they can be employed without incurring hiring or search costs, are some of the main reasons for the superiority of family over large-scale wage operations.

Indeed empirical evidence indicates that hired labor is not only less productive than family labor, but also that the intensity of supervision matters (Frisvold 1994). A large number of studies based on aggregate or cross-sectional data confirm the existence of a negative farm-size productivity relationship for all but the smallest farm size classes (Berry and Cline 1979; Carter 1984; Benjamin 1995; Newell, Pandya, and Symons 1997; Kutcher and Scandizzo 1981). The relationship weakens if adjustments for soil quality are made (Bhalla and Roy 1988; Benjamin 1995). However, a number of studies using panel data with household- or plot-specific effects confirm the existence of a negative farm size productivity relationship (Burgess 1997; Olinto 1995; Udry 1996).

One implication from the above that is clearly recognized in the LRPP is that collective farms are not an efficient form of production. The three main reasons for their inferior performance are that (1) members do not receive the full benefits from increased effort supply (free rider problem); (2) investment incentives are diminished because members' ability to benefit from the collective's assets ends with the termination of membership; and (3) there is an incentive to gradually reduce the number of members —often coupled with the utilization of government subsidies to embark on a capital-intensive path of development—which implies that collectives generate much less employment than small (or even large) farms would. This is supported by the fact that, all over the world, collectives performed very badly (Peru, Vietnam, Ethiopia, Nicaragua, Cuba, China) and steps were taken to replace them with increased individual responsibility for production. Progress towards the establishment of individual farms is uneven; the two main determinants being initial conditions (individual land title; experience with farming), and the degree to which markets for inputs and outputs, credit, and services exist and are accessible to small cultivators.

Desirability of efficiency enhancing transfers

The LRPP is very clear about the fact that transfers of land from less to more productive users provide the justification for interventions aimed at improved functioning of land markets. However, this recommendation does not appropriately account for the imperfections commonly encountered in rural areas of developing countries, which would imply that actually observed market outcomes might deviate considerably from the ideal world of perfect markets. Indeed, the supervision cost advantage of small farmers could easily be overturned if they are either completely rationed out of credit markets or face higher credit costs. In this case, land sales markets could lead to efficiency- and equity-*reducing* transfers. As land rental markets would be less affected by issues related to access to credit, increased reliance on rental markets might be more effective in promoting goals of efficiency and equity.[2]

In cases where access to capital markets is imperfect, the disadvantage of small farms in accessing markets for credit and insurance, and their more limited ability to cope with risk, could offset the supervision cost advantage of small family farms. Indeed, empirical evidence points to a wide variety of conditions, depending largely on small farmers' ability to access capital markets. For example in the Sudan, capital market imperfections together with reasonably functioning land and labor markets, and a technology that was not too supervision-intensive led to the emergence of a positive farm-size productivity relationship (Kevane 1996). By contrast, in panel data from Burkina Faso an inverse farm size-productivity relationship remains, even though the positive correlation between yields and cash inflows from non-agricultural employment points towards the importance of capital market imperfections (Udry 1996). Combining the labor market advantage of agricultural operations based on family labor with the credit cost advantage of land ownership can lead to the emergence of an optimum farm size, as demonstrated in Latin America (Carter and Mesbah 1993).

Small producers' inability to access formal markets for credit and insurance often forces them to adopt costly (and relatively inefficient) insurance substitutes, one of which is the adjustment of crop and asset portfolios to a low return–low risk combination, a behavioral reaction that would clearly have implications for the relative efficiency of different farm units and, as an implication, the type of transactions observed in land sales and rental markets. If they do not have access to markets for credit and insurance, small farmers will be forced to adjust their asset portfolio so as to facilitate adjustment to unexpected productivity, as well as idiosyncratic shocks. This will affect the desired composition of their asset portfolios, in particular the amount of land they will want to hold. In order to ensure satisfaction of a minimum subsistence requirement during periods of distress, credit-constrained producers will tend to hold a portfolio of less risky but also less productive assets than unconstrained producers. Thus the degree to which farmers have access to low-cost means for credit and insurance will have implications for producers' desired asset portfolio, the timing of their participation in the markets for asset sales, and their productive performance.

Indeed, it has been observed that the desire to diversify against risk in the presence of credit market imperfections can explain a number of familiar characteristics of rural

[2] The scope for linkages between land and credit markets to lead to use of land market transactions as a credit market substitute in a model of 'interim' land transactions was first discussed by Basu (1986). He notes that, the supply of land for sale increases the probability of being able to buy back the land, the attractiveness of other (financial) assets as compared to land, and the need for liquidity. Depending on expectations, different equilibria are possible and benefits increase in the amount of turnover in the land sales market.

areas such as fragmentation of fields and strip-cropping (Fenoaltea 1976; Townsend 1995), long-distance marriages (Rosenzweig and Stark 1989), gift-giving, and patron–client relationships that have often been postulated to be at the root of a distinct 'peasant rationality' (Fafchamps 1992). For India, Rosenzweig and Wolpin (1993) show that the lack of insurance substitutes affects farmers' investment patterns. However, while small farmers' asset portfolio differs from the optimal allocation of assets, they are still more productive than large farmers (Rosenzweig and Binswanger 1993). For Africa, the level of liquid assets and capital available to the household will determine its ability to enter into high risk but high return activities (Dercon 1996; Dercon and Krishnan 1996).

Studies indicate that the impact of such arrangements can be quantitatively important, and that whether or to what degree credit market imperfections are strong enough to offset small farmers' supervision cost advantage are essentially empirical questions. Rosenzweig and Binswanger (1993), for example, show that just to mitigate risks, small farmers in India adopt crop portfolios that provide them with an income that is 45% lower than that of large farmers who, due to their access to markets for credit and insurance, can adopt profit maximizing crop portfolios. The ability to access formal financial institutions has a significant impact on peasants' savings behavior. Positive shocks led farmers close to a bank branch to save more, while those at a greater distance resorted to gift-giving—a distinctly less efficient method of insurance (Behrman, Foster, and Rosenzweig 1997).

The ability to acquire land and thereby gain access to credit could have a significant impact on equilibrium land prices. With imperfect inter-temporal markets, the value associated with the ability to use land as collateral in formal credit markets will be capitalized into land prices, and the equilibrium price of land will exceed the present discounted value of the income stream that can be produced from the land. If the poor have to borrow to buy land at its present value, the only income stream available for consumption is the imputed value of family labor, while the remainder of the profits has to be used to pay for the loan. This would reduce the purchasers' utility below what could be achieved, for example, in the labor market. Land purchases will thus normally have to be financed out of household savings, precluding widespread participation of the poor in the land purchase market.

This implies that completely mortgage-based acquisition of land is unlikely to lead to redistribution in favor of landless households, even if these had perfect credit access (Binswanger and Elgin 1990) in what has been called the 'fundamental financing problem of the poor' (Carter and Mesbah 1993). As mortgaged land cannot be used as collateral for working capital, the owner does not reap the production credit advantage and thus will be unable to repay a loan merely out of increased income from the agricultural production.

Even if imperfections in markets for credit and insurance reduce the scope for the land sales market to effect efficiency-enhancing land transfers from large to small producers, such transactions should—in a frictionless world—be effected through the land rental market. One possibility would be an interlinked contract whereby the landlord uses the credit access provided by land ownership to provide the tenant with working capital as part of the rental contract. Land rental markets are unlikely to achieve full efficiency because the tenant has limited incentives for investment and any tenancy contract involves an incentive to undersupply non-contractible inputs such as work effort.

Desirability (and difficulty) of land reform

If common market imperfections prevent land sales and rental markets from achieving a fully efficient resource allocation, redistributive land reform may be warranted for both equity and efficiency reasons. Indeed, the LRPP strongly supports the case for land reform, pointing to the successful experience of Asian land redistribution and the Bank's supportive role in the Kenyan 'million-acre scheme' that successfully redistributed this amount from European settlers to African farmers.

The ease of actually implementing land reform has varied considerably between 'landlord estates' that had already been cultivated by tenants and 'haciendas' where tenants received a small home plot in return for working on the landlord's home farm. In landlord estates, all that was required was a reassignment of property rights; land reform was generally easy and stable systems of production emerged. Since the end of World War II, landlord estates in Bolivia, large areas of China, Eastern India, Ethiopia, Iran, Japan, Korea, and Taiwan have been transferred to tenants in the course of successful land reforms. The productivity gains associated with this measure were modest in cases where security of tenure had already been high, cash-rent (rather than share rent) contracts had prevailed before the reform, and where landlords had provided tenants with market access and no arrangements to substitute for this were available. Both welfare and productivity increased where investment opportunities were available (Callison 1983; Koo 1968; King 1977); where land ownership enabled the new owners to access markets for credit and insurance that had previously been beyond their reach (Dorner and Thiesenhusen 1990); and where new technology could be readily adopted (Otsuka, Chuma, and Hayami 1992).

By contrast, land reform in *hacienda* systems, i.e., where tenants had a small house-plot for subsistence but worked the majority of the time on the landlord's home farm, has been very difficult, up to the point where the 'game of Latin American Land Reform' was declared lost (de Janvry and Sadoulet 1989). In the large majority of these systems, large landowners responded to the threat of land reform by reducing their reliance on hired workers or tenants who could have made claims to land ownership under a possible reform program through large-scale tenant evictions. They either resumed extensive livestock production and ranching or—aided by significant credit subsidies—started highly mechanized self-cultivation (Binswanger, Deininger, and Feder 1995). This not only reduced tenant welfare, but also depopulated farms and created further difficulties for redistributive land reform. Against this background, the failure to implement more effective land reform programs can be attributed to several factors.

One set of issues relates to the productive use of the farm, of which three points are of relevance. First, the transfer from large to small farmers generally requires a change in the pattern of production, subdivision of the farm, and construction of complementary infrastructure. Second, as the main productivity advantage from land reform is linked to the increased incentives by owner-operators, realization of the full social benefit from such an intervention requires a mechanism to settle additional beneficiaries—over and above the workers that may already work on the farm. Lack of family labor and/or capital in most cases prevented beneficiaries from significantly increasing efficiency of production—and may, in the case of well-run plantations, even have reduced productive efficiency (Hayami, Adriano, and Quisumbing 1990). Third, beneficiaries, even if they are workers of the former farm, are generally not accustomed to making independent entrepreneurial decisions, a constraint that is particularly important if realization of the benefits from land reform requires significant modifications in the farm's cropping pattern. In the many cases where the farms acquired for land reform were not farmed at full capacity, run down and decapitalized, or highly mechanized, neglect of simple works (cleaning of pastures, fencing, construction of basic infrastructure, etc.) or the need for some startup capital can often be linked to beneficiary failure and eventually desertion. Similarly, programs that were limited to the mere transfer of land to existing workers, without complementary investment, training, technical assistance, and provision of resources beyond the mere land, were generally associated with very limited equity and efficiency benefits.

A second set of issues relates to the fact that without access to credit markets, land reform 'beneficiaries' might be worse off than before, when the landlord provided them with inputs and possibly even credit for consumption smoothing. A large-scale land reform program in Ireland actually *worsened* access to credit by limiting the ability of new landowners to mortgage land while at the same time cutting off informal credit they had earlier obtained from the landlord (Guinnane and Miller 1997). Similarly severely restricted access to credit, together with insecure property rights, have led to widespread selling of land by former land reform beneficiaries in Nicaragua as well as the Philippines—often at prices far below the productive value of the land (Jonakin 1996). To avoid such an outcome, beneficiaries' ability to access output and financial markets is key.[3] Arrangements akin to outgrower schemes, where financial intermediaries supervise production, can provide input credit in kind and help in the organization of marketing, and, in some cases, can enable reform beneficiaries to overcome obstacles posed by these market imperfections, at least during the establishment phase.

Implications for implementation

Tenure security

Communal tenure

Communal tenure systems or variations thereof are dominant in most countries of Africa, in indigenous areas of many Latin American countries, the Mexican *ejidos*, and in China.

[3] This is in line with the observation that, in situations where other markets are highly incomplete, the inability to access other markets has proven to be a potent obstacle for the initiation and success of independent small farming operations (Brooks and Lerman 1994).

Under communal tenure, land is held by the community rather than the individual and, based on population growth, periodically redistributed among members (normally by the village chief). While individuals who are members of the community have very secure and normally inheritable rights to receive land even after a period of absence, they do not have permanent property rights to a specific plot, a limitation that is likely to reduce investment incentives.

Traditionally, communal tenure arrangements have often been considered an economically 'inferior' arrangement equivalent to collective cultivation. To facilitate economic growth and prevent the static and dynamic efficiency losses that were assumed to be associated with this tenure arrangement, establishment of freehold and the subdivision of the commons were proposed as the most appropriate solution. However, results of indiscriminate application of this method often failed to bring about the desired benefits because the links to other markets were not sufficiently taken into account. More intensive study of communal tenure systems in a broader framework and recognition of the multiple functions these systems may perform have led to a reassessment of the recommendations.

The efficiency losses associated with communal tenure systems may be more modest than generally assumed for several reasons. First, arable land (in contrast to pasture, forest, or fishing grounds which are enjoyed by the whole community) is, in the large majority of communal tenure systems, cultivated individually and in many cases individuals do receive inheritable rights. Second, communal resource ownership is often maintained because it provides public goods or allows the advantage of synergies, which would be difficult to provide under fully individualized cultivation. Examples include risk reduction through diversification in highly variable environments (Nugent and Sanchez 1993; McCloskey 1991), the utilization of economies of scale to break seasonal labor bottlenecks (Beard 1996; Mearns 1996), or investment in community-level infrastructure (Boserup 1965; Dong 1996). Given the individual cultivation, there is little or no static efficiency loss from communal tenure. Third, under conditions of low population density, when payoffs from land-related investments are limited, the investment disincentives associated with communal tenure are likely to be low as people tend not to invest under either system of tenure. As the scarcity of land increases, many communal tenure systems do recognize property rights to land improvements (e.g. trees), or compensate for improvements made upon redistribution of land thus attenuating tenure-related investment-disincentives (Sjaastad and Bromley 1997). Fourth, while communal systems prohibit land transactions with outsiders, rental and often even sale within the community are normally allowed and provide scope for efficiency-enhancing transfers. Note that communal tenure arrangements of this sort provide much greater flexibility and scope for efficiency-enhancing transfers than many of the closed 'joint stock companies' founded in Eastern European countries, where members can often neither physically identify their share nor rent it out internally to a more efficient producer.

In situations characterized by low population density and limited access to infrastructure and markets, the *costs* of delimiting and enforcing boundaries to individual plots would be prohibitively high. In this context, individualized titling may not be the most cost-effective solution. There are many cases where the benefits of full-blown titling will not be enough to justify the costs (which include not only the establishment but also the maintenance of registries). Titles that have been generated at high cost may easily become worthless if landowners do not have an incentive to update them, as happened for example in Kenya. In this case, and as long as there is effective governance, communal tenure systems can constitute a low-cost way of providing tenure security (Heath 1992). One benefit is that, if the administration is at the local level, communal titles can be established and administered at a fraction of the cost of individual titles because there is no need for sophisticated demarcation of individual plots. A second benefit is that, as indicated above, communal land ownership that uses a fallow reserve to help adjust land area to family size can provide an incentive compatible with social safety that can substitute for more costly mechanisms to achieve the same goal. Historically, societies appear to have maintained communal forms of land ownership even when they were aware of the costs in terms of reduced investment incentives, suggesting that—according to their subjective assessment—efficiency losses were more than outweighed by the insurance benefits provided.

This fact implies that, instead of posing an unrealistic and often artificial dichotomy between private and communal title, policy makers' attention should focus on ways to enhance security and effectiveness of property rights can be enhanced under existing arrangements. The literature indicates that communal tenure systems can break down, with negative consequences for vulnerable households (Andre and Platteau 1996), and that the threat of arbitrary redistribution by the village chief may eliminate investment incentives, with significant impacts on productivity under high population density (Carter and Yao 1998). However, in many such situations, private titling is not a realistic alternative. The challenge is to find ways to increase tenure security and protect individuals against arbitrariness in a way that facilitates gradual evolution of the system in a cost-effective manner.

One illustration for the insufficiency of communal tenure systems, even under land abundance, is Zambia (with a population density of 12 persons per km^2 and 75% of the land suitable for agriculture). There, almost 50% of farmers feel their land tenure to be insecure and would be willing to pay (US \$40 on average) for land titles (Deininger *et al.* 1998). If internal arrangements within the community function reasonably well, clarification of community boundaries and recognition of community rights to specific tracts of land, possibly through formal certificates at the community level, can be an effective means to limit encroachment by outsiders. If arbitrary actions by local chiefs and headmen are at the root of the problem, the establishment of accessible mechanisms for dispute resolution and enforcement to increase the accountability of local authorities would be needed. All of these are based on the communities' scope for autonomous arrangements within a community, in line with a set of officially approved 'by-laws.'

The fact that many countries now have land laws that provide formal recognition for communal forms of land tenure represents significant progress over earlier situations where such communities often did not even have a legal basis to protect their rights. However, the need for the gradual evolution of land rights systems suggests that such protection needs to be combined with internal flexibility. Rigorous codification of a 'communal land' category that does not specify a process for a community to lift some or all of the associated restrictions, may prevent the gradual evolution of land tenure systems in response to economic needs, and be associated with efficiency losses and/or unsustainable practices.

One example that illustrates both the scope for such efficiency losses and a way to deal with them is the case of Mexico. In the aftermath of the 1915 Revolution, *haciendas* and latifundia were eliminated and about half of the national land area was granted to communities (*ejidos)* under communal title. Well-intended restrictions that established that *ejido* land could not be alienated, rented, or mortgaged, and that made usufructuary rights to land contingent on occupation and cultivation—prohibiting even hiring of labor in the process—proved to be highly restrictive. Although farmers invented ingenuous ways to circumvent these restrictions (Heath 1992), it was very difficult for *ejiditarios* to obtain commercial credit and the transaction costs imposed by the various restrictions were high, involving among others the threat of loss of land. In areas where non-agricultural opportunities had increased and farmers engaged in seasonal migration, communal tenure became increasingly dysfunctional and large tracts of land lay either fallow or remained underutilized, thus causing significant efficiency losses.

This issue was addressed through a revision of Article 27 of the 1992 Constitution that stipulates two main regulations. First, the restrictions on internal transferability of *ejido* land is lifted, i.e., members can freely alienate lands within the community, subject only to an upper limit.[4] Second, *ejidos* can regulate internal matters, among others, the admission of members and the tenure regime under which they will exploit their lands through the general assembly by choosing from a menu of options. In this context, they can decide to farm under communal tenure, to contribute part of the common lands to a corporation or a joint venture with outsiders, to parcel all or part of the land out to members under freehold title, or even to convert the whole *ejido* from communal into freehold tenure. All that is required is a qualified majority in the general assembly. Contrary to some fears, the law has not led to a widespread sell-off and pauperization of the majority of *ejido* members. Instead, by allowing communities for whom existing regulations had increasingly become a constraint, the ability to shift towards a different tenure regime increased flexibility without giving up the core principles (and the advantages, such as the insurance function provided by joint land ownership) associated with communal types of tenure (Key *et al.* 1998).

Formal titling

In line with a classical paradigm, the LRPP has viewed land registration and titling as the main instrument to increase individuals' tenure security, to contribute to a flourishing land market (both for sales and rental), and to facilitate the use of land as collateral in credit markets. Experience has led to a considerable revision of this assessment.

While numerous studies have confirmed the positive impact of titling, experience with Bank projects has also demonstrated that titling is unlikely to be a panacea to achieve

[4] No member can hold more than 5% of the total area of the *ejido*.

these goals. Even if there is a case for titling, it is important to consider the situation before titling (collective, communal, or squatting) to decide on the most appropriate policy interventions. One reason is that lack of title is rarely a constraint on efficiency-enhancing land transactions. All over the world, but most clearly in the recent past in many Eastern European countries, land rental and even sales transactions emerged long before individuals were able to obtain formal land title. By contrast, in many countries, government regulations that limited the operation of rental and sales markets precluded the operation of an efficiency-enhancing land market, even in situations where individuals had formal title to their land. Also, where the underlying rights lack legitimacy, title will do little to increase tenure security, as is most clearly demonstrated in African countries where formal titles are not enforceable and land continues to be allocated along lineages (Atwood 1990). Finally, title alone is not sufficient to jump-start a formal credit market because banks are unlikely to accept land that cannot be repossessed as collateral. Even in cases where repossession is feasible, title reduces the risk but not the transaction costs associated with lending to small producers, and would therefore rarely lead to expanded availability of credit. Through experience, the World Bank has identified a number of preconditions for titling to be useful.

First, studies show that the main benefit from *formal* title is the access to formal credit it provides. This implies that establishing individual property rights through titling is most useful where a formal credit market permitting use of title as collateral already exists, and where profitable investment opportunities are available. As titles do not reduce the transaction costs associated with disbursement of credit, they are unlikely to have much effect if transaction costs to deal with rural clients are too high. An enforceable title increases a bank's ability to repossess in case of default; it has little impact on the transaction costs associated with making loans to small borrowers.

If, for whatever reasons, these transaction costs are too high even with title, even formal title may not alleviate small farmers' credit constraints, and if it increases large farmers' willingness to buy land, may even have negative equity implications. In Paraguay, for example, although title increased credit supply for all farms, producers below 20 hectares remained rationed out of the credit market and therefore did not benefit at all from the credit-supply effect of title (Carter and Olinto 1996). For titling to contribute to broad-based growth, it is therefore essential that concurrent measures be taken to increase access to and improve the functioning of credit markets, that expected costs and benefits be quantified, and that this information be used to establish cost recovery mechanisms.

Second, titling will not have much impact if there are other (cultural, political, or social) restrictions that prevent the emergence of a land sales market. If there are no disputes and traditional systems function reasonably well, it will be difficult to replace them by formal title. Even where there is a demand for formal credit and the use of land as collateral, it is only the ability to effectively foreclose on defaulters that will persuade banks to accept land as collateral for loans, as the example of Kenya illustrates. If political interference (often in favor of big landowners) precludes them from doing so, title will not improve banks' security and would therefore have no effect on formal credit supply. Similarly, if buying and mortgaging of land is restricted, title will not have much usefulness as collateral. In all of these cases, clear quantitative evidence on the inadequacy of current tenure arrangements should be made to justify such an intervention. Indicators to be used are the cost of disputes, the efficiency loss imposed by preventing cross-community transfers, or the productivity losses arising from investment disincentives.

Third, it is not wise to embark on a titling project in the absence of a clear legal base and an agreed and streamlined institutional infrastructure that is capable of administering the process efficiently. A large number of Bank projects have either underestimated the complexity of technical issues involved in titling, or assumed that titling could be initiated even if agreement over complex policy issues—in particular, how conflicting rights over the same piece of land will be settled—was not yet reached. Many countries are characterized by a plethora of institutions, programs, and projects—often with overlapping competencies and responsibilities, contradictory approaches, and high resource requirements to ensure interinstitutional coordination. Without streamlining the institutional infrastructure and the regulatory environment, it will be impossible to effectively administer a titling program or to instill confidence in the validity of the titles received by beneficiaries. In such a system, updating of titles would be very costly, thus undermining the sustainability of the effort.

Fourth, land titling must be systematic and area-based rather than 'on demand' for a number of reasons. An area-based program with complete coverage will be able to utilize considerable economies of scale in measurement, adjudication, and an effective and just process for conflict resolution. This would not only reduce the cost of program implementation but, by speeding up the process, would allow earlier access to the benefits from secure land title, thereby increasing the discounted benefits from the program. Experience in Thailand, El Salvador, Bolivia, and other countries demonstrates that the most practical way to accomplish this is to combine titling with a mechanism for dispute resolution on the spot, and a publicity campaign that would explain the legal background, the mechanisms utilized, the rights of different parties, and the rules of evidence utilized for dispute resolution as well as mechanisms for appeal. Furthermore, titling will reduce the transaction costs associated with land sales and rentals only if potential buyers can be assured of the integrity of the title they are acquiring (and the absence of overlapping claims to the same piece of land).

If individual parcels are titled on demand, it will still be necessary to investigate the status of individual plots on a case-by-case basis, and the reduction of transaction costs associated with titling will be minimal. Measures to ensure that beneficiaries from titling efforts have access to credit markets—which will be critical for the poverty impact of such a program—are much easier and much less costly in area-based programs. Finally, in addition to being costly, titling on demand has often had disastrous equity consequences. It allows individuals with good political connections to speed up the process, bypassing the need to thoroughly investigate existing claims to the same land, with the consequence of permanently eliminating land rights of indigenous people, women, or other vulnerable groups.

Fifth, there is a clear awareness in the literature that award of titles may, by codifying social and property relations that were hitherto only implicit, permanently reduce the asset-endowment of vulnerable groups and individuals with inadequate access to political power (Platteau 1996). This danger is particularly acute with respect to public lands, which have, in the past, often been acquired by powerful individuals in violation of government regulations or long-established rights of indigenous communities. Indeed, in many African countries the most deleterious equity implications of titling programs came about not through operation of a land sales market *after* titles had been issued, but through land-grabbing by influential individuals *during* the titling process (Bruce 1988). This implies that titling programs are advisable only where the legal basis for land ownership by historically disenfranchised groups (e.g., women) is satisfactory (see Gopal and Salim 1998 and Deere and León 1997 for examples) an equitable and quick procedure exists, and there are mechanisms for conflict resolution that provide for the return of illegitimately acquired land to the legitimate owner.

The case of Bolivia illustrates some of these issues. Bolivia has been characterized by a long history of arbitrary allocation of frontier lands to influential individuals, often in huge chunks of many square kilometers. Corruption within the responsible agencies resulted in double titling and superposition of conflicting rights, which created considerable tenure insecurity. This was exacerbated by a 'proper use clause' (stating that land that is not properly cultivated will revert to the state) that gave rise to manipulation and blackmail. Titling was highly arbitrary (taking more than twelve years for the average individual without political connections) with the poorest groups (including the indigenous population) being least able to protect their rights. Thus, before any more specific interventions could be undertaken, a thorough reorientation of the legal framework and the overall institutional environment was needed. Given the political sensitivity of the issues and the need to develop a broad consensus on how to proceed, this was a time-consuming and difficult process that took about three years and required high-level political support, including presidential intervention (Munoz and Lavadenz 1997). Two areas of the resulting legislation are of particular interest.

On the one hand, the law recognizes that there are multiple possible claims on land and, to cater to this need, establishes three classes of property rights, namely private homesteads, communal lands, and land under private freehold title. Rights to *homesteads*, i.e., family residences with an extension up to half a hectare, are restricted (neither mortgaging nor subdivision are allowed) and, as long as there are no conflicting claims, owners can receive title merely through proof of possession and occupancy in a relatively simple and quick process. Title to *communal lands* is awarded to land that has been permanently occupied and continuously used by a community or indigenous group. To receive title and have boundaries officially demarcated, the community has to acquire legal status and specify by-laws to govern internal matters as they wish.[5] *Private agricultural properties* under freehold can be established on the remainder of the lands. In addition, public lands will, with priority, be allocated for free to indigenous communities and landless peasants or, if there is no demand from these groups, sold

[5] As in the case of Mexico, communities can decide to subdivide the communal lands and distribute parcels to individual members under freehold title if they so wish, subject to an upper size limit on the holding of any individual in the group and the adherence to proper processes in doing so.

off at market prices through a competitive auction. All land titles that have been acquired illegally are declared null and void.

A second issue of interest is the way in which conflicting claims are adjudicated, land rights regularized, and a legal cadastre established. The administration of this process is handled by a newly established special institution. Recognizing that it is administratively impossible to cover the whole country at once, priority areas are selected on the basis of existing land conflicts and demand for regularization. Once this is done, a desk investigation, based on existing registry information and aerial photography, is carried out. This is followed by an elaborate publicity campaign that leads to a detailed and thorough field investigation that involves participation by the affected communities and all other claimants. During the fieldwork, juridical aspects (e.g., the presence of certificates, length of tenure, etc.) are clarified, physical boundaries identified and demarcated, and a preliminary cadastral survey conducted. The results of the field investigation are then cross-checked with the land records to produce a list of current owners with the associated cadastral map that is publicized in the communities with the goal of eliciting complaints and objections. Such complaints will be investigated by local offices involving community leaders and be referred to higher levels only if resolution at the local level is impossible. Once complaints arising from the community level have been attended to, the results from the process are advertised and posted publicly for two months when, assuming that no further complaints are being lodged, the rights are finally registered. Experience thus far suggests that all but a tiny minority of claims can actually be regularized using this process, and that large landowners are happy to cede illegally acquired parts of their 'property' in exchange for legally recognized title to the rest.

Land sales markets

The World Bank's 1975 LRPP has focused on land sales markets as the main institution to achieve efficiency-enhancing transfers from bad to better managers. This advice was based on economic theory suggesting that, due to the 'Marshallian inefficiency' and dynamic investment disincentives, land rental will be associated with static and dynamic efficiency losses. Evidence that has become available since then suggests that, in situations where other markets are imperfect, land sales markets may be even less efficiency-enhancing than land rental markets and may achieve only a second or third best outcome, with efficiency and equity implications that may be decidedly worse than what would be achieved by land rental. In these cases, attempts to make land sales markets more fluid may not be efficiency-enhancing and possibly leave society worse off, an illustration of the theorem of the second-best.

One major reason for land sales markets not leading to a first-best allocation is that, as discussed earlier, with imperfect inter-temporal markets, the value of the ability to use land as collateral in formal credit markets will be capitalized into land prices. As a consequence, the equilibrium price of land at given credit costs will exceed the present discounted value of the income stream that can be produced from the land (Binswanger and Elgin 1990; Just and Miranowski 1988). The same is true for expected appreciation of land values which may be capitalized in land prices but which can be realized only upon sale of the property. Policy distortions, such as the use of land as an inflation hedge, credit subsidies, and tax advantages that allow using agriculture as a tax shelter, will have the same effect (Gunjal, Williams, and Romain 1996). All these factors would make it more difficult for small producers to acquire land, and thus militate against an equity-enhancing operation of the land sales market to redistribute land to landless or marginal land-owning households that could have a productivity advantage as family farmers.

A second reason is that, where access to markets for credit and insurance is imperfect, shocks may force the poor to sell off land in periods of distress. To the degree that such shocks are covariate, they may be associated with significant fluctuation of land prices over time, forcing the poor to sell off at low prices during disaster and leaving them unable to re-purchase their asset later. The possibility of transactions in the land sales market being driven by lack of access to markets for credit and insurance, rather than cultivators' productive efficiency, is illustrated by Cain (1981). He compares land transactions in Indian and Bangladeshi villages with very different access to risk-coping mechanisms over the 1960–80 period. In villages that had access to a safety net program, the land sales market did actually contribute to an equalization of the land-ownership distribution, suggesting that the poor were able to use the land market to augment their land holdings. The main pattern of land sales was that richer farmers sold land to undertake productivity-enhancing investments (digging of wells, purchase of pumpsets, children's education and marriages). By contrast, where such consumption-smoothing devices were absent, the majority of land sales market activity was accounted for by distress sales (to obtain food and medicine) that led to a marked disequalization of the land-ownership distribution. Indeed distress sales have not only played a major role historically,[6] but are also linked to the elimination of traditional mechanisms for coping with risk in the literature (Kranton and Swamy 1997; Brockett 1984). This is of relevance as covariance of weather risks would imply that land prices fluctuate widely over time and tend to be low (due to insignificant effective demand and high supply) during bad crop years (Bidinger *et al.* 1991), implying that it is hard or impossible to recover those asset losses.

A further factor that might prevent land markets from achieving a first-best allocation is the transaction costs associated with land sales and rentals. It has often been observed (see, for example, Balcazar 1990; Carter and Zegarra 1995) that, especially in countries with a dualistic distribution of land ownership, land *sales* markets are highly segmented in the sense that—despite a considerable amount of land transactions within farm size groups (i.e., large or small farmer)—land sales across farm-size class-boundaries are virtually absent. One explanation is that it is costly to subdivide large farms so as to make them suitable for smallholder cultivation (or the other way round). Similarly, the fact that certain costs (e.g., formal registration) associated with land transactions are independent of the size of the purchase creates indivisibilities that would

[6] Distress sales have been important in China (Shih 1992), in early Japan (Takekoshi 1967), in the Indian Punjab (Hamid 1982), and in Latin America following the abolition of communal tenure (Brockett 1984).

either discourage small land transactions or drive them into informality where such costs are not incurred.

To improve the functioning of land sales markets, governments can (in order of priority) eliminate remaining policy distortions and take measures to reduce transaction costs in land rental and sales markets, establish a decentralized land tax, and review the appropriateness of remaining restrictions on the operation of land sales markets. One essential step, in addition to elimination of remaining distortions, is the establishment of a market information system that would reduce transaction costs and improve information about land prices and the functioning of land markets (for rental and sales). This would help individuals form realistic expectations about the functioning of these markets, improve the basis for their participation in these markets, and prevent them from being cheated. It would also help to devise, fine tune, and evaluate the broader land policy framework. In particular, it would help to assess to what degree distortions continue to affect land markets, identify the participants in these markets, and determine to what degree markets achieve efficiency-enhancing transfers, and the interaction between land and credit markets. Such information could help put land policy into the broader context of the functioning of factor markets, compare rental and sales markets, and gauge to what degree policy interventions have had their expected impact.

A land tax, to be enforced at the municipal level, could be of relevance not only to increase large landowners' incentive to utilize their land more productively, but would also make an important contribution to decentralization. On the one hand, taxation of land is one of the few cases of a lump sum tax where, using asset rather than production values, the effective tax rate does decrease with the income generated from the land, thus encouraging more productive resource use. A flat tax rate could possibly be used by local governments to leverage access to other sources of financing. This mechanism has proven to be feasible in a wide range of urban contexts in developing countries and—if accompanied by appropriate institutions to help with accounting and implementation—should be feasible in rural ones as well.[7] As the value of land tax revenues in any given municipality is linked to land values, potential land tax revenues will obviously be meager in remote and poor rural municipalities. Land taxes, therefore, cannot serve as a tool to achieve redistribution from rich to poor neighborhoods, implying that the interest of horizontal equity will require providing local governments with additional sources of finance.

Governments in many developing countries do maintain regulations, in particular restrictions on the transferability and use of land, and limits on the amount of land that can be owned by a given individual (land-ownership ceilings). These restrictions have a profound impact on the functioning of land sales markets. In many cases these restrictions have been adopted as a second-best policy instrument under a highly distorted policy, and a re-assessment and re-direction of those measures might be appropriate.

[7] Effective imposition of progressive land taxes has been frustrated by political difficulties and resistance in countries as diverse as Argentina, Bangladesh, Brazil, Colombia, and Jamaica (Strasma *et al.* 1987; Bird 1974). While one of the reasons was the fact that the main purpose of these taxes was to encourage subdivision in a highly distorted environment, a flat tax rate is more advisable.

Restrictions on transferability of land have often been imposed on beneficiaries of land reform or settlers on formerly state-owned land, preventing them from selling or mortgaging their land. Imposed with the intention of preventing them from selling out, this has also deprived beneficiaries from accessing credit—often in the establishment phase when credit would be most needed. Farmers have been forced to substitute more inefficient arrangements (e.g., usufruct-mortgaging and the associated use of wage labor contracts) to gain access to credit (Hayami and Otsuka 1993). The desirable goal of preventing land reform beneficiaries from selling out in response to temporary shocks would be better served by adequate training and preparation, and by ensuring that they have access to output and credit markets. Permanently precluding land reform beneficiaries from rental or sales is likely to reduce efficiency—by permitting the existence of large tracts of uncultivated or less than optimally utilized land reform land; allowing for some adjustments in response to differential settler ability may be preferable to the losses. While a moratorium on land sales might be justifiable as a second-best solution at the frontier in order to discourage speculative land acquisition, more rigorous evaluation of the experience thus far and the alternatives available (e.g., limiting the size of titles that are allocated to individual applicants, or requiring actual cultivation for title applications to be approved) would be useful.

Another restriction intended to facilitate the breakup of large farms and the associated sales of land to small producers has been the imposition of land ownership ceilings. While recent evidence suggests that such land reform legislation may have been effective in reducing poverty (Besley and Burgess 1998), the instrument appears to have been clearly second best, with the goal being achieved in a highly inefficient way. Even in the most favorable case such ceilings would constitute a temporary second-best measure to allow government to deal with the problem in a more thorough way. Ceiling laws have been expensive to enforce, imposed costs on landowners who took measures to avoid them, and generated arbitrariness, corruption, and red tape where bureaucrats had to decide on exceptions to this rule to allow utilization of economies of scale in plantation crops. If, as suggested by the evidence, the reason for land concentration is not the relative inefficiency of small farms, but rather imperfections in product and financial markets, and the inability of small farmers to self-insure due to limited endowments, it might well be more effective for government to focus on the root of the problem rather than trying to deal with the symptoms. If there is concern about potential adverse equity impacts of land sales, governments should help small farmers to compete, take measures to improve the functioning of financial markets, and provide quick and effective relief during disasters to avoid distress sales. To the degree that land use patterns are deemed inappropriate (either because of high levels of fragmentation of because of zoning), effective regulation together with an approach compatible with market forces (e.g., a transaction cost subsidy to specific types of transaction or a land purchase grant as discussed below) might be more appropriate.

Land rental markets

Even if imperfections in markets for credit and insurance reduce the scope for the land sales market to effect efficiency-enhancing land transfers from large to small producers, such transactions should—in a frictionless world—still be effected through the land rental market. The reason is that, by renting out, landowners would not forgo the credit access associated with land ownership (and could even advance the credit thus obtained to a credit-constrained tenant under an interlinked contract) but would at the same time be able to utilize the efficiency advantage of tenants' family labor.

However, compared to the positive stance towards land sales markets, the LRPP's attitude towards land rental markets is decidedly negative. Such a stance was justified by the static efficiency losses of share tenancy associated with the 'Marshallian inefficiency,' whereby tenants who receive only a share of their marginal product would have less incentive to exert effort. Experience and theoretical research that have become available in the interim suggest that such a negative assessment of land rental markets was premature. Rigorous measurement of the static efficiency losses from share tenancy suggests that these losses are relatively modest and can be further reduced by mechanisms of social control at the village level. Theoretical models that embed the choice of share tenancy contract in a broader framework of bargaining between landlord and tenant have pointed towards the crucial role of potential tenants' reservation utility as a determinant for the efficiency and equity of the resulting contract.

The analytical literature does suggest that the main factor underlying the adoption of share tenancy contracts is the lack of tenant wealth that creates the possibility for opportunistic behavior (i.e., strategic default) by the tenant (Shetty 1988). This has been further elaborated by explicitly incorporating the tenant's reservation utility in a bargaining game between tenant and landlord on a land-cum credit contract (Bardhan, Bowles, and Gintis 1998). These models clearly illustrate that the parameters of the contract do reflect the bargaining power of the two parties, and therefore, that measures (from land redistribution to provision of education and off-farm opportunities) that increase potential tenants' reservation utility will be more effective in changing the contractual outcome than administrative restrictions. An important point is that, since effort is not contractible, such increases in tenants' reservation utility will increase not only equity, but also through the better contract terms and the higher incentives they convey, efficiency of agricultural production. One implication is that redistribution of land, even though it would never come about through the market, would increase efficiency (Mookherjee 1997). Empirical evidence supports these conclusions and suggests that, indeed, share tenancy contracts will be adopted only if tenants' wealth constraints make fixed rent contracts (which would not be associated with any static efficiency loss) infeasible (Laffont and Matoussi 1995). Landlords do rank possible tenants according to wealth or their inherent productivity (Olson-Lanjouw 1995). Furthermore, to the degree that it has been effective in improving the reservation utility of tenants, tenant protection can be shown to have a significant productivity effect (Banerjee and Ghatak 1996).

This would imply that, in the large majority of situations, the policy advice of the LRPP has to be changed in the sense that activation of land rental markets would be more desirable than activation of land sales markets. While there is no doubt that, due to limitations in tenants' endowment, a second-best share rental arrangement rather than a first-best fixed rent contract will be chosen, administrative restrictions may well lead to a third-best wage labor outcome, which would further reduce efficiency and equity. Policies that aim at increasing potential tenants' reservation utility will improve both, and would therefore be much more desirable in the long term.

While theoretical reasoning suggests that share tenancy will be adopted only if other options are not feasible, empirical evidence from actual share tenancy contracts indicates that, in many cases, the associated efficiency losses are rather modest. Comparing sharecropped and owned (or cash-rented) plots for the same household indicates that, on average, share tenancy was associated with a 32% loss in output, a figure that declined to 16% once adjustments were made for differences in land quality. By contrast, there was no efficiency loss associated with fixed rent tenancy (Shaban 1987). Even where share tenancy is the only feasible option, the associated efficiency losses can be further reduced through other mechanisms. Embedding contractual arrangements in a long-term relationship, for example, offers further potential to attenuate the disincentives and productivity losses associated with share contracts. Indeed, for share tenancy contracts between kin (but not between all others), empirical evidence supports neither a disincentive effect nor a reduction in output as compared to fixed rent or owner-operation (Sadoulet, de Janvry, and Fukui 1997). This can be explained in an intertemporal setting by provision of implicit insurance through the landlord, and is in line with other evidence (Otsuka 1991).[8]

While land rental markets may not be able to achieve a first-best allocation, they have a number of potential advantages over sales markets, namely that credit market imperfections have a much stronger impact on land sales than on land rental markets; that transaction costs are lower than in land sales markets; and that there is considerable scope for generating positive externalities by facilitating acquisition of agricultural knowledge by the tenant through rental rather than sales. Especially in view of the finding that land rental markets may be more efficiency-enhancing than land sales markets (Olinto 1995), governments should promote the emergence of rental markets, and create a legal and institutional framework to efficiently resolve whatever disputes might arise, instead of trying to restrict tenancy.

The conclusion that administrative restrictions of land rental markets are rarely justified is further reinforced by the negative impact that was historically associated with such restrictions. Literature from Asia clearly shows that fixed wage permanent contracts will not be chosen unless tenancy is prohibited. The associated permanent labor contracts are much less efficient than tenancy or owner operated farming and may even lead to inefficient factor substitution away from labor (Otsuka 1991). Examples where land reform legislation has led to widespread and inefficient adoption of wage labor include, among others, India and the Philippines. Similarly in Latin America, the

[8] Otsuka and Hayami (1988) found a large number of studies equally split between efficiency and inefficiency of sharecropping contracts. Studies that did not find a disincentive effect of sharecropping were generally conducted in environments where such a contract was embedded in enduring family and patron-client relationships, or where effort was easily monitored. By contrast, studies that find sharecropping associated with large efficiency losses were often conducted where share contracts had been adopted as a result of exogenous tenancy regulations that prohibited tenant evictions even in clear cases of shirking, or where regulations had eliminated the fixed rent contracts from the menu of options open to the landlord.

imposition of explicit or implicit limitations on land rental markets, together with the threat of land reform, has severely reduced efficiency. In the majority of cases, landlords responded to attempts to increase tenants' security of tenure by large-scale evictions and a shift to ranching, highly mechanized forms of cultivation, or use of wage labor. Elimination of such restrictions (and the threat of losing property rights if renting out), together with provision of a clear regulatory framework for land rental markets could do much to improve agricultural efficiency and the welfare of potential tenants.

A second conclusion is that an appropriate analysis of contractual outcomes cannot be restricted only to one factor market. This requires consideration of a much broader set of policy instruments than only those that affect functioning of the land market directly. If indeed any change in tenants' reservation utility will affect the outcome of the bargaining between landlord and potential tenants, creation of off-farm opportunities, infrastructure, investments, and other components of an overall rural development strategy will affect the contractual outcome, and their costs and benefits need to be compared to tenancy restrictions.

Redistributive land reform

Long-standing distortions in land, labor, and product markets, many of which date back to colonial days, imply that in many countries the distribution of land is highly unequal, with large tracts of productive land lying idle while small peasants have to eke out a living on marginal and often environmentally fragile lands. Such unequal distribution of land ownership not only affects productivity, but also is often also linked to social unrest and violence. The LRPP clearly supports land reform as a mechanism that can, in countries where the historical legacy has led to a very unequal distribution of land ownership, increase efficiency as well as equity. In view of the political sensitivity of the topic and the difficulties of existing approaches, the LRPP recommended a focus on alternative mechanisms and, where necessary, financing of complementary investments associated with land reform implementation.

While the decision to make a more active involvement in this area contingent on a depolarization of the issue was probably right, the three alternative mechanisms considered have proven to be ineffective. Land Banks were not viable wherever they were established due to the collateral value of land.[9] Frontier settlement is no longer seen as a way to equalize the land distribution—in addition to its high administrative cost and the associated environmental hazards, it has reinforced rather than eliminated unequal land-ownership patterns in many countries. Finally, expropriative land reforms were more successful in creating bureaucratic behemoths than in redistributing land. In addition, selection of land and beneficiaries were highly politicized, significantly reducing (or even eliminating) potential efficiency gains. This is due to three main reasons, further to the conceptual issues discussed earlier.

[9] Expecting beneficiaries to repay the full price of land has resulted in widespread default and non-recoverable loans, while provision of credit at subsidized rates has generally undermined the ability to target the poor.

First, instead of aiming to increase productivity and sustainably reduce poverty, past land reforms in many countries aimed more at calming social unrest and allaying political pressures by peasant organizations.[10] Many land reform programs in Africa and Latin America were initiated in response to political pressure (or to divert attention from other problems) rather than as part of a long-term rural development strategy.[11] As a consequence, they were often designed ad hoc, bore little relation to actual needs on the ground, and commitment to them faltered once social emergencies had subsided. Moreover, individuals targeted to benefit from these programs were often well-connected and the most vocal politically, rather than those with the best ability to make productive use of the land, or the most deserving on poverty grounds.[12]

Second, the costs of carrying out land reform were often increased by the continued existence of implicit and explicit distortions that drove land prices above the capitalized value of agricultural profits. Experience has shown that the continued existence of such distortions will not only increase the fiscal cost of carrying out land reform, but also will reduce the sustainability of such an intervention, and—by encouraging land reform beneficiaries to sell out to large farmers—will contribute to a reconcentration of holdings. Attempts to limit beneficiary desertion through imposition of legal restrictions and severe punishment in cases of contravention often made matters worse. There is considerable anecdotal evidence on land sales by reform beneficiaries in Nicaragua, Colombia, and El Salvador, and in a recent census of Brazilian land reform settlements, only about 60% of land reform beneficiaries were actually found tilling their land (*Correiro Brazilense* 1997).

Third, instead of aiming to create conditions that would improve the functioning of land rental and sales markets and thus allow integration and utilization of these markets to complement government efforts at redistribution of agricultural land, past land reform programs have often been substitutes for these markets. This has resulted in complex regulations and a cumbersome and centralized implementation process that has stretched available administrative capacity (Lipton 1974). Centralized government bureaucracies—justified by the need to provide technical assistance and other support services to beneficiaries—proved to be expensive, ineffective in responding to beneficiary demands, and often corrupt.

Due to these difficulties, and the fact that land reform was a highly politicized topic, many of the land reforms that have been undertaken since the 1960s have not achieved their stated objectives. Evidence on the longer-term impact of land reform

[10] Of course, this would be consistent with the interpretation of land reform as a piecemeal strategy by the rich to avoid the imminent threat of revolt, with backtracking as soon as the threat weakens, as modeled by Horowitz (1993).

[11] Even with a genuine commitment to breaking the power of landed élites, agrarian reforms were generally designed by urban intellectuals, with little idea of the realities of agricultural production and a sound suspicion of the ability of small-scale cultivators to manage on their own, let alone be able to increase productivity (Barraclough 1970).

[12] This is in line with evidence from a number of Eastern European countries where political constraints generally led to a relatively 'inefficient' way of implementing land reform—through physical restitution of plots rather than compensation of former owners through fungible cash payments (Swinnen, this volume).

on poverty and productivity is more limited than desirable.[13] However, in countries (e.g. Zimbabwe, Malawi, South Africa, Brazil, Colombia, and the Philippines, among others) that continue to be characterized by a concentration of underutilized tracts of land in large farms, along with a pervasive lack of land access for poor and landless, macro-economic reforms have altered the rules of the game. A reduction in land prices, associated with the loss of privileges that have historically been conferred on large farms by discriminatory laws, trade protection, and credit subsidies, might make it easier to utilize the market for a type of land redistribution aimed at increasing productivity and equity.

To this end, a number of countries (Brazil, Colombia, South Africa) are in the process of implementing a new model of 'negotiated' land reform. Key elements of this approach are: (1) an emphasis on sustainable poverty reduction through elaboration of integrated farm projects by the poor (which are then supported by a land purchase grant); (2) decentralized execution and integration into development objectives at the local level, with an overarching emphasis on beneficiary training and human capital formation; (3) and private sector involvement in project development, financing, and implementation. Obviously, mere adoption of a 'negotiated' mode is not immune from the shortcomings that have plagued earlier land reform attempts.[14] However, initial evidence, from pilots that have aimed to integrate land reform into a more comprehensive package of support, suggests that the new approach is perceived to be significantly different from earlier land reform attempts. While this points towards a scope to reduce poverty, and increases agricultural productivity and a positive social rate of return, the degree to which this potential is actually realized needs to be assessed through careful monitoring in the future.

Challenges ahead

The discussion above illustrates that, since the 1970s, there have been significant advances in understanding the principles underlying land relations and in the way in which specific policy interventions aimed at growth and poverty reduction are implemented. At the same time, the agenda of issues to be tackled has grown considerably as both the number of countries where land relations are of importance and the range of topics has expanded.

- In many countries, indigenous communities lack secure or clearly defined and exchangeable property rights; the challenge to establish such rights and facilitate economically rational use of the land involved persists—for the group as well as the

[13] One example is the study by Scott (1976). While it illustrates that land reform can have a positive social rate of return, it is based on data gathered in the immediate aftermath of the reforms after which data collection was obviously discontinued.

[14] Due to a lack of poverty targeting, an exclusive focus on land purchases but not complementary investments, and a high (75%) level of subsidy, a 'negotiated' program of land reform that was carried out in Italy during the 1948 to 1970 period had only a limited impact on poverty reduction and was characterized by relatively high costs (Shearer and Barbero 1993).

individual. Group titles that specify boundaries and thus limit encroachment by outsiders are a promising solution, but more efforts are required to develop rules of accountability to guide the administration of such rights within the community, and to ensure a smooth and decentralized transition towards full private property rights at the appropriate moment.

- It has long been known that problems of environmental degradation at the frontier cannot be understood—let alone solved—without tackling the issues of sustainable resource use and land rights within the frontier. This vindicates the Bank's emphasis on a national policy dialogue rather than isolated ad hoc interventions. A number of countries have imposed size limits on the land to which title can be awarded at the frontier, and at the same time have taken complementary measures to facilitate sustainable intensification of existing settlements. Evaluation of these experiences could provide valuable hints regarding its replicability in other situations.
- There are many countries where, due to a history of conflict, war, collectivization, or expropriation, multiple overlapping claims to the same plot of land do exist and prevent ownership security and long-term investment (e.g. in Uganda, the FSU, and Central American countries). The elimination of these sources of insecurity, by providing a consistent legal framework, helping to resolve conflicts quickly and efficiently, and establishing the administrative infrastructure necessary for its implementation, is a key challenge in many cases of post-conflict and post-communist development.
- Ensuring access to land for the landless is not only a key political demand but could also provide a starting point for sustained improvements in the ability of the poor to accumulate assets and increase the equality of opportunity. Elimination of credit subsidies and agricultural protection have caused precipitous drops in land prices and greatly increased the supply of land from large landowners (e.g., in Brazil, Malawi, and South Africa).

Adaptation of the models of negotiated land reform could provide one way of addressing this demand. To deal with these challenges, a few key principles are of importance:

- The large majority of the evidence quoted in this review indicates that attempts to view the land market in isolation from the broader institutional context and the remainder of factor markets in rural areas may give rise to inappropriate policy advice. This is the basis for the Bank's insistence on placing land issues in a policy framework that integrates land market issues with the broader rural development strategy.
- The fact that land-related interventions do often require significant changes in the existing institutional framework, together with the political sensitivity of the issue, and the need to account for location-specific issues makes the use of pilots mandatory. Pilots are of importance not only to ascertain the viability of proposed approaches, but also to provide feedback on key design features and, most importantly, to demonstrate that decentralized alternatives to the existing institutional arrangements are actually workable.

- The experience of the past twenty years has caused the Bank to appreciate the importance of policy dialogue and client demand in an area that is as politically sensitive as land. While outside donors and the Bank can enrich the policy dialogue by providing access to broader experience, land policy initiatives that do not have a strong constituency (or respond to political demands) are unlikely to be sustainable. Local groups are indispensable to maintain the policy dialogue, conduct analysis, and generate a national debate about critical policy issues, in addition to their crucial importance for the implementation of specific policy initiatives.
- The World Bank also needs to place increased emphasis on partnerships in the international arena. Strategic alliances with other bi- and multilateral donors that are based on an analysis of each of the partners' comparative advantages will be of great importance. Increasingly, this will probably be complemented by the exchange of experiences between countries implementing specific programs.

REFERENCES

Alston, Lee J., Thrainn Eggertsson, and Douglas C. North. 1996. *Empirical Studies in Institutional Change*. New York: Cambridge University Press.

Andre, Catherine and Jean-Philippe Platteau. 1996. 'Land Relations under Unbearable Stress: Rwanda Caught in the Malthusian Trap.' Working paper, Centre de Recherche en Economie du Développement (CRED), Namur, Belgium.

Atwood, D.A. 1990. 'Land Registration in Africa: The Impact on Agricultural Production.' *World Development* 18(5): 659–71.

Baland, Jean-Marie and Jean-Philippe Platteau. 1996. *Halting Degradation of Natural Resources: Is There a Role for Rural Communities?* New York: FAO, Clarendon Press, Oxford University Press.

Balcazar, Alvaro. 1990. 'Tanaño de Finca, Dinamica Tecnologia y Rendimientos Agricolas.' *Coyuntura Agropecuaria* 7(3): 107–25.

Banerjee, Abhijit V. and Maitreesh Ghatak. 1996. 'Empowerment and Efficiency: The Economics of Tenancy Reform.' Working paper, Massachusetts Institute of Technology (MIT) and Harvard University, Cambridge, MA.

Banerjee, Abhijit V., Paul J. Gertler, and Maitreesh Ghatak. 1998. 'Empowerment and Efficiency: The Economics of Agrarian Reform.' Working paper, Department of Economics, University of Chicago, Chicago, IL.

Banerjee, Abhijit, Dilip Mookherjee, Kaivan Munshi, and Debraj Ray. 1997. 'Inequality, Control Rights and Rent Seeking: A Theoretical and Empirical Analysis of Sugar Cooperatives in Maharashtra.' Working paper, Department of Economics, Boston University, Boston, MA.

Bardhan, Pranab, Samuel Bowles, and Herbert Gintis. 1998. 'Wealth Inequality, Wealth Constraints and Economic Performance.' Working Paper No. C98-097, Center for International and Development Economics, Department of Economics, University of California, Berkeley, CA.

Barham, Bradford, Michael R. Carter, and Wayne Sigelko. 1995. 'Agro-Export Production and Peasant Land Access: Examining the Dynamic between Adoption and Accumulation.' *Journal of Development Economics* 46(1): 85–107.

Barraclough, S.L. 1970. 'Agricultural Policy and Land Reform.' *Journal of Political Economy* 78(4): 906–47.

Basu, Kaushik. 1986. 'The Market for Land: An Analysis of Interim Transactions.' *Journal of Development Economics* 20(1): 163–77.

Beard, Rodney. 1996. 'The Economic Theory of Extensive Patoralism.' Working paper, University of Queensland, Queensland.

Behrman, Jere R., Andrew Foster, and Mark R. Rosenzweig. 1997. 'Dynamic Savings Decisions in Agricultural Environments with Incomplete Markets.' *Journal of Business and Economic Statistics* 15(2): 282–92.

Benjamin, Dwayne. 1995. 'Can Unobserved Land Quality Explain the Inverse Productivity Relationship?' *Journal of Development Economics* 46(1): 51–84.

Berry, R.A. and W.R. Cline. 1979. *Agrarian Structure and Productivity in Developing Countries.* Geneva: International Labor Organization.

Besley, Timothy. 1995. 'Property Rights and Investment Incentives: Theory and Evidence from Ghana.' *Journal of Political Economy* 103(5): 903–37.

Besley, Timothy and Robin Burgess. 1998. 'Land Reform, Poverty Reduction, and Growth: Evidence from India.' Working paper, London School of Economics, London.

Bhalla, S.S. and P. Roy. 1988. 'Mis-specification in Farm Productivity Analysis: The Role of Land Quality.' *Oxford Economic Papers* 40(1): 55–73.

Bidinger, P.D., T.S. Walker, B. Sarkar, A.R. Murty, and P. Babu. 1991. 'Consequences of mid-1980s Drought: Longitudinal Evidence from Mahbubnagar.' *Economic and Political Weekly* 26: A105–A114.

Binswanger, Hans P. 1991. 'Brazilian Policies that Encourage Deforestation in the Amazon.' *World Development* 19(7): 821–9.

Binswanger, Hans P. and Klaus Deininger. 1997. 'Explaining Agricultural and Agrarian Policies in Developing Countries.' *Journal of Economic Literature* 35(4): 1958–2005.

Binswanger, Hans P. and Miranda Elgin. 1990. 'What Are the Prospects for Land Reform?' In *Agriculture and Governments in an Independent World*, Allen Maunder and Alberto Valdés (eds.). Proceedings of the Twentieth International Conference of Agricultural Economists, August 1988, Buenos Aires, Argentina. Aldershot: Dartmouth Publishing Company.

Binswanger, Hans P. and Mark R. Rosenzweig. 1981. *Contractual Arrangements, Employment, and Wages in Rural Labor Markets: A Critical Review*. New York: Agricultural Development Council.

Binswanger, Hans P., Klaus Deininger, and Gershon Feder. 1995. 'Power, Distortions, Revolt and Reform in Agricultural Land Relations.' In *Handbook of Development Economics*, Volume 3B, Jere Behrman and T.N. Srinivasan (eds.). Amsterdam: Elsevier Science BV.

Bird, R. 1974. *Taxing Agricultural Land in Developing Countries.* Cambridge, MA: Harvard University Press.

Birdsall, Nancy and Juan Luis Londoño. 1997. 'Asset Inequality Matters: An Assessment of the World Bank's Approach to Poverty Reduction.' The World Bank, *AEA Papers and Proceedings* 87(2): 32–7.

Blarel, B., P. Hazell, F. Place, and J. Quiggin. 1992. 'The Economics of Farm Fragmentation: Evidence from Ghana and Rwanda.' *World Bank Economic Review* 6(2): 233–54.

Boserup, Ester. 1965. *Conditions of Agricultural Growth: The Economics of Agrarian Change Under Population Pressure*. New York: Aldine Publishing Co.

Brasselle, Anne-Sophie, Frederic Gaspart, and Jean-Philippe Platteau. 1997. 'Land Tenure Security and Investment Incentives: Some Further Puzzling Evidence from Burkina Faso.' Working paper, CRED, Namur, Belgium.

Brockett, C.D. 1984. 'Malnutrition, Public Policy and Agrarian Change in Guatemala.' *Journal of Interamerican Studies and World Affairs* 26(4): 477–97.

Brooks, K. and Zvi Lehrman. 1994. 'Land Reform and Farm Restructuring in Russia.' World Bank Discussion Paper No. 233, The World Bank, Washington DC.

Bruce, J.W. 1988. 'A Perspective on Indigenous Land Tenure Systems and Land Concentration.' In *Land and Society in Contemporary Africa*, R.W. Downs and S.P. Reyna (eds.). Hanover and London: Published for University of New Hampshire by University Press of New England.

Bruce, J.W. and S. Migot-Adholla. 1994. *Searching for Land Tenure Security in Africa*. Dubuque, IA: Kendall Hunt Publishing Company.

Burgess, Robin. 1997. 'Land, Welfare and Efficiency in Rural China.' Working paper, London School of Economics, London.

Cain, M. 1981. 'Risk and Insurance: Perspectives on Fertility and Agrarian Change in India and Bangladesh.' *Population and Development Review* 7(3): 435–74.

Callison, C.S. 1983. *Land to the Tiller in the Mekong Delta: Economic, Social and Political Consequences of Land Reform in Four Villages of South Vietnam*. Bloomington, IN: University Press of America.

Carter, Michael R. 1984. 'Identification of the Inverse Relationship between Farm Size and Productivity: An Empirical Analysis of Peasant Agricultural Production.' *Oxford Economic Papers* 36(1): 131–45.

Carter, Michael R. and Dina Mesbah. 1993. 'State-Mandated and Market-Mediated Land Reform in Latin America.' In *Including the Poor*, Michael Lipton and Jacques van der Gaag (eds.). Proceedings of a Symposium organized by the World Bank and the International Food Policy Research Institute. Washington DC: World Bank.

Carter, Michael R. and Pedro Olinto. 1996. 'Does Land Titling Activate a Productivity-Promoting Land Market? Econometric Evidence from Rural Paraguay.' Working paper, Department of Agricultural Economics, University of Wisconsin, Madison, WI.

Carter, M.R. and K.D. Wiebe. 1990. 'Access to Capital and its Impact on Agrarian Structure and Productivity in Kenya.' *American Journal of Agricultural Economics* 72(5): 1146–50.

Carter, M.R. and Yang Yao. 1998. 'Property Rights and Agricultural Productivity in an Industrializing Economy: Theory and Evidence from China.' Working paper, University of Wisconsin, Madison, WI.

Carter, Michael R. and Eduardo Zegarra. 1995. 'Reshaping Class Competitiveness and the Trajectory of Agrarian Growth with Well-Sequenced Policy Reform.' Agricultural Economics Staff Paper Series No. 379, University of Wisconsin, Madison, WI.

Carter, M.R., B.L. Barham, and D. Mesbah. 1996. 'Agricultural Export Booms and the Rural Poor in Chile, Guatemala and Paraguay.' *Latin American Research Review* 31(1): 33–65.

Carter, Michael R., Shouying Liu, Michael Roth, and Yang Yao. 1996. 'An Induced Institutional Innovation Perspective on the Evolution of Property Rights in Post-Reform Rural China.' Working paper, Department of Agricultural Economics, University of Wisconsin, Madison, WI.

Chavas, J.P. and T.L. Cox. 1994. 'Primal-Dual Approach to Nonparametric Productivity Analysis. The Case of U.S. Agriculture.' *Journal of Productivity Analysis* 5(4): 359–73.

Collier, P. 1989. 'Contractual Constraints on Labour Exchange in Rural Kenya.' *International Labour Review* 128(6): 745–68.

Correiro Brazilense. 1997. 'Censo do INCRA Revela Atraso no Campo.' 29 June 1997, p. 14.

de Janvry, A. and E. Sadoulet. 1989. 'A Study in Resistance to Institutional Change: The Lost Game of Latin American Land Reform.' *World Development* 17(9): 1397–1407.

de Janvry, A., Gustavo Gordillo, and Elisabeth Sadoulet. 1997. *Mexico's Second Agrarian Reform: Household and Community Responses, 1990–1994*. La Jolla, CA: University of California Center for U.S.-Mexican Studies.

de Meza, D. and J.R. Gould. 1992. 'The Social Efficiency of Private Decisions to Enforce Property Rights.' *Journal of Political Economy* 100(3): 561–80.

de Soto, Hernando. 1989. *The Other Path: The Invisible Revolution in the Third World*. New York: Harper and Row.

Deere, Carmen Diana and Magdalena León. 1997. 'Women and Land Rights in the Latin American Neo-Liberal Counter-Reforms.' Working Paper No. 264, Women in International Development Working Paper Series, Michigan State University, East Lansing, MI.

Deininger, Klaus and Lyn Squire. 1998. 'New Ways of Looking at Old Issues: Inequality and Growth.' *Journal of Development Economics* 57(2): 257–85.

Deininger, K., P. Olinto, M. Wamulume, and D. Chiwele. 1998. 'Agricultural Sector Performance in a Post-Reform Environment: Implications for Second-Generation Reforms in Zambia.' Working paper, The World Bank, Washington DC.

Dercon, Stefan. 1996. 'Risk, Crop Choice, and Savings: Evidence from Tanzania.' *Economic Development and Cultural Change* 44(3): 485–513.

Dercon, Stefan and Pramila Krishnan. 1996. 'Income Portfolios in Rural Ethiopia and Tanzania: Choices and Constraints.' *The Journal of Development Studies* 32(6): 850–75.

Dong, Xiao-Yuan. 1996. 'Two-Tier Land Tenure System and Sustained Economic Growth in post-1978 Rural China.' *World Development* 24(5): 915–28.

Dorner, P. and W.C. Thiesenhusen. 1990. 'Selected Land Reforms in East and Southeast Asia: Their Origins and Impacts.' *Asian Pacific Economic Literature* 4(1): 69–95.

Eckstein, Zvi and Itzhak Zilcha. 1994. 'The Effects of Compulsory Schooling on Growth Income Distribution and Welfare.' *Journal of Public Economics* 54(3): 339–59.

Edwards, Sebastian. 1997. 'Latin America's Underperformance.' *Foreign Affairs* 76(2): 93–103.

Eswaran, M. and A. Kotwal. 1985. 'A Theory of Contractual Structure in Agriculture.' *American Economic Review* 75(3): 352–67.

Fafchamps, Marcel. 1992. 'Solidarity Networks in Preindustrial Societies: Rational Peasants with a Moral Economy.' *Economic Development and Cultural Change* 41(1): 147–74.

Fafchamps, Marcel and John Pender. 1997. 'Precautionary Saving, Credit Constraints, and Irreversible Investment: Theory and Evidence from Semi-Arid India.' *Journal of Business and Economic Statistics* 15(2): 180–94.

Fajnzylber, P., D. Lederman, and N. Loayza. 1998. 'What Causes Violent Crime?' Working paper, The World Bank, Washington DC.

Feder, G. 1985. 'The Relation Between Farm Size and Farm Productivity: The Role of Family Labor, Supervision, and Credit Constraints.' *Journal of Development Economics* 18(2–3): 297–313.

Feder, G. and D. Feeny. 1991. 'Land Tenure and Property Rights: Theory and Implications for Development Policy.' *World Bank Economic Review* 5(1): 135–55.

Feder, G., T. Onchan, and T. Raparla. 1988. 'Collateral, Guarantees and Rural Credit in Developing Countries: Evidence from Asia.' *Agricultural Economics* 2: 231–45.

Feder, G., L.J. Lau, J.Y. Lin, and L. Xiaopeng. 1989. 'Agricultural Credit and Farm Performance in China.' *Journal of Comparative Economics* 13(4): 508–26.

Fenoaltea, S. 1976. 'Risk, Transaction Costs, and the Organization of Medieval Agriculture.' *Explorations in Economic History* 13(2): 129–75.

Frisvold, George B. 1994. 'Does Supervision Matter? Some Hypothesis Tests Using Indian Farm-Level Data.' *Journal of Development Economics* 43(2): 217–38.

Galor, Oded and Joseph Zeira. 1993. 'Income Distribution and Macroeconomics.' *Review of Economic Studies* 60(1): 35–52.

Gavian, Sarah and Marcel Fafchamps. 1996. 'Land Tenure and Allocative Efficiency in Niger.' *American Journal of Agricultural Economics* 78(2): 460–71.

Glover, D. 1990. 'Contract Farming and Outgrower Schemes in East and Southern Africa.' *Journal of Agricultural Economics* 41(3): 303–15.

Gopal, G. and M. Salim (eds.). 1998. *Gender and Law: Eastern Africa Speaks. Directions in Development*. Washington DC: The World Bank.

Guinnane, Timothy W. and Ronald I. Miller. 1997. 'The Limits to Land Reform: The Land Acts in Ireland, 1870–1909.' *Economic Development and Cultural Change* 45(3): 591–612.

Gunjal, Kisan, Sarah Williams, and Robert Romain. 1996. 'Agricultural Credit Subsidies and Farmland Values in Canada.' *Canadian Journal of Agricultural Economics* 44(1): 39–52.

Hamid, N. 1982. 'Dispossession and Differentiation of the Peasantry in the Punjab During Colonial Rule.' *Journal of Peasant Studies* 10(1): 52–72.

Hayami, Yujiro and Keijiro Otsuka. 1993. *The Economics of Contract Choice: An Agrarian Perspective*. Oxford: Oxford University Press.

Hayami, Yuiro, L.S. Adriano, and M.A.R. Quisumbing. 1990. *Toward an Alternative Land Reform Paradigm. A Philippine Perspective*. Manila: Ateneo de Manila University Press.

Heath, J.R. 1992. 'Evaluating the Impact of Mexico's Land Reform on Agricultural Productivity.' *World Development* 20(5): 695–711.

Hoff, Karla and Andrew B. Lyon. 1994. 'Non-Leaky Buckets: Optimal Redistributive Taxation and Agency Costs.' NBER Working Paper Series No. 4652, National Bureau of Economic Research, Cambridge, MA.

Horowitz, Andrew W. 1993. 'Time Paths of Land Reform: A Theoretical Model of Reform Dynamics.' *The American Economic Review* 83(4): 1003–10.

Jalan, Jyotsna and Martin Ravallion. 1997. 'Are the Poor Less Well Insured? Evidence on Vulnerability to Income Risk in Rural China.' Working paper, The World Bank, Washington DC.

Jensen, M.C. and W.H. Meckling. 1976. 'Theory of the Firm: Managerial Behavior, Agency Costs, and Ownership Structure.' *Journal of Financial Economics* 3(4): 305–60.

Jodha, N.S. 1984. 'Agricultural Tenancy in Semiarid Tropical India.' In *Contractual Arrangements, Employment, and Wages in Rural Labor Markets in Asia*, H.P. Binswanger and M.R. Rosenzweig (eds.). New Haven, CT: Yale University Press.

Jonakin, Jon. 1996. 'The Impact of Structural Adjustment and Property Rights Conflicts on Nicaraguan Agrarian Reform Beneficiaries.' *World Development* 24(7): 1179–91.

Just, R.E. and J.A. Miranowski. 1988. 'U.S. Land Prices: Trends and Determinants.' In *Agriculture and Governments in an Interdependent World*, A. Maunder and A. Valdes (eds.). Proceedings of the Twentieth International Conference of Agricultural Economists, 1988.

Kevane, Michael. 1996. 'Agrarian Structure and Agricultural Practice: Typology and Application to Western Sudan.' *American Journal of Agricultural Economics* 78(1): 236–45.

Key, Nigel, Carlos Muñoz-Piña, Alain de Janvry, and Elisabeth Sadoulet. 1998. 'Social and Environmental Consequences of the Mexican Reforms: Common Pool Resources in the Ejido Sector.' Working paper, Department of Agricultural and Resource Economics, University of California, Berkeley, CA.

King, R. 1977. *Land Reform: A World Survey*. London: G. Bell and Sons.

Kislev, Y. and W. Peterson. 1982. 'Prices, Technology, and Farm Size.' *Journal of Political Economy* 90(3): 578–95.

Koo, A.Y.C. 1968. *Land Reform and Economic Development: A Case Study of Taiwan*. New York: Praeger.

Kranton, Rachel E. and Anand V. Swamy. 1997. 'The Hazards of Piecemeal Reform: British Civil Courts and the Credit Market in Colonial India.' Washington DC: The World Bank.

Kutcher, G.P. and P.L. Scandizzo. 1981. *The Agricultural Economy of Northeast Brazil*. Washington DC: The World Bank.

Laffont, Jean-Jacques and Mohamed-Salah Matoussi. 1995. 'Moral Hazard, Financial Constraints and Sharecropping in El Oulja.' *Review of Economic Studies* 62(3): 381–99.

Lin, J.Y. 1992. 'Rural Reforms and Agricultural Growth in China.' *American Economic Review* 82(1): 34–51.

Lipton, Michael. 1974. 'Towards a Theory of Land Reform.' In *Peasants, Landlords and Governments: Agrarian Reform in the Third World*, D. Lehman (ed.). New York: Holmes & Meyer.

Lopez, Ramon. 1997. 'Tenure Security and Investment in Honduras.' Working paper, The World Bank, Washington DC.

Malik, A. and R.M. Schwab. 1991. 'Optimal Investments to Establish Property Rights in Land.' *Journal of Urban Economics* 29(3): 295–309.

McCarthy, Nancy, Alain de Janvry, and Elisabeth Sadoulet. 1998. 'Land Allocation under Dual Individual-Collective Use in Mexico.' *Journal of Development Economics* 56(2): 239–64.

McCloskey, D.N. 1991. 'The Prudent Peasant: New Findings On Open Fields.' *Journal of Economic History* 51(2): 343–55.

McMillan, J., J. Whalley, and L. Zhu. 1989. 'The Impact of China's Economic Reforms on Agricultural Productivity Growth.' *Journal of Political Economy* 97(4): 781–807.

Mearns, Robin. 1996. 'Community, Collective Action and Common Grazing: The Case of Post-Socialist Mongolia.' *Journal of Development Studies* 32(3): 297–339.

Migot-Adholla, S., P. Hazell, B. Blarel, and F. Place. 1991. 'Indigenous Land Rights Systems in Sub-Saharan Africa: A Constraint on Productivity?' *World Bank Economic Review* 5(1): 155–75.

Mookherjee, Dilip. 1997. 'Informational Rents and Property Rights in Land.' In *Property Rights, Incentives & Welfare*, J. Roemer (ed.). London: Macmillan Press.

Munoz, Jorge A. and Isabel Lavadenz. 1997. 'Reforming the Agrarian Reform in Bolivia.' Harvard Institute of International Development (HIID) Discussion Paper, Harvard University, Cambridge, MA.

Newell, Andrew, Kiran Pandya, and James Symons. 1997. 'Farm Size and the Intensity of Land Use in Gujarat.' *Oxford Economic Papers* 49(2): 307–15.

Nugent, Jeffrey and Nicolas Sanchez. 1993. 'Tribes, Chiefs, and Transhumance: A Comparative Institutional Analysis.' *Economic Development and Cultural Change* 42(1): 87–113.

Olinto, Pedro V. 1995. 'Land Quality and the Inverse Relationship between Farm Size and Productivity: A Panel Data Analysis of Paraguayan Farm Households.' Working paper, Department of Agricultural Economics, University of Wisconsin, Madison, WI.

Olson-Lanjouw, Jean. 1995. 'Information and the Operation of Markets: Tests Based on a General Equilibrium Model of Land Leasing in India.' Economic Growth Center Discussion Paper no. 727, Yale University, New Haven, CT.

Otsuka, K. 1991. 'Determinants and Consequences of Land Reform Implementation in the Philippines.' *Journal of Development Economics* 35(2): 339–55.

Otsuka, K. and Y. Hayami. 1988. 'Theories of Share Tenancy: A Critical Survey.' *Economic Development and Cultural Change* 37(1): 31–68.

Otsuka, K., H. Chuma, and Y. Hayami. 1992. 'Land and Labor Contracts in Agrarian Economies: Theories and Facts.' *Journal of Economic Literature* 30(4): 1965–2018.

Pender, John L. and J.M. Kerr. 1994. 'The Effect of Transferable Land Rights on Credit, Land Investment and Use: Evidence from South India.' Working paper, Department of Economics, Brigham Young University, Provo, UT.

Platteau, Jean-Philippe. 1996. 'The Evolutionary Theory of Land Rights as Applied to Sub-Saharan Africa: A Critical Assessment.' *Development and Change* 27(1): 29–86.

Platteau, Jean-Philippe. 1998. 'Property Rights in Land, Part II: Individualization of Tenure.' Working paper, University of Namur, Namur, Belgium.

Rodrik, Dani. 1998. 'Where Did All the Growth Go? External Shocks, Social Conflict, and Growth Collapses.' Working paper, Harvard University, Cambridge, MA.

Rosenzweig, M.R. and H.P. Binswanger. 1993. 'Wealth, Weather Risk and the Composition and Profitability of Agricultural Investments.' *Economic Journal* 103(416): 56–8.

Rosenzweig, M.R. and O. Stark. 1989. 'Consumption Smoothing, Migration, and Marriage: Evidence from Rural India.' *Journal of Political Economy* 97(4): 905–26.

Rosenzweig, M.R. and K.I. Wolpin. 1993. 'Credit Market Constraints, Consumption Smoothing, and the Accumulation of Durable Production Assets in Low-Income Countries. Investments in Bullocks in India.' *Journal of Political Economy* 101(2): 223–44.

Rozelle, Scott, Li Guo, and Loren Brandt. 1996. 'Land Tenure, Property Rights, and Productivity in China's Agricultural Sector.' Working paper, Food Research Institute, Stanford University, Stanford, CA.

Sadoulet, Elisabeth, Alain de Janvry, and Seiichi Fukui. 1997. 'The Meaning of Kinship in Sharecropping Contracts.' *American Journal of Agricultural Economics* 79(2): 394–406.

Scott, J.C. 1976. *The Moral Economy of the Peasant: Rebellion and Subsistence in Southeast Asia.* New Haven, CT: Yale University Press.

Shaban, R.A. 1987. 'Testing between Competing Models of Sharecropping.' *Journal of Political Economy* 95(5): 893–920.

Shearer, Eric B. and Giuseppe Barbero. 1993. 'Public Policy for the Promotion of Family Farms in Italy.' World Bank Discussion Paper 262, The World Bank, Washington DC.

Shetty, S. 1988. 'Limited Liability, Wealth Differences and Tenancy Contracts in Agrarian Economics.' *Journal of Development Economics* 29(1): 1–22.

Shih, H. 1992. *Chinese Rural Society in Transition: A Case Study of the Lake Tai Area, 1368–1800.* Berkeley, CA: University of California Press.

Sjaastad, Espen and Daniel Bromley. 1997. 'Indigenous Land Rights in Sub-Saharan Africa: Appropriation, Security and Investment Demand.' *World Development* 25(4): 549–62.

Skoufias, Emmanuel. 1995. 'Household Resources, Transaction Costs, and Adjustment through Land Tenancy.' *Land Economics* 71(1): 42–56.

Strasma, J., J. Alsm, E. Shearer, and A. Waldstein. 1987. 'Impact of Agricultural Land Revenue Systems on Agricultural Land Usage.' Working paper, Land Tenure Center, Madison, WI.

Takekoshi, Y. 1967. *The Economic Aspects of the History of the Civilization of Japan.* London: Dawsons of Pall Mall.

Townsend, Robert M. 1995. 'Consumption Insurance: An Evaluation of Risk-Bearing Systems in Low-Income Economies.' *Journal of Economic Perspectives* 9(3): 83–102.

Udry, Christopher. 1996. 'Efficiency and Market Structure: Testing for Profit Maximization in African Agriculture.' Working paper, Northwestern University, Evanston, IL.

Yao, Yang. 1996. 'Three Essays on the Implications of Imperfect Markets in Rural China.' Ph.D. Dissertation, University of Wisconsin, Madison, WI.

INDEX